THE LAW OF DISABILITY DISCRIMINATION HANDBOOK

SIXTH EDITION

RUTH COLKER
Heck-Faust Memorial Chair of Constitutional Law
Michael E. Moritz College of Law
The Ohio State University

LexisNexis

ISBN#: 1-4224-1814-6

This publication is designed to provide accurate and authoritative information in regard to the subject matter covered. It is sold with the understanding that the publisher is not engaged in rendering legal, accounting, or other professional services. If legal advice or other expert assistance is required, the services of a competent professional should be sought.

LexisNexis, the knowledge burst logo, and Michie are trademarks of Reed Elsevier Properties Inc., used under license. Matthew Bender is a registered trademark of Matthew Bender Properties Inc.

Copyright © 2007 Matthew Bender & Company, Inc., one of the LEXIS Publishing companies.

All Rights Reserved.

No copyright is claimed in the text of statutes, regulations, and excerpts from court opinions quoted within this work. Permission to copy material exceeding fair use, 17 U.S.C. § 107, may be licensed for a fee of 10¢ per page per copy from the Copyright Clearance Center, 222 Rosewood Drive, Danvers, Mass. 01923, telephone (978) 750-8400.

Editorial Offices
744 Broad Street, Newark, NJ 07102 (973) 820-2000
201 Mission St., San Francisco, CA 94105-1831 (415) 908-3200
701 East Water Street, Charlottesville, VA 22902-7587 (804) 972-7600

(Pub.3554)

SUMMARY OF CONTENTS

ADA GENERAL PROVISIONS
ADA GENERAL PROVISIONS 1

ADA TITLE I
ADA TITLE I 2
ADA TITLE I EEOC REGULATIONS 7
ADA TITLE I EEOC INTERPRETIVE GUIDANCE 15

ADA TITLE II
ADA TITLE II 41
ADA TITLE II DOJ REGULATIONS 49
ADA TITLE II DOJ INTERPRETIVE GUIDANCE 57

ADA TITLE III
ADA TITLE III 77
ADA TITLE III DOJ REGULATIONS 85
ADA TITLE III DOJ INTERPRETIVE GUIDANCE 101

ADA TITLE IV
ADA TITLE IV 167

ADA TITLE V
ADA TITLE V 169

REHABILITATION ACT
SECTIONS 501, 503, AND 504 OF THE REHABILITATION ACT OF 1973 175
REHABILITATION ACT REGULATIONS 187

FAIR HOUSING
FAIR HOUSING ACT AMENDMENTS OF 1988 197
FAIR HOUSING ACT AMENDMENTS HUD REGULATIONS 203

DAMAGES
CIVIL RIGHTS ACT OF 1991 215

INDIVIDUALS WITH DISABILITIES EDUCATION ACT
INDIVIDUALS WITH DISABILITIES EDUCATION ACT 217
IDEA DEPARTMENT OF EDUCATION REGULATIONS. 325
CONVENTION ON THE RIGHTS OF PERSONS WITH DISABILITIES. 387

TABLE OF CONTENTS

Page

Summary of Contents iii

Preface xvii

Acknowledgments xix

ADA GENERAL PROVISIONS

42 U.S.C. §
- 12101 Findings and Purposes 1
- 12102 Definitions 1

ADA TITLE I

ADA TITLE I 2

EMPLOYMENT

42 U.S.C. §
- 12111 Definitions 2
- 12112 Discrimination 3
- 12113 Defenses 4
- 12114 Illegal Use of Drugs and Alcohol 5
- 12115 Posting Notices 6
- 12116 Regulations 6
- 12117 Enforcement 6

ADA TITLE I EEOC REGULATIONS 7

29 C.F.R. §
- 1630.1 Purpose, Applicability and Construction 7
- 1630.2 Definitions 7
- 1630.3 Exceptions to the Definitions of "Disability" and "Qualified Individual with a Disability" 10
- 1630.4 Discrimination Prohibited 10
- 1630.5 Limiting, Segregating and Classifying 10
- 1630.6 Contractual or Other Arrangements 10
- 1630.7 Standards, Criteria, or Methods of Administration 11
- 1630.8 Relationship or Association with an Individual with a Disability 11
- 1630.9 Not Making Reasonable Accommodation 11
- 1630.10 Qualification Standards, Tests, and Other Selection Criteria 11
- 1630.11 Administration of Tests 11
- 1630.12 Retaliation and Coercion 11
- 1630.13 Prohibited Medical Examinations and Inquiries 12
- 1630.14 Medical Examinations and Inquiries Specifically Permitted 12
- 1630.15 Defenses 13
- 1630.16 Specific Activities Permitted 13

vi TABLE OF CONTENTS

ADA TITLE I EEOC INTERPRETIVE GUIDANCE 15
  Background 15
  Introduction 16
Interpreting 29 C.F.R. §
  1630.1 Purpose, Applicability and Construction 16
    (a) Purpose 16
    (b) and (c) Applicability and Construction 16
  1630.2(a)-(f) Commission, Covered Entity, etc. 17
    (g) Disability 17
    (h) Physical or Mental Impairment 17
    (i) Major Life Activities 17
    (j) Substantially Limits 18
    (k) Record of a Substantially Limiting Condition 19
    (l) Regarded as Substantially Limited in a Major Life Activity 20
    (m) Qualified Individual with a Disability 21
    (n) Essential Functions 21
    (o) Reasonable Accommodation 22
    (p) Undue Hardship 24
    (r) Direct Threat 25
  1630.3 Exceptions to the Definitions of "Disability" and "Qualified Individual
        with a Disability" 26
        (a) through (c) Illegal Use of Drugs 26
  1630.4 Discrimination Prohibited 26
  1630.5 Limiting, Segregating and Classifying 26
  1630.6 Contractual or Other Arrangements 27
  1630.8 Relationship or Association with an Individual with a Disability 28
  1630.9 Not Making Reasonable Accommodation 28
        Process of Determining the Appropriate Reasonable Accommodation 30
        Reasonable Accommodation Process Illustrated 31
    (b) 31
    (d) 32
  1630.10 Qualification Standards, Tests, and Other Selection Criteria 32
  1630.11 Administration of Tests 32
  1630.13 Prohibited Medical Examinations and Inquiries 33
    (a) Pre-Employment Examination or Inquiry 33
    (b) Examination or Inquiry of Employees 33
  1630.14 Medical Examinations and Inquiries Specifically Permitted 34
    (a) Pre-Employment Inquiry 34
    (b) Employment Entrance Examination 35
    (c) Examination of Employees 35
    (d) Other Acceptable Examinations and Inquiries 35
  1630.15 Defenses 36
    (a) Disparate Treatment Defenses 36
    (b) and (c) Disparate Impact Defenses 36
    (d) Defense to Not Making Reasonable Accommodation 37
    (e) Defense—Conflicting Federal Laws and Regulations 38
  1630.16 Specific Activities Permitted 38
    (a) Religious Entities 38

	(b)	Regulation of Alcohol and Drugs 38
	(c)	Drug Testing 38
	(e)	Infectious and Communicable Diseases; Food Handling Jobs 38
	(f)	Health Insurance, Life Insurance, and Other Benefit Plans 38

ADA TITLE II

ADA TITLE II 41

PUBLIC SERVICES

PROHIBITION AGAINST DISCRIMINATION AND OTHER GENERALLY APPLICABLE PROVISIONS

42 U.S.C. §

12131	Definition 41
12132	Discrimination 41
12133	Enforcement 41
12134	Regulations 41

ACTIONS APPLICABLE TO PUBLIC TRANSPORTATION PROVIDED BY PUBLIC ENTITIES CONSIDERED DISCRIMINATORY
Public Transportation Other Than by Aircraft or Certain Rail Operations

12141	Definitions 42
12142	Public Entities Operating Fixed Route Systems 42
12143	Paratransit as a Complement to Fixed Route Service 43
12144	Public Entity Operating a Demand Responsive System 45
12145	Temporary Relief Where Lifts Are Unavailable 45
12146	New Facilities 45
12147	Alterations of Existing Facilities 45
12148	Public Transportation Programs and Activities in Existing Facilities and One Car per Train Rule 46
12149	Regulations 46
12150	Interim Accessibility Requirements 47

ADA TITLE II DOJ REGULATIONS 49

28 C.F.R. §

Subpart A—General

35.102	Application 49
35103	Relationship to Other Laws 49
35.104	Definitions 49

Subpart B—General Requirements

35.130	General Prohibitions Against Discrimination 51
35.131	Illegal Use of Drugs 52
35.132	Smoking 52
35.133	Maintenance of Accessible Features 52

viii TABLE OF CONTENTS

35.134   Retaliation or Coercion 52
35.135   Personal Devices and Services 53

Subpart C—Employment

35.140   Employment Discrimination Prohibited 53

Subpart D—Program Accessibility

35.149   Discrimination Prohibited 53
35.150   Existing Facilities 53
35.151   New Construction and Alterations 54

Suppart E—Communications

35.160   General 55
35.161   Telecommunication devices for the deaf (TDD's) 55
35.162   Telephone emergency services 55
35.163   Information and signage 55
35.164   Duties 55

Subpart F—Compliance Procedures

35.178   State Immunity 55

ADA TITLE II DOJ INTERPRETIVE GUIDANCE 57

28 C.F.R §

Subpart A—General

35.104   Definitions 57

Subpart B—General Requirements

35.130   General Prohibitions Against Discrimination 63
35.131   Illegal Use of Drugs 68
35.132   Smoking 70
35.133   Maintenance of Accessible Features 70
35.134   Retaliation or Coercion 70
35.135   Personal Devices and Services 71

Subpart C—Employment

35.140   Employment Discrimination Prohibited 71

Subpart D—Program Accessibility

35.149   Discrimination Prohibited 72
35.150   Existing Facilities 72
35.151   New Construction and Alterations 73
35.178   State Immunity 75

ADA TITLE III

ADA TITLE III 77

PUBLIC ACCOMMODATIONS AND SERVICES OPERATED BY PRIVATE ENTITIES

42 U.S.C. §

12181	Definitions	.77
12182	Prohibition of Discrimination by Public Accommodations	.78
12183	New Construction and Alterations in Public Accommodations and Commercial Facilities	.80
12184	Prohibition of Discrimination in Specified Public Transportation Services Provided by Private Entities	.80
12185	Study	.81
12186	Regulations	.82
12187	Exemptions for Private Clubs and Religious Organizations	.83
12188	Enforcement	.83
12189	Examinations and Courses	.84

ADA TITLE III DOJ REGULATIONS 85

28 C.F.R. §

Subpart A—General

36.104	Definitions	.85

Subpart B—General Requirements

36.201	General	.87
36.202	Activities	.88
36.203	Integrated Settings	.88
36.204	Administrative Methods	.88
36.205	Association	.88
36.206	Retaliation or Coercion	.88
36.207	Places of Public Accommodation Located in Private Residences	.89
36.208	Direct Threat	.89
36.209	Illegal Use of Drugs	.89
36.210	Smoking	.89
36.211	Maintenance of Accessible Features	.89
36.212	Insurance	.90

Subpart C—Specific Requirements

36.301	Eligibility Criteria	.90
36.302	Modification in Policies, Practices, or Procedures	.90
36.303	Auxilliary Aids and Services	.91
36.304	Removal of Barriers	.91
36.305	Alternatives to Barrier Removal	.92
36.306	Personal Devices and Services	.93
36.307	Accessible or Special Goods	.93
36.308	Seating in Assembly Areas	.93
36.309	Examinations and Courses	.93

x   TABLE OF CONTENTS

Subpart D—New Construction and Alterations

36.401	New Construction	94
36.402	Alterations	95
36.403	Alterations: Path of Travel	96
36.404	Alterations: Elevator Exemption	97
36.405	Alterations: Historic Preservation	97
36.406	Standards for New Construction and Alterations	97

Subpart E—Enforcement

36.501	Private Suits	98
36.502	Investigations and Compliance Reviews	98
36.503	Suit by the Attorney General	98
36.504	Relief	98
36.505	Attorney Fees	99

ADA TITLE III DOJ INTERPRETIVE GUIDANCE 101

Interpreting 28 C.F.R. §

Subpart A—General

36.101	Purpose	101
36.102	Application	101
36.103	Relationship to Other Laws	101
36.104	Definitions	102

Subpart B—General Requirements

36.201	General	113
36.202	Activities	116
36.203	Integrated Settings	116
36.204	Administrative Methods	118
36.205	Association	118
36.206	Retaliation or Coercion	119
36.207	Places of Public Accommodation Located in Private Residences	119
36.208	Direct Threat	120
36.209	Illegal Use of Drugs	122
36.210	Smoking	123
36.211	Maintenance of Accessible Features	123
36.212	Insurance	124
36.213	Relationship of Subpart 8 to Subparts C and D	125

Subpart C—Specific Requirements

36.301	Eligibility Criteria	126
36.302	Modification in Policies, Practices, or Procedures	127
36.303	Auxilliary Aids and Services	128
36.304	Removal of Barriers	131
36.305	Alternatives to Barrier Removal	135
36.306	Personal Devices and Services	135
36.307	Accessible or Special Goods	136
36.308	Seating in Assembly Areas	136
36.309	Purchase of Furniture and Equipment	137

| 36.309 | Examinations and Courses | 137 |
| 36.310 | Transportation Provided by Public Accommodations | 140 |

Subpart D—New Construction and Alterations

36.401	New Construction	141
36.402	Alterations	149
36.403	Alterations: Path of Travel	151
36.404	Alterations: Elevator Exemption	154
36.405	Alterations: Historic Preservation	154
36.406	Standards for New Construction and Alterations	155

Subpart E—Enforcement 161

| 36.305 | Effective Date | 163 |

Subpart F—Certification of State Labs or Local Building Codes 163

ADA TITLE IV

ADA TITLE IV 167

42 U.S.C. § 225 Telecommunications Services for Hearing-Impaired and Speech-Impaired Individuals 167

ADA TITLE V

ADA TITLE V 169

MISCELLANEOUS PROVISIONS

42 U.S.C. §

12201	Construction	169
12202	State Immunity	169
12203	Prohibition Against Retaliation and Coercion	169
12204	Regulations by the Architectural and Transportation Barriers Compliance Board	170
12205	Attorney's Fees	170
12206	Technical Assistance	170
12207	Federal Wilderness Areas	171
12208	Transvestites	171
12209	Instrumentalities of the Congress	171
12210	Illegal Use of Drugs	172
12211	Definitions	172
12212	Alternative Means of Dispute Resolution	173
12213	Severability	173

xii TABLE OF CONTENTS

REHABILITATION ACT

SECTIONS 501, 503, AND 504 OF THE REHABILITATION ACT OF 1973 175

29 U.S.C. §

705	Definitions	175
791	Employment of Individuals with Disabilities	182
793	Employment Under Federal Contracts	183
794	Nondiscrimination under Federal Grants and Programs	184
794a	Remedies and Attorney Fees	185

REHABILITATION ACT REGULATIONS 187

29 C.F.R §

Subpart A—General Provisions

32.1	Purpose	187
32.2	Applicaion	187
32.3	Definitions	187
32.4	Discrimination prohibited	189
32.5	Assurances Required	190
32.6	Remedial Action, Voluntary Action, and Self-Evaluation	191
32.7	Designation of Responsible Employee	191
32.8	Notice	191
32.9	Administrative Requirements for Small Recipients	192
32.10	Effect of State or Local Law or Other Requirements and Effect of Employment Opportunities	192

Subpart B—Employment Practices and Employment Related Training Program Participation

32.12	Discrimination Prohibited	192
32.13	Reasonable Accomodation	193
32.14	Job Qualifications	193
32.15	Preemployment Inquiries	193
32.16	Listing of Employment Openings	194
32.17	Labor Unions and Recruiting and Training Agencies	194

Subpart C—Program Accessibility

32.26	Discrimination Prohibited	195
32.27	Access to Programs	195
32.28	Architectural Standards	196

FAIR HOUSING

FAIR HOUSING ACT AMENDMENTS OF 1988 197

42 U.S.C. §

3601	Declaration of Policy	197
3602	Definitions	197

3603	Effective Dates of Certain Prohibitions	197
3604	Discrimination in the Sale or Rental of Housing and Other Prohibited Practices	198
3605	Discrimination in Residential Real Estate-Related Transactions	200
3606	Discrimination in Provision of Brokerage Services	200
3607	Exemption	200

FAIR HOUSING ACT AMENDMENTS HUD REGULATIONS 203

24 C.F.R §

Subpart A—General

100.1	Authority	203
100.5	Scope	203
100.10	Exemptions	203
100.20	Definitions	204

Subpart B—Discriminatory Housing Practices

100.50	Real Estate Practices Prohibited	205
100.60	Unlawful Refusal to Sell or Rent or to Negotiate for the Sale or Rental	205
100.65	Discrimination in Terms, Conditions and Privileges and in Services and Facilities	205
100.70	Other Prohibited Sale and Rental Conduct	206
100.75	Discriminatory Advertisements, Statements and Notices	206
100.80	Discriminatory Representations on the Availability of Dwellings	207
100.85	Blockbusting	207
100.90	Discrimination in the Provision of Brokerage Services	207

Subpart C—Discrimination in Residential Real Estate-Related Transactions

100.110	Discriminatory Practices in Residential Real Estate-Related Transactions	208
100.115	Residential Real Estate-Related Transactions	208
100.120	Discrimination in the Making of Loans and in the Provision of Other Financial Assistance	208
100.125	Discrimination in the Purchasing of Loans	208
100.130	Discrimination in the Terms and Conditions for Making Available Loans or Other Financial Assistance	209
100.135	Unlawful Practices in the Selling, Brokering, or Appraising of Residential Real Property	209

Subpart D—Prohibition Against Discrimination Because of Handicap

100.200	Purpose	209
100.201	Definitions	209
100.202	General Prohibitions Against Discrimination Because of Handicap	211
100.203	Reasonable Modifications of Existing Premises	211
100.204	Reasonable Accommodations	212
100.205	Design and Construction Requirements	212

DAMAGES

CIVIL RIGHTS ACT OF 1991 215

42 U.S.C. §
   1981a Damages in Cases of Intentional Discrimination in Employment 215

INDIVIDUALS WITH DISABILITIES EDUCATION ACT

INDIVIDUALS WITH DISABILITIES EDUCATION ACT 217

Part A—General Provisions

20 U.S.C. §
   1400 Short title; Table of Contents; Findings; Purposes 217
   1401 Definitions 217
   1402 Office of Special Education Programs 222
   1403 Abrogation of State Sovereign Immunity 223
   1404 Acquisition of Equipment; Construction or Alteration of Facilities 223
   1405 Employment of Individuals with Disabilities 223
   1406 Requirements for Prescribing Regulations 223
   1407 State Administration 224
   1408 Paperwork Reduction 224
   1409 Freely Associated States 225

Part B—Assistance for Education
of All Children with Disabilities

20 U.S.C. §
   1411 Authorization; Allotment; Use of Funds; Authorization of Appropriations 226
   1412 State Eligibility 235
   1413 Local Educational Agency Eligibility 248
   1414 Evaluations, Eligibility Determinations, Individualized Education Programs, and Educational Placements 253
   1415 Procedural Safeguards 262
   1416 Withholding and Judicial Review 273
   1417 Administration 278
   1418 Program Information 278
   1419 Preschool Grants 280

Part C—Infants and Toddlers with Disabilities

20 U.S.C §
   1431 Findings and Policy 283
   1432 Definitions 283
   1433 General Authority 284
   1434 Eligibility 285
   1435 Requirements for Statewide System 285
   1436 Individualized Family Service Plan 288

1437 State Application and Assurances 289
1438 Uses of Funds 291
1439 Procedural Safeguards 291
1440 Payor of Last Resort 292
1441 State Interagency Coordinating Council 293
1442 Federal Administration 294
1443 Allocation of Funds 295
1444 Authorization of Appropriations 296

Part D—National Activities to Improve Education of Children with Disabilities

20 U.S.C. §
1450 Findings and Purpose 297

Subpart 1—State Personnel Development Grants

20 U.S.C. §
1451 Purpose; Definition of Personnel; Program Authority 298
1452 Eligibility and Collaborative Process 300
1453 Applications 300
1454 Use of Funds 302
1455 Authorization of Appropriations 305

Subpart 2— Personnel Preparation, Technical Assistance, Model Demonstration Projects and Dissemination of Information

20 U.S.C. §
1461 Purpose; Definition of Eligible Entity 305
1462 Personnel Development to Improve Services and Results for Children with Disabilities 306
1463 Technical Assistance, Demonstration Projects, Dissemination of Information, and Implementation of Scientifically Based Research 310
1464 Studies and Evaluations 312
1465 Interim Alternative Educational Settings, Behavioral Supports, and Systemic School Interventions 314
1466 Authorization of Appropriations 315

Subpart 3—Supports to Improve Results for Children with Disabilities

20 U.S.C. §
1470 Findings and Purposes 315
1471 Parent Training and Information Centers 316
1472 Community Parent Resource Centers 318
1473 Technical Assistance for Parent Training and Information Centers 318
1474 Technology Development, Demonstration, and Utilization; Media Services; and Instructional Materials 319
1475 Authorization of Appropriations 321

Subpart 4—General Provisions

20 U.S.C. §

1481 Comprehensve Plan for Suparts 2 and 3 321
1482 Administrative Provisions 323

IDEA DEPARTMENT OF EDUCATION REGULATIONS 325

34 CFR §

300.1 Purposes 325
300.2 Applicability of this part to State and local agencies 325
Definitions Used in This Part 325
300.4 Act 325
300.5 Assistive technology device 325
300.6 Assistive technology service 325
300.7 Charter school 326
300.8 Child with a disability 326
300.9 Consent 328
300.10 Core academic subjects 328
300.11 Day; business day; school day 328
300.12 Educational service agency 328
300.13 Elementary school 328
300.14 Equipment 328
300.15 Evaluation 328
300.16 Excess costs 328
300.17 Free appropriate public education 329
300.18 Highly qualified special education teachers 329
300.19 Homeless children 331
300.20 Include 331
300.21 Indian and Indian tribe 331
300.22 Individualized education program 331
300.23 Individualized education program team 331
300.24 Individualized family service plan 331
300.25 Infant or toddler with a disability 331
300.26 Institution of higher education 331
300.27 Limited English proficient 331
300.28 Local educational agency 331
300.29 Native language 332
300.30 Parent 332
300.31 Parent training and information center 332
300.32 Personally identifiable 332
300.33 Public agency 333
300.34 Related services 333
300.35 Scientifically based research 335
300.36 Secondary school 335
300.37 Services plan 335
300.38 Secretary 335
300.39 Special education 335
300.40 State 336
300.41 State educational agency 336

300.42 Supplementary aids and services 336
300.43 Transition services 336
300.44 Universal design 336
300.45 Ward of the State 336
300.100 Eligibility for assistance 336
FAPE Requirements 337
300.101 Free appropriate public education (FAPE) 337
300.102 Limitation—exception to FAPE for certain ages 337
Other FAPE Requirements 337
300.103 FAPE—methods and payments 337
300.104 Residential placement 338
300.105 Assistive technology 338
300.106 Extended school year services 338
300.107 Nonacademic services 338
300.108 Physical education 338
300.109 Full educational opportunity goal (FEOG) 339
300.110 Program options 339
300.111 Child find 339
300.112 Individualized education programs (IEP) 339
300.113 Routine checking of hearing aids and external components
     of surgically implanted medical devices 339
Least Restrictive Environment (LRE) 340
300.114 LRE requirements 340
300.115 Continuum of alternative placements 340
300.116 Placements 340
300.117 Nonacademic settings 341
300.118 Children in public or private institutions 341
300.119 Technical assistance and training activities 341
300.120 Monitoring activities 341
Additional Eligibility Requirements 341
300.121 Procedural safeguards 341
300.122 Evaluation 341
300.123 Confidentiality of personally identifiable information 341
300.124 Transition of children from the Part C program to preschool programs 341
300.125 to 300.128 [Reserved] 341
Children in Private Schools 342
300.129 State responsibility regarding children in private schools 342
Children with Disabilities Enrolled by Their Parents in Private Schools 342
300.130 Definition of parentally-placed private school children with disabilities 342
300.131 Child find for parentally-placed private school children with disabilities 342
300.132 Provision of services for parentally-placed private school children with
     disabilities—basic requirement 342
300.133 Expenditures 342
300.134 Consultation 343
300.135 Written affirmation 344
300.136 Compliance 344
300.137 Equitable services determined 344
300.138 Equitable services provided 345
300.139 Location of services and transportation 345

300.140 Due process complaints and State complaints 345
300.141 Requirement that funds not benefit a private school 346
300.142 Use of personnel 346
300.143 Separate classes prohibited 346
300.144 Property, equipment, and supplies 346
Children with Disabilities in Private Schools Placed or Referred by Public Agencies 346
300.145 Applicability of 300.146 through 300.147 346
300.146 Responsibility of SEA 347
300.147 Implementation by SEA 347
Children with Disabilities Enrolled by Their Parents in Private Schools
  When FAPE is at Issue 347
300.148 Placement of children by parents when FAPE is at issue 347
SEA Responsibility for General Supervision and Implementation
  of Procedural Safeguards 348
300.149 SEA responsibility for general supervision 348
300.150 SEA implementation of procedural safeguards 348
State Complaint Procedures 348
300.151 Adoption of State complaint procedures 348
300.152 Minimum State complaint procedures 349
300.153 Filing a complaint 349
Methods of Ensuring Service 350
300.154 Methods of ensuring services 350
300.155 Hearings relating to LEA eligibility 352
300.156 Personnel qualifications 352
300.157 Performance goals and indicators 353
 300.158 to 300.161 [Reserved] 353
300.162 to 300.173 [omitted] 353
300.174 Prohibition on mandatory medication 353
300.175 to 300.186 [omitted] 353
By-pass for Children in Private Schools 353
300.190 By-pass—general 353
300.191 Provisions for services under a by-pass 353
300.192 Notice of intent to implement a by-pass 354
300.193 Request to show cause 354
300.194 Show cause hearing 354
300.195 Decision 355
300.196 Filing requirements 355
300.197 Judicial review 355
300.198 Continuation of a by-pass 355
300.199 to 300.208 [omitted] 355
300.209 Treatment of charter schools and their students 355
300.210 Purchase of instructional materials 356
300.211 Information for SEA 356
300.212 Public information 356
300.213 Records regarding migratory children with disabilities 356
 300.214 to 300.219 [Reserved] 356
300.220 to 300.230 [omitted] 356

Subpart D. Evaluations, Eligibility Determinations, Individualized Education Programs, and Educational Placements

Parental Consent 356
300.300 Parental consent 356
Evaluations and Reevaluations 358
300.301 Initial evaluations 358
300.302 Screening for instructional purposes is not evaluation 358
300.303 Reevaluations 359
300.304 Evaluation procedures 359
300.305 Additional requirements for evaluations and reevaluations 360
300.306 Determination of eligibility 361
Additional Procedures for Identifying Children with Specific Learning Disabilities 361
300.307 Specific learning disabilities 361
300.308 Additional group members 361
300.309 Determining the existence of a specific learning disability 361
300.310 Observation 362
300.311 Specific documentation for the eligibility determination 362
Individualized Education Programs 363
300.320 Definition of individualized education program 363
300.321 IEP Team 364
300.322 Parent participation 365
300.323 When IEPs must be in effect 366
Development of IEP 367
300.324 Development, review, and revision of IEP 367
300.325 Private school placements by public agencies 369
300.326 [Reserved] 369
300.327 Educational placements 369
300.328 Alternative means of meeting participation 369
Subpart E. Procedural Safeguards 369
Due Process Procedures for Parents and Children 369
300.500 Responsibility of SEA and other public agencies 369
300.501 Opportunity to examine records; parent participation in meetings 369
300.502 Independent educational evaluation 370
300.503 Prior notice by the public agency; content of notice 371
300.504 Procedural safeguards notice 372
300.505 Electronic mail 372
300.506 Mediation 372
300.507 Filing a due process complaint 373
300.508 Due process complaint 373
300.509 Model forms 374
300.510 Resolution process 375
300.511 Impartial due process hearing 376
300.512 Hearing rights 376
300.513 Hearing decisions 377
300.514 Finality of decision; appeal; impartial review 377
300.515 Timelines and convenience of hearings and reviews 378
300.516 Civil action 378
300.517 Attorneys' fees 378

300.518 Child's status during proceedings 380
300.519 Surrogate parents 380
300.520 Transfer of parental rights at age of majority 381
300.521 to 300.529 [Reserved] 381
Discipline Procedures 381
300.530 Authority of school personnel 381
300.531 Determination of setting 383
300.532 Appeal 383
300.533 Placement during appeals 384
300.534 Protections for children not determined eligible for special education and related services 384
300.535 Referral to and action by law enforcement and judicial authorities 384
300.536 Change of placement because of disciplinary removals 385
300.537 State enforcement mechanisms 385
300.538 to 300.599 [Reserved] 385

UNITED NATIONS CONVENTION ON THE RIGHTS OF PERSONS WITH DISABILITIES

Annex I Convention on the Rights of Persons with Disabilities 387
Preamble 387
Article 1 Purpose 389
Article 2 Definitions 389
Article 3 General principles 390
Article 4 General obligation 390
Article 5 Equality and non-discrimination 391
Article 6 Women with disabilities 391
Article 7 Children with disabilities 391
Article 8 Awareness-raising 391
Article 9 Accessibility 392
Article 10 Right to life 392
Article 11 Situations of risk and humanitarian emergencies 392
Article 12 Equal recognition before the law 392
Article 13 Access to justice 393
Article 14 Liberty and security of person 393
Article 15 Freedom from torture or cruel, inhuman or degrading treatment or punishment 393
Article 16 Freedom from exploitation, violence or abuse 393
Article 17 Protecting the integrity of the person 394
Article 18 Liberty of movement and nationality 394
Article 19 Living independently and being included in the community 394
Article 20 Personal mobility 394
Article 21 Freedom of expression of opinion and access to information 394
Article 22 Respect for privacy 395
Article 23 Respect for home and the family 395
Article 24 Education 395
Article 25 Health 396

Article 26 Habilitation and rehabilitation 397
Article 27 Work and employment 397
Article 28 Adequate standard of living and social protection 398
Article 29 Participation in political and public life 398
Article 30 Participation in cultural life 399
Article 31 Statistics and data collection 399
Article 32 International cooperation 399
Article 33 National implementation and monitoring 400
Article 34 Committee on the Rights of Persons with Disabilities 400
Article 35 Reports by States Parties 401
Article 36 Consideration of reports 401
Article 37 Cooperation between States Parties and the Committee 402
Article 38 Relationship of the Committee to other bodies 402
Article 39 Report of the Committee 402
Article 40 Conference of States Parties 402
Article 41 Depositary 402
Article 42 Signature 402
Article 43 Consent to be bound 403
Article 44 Regional integration organizations 403
Article 45 Entry into force 403
Article 46 Reservations 403
Article 47 Amendments 403
Article 48 Denunciation 404
Article 49 Accessible formation 404
Article 50 Authentic texts 404
ANNEX II Optional Protocol to the Convention on the Rights of Persons with Disabilities 404

PREFACE

This Handbook includes reference material relevant to interpreting federal law prohibiting discrimination on the basis of disability. The Sixth Edition also includes the recently adopted United Nations Convention on the Rights of Individuals with Disabilities.

The Handbook begins by including reference material relevant to interpreting the Americans with Disabilities Act of 1990 ("the ADA"). After the statutory language of each Title of the ADA, the Handbook includes the regulations and interpretive guidance promulgated by the lead regulatory agency. Prior editions of the Handbook also contained other guidance and material from the Technical Assistance Manual. In the interests of saving space, this and other relevant material has been omitted but can be found at www.eeoc.gov.

The Handbook next contains the statutory language of Section 504 of the Rehabilitation Act and some of the regulations promulgated to enforce Section 504.

The Handbook also contains the Fair Housing Act Amendments of 1988 ("FHAA") and the regulations promulgated by the Department of Housing and Urban Development to enforce the FHAA. It also contains excerpts from the Civil Rights Act of 1991 which relate to the issue of damages in employment discrimination actions.

The Handbook next contains the Individuals with Disabilities Education Act, including the amendments made as part of the reauthorization in late 2004. Excerpts from the regulations promulgated by the United States Department of Education to enforce the IDEA are also included. This material is new to the Sixth Edition.

Finally, the Handbook contains the text of the United Nations Convention on the Rights of Individuals with Disabilities.

A disk version of this volume will be made available upon request to individuals with disabilities who are unable to utilize the written version.

Ruth Colker
May 2007

ACKNOWLEDGMENTS

The Sixth Edition of this Handbook was made possible, in part, by generous research assistance support at the Ohio State University Moritz College of Law. I appreciate the effort that Adam Milani made in adding the IDEA to the prior edition of this Handbook. I thank Katherine Hall, at the Moritz Law Library, who helped me update this Edition with the IDEA regulations and the United Nations Convention of the Rights of Individuals with Disabilities. Megan St. Ledger and Traci Martinez helped me correct some errors in prior editions.

ADA GENERAL PROVISIONS

42 U.S.C. §
- 12101 Findings and purposes
- 12102 Definitions

ADA GENERAL PROVISIONS

§ 12101. Findings and purposes

(a) Findings

The Congress finds that—

(1) some 43,000,000 Americans have one or more physical or mental disabilities, and this number is increasing as the population as a whole is growing older;

(2) historically, society has tended to isolate and segregate individuals with disabilities, and, despite some improvements, such forms of discrimination against individuals with disabilities continue to be a serious and pervasive social problem;

(3) discrimination against individuals with disabilities persists in such critical areas as employment, housing, public accommodations, education, transportation, communication, recreation, institutionalization, health services, voting, and access to public services;

(4) unlike individuals who have experienced discrimination on the basis of race, color, sex, national origin, religion, or age, individuals who have experienced discrimination on the basis of disability have often had no legal recourse to redress such discrimination;

(5) individuals with disabilities continually encounter various forms of discrimination, including outright intentional exclusion, the discriminatory effects of architectural, transportation, and communication barriers, overprotective rules and policies, failure to make modifications to existing facilities and practices, exclusionary qualification standards and criteria, segregation, and relegation to lesser services, programs, activities, benefits, jobs, or other opportunities;

(6) census data, national polls, and other studies have documented that people with disabilities, as a group, occupy an inferior status in our society, and are severely disadvantaged socially, vocationally, economically, and educationally;

(7) individuals with disabilities are a discrete and insular minority who have been faced with restrictions and limitations, subjected to a history of purposeful unequal treatment, and relegated to a position of political powerlessness in our society, based on characteristics that are beyond the control of such individuals and resulting from stereotypic assumptions not truly indicative of the individual ability of such individuals to participate in, and contribute to, society;

(8) the Nation's proper goals regarding individuals with disabilities are to assure equality of opportunity, full participation, independent living, and economic self-sufficiency for such individuals; and

(9) the continuing existence of unfair and unnecessary discrimination and prejudice denies people with disabilities the opportunity to compete on an equal basis and to pursue those opportunities for which our free society is justifiably famous, and costs the United States billions of dollars in unnecessary expenses resulting from dependency and nonproductivity.

(b) Purpose

It is the purpose of this chapter—

(1) to provide a clear and comprehensive national mandate for the elimination of discrimination against individuals with disabilities;

(2) to provide clear, strong, consistent, enforceable standards addressing discrimination against individuals with disabilities;

(3) to ensure that the Federal Government plays a central role in enforcing the standards established in this chapter on behalf of individuals with disabilities; and

(4) to invoke the sweep of congressional authority, including the power to enforce the fourteenth amendment and to regulate commerce, in order to address the major areas of discrimination faced day-to-day by people with disabilities.

§ 12102. Definitions

As used in this chapter:

(1) Auxiliary aids and services

The term "auxiliary aids and services" includes—

(A) qualified interpreters or other effective methods of making aurally delivered materials available to individuals with hearing impairments;

(B) qualified readers, taped texts, or other effective methods of making visually delivered materials available to individuals with visual impairments;

(C) acquisition or modification of equipment or devices; and

(D) other similar services and actions.

(2) Disability

The term "disability" means, with respect to an individual—

(A) a physical or mental impairment that substantially limits one or more of the major life activities of such individual;

    (B) a record of such an impairment; or

    (C) being regarded as having such an impairment.

(3) State

The term "State" means each of the several States, the District of Columbia, the Commonwealth of Puerto Rico, Guam, American Samoa, the Virgin Islands, the Trust Territory of the Pacific Islands, and the Commonwealth of the Northern Mariana Islands.

ADA TITLE I
EMPLOYMENT

42 U.S.C. §

12111	Definitions
12112	Discrimination
12113	Defenses
12114	Illegal use of drugs and alcohol
12115	Posting notices
12116	Regulations
12117	Enforcement

ADA TITLE I
EMPLOYMENT

§ 12111. Definitions

As used in this subchapter:

(1) Commission

The term "Commission" means the Equal Employment Opportunity Commission established by section 2000e-4 of this title.

(2) Covered entity

The term "covered entity" means an employer, employment agency, labor organization, or joint labor-management committee.

(3) Direct threat

The term "direct threat" means a significant risk to the health or safety of others that cannot be eliminated by reasonable accommodation.

(4) Employee

The term "employee" means an individual employed by an employer. With respect to employment in a foreign country, such term includes an individual who is a citizen of the United States.

(5) Employer

    (A) In general

The term "employer" means a person engaged in an industry affecting commerce who has 15 or more employees for each working day in each of 20 or more calendar weeks in the current or preceding calendar year, and any agent of such person, except that, for two years following the effective date of this subchapter, an employer means a person engaged in an industry affecting commerce who has 25 or more employees for each working day in each of 20 or more calendar weeks in the current or preceding year, and any agent of such person.

    (B) Exceptions

The term "employer" does not include—

    (i) the United States, a corporation wholly owned by the government of the United States, or an Indian tribe; or

    (ii) a bona fide private membership club (other than a labor organization) that is exempt from taxation under section 501(c) of Title 26.

(6) Illegal use of drugs

    (A) In general

The term "illegal use of drugs" means the use of drugs, the possession or distribution of which is unlawful under the Controlled Substances Act (21 U.S.C. 812). Such term does not include the use of a drug taken under supervision by a licensed health care professional, or other uses authorized by the Controlled Substances Act [21 U.S.C.A. § 801 et seq.] or other provisions of Federal law.

    (B) Drugs

The term "drug" means a controlled substance, as defined in schedules I through V of section 202 of the Controlled Substances Act [21 U.S.C.A. § 812].

(7) Person, etc.

The terms "person", "labor organization", "employment agency", "commerce", and "industry affecting commerce", shall have the same meaning given such terms in section 2000e of this title.

(8) Qualified individual with a disability

The term "qualified individual with a disability" means an individual with a disability who, with or without reasonable accommodation, can perform the essential functions of the employment position that such individual holds or desires. For the purposes of this subchapter, consideration shall be given to the employer's judgment as to what functions of a job are essential, and if an employer has prepared a written description before advertising or interviewing applicants for the job, this description shall be considered evidence of the essential functions of the job.

(9) Reasonable accommodation

The term "reasonable accommodation" may include—

    (A) making existing facilities used by employees readily accessible to and usable by individuals with disabilities; and

    (B) job restructuring, part-time or modified work schedules, reassignment to a vacant position, acquisition or modification of equipment or devices, appropriate adjustment or modifications of examinations, training materials or policies, the provision of qualified readers or interpreters, and other similar accommodations for individuals with disabilities.

(10) Undue hardship

(A) In general

The term "undue hardship" means an action requiring significant difficulty or expense, when considered in light of the factors set forth in subparagraph (B).

(B) Factors to be considered

In determining whether an accommodation would impose an undue hardship on a covered entity, factors to be considered include—

(i) the nature and cost of the accommodation needed under this chapter;

(ii) the overall financial resources of the facility or facilities involved in the provision of the reasonable accommodation; the number of persons employed at such facility; the effect on expenses and resources, or the impact otherwise of such accommodation upon the operation of the facility;

(iii) the overall financial resources of the covered entity; the overall size of the business of a covered entity with respect to the number of its employees; the number, type, and location of its facilities; and

(iv) the type of operation or operations of the covered entity, including the composition, structure, and functions of the work force of such entity; the geographic separateness, administrative, or fiscal relationship of the facility or facilities in question to the covered entity.

§ 12112. Discrimination

(a) General rule

No covered entity shall discriminate against a qualified individual with a disability because of the disability of such individual in regard to job application procedures, the hiring, advancement, or discharge of employees, employee compensation, job training, and other terms, conditions, and privileges of employment.

(b) Construction

As used in subsection (a) of this section, the term "discriminate" includes—

(1) limiting, segregating, or classifying a job applicant or employee in a way that adversely affects the opportunities or status of such applicant or employee because of the disability of such applicant or employee;

(2) participating in a contractual or other arrangement or relationship that has the effect of subjecting a covered entity's qualified applicant or employee with a disability to the discrimination prohibited by this subchapter (such relationship includes a relationship with an employment or referral agency, labor union, an organization providing fringe benefits to an employee of the covered entity, or an organization providing training and apprenticeship programs);

(3) utilizing standards, criteria, or methods of administration—

(A) that have the effect of discrimination on the basis of disability; or

(B) that perpetuate the discrimination of others who are subject to common administrative control;

(4) excluding or otherwise denying equal jobs or benefits to a qualified individual because of the known disability of an individual with whom the qualified individual is known to have a relationship or association;

(5) (A) not making reasonable accommodations to the known physical or mental limitations of an otherwise qualified individual with a disability who is an applicant or employee, unless such covered entity can demonstrate that the accommodation would impose an undue hardship on the operation of the business of such covered entity; or

(B) denying employment opportunities to a job applicant or employee who is an otherwise qualified individual with a disability, if such denial is based on the need of such covered entity to make reasonable accommodation to the physical or mental impairments of the employee or applicant;

(6) using qualification standards, employment tests or other selection criteria that screen out or tend to screen out an individual with a disability or a class of individuals with disabilities unless the standard, test or other selection criteria, as used by the covered entity, is shown to be job-related for the position in question and is consistent with business necessity; and

(7) failing to select and administer tests concerning employment in the most effective manner to ensure that, when such test is administered to a job applicant or employee who has a disability that impairs sensory, manual, or speaking skills, such test results accurately reflect the skills, aptitude, or whatever other factor of such applicant or employee that such test purports to measure, rather than reflecting the impaired sensory, manual, or speaking skills of such employee or applicant (except where such skills are the factors that the test purports to measure).

(c) Covered entities in foreign countries

(1) In general

It shall not be unlawful under this section for a covered entity to take any action that constitutes discrimination under this section with respect to an employee in a workplace in a foreign country if compliance with this section would cause such covered entity to violate the law of the foreign country in which such workplace is located.

(2) Control of corporation

(A) Presumption

If an employer controls a corporation whose place of incorporation is a foreign country, any practice that constitutes discrimination under this section and is engaged in by such corporation shall be presumed to be engaged in by such employer.

(B) Exception

This section shall not apply with respect to the foreign operations of an employer that is a foreign person not controlled by an American employer.

(C) Determination

For purposes of this paragraph, the determination of whether an employer controls a corporation shall be based on—

(i) the interrelation of operations;

(ii) the common management;

(iii) the centralized control of labor relations; and

(iv) the common ownership or financial control, of the employer and the corporation.

(d) Medical examinations and inquiries

(1) In general

The prohibition against discrimination as referred to in subsection (a) of this section shall include medical examinations and inquiries.

(2) Pre-employment

(A) Prohibited examination or inquiry

Except as provided in paragraph (3), a covered entity shall not conduct a medical examination or make inquiries of a job applicant as to whether such applicant is an individual with a disability or as to the nature or severity of such disability.

(B) Acceptable inquiry

A covered entity may make pre-employment inquiries into the ability of an applicant to perform job-related functions.

(3) Employment entrance examination

A covered entity may require a medical examination after an offer of employment has been made to a job applicant and prior to the commencement of the employment duties of such applicant, and may condition an offer of employment on the results of such examination, if—

(A) all entering employees are subjected to such an examination regardless of disability;

(B) information obtained regarding the medical condition or history of the applicant is collected and maintained on separate forms and in separate medical files and is treated as a confidential medical record, except that—

(i) supervisors and managers may be informed regarding necessary restrictions on the work or duties of the employee and necessary accommodations;

(ii) first aid and safety personnel may be informed, when appropriate, if the disability might require emergency treatment; and

(iii) government officials investigating compliance with this chapter shall be provided relevant information on request; and

(C) the results of such examination are used only in accordance with this subchapter.

(4) Examination and inquiry

(A) Prohibited examinations and inquiries

A covered entity shall not require a medical examination and shall not make inquiries of an employee as to whether such employee is an individual with a disability or as to the nature or severity of the disability, unless such examination or inquiry is shown to be job-related and consistent with business necessity.

(B) Acceptable examinations and inquiries

A covered entity may conduct voluntary medical examinations, including voluntary medical histories, which are part of an employee health program available to employees at that work site. A covered entity may make inquiries into the ability of an employee to perform job-related functions.

(C) Requirement

Information obtained under subparagraph (B) regarding the medical condition or history of any employee are subject to the requirements of subparagraphs (B) and (C) of paragraph (3).

§ 12113. Defenses

(a) In general

It may be a defense to a charge of discrimination under this chapter that an alleged application of qualification standards, tests, or selection criteria that screen out or tend to screen out or otherwise deny a job or benefit to an individual with a disability has been shown to be job-related and consistent with business necessity, and such performance cannot be accomplished by reasonable accommodation, as required under this subchapter.

(b) Qualification standards

The term "qualification standards" may include a requirement that an individual shall not pose a direct threat to the health or safety of other individuals in the workplace.

(c) Religious entities

(1) In general

This subchapter shall not prohibit a religious corporation, association, educational institution, or society from giving preference in employment to individuals of a particular religion to perform work connected with the carrying on by such corporation, association, educational institution, or society of its activities.

(2) Religious tenets requirement

Under this subchapter, a religious organization may require that all applicants and employees conform to the religious tenets of such organization.

(d) List of infectious and communicable diseases

(1) In general

The Secretary of Health and Human Services, not later than 6 months after July 26, 1990, shall—

(A) review all infectious and communicable diseases which may be transmitted through handling the food supply;

(B) publish a list of infectious and communicable diseases which are transmitted through handling the food supply;

(C) publish the methods by which such diseases are transmitted; and

(D) widely disseminate such information regarding the list of diseases and their modes of transmissibility to the general public.

Such list shall be updated annually.

(2) Applications

In any case in which an individual has an infectious or communicable disease that is transmitted to others through the handling of food, that is included on the list developed by the Secretary of Health and Human Services under paragraph (1), and which cannot be eliminated by reasonable accommodation, a covered entity may refuse to assign or continue to assign such individual to a job involving food handling.

(3) Construction

Nothing in this chapter shall be construed to preempt, modify, or amend any State, county, or local law, ordinance, or regulation applicable to food handling which is designed to protect the public health from individuals who pose a significant risk to the health or safety of others, which cannot be eliminated by reasonable accommodation, pursuant to the list of infectious or communicable diseases and the modes of transmissibility published by the Secretary of Health and Human Services.

§ 12114. Illegal use of drugs and alcohol

(a) Qualified individual with a disability

For purposes of this subchapter, the term "qualified individual with a disability" shall not include any employee or applicant who is currently engaging in the illegal use of drugs, when the covered entity acts on the basis of such use.

(b) Rules of construction

Nothing in subsection (a) of this section shall be construed to exclude as a qualified individual with a disability an individual who—

(1) has successfully completed a supervised drug rehabilitation program and is no longer engaging in the illegal use of drugs, or has otherwise been rehabilitated successfully and is no longer engaging in such use;

(2) is participating in a supervised rehabilitation program and is no longer engaging in such use; or

(3) is erroneously regarded as engaging in such use, but is not engaging in such use;

except that it shall not be a violation of this chapter for a covered entity to adopt or administer reasonable policies or procedures, including but not limited to drug testing, designed to ensure that an individual described in paragraph (1) or (2) is no longer engaging in the illegal use of drugs.

(c) Authority of covered entity

A covered entity—

(1) may prohibit the illegal use of drugs and the use of alcohol at the workplace by all employees;

(2) may require that employees shall not be under the influence of alcohol or be engaging in the illegal use of drugs at the workplace;

(3) may require that employees behave in conformance with the requirements established under the Drug-Free Workplace Act of 1988 (41 U.S.C. 701 et seq.);

(4) may hold an employee who engages in the illegal use of drugs or who is an alcoholic to the same qualification standards for employment or job performance and behavior that such entity holds other employees, even if any unsatisfactory performance or behavior is related to the drug use or alcoholism of such employee; and

(5) may, with respect to Federal regulations regarding alcohol and the illegal use of drugs, require that—

(A) employees comply with the standards established in such regulations of the Department of Defense, if the employees of the covered entity are employed in an industry subject to such regulations, including complying with regulations (if any) that apply to employment in sensitive positions in such an industry, in the case of employees of the covered entity who are employed in such positions (as defined in the regulations of the Department of Defense);

(B) employees comply with the standards established in such regulations of the Nuclear Regulatory Commission, if the employees of the covered entity are employed in an industry subject to such regulations, including complying with regulations (if any) that apply to employment in sensitive positions in such an industry, in the case of employees of the covered entity who are employed in such positions (as defined in the regulations of the Nuclear Regulatory Commission); and

(C) employees comply with the standards established in such regulations of the Department of Transportation, if the employees of the covered entity are employed in a transportation industry subject to such regulations, including complying with such regulations (if any) that apply to employment in sensitive positions in such an industry, in the case of employees of the covered entity who are employed in such positions (as defined in the regulations of the Department of Transportation).

(d) Drug testing

(1) In general

For purposes of this subchapter, a test to determine the illegal use of drugs shall not be considered a medical examination.

(2) Construction

Nothing in this subchapter shall be construed to encourage, prohibit, or authorize the conducting of drug testing for the illegal use of drugs by job applicants or employees or making employment decisions based on such test results.

(e) Transportation employees

Nothing in this subchapter shall be construed to encourage, prohibit, restrict, or authorize the otherwise lawful exercise by entities subject to the jurisdiction of the Department of Transportation of authority to—

(1) test employees of such entities in, and applicants for, positions involving safety-sensitive duties for the illegal use of drugs and for on-duty impairment by alcohol; and

(2) remove such persons who test positive for illegal use of drugs and on-duty impairment by alcohol pursuant to paragraph (1) from safety-sensitive duties in implementing subsection (c) of this section.

§ 12115. Posting notices

Every employer, employment agency, labor organization, or joint labor-management committee covered under this title shall post notices in an accessible format to applicants, employees, and members describing the applicable provisions of this Act, in the manner prescribed by section 711 of the Civil Rights Act of 1964 (42 U.S.C. 2000e-10).

§ 12116. Regulations

Not later than 1 year after the date of enactment of this Act [enacted July 26, 1990], the Commission shall issue regulations in an accessible format to carry out this title in accordance with subchapter II of chapter 5 of title 5, United States Code [5 USCS §§ 551 et seq.].

§ 12117. Enforcement

(a) Powers, remedies, and procedures

The powers, remedies, and procedures set forth in sections 2000e-4, 2000e-5, 2000e-6, 2000e-8, and 2000e-9 of this title shall be the powers, remedies, and procedures this subchapter provides to the Commission, to the Attorney General, or to any person alleging discrimination on the basis of disability in violation of any provision of this chapter, or regulations promulgated under section 12116 of this title, concerning employment.

(b) Coordination

The agencies with enforcement authority for actions which allege employment discrimination under this subchapter and under the Rehabilitation Act of 1973 [29 U.S.C.A. § 701 et seq.] shall develop procedures to ensure that administrative complaints filed under this subchapter and under the Rehabilitation Act of 1973 [29 U.S.C.A. § 701 et seq.] are dealt with in a manner that avoids duplication of effort and prevents imposition of inconsistent or conflicting standards for the same requirements under this subchapter and the Rehabilitation Act of 1973 [29 U.S.C.A. § 701 et seq.]. The Commission, the Attorney General, and the Office of Federal Contract Compliance Programs shall establish such coordinating mechanisms (similar to provisions contained in the joint regulations promulgated by the Commission and the Attorney General at part 42 of title 28 and part 1691 of title 29, Code of Federal Regulations, and the Memorandum of Understanding between the Commission and the Office of Federal Contract Compliance Programs dated January 16, 1981 (46 Fed. Reg. 7435, January 23, 1981)) in regulations implementing this subchapter and Rehabilitation Act of 1973 [29 U.S.C.A. § 701 et seq.] not later than 18 months after July 26, 1990.

ADA TITLE I
EEOC REGULATIONS

29 C.F.R. §
- 1630.1 Purpose, applicability and construction
- 1630.2 Definitions
- 1630.3 Exceptions to the definitions of "Disability" and "Qualified Individual with a Disability"
- 1630.4 Discrimination Prohibited
- 1630.5 Limiting, Segregating and Classifying
- 1630.6 Contractual or Other Arrangements
- 1630.7 Standards, criteria, or methods of administration
- 1630.8 Relationship or Association With an Individual With a Disability
- 1630.9 Not Making Reasonable Accommodation
- 1630.10 Qualification Standards, Tests, and Other Selection Criteria
- 1630.11 Administration of Tests
- 1630.12 Retaliation and coercion
- 1630.13 Prohibited Medical Examinations and Inquiries
- 1630.14 Medical Examinations and Inquiries Specifically Permitted
- 1630.15 Defenses
- 1630.16 Specific Activities Permitted

ADA TITLE I
EEOC REGULATIONS

§ 1630.1 Purpose, applicability, and construction.

(a) Purpose. The purpose of this part is to implement title I of the Americans with Disabilities Act (42 U.S.C. 12101, et seq.) (ADA), requiring equal employment opportunities for qualified individuals with disabilities, and sections 3(2), 3(3), 501, 503, 506(e), 508, 510, and 511 of the ADA as those sections pertain to the employment of qualified individuals with disabilities.

(b) Applicability. This part applies to "covered entities" as defined at § 1630.2(b).

(c) Construction—

(1) In general. Except as otherwise provided in this part, this part does not apply a lesser standard than the standards applied under title V of the Rehabilitation Act of 1973 (29 U.S.C. 790-794a), or the regulations issued by Federal agencies pursuant to that title.

(2) Relationship to other laws. This part does not invalidate or limit the remedies, rights, and procedures of any Federal law or law of any State or political subdivision of any State or jurisdiction that provides greater or equal protection for the rights of individuals with disabilities than are afforded by this part.

§ 1630.2 Definitions.

(a) Commission means the Equal Employment Opportunity Commission established by section 705 of the Civil Rights Act of 1964 (42 U.S.C. 2000e-4).

(b) Covered Entity means an employer, employment agency, labor organization, or joint labor management committee.

(c) Person, labor organization, employment agency, commerce and industry affecting commerce shall have the same meaning given those terms in section 701 of the Civil Rights Act of 1964 (42 U.S.C. 2000e).

(d) State means each of the several States, the District of Columbia, the Commonwealth of Puerto Rico, Guam, American Samoa, the Virgin Islands, the Trust Territory of the Pacific Islands, and the Commonwealth of the Northern Mariana Islands.

(e) Employer—

(1) In general. The term employer means a person engaged in an industry affecting commerce who has 15 or more employees for each working day in each of 20 or more calendar weeks in the current or preceding calendar year, and any agent of such person, except that, from July 26, 1992 through July 25, 1994, an employer means a person engaged in an industry affecting commerce who has 25 or more employees for each working day in each of 20 or more calendar weeks in the current or preceding year and any agent of such person.

(2) Exceptions. The term employer does not include—

(i) The United States, a corporation wholly owned by the government of the United States, or an Indian tribe; or

(ii) A bona fide private membership club (other than a labor organization) that is exempt from taxation under section 501(c) of the Internal Revenue Code of 1986.

(f) Employee means an individual employed by an employer.

(g) Disability means, with respect to an individual—

(1) A physical or mental impairment that substantially limits one or more of the major life activities of such individual;

(2) A record of such an impairment; or

(3) being regarded as having such an impairment.

(See § 1630.3 for exceptions to this definition.)

(h) Physical or mental impairment means:

(1) Any physiological disorder, or condition, cosmetic disfigurement, or anatomical loss affecting one or more of the following body systems: neurological, musculoskeletal, special sense organs, respiratory (including speech organs), cardiovascular, reproductive, digestive, genito-urinary, hemic and lymphatic, skin, and endocrine; or

(2) Any mental or psychological disorder, such as mental retardation, organic brain syndrome, emotional or mental illness, and specific learning disabilities.

(i) Major Life Activities means functions such as caring for oneself, performing manual tasks, walking, seeing, hearing, speaking, breathing, learning, and working.

(j) Substantially limits—

(1) The term substantially limits means:

(i) Unable to perform a major life activity that the average person in the general population can perform; or

(ii) Significantly restricted as to the condition, manner or duration under which an individual can perform a particular major life activity as compared to the condition, manner, or duration under which the average person in the general population can perform that same major life activity.

(2) The following factors should be considered in determining whether an individual is substantially limited in a major life activity:

(i) The nature and severity of the impairment;

(ii) The duration or expected duration of the impairment; and

(iii) The permanent or long term impact, or the expected permanent or long term impact of or resulting from the impairment.

(3) With respect to the major life activity of working—

(i) The term substantially limits means significantly restricted in the ability to perform either a class of jobs or a broad range of jobs in various classes as compared to the average person having comparable training, skills and abilities. The inability to perform a single, particular job does not constitute a substantial limitation in the major life activity of working.

(ii) In addition to the factors listed in paragraph (j)(2) of this section, the following factors may be considered in determining whether an individual is substantially limited in the major life activity of "working":

(A) The geographical area to which the individual has reasonable access;

(B) The job from which the individual has been disqualified because of an impairment, and the number and types of jobs utilizing similar training, knowledge, skills or abilities, within that geographical area, from which the individual is also disqualified because of the impairment (class of jobs); and/or

(C) The job from which the individual has been disqualified because of an impairment, and the number and types of other jobs not utilizing similar training, knowledge, skills or abilities, within that geographical area, from which the individual is also disqualified because of the impairment (broad range of jobs in various classes).

(k) Has a record of such impairment means has a history of, or has been misclassified as having, a mental or physical impairment that substantially limits one or more major life activities.

(l) Is regarded as having such an impairment means:

(1) Has a physical or mental impairment that does not substantially limit major life activities but is treated by a covered entity as constituting such limitation;

(2) Has a physical or mental impairment that substantially limits major life activities only as a result of the attitudes of others toward such impairment; or

(3) Has none of the impairments defined in paragraphs (h) (1) or (2) of this section but is treated by a covered entity as having a substantially limiting impairment.

(m) Qualified individual with a disability means an individual with a disability who satisfies the requisite skill, experience, education and other job-related requirements of the employment position such individual holds or desires, and who, with or without reasonable accommodation, can perform the essential functions of such position. (See § 1630.3 for exceptions to this definition).

(n) Essential functions.—

(1) In general. The term essential functions means the fundamental job duties of the employment position the individual with a disability holds or desires. The term "essential functions" does not include the marginal functions of the position.

(2) A job function may be considered essential for any of several reasons, including but not limited to the following:

(i) The function may be essential because the reason the position exists is to perform that function;

(ii) The function may be essential because of the limited number of employees available among whom the performance of that job function can be distributed; and/or

(iii) The function may be highly specialized so that the incumbent in the position is hired for his or her expertise or ability to perform the particular function.

(3) Evidence of whether a particular function is essential includes, but is not limited to:

(i) The employer's judgment as to which functions are essential;

(ii) Written job descriptions prepared before advertising or interviewing applicants for the job;

(iii) The amount of time spent on the job performing the function;

(iv) The consequences of not requiring the incumbent to perform the function;

(v) The terms of a collective bargaining agreement;

(vi) The work experience of past incumbents in the job; and/or

(vii) The current work experience of incumbents in similar jobs.

(o) Reasonable accommodation.

(1) The term reasonable accommodation means:

(i) Modifications or adjustments to a job application process that enable a qualified applicant with a disability to be considered for the position such qualified applicant desires; or

(ii) Modifications or adjustments to the work environment, or to the manner or circumstances under which the position held or desired is customarily performed, that enable a qualified individual with a disability to perform the essential functions of that position; or

(iii) Modifications or adjustments that enable a covered entity's employee with a disability to enjoy equal benefits and privileges of employment as are enjoyed by its other similarly situated employees without disabilities.

(2) Reasonable accommodation may include but is not limited to:

(i) Making existing facilities used by employees readily accessible to and usable by individuals with disabilities; and

(ii) Job restructuring; part-time or modified work schedules; reassignment to a vacant position; acquisition or modifications of equipment or devices; appropriate adjustment or modifications of examinations, training materials, or policies; the provision of qualified readers or interpreters; and other similar accommodations for individuals with disabilities.

(3) To determine the appropriate reasonable accommodation it may be necessary for the covered entity to initiate an informal, interactive process with the qualified individual with a disability in need of the accommodation. This process should identify the precise limitations resulting from the disability and potential reasonable accommodations that could overcome those limitations.

(p) Undue hardship—

(1) In general. Undue hardship means, with respect to the provision of an accommodation, significant difficulty or expense incurred by a covered entity, when considered in light of the factors set forth in paragraph (p)(2) of this section.

(2) Factors to be considered. In determining whether an accommodation would impose an undue hardship on a covered entity, factors to be considered include:

(i) The nature and net cost of the accommodation needed under this part, taking into consideration the availability of tax credits and deductions, and/or outside funding;

(ii) The overall financial resources of the facility or facilities involved in the provision of the reasonable accommodation, the number of persons employed at such facility, and the effect on expenses and resources;

(iii) The overall financial resources of the covered entity, the overall size of the business of the covered entity with respect to the number of its employees, and the number, type and location of its facilities;

(iv) The type of operation or operations of the covered entity, including the composition, structure and functions of the work force of such entity, and the geographic separateness and administrative or fiscal relationship of the facility or facilities in question to the covered entity; and

(v) The impact of the accommodation upon the operation of the facility, including the impact on the ability of other employees to perform their duties and the impact on the facility's ability to conduct business.

(q) Qualification standards means the personal and professional attributes including the skill, experience, education, physical, medical, safety and other requirements established by a covered entity as requirements which an individual must meet in order to be eligible for the position held or desired.

(r) Direct Threat means a significant risk of substantial harm to the health or safety of the individual or others that cannot be eliminated or reduced by reasonable accommodation. The determination that an individual poses a "direct threat" shall be based on an individualized assessment of the individual's present ability to safely perform the essential functions of the job. This assessment shall be based on a reasonable medical judgment that relies on the most current medical knowledge and/or on the best available objective evidence. In determining whether an individual would pose a direct threat, the factors to be considered include:

(1) The duration of the risk;

(2) The nature and severity of the potential harm;

(3) The likelihood that the potential harm will occur; and

(4) The imminence of the potential harm.

§ 1630.3 Exceptions to the definitions of "Disability" and "Qualified Individual with a Disability."

(a) The terms disability and qualified individual with a disability do not include individuals currently engaging in the illegal use of drugs, when the covered entity acts on the basis of such use.

(1) Drug means a controlled substance, as defined in schedules I through V of Section 202 of the Controlled Substances Act (21 U.S.C. 812)

(2) Illegal use of drugs means the use of drugs the possession or distribution of which is unlawful under the Controlled Substances Act, as periodically updated by the Food and Drug Administration. This term does not include the use of a drug taken under the supervision of a licensed health care professional, or other uses authorized by the Controlled Substances Act or other provisions of Federal law.

(b) However, the terms disability and qualified individual with a disability may not exclude an individual who:

(1) Has successfully completed a supervised drug rehabilitation program and is no longer engaging in the illegal use of drugs, or has otherwise been rehabilitated successfully and is no longer engaging in the illegal use of drugs; or

(2) Is participating in a supervised rehabilitation program and is no longer engaging in such use; or

(3) Is erroneously regarded as engaging in such use, but is not engaging in such use.

(c) It shall not be a violation of this part for a covered entity to adopt or administer reasonable policies or procedures, including but not limited to drug testing, designed to ensure that an individual described in paragraph (b) (1) or (2) of this section is no longer engaging in the illegal use of drugs. (See § 1630.16(c) Drug testing).

(d) Disability does not include:

(1) Transvestism, transsexualism, pedophilia, exhibitionism, voyeurism, gender identity disorders not resulting from physical impairments, or other sexual behavior disorders;

(2) Compulsive gambling, kleptomania, or pyromania; or

(3) Psychoactive substance use disorders resulting from current illegal use of drugs.

(e) Homosexuality and bisexuality are not impairments and so are not disabilities as defined in this part.

§ 1630.4 Discrimination prohibited.

It is unlawful for a covered entity to discriminate on the basis of disability against a qualified individual with a disability in regard to:

(a) Recruitment, advertising, and job application procedures;

(b) Hiring, upgrading, promotion, award of tenure, demotion, transfer, layoff, termination, right of return from layoff, and rehiring;

(c) Rates of pay or any other form of compensation and changes in compensation;

(d) Job assignments, job classifications, organizational structures, position descriptions, lines of progression, and seniority lists;

(e) Leaves of absence, sick leave, or any other leave;

(f) Fringe benefits available by virtue of employment, whether or not administered by the covered entity;

(g) Selection and financial support for training, including: apprenticeships, professional meetings, conferences and other related activities, and selection for leaves of absence to pursue training;

(h) Activities sponsored by a covered entity including social and recreational programs; and

(i) Any other term, condition, or privilege of employment.

The term discrimination includes, but is not limited to, the acts described in §§ 1630.5 through 1630.13 of this part.

§ 1630.5 Limiting segregating, and classifying.

It is unlawful for a covered entity to limit, segregate, or classify a job applicant or employee in a way that adversely affects his or her employment opportunities or status on the basis of disability.

§ 1630.6 Contractual or other arrangements.

(a) In general. It is unlawful for a covered entity to participate in a contractual or other arrangement or relationship that has the effect of subjecting the covered entity's own qualified applicant or employee with a disability to the discrimination prohibited by this part.

(b) Contractual or other arrangement defined. The

phrase contractual or other arrangement or relationship includes, but is not limited to, a relationship with an employment or referral agency; labor union, including collective bargaining agreements; an organization providing fringe benefits to an employee of the covered entity; or an organization providing training and apprenticeship programs.

(c) Application. This section applies to a covered entity, with respect to its own applicants or employees, whether the entity offered the contract or initiated the relationship, or whether the entity accepted the contract or acceded to the relationship. A covered entity is not liable for the actions of the other party or parties to the contract which only affect that other party's employees or applicants.

§ 1630.7 Standards, criteria, or methods of administration.

It is unlawful for a covered entity to use standards, criteria, or methods of administration, which are not job-related and consistent with business necessity, and:

(a) That have the effect of discriminating on the basis of disability; or

(b) That perpetuate the discrimination of others who are subject to common administrative control.

§ 1630.8 Relationship or association with an individual with a disability.

It is unlawful for a covered entity to exclude or deny equal jobs or benefits to, or otherwise discriminate against, a qualified individual because of the known disability of an individual with whom the qualified individual is known to have a family, business, social or other relationship or association.

§ 1630.9 Not making reasonable accommodation.

(a) It is unlawful for a covered entity not to make reasonable accommodation to the known physical or mental limitations of an otherwise qualified applicant or employee with a disability, unless such covered entity can demonstrate that the accommodation would impose an undue hardship on the operation of its business.

(b) It is unlawful for a covered entity to deny employment opportunities to an otherwise qualified job applicant or employee with a disability based on the need of such covered entity to make reasonable accommodation to such individual's physical or mental impairments.

(c) A covered entity shall not be excused from the requirements of this part because of any failure to receive technical assistance authorized by section 506 of the ADA, including any failure in the development or dissemination of any technical assistance manual authorized by that Act.

(d) A qualified individual with a disability is not required to accept an accommodation, aid, service, opportunity or benefit which such qualified individual chooses not to accept. However, if such individual rejects a reasonable accommodation, aid, service, opportunity or benefit that is necessary to enable the individual to perform the essential functions of the position held or desired, and cannot, as a result of that rejection, perform the essential functions of the position, the individual will not be considered a qualified individual with a disability.

§ 1630.10 Qualification standards, tests, and other selection criteria.

It is unlawful for a covered entity to use qualification standards, employment tests or other selection criteria that screen out or tend to screen out an individual with a disability or a class of individuals with disabilities, on the basis of disability, unless the standard, test or other selection criteria, as used by the covered entity, is shown to be job-related for the position in question and is consistent with business necessity.

§ 1630.11 Administration of tests.

It is unlawful for a covered entity to fail to select and administer tests concerning employment in the most effective manner to ensure that, when a test is administered to a job applicant or employee who has a disability that impairs sensory, manual or speaking skills, the test results accurately reflect the skills, aptitude, or whatever other factor of the applicant or employee that the test purports to measure, rather than reflecting the impaired sensory, manual, or speaking skills of such employee or applicant (except where such skills are the factors that the test purports to measure).

§ 1630.12 Retaliation and coercion.

(a) Retaliation. It is unlawful to discriminate against any individual because that individual has opposed any act or practice made unlawful by this part or because that individual made a charge, testified, assisted, or participated in any manner in an investigation, proceeding, or hearing to enforce any provision contained in this part.

(b) Coercion, interference or intimidation. It is unlawful to coerce, intimidate, threaten, harass or interfere with any individual in the exercise or enjoyment of, or because that individual aided or encouraged any other individual in the exercise of, any right granted or protected by this part.

§ 1630.13 Prohibited medical examinations and inquiries.

(a) Pre-employment examination or inquiry. Except as permitted by § 1630.14, it is unlawful for a covered entity to conduct a medical examination of an applicant or to make inquiries as to whether an applicant is an individual with a disability or as to the nature or severity of such disability.

(b) Examination or inquiry of employees. Except as permitted by § 1630.14, it is unlawful for a covered entity to require a medical examination of an employee or to make inquiries as to whether an employee is an individual with a disability or as to the nature or severity of such disability.

§ 1630.14 Medical examinations and inquiries specifically permitted.

(a) Acceptable pre-employment inquiry. A covered entity may make pre-employment inquiries into the ability of an applicant to perform job-related functions, and/or may ask an applicant to describe or to demonstrate how, with or without reasonable accommodation, the applicant will be able to perform job-related functions.

(b) Employment entrance examination. A covered entity may require a medical examination (and/or inquiry) after making an offer of employment to a job applicant and before the applicant begins his or her employment duties, and may condition an offer of employment on the results of such examination (and/or inquiry), if all entering employees in the same job category are subjected to such an examination (and/or inquiry) regardless of disability.

(1) Information obtained under paragraph (b) of this section regarding the medical condition or history of the applicant shall be collected and maintained on separate forms and in separate medical files and be treated as a confidential medical record, except that:

(i) Supervisors and managers may be informed regarding necessary restrictions on the work or duties of the employee and necessary accommodations;

(ii) First aid and safety personnel may be informed, when appropriate, if the disability might require emergency treatment; and

(iii) Government officials investigating compliance with this part shall be provided relevant information on request.

(2) The results of such examination shall not be used for any purpose inconsistent with this part.

(3) Medical examinations conducted in accordance with this section do not have to be job-related and consistent with business necessity. However, if certain criteria are used to screen out an employee or employees with disabilities as a result of such an examination or inquiry, the exclusionary criteria must be job-related and consistent with business necessity, and performance of the essential job functions cannot be accomplished with reasonable accommodation as required in this part. (See § 1630.15(b) Defenses to charges of discriminatory application of selection criteria.)

(c) Examination of employees. A covered entity may require a medical examination (and/or inquiry) of an employee that is job-related and consistent with business necessity. A covered entity may make inquiries into the ability of an employee to perform job-related functions.

(1) Information obtained under paragraph (c) of this section regarding the medical condition or history of any employee shall be collected and maintained on separate forms and in separate medical files and be treated as a confidential medical record, except that:

(i) Supervisors and managers may be informed regarding necessary restrictions on the work or duties of the employee and necessary accommodations;

(ii) First aid and safety personnel may be informed, when appropriate, if the disability might require emergency treatment; and

(iii) Government officials investigating compliance with this part shall be provided relevant information on request.

(2) Information obtained under paragraph (c) of this section regarding the medical condition or history of any employee shall not be used for any purpose inconsistent with this part.

(d) Other acceptable examinations and inquiries. A covered entity may conduct voluntary medical examinations and activities, including voluntary medical histories, which are part of an employee health program available to employees at the work site.

(1) Information obtained under paragraph (d) of this section regarding the medical condition or history of any employee shall be collected and maintained on separate forms and in separate medical files and be treated as a confidential medical record, except that:

(i) Supervisors and managers may be informed regarding necessary restrictions on the work or duties of the employee and necessary accommodations;

(ii) First aid and safety personnel may be informed, when appropriate, if the disability might require emergency treatment; and

(iii) Government officials investigating compliance with this part shall be provided relevant information on request.

(2) Information obtained under paragraph (d) of this section regarding the medical condition or history of any employee shall not be used for any purpose inconsistent with this part.

§ 1630.15 Defenses.

Defenses to an allegation of discrimination under this part may include, but are not limited to, the following:

(a) Disparate treatment charges. It may be a defense to a charge of disparate treatment brought under §§ 1630.4 through 1630.8 and 1630.11 through 1630.12 that the challenged action is justified by a legitimate, nondiscriminatory reason.

(b) Charges of discriminatory application of selection criteria—

(1) In general. It may be a defense to a charge of discrimination, as described in § 1630.10, that an alleged application of qualification standards, tests, or selection criteria that screens out or tends to screen out or otherwise denies a job or benefit to an individual with a disability has been shown to be job-related and consistent with business necessity, and such performance cannot be accomplished with reasonable accommodation, as required in this part.

(2) Direct threat as a qualification standard. The term "qualification standard" may include a requirement that an individual shall not pose a direct threat to the health or safety of the individual or others in the workplace. (See § 1630.2(r) defining direct threat.)

(c) Other disparate impact charges. It may be a defense to a charge of discrimination brought under this part that a uniformly applied standard, criterion, or policy has a disparate impact on an individual with a disability or a class of individuals with disabilities that the challenged standard, criterion or policy has been shown to be job-related and consistent with business necessity, and such performance cannot be accomplished with reasonable accommodation, as required in this part.

(d) Charges of not making reasonable accommodation. It may be a defense to a charge of discrimination, as described in § 1630.9, that a requested or necessary accommodation would impose an undue hardship on the operation of the covered entity's business.

(e) Conflict with other federal laws. It may be a defense to a charge of discrimination under this part that a challenged action is required or necessitated by another Federal law or regulation, or that another Federal law or regulation prohibits an action (including the provision of a particular reasonable accommodation) that would otherwise be required by this part.

(f) Additional defenses. It may be a defense to a charge of discrimination under this part that the alleged discriminatory action is specifically permitted by §§ 1630.14 or 1630.16.

§ 1630.16 Specific activities permitted.

(a) Religious entities. A religious corporation, association, educational institution, or society is permitted to give preference in employment to individuals of a particular religion to perform work connected with the carrying on by that corporation, association, educational institution, or society of its activities. A religious entity may require that all applicants and employees conform to the religious tenets of such organization. However, a religious entity may not discriminate against a qualified individual, who satisfies the permitted religious criteria, because of his or her disability.

(b) Regulation of alcohol and drugs. A covered entity:

(1) May prohibit the illegal use of drugs and the use of alcohol at the workplace by all employees;

(2) May require that employees not be under the influence of alcohol or be engaging in the illegal use of drugs at the workplace;

(3) May require that all employees behave in conformance with the requirements established under the Drug-Free Workplace Act of 1988 (41 U.S.C. 701 et seq.);

(4) May hold an employee who engages in the illegal use of drugs or who is an alcoholic to the same qualification standards for employment or job performance and behavior to which the entity holds its other employees, even if any unsatisfactory performance or behavior is related to the employee's drug use or alcoholism;

(5) May require that its employees employed in an industry subject to such regulations comply with the standards established in the regulations (if any) of the Departments of Defense and Transportation, and of the Nuclear Regulatory Commission, regarding alcohol and the illegal use of drugs; and

(6) May require that employees employed in sensitive positions comply with the regulations (if any) of the Departments of Defense and Transportation and of the Nuclear Regulatory Commission that apply to employment in sensitive positions subject to such regulations.

(c) Drug testing—

(1) General policy. For purposes of this part, a test to determine the illegal use of drugs is not consid-

ered a medical examination. Thus, the administration of such drug tests by a covered entity to its job applicants or employees is not a violation of § 1630.13 of this part. However, this part does not encourage, prohibit, or authorize a covered entity to conduct drug tests of job applicants or employees to determine the illegal use of drugs or to make employment decisions based on such test results.

(2) Transportation Employees. This part does not encourage, prohibit, or authorize the otherwise lawful exercise by entities subject to the jurisdiction of the Department of Transportation of authority to:

(i) Test employees of entities in, and applicants for, positions involving safety sensitive duties for the illegal use of drugs or for on-duty impairment by alcohol; and

(ii) Remove from safety-sensitive positions persons who test positive for illegal use of drugs or on-duty impairment by alcohol pursuant to paragraph (c)(2)(i) of this section.

(3) Confidentiality. Any information regarding the medical condition or history of any employee or applicant obtained from a test to determine the illegal use of drugs, except information regarding the illegal use of drugs, is subject to the requirements of § 1630.14(b) (2) and (3) of this part.

(d) Regulation of smoking. A covered entity may prohibit or impose restrictions on smoking in places of employment. Such restrictions do not violate any provision of this part.

(e) Infectious and communicable diseases; food handling jobs—

(1) In general. Under title I of the ADA, section 103(d)(1), the Secretary of Health and Human Services is to prepare a list, to be updated annually, of infectious and communicable diseases which are transmitted through the handling of food. (Copies may be obtained from Center for Infectious Diseases, Centers for Disease Control, 1600 Clifton Road, NE., Mailstop C09, Atlanta, GA 30333.) If an individual with a disability is disabled by one of the infectious or communicable diseases included on this list, and if the risk of transmitting the disease associated with the handling of food cannot be eliminated by reasonable accommodation, a covered entity may refuse to assign or continue to assign such individual to a job involving food handling. However, if the individual with a disability is a current employee, the employer must consider whether he or she can be accommodated by reassignment to a vacant position not involving food handling.

(2) Effect on state or other laws. This part does not preempt, modify, or amend any State, county, or local law, ordinance or regulation applicable to food handling which:

(i) Is in accordance with the list, referred to in paragraph (e)(1) of this section, of infectious or communicable diseases and the modes of transmissibility published by the Secretary of Health and Human Services; and

(ii) Is designed to protect the public health from individuals who pose a significant risk to the health or safety of others, where that risk cannot be eliminated by reasonable accommodation.

(f) Health insurance, life insurance, and other benefit plans—

(1) An insurer, hospital, or medical service company, health maintenance organization, or any agent or entity that administers benefit plans, or similar organizations may underwrite risks, classify risks, or administer such risks that are based on or not inconsistent with State law.

(2) A covered entity may establish, sponsor, observe or administer the terms of a bona fide benefit plan that are based on underwriting risks, classifying risks, or administering such risks that are based on or not inconsistent with State law.

(3) A covered entity may establish, sponsor, observe, or administer the terms of a bona fide benefit plan that is not subject to State laws that regulate insurance.

(4) The activities described in paragraphs (f)(1), (2), and (3) of this section are permitted unless these activities are being used as a subterfuge to evade the purposes of this part.

ADA TITLE I
EEOC INTERPRETIVE GUIDANCE

Background
Introduction
1630.1 Purpose, Applicability and Construction
  (a) Purpose
  (b) and (c) Applicability and Construction
1630.2(a)-(f) Commission, Covered Entity, etc.
  (g) Disability
  (h) Physical or Mental Impairment
  (i) Major Life Activities
  (j) Substantially Limits
  (k) Record of a Substantially Limiting Condition
  (l) Regarded as Substantially Limited in a Major Life Activity
  (m) Qualified Individual With a Disability
  (n) Essential Functions
  (o) Reasonable Accommodation
  (p) Undue Hardship
  (r) Direct Threat
1630.3 Exceptions to the Definitions of "Disability" and "Qualified Individual with a Disability"
  (a) through (c) Illegal Use of Drugs
1630.4 Discrimination Prohibited
1630.5 Limiting, Segregating and Classifying
1630.6 Contractual or Other Arrangements
1630.8 Relationship or Association With an Individual With a Disability
1630.9 Not Making Reasonable Accommodation
  Process of Determining the Appropriate Reasonable Accommodation
  Reasonable Accommodation Process Illustrated
  (b)
  (d)
1630.10 Qualification Standards, Tests, and Other Selection Criteria
1630.11 Administration of Tests
1630.13 Prohibited Medical Examinations and Inquiries
  (a) Pre-employment Examination or Inquiry
  (b) Examination or Inquiry of Employees
1630.14 Medical Examinations and Inquiries Specifically Permitted
  (a) Pre-Employment Inquiry
  (b) Employment Entrance Examination
  (c) Examination of Employees
  (d) Other Acceptable Examinations and Inquiries
1630.15 Defenses
  (a) Disparate Treatment Defenses
  (b) and (c) Disparate Impact Defenses
  (d) Defense to Not Making Reasonable Accommodation
  (e) Defense—Conflicting Federal Laws and Regulations
1630.16 Specific Activities Permitted
  (a) Religious Entities
  (b) Regulation of Alcohol and Drugs
  (c) Drug Testing
  (e) Infectious and Communicable Diseases; Food Handling Jobs
  (f) Health Insurance, Life Insurance, and Other Benefit Plans

ADA TITLE I
EEOC INTERPRETIVE GUIDANCE

Background

The ADA is a federal anti-discrimination statute de-signed to remove barriers which prevent qualified individuals with disabilities from enjoying the same employment opportunities that are available to persons without disabilities.

Like the Civil Rights Act of 1964 that prohibits discrimination on the bases of race, color, religion, national origin, and sex, the ADA seeks to ensure access to equal employment opportunities based on merit. It does not guarantee equal results, establish quotas, or require preferences favoring individuals with disabilities over those without disabilities.

However, while the Civil Rights Act of 1964 prohibits any consideration of personal characteristics such as race or national origin, the ADA necessarily takes a different approach. When an individual's disability creates a barrier to employment opportunities, the ADA requires employers to consider whether reasonable accommodation could remove the barrier.

The ADA thus establishes a process in which the employer must assess a disabled individual's ability to perform the essential functions of the specific job held or desired. While the ADA focuses on eradicating barriers, the ADA does not relieve a disabled employee or applicant from the obligation to perform the essential functions of the job. To the contrary, the ADA is intended to enable disabled persons to compete in the workplace based on the same performance standards and requirements that employers expect of persons who are not disabled.

However, where that individual's functional limitation impedes such job performance, an employer must take steps to reasonably accommodate, and thus help overcome the particular impediment, unless to do so would impose an undue hardship. Such accommodations usually take the form of adjustments to the way a job customarily is performed, or to the work environment itself.

This process of identifying whether, and to what extent, a reasonable accommodation is required should be flexible and involve both the employer and the individual with a disability. Of course, the determination of whether an individual is qualified for a particular position must necessarily be made on a case-by-case basis. No specific form of accommodation is guaranteed for all individuals with a particular disability. Rather, an accommodation must be tailored to match the needs of the disabled individual with the needs of the job's essential functions.

This case-by-case approach is essential if qualified individuals of varying abilities are to receive equal opportunities to compete for an infinitely diverse range of jobs. For this reason, neither the ADA nor this part can supply the "correct" answer in advance for each employment decision concerning an individual with a disability. Instead, the ADA simply establishes parameters to guide employers in how to consider, and take into account, the disabling condition involved.

Introduction

The Equal Employment Opportunity Commission (the Commission or EEOC) is responsible for enforcement of title I of the Americans with Disabilities Act (ADA), 42 U.S.C. 12101 et seq. (1990), which prohibits employment discrimination on the basis of disability. The Commission believes that it is essential to issue interpretive guidance concurrently with the issuance of this part in order to ensure that qualified individuals with disabilities understand their rights under this part and to facilitate and encourage compliance by covered entities. This appendix represents the Commission's interpretation of the issues discussed, and the Commission will be guided by it when resolving charges of employment discrimination. The appendix addresses the major provisions of this part and explains the major concepts of disability rights.

The terms "employer" or "employer or other covered entity" are used interchangeably throughout the appendix to refer to all covered entities subject to the employment provisions of the ADA.

Section 1630.1
Purpose, Applicability and Construction

Section 1630.1(a)
Purpose

The Americans with Disabilities Act was signed into law on July 26, 1990. It is an anti-discrimination statute that requires that individuals with disabilities be given the same consideration for employment that individuals without disabilities are given. An individual who is qualified for an employment opportunity cannot be denied that opportunity because of the fact that the individual is disabled. The purpose of title I and this part is to ensure that qualified individuals with disabilities are protected from discrimination on the basis of disability.

The ADA uses the term "disabilities" rather than the term "handicaps" used in the Rehabilitation Act of 1973, 29 U.S.C. 701-796. Substantively, these terms are equivalent. As noted by the House Committee on the Judiciary, "[t]he use of the term 'disabilities' instead of the term 'handicaps' reflects the desire of the Committee to use the most current terminology. It reflects the preference of persons with disabilities to use that term rather than 'handicapped' as used in previous laws, such as the Rehabilitation Act of 1973 * * *." H.R. Rep. No. 485 part 3, 101st Cong., 2d Sess. 26-27 (1990) (hereinafter House Judiciary Report); see also S. Rep. No. 116, 101st Cong., 1st Sess. 21 (1989) (hereinafter Senate Report); H.R. Rep. No. 485 part 2, 101st Cong., 2d Sess. 50-51 (1990) [hereinafter House Labor Report].

The use of the term "Americans" in the title of the ADA is not intended to imply that the Act only applies to United States citizens. Rather, the ADA protects all qualified individuals with disabilities, regardless of their citizenship status or nationality.

Section 1630.1(b) and (c)
Applicability and Construction

Unless expressly stated otherwise, the standards applied in the ADA are not intended to be lesser than the standards applied under the Rehabilitation Act of 1973.

The ADA does not preempt any Federal law, or any state or local law, that grants to individuals with disabilities protection greater than or equivalent to that provided by the ADA. This means that the existence of a lesser standard of protection to individuals with disabilities under the ADA will not provide a defense to failing to meet a higher standard under another law. Thus, for example, title I of the ADA would not be a defense to failing to collect information required to satisfy the affirmative action requirements of section 503 of the Rehabilitation Act. On the other hand, the existence of a lesser standard under another law will not provide a defense to failing to meet a higher standard under the ADA. See House Labor Report at 135; House Judiciary Report at 69-70.

This also means that an individual with a disability could choose to pursue claims under a state discrimination or tort law that does not confer greater substantive rights, or even confers fewer substantive rights, if the potential available remedies would be greater than those available under the ADA and this part. The ADA does not restrict an individual with a disability from pursuing such claims in addition to charges brought under this part. House Judiciary at 69-70.

The ADA does not automatically preempt medical standards or safety requirements established by Federal law or regulations. It does not preempt State, county, or local laws, ordinances or regulations that are consistent with this part, and are designed to protect the public health from individuals who pose a direct threat, that cannot be eliminated or reduced by reasonable accommodation, to the health or safety of others. However, the ADA does preempt inconsistent requirements established by state or local law for safety or security sensitive positions. See Senate Report at 27; House Labor Report at 57.

An employer allegedly in violation of this part cannot successfully defend its actions by relying on the obligation to comply with the requirements of any state or local law that imposes prohibitions or limitations on the eligibility of qualified individuals with disabilities to practice any occupation or profession. For example, suppose a municipality has an ordinance that prohibits individuals with tuberculosis from teaching school children. If an individual with dormant tuberculosis challenges a private school's refusal to hire him or her because of the tuberculosis, the private school would not be able to rely on the city ordinance as a defense under the ADA.

Section 1630.2(a)-(f)
Commission, Covered Entity, etc.

The definitions section of part 1630 includes several terms that are identical, or almost identical, to the terms found in title VII of the Civil Rights Act of 1964. Among these terms are "Commission," "Person," "State," and "Employer." These terms are to be given the same meaning under the ADA that they are given under title VII.

In general, the term "employee" has the same meaning that is given under title VII. However, the ADA's definition of "employee" does not contain an exception, as does title VII, for elected officials and their personal staffs. It should be further noted that all state and local governments are covered by title II of the ADA whether or not they are also covered by this part. Title II, which is enforced by the Department of Justice, becomes effective on January 26, 1992. See 28 CFR part 35.

The term "covered entity" is not found in title VII. However, the title VII definitions of the entities included in the term "covered entity" (e.g., employer, employment agency, etc.) are applicable to the ADA.

Section 1630.2(g) Disability

In addition to the term "covered entity," there are several other terms that are unique to the ADA. The first of these is the term "disability." Congress adopted the definition of this term from the Rehabilitation Act definition of the term "individual with handicaps." By so doing, Congress intended that the relevant caselaw developed under the Rehabilitation Act be generally applicable to the term "disability" as used in the ADA. Senate Report at 21; House Labor Report at 50; House Judiciary Report at 27.

The definition of the term "disability" is divided into three parts. An individual must satisfy at least one of these parts in order to be considered an individual with a disability for purposes of this part. An individual is considered to have a "disability" if that individual either (1) has a physical or mental impairment which substantially limits one or more of that person's major life activities, (2) has a record of such an impairment, or, (3) is regarded by the covered entity as having such an impairment. To understand the meaning of the term "disability," it is necessary to understand, as a preliminary matter, what is meant by the terms "physical or mental impairment," "major life activity," and "substantially limits." Each of these terms is discussed below.

Section 1630.2(h)
Physical or Mental Impairment

This term adopts the definition of the term "physical or mental impairment" found in the regulations implementing section 504 of the Rehabilitation Act at 34 CFR part 104. It defines physical or mental impairment as any physiological disorder or condition, cosmetic disfigurement, or anatomical loss affecting one or more of several body systems, or any mental or psychological disorder.

Section 1630.2(i) Major Life Activities

This term adopts the definition of the term "major life activities" found in the regulations implementing section 504 of the Rehabilitation Act at 34 CFR part 104. "Major life activities" are those basic activities that the average person in the general population can perform with little or no difficulty. Major life activities include caring for oneself, performing manual tasks, walking, seeing, hearing, speaking, breathing, learning, and working. This list is not exhaustive. For example, other major life activities include, but are not limited to, sitting, standing, lifting, reaching. See Senate Report at 22; House Labor Report at 52; House

Judiciary Report at 28.

Section 1630.2(j) Substantially Limits

Determining whether a physical or mental impairment exists is only the first step in determining whether or not an individual is disabled. Many impairments do not impact an individual's life to the degree that they constitute disabling impairments. An impairment rises to the level of disability if the impairment substantially limits one or more of the individual's major life activities. Multiple impairments that combine to substantially limit one or more of an individual's major life activities also constitute a disability.

The ADA and this part, like the Rehabilitation Act of 1973, do not attempt a "laundry list" of impairments that are "disabilities." The determination of whether an individual has a disability is not necessarily based on the name or diagnosis of the impairment the person has, but rather on the effect of that impairment on the life of the individual. Some impairments may be disabling for particular individuals but not for others, depending on the stage of the disease or disorder, the presence of other impairments that combine to make the impairment disabling or any number of other factors.

Other impairments, however, such as HIV infection, are inherently substantially limiting.

On the other hand, temporary, non-chronic impairments of short duration, with little or no long term or permanent impact, are usually not disabilities. Such impairments may include, but are not limited to, broken limbs, sprained joints, concussions, appendicitis, and influenza. Similarly, except in rare circumstances, obesity is not considered a disabling impairment.

An impairment that prevents an individual from performing a major life activity substantially limits that major life activity. For example, an individual whose legs are paralyzed is substantially limited in the major life activity of walking because he or she is unable, due to the impairment, to perform that major life activity.

Alternatively, an impairment is substantially limiting if it significantly restricts the duration, manner or condition under which an individual can perform a particular major life activity as compared to the average person in the general population's ability to perform that same major life activity. Thus, for example, an individual who, because of an impairment, can only walk for very brief periods of time would be substantially limited in the major life activity of walking. It should be noted that the term "average person" is not intended to imply a precise mathematical "average."

Part 1630 notes several factors that should be considered in making the determination of whether an impairment is substantially limiting. These factors are (1) the nature and severity of the impairment, (2) the duration or expected duration of the impairment, and (3) the permanent or long term impact, or the expected permanent or long term impact of, or resulting from, the impairment. The term "duration," as used in this context, refers to the length of time an impairment persists, while the term "impact" refers to the residual effects of an impairment. Thus, for example, a broken leg that takes eight weeks to heal is an impairment of fairly brief duration. However, if the broken leg heals improperly, the "impact" of the impairment would be the resulting permanent limp. Likewise, the effect on cognitive functions resulting from traumatic head injury would be the "impact" of that impairment.

The determination of whether an individual is substantially limited in a major life activity must be made on a case by case basis. An individual is not substantially limited in a major life activity if the limitation, when viewed in light of the factors noted above, does not amount to a significant restriction when compared with the abilities of the average person. For example, an individual who had once been able to walk at an extraordinary speed would not be substantially limited in the major life activity of walking if, as a result of a physical impairment, he or she were only able to walk at an average speed, or even at moderately below average speed.

It is important to remember that the restriction on the performance of the major life activity must be the result of a condition that is an impairment. As noted earlier, advanced age, physical or personality characteristics, and environmental, cultural, and economic disadvantages are not impairments. Consequently, even if such factors substantially limit an individual's ability to perform a major life activity, this limitation will not constitute a disability. For example, an individual who is unable to read because he or she was never taught to read would not be an individual with a disability because lack of education is not an impairment. However, an individual who is unable to read because of dyslexia would be an individual with a disability because dyslexia, a learning disability, is an impairment.

If an individual is not substantially limited with respect to any other major life activity, the individual's ability to perform the major life activity of working should be considered. If an individual is substantially limited in any other major life activity, no determination should be made as to whether the individual is substantially limited in working. For example, if an individual is blind, i.e., substantially limited in the major life activity of seeing, there is no need to determine whether the individual is also substantially limited in the major life activity of working. The determination of whether an individual is substantially limited in working must also be made on a case by case basis.

This part lists specific factors that may be used in making the determination of whether the limitation in working is "substantial." These factors are:

(1) The geographical area to which the individual has reasonable access;

(2) The job from which the individual has been disqualified because of an impairment, and the number and types of jobs utilizing similar training, knowledge, skills or abilities, within that geographical area, from which the individual is also disqualified because of the impairment (class of jobs); and/or

(3) The job from which the individual has been disqualified because of an impairment, and the number and types of other jobs not utilizing similar training, knowledge, skills or abilities, within that geographical area, from which the individual is also disqualified because of the impairment (broad range of jobs in various classes).

Thus, an individual is not substantially limited in working just because he or she is unable to perform a particular job for one employer, or because he or she is unable to perform a specialized job or profession requiring extraordinary skill, prowess or talent. For example, an individual who cannot be a commercial airline pilot because of a minor vision impairment, but who can be a commercial airline co-pilot or a pilot for a courier service, would not be substantially limited in the major life activity of working. Nor would a professional baseball pitcher who develops a bad elbow and can no longer throw a baseball be considered substantially limited in the major life activity of working. In both of these examples, the individuals are not substantially limited in the ability to perform any other major life activity and, with regard to the major life activity of working, are only unable to perform either a particular specialized job or a narrow range of jobs. See *Forrisi v. Bowen*, 794 F.2d 931 (4th Cir. 1986); *Jasany v. U.S. Postal Service*, 755 F.2d 1244 (6th Cir. 1985); *E.E. Black, Ltd. v. Marshall*, 497 F. Supp. 1088 (D. Hawaii 1980).

On the other hand, an individual does not have to be totally unable to work in order to be considered substantially limited in the major life activity of working. An individual is substantially limited in working if the individual is significantly restricted in the ability to perform a class of jobs or a broad range of jobs in various classes, when compared with the ability of the average person with comparable qualifications to perform those same jobs. For example, an individual who has a back condition that prevents the individual from performing any heavy labor job would be substantially limited in the major life activity of working because the individual's impairment eliminates his or her ability to perform a class of jobs. This would be so even if the individual were able to perform jobs in another class, e.g., the class of semi-skilled jobs. Similarly, suppose an individual has an allergy to a substance found in most high rise office buildings, but seldom found elsewhere, that makes breathing extremely difficult. Since this individual would be substantially limited in the ability to perform the broad range of jobs in various classes that are conducted in high rise office buildings within the geographical area to which he or she has reasonable access, he or she would be substantially limited in working.

The terms "number and types of jobs" and "number and types of other jobs," as used in the factors discussed above, are not intended to require an onerous evidentiary showing. Rather, the terms only require the presentation of evidence of general employment demographics and/or of recognized occupational classifications that indicate the approximate number of jobs (e.g., "few," "many," "most") from which an individual would be excluded because of an impairment.

If an individual has a "mental or physical impairment" that "substantially limits" his or her ability to perform one or more "major life activities," that individual will satisfy the first part of the regulatory definition of "disability" and will be considered an individual with a disability. An individual who satisfies this first part of the definition of the term "disability" is not required to demonstrate that he or she satisfies either of the other parts of the definition. However, if an individual is unable to satisfy this part of the definition, he or she may be able to satisfy one of the other parts of the definition.

Section 1630.2(k)
Record of a Substantially Limiting Condition

The second part of the definition provides that an individual with a record of an impairment that substantially limits a major life activity is an individual with a disability. The intent of this provision, in part, is to ensure that people are not discriminated against because of a history of disability. For example, this provision protects former cancer patients from discrimination based on their prior medical history. This provision also ensures that individuals are not discriminated against because they have been misclassified as disabled. For example, individuals misclassified as learning disabled are protected from discrimination on the basis of that erroneous classification. Senate Report at 23; House Labor Report at 52-53; House Judiciary Report at 29.

This part of the definition is satisfied if a record relied on by an employer indicates that the individual has or has had a substantially limiting impairment. The impairment indicated in the record must be an impairment that would substantially limit one or more of the individual's major life activities. There are many types of records that could potentially contain this information, including but not limited to, education, medical, or employment records.

The fact that an individual has a record of being a disabled veteran, or of disability retirement, or is classified as disabled for other purposes does not guarantee that the individual will satisfy the definition of "disability" under part 1630. Other statutes, regulations and programs may have a definition of "disability" that is not the same as the definition set forth in the ADA and contained in part 1630. Accordingly, in order for an individual who has been classified in a record as "disabled" for some other purpose to be considered disabled for purposes of part 1630, the impairment indicated in the record must be a physical or mental impairment that substantially limits one or more of the individual's major life activities.

Section 1630.2(l)
Regarded as Substantially Limited in a Major Life Activity

If an individual cannot satisfy either the first part of the definition of "disability" or the second "record of" part of the definition, he or she may be able to satisfy the third part of the definition. The third part of the definition provides that an individual who is regarded by an employer or other covered entity as having an impairment that substantially limits a major life activity is an individual with a disability.

There are three different ways in which an individual may satisfy the definition of "being regarded as having a disability":

(1) The individual may have an impairment which is not substantially limiting but is perceived by the employer or other covered entity as constituting a substantially limiting impairment;

(2) The individual may have an impairment which is only substantially limiting because of the attitudes of others toward the impairment; or

(3) The individual may have no impairment at all but is regarded by the employer or other covered entity as having a substantially limiting impairment.

Senate Report at 23; House Labor Report at 53; House Judiciary Report at 29.

An individual satisfies the first part of this definition if the individual has an impairment that is not substantially limiting, but the covered entity perceives the impairment as being substantially limiting. For example, suppose an employee has controlled high blood pressure that is not substantially limiting. If an employer reassigns the individual to less strenuous work because of unsubstantiated fears that the individual will suffer a heart attack if he or she continues to perform strenuous work, the employer would be regarding the individual as disabled.

An individual satisfies the second part of the "regarded as" definition if the individual has an impairment that is only substantially limiting because of the attitudes of others toward the condition. For example, an individual may have a prominent facial scar or disfigurement, or may have a condition that periodically causes an involuntary jerk of the head but does not limit the individual's major life activities. If an employer discriminates against such an individual because of the negative reactions of customers, the employer would be regarding the individual as disabled and acting on the basis of that perceived disability. See Senate Report at 24; House Labor Report at 53; House Judiciary Report at 30-31.

An individual satisfies the third part of the "regarded as" definition of "disability" if the employer or other covered entity erroneously believes the individual has a substantially limiting impairment that the individual actually does not have. This situation could occur, for example, if an employer discharged an employee in response to a rumor that the employee is infected with Human Immunodeficiency Virus (HIV). Even though the rumor is totally unfounded and the individual has no impairment at all, the individual is considered an individual with a disability because the employer perceived of this individual as being disabled. Thus, in this example, the employer, by discharging this employee, is discriminating on the basis of disability.

The rationale for the "regarded as" part of the definition of disability was articulated by the Supreme Court in the context of the Rehabilitation Act of 1973 in *School Board of Nassau County v. Arline*, 480 U.S. 273 (1987). The Court noted that, although an individual may have an impairment that does not in fact substantially limit a major life activity, the reaction of others may prove just as disabling. "Such an impairment might not diminish a person's physical or mental capabilities, but could nevertheless substantially limit that person's ability to work as a result of the negative reactions of others to the impairment." 480 U.S. at 283. The Court concluded that by including "regarded as" in the Rehabilitation Act's definition, "Congress acknowledged that society's accumulated myths and fears about disability and diseases are as handicapping as are the physical limitations that flow from actual impairment." 480 U.S. at 284.

An individual rejected from a job because of the "myths, fears and stereotypes" associated with disabilities would be covered under this part of the definition of disability, whether or not the employer's or other covered entity's perception were shared by others in the field and whether or not the individual's actual physical or mental condition would be considered a disability under the first or second part of this definition. As the legislative history notes, sociologists have identified common attitudinal barriers that frequently result in employers excluding individuals with disabilities. These include concerns regarding productivity, safety, insurance, liability, attendance, cost of accommodation and accessibility, workers' compensation costs, and acceptance by coworkers and customers.

Therefore, if an individual can show that an employer or other covered entity made an employment decision because of a perception of disability based on "myth, fear or stereotype," the individual will satisfy the "regarded as" part of the definition of disability. If the employer cannot articulate a non-discriminatory reason for the employment action, an inference that the employer is acting on the basis of "myth, fear or stereotype" can be drawn.

Section 1630.2(m)
Qualified Individual With a Disability

The ADA prohibits discrimination on the basis of disability against qualified individuals with disabilities. The determination of whether an individual with a disability is "qualified" should be made in two steps. The first step is to determine if the individual satisfies the prerequisites for the position, such as possessing the appropriate educational background, employment experience, skills, licenses, etc. For example, the first step in determining whether an accountant who is paraplegic is qualified for a certified public accountant (CPA) position is to examine the individual's credentials to determine whether the individual is a licensed CPA. This is sometimes referred to in the Rehabilitation Act caselaw as determining whether the individual is "otherwise qualified" for the position. See Senate Report at 33; House Labor Report at 64-65. (See § 1630.9 Not Making Reasonable Accommodation).

The second step is to determine whether or not the individual can perform the essential functions of the position held or desired, with or without reasonable accommodation. The purpose of this second step is to ensure that individuals with disabilities who can perform the essential functions of the position held or desired are not denied employment opportunities because they are not able to perform marginal functions of the position. House Labor Report at 55.

The determination of whether an individual with a disability is qualified is to be made at the time of the employment decision. This determination should be based on the capabilities of the individual with a disability at the time of the employment decision, and should not be based on speculation that the employee may become unable in the future or may cause increased health insurance premiums or workers compensation costs.

Section 1630.2(n) Essential Functions

The determination of which functions are essential may be critical to the determination of whether or not the individual with a disability is qualified. The essential functions are those functions that the individual who holds the position must be able to perform unaided or with the assistance of a reasonable accommodation.

The inquiry into whether a particular function is essential initially focuses on whether the employer actually requires employees in the position to perform the functions that the employer asserts are essential. For example, an employer may state that typing is an essential function of a position. If, in fact, the employer has never required any employee in that particular position to type, this will be evidence that typing is not actually an essential function of the position.

If the individual who holds the position is actually required to perform the function the employer asserts is an essential function, the inquiry will then center around whether removing the function would fundamentally alter that position. This determination of whether or not a particular function is essential will generally include one or more of the following factors listed in part 1630.

The first factor is whether the position exists to perform a particular function. For example, an individual may be hired to proofread documents. The ability to proofread the documents would then be an essential function, since this is the only reason the position exists.

The second factor in determining whether a function is essential is the number of other employees available to perform that job function or among whom the performance of that job function can be distributed. This may be a factor either because the total number of available employees is low, or because of the fluctuating demands of the business operation. For example, if an employer has a relatively small number of available employees for the volume of work to be performed, it may be necessary that each employee perform a multitude of different functions. Therefore, the performance of those functions by each employee becomes more critical and the options for reorganizing the work become more limited. In such a situation, functions that might not be essential if there were a larger staff may become essential because the staff size is small compared to the volume of work that has to be done. See *Treadwell v. Alexander*, 707 F.2d 473 (11th Cir. 1983).

A similar situation might occur in a larger work force if the work flow follows a cycle of heavy demand for labor intensive work followed by low demand periods. This type of workflow might also make the performance of each function during the peak periods more critical and might limit the employer's flexibility in reorganizing operating procedures. See *Dexler v. Tisch*, 660 F. Supp. 1418 (D. Conn. 1987).

The third factor is the degree of expertise or skill required to perform the function. In certain professions and highly skilled positions the employee is hired for his or her expertise or ability to perform the particular function. In such a situation, the performance of that specialized task would be an essential function.

Whether a particular function is essential is a factual determination that must be made on a case by case basis. In determining whether or not a particular function is essential, all relevant evidence should be considered. Part 1630 lists various types of evidence, such as an established job description, that should be considered in determining whether a particular function is essential. Since the list is not exhaustive, other relevant evidence may also be presented. Greater weight will not be granted to the types of evidence included on the list than to the types of evidence not listed.

Although part 1630 does not require employers to develop or maintain job descriptions, written job descriptions prepared before advertising or interviewing applicants for the job, as well as the employer's judgment as to what functions are essential are among the relevant evidence to be considered in determining whether a particular function is essential. The terms of a collective bargaining agreement are also relevant to the determination of whether a particular function is essential. The work experience of past employees in the job or of current employees in similar jobs is likewise relevant to the determination of whether a particular function is essential. See H.R. Conf. Rep. No. 101-596, 101st Cong., 2d Sess. 58 (1990) [hereinafter Conference Report]; House Judiciary Report at 33-34. See also *Hall v. U.S. Postal Service*, 857 F.2d 1073 (6th Cir. 1988). The time spent performing the particular function may also be an indicator of whether that function is essential. For example, if an employee spends the vast majority of his or her time working at a cash register, this would be evidence that operating the cash register is an essential function. The consequences of failing to require the employee to perform the function may be another indicator of whether a particular function is essential. For example, although a firefighter may not regularly have to carry an unconscious adult out of a burning building, the consequence of failing to require the firefighter to be able to perform this function would be serious.

It is important to note that the inquiry into essential functions is not intended to second guess an employer's business judgment with regard to production standards, whether qualitative or quantitative, nor to require employers to lower such standards. (See § 1630.10 Qualification Standards, Tests and Other Selection Criteria). If an employer requires its typists to be able to accurately type 75 words per minute, it will not be called upon to explain why an inaccurate work product, or a typing speed of 65 words per minute, would not be adequate. Similarly, if a hotel requires its service workers to thoroughly clean 16 rooms per day, it will not have to explain why it requires thorough cleaning, or why it chose a 16 room rather than a 10 room requirement. However, if an employer does require accurate 75 word per minute typing or the thorough cleaning of 16 rooms, it will have to show that it actually imposes such requirements on its employees in fact, and not simply on paper. It should also be noted that, if it is alleged that the employer intentionally selected the particular level of production to exclude individuals with disabilities, the employer may have to offer a legitimate, nondiscriminatory reason for its selection.

Section 1630.2(o) Reasonable Accommodation

An individual is considered a "qualified individual with a disability" if the individual can perform the essential functions of the position held or desired with or without reasonable accommodation. In general, an accommodation is any change in the work environment or in the way things are customarily done that enables an individual with a disability to enjoy equal employment opportunities. There are three categories of reasonable accommodation. These are (1) accommodations that are required to ensure equal opportunity in the application process; (2) accommodations that enable the employer's employees with disabilities to perform the essential functions of the position held or desired; and (3) accommodations that enable the employer's employees with disabilities to enjoy equal benefits and privileges of employment as are enjoyed by employees without disabilities. It should be noted that nothing in this part prohibits employers or other covered entities from providing accommodations beyond those required by this part.

Part 1630 lists the examples, specified in title I of the ADA, of the most common types of accommodation that an employer or other covered entity may be required to provide. There are any number of other specific accommodations that may be appropriate for particular situations but are not specifically mentioned in this listing. This listing is not intended to be exhaustive of accommodation possibilities. For example, other accommodations could include permitting the use of accrued paid leave or providing additional unpaid leave for necessary treatment, making employer provided transportation accessible, and providing reserved parking spaces. Providing personal assistants, such as a page turner for an employee with no hands or a travel attendant to act as a sighted guide to assist a blind employee on occasional business trips, may also be a reasonable accommodation. Senate Report at 31; House Labor Report at 62; House Judiciary Report at 39.

It may also be a reasonable accommodation to permit an individual with a disability the opportunity to provide and utilize equipment, aids or services that an employer is not required to provide as a reasonable accommodation. For example, it would be a reasonable accommodation for an employer to permit an individual who is blind to use a guide dog at work, even though the employer would not be required to provide a guide dog for the employee.

The accommodations included on the list of reasonable accommodations are generally self explanatory. However, there are a few that require further explanation. One of these is the accommodation of making existing facilities used by employees readily accessible to, and usable by, individuals with disabilities. This accommodation includes both those areas that must be accessible for the employee to perform essential job functions, as well as non-work areas used by the employer's employees for other purposes. For example, accessible break rooms, lunch rooms, training rooms, restrooms etc., may be required as reasonable accommodations.

Another of the potential accommodations listed is "job restructuring." An employer or other covered entity may restructure a job by reallocating or redistributing nonessential, marginal job functions. For example, an employer may have two jobs, each of which entails the performance of a number of marginal functions. The employer hires a qualified individual with a disability who is able to perform some of the marginal functions of each job but not all of the marginal functions of either job. As an accommodation, the employer may redistribute the marginal functions so that all of the marginal functions that the qualified individual with a disability can perform are made a part of the position to be filled by the qualified individual with a disability. The remaining marginal functions that the individual with a disability cannot perform would then be transferred to the other position. See Senate Report at 31; House Labor Report at 62.

An employer or other covered entity is not required to reallocate essential functions. The essential functions are by definition those that the individual who holds the job would have to perform, with or without reasonable accommodation, in order to be considered qualified for the position. For example, suppose a security guard position requires the individual who holds the job to inspect identification cards. An employer would not have to provide an individual who is legally blind with an assistant to look at the identification cards for the legally blind employee. In this situation the assistant would be performing the job for the individual with a disability rather than assisting the individual to perform the job. See *Coleman v. Darden*, 595 F.2d 533 (10th Cir. 1979).

An employer or other covered entity may also restructure a job by altering when and/or how an essential function is performed. For example, an essential function customarily performed in the early morning hours may be rescheduled until later in the day as a reasonable accommodation to a disability that precludes performance of the function at the customary hour. Likewise, as a reasonable accommodation, an employee with a disability that inhibits the ability to write, may be permitted to computerize records that were customarily maintained manually.

Reassignment to a vacant position is also listed as a potential reasonable accommodation. In general, reassignment should be considered only when accommodation within the individual's current position would pose an undue hardship. Reassignment is not available to applicants. An applicant for a position must be qualified for, and be able to perform the essential functions of, the position sought with or without reasonable accommodation.

Reassignment may not be used to limit, segregate, or otherwise discriminate against employees with disabilities by forcing reassignments to undesirable positions or to designated offices or facilities. Employers should reassign the individual to an equivalent position, in terms of pay, status, etc., if the individual is qualified, and if the position is vacant within a reasonable amount of time. A "reasonable amount of time" should be determined in light of the totality of the circumstances. As an example, suppose there is no vacant position available at the time that an individual with a disability requests reassignment as a reasonable accommodation. The employer, however, knows that an equivalent position for which the individual is qualified, will become vacant next week. Under these circumstances, the employer should reassign the individual to the position when it becomes available.

An employer may reassign an individual to a lower graded position if there are no accommodations that would enable the employee to remain in the current position and there are no vacant equivalent positions for which the individual is qualified with or without reasonable accommodation. An employer, however, is not required to maintain the reassigned individual with a disability at the salary of the higher graded position if it does not so maintain reassigned employees who are not disabled. It should also be noted that an employer is not required to promote an individual with a disability as an accommodation. See Senate Report at 31-32; House Labor Report at 63.

The determination of which accommodation is appropriate in a particular situation involves a process in which the employer and employee identify the precise limitations imposed by the disability and explore potential accommodations that would overcome those limitations. This process is discussed more fully in § 1630.9 Not Making Reasonable Accommodation.

Section 1630.2(p) Undue Hardship

An employer or other covered entity is not required to provide an accommodation that will impose an undue hardship on the operation of the employer's or other covered entity's business. The term "undue hardship" means significant difficulty or expense in, or resulting from, the provision of the accommodation. The "undue hardship" provision takes into account the financial realities of the particular employer or other covered entity. However, the concept of undue hardship is not limited to financial difficulty. "Undue hardship" refers to any accommodation that would be unduly costly, extensive, substantial, or disruptive, or that would fundamentally alter the nature or operation of the business. See Senate Report at 35; House Labor Report at 67.

For example, suppose an individual with a disabling visual impairment that makes it extremely difficult to see in dim lighting applies for a position as a waiter in a nightclub and requests that the club be brightly lit as a reasonable accommodation. Although the individual may be able to perform the job in bright lighting, the nightclub will probably be able to demonstrate that that particular accommodation, though inexpensive, would impose an undue hardship if the bright lighting would destroy the ambience of the nightclub and/or make it difficult for the customers to see the stage show. The fact that that particular accommodation poses an undue hardship, however, only means that the employer is not required to provide that accommodation. If there is another accommodation that will not create an undue hardship, the employer would be required to provide the alternative accommodation.

An employer's claim that the cost of a particular accommodation will impose an undue hardship will be analyzed in light of the factors outlined in part 1630. In part, this analysis requires a determination of whose financial resources should be considered in deciding whether the accommodation is unduly costly. In some cases the financial resources of the employer or other covered entity in its entirety should be considered in determining whether the cost of an accommodation poses an undue hardship. In other cases, consideration of the financial resources of the employer or other covered entity as a whole may be inappropriate because it may not give an accurate picture of the financial resources available to the particular facility that will actually be required to provide the accommodation. See House Labor Report at 68-69; House Judiciary Report at 40-41; see also Conference Report at 56-57.

If the employer or other covered entity asserts that only the financial resources of the facility where the individual will be employed should be considered, part 1630 requires a factual determination of the relationship between the employer or other covered entity and the facility that will provide the accommodation. As an example, suppose that an independently owned fast food franchise that receives no money from the franchisor refuses to hire an individual with a hearing impairment because it asserts that it would be an undue hardship to provide an interpreter to enable the individual to participate in monthly staff meetings. Since the financial relationship between the franchisor and the franchise is limited to payment of an annual franchise fee, only the financial resources of the franchise would be considered in determining whether or not providing the accommodation would be an undue hardship. See House Labor Report at 68; House Judiciary Report at 40.

If the employer or other covered entity can show that the cost of the accommodation would impose an undue hardship, it would still be required to provide the accommodation if the funding is available from another source, e.g., a State vocational rehabilitation agency, or if Federal, State or local tax deductions or tax credits are available to offset the cost of the accommodation. If the employer or other covered entity receives, or is eligible to receive, monies from an external source that would pay the entire cost of the accommodation, it cannot claim cost as an undue hardship. In the absence of such funding, the individual with a disability requesting the accommodation should be given the option of providing the accommodation or of paying that portion of the cost which constitutes the undue hardship on the operation of the business. To the extent that such monies pay or would pay for only part of the cost of the accommodation, only that portion of the cost of the accommodation that could not be recovered—the final net cost to the entity—may be considered in determining undue hardship. (See § 1630.9 Not Making Reasonable Accommodation). See Senate Report at 36; House Labor Report at 69.

Section 1630.2(r) Direct Threat

An employer may require, as a qualification standard, that an individual not pose a direct threat to the health or safety of himself/herself or others. Like any other qualification standard, such a standard must apply to all applicants or employees and not just to individuals with disabilities. If, however, an individual poses a direct threat as a result of a disability, the employer must determine whether a reasonable accommodation would either eliminate the risk or reduce it to an acceptable level. If no accommodation exists that would either eliminate or reduce the risk, the employer may refuse to hire an applicant or may discharge an employee who poses a direct threat.

An employer, however, is not permitted to deny an employment opportunity to an individual with a disability merely because of a slightly increased risk. The risk can only be considered when it poses a significant risk, i.e., high probability, of substantial harm; a speculative or remote risk is insufficient. See Senate Report at 27; House Report Labor Report at 56-57; House Judiciary Report at 45.

Determining whether an individual poses a significant risk of substantial harm to others must be made on a case by case basis. The employer should identify the specific risk posed by the individual. For individuals with mental or emotional disabilities, the employer must identify the specific behavior on the part of the individual that would pose the direct threat. For individuals with physical disabilities, the employer must identify the aspect of the disability that would pose the direct threat. The employer should then consider the four factors listed in part 1630:

(1) The duration of the risk;

(2) The nature and severity of the potential harm;

(3) The likelihood that the potential harm will occur; and

(4) The imminence of the potential harm.

Such consideration must rely on objective, factual evidence—not on subjective perceptions, irrational fears, patronizing attitudes, or stereotypes—about the nature or effect of a particular disability, or of disability generally. See Senate Report at 27; House Labor Report at 56-57; House Judiciary Report at 45-46. See also *Strathie v. Department of Transportation*, 716 F.2d 227 (3d Cir. 1983). Relevant evidence may include input from the individual with a disability, the experience of the individual with a disability in previous similar positions, and opinions of medical doctors, rehabilitation counselors, or physical therapists who have expertise in the disability involved and/or direct knowledge of the individual with the disability.

An employer is also permitted to require that an individual not pose a direct threat of harm to his or her own safety or health. If performing the particular functions of a job would result in a high probability of substantial harm to the individual, the employer could reject or discharge the individual unless a reasonable accommodation that would not cause an undue hardship would avert the harm. For example, an employer would not be required to hire an individual, disabled by narcolepsy, who frequently and unexpectedly loses consciousness for a carpentry job the essential functions of which require the use of power saws and other dangerous equipment, where no accommodation exists that will reduce or eliminate the risk.

The assessment that there exists a high probability of substantial harm to the individual, like the assessment that there exists a high probability of substantial harm to others, must be strictly based on valid medical analyses and/or on other objective evidence. This determination must be based on individualized factual data, using the factors discussed above, rather than on stereotypic or patronizing assumptions and must consider potential reasonable accommodations. Generalized fears about risks from the employment environment, such as exacerbation of the disability caused by stress, cannot be used by an employer to disqualify an individual with a disability. For example, a law firm could not reject an applicant with a history of disabling mental illness based on a generalized fear that the stress of trying to make partner might trigger a relapse of the individual's mental illness. Nor can generalized fears about risks to individuals with disabilities in the event of an evacuation or other emergency be used by an employer to disqualify an individual with a disability. See Senate Report at 56; House Labor Report at 73-74; House Judiciary Report at 45. See also *Mantolete v. Bolger*, 767 F.2d 1416 (9th Cir. 1985); *Bentivegna v. U.S. Department of Labor*, 694 F.2d 619 (9th Cir. 1982).

1630.3 Exceptions to the Definitions of "Disability" and "Qualified Individual with a Disability"

Section 1630.3 (a) through (c) Illegal Use of Drugs

Part 1630 provides that an individual currently engaging in the illegal use of drugs is not an individual with a disability for purposes of this part when the employer or other covered entity acts on the basis of such use. Illegal use of drugs refers both to the use of unlawful drugs, such as cocaine, and to the unlawful use of prescription drugs.

Employers, for example, may discharge or deny employment to persons who illegally use drugs, on the basis of such use, without fear of being held liable for discrimination. The term "currently engaging" is not intended to be limited to the use of drugs on the day of, or within a matter of days or weeks before, the employment action in question. Rather, the provision is intended to apply to the illegal use of drugs that has occurred recently enough to indicate that the individual is actively engaged in such conduct. See Conference Report at 64.

Individuals who are erroneously perceived as engaging in the illegal use of drugs, but are not in fact illegally using drugs are not excluded from the definitions of the terms "disability" and "qualified individual with a disability." Individuals who are no longer illegally using drugs and who have either been rehabilitated successfully or are in the process of completing a rehabilitation program are, likewise, not excluded from the definitions of those terms. The term "rehabilitation program" refers to both in-patient and out-patient programs, as well as to appropriate employee assistance programs, professionally recognized self-help programs, such as Narcotics Anonymous, or other programs that provide professional (not necessarily medical) assistance and counseling for individuals who illegally use drugs. See Conference Report at 64; see also House Labor Report at 77; House Judiciary Report at 47.

It should be noted that this provision simply provides that certain individuals are not excluded from the definitions of "disability" and "qualified individual with a disability." Consequently, such individuals are still required to establish that they satisfy the requirements of these definitions in order to be protected by the ADA and this part. An individual erroneously regarded as illegally using drugs, for example, would have to show that he or she was regarded as a drug addict in order to demonstrate that he or she meets the definition of "disability" as defined in this part.

Employers are entitled to seek reasonable assurances that no illegal use of drugs is occurring or has occurred recently enough so that continuing use is a real and ongoing problem. The reasonable assurances that employers may ask applicants or employees to provide include evidence that the individual is participating in a drug treatment program and/or evidence, such as drug test results, to show that the individual is not currently engaging in the illegal use of drugs. An employer, such as a law enforcement agency, may also be able to impose a qualification standard that excludes individuals with a history of illegal use of drugs if it can show that the standard is job-related and consistent with business necessity. (See § 1630.10 Qualification Standards, Tests and Other Selection Criteria) See Conference Report at 64.

Section 1630.4 Discrimination Prohibited

This provision prohibits discrimination against a qualified individual with a disability in all aspects of the employment relationship. The range of employment decisions covered by this nondiscrimination mandate is to be construed in a manner consistent with the regulations implementing section 504 of the Rehabilitation Act of 1973.

Part 1630 is not intended to limit the ability of covered entities to choose and maintain a qualified work force. Employers can continue to use job-related criteria to select qualified employees, and can continue to hire employees who can perform the essential functions of the job.

Section 1630.5
Limiting, Segregating and Classifying

This provision and the several provisions that follow describe various specific forms of discrimination that are included within the general prohibition of § 1630.4. Covered entities are prohibited from restricting the employment opportunities of qualified individuals with disabilities on the basis of stereotypes and myths about the individual's disability. Rather, the capabilities of qualified individuals with disabilities must be determined on an individualized, case by case basis. Covered entities are also prohibited from segregating qualified employees with disabilities into separate work areas or into separate lines of advancement.

Thus, for example, it would be a violation of this part for an employer to limit the duties of an employee with a disability based on a presumption of what is best for an individual with such a disability, or on a presumption about the abilities of an individual with such a disability. It would be a violation of this part for an employer to adopt a separate track of job promotion or progression for employees with disabilities based on a presumption that employees with disabilities are uninterested in, or incapable of, performing particular jobs. Similarly, it would be a violation for an employer to assign or reassign (as a reasonable accommodation) employees with disabilities to one particular office or installation, or to require that employees with disabilities only use particular employer provided non-work facilities such as segregated break-rooms, lunch rooms, or lounges. It would also be a violation of this part to deny employment to an applicant or employee with a disability based on generalized fears about the safety of an individual with such a disability, or based on generalized assumptions about the absenteeism rate of an individual with such a disability.

In addition, it should also be noted that this part is intended to require that employees with disabilities be accorded equal access to whatever health insurance coverage the employer provides to other employees. This part does not, however, affect pre-existing condition clauses included in health insurance policies offered by employers. Consequently, employers may continue to offer policies that contain such clauses, even if they adversely affect individuals with disabilities, so long as the clauses are not used as a subterfuge to evade the purposes of this part.

So, for example, it would be permissible for an employer to offer an insurance policy that limits coverage for certain procedures or treatments to a specified number per year. Thus, if a health insurance plan provided coverage for five blood transfusions a year to all covered employees, it would not be discriminatory to offer this plan simply because a hemophiliac employee may require more than five blood transfusions annually. However, it would not be permissible to limit or deny the hemophiliac employee coverage for other procedures, such as heart surgery or the setting of a broken leg, even though the plan would not have to provide coverage for the additional blood transfusions that may be involved in these procedures. Likewise, limits may be placed on reimbursements for certain procedures or on the types of drugs or procedures covered (e.g., limits on the number of permitted X-rays or non-coverage of experimental drugs or procedures), but that limitation must be applied equally to individuals with and without disabilities. See Senate Report at 28-29; House Labor Report at 58-59; House Judiciary Report at 36.

Leave policies or benefit plans that are uniformly applied do not violate this part simply because they do not address the special needs of every individual with a disability. Thus, for example, an employer that reduces the number of paid sick leave days that it will provide to all employees, or reduces the amount of medical insurance coverage that it will provide to all employees, is not in violation of this part, even if the benefits reduction has an impact on employees with disabilities in need of greater sick leave and medical coverage. Benefits reductions adopted for discriminatory reasons are in violation of this part. See *Alexander v. Choate,* 469 U.S. 287 (1985). See Senate Report at 85; House Labor Report at 137. (See also, the discussion at § 1630.16(f) Health Insurance, Life Insurance, and Other Benefit Plans).

Section 1630.6
Contractual or Other Arrangements

An employer or other covered entity may not do through a contractual or other relationship what it is prohibited from doing directly. This provision does not affect the determination of whether or not one is a "covered entity" or "employer" as defined in § 1630.2.

This provision only applies to situations where an employer or other covered entity has entered into a contractual relationship that has the effect of discriminating against its own employees or applicants with disabilities. Accordingly, it would be a violation for an employer to participate in a contractual relationship that results in discrimination against the employer's employees with disabilities in hiring, training, promotion, or in any other aspect of the employment relationship. This provision applies whether or not the employer or other covered entity intended for the contractual relationship to have the discriminatory effect.

Part 1630 notes that this provision applies to parties on either side of the contractual or other relationship. This is intended to highlight that an employer whose employees provide services to others, like an employer whose employees receive services, must ensure that those employees are not discriminated against on the basis of disability. For example, a copier company whose service representative is a dwarf could be required to provide a step stool, as a reasonable accommodation, to enable him to perform the necessary repairs. However, the employer would not be required, as a reasonable accommodation, to make structural changes to its customer's inaccessible premises.

The existence of the contractual relationship adds no new obligations under part 1630. The employer, therefore, is not liable through the contractual arrangement for any discrimination by the contractor against the contractors own employees or applicants, although the contractor, as an employer, may be liable for such discrimination.

An employer or other covered entity, on the other hand, cannot evade the obligations imposed by this part by engaging in a contractual or other relationship. For example, an employer cannot avoid its responsibility to make reasonable accommodation subject to the undue hardship limitation through a contractual arrangement. See Conference Report at 59; House Labor Report at 59-61; House Judiciary Report at 36-37.

To illustrate, assume that an employer is seeking to contract with a company to provide training for its employees. Any responsibilities of reasonable accommodation applicable to the employer in providing the training remain with that employer even if it contracts with another company for this service. Thus, if the training company were planning to conduct the training at an inaccessible location, thereby making it impossible for an employee who uses a wheelchair to attend, the employer would have a duty to make reasonable accommodation unless to do so would impose an undue hardship. Under these circumstances, appropriate accommodations might include (1) having the training company identify accessible training sites and relocate the training program; (2) having the training company make the training site accessible; (3) directly making the training site accessible or providing the training company with the means by which to make the site accessible; (4) identifying and contracting with another training company that uses accessible sites; or (5) any other accommodation that would result in making the training available to the employee.

As another illustration, assume that instead of contracting with a training company, the employer contracts with a hotel to host a conference for its employees. The employer will have a duty to ascertain and ensure the accessibility of the hotel and its conference facilities. To fulfill this obligation the employer could, for example, inspect the hotel first-hand or ask a local disability group to inspect the hotel. Alternatively, the employer could ensure that the contract with the hotel specifies it will provide accessible guest rooms for those who need them and that all rooms to be used for the conference, including exhibit and meeting rooms, are accessible. If the hotel breaches this accessibility provision, the hotel may be liable to the employer, under a non-ADA breach of contract theory, for the cost of any accommodation needed to provide access to the hotel and conference, and for any other costs accrued by the employer. (In addition, the hotel may also be independently liable under title III of the ADA). However, this would not relieve the employer of its responsibility under this part nor shield it from charges of discrimination by its own employees. See House Labor Report at 40; House Judiciary Report at 37.

Section 1630.8
Relationship or Association With an Individual With a Disability

This provision is intended to protect any qualified individual, whether or not that individual has a disability, from discrimination because that person is known to have an association or relationship with an individual who has a known disability. This protection is not limited to those who have a familial relationship with an individual with a disability.

To illustrate the scope of this provision, assume that a qualified applicant without a disability applies for a job and discloses to the employer that his or her spouse has a disability. The employer thereupon declines to hire the applicant because the employer believes that the applicant would have to miss work or frequently leave work early in order to care for the spouse. Such a refusal to hire would be prohibited by this provision. Similarly, this provision would prohibit an employer from discharging an employee because the employee does volunteer work with people who have AIDS, and the employer fears that the employee may contract the disease.

This provision also applies to other benefits and privileges of employment. For example, an employer that provides health insurance benefits to its employees for their dependents may not reduce the level of those benefits to an employee simply because that employee has a dependent with a disability. This is true even if the provision of such benefits would result in increased health insurance costs for the employer.

It should be noted, however, that an employer need not provide the applicant or employee without a disability with a reasonable accommodation because that duty only applies to qualified applicants or employees with disabilities. Thus, for example, an employee would not be entitled to a modified work schedule as an accommodation to enable the employee to care for a spouse with a disability. See Senate Report at 30; House Labor Report at 61-62; House Judiciary Report at 38-39.

Section 1630.9
Not Making Reasonable Accommodation

The obligation to make reasonable accommodation is a form of non-discrimination. It applies to all employment decisions and to the job application process. This obligation does not extend to the provision of adjustments or modifications that are primarily for the personal benefit of the individual with a disability. Thus, if an adjustment or modification is job-related, e.g., specifically assists the individual in performing the duties of a particular job, it will be considered a type of reasonable accommodation. On the other hand, if an adjustment or modification assists the individual throughout his or her daily activities, on and off the job, it will be considered a personal item that the employer is not required to provide. Accordingly, an employer would generally not be required to provide an employee with a disability with a prosthetic limb, wheelchair, or eyeglasses. Nor would an employer have to provide as an accommodation any amenity or convenience that is not job-related, such as a private hot plate, hot pot or refrigerator that is not provided to employees without disabilities. See Senate Report at 31; House Labor Report at 62.

It should be noted, however, that the provision of such items may be required as a reasonable accommodation where such items are specifically designed or required to meet job-related rather than personal needs. An employer, for example, may have to provide an individual with a disabling visual impairment with eyeglasses specifically designed to enable the individual to use the office computer monitors, but that are not otherwise needed by the individual outside of the office.

The term "supported employment," which has been applied to a wide variety of programs to assist individuals with severe disabilities in both competitive and non-competitive employment, is not synonymous with reasonable accommodation. Examples of supported employment include modified training materials, restructuring essential functions to enable an individual to perform a job, or hiring an outside professional ("job coach") to assist in job training. Whether a particular form of assistance would be required as a reasonable accommodation must be determined on an individualized, case by case basis without regard to whether that assistance is referred to as "supported employment." For example, an employer, under certain circumstances, may be required to provide modified training materials or a temporary "job coach" to assist in the training of a qualified individual with a disability as a reasonable accommodation. However, an employer would not be required to restructure the essential functions of a position to fit the skills of an individual with a disability who is not otherwise qualified to perform the position, as is done in certain supported employment programs. See 34 CFR part 363. It should be noted that it would not be a violation of this part for an employer to provide any of these personal modifications or adjustments, or to engage in supported employment or similar rehabilitative programs.

The obligation to make reasonable accommodation applies to all services and programs provided in connection with employment, and to all non-work facilities provided or maintained by an employer for use by its employees. Accordingly, the obligation to accommodate is applicable to employer sponsored placement or counseling services, and to employer provided cafeterias, lounges, gymnasiums, auditoriums, transportation and the like.

The reasonable accommodation requirement is best understood as a means by which barriers to the equal employment opportunity of an individual with a disability are removed or alleviated. These barriers may, for example, be physical or structural obstacles that inhibit or prevent the access of an individual with a disability to job sites, facilities or equipment. Or they may be rigid work schedules that permit no flexibility as to when work is performed or when breaks may be taken, or inflexible job procedures that unduly limit the modes of communication that are used on the job, or the way in which particular tasks are accomplished.

The term "otherwise qualified" is intended to make clear that the obligation to make reasonable accommodation is owed only to an individual with a disability who is qualified within the meaning of § 1630.2(m) in that he or she satisfies all the skill, experience, education, and other job-related selection criteria. An individual with a disability is "otherwise qualified," in other words, if he or she is qualified for a job, except that, because of the disability, he or she needs a reasonable accommodation to be able to perform the job's essential functions.

For example, if a law firm requires that all incoming lawyers have graduated from an accredited law school and have passed the bar examination, the law firm need not provide an accommodation to an individual with a visual impairment who has not met these selection criteria. That individual is not entitled to a reasonable accommodation because the individual is not "otherwise qualified" for the position.

On the other hand, if the individual has graduated from an accredited law school and passed the bar examination, the individual would be "otherwise qualified." The law firm would thus be required to provide a reasonable accommodation, such as a machine that magnifies print, to enable the individual to perform the essential functions of the attorney position, unless the necessary accommodation would impose an undue hardship on the law firm. See Senate Report at 33-34; House Labor Report at 64-65.

The reasonable accommodation that is required by this part should provide the qualified individual with a disability with an equal employment opportunity. Equal employment opportunity means an opportunity to attain the same level of performance, or to enjoy the same level of benefits and privileges of employment as are available to the average similarly situated employee without a disability. Thus, for example, an accommodation made to assist an employee with a disability in the performance of his or her job must be adequate to enable the individual to perform the essential functions of the relevant position. The accommodation, however, does not have to be the "best" accommodation possible, so long as it is sufficient to meet the job-related needs of the individual being accommodated. Accordingly, an employer would not have to provide an employee disabled by a back impairment with a state-of-the art mechanical lifting device if it provided the employee with a less expensive or more readily available device that enabled the employee to perform the essential functions of the job. See Senate Report at 35; House Labor Report at 66; see also *Carter v. Bennett*, 840 F.2d 63 (D.C. Cir. 1988). Employers are obligated to make reasonable accommodation only to the physical or mental limitations resulting from the disability of a qualified individual with a disability that is known to the employer. Thus, an employer would not be expected to accommodate disabilities of which it is unaware. If an employee with a known disability is having difficulty performing his or her job, an employer may inquire whether the employee is in need of a reasonable accommodation. In general, however, it is the responsibility of the individual with a disability to inform the employer that an accommodation is needed. When the need for an accommodation is not obvious, an employer, before providing a reasonable accommodation, may require that the individual with a disability provide documentation of the need for accommodation.

See Senate Report at 34; House Labor Report at 65.

Process of Determining the Appropriate Reasonable Accommodation

Once a qualified individual with a disability has requested provision of a reasonable accommodation, the employer must make a reasonable effort to determine the appropriate accommodation. The appropriate reasonable accommodation is best determined through a flexible, interactive process that involves both the employer and the qualified individual with a disability. Although this process is described below in terms of accommodations that enable the individual with a disability to perform the essential functions of the position held or desired, it is equally applicable to accommodations involving the job application process, and to accommodations that enable the individual with a disability to enjoy equal benefits and privileges of employment. See Senate Report at 34-35; House Labor Report at 65-67.

When a qualified individual with a disability has requested a reasonable accommodation to assist in the performance of a job, the employer, using a problem solving approach, should:

(1) Analyze the particular job involved and determine its purpose and essential functions;

(2) Consult with the individual with a disability to ascertain the precise job-related limitations imposed by the individual's disability and how those limitations could be overcome with a reasonable accommodation;

(3) In consultation with the individual to be accommodated, identify potential accommodations and assess the effectiveness each would have in enabling the individual to perform the essential functions of the position; and

(4) Consider the preference of the individual to be accommodated and select and implement the accommodation that is most appropriate for both the employee and the employer.

In many instances, the appropriate reasonable accommodation may be so obvious to either or both the employer and the qualified individual with a disability that it may not be necessary to proceed in this step-by-step fashion. For example, if an employee who uses a wheelchair requests that his or her desk be placed on blocks to elevate the desktop above the arms of the wheelchair and the employer complies, an appropriate accommodation has been requested, identified, and provided without either the employee or employer being aware of having engaged in any sort of "reasonable accommodation process."

However, in some instances neither the individual requesting the accommodation nor the employer can readily identify the appropriate accommodation. For example, the individual needing the accommodation may not know enough about the equipment used by the employer or the exact nature of the work site to suggest an appropriate accommodation. Likewise, the employer may not know enough about the individual's disability or the limitations that disability would impose on the performance of the job to suggest an appropriate accommodation. Under such circumstances, it may be necessary for the employer to initiate a more defined problem solving process, such as the step-by-step process described above, as part of its reasonable effort to identify the appropriate reasonable accommodation.

This process requires the individual assessment of both the particular job at issue, and the specific physical or mental limitations of the particular individual in need of reasonable accommodation. With regard to assessment of the job, "individual assessment" means analyzing the actual job duties and determining the true purpose or object of the job. Such an assessment is necessary to ascertain which job functions are the essential functions that an accommodation must enable an individual with a disability to perform.

After assessing the relevant job, the employer, in consultation with the individual requesting the accommodation, should make an assessment of the specific limitations imposed by the disability on the individual's performance of the job's essential functions. This assessment will make it possible to ascertain the precise barrier to the employment opportunity which, in turn, will make it possible to determine the accommodation(s) that could alleviate or remove that barrier. If consultation with the individual in need of the accommodation still does not reveal potential appropriate accommodations, then the employer, as part of this process, may find that technical assistance is helpful in determining how to accommodate the particular individual in the specific situation. Such assistance could be sought from the Commission, from state or local rehabilitation agencies, or from disability constituent organizations. It should be noted, however, that, as provided in § 1630.9(c) of this part, the failure to obtain or receive technical assistance from the federal agencies that administer the ADA will not excuse the employer from its reasonable accommodation obligation.

Once potential accommodations have been identified, the employer should assess the effectiveness of each potential accommodation in assisting the individual in need of the accommodation in the performance of the essential functions of the position. If more than one of these accommodations will enable the individual to perform the essential functions or if the individual would prefer to provide his or her own accommodation, the preference of the individual with a disability should be given primary consideration. However, the employer providing the accommodation has the ultimate discretion to choose between effective accommodations, and may choose the less expensive accommodation or the accommodation that is easier for it to provide. It should also be noted that the individual's willingness to provide his or her own accommodation does not relieve the employer of the duty to provide the accommodation should the individual for any reason be unable or unwilling to continue to provide the accommodation.

Reasonable Accommodation
Process Illustrated

The following example illustrates the informal reasonable accommodation process. Suppose a Sack Handler position requires that the employee pick up fifty pound sacks and carry them from the company loading dock to the storage room, and that a sack handler who is disabled by a back impairment requests a reasonable accommodation. Upon receiving the request, the employer analyzes the Sack Handler job and determines that the essential function and purpose of the job is not the requirement that the job holder physically lift and carry the sacks, but the requirement that the job holder cause the sack to move from the loading dock to the storage room.

The employer then meets with the sack handler to ascertain precisely the barrier posed by the individual's specific disability to the performance of the job's essential function of relocating the sacks. At this meeting the employer learns that the individual can, in fact, lift the sacks to waist level, but is prevented by his or her disability from carrying the sacks from the loading dock to the storage room. The employer and the individual agree that any of a number of potential accommodations, such as the provision of a dolly, hand truck, or cart, could enable the individual to transport the sacks that he or she has lifted.

Upon further consideration, however, it is determined that the provision of a cart is not a feasible effective option. No carts are currently available at the company, and those that can be purchased by the company are the wrong shape to hold many of the bulky and irregularly shaped sacks that must be moved. Both the dolly and the hand truck, on the other hand, appear to be effective options. Both are readily available to the company, and either will enable the individual to relocate the sacks that he or she has lifted. The sack handler indicates his or her preference for the dolly. In consideration of this expressed preference, and because the employer feels that the dolly will allow the individual to move more sacks at a time and so be more efficient than would a hand truck, the employer ultimately provides the sack handler with a dolly in fulfillment of the obligation to make reasonable accommodation.

Section 1630.9(b)

This provision states that an employer or other covered entity cannot prefer or select a qualified individual without a disability over an equally qualified individual with a disability merely because the individual with a disability will require a reasonable accommodation. In other words, an individual's need for an accommodation cannot enter into the employer's or other covered entity's decision regarding hiring, discharge, promotion, or other similar employment decisions, unless the accommodation would impose an undue hardship on the employer. See House Labor Report at 70.

Section 1630.9(d)

The purpose of this provision is to clarify that an employer or other covered entity may not compel a qualified individual with a disability to accept an accommodation, where that accommodation is neither requested nor needed by the individual. However, if a necessary reasonable accommodation is refused, the individual may not be considered qualified. For example, an individual with a visual impairment that restricts his or her field of vision but who is able to read unaided would not be required to accept a reader as an accommodation. However, if the individual were not able to read unaided and reading was an essential function of the job, the individual would not be qualified for the job if he or she refused a reasonable accommodation that would enable him or her to read. See Senate Report at 34; House Labor Report at 65; House Judiciary Report at 71-72.

Section 1630.10
Qualification Standards, Tests, and Other Selection Criteria

The purpose of this provision is to ensure that individuals with disabilities are not excluded from job opportunities unless they are actually unable to do the job. It is to ensure that there is a fit between job criteria and an applicant's (or employee's) actual ability to do the job. Accordingly, job criteria that even unintentionally screen out, or tend to screen out, an individual with a disability or a class of individuals with disabilities because of their disability may not be used unless the employer demonstrates that that criteria, as used by the employer, are job-related to the position to which they are being applied and are consistent with business necessity. The concept of "business necessity" has the same meaning as the concept of "business necessity" under section 504 of the Rehabilitation Act of 1973.

Selection criteria that exclude, or tend to exclude, an individual with a disability or a class of individuals with disabilities because of their disability but do not concern an essential function of the job would not be consistent with business necessity.

The use of selection criteria that are related to an essential function of the job may be consistent with business necessity. However, selection criteria that are related to an essential function of the job may not be used to exclude an individual with a disability if that individual could satisfy the criteria with the provision of a reasonable accommodation. Experience under a similar provision of the regulations implementing section 504 of the Rehabilitation Act indicates that challenges to selection criteria are, in fact, most often resolved by reasonable accommodation. It is therefore anticipated that challenges to selection criteria brought under this part will generally be resolved in a like manner.

This provision is applicable to all types of selection criteria, including safety requirements, vision or hearing requirements, walking requirements, lifting requirements, and employment tests. See Senate Report at 37-39; House Labor Report at 70-72; House Judiciary Report at 42. As previously noted, however, it is not the intent of this part to second guess an employer's business judgment with regard to production standards. (See section 1630.2(n) Essential Functions). Consequently, production standards will generally not be subject to a challenge under this provision.

The Uniform Guidelines on Employee Selection Procedures (UGESP) 29 CFR part 1607 do not apply to the Rehabilitation Act and are similarly inapplicable to this part.

Section 1630.11 Administration of Tests

The intent of this provision is to further emphasize that individuals with disabilities are not to be excluded from jobs that they can actually perform merely because a disability prevents them from taking a test, or negatively influences the results of a test, that is a prerequisite to the job. Read together with the reasonable accommodation requirement of section 1630.9, this provision requires that employment tests be administered to eligible applicants or employees with disabilities that impair sensory, manual, or speaking skills in formats that do not require the use of the impaired skill.

The employer or other covered entity is, generally, only required to provide such reasonable accommodation if it knows, prior to the administration of the test, that the individual is disabled and that the disability impairs sensory, manual or speaking skills. Thus, for example, it would be unlawful to administer a written employment test to an individual who has informed the employer, prior to the administration of the test, that he is disabled with dyslexia and unable to read. In such a case, as a reasonable accommodation and in accordance with this provision, an alternative oral test should be administered to that individual. By the same token, a written test may need to be substituted for an oral test if the applicant taking the test is an individual with a disability that impairs speaking skills or impairs the processing of auditory information.

Occasionally, an individual with a disability may not realize, prior to the administration of a test, that he or she will need an accommodation to take that particular test. In such a situation, the individual with a disability, upon becoming aware of the need for an accommodation, must so inform the employer or other covered entity. For example, suppose an individual with a disabling visual impairment does not request an accommodation for a written examination because he or she is usually able to take written tests with the aid of his or her own specially designed lens. When the test is distributed, the individual with a disability discovers that the lens is insufficient to distinguish the words of the test because of the unusually low color contrast between the paper and the ink, the individual would be entitled, at that point, to request an accommodation. The employer or other covered entity would, thereupon, have to provide a test with higher contrast, schedule a retest, or provide any other effective accommodation unless to do so would impose an undue hardship.

Other alternative or accessible test modes or formats include the administration of tests in large print or braille, or via a reader or sign interpreter. Where it is not possible to test in an alternative format, the employer may be required, as a reasonable accommodation, to evaluate the skill to be tested in another manner (e.g., through an interview, or through education license, or work experience requirements). An employer may also be required, as a reasonable accommodation, to allow more time to complete the test. In addition, the employer's obligation to make reasonable accommodation extends to ensuring that the test site is accessible. (See § 1630.9 Not Making Reasonable Accommodation) See Senate Report at 37-38; House Labor Report at 70-72; House Judiciary Report at 42; see also *Stutts v. Freeman*, 694 F.2d 666 (11th Cir. 1983); *Crane v. Dole*, 617 F. Supp. 156 (D.D.C. 1985).

This provision does not require that an employer offer every applicant his or her choice of test format. Rather, this provision only requires that an employer provide, upon advance request, alternative, accessible tests to individuals with disabilities that impair sensory, manual, or speaking skills needed to take the test.

This provision does not apply to employment tests that require the use of sensory, manual, or speaking skills where the tests are intended to measure those skills. Thus, an employer could require that an applicant with dyslexia take a written test for a particular position if the ability to read is the skill the test is designed to measure. Similarly, an employer could require that an applicant complete a test within established time frames if speed were one of the skills for which the applicant was being tested. However, the results of such a test could not be used to exclude an individual with a disability unless the skill was necessary to perform an essential function of the position and no reasonable accommodation was available to enable the individual to perform that function, or the necessary accommodation would impose an undue hardship.

Section 1630.13 Prohibited
Medical Examinations and Inquiries

Section 1630.13(a)
Pre-employment Examination or Inquiry

This provision makes clear that an employer cannot inquire as to whether an individual has a disability at the pre-offer stage of the selection process. Nor can an employer inquire at the pre-offer stage about an applicant's workers' compensation history.

Employers may ask questions that relate to the applicant's ability to perform job-related functions. However, these questions should not be phrased in terms of disability. An employer, for example, may ask whether the applicant has a driver's license, if driving is a job function, but may not ask whether the applicant has a visual disability. Employers may ask about an applicant's ability to perform both essential and marginal job functions. Employers, though, may not refuse to hire an applicant with a disability because the applicant's disability prevents him or her from performing marginal functions. See Senate Report at 39; House Labor Report at 72-73; House Judiciary Report at 42-43.

Section 1630.13(b)
Examination or Inquiry of Employees

The purpose of this provision is to prevent the administration to employees of medical tests or inquiries that do not serve a legitimate business purpose. For example, if an employee suddenly starts to use increased amounts of sick leave or starts to appear sickly, an employer could not require that employee to be tested for AIDS, HIV infection, or cancer unless the employer can demonstrate that such testing is job-related and consistent with business necessity. See Senate Report at 39; House Labor Report at 75; House Judiciary Report at 44.

Section 1630.14 Medical Examinations and Inquiries Specifically Permitted

Section 1630.14(a) Pre-employment Inquiry

Employers are permitted to make pre-employment inquiries into the ability of an applicant to perform job-related functions. This inquiry must be narrowly tailored. The employer may describe or demonstrate the job function and inquire whether or not the applicant can perform that function with or without reasonable accommodation. For example, an employer may explain that the job requires assembling small parts and ask if the individual will be able to perform that function, with or without reasonable accommodation. See Senate Report at 39; House Labor Report at 73; House Judiciary Report at 43.

An employer may also ask an applicant to describe or to demonstrate how, with or without reasonable accommodation, the applicant will be able to perform job-related functions. Such a request may be made of all applicants in the same job category regardless of disability. Such a request may also be made of an applicant whose known disability may interfere with or prevent the performance of a job-related function, whether or not the employer routinely makes such a request of all applicants in the job category. For example, an employer may ask an individual with one leg who applies for a position as a home washing machine repairman to demonstrate or to explain how, with or without reasonable accommodation, he would be able to transport himself and his tools down basement stairs. However, the employer may not inquire as to the nature or severity of the disability. Therefore, for example, the employer cannot ask how the individual lost the leg or whether the loss of the leg is indicative of an underlying impairment.

On the other hand, if the known disability of an applicant will not interfere with or prevent the performance of a job-related function, the employer may only request a description or demonstration by the applicant if it routinely makes such a request of all applicants in the same job category. So, for example, it would not be permitted for an employer to request that an applicant with one leg demonstrate his ability to assemble small parts while seated at a table, if the employer does not routinely request that all applicants provide such a demonstration.

An employer that requires an applicant with a disability to demonstrate how he or she will perform a job-related function must either provide the reasonable accommodation the applicant needs to perform the function or permit the applicant to explain how, with the accommodation, he or she will perform the function. If the job-related function is not an essential function, the employer may not exclude the applicant with a disability because of the applicant's inability to perform that function. Rather, the employer must, as a reasonable accommodation, either provide an accommodation that will enable the individual to perform the function, transfer the function to another position, or exchange the function for one the applicant is able to perform.

An employer may not use an application form that lists a number of potentially disabling impairments and ask the applicant to check any of the impairments he or she may have. In addition, as noted above, an employer may not ask how a particular individual became disabled or the prognosis of the individual's disability. The employer is also prohibited from asking how often the individual will require leave for treatment or use leave as a result of incapacitation because of the disability. However, the employer may state the attendance requirements of the job and inquire whether the applicant can meet them.

An employer is permitted to ask, on a test announcement or application form, that individuals with disabilities who will require a reasonable accommodation in order to take the test so inform the employer within a reasonable established time period prior to the administration of the test. The employer may also request that documentation of the need for the accommodation accompany the request. Requested accommodations may include accessible testing sites, modified testing conditions and accessible test formats. (See § 1630.11 Administration of Tests).

Physical agility tests are not medical examinations and so may be given at any point in the application or employment process. Such tests must be given to all similarly situated applicants or employees regardless of disability. If such tests screen out or tend to screen out an individual with a disability or a class of individuals with disabilities, the employer would have to demonstrate that the test is job-related and consistent with business necessity and that performance cannot be achieved with reasonable accommodation. (See § 1630.9 Not Making Reasonable Accommodation: Process of Determining the Appropriate Reasonable Accommodation).

As previously noted, collecting information and inviting individuals to identify themselves as individuals with disabilities as required to satisfy the affirmative action requirements of Section 503 of the Rehabilitation Act is not restricted by this part. (See § 1630.1 (b) and (c) Applicability and Construction).

Section 1630.14(b)
Employment Entrance Examination

An employer is permitted to require post-offer medical examinations before the employee actually starts working. The employer may condition the offer of employment on the results of the examination, provided that all entering employees in the same job category are subjected to such an examination, regardless of disability, and that the confidentiality requirements specified in this part are met.

This provision recognizes that in many industries, such as air transportation or construction, applicants for certain positions are chosen on the basis of many factors including physical and psychological criteria, some of which may be identified as a result of post-offer medical examinations given prior to entry on duty. Only those employees who meet the employer's physical and psychological criteria for the job, with or without reasonable accommodation, will be qualified to receive confirmed offers of employment and begin working.

Medical examinations permitted by this section are not required to be job-related and consistent with business necessity. However, if an employer withdraws an offer of employment because the medical examination reveals that the employee does not satisfy certain employment criteria, either the exclusionary criteria must not screen out or tend to screen out an individual with a disability or a class of individuals with disabilities, or they must be job-related and consistent with business necessity. As part of the showing that an exclusionary criteria is job-related and consistent with business necessity, the employer must also demonstrate that there is no reasonable accommodation that will enable the individual with a disability to perform the essential functions of the job. See Conference Report at 59-60; Senate Report at 39; House Labor Report at 73-74; House Judiciary Report at 43.

As an example, suppose an employer makes a conditional offer of employment to an applicant, and it is an essential function of the job that the incumbent be available to work every day for the next three months. An employment entrance examination then reveals that the applicant has a disabling impairment that, according to reasonable medical judgment that relies on the most current medical knowledge, will require treatment that will render the applicant unable to work for a portion of the three month period. Under these circumstances, the employer would be able to withdraw the employment offer without violating this part.

The information obtained in the course of a permitted entrance examination or inquiry is to be treated as a confidential medical record and may only be used in a manner not inconsistent with this part. State workers' compensation laws are not preempted by the ADA or this part. These laws require the collection of information from individuals for state administrative purposes that do not conflict with the ADA or this part. Consequently, employers or other covered entities may submit information to state workers' compensation offices or second injury funds in accordance with state workers' compensation laws without violating this part.

Consistent with this section and with § 1630.16(f) of this part, information obtained in the course of a permitted entrance examination or inquiry may be used for insurance purposes described in § 1630.16(f).

Section 1630.14(c)
Examination of Employees

This provision permits employers to make inquiries or require medical examinations (fitness for duty exams) when there is a need to determine whether an employee is still able to perform the essential functions of his or her job. The provision permits employers or other covered entities to make inquiries or require medical examinations necessary to the reasonable accommodation process described in this part. This provision also permits periodic physicals to determine fitness for duty or other medical monitoring if such physicals or monitoring are required by medical standards or requirements established by Federal, state, or local law that are consistent with the ADA and this part (or in the case of a federal standard, with section 504 of the Rehabilitation Act) in that they are job-related and consistent with business necessity.

Such standards may include federal safety regulations that regulate bus and truck driver qualifications, as well as laws establishing medical requirements for pilots or other air transportation personnel. These standards also include health standards promulgated pursuant to the Occupational Safety and Health Act of 1970, the Federal Coal Mine Health and Safety Act of 1969, or other similar statutes that require that employees exposed to certain toxic and hazardous substances be medically monitored at specific intervals. See House Labor Report at 74-75.

The information obtained in the course of such examination or inquiries is to be treated as a confidential medical record and may only be used in a manner not inconsistent with this part.

Section 1630.14(d) Other
Acceptable Examinations and Inquiries

Part 1630 permits voluntary medical examinations, including voluntary medical histories, as part of employee health programs. These programs often include, for example, medical screening for high blood pressure, weight control counseling, and cancer detection. Voluntary activities, such as blood pressure monitoring and the administering of prescription drugs, such as insulin, are also permitted. It should be noted, however, that the medical records developed in the course of such activities must be maintained in the confidential manner required by this part and must not be used for any purpose in violation of this part, such as limiting health insurance eligibility. House Labor Report at 75; House Judiciary Report at 43-44.

Section 1630.15 Defenses

The section on defenses in part 1630 is not intended to be exhaustive. However, it is intended to inform employers of some of the potential defenses available to a charge of discrimination under the ADA and this part.

Section 1630.15(a)
Disparate Treatment Defenses

The "traditional" defense to a charge of disparate treatment under title VII, as expressed in *McDonnell Douglas Corp. v. Green*, 411 U.S. 792 (1973), *Texas Department of Community Affairs v. Burdine*, 450 U.S. 248 (1981), and their progeny, may be applicable to charges of disparate treatment brought under the ADA. See *Prewitt v. U.S. Postal Service*, 662 F.2d 292 (5th Cir. 1981). Disparate treatment means, with respect to title I of the ADA, that an individual was treated differently on the basis of his or her disability. For example, disparate treatment has occurred where an employer excludes an employee with a severe facial disfigurement from staff meetings because the employer does not like to look at the employee. The individual is being treated differently because of the employer's attitude towards his or her perceived disability. Disparate treatment has also occurred where an employer has a policy of not hiring individuals with AIDS regardless of the individuals' qualifications.

The crux of the defense to this type of charge is that the individual was treated differently not because of his or her disability but for a legitimate nondiscriminatory reason such as poor performance unrelated to the individual's disability. The fact that the individual's disability is not covered by the employer's current insurance plan or would cause the employer's insurance premiums or workers' compensation costs to increase, would not be a legitimate nondiscriminatory reason justifying disparate treatment of an individual with a disability. Senate Report at 85; House Labor Report at 136 and House Judiciary Report at 70. The defense of a legitimate nondiscriminatory reason is rebutted if the alleged nondiscriminatory reason is shown to be pretextual.

Section 1630.15 (b) and (c)
Disparate Impact Defenses

Disparate impact means, with respect to title I of the ADA and this part, that uniformly applied criteria have an adverse impact on an individual with a disability or a disproportionately negative impact on a class of individuals with disabilities. Section 1630.15(b) clarifies that an employer may use selection criteria that have such a disparate impact, i.e., that screen out or tend to screen out an individual with a disability or a class of individuals with disabilities only when they are job-related and consistent with business necessity.

For example, an employer interviews two candidates for a position, one of whom is blind. Both are equally qualified. The employer decides that while it is not essential to the job it would be convenient to have an employee who has a driver's license and so could occasionally be asked to run errands by car. The employer hires the individual who is sighted because this individual has a driver's license. This is an example of a uniformly applied criterion, having a driver's permit, that screens out an individual who has a disability that makes it impossible to obtain a driver's permit. The employer would, thus, have to show that this criterion is job-related and consistent with business necessity. See House Labor Report at 55.

However, even if the criterion is job-related and consistent with business necessity, an employer could not exclude an individual with a disability if the criterion could be met or job performance accomplished with a reasonable accommodation. For example, suppose an employer requires, as part of its application process, an interview that is job-related and consistent with business necessity. The employer would not be able to refuse to hire a hearing impaired applicant because he or she could not be interviewed. This is so because an interpreter could be provided as a reasonable accommodation that would allow the individual to be interviewed, and thus satisfy the selection criterion.

With regard to safety requirements that screen out or tend to screen out an individual with a disability or a class of individuals with disabilities, an employer must demonstrate that the requirement, as applied to the individual, satisfies the "direct threat" standard in § 1630.2(r) in order to show that the requirement is job-related and consistent with business necessity.

Section 1630.15(c) clarifies that there may be uniformly applied standards, criteria and policies not relating to selection that may also screen out or tend to screen out an individual with a disability or a class of individuals with disabilities. Like selection criteria that have a disparate impact, non-selection criteria having such an impact may also have to be job-related and consistent with business necessity, subject to consideration of reasonable accommodation.

It should be noted, however, that some uniformly applied employment policies or practices, such as leave policies, are not subject to challenge under the adverse impact theory. "No-leave" policies (e.g., no leave during the first six months of employment) are likewise not subject to challenge under the adverse impact theory. However, an employer, in spite of its "no-leave" policy, may, in appropriate circumstances, have to consider the provision of leave to an employee with a disability as a reasonable accommodation, unless the provision of leave would impose an undue hardship. See discussion at § 1630.5 Limiting, Segregating and Classifying, and § 1630.10 Qualification Standards, Tests, and Other Selection Criteria.

Section 1630.15(d) Defense to Not Making Reasonable Accommodation

An employer or other covered entity alleged to have discriminated because it did not make a reasonable accommodation, as required by this part, may offer as a defense that it would have been an undue hardship to make the accommodation.

It should be noted, however, that an employer cannot simply assert that a needed accommodation will cause it undue hardship, as defined in § 1630.2(p), and thereupon be relieved of the duty to provide accommodation. Rather, an employer will have to present evidence and demonstrate that the accommodation will, in fact, cause it undue hardship. Whether a particular accommodation will impose an undue hardship for a particular employer is determined on a case by case basis. Consequently, an accommodation that poses an undue hardship for one employer at a particular time may not pose an undue hardship for another employer, or even for the same employer at another time. Likewise, an accommodation that poses an undue hardship for one employer in a particular job setting, such as a temporary construction work site, may not pose an undue hardship for another employer, or even for the same employer at a permanent worksite. See House Judiciary Report at 42.

The concept of undue hardship that has evolved under Section 504 of the Rehabilitation Act and is embodied in this part is unlike the "undue hardship" defense associated with the provision of religious accommodation under title VII of the Civil Rights Act of 1964. To demonstrate undue hardship pursuant to the ADA and this part, an employer must show substantially more difficulty or expense than would be needed to satisfy the "de minimis" title VII standard of undue hardship. For example, to demonstrate that the cost of an accommodation poses an undue hardship, an employer would have to show that the cost is undue as compared to the employer's budget. Simply comparing the cost of the accommodation to the salary of the individual with a disability in need of the accommodation will not suffice. Moreover, even if it is determined that the cost of an accommodation would unduly burden an employer, the employer cannot avoid making the accommodation if the individual with a disability can arrange to cover that portion of the cost that rises to the undue hardship level, or can otherwise arrange to provide the accommodation. Under such circumstances, the necessary accommodation would no longer pose an undue hardship. See Senate Report at 36; House Labor Report at 68-69; House Judiciary Report at 40-41. Excessive cost is only one of several possible bases upon which an employer might be able to demonstrate undue hardship. Alternatively, for example, an employer could demonstrate that the provision of a particular accommodation would be unduly disruptive to its other employees or to the functioning of its business. The terms of a collective bargaining agreement may be relevant to this determination. By way of illustration, an employer would likely be able to show undue hardship if the employer could show that the requested accommodation of the upward adjustment of the business' thermostat would result in it becoming unduly hot for its other employees, or for its patrons or customers. The employer would thus not have to provide this accommodation. However, if there were an alternate accommodation that would not result in undue hardship, the employer would have to provide that accommodation.

It should be noted, moreover, that the employer would not be able to show undue hardship if the disruption to its employees were the result of those employees fears or prejudices toward the individual's disability and not the result of the provision of the accommodation. Nor would the employer be able to demonstrate undue hardship by showing that the provision of the accommodation has a negative impact on the morale of its other employees but not on the ability of these employees to perform their jobs.

Section 1630.15(e) Defense—Conflicting Federal Laws and Regulations

There are several Federal laws and regulations that address medical standards and safety requirements. If the alleged discriminatory action was taken in compliance with another Federal law or regulation, the employer may offer its obligation to comply with the conflicting standard as a defense. The employer's defense of a conflicting Federal requirement or regulation may be rebutted by a showing of pretext, or by showing that the Federal standard did not require the discriminatory action, or that there was a non-exclusionary means to comply with the standard that would not conflict with this part. See House Labor Report at 74.

Section 1630.16 Specific Activities Permitted

Section 1630.16(a) Religious Entities

Religious organizations are not exempt from title I of the ADA or this part. A religious corporation, association, educational institution, or society may give a preference in employment to individuals of the particular religion, and may require that applicants and employees conform to the religious tenets of the organization. However, a religious organization may not discriminate against an individual who satisfies the permitted religious criteria because that individual is disabled. The religious entity, in other words, is required to consider qualified individuals with disabilities who satisfy the permitted religious criteria on an equal basis with qualified individuals without disabilities who similarly satisfy the religious criteria. See Senate Report at 42; House Labor Report at 76-77; House Judiciary Report at 46.

Section 1630.16(b) Regulation of Alcohol and Drugs

This provision permits employers to establish or comply with certain standards regulating the use of drugs and alcohol in the workplace. It also allows employers to hold alcoholics and persons who engage in the illegal use of drugs to the same performance and conduct standards to which it holds all of its other employees. Individuals disabled by alcoholism are entitled to the same protections accorded other individuals with disabilities under this part. As noted above, individuals currently engaging in the illegal use of drugs are not individuals with disabilities for purposes of part 1630 when the employer acts on the basis of such use.

Section 1630.16(c) Drug Testing

This provision reflects title I's neutrality toward testing for the illegal use of drugs. Such drug tests are neither encouraged, authorized nor prohibited. The results of such drug tests may be used as a basis for disciplinary action. Tests for the illegal use of drugs are not considered medical examinations for purposes of this part. If the results reveal information about an individual's medical condition beyond whether the individual is currently engaging in the illegal use of drugs, this additional information is to be treated as a confidential medical record. For example, if a test for the illegal use of drugs reveals the presence of a controlled substance that has been lawfully prescribed for a particular medical condition, this information is to be treated as a confidential medical record. See House Labor Report at 79; House Judiciary Report at 47.

1630.16(e) Infectious and Communicable Diseases; Food Handling Jobs

This provision addressing food handling jobs applies the "direct threat" analysis to the particular situation of accommodating individuals with infectious or communicable diseases that are transmitted through the handling of food. The Department of Health and Human Services is to prepare a list of infectious and communicable diseases that are transmitted through the handling of food. If an individual with a disability has one of the listed diseases and works in or applies for a position in food handling, the employer must determine whether there is a reasonable accommodation that will eliminate the risk of transmitting the disease through the handling of food. If there is an accommodation that will not pose an undue hardship, and that an individual is an applicant for a food handling position the employer is not required to hire the individual. However, if the individual is a current employee, the employer would be required to consider the accommodation of reassignment to a vacant position not involving food handling for which the individual is qualified. Conference Report at 61-63. (See § 1630.2(r) Direct Threat).

1630.16(f) Health Insurance, Life Insurance, and Other Benefit Plans

This provision is a limited exemption that is only applicable to those who establish, sponsor, observe or administer benefit plans, such as health and life insurance plans. It does not apply to those who establish, sponsor, observe or administer plans not involving benefits, such as liability insurance plans.

The purpose of this provision is to permit the development and administration of benefit plans in accordance with accepted principles of risk assessment. This provision is not intended to disrupt the current regulatory structure for self-insured employers. These employers may establish, sponsor, observe, or administer the terms of a bona fide benefit plan not subject to state laws that regulate insurance. This provision is also not intended to disrupt the current nature of insurance underwriting, or current insurance industry practices in sales, underwriting, pricing, administrative and other services, claims and similar insurance related activities based on classification of risks as regulated by the States.

The activities permitted by this provision do not violate part 1630 even if they result in limitations on individuals with disabilities, provided that these activities are not used as a subterfuge to evade the purposes of this part. Whether or not these activities are being used as a subterfuge is to be determined without regard to the date the insurance plan or employee benefit plan was adopted.

However, an employer or other covered entity cannot deny a qualified individual with a disability equal access to insurance or subject a qualified individual with a disability to different terms or conditions of insurance based on disability alone, if the disability does not pose increased risks. Part 1630 requires that decisions not based on risk classification be made in conformity with non-discrimination requirements. See Senate Report at 84-86; House Labor Report at 136-138; House Judiciary Report at 70-71. See the discussion of § 1630.5 Limiting, Segregating and Classifying.

ADA TITLE II

PUBLIC SERVICES

PROHIBITION AGAINST DISCRIMINATION AND OTHER GENERALLY APPLICABLE PROVISIONS

42 U.S.C. §
- 12131 Definition
- 12132 Discrimination
- 12133 Enforcement
- 12134 Regulations

ACTIONS APPLICABLE TO PUBLIC TRANSPORTATION PROVIDED BY PUBLIC ENTITIES CONSIDERED DISCRIMINATORY

Public Transportation Other Than by Aircraft or Certain Rail Operations

- 12141 Definition
- 12142 Public entities operating fixed route systems
- 12143 Paratransit as a complement to fixed route service
- 12144 Public entity operating a demand responsive system
- 12145 Temporary relief where lifts are unavailable
- 12146 New facilities
- 12147 Alterations of existing facilities
- 12148 Public transportation programs and activities in existing facilities and one car per train rule
- 12149 Regulations
- 12150 Interim accessibility requirements

ADA TITLE II

PUBLIC SERVICES

PROHIBITION AGAINST DISCRIMINATION AND OTHER GENERALLY APPLICABLE PROVISIONS

§ 12131. Definition

As used in this subchapter:

(1) Public entity

The term "public entity" means—

(A) any State or local government;

(B) any department, agency, special purpose district, or other instrumentality of a State or States or local government; and

(C) the National Railroad Passenger Corporation, and any commuter authority (as defined in section 502(8) of Title 45).

(2) Qualified individual with a disability

The term "qualified individual with a disability" means an individual with a disability who, with or without reasonable modifications to rules, policies, or practices, the removal of architectural, communication, or transportation barriers, or the provision of auxiliary aids and services, meets the essential eligibility requirements for the receipt of services or the participation in programs or activities provided by a public entity.

§ 12132. Discrimination

Subject to the provisions of this subchapter, no qualified individual with a disability shall, by reason of such disability, be excluded from participation in or be denied the benefits of the services, programs, or activities of a public entity, or be subjected to discrimination by any such entity.

§ 12133. Enforcement

The remedies, procedures, and rights set forth in section 794a of Title 29 shall be the remedies, procedures, and rights this subchapter provides to any person alleging discrimination on the basis of disability in violation of section 12132 of this title.

§ 12134. Regulations

(a) In general. Not later than 1 year after the date of enactment of this Act [enacted July 26, 1990], the Attorney General shall promulgate regulations in an accessible format that implement this subtitle. Such regulations shall not include any matter within the scope of the authority of the Secretary of Transportation under section 223, 229, or 244 [42 USCS § 12143, 12149, or 12164].

(b) Relationship to other regulations. Except for "program accessibility, existing facilities", and "communications", regulations under subsection (a) shall be consistent with this Act and with the coordination regulations under part 41 of title 28, Code of Federal Regulations (as promulgated by the Department of Health, Education, and Welfare on January 13, 1978), applicable to recipients of Federal financial assistance under section 504 of the Rehabilitation Act of 1973 (29 U.S.C. 794). With respect to "program accessibility, existing facilities", and "communications", such regulations shall be consistent with regulations and analysis as in part 39 of title 28 of the Code of Federal

Regulations, applicable to federally conducted activities under such section 504.

(c) Standards. Regulations under subsection (a) shall include standards applicable to facilities and vehicles covered by this subtitle, other than facilities, stations, rail passenger cars, and vehicles covered by subtitle B. Such standards shall be consistent with the minimum guidelines and requirements issued by the Architectural and Transportation Barriers Compliance Board in accordance with section 504(a) of this Act [42 USCS § 12204(a)].

ACTIONS APPLICABLE TO PUBLIC TRANSPORTATION PROVIDED BY PUBLIC ENTITIES CONSIDERED DISCRIMINATORY
Public Transportation Other Than by Aircraft or Certain Rail Operations

§ 12141. Definitions

As used in this sub-part:

(1) Demand responsive system

The term "demand responsive system" means any system of providing designated public transportation which is not a fixed route system.

(2) Designated public transportation

The term "designated public transportation" means transportation (other than public school transportation) by bus, rail, or any other conveyance (other than transportation by aircraft or intercity or commuter rail transportation (as defined in section 12161 of this title) that provides the general public with general or special service (including charter service) on a regular and continuing basis.

(3) Fixed route system

The term "fixed route system" means a system of providing designated public transportation on which a vehicle is operated along a prescribed route according to a fixed schedule.

(4) Operates

The term "operates", as used with respect to a fixed route system or demand responsive system, includes operation of such system by a person under a contractual or other arrangement or relationship with a public entity.

(5) Public school transportation

The term "public school transportation" means transportation by school bus vehicles of schoolchildren, personnel, and equipment to and from a public elementary or secondary school and school-related activities.

(6) Secretary

The term "Secretary" means the Secretary of Transportation.

§ 12142. Public entities operating fixed route systems

(a) Purchase and lease of new vehicles

It shall be considered discrimination for purposes of section 12132 of this title and section 794 of Title 29 for a public entity which operates a fixed route system to purchase or lease a new bus, a new rapid rail vehicle, a new light rail vehicle, or any other new vehicle to be used on such system, if the solicitation for such purchase or lease is made after the 30th day following July 26, 1990, and if such bus, rail vehicle, or other vehicle is not readily accessible to and usable by individuals with disabilities, including individuals who use wheelchairs.

(b) Purchase and lease of used vehicles

Subject to subsection (c)(1) of this section, it shall be considered discrimination for purposes of section 12132 of this title and section 794 of Title 29 for a public entity which operates a fixed route system to purchase or lease, after the 30th day following July 26, 1990, a used vehicle for use on such system unless such entity makes demonstrated good faith efforts to purchase or lease a used vehicle for use on such system that is readily accessible to and usable by individuals with disabilities, including individuals who use wheelchairs.

(c) Remanufactured vehicles

(1) General rule

Except as provided in paragraph (2), it shall be considered discrimination for purposes of section 12132 of this title and section 794 of Title 29 for a public entity which operates a fixed route system—

(A) to remanufacture a vehicle for use on such system so as to extend its usable life for 5 years or more, which remanufacture begins (or for which the solicitation is made) after the 30th day following July 26, 1990; or

(B) to purchase or lease for use on such system a remanufactured vehicle which has been remanufactured so as to extend its usable life for 5 years or more, which purchase or lease occurs after such 30th day and during the period in which the usable life is extended; unless, after remanufacture, the vehicle is, to the maximum extent feasible, readily accessible to and usable by individuals with disabilities, including individuals who use wheelchairs.

(2) Exception for historic vehicles
    (A) General rule
If a public entity operates a fixed route system any segment of which is included on the National Register of Historic Places and if making a vehicle of historic character to be used solely on such segment readily accessible to and usable by individuals with disabilities would significantly alter the historic character of such vehicle, the public entity only has to make (or to purchase or lease a remanufactured vehicle with) those modifications which are necessary to meet the requirements of paragraph (1) and which do not significantly alter the historic character of such vehicle.
    (B) Vehicles of historic character defined by regulations
For purposes of this paragraph and section 12148(b) of this title, a vehicle of historic character shall be defined by the regulations issued by the Secretary to carry out this subsection.

§ 12143. Paratransit as a complement to fixed route service

(a) General rule

It shall be considered discrimination for purposes of section 12132 of this title and section 794 of Title 29 for a public entity which operates a fixed route system (other than a system which provides solely commuter bus service) to fail to provide with respect to the operations of its fixed route system, in accordance with this section, paratransit and other special transportation services to individuals with disabilities, including individuals who use wheelchairs, that are sufficient to provide to such individuals a level of service (1) which is comparable to the level of designated public transportation services provided to individuals without disabilities using such system; or (2) in the case of response time, which is comparable, to the extent practicable, to the level of designated public transportation services provided to individuals without disabilities using such system.

(b) Issuance of regulations

Not later than 1 year after July 26, 1990, the Secretary shall issue final regulations to carry out this section.

(c) Required contents of regulations
    (1) Eligible recipients of service
The regulations issued under this section shall require each public entity which operates a fixed route system to provide the paratransit and other special transportation services required under this section—
    (A)(i) to any individual with a disability who is unable, as a result of a physical or mental impairment (including a vision impairment) and without the assistance of another individual (except an operator of a wheelchair lift or other boarding assistance device), to board, ride, or disembark from any vehicle on the system which is readily accessible to and usable by individuals with disabilities;
    (ii) to any individual with a disability who needs the assistance of a wheelchair lift or other boarding assistance device (and is able with such assistance) to board, ride, and disembark from any vehicle which is readily accessible to and usable by individuals with disabilities if the individual wants to travel on a route on the system during the hours of operation of the system at a time (or within a reasonable period of such time) when such a vehicle is not being used to provide designated public transportation on the route; and
    (iii) to any individual with a disability who has a specific impairment-related condition which prevents such individual from traveling to a boarding location or from a disembarking location on such system;
    (B) to one other individual accompanying the individual with the disability; and
    (C) to other individuals, in addition to the one individual described in subparagraph (B), accompanying the individual with a disability provided that space for these additional individuals is available on the paratransit vehicle carrying the individual with a disability and that the transportation of such additional individuals will not result in a denial of service to individuals with disabilities.
For purposes of clauses (i) and (ii) of subparagraph (A), boarding or disembarking from a vehicle does not include travel to the boarding location or from the disembarking location.
    (2) Service area
The regulations issued under this section shall require the provision of paratransit and special transportation services required under this section in the service area of each public entity which operates a fixed route system, other than any portion of the service area in which the public entity solely provides commuter bus service.
    (3) Service criteria
Subject to paragraphs (1) and (2), the regulations issued under this section shall establish minimum service criteria for determining the level of services to be required under this section.
    (4) Undue financial burden limitation
The regulations issued under this section shall provide that, if the public entity is able to demonstrate to the satisfaction of the Secretary that the provision of paratransit and other special transportation services

otherwise required under this section would impose an undue financial burden on the public entity, the public entity, notwithstanding any other provision of this section (other than paragraph (5)), shall only be required to provide such services to the extent that providing such services would not impose such a burden.

(5) Additional services

The regulations issued under this section shall establish circumstances under which the Secretary may require a public entity to provide, notwithstanding paragraph (4), paratransit and other special transportation services under this section beyond the level of paratransit and other special transportation services which would otherwise be required under paragraph (4).

(6) Public participation

The regulations issued under this section shall require that each public entity which operates a fixed route system hold a public hearing, provide an opportunity for public comment, and consult with individuals with disabilities in preparing its plan under paragraph (7).

(7) Plans

The regulations issued under this section shall require that each public entity which operates a fixed route system—

(A) within 18 months after July 26, 1990, submit to the Secretary, and commence implementation of, a plan for providing paratransit and other special transportation services which meets the requirements of this section; and

(B) on an annual basis thereafter, submit to the Secretary, and commence implementation of, a plan for providing such services.

(8) Provision of services by others

The regulations issued under this section shall—

(A) require that a public entity submitting a plan to the Secretary under this section identify in the plan any person or other public entity which is providing a paratransit or other special transportation service for individuals with disabilities in the service area to which the plan applies; and

(B) provide that the public entity submitting the plan does not have to provide under the plan such service for individuals with disabilities.

(9) Other provisions

The regulations issued under this section shall include such other provisions and requirements as the Secretary determines are necessary to carry out the objectives of this section.

(d) Review of plan

(1) General rule

The Secretary shall review a plan submitted under this section for the purpose of determining whether or not such plan meets the requirements of this section, including the regulations issued under this section.

(2) Disapproval

If the Secretary determines that a plan reviewed under this subsection fails to meet the requirements of this section, the Secretary shall disapprove the plan and notify the public entity which submitted the plan of such disapproval and the reasons therefor.

(3) Modification of disapproved plan

Not later than 90 days after the date of disapproval of a plan under this subsection, the public entity which submitted the plan shall modify the plan to meet the requirements of this section and shall submit to the Secretary, and commence implementation of, such modified plan.

(e) Discrimination defined

As used in subsection (a) of this section, the term "discrimination" includes—

(1) a failure of a public entity to which the regulations issued under this section apply to submit, or commence implementation of, a plan in accordance with subsections (c)(6) and (c)(7) of this section;

(2) a failure of such entity to submit, or commence implementation of, a modified plan in accordance with subsection (d)(3) of this section;

(3) submission to the Secretary of a modified plan under subsection (d)(3) of this section which does not meet the requirements of this section; or

(4) a failure of such entity to provide paratransit or other special transportation services in accordance with the plan or modified plan the public entity submitted to the Secretary under this section.

(f) Statutory construction

Nothing in this section shall be construed as preventing a public entity—

(1) from providing paratransit or other special transportation services at a level which is greater than the level of such services which are required by this section,

(2) from providing paratransit or other special transportation services in addition to those paratransit and special transportation services required by this section, or

(3) from providing such services to individuals in addition to those individuals to whom such services are required to be provided by this section.

§ 12144. Public entity operating a demand responsive system

If a public entity operates a demand responsive system, it shall be considered discrimination, for purposes of section 12132 of this title and section 794 of Title 29, for such entity to purchase or lease a new vehicle for use on such system, for which a solicitation is made after the 30th day following July 26, 1990, that is not readily accessible to and usable by individuals with disabilities, including individuals who use wheelchairs, unless such system, when viewed in its entirety, provides a level of service to such individuals equivalent to the level of service such system provides to individuals without disabilities.

§ 12145. Temporary relief where lifts are unavailable

(a) Granting

With respect to the purchase of new buses, a public entity may apply for, and the Secretary may temporarily relieve such public entity from the obligation under section 12142(a) or 12144 of this title to purchase new buses that are readily accessible to and usable by individuals with disabilities if such public entity demonstrates to the satisfaction of the Secretary—

(1) that the initial solicitation for new buses made by the public entity specified that all new buses were to be lift-equipped and were to be otherwise accessible to and usable by individuals with disabilities;

(2) the unavailability from any qualified manufacturer of hydraulic, electromechanical, or other lifts for such new buses;

(3) that the public entity seeking temporary relief has made good faith efforts to locate a qualified manufacturer to supply the lifts to the manufacturer of such buses in sufficient time to comply with such solicitation; and

(4) that any further delay in purchasing new buses necessary to obtain such lifts would significantly impair transportation services in the community served by the public entity.

(b) Duration and notice to Congress

Any relief granted under subsection (a) of this section shall be limited in duration by a specified date, and the appropriate committees of Congress shall be notified of any such relief granted.

(c) Fraudulent application

If, at any time, the Secretary has reasonable cause to believe that any relief granted under subsection (a) of this section was fraudulently applied for, the Secretary shall—

(1) cancel such relief if such relief is still in effect; and

(2) take such other action as the Secretary considers appropriate.

§ 12146. New facilities

For purposes of section 12132 of this title and section 794 of Title 29, it shall be considered discrimination for a public entity to construct a new facility to be used in the provision of designated public transportation services unless such facility is readily accessible to and usable by individuals with disabilities, including individuals who use wheelchairs.

§ 12147. Alterations of existing facilities

(a) General rule

With respect to alterations of an existing facility or part thereof used in the provision of designated public transportation services that affect or could affect the usability of the facility or part thereof, it shall be considered discrimination, for purposes of section 12132 of this title and section 794 of Title 29, for a public entity to fail to make such alterations (or to ensure that the alterations are made) in such a manner that, to the maximum extent feasible, the altered portions of the facility are readily accessible to and usable by individuals with disabilities, including individuals who use wheelchairs, upon the completion of such alterations. Where the public entity is undertaking an alteration that affects or could affect usability of or access to an area of the facility containing a primary function, the entity shall also make the alterations in such a manner that, to the maximum extent feasible, the path of travel to the altered area and the bathrooms, telephones, and drinking fountains serving the altered area, are readily accessible to and usable by individuals with disabilities, including individuals who use wheelchairs, upon completion of such alterations, where such alterations to the path of travel or the bathrooms, telephones, and drinking fountains serving the altered area are not disproportionate to the overall alterations in terms of cost and scope (as determined under criteria established by the Attorney General).

(b) Special rule for stations

(1) General rule

For purposes of section 12132 of this title and section 794 of Title 29, it shall be considered discrimination for a public entity that provides designated public transportation to fail, in accordance with the provisions of this subsection, to make key stations (as determined under criteria established by the Secretary by regulation) in rapid rail and light rail systems readily accessible to and usable by individuals with disabilities, including individuals who use wheelchairs.

(2) Rapid rail and light rail key stations

(A) Accessibility

Except as otherwise provided in this paragraph, all key stations (as determined under criteria established by the Secretary by regulation) in rapid rail and light rail systems shall be made readily accessible to and usable by individuals with disabilities, including individuals who use wheelchairs, as soon as practicable but in no event later than the last day of the 3-year period beginning on July 26, 1990.

(B) Extension for extraordinarily expensive structural changes

The Secretary may extend the 3-year period under subparagraph (A) up to a 30-year period for key stations in a rapid rail or light rail system which stations need extraordinarily expensive structural changes to, or replacement of, existing facilities; except that by the last day of the 20th year following July 26, 1990, at least 2/3 of such key stations must be readily accessible to and usable by individuals with disabilities.

(3) Plans and milestones

The Secretary shall require the appropriate public entity to develop and submit to the Secretary a plan for compliance with this subsection—

(A) that reflects consultation with individuals with disabilities affected by such plan and the results of a public hearing and public comments on such plan, and

(B) that establishes milestones for achievement of the requirements of this subsection.

§ 12148. Public transportation programs and activities in existing facilities and one car per train rule

(a) Public transportation programs and activities in existing facilities

(1) In general

With respect to existing facilities used in the provision of designated public transportation services, it shall be considered discrimination, for purposes of section 12132 of this title and section 794 of Title 29, for a public entity to fail to operate a designated public transportation program or activity conducted in such facilities so that, when viewed in the entirety, the program or activity is readily accessible to and usable by individuals with disabilities.

(2) Exception

Paragraph (1) shall not require a public entity to make structural changes to existing facilities in order to make such facilities accessible to individuals who use wheelchairs, unless and to the extent required by section 12147(a) of this title (relating to alterations) or section 12147(b) of this title (relating to key stations).

(3) Utilization

Paragraph (1) shall not require a public entity to which paragraph (2) applies, to provide to individuals who use wheelchairs services made available to the general public at such facilities when such individuals could not utilize or benefit from such services provided at such facilities.

(b) One car per train rule

(1) General rule

Subject to paragraph (2), with respect to 2 or more vehicles operated as a train by a light or rapid rail system, for purposes of section 12132 of this title and section 794 of Title 29, it shall be considered discrimination for a public entity to fail to have at least 1 vehicle per train that is accessible to individuals with disabilities, including individuals who use wheelchairs, as soon as practicable but in no event later than the last day of the 5-year period beginning on the effective date of this section.

(2) Historic trains

In order to comply with paragraph (1) with respect to the remanufacture of a vehicle of historic character which is to be used on a segment of a light or rapid rail system which is included on the National Register of Historic Places, if making such vehicle readily accessible to and usable by individuals with disabilities would significantly alter the historic character of such vehicle, the public entity which operates such system only has to make (or to purchase or lease a remanufactured vehicle with) those modifications which are necessary to meet the requirements of section 12142(c)(1) of this title and which do not significantly alter the historic character of such vehicle.

§ 12149. Regulations

(a) In general. Not later than 1 year after the date of enactment of this Act [enacted July 26, 1990], the Secretary of Transportation shall issue regulations, in an accessible format, necessary for carrying out this part [42 USCS §§ 12141 et seq.] (other than section 223).

(b) Standards. The regulations issued under this section and section 223 [42 USCS § 12143] shall include standards applicable to facilities and vehicles covered by this subtitle [42 USCS §§ 12141 et seq.]. The standards shall be consistent with the minimum guidelines and requirements issued by the Architectural and Transportation Barriers Compliance Board in accordance with section 504 of this Act [42 USCS § 12204].

§ 12150. Interim accessibility requirements

If final regulations have not been issued pursuant to section 229 [42 USCS § 12149] for new construction or alterations for which a valid and appropriate State or local building permit is obtained prior to the issuance of final regulations under such section, and for which the construction or alteration authorized by such permit begins within one year of the receipt of such permit and is completed under the terms of such permit, compliance with the Uniform Federal Accessibility Standards in effect at the time the building permit is issued shall suffice to satisfy the requirement that facilities be readily accessible to and usable by persons with disabilities as required under sections 226 and 227 [42 USCS §§ 12146, 12147], except that, if such final regulations have not been issued one year after the Architectural and Transportation Barriers Compliance Board has issued the supplemental minimum guidelines required under section 504(a) of this Act [42 USCS § 12204(a)], compliance with such supplemental minimum guidelines shall be necessary to satisfy the requirement that facilities be readily accessible to and usable by persons with disabilities prior to issuance of the final regulations.

ADA TITLE II DOJ REGULATIONS

28 C.F.R. §

Subpart A—General

35.102 Application
35.103 Relationship to other laws
35.104 Definitions

Subpart B—General Requirements

35.130 General prohibitions against discrimination
35.131 Illegal use of drugs
35.132 Smoking
35.133 Maintenance of accessible features
35.134 Retaliation or coercion
35.135 Personal devices and services

Subpart C—Employment

35.140 Employment discrimination prohibited

Subpart D—Program Accessibility

35.149 Discrimination prohibited
35.150 Existing facilities
35.151 New construction and alterations

Subpart E—Communications

35.160 General
35.161 Telecommunication devices for the deaf (TDD's)
35.162 Telephone emergency services
35.163 Information and signage

Subpart F—Compliance Procedures

35.178 State immunity

ADA TITLE II DOJ REGULATIONS

Subpart A—General

§ 35.102 Application.

(a) Except as provided in paragraph (b) of this section, this part applies to all services, programs, and activities provided or made available by public entities.

(b) To the extent that public transportation services, programs, and activities of public entities are covered by subtitle B of title II of the ADA (42 U.S.C. 12141), they are not subject to the requirements of this part.

§ 35.103 Relationship to other laws.

(a) Rule of interpretation. Except as otherwise provided in this part, this part shall not be construed to apply a lesser standard than the standards applied under title V of the Rehabilitation Act of 1973 (29 U.S.C. 791) or the regulations issued by Federal agencies pursuant to that title.

(b) Other laws. This part does not invalidate or limit the remedies, rights, and procedures of any other Federal laws, or State or local laws (including State common law) that provide greater or equal protection for the rights of individuals with disabilities or individuals associated with them.

§ 35.104 Definitions.

For purposes of this part, the term—

Act means the Americans with Disabilities Act (Pub. L. 101-336, 104 Stat. 327, 42 U.S.C. 12101-12213 and 47 U.S.C. 225 and 611).

Assistant Attorney General means the Assistant Attorney General, Civil Rights Division, United States Department of Justice.

Auxiliary aids and services includes—

(1) Qualified interpreters, note takers, transcription services, written materials, telephone handset amplifiers, assistive listening devices, assistive listening systems, telephones compatible with hearing aids, closed caption decoders, open and closed captioning, telecommunications devices for deaf persons (TDD's), videotext displays, or other effective methods of making aurally delivered materials available to individuals with hearing impairments;

(2) Qualified readers, taped texts, audio recordings, Brailled materials, large print materials, or other effective methods of making visually delivered materials available to individuals with visual impairments;

(3) Acquisition or modification of equipment or devices; and

(4) Other similar services and actions.

Complete complaint means a written statement that contains the complainant's name and address and describes the public entity's alleged discriminatory action in sufficient detail to inform the agency of the nature and date of the alleged violation of this part. It shall be signed by the complainant or by someone authorized to do so on his or her behalf. Complaints filed on behalf of classes or third parties shall describe or identify (by name, if possible) the alleged victims of discrimination.

Current illegal use of drugs means illegal use of drugs that occurred recently enough to justify a reasonable belief that a person's drug use is current or that continuing use is a real and ongoing problem.

Designated agency means the Federal agency designated under sub-part G of this part to oversee compliance activities under this part for particular components of State and local governments.

Disability means, with respect to an individual, a physical or mental impairment that substantially limits one or more of the major life activities of such individual; a record of such an impairment; or being regarded as having such an impairment.

(1)(i) The phrase physical or mental impairment means—

(A) Any physiological disorder or condition, cosmetic disfigurement, or anatomical loss affecting one or more of the following body systems: Neurological, musculoskeletal, special sense organs, respiratory (including speech organs); cardiovascular, reproductive, digestive, genitourinary, hemic and lymphatic, skin, and endocrine;

(B) Any mental or psychological disorder such as mental retardation, organic brain syndrome, emotional or mental illness, and specific learning disabilities.

(ii) The phrase physical or mental impairment includes, but is not limited to, such contagious and noncontagious diseases and conditions as orthopedic, visual, speech and hearing impairments, cerebral palsy, epilepsy, muscular dystrophy, multiple sclerosis, cancer, heart disease, diabetes, mental retardation, emotional illness, specific learning disabilities, HIV disease (whether symptomatic or asymptomatic), tuberculosis, drug addiction, and alcoholism.

(iii) The phrase physical or mental impairment does not include homosexuality or bisexuality.

(2) The phrase major life activities means functions such as caring for one's self, performing manual tasks, walking, seeing, hearing, speaking, breathing, learning, and working.

(3) The phrase has a record of such an impairment means has a history of, or has been misclassified as having, a mental or physical impairment that substantially limits one or more major life activities.

(4) The phrase is regarded as having an impairment means—

(i) Has a physical or mental impairment that does not substantially limit major life activities but that is treated by a public entity as constituting such a limitation;

(ii) Has a physical or mental impairment that substantially limits major life activities only as a result of the attitudes of others toward such impairment; or

(iii) Has none of the impairments defined in paragraph (1) of this definition but is treated by a public entity as having such an impairment.

(5) The term disability does not include—

(i) Transvestism, transsexualism, pedophilia, exhibitionism, voyeurism, gender identity disorders not resulting from physical impairments, or other sexual behavior disorders;

(ii) Compulsive gambling, kleptomania, or pyromania; or

(iii) Psychoactive substance use disorders resulting from current illegal use of drugs.

Drug means a controlled substance, as defined in schedules I through V of section 202 of the Controlled Substances Act (21 U.S.C. 812).

Facility means all or any portion of buildings, structures, sites, complexes, equipment, rolling stock or other conveyances, roads, walks, passageways, parking lots, or other real or personal property, including the site where the building, property, structure, or equipment is located.

Historic preservation programs means programs conducted by a public entity that have preservation of historic properties as a primary purpose.

Historic Properties means those properties that are listed or eligible for listing in the National Register of Historic Places or properties designated as historic under State or local law.

Illegal use of drugs means the use of one or more drugs, the possession or distribution of which is unlawful under the Controlled Substances Act (21 U.S.C. 812). The term illegal use of drugs does not include the use of a drug taken under supervision by a licensed health care professional, or other uses authorized by the Controlled Substances Act or other provisions of Federal law.

Individual with a disability means a person who has a disability. The term individual with a disability does not include an individual who is currently engaging in the illegal use of drugs, when the public entity acts on the basis of such use.

Public entity means—

(1) Any State or local government;

(2) Any department, agency, special purpose district, or other instrumentality of a State or States or local government; and

(3) The National Railroad Passenger Corporation, and any commuter authority (as defined in section 103(8) of the Rail Passenger Service Act).

Qualified individual with a disability means an individual with a disability who, with or without reasonable modifications to rules, policies, or practices, the removal of architectural, communication, or transportation barriers, or the provision of auxiliary aids and services, meets the essential eligibility requirements for the receipt of services or the participation in programs or activities provided by a public entity.

Qualified interpreter means an interpreter who is able to interpret effectively, accurately, and impartially both receptively and expressively, using any necessary specialized vocabulary.

Section 504 means section 504 of the Rehabilitation Act of 1973 (Pub. L. 93-112, 87 Stat. 394 (29 U.S.C. 794)), as amended.

State means each of the several States, the District of Columbia, the Commonwealth of Puerto Rico, Guam, American Samoa, the Virgin Islands, the Trust Territory of the Pacific Islands, and the Commonwealth of the Northern Mariana Islands.

Subpart B—General Requirements

§ 35.130 General prohibitions against discrimination.

(a) No qualified individual with a disability shall, on the basis of disability, be excluded from participation in or be denied the benefits of the services, programs, or activities of a public entity, or be subjected to discrimination by any public entity.

(b)(1) A public entity, in providing any aid, benefit, or service, may not, directly or through contractual, licensing, or other arrangements, on the basis of disability—

(i) Deny a qualified individual with a disability the opportunity to participate in or benefit from the aid, benefit, or service;

(ii) Afford a qualified individual with a disability an opportunity to participate in or benefit from the aid, benefit, or service that is not equal to that afforded others;

(iii) Provide a qualified individual with a disability with an aid, benefit, or service that is not as effective in affording equal opportunity to obtain the same result, to gain the same benefit, or to reach the same level of achievement as that provided to others;

(iv) Provide different or separate aids, benefits, or services to individuals with disabilities or to any class of individuals with disabilities than is provided to others unless such action is necessary to provide qualified individuals with disabilities with aids, benefits, or services that are as effective as those provided to others;

(v) Aid or perpetuate discrimination against a qualified individual with a disability by providing significant assistance to an agency, organization, or person that discriminates on the basis of disability in providing any aid, benefit, or service to beneficiaries of the public entity's program;

(vi) Deny a qualified individual with a disability the opportunity to participate as a member of planning or advisory boards;

(vii) Otherwise limit a qualified individual with a disability in the enjoyment of any right, privilege, advantage, or opportunity enjoyed by others receiving the aid, benefit, or service.

(2) A public entity may not deny a qualified individual with a disability the opportunity to participate in services, programs, or activities that are not separate or different, despite the existence of permissibly separate or different programs or activities.

(3) A public entity may not, directly or through contractual or other arrangements, utilize criteria or methods of administration:

(i) That have the effect of subjecting qualified individuals with disabilities to discrimination on the basis of disability;

(ii) That have the purpose or effect of defeating or substantially impairing accomplishment of the objectives of the public entity's program with respect to individuals with disabilities; or

(iii) That perpetuate the discrimination of another public entity if both public entities are subject to common administrative control or are agencies of the same State.

(4) A public entity may not, in determining the site or location of a facility, make selections—

(i) That have the effect of excluding individuals with disabilities from, denying them the benefits of, or otherwise subjecting them to discrimination; or

(ii) That have the purpose or effect of defeating or substantially impairing the accomplishment of the objectives of the service, program, or activity with respect to individuals with disabilities.

(5) A public entity, in the selection of procurement contractors, may not use criteria that subject qualified individuals with disabilities to discrimination on the basis of disability.

(6) A public entity may not administer a licensing or certification program in a manner that subjects qualified individuals with disabilities to discrimination on the basis of disability, nor may a public entity establish requirements for the programs or activities of licensees or certified entities that subject qualified individuals with disabilities to discrimination on the

basis of disability. The programs or activities of entities that are licensed or certified by a public entity are not, themselves, covered by this part.

(7) A public entity shall make reasonable modifications in policies, practices, or procedures when the modifications are necessary to avoid discrimination on the basis of disability, unless the public entity can demonstrate that making the modifications would fundamentally alter the nature of the service, program, or activity.

(8) A public entity shall not impose or apply eligibility criteria that screen out or tend to screen out an individual with a disability or any class of individuals with disabilities from fully and equally enjoying any service, program, or activity, unless such criteria can be shown to be necessary for the provision of the service, program, or activity being offered.

(c) Nothing in this part prohibits a public entity from providing benefits, services, or advantages to individuals with disabilities, or to a particular class of individuals with disabilities beyond those required by this part.

(d) A public entity shall administer services, programs, and activities in the most integrated setting appropriate to the needs of qualified individuals with disabilities.

(e)(1) Nothing in this part shall be construed to require an individual with a disability to accept an accommodation, aid, service, opportunity, or benefit provided under the ADA or this part which such individual chooses not to accept.

(2) Nothing in the Act or this part authorizes the representative or guardian of an individual with a disability to decline food, water, medical treatment, or medical services for that individual.

(f) A public entity may not place a surcharge on a particular individual with a disability or any group of individuals with disabilities to cover the costs of measures, such as the provision of auxiliary aids or program accessibility, that are required to provide that individual or group with the nondiscriminatory treatment required by the Act or this part.

(g) A public entity shall not exclude or otherwise deny equal services, programs, or activities to an individual or entity because of the known disability of an individual with whom the individual or entity is known to have a relationship or association.

§ 35.131 Illegal use of drugs.

(a) General.

(1) Except as provided in paragraph (b) of this section, this part does not prohibit discrimination against an individual based on that individual's current illegal use of drugs.

(2) A public entity shall not discriminate on the basis of illegal use of drugs against an individual who is not engaging in current illegal use of drugs and who—

(i) Has successfully completed a supervised drug rehabilitation program or has otherwise been rehabilitated successfully;

(ii) Is participating in a supervised rehabilitation program; or

(iii) Is erroneously regarded as engaging in such use.

(b) Health and drug rehabilitation services.

(1) A public entity shall not deny health services, or services provided in connection with drug rehabilitation, to an individual on the basis of that individual's current illegal use of drugs, if the individual is otherwise entitled to such services.

(2) A drug rehabilitation or treatment program may deny participation to individuals who engage in illegal use of drugs while they are in the program.

(c) Drug testing.

(1) This part does not prohibit a public entity from adopting or administering reasonable policies or procedures, including but not limited to drug testing, designed to ensure that an individual who formerly engaged in the illegal use of drugs is not now engaging in current illegal use of drugs.

(2) Nothing in paragraph (c) of this section shall be construed to encourage, prohibit, restrict, or authorize the conduct of testing for the illegal use of drugs.

§ 35.132 Smoking.

This part does not preclude the prohibition of, or the imposition of restrictions on, smoking in transportation covered by this part.

§ 35.133 Maintenance of accessible features.

(a) A public entity shall maintain in operable working condition those features of facilities and equipment that are required to be readily accessible to and usable by persons with disabilities by the Act or this part.

(b) This section does not prohibit isolated or temporary interruptions in service or access due to maintenance or repairs.

§ 35.134 Retaliation or coercion.

(a) No private or public entity shall discriminate against any individual because that individual has opposed any act or practice made unlawful by this part, or because that individual made a charge, testified, assisted, or participated in any manner in an investigation, proceeding, or hearing under the Act or this part.

(b) No private or public entity shall coerce, intimidate, threaten, or interfere with any individual in the exercise or enjoyment of, or on account of his or her having exercised or enjoyed, or on account of his or her having aided or encouraged any other individual in the exercise or enjoyment of, any right granted or protected by the Act or this part.

§ 35.135 Personal devices and services.

This part does not require a public entity to provide to individuals with disabilities personal devices, such as wheelchairs; individually prescribed devices, such as prescription eyeglasses or hearing aids; readers for personal use or study; or services of a personal nature including assistance in eating, toileting, or dressing.

Subpart C—Employment

§ 35.140 Employment discrimination prohibited.

(a) No qualified individual with a disability shall, on the basis of disability, be subjected to discrimination in employment under any service, program, or activity conducted by a public entity.

(b)(1) For purposes of this part, the requirements of title I of the Act, as established by the regulations of the Equal Employment Opportunity Commission in 29 CFR part 1630, apply to employment in any service, program, or activity conducted by a public entity if that public entity is also subject to the jurisdiction of title I.

(2) For the purposes of this part, the requirements of section 504 of the Rehabilitation Act of 1973, as established by the regulations of the Department of Justice in 28 CFR part 41, as those requirements pertain to employment, apply to employment in any service, program, or activity conducted by a public entity if that public entity is not also subject to the jurisdiction of title I

Subpart D—Program Accessibility

§ 35.149 Discrimination prohibited.

Except as otherwise provided in § 35.150, no qualified individual with a disability shall, because a public entity's facilities are inaccessible to or unusable by individuals with disabilities, be excluded from participation in, or be denied the benefits of the services, programs, or activities of a public entity, or be subjected to discrimination by any public entity.

§ 35.150 Existing facilities.

(a) General. A public entity shall operate each service, program, or activity so that the service, program, or activity, when viewed in its entirety, is readily accessible to and usable by individuals with disabilities. This paragraph does not—

(1) Necessarily require a public entity to make each of its existing facilities accessible to and usable by individuals with disabilities;

(2) Require a public entity to take any action that would threaten or destroy the historic significance of an historic property; or

(3) Require a public entity to take any action that it can demonstrate would result in a fundamental alteration in the nature of a service, program, or activity or in undue financial and administrative burdens. In those circumstances where personnel of the public entity believe that the proposed action would fundamentally alter the service, program, or activity or would result in undue financial and administrative burdens, a public entity has the burden of proving that compliance with § 35.150(a) of this part would result in such alteration or burdens. The decision that compliance would result in such alteration or burdens must be made by the head of a public entity or his or her designee after considering all resources available for use in the funding and operation of the service, program, or activity, and must be accompanied by a written statement of the reasons for reaching that conclusion. If an action would result in such an alteration or such burdens, a public entity shall take any other action that would not result in such an alteration or such burdens but would nevertheless ensure that individuals with disabilities receive the benefits or services provided by the public entity.

(b) Methods—

(1) General. A public entity may comply with the requirements of this section through such means as redesign of equipment, reassignment of services to accessible buildings, assignment of aides to beneficiaries, home visits, delivery of services at alternate accessible sites, alteration of existing facilities and construction of new facilities, use of accessible rolling stock or other conveyances, or any other methods that result in making its services, programs, or activities readily accessible to and usable by individuals with disabilities. A public entity is not required to make

structural changes in existing facilities where other methods are effective in achieving compliance with this section. A public entity, in making alterations to existing buildings, shall meet the accessibility requirements of § 35.151. In choosing among available methods for meeting the requirements of this section, a public entity shall give priority to those methods that offer services, programs, and activities to qualified individuals with disabilities in the most integrated setting appropriate.

(2) Historic preservation programs. In meeting the requirements of § 35.150(a) in historic preservation programs, a public entity shall give priority to methods that provide physical access to individuals with disabilities. In cases where a physical alteration to an historic property is not required because of paragraph (a)(2) or (a)(3) of this section, alternative methods of achieving program accessibility include—

(i) Using audio-visual materials and devices to depict those portions of an historic property that cannot otherwise be made accessible;

(ii) Assigning persons to guide individuals with handicaps into or through portions of historic properties that cannot otherwise be made accessible; or

(iii) Adopting other innovative methods.

(c) Time period for compliance. Where structural changes in facilities are undertaken to comply with the obligations established under this section, such changes shall be made within three years of January 26, 1992, but in any event as expeditiously as possible.

(d) Transition plan.

(1) In the event that structural changes to facilities will be undertaken to achieve program accessibility, a public entity that employs 50 or more persons shall develop, within six months of January 26, 1992, a transition plan setting forth the steps necessary to complete such changes. A public entity shall provide an opportunity to interested persons, including individuals with disabilities or organizations representing individuals with disabilities, to participate in the development of the transition plan by submitting comments. A copy of the transition plan shall be made available for public inspection.

(2) If a public entity has responsibility or authority over streets, roads, or walkways, its transition plan shall include a schedule for providing curb ramps or other sloped areas where pedestrian walks cross curbs, giving priority to walkways serving entities covered by the Act, including State and local government offices and facilities, transportation, places of public accommodation, and employers, followed by walkways serving other areas.

(3) The plan shall, at a minimum—

(i) Identify physical obstacles in the public entity's facilities that limit the accessibility of its programs or activities to individuals with disabilities;

(ii) Describe in detail the methods that will be used to make the facilities accessible;

(iii) Specify the schedule for taking the steps necessary to achieve compliance with this section and, if the time period of the transition plan is longer than one year, identify steps that will be taken during each year of the transition period; and

(iv) Indicate the official responsible for implementation of the plan.

(4) If a public entity has already complied with the transition plan requirement of a Federal agency regulation implementing section 504 of the Rehabilitation Act of 1973, then the requirements of this paragraph (d) shall apply only to those policies and practices that were not included in the previous transition plan.

(Approved by the Office of Management and Budget under control number 1190-0004)

§ 35.151 New construction and alterations.

(a) Design and construction. Each facility or part of a facility constructed by, on behalf of, or for the use of a public entity shall be designed and constructed in such manner that the facility or part of the facility is readily accessible to and usable by individuals with disabilities, if the construction was commenced after January 26, 1992.

(b) Alteration. Each facility or part of a facility altered by, on behalf of, or for the use of a public entity in a manner that affects or could affect the usability of the facility or part of the facility shall, to the maximum extent feasible, be altered in such manner that the altered portion of the facility is readily accessible to and usable by individuals with disabilities, if the alteration was commenced after January 26, 1992.

(c) Accessibility standards. Design, construction, or alteration of facilities in conformance with the Uniform Federal Accessibility Standards (UFAS) (Appendix A to 41 CFR part 101-19.6) or with the Americans with Disabilities Act Accessibility Guidelines for Buildings and Facilities (ADAAG) (Appendix A to 28 CFR part 36) shall be deemed to comply with the requirements of this section with respect to those facilities, except that the elevator exemption contained at section 4.1.3(5) and section 4.1.6(1)(k) of ADAAG shall not apply. Departures from particular requirements of either standard by the use of other methods shall be permitted when it is clearly evident that equivalent access to the facility or part of the facility is thereby provided.

(d) Alterations: Historic properties.

(1) Alterations to historic properties shall comply, to the maximum extent feasible, with section 4.1.7 of UFAS or section 4.1.7 of ADAAG.

(2) If it is not feasible to provide physical access to an historic property in a manner that will not threaten or destroy the historic significance of the building or facility, alternative methods of access shall be provided pursuant to the requirements of § 35.150.

(e) Curb ramps.

(1) Newly constructed or altered streets, roads, and highways must contain curb ramps or other sloped areas at any intersection having curbs or other barriers to entry from a street level pedestrian walkway.

(2) Newly constructed or altered street level pedestrian walkways must contain curb ramps or other sloped areas at intersections to streets, roads, or highways.

Subpart E—Communications

§ 35.160 General.

(a) A public entity shall take appropriate steps to ensure that communications with applicants, participants, and members of the public with disabilities are as effective as communications with others.

(b)(1) A public entity shall furnish appropriate auxiliary aids and services where necessary to afford an individual with a disability an equal opportunity to participate in, and enjoy the benefits of, a service, program, or activity conducted by a public entity.

(2) In determining what type of auxiliary aid and service is necessary, a public entity shall give primary consideration to the requests of the individual with disabilities.

§ 35.161 Telecommunication devices for the deaf (TDD's).

Where a public entity communicates by telephone with applicants and beneficiaries, TDD's or equally effective telecommunication systems shall be used to communicate with individuals with impaired hearing or speech.

§ 35.162 Telephone emergency services.

Telephone emergency services, including 911 services, shall provide direct access to individuals who use TDD's and computer modems.

§ 35.163 Information and signage.

(a) A public entity shall ensure that interested persons, including persons with impaired vision or hearing, can obtain information as to the existence and location of accessible services, activities, and facilities.

(b) A public entity shall provide signage at all inaccessible entrances to each of its facilities, directing users to an accessible entrance or to a location at which they can obtain information about accessible facilities. The international symbol for accessibility shall be used at each accessible entrance of a facility.

§ 35.164 Duties.

This subpart does not require a public entity to take any action that it can demonstrate would result in a fundamental alteration in the nature of a service, program, or activity or in undue financial and administrative burdens. In those circumstances where personnel of the public entity believe that the proposed action would fundamentally alter the service, program, or activity or would result in undue financial and administrative burdens, a public entity has the burden of proving that compliance with this subpart would result in such alteration or burdens. The decision that compliance would result in such alteration or burdens must be made by the head of the public entity or his or her designee after considering all resources available for use in the funding and operation of the service, program, or activity and must be accompanied by a written statement of the reasons for reaching that conclusion. If an action required to comply with this subpart would result in such an alteration or such burdens, a public entity shall take any other action that would not result in such an alteration or such burdens but would nevertheless ensure that, to the maximum extent possible, individuals with disabilities receive the benefits or services provided by the public entity.

Subpart F—Compliance Procedures

§ 35.178 State immunity.

A State shall not be immune under the eleventh amendment to the Constitution of the United States from an action in Federal or State court of competent jurisdiction for a violation of this Act. In any action against a State for a violation of the requirements of this Act, remedies (including remedies both at law and in equity) are available for such a violation to the same extent as such remedies are available for such a violation in an action against any public or private entity other than a State.

ADA TITLE II
DOJ INTERPRETIVE GUIDANCE

28 C.F.R §

Subpart A—General

35.104 Definitions

Subpart B—General Requirements

35.150 General Prohibitions Against Discrimination
35.131 Illegal Use of Drugs
35.132 Smoking
35.133 Maintenance of Accessible Features
35.134 Retaliation or Coercion
35.135 Personal Devices and Services

Subpart C—Employment

35.140 Employment Discrimination Prohibited

Subpart D—Program Accessibility

35.149 Discrimination Prohibited
35.150 Existing Facilities
35.151 New Construction and Alterations
35.178 State Immunity

ADA TITLE II
DOJ INTERPRETIVE GUIDANCE

Subpart A—General

Section 35.104 Definitions

"Act." The word "Act" is used in this part to refer to the Americans with Disabilities Act of 1990, Public Law 101-336, which is also referred to as the "ADA."

"Assistant Attorney General." The term "Assistant Attorney General" refers to the Assistant Attorney General of the Civil Rights Division of the Department of Justice.

"Auxiliary aids and services." Auxiliary aids and services include a wide range of services and devices for ensuring effective communication. The proposed definition in § 35.104 provided a list of examples of auxiliary aids and services that were taken from the definition of auxiliary aids and services in section 3(1) of the ADA and were supplemented by examples from regulations implementing section 504 in federally conducted programs (see 28 CFR 39.103).

A substantial number of commenters suggested that additional examples be added to this list. The Department has added several items to this list but wishes to clarify that the list is not an all-inclusive or exhaustive catalogue of possible or available auxiliary aids or services. It is not possible to provide an exhaustive list, and an attempt to do so would omit the new devices that will become available with emerging technology.

Subparagraph (1) lists several examples, which would be considered auxiliary aids and services to make aurally delivered materials available to individuals with hearing impairments. The Department has changed the phrase used in the proposed rules, "orally delivered materials," to the statutory phrase, "aurally delivered materials," to track section 3 of the ADA and to include non-verbal sounds and alarms, and computer generated speech.

The Department has added videotext displays, transcription services, and closed and open captioning to the list of examples. Videotext displays have become an important means of accessing auditory communications through a public address system. Transcription services are used to relay aurally delivered material almost simultaneously in written form to persons who are deaf or hearing-impaired. This technology is often used at conferences, conventions, and hearings. While the proposed rule expressly included television decoder equipment as an auxiliary aid or service, it did not mention captioning itself. The final rule rectifies this omission by mentioning both closed and open captioning.

Several persons and organizations requested that the Department replace the term "telecommunications devices for deaf persons" or "TDD's" with the term "text telephone." The Department has declined to do so. The Department is aware that the Architectural and Transportation Barriers Compliance Board (ATBCB) has used the phrase "text telephone" in lieu of the statutory term "TDD" in its final accessibility guidelines. Title IV of the ADA, however, uses the term "Telecommunications Device for the Deaf" and the Department believes it would be inappropriate to abandon this statutory term at this time.

Several commenters urged the Department to include in the definition of "auxiliary aids and services" devices that are now available or that may become available with emerging technology. The Department declines to do so in the rule. The Department, however, emphasizes that, although the definition would include "state of the art" devices, public entities are not required to use the newest or most advanced technologies as long as the auxiliary aid or service that is selected affords effective communication.

Subparagraph (2) lists examples of aids and services for making visually delivered materials accessible to persons with visual impairments. Many commenters proposed additional examples, such as signage or mapping, audio description services, secondary auditory programs, telebraillers, and reading machines. While the Department declines to add these items to the list, they are auxiliary aids and services and may be appropriate depending on the circumstances.

Subparagraph (3) refers to acquisition or modification of equipment or devices. Several commenters suggested the addition of current technological innovations in microelectronics and computerized control systems (e.g., voice recognition systems, automatic dialing telephones, and infrared elevator and light control systems) to the list of auxiliary aids. The Department interprets auxiliary aids and services as those aids and services designed to provide effective communications, i.e., making aurally and visually delivered information available to persons with hearing, speech, and vision impairments. Methods of making services, programs, or activities accessible to, or usable by, individuals with mobility or manual dexterity impairments are addressed by other sections of this part, including the provision for modifications in policies, practices, or procedures (s 35.130 (b)(7)).

Paragraph (b)(4) deals with other similar services and actions. Several commenters asked for clarification that "similar services and actions" include retrieving items from shelves, assistance in reaching a marginally accessible seat, pushing a barrier aside in order to provide an accessible route, or assistance in removing a sweater or coat. While retrieving an item from a shelf might be an "auxiliary aid or service" for a blind person who could not locate the item without assistance, it might be a method of providing program access for a person using a wheelchair who could not reach the shelf, or a reasonable modification to a self-service policy for an individual who lacked the ability to grasp the item. As explained above, auxiliary aids and services are those aids and services required to provide effective communications. Other forms of assistance are more appropriately addressed by other provisions of the final rule.

"Complete complaint." "Complete complaint" is defined to include all the information necessary to enable the Federal agency designated under subpart G as responsible for investigation of a complaint to initiate its investigation.

"Current illegal use of drugs." The phrase "current illegal use of drugs" is used in § 35.131. Its meaning is discussed in the preamble for that section.

"Designated agency." The term "designated agency" is used to refer to the Federal agency designated under subpart G of this rule as responsible for carrying out the administrative enforcement responsibilities established by subpart F of the rule.

"Disability." The definition of the term "disability" is the same as the definition in the title III regulation codified at 28 CFR part 36. It is comparable to the definition of the term "individual with handicaps" in section 7(8) of the Rehabilitation Act and section 802(h) of the Fair Housing Act. The Education and Labor Committee report makes clear that the analysis of the term "individual with handicaps" by the Department of Health, Education, and Welfare (HEW) in its regulations implementing section 504 (42 FR 22685 (May 4, 1977)) and the analysis by the Department of Housing and Urban Development in its regulation implementing the Fair Housing Amendments Act of 1988 (54 FR 3232 (Jan. 23, 1989)) should also apply fully to the term "disability" (Education and Labor report at 50).

The use of the term "disability" instead of "handicap" and the term "individual with a disability" instead of "individual with handicaps" represents an effort by Congress to make use of up-to-date, currently accepted terminology. As with racial and ethnic epithets, the choice of terms to apply to a person with a disability is overlaid with stereotypes, patronizing attitudes, and other emotional connotations. Many individuals with disabilities, and organizations representing such individuals, object to the use of such terms as "handicapped person" or "the handicapped." In other recent legislation, Congress also recognized this shift in terminology, e.g., by changing the name of the National Council on the Handicapped to the National Council on Disability (Pub. L. 100-630).

In enacting the Americans with Disabilities Act, Congress concluded that it was important for the current legislation to use terminology most in line with the sensibilities of most Americans with disabilities. No change in definition or substance is intended nor should one be attributed to this change in phraseology. The term "disability" means, with respect to an individual—

(A) A physical or mental impairment that substantially limits one or more of the major life activities of such individual;

(B) A record of such an impairment; or

(C) Being regarded as having such an impairment.

If an individual meets any one of these three tests, he or she is considered to be an individual with a disability for purposes of coverage under the Americans with Disabilities Act.

Congress adopted this same basic definition of "disability," first used in the Rehabilitation Act of 1973 and in the Fair Housing Amendments Act of 1988, for a number of reasons. First, it has worked well since it was adopted in 1974. Second, it would not be possible to guarantee comprehensiveness by providing a list of specific disabilities, especially because new disorders may be recognized in the future, as they have since the definition was first established in 1974.

Test A—A physical or mental impairment that substantially limits one or more of the major life activities of such individual

Physical or mental impairment. Under the first test, an individual must have a physical or mental impairment. As explained in paragraph (1)(i) of the definition, "impairment" means any physiological disorder or condition, cosmetic disfigurement, or anatomical loss affecting one or more of the following body systems: neurological; musculoskeletal; special sense organs (which would include speech organs that are not respiratory such as vocal cords, soft palate, tongue, etc.); respiratory, including speech organs; cardiovascular; reproductive; digestive; genitourinary; hemic and lymphatic; skin; and endocrine. It also means any mental or psychological disorder, such as mental retardation, organic brain syndrome, emotional or mental illness, and specific learning disabilities. This list closely tracks the one used in the regulations for section 504 of the Rehabilitation Act of 1973 (see, e.g., 45 CFR 84.3(j)(2)(i)).

Many commenters asked that "traumatic brain injury" be added to the list in paragraph (1)(i). Traumatic brain injury is already included because it is a physiological condition affecting one of the listed body systems, i.e., "neurological." Therefore, it was unnecessary to add the term to the regulation, which only provides representative examples of physiological disorders.

It is not possible to include a list of all the specific conditions, contagious and noncontagious diseases, or infections that would constitute physical or mental impairments because of the difficulty of ensuring the comprehensiveness of such a list, particularly in light of the fact that other conditions or disorders may be identified in the future. However, the list of examples in paragraph (1)(ii) of the definition includes: orthopedic, visual, speech and hearing impairments, cerebral palsy, epilepsy, muscular dystrophy, multiple sclerosis, cancer, heart disease, diabetes, mental retardation, emotional illness, specific learning disabilities, HIV disease (symptomatic or asymptomatic), tuberculosis, drug addiction, and alcoholism. The phrase "symptomatic or asymptomatic" was inserted in the final rule after "HIV disease" in response to commenters who suggested the clarification was necessary.

The examples of "physical or mental impairments" in paragraph (1)(ii) are the same as those contained in many section 504 regulations, except for the addition of the phrase "contagious and noncontagious" to describe the types of diseases and conditions included, and the addition of "HIV disease (symptomatic or asymptomatic)" and "tuberculosis" to the list of examples. These additions are based on the committee reports, caselaw, and official legal opinions interpreting section 504. In *School Board of Nassau County v. Arline*, 480 U.S. 273 (1987), a case involving an individual with tuberculosis, the Supreme Court held that people with contagious diseases are entitled to the protections afforded by section 504. Following the Arline decision, this Department's Office of Legal Counsel issued a legal opinion that concluded that symptomatic HIV disease is an impairment that substantially limits a major life activity; therefore it has been included in the definition of disability under this part. The opinion also concluded that asymptomatic HIV disease is an impairment that substantially limits a major life activity, either because of its actual effect on the individual with HIV disease or because the reactions of other people to individuals with HIV disease cause such individuals to be treated as though they are disabled. See Memorandum from Douglas W. Kmiec, Acting Assistant Attorney General, Office of Legal Counsel, Department of Justice, to Arthur B. Culvahouse, Jr., Counsel to the President (Sept. 27, 1988), reprinted in Hearings on S. 933, the Americans with Disabilities Act, Before the Subcomm. on the Handicapped of the Senate Comm. on Labor and Human Resources, 101st. Cong., 1st Sess. 346 (1989).

Paragraph (1)(iii) states that the phrase "physical or mental impairment" does not include homosexuality or bisexuality. These conditions were never considered impairments under other Federal disability laws. Section 511(a) of the statute makes clear that they are likewise not to be considered impairments under the Americans with Disabilities Act.

Physical or mental impairment does not include simple physical characteristics, such as blue eyes or black hair. Nor does it include environmental, cultural, economic, or other disadvantages, such as having a prison record, or being poor. Nor is age a disability. Similarly, the definition does not include common personality traits such as poor judgment or a quick temper where these are not symptoms of a mental or psychological disorder. However, a person who has these characteristics and also has a physical or mental impairment may be considered as having a disability for purposes of the Americans with Disabilities Act based on the impairment. Substantial Limitation of a Major Life Activity. Under Test A, the impairment must be one that "substantially limits a major life activity." Major life activities include such things as caring for one's self, performing manual tasks, walking, seeing, hearing, speaking, breathing, learning, and working.

For example, a person who is paraplegic is substantially limited in the major life activity of walking, a person who is blind is substantially limited in the major life activity of seeing, and a person who is mentally retarded is substantially limited in the major life activity of learning. A person with traumatic brain injury is substantially limited in the major life activities of caring for one's self, learning, and working because of memory deficit, confusion, contextual difficulties, and inability to reason appropriately.

A person is considered an individual with a disability for purposes of Test A, the first prong of the definition, when the individual's important life activities are restricted as to the conditions, manner, or duration under which they can be performed in comparison to most people. A person with a minor, trivial impairment, such as a simple infected finger, is not impaired in a major life activity. A person who can walk for 10 miles continuously is not substantially limited in walking merely because, on the eleventh mile, he or she begins to experience pain, because most people would not be able to walk eleven miles without experiencing some discomfort.

The Department received many comments on the proposed rule's inclusion of the word "temporary" in the definition of "disability." The preamble indicated that impairments are not necessarily excluded from the definition of "disability" simply because they are temporary, but that the duration, or expected duration, of an impairment is one factor that may properly be considered in determining whether the impairment substantially limits a major life activity. The preamble recognized, however, that temporary impairments, such as a broken leg, are not commonly regarded as disabilities, and only in rare circumstances would the degree of the limitation and its expected duration be substantial. Nevertheless, many commenters objected to inclusion of the word "temporary" both because it is not in the statute and because it is not contained in the definition of "disability" set forth in the title I regulations of the Equal Employment Opportunity Commission (EEOC). The word "temporary" has been deleted from the final rule to conform with the statutory language.

The question of whether a temporary impairment is a disability must be resolved on a case-by-case basis, taking into consideration both the duration (or expected duration) of the impairment and the extent to which it actually limits a major life activity of the affected individual.

The question of whether a person has a disability should be assessed without regard to the availability of mitigating measures, such as reasonable modification or auxiliary aids and services. For example, a person with hearing loss is substantially limited in the major life activity of hearing, even though the loss may be improved through the use of a hearing aid. Likewise, persons with impairments, such as epilepsy or diabetes, that substantially limit a major life activity, are covered under the first prong of the definition of disability, even if the effects of the impairment are controlled by medication.

Many commenters asked that environmental illness (also known as multiple chemical sensitivity) as well as allergy to cigarette smoke be recognized as disabilities. The Department, however, declines to state categorically that these types of allergies or sensitivities are disabilities, because the determination as to whether an impairment is a disability depends on whether, given the particular circumstances at issue, the impairment substantially limits one or more major life activities (or has a history of, or is regarded as having such an effect).

Sometimes respiratory or neurological functioning is so severely affected that an individual will satisfy the requirements to be considered disabled under the regulation. Such an individual would be entitled to all of the protections afforded by the Act and this part. In other cases, individuals may be sensitive to environmental elements or to smoke but their sensitivity will not rise to the level needed to constitute a disability. For example, their major life activity of breathing may be somewhat, but not substantially, impaired. In such circumstances, the individuals are not disabled and are not entitled to the protections of the statute despite their sensitivity to environmental agents.

In sum, the determination as to whether allergies to cigarette smoke, or allergies or sensitivities characterized by the commenters as environmental illness are disabilities covered by the regulation must be made using the same case-by-case analysis that is applied to all other physical or mental impairments. Moreover, the addition of specific regulatory provisions relating to environmental illness in the final rule would be inappropriate at this time pending future consideration of the issue by the Architectural and Transportation Barriers Compliance Board, the Environmental Protection Agency, and the Occupational Safety and Health Administration of the Department of Labor.

Test B—A record of such an impairment

This test is intended to cover those who have a record of an impairment. As explained in paragraph (3) of the rule's definition of disability, this includes a person who has a history of an impairment that substantially limited a major life activity, such as someone who has recovered from an impairment. It also includes persons who have been misclassified as having an impairment.

This provision is included in the definition in part to protect individuals who have recovered from a physical or mental impairment that previously substantially limited them in a major life activity. Discrimination on the basis of such a past impairment is prohibited. Frequently occurring examples of the first group (those who have a history of an impairment) are persons with histories of mental or emotional illness, heart disease, or cancer; examples of the second group (those who have been misclassified as having an impairment) are persons who have been misclassified as having mental retardation or mental illness.

Test C—Being regarded as having such an impairment

This test, as contained in paragraph (4) of the definition, is intended to cover persons who are treated by a public entity as having a physical or mental impairment that substantially limits a major life activity. It applies when a person is treated as if he or she has an impairment that substantially limits a major life activity, regardless of whether that person has an impairment.

The Americans with Disabilities Act uses the same "regarded as" test set forth in the regulations implementing section 504 of the Rehabilitation Act. See, e.g., 28 CFR 42.540(k)(2)(iv), which provides:

(iv) "Is regarded as having an impairment" means (A) Has a physical or mental impairment that does not substantially limit major life activities but that is treated by a recipient as constituting such a limitation; (B) Has a physical or mental impairment that substantially limits major life activities only as a result of the attitudes of others toward such impairment; or (C) Has none of the impairments defined in paragraph (k)(2)(i) of this section but is treated by a recipient as having such an impairment.

The perception of the covered entity is a key element of this test. A person who perceives himself or herself to have an impairment, but does not have an impairment, and is not treated as if he or she has an impairment, is not protected under this test.

A person would be covered under this test if a public entity refused to serve the person because it perceived that the person had an impairment that limited his or her enjoyment of the goods or services being offered.

For example, persons with severe burns often encounter discrimination in community activities, resulting in substantial limitation of major life activities. These persons would be covered under this test based on the attitudes of others towards the impairment, even if they did not view themselves as "impaired."

The rationale for this third test, as used in the Rehabilitation Act of 1973, was articulated by the Supreme Court in *Arline,* 480 U.S. 273 (1987). The Court noted that although an individual may have an impairment that does not in fact substantially limit a major life activity, the reaction of others may prove just as disabling. "Such an impairment might not diminish a person's physical or mental capabilities, but could nevertheless substantially limit that person's ability to work as a result of the negative reactions of others to the impairment." *Id.* at 283. The Court concluded that, by including this test in the Rehabilitation Act's definition, "Congress acknowledged that society's accumulated myths and fears about disability and diseases are as handicapping as are the physical limitations that flow from actual impairment." *Id.* at 284.

Thus, a person who is denied services or benefits by a public entity because of myths, fears, and stereotypes associated with disabilities would be covered under this third test whether or not the person's physical or mental condition would be considered a disability under the first or second test in the definition.

If a person is refused admittance on the basis of an actual or perceived physical or mental condition, and the public entity can articulate no legitimate reason for the refusal (such as failure to meet eligibility criteria), a perceived concern about admitting persons with disabilities could be inferred and the individual would qualify for coverage under the "regarded as" test. A person who is covered because of being regarded as having an impairment is not required to show that the public entity's perception is inaccurate (e.g., that he will be accepted by others) in order to receive benefits from the public entity.

Paragraph (5) of the definition lists certain conditions that are not included within the definition of "disability." The excluded conditions are: Transvestism, transsexualism, pedophilia, exhibitionism, voyeurism, gender identity disorders not resulting from physical impairments, other sexual behavior disorders, compulsive gambling, kleptomania, pyromania, and psychoactive substance use disorders resulting from current illegal use of drugs. Unlike homosexuality and bisexuality, which are not considered impairments under either section 504 or the Americans with Disabilities Act (see the definition of "disability," paragraph (1)(iv)), the conditions listed in paragraph (5), except for transvestism, are not necessarily excluded as impairments under section 504. (Transvestism was excluded from the definition of disability for section 504 by the Fair Housing Amendments Act of 1988, Pub. L. 100-430, section 6(b)).

"Drug." The definition of the term "drug" is taken from section 510(d)(2) of the ADA.

"Facility." "Facility" means all or any portion of buildings, structures, sites, complexes, equipment, rolling stock or other conveyances, roads, walks, passageways, parking lots, or other real or personal property, including the site where the building, property, structure, or equipment is located. It includes both indoor and outdoor areas where human-constructed improvements, structures, equipment, or property have been added to the natural environment.

Commenters raised questions about the applicability of this part to activities operated in mobile facilities, such as bookmobiles or mobile health screening units. Such activities would be covered by the requirement for program accessibility in § 35.150, and would be included in the definition of "facility" as "other real or personal property," although standards for new construction and alterations of such facilities are not yet included in the accessibility standards adopted by § 35.151. Sections 35.150 and 35.151 specifically address the obligations of public entities to ensure accessibility by providing curb ramps at pedestrian walkways.

"Historic preservation programs" and "Historic properties" are defined in order to aid in the interpretation of §§ 35.150 (a)(2) and (b)(2), which relate to accessibility of historic preservation programs, and § 35.151(d), which relates to the alteration of historic properties.

"Illegal use of drugs." The definition of "illegal use of drugs" is taken from section 510(d)(1) of the Act and clarifies that the term includes the illegal use of one or more drugs.

"Individual with a disability" means a person who has a disability but does not include an individual who is currently illegally using drugs, when the public entity acts on the basis of such use. The phrase "current illegal use of drugs" is explained in § 35.131.

"Public entity." The term "public entity" is defined in accordance with section 201(1) of the ADA as any State or local government; any department, agency, special purpose district, or other instrumentality of a State or States or local government; or the National Railroad Passenger Corporation, and any commuter authority (as defined in section 103(8) of the Rail Passenger Service Act).

"Qualified individual with a disability." The definition of "qualified individual with a disability" is taken from section 201(2) of the Act, which is derived from the definition of "qualified handicapped person" in the Department of Health and Human Services' regulation implementing section 504 (45 CFR § 84.3(k)). It combines the definition at 45 CFR 84.3(k)(1) for employment ("a handicapped person who, with reasonable accommodation, can perform the essential functions of the job in question") with the definition for other services at 45 CFR 84.3(k)(4) ("a handicapped person who meets the essential eligibility requirements for the receipt of such services").

Some commenters requested clarification of the term "essential eligibility requirements." Because of the variety of situations in which an individual's qualifications will be at issue, it is not possible to include more specific criteria in the definition. The "essential eligibility requirements" for participation in some activities covered under this part may be minimal. For example, most public entities provide information about their operations as a public service to anyone who requests it. In such situations, the only "eligibility requirement" for receipt of such information would be the request for it. Where such information is provided by telephone, even the ability to use a voice telephone is not an "essential eligibility requirement," because § 35.161 requires a public entity to provide equally effective telecommunication systems for individuals with impaired hearing or speech.

For other activities, identification of the "essential eligibility requirements" may be more complex. Where questions of safety are involved, the principles established in § 36.208 of the Department's regulation implementing title III of the ADA, to be codified at 28 CFR, part 36, will be applicable. That section implements section 302(b)(3) of the Act, which provides that a public accommodation is not required to permit an individual to participate in or benefit from the goods, services, facilities, privileges, advantages and accommodations of the public accommodation, if that individual poses a direct threat to the health or safety of others.

A "direct threat" is a significant risk to the health or safety of others that cannot be eliminated by a modification of policies, practices, or procedures, or by the provision of auxiliary aids or services. In *School Board of Nassau County v. Arline*, 480 U.S. 273 (1987), the Supreme Court recognized that there is a need to balance the interests of people with disabilities against legitimate concerns for public safety. Although persons with disabilities are generally entitled to the protection of this part, a person who poses a significant risk to others will not be "qualified," if reasonable modifications to the public entity's policies, practices, or procedures will not eliminate that risk.

The determination that a person poses a direct threat to the health or safety of others may not be based on generalizations or stereotypes about the effects of a particular disability. It must be based on an individualized assessment, based on reasonable judgment that relies on current medical evidence or on the best available objective evidence, to determine: the nature, duration, and severity of the risk; the probability that the potential injury will actually occur; and whether reasonable modifications of policies, practices, or procedures will mitigate the risk. This is the test established by the Supreme Court in Arline. Such an inquiry is essential if the law is to achieve its goal of protecting disabled individuals from discrimination based on prejudice, stereotypes, or unfounded fear, while giving appropriate weight to legitimate concerns, such as the need to avoid exposing others to significant health and safety risks. Making this assessment will not usually require the services of a physician. Sources for medical knowledge include guidance from public health authorities, such as the U.S. Public Health Service, the Centers for Disease Control, and the National Institutes of Health, including the National Institute of Mental Health.

"Qualified interpreter." The Department received substantial comment regarding the lack of a definition of "qualified interpreter." The proposed rule defined auxiliary aids and services to include the statutory term, "qualified interpreters" (§ 35.104), but did not define it. Section 35.160 requires the use of auxiliary aids including qualified interpreters and commenters stated that a lack of guidance on what the term means would create confusion among those trying to secure interpreting services and often result in less than effective communication.

Many commenters were concerned that, without clear guidance on the issue of "qualified" interpreter, the rule would be interpreted to mean "available, rather than qualified" interpreters. Some claimed that few public entities would understand the difference between a qualified interpreter and a person who simply knows a few signs or how to fingerspell.

In order to clarify what is meant by "qualified interpreter" the Department has added a definition of the term to the final rule. A qualified interpreter means an interpreter who is able to interpret effectively, accurately, and impartially both receptively and expressively, using any necessary specialized vocabulary. This definition focuses on the actual ability of the interpreter in a particular interpreting context to facilitate effective communication between the public entity and the individual with disabilities.

Public comment also revealed that public entities have at times asked persons who are deaf to provide family members or friends to interpret. In certain circumstances, notwithstanding that the family member of friend is able to interpret or is a certified interpreter, the family member or friend may not be qualified to render the necessary interpretation because of factors such as emotional or personal involvement or considerations of confidentiality that may adversely affect the ability to interpret "effectively, accurately, and impartially."

The definition of "qualified interpreter" in this rule does not invalidate or limit standards for interpreting services of any State or local law that are equal to or more stringent than those imposed by this definition. For instance, the definition would not supersede any requirement of State law for use of a certified interpreter in court proceedings.

"Section 504." The Department added a definition of "section 504" because the term is used extensively in subpart F of this part.

"State." The definition of "State" is identical to the statutory definition in section 3(3) of the ADA.

Subpart B—General Requirements

Section 35.130 General Prohibitions Against Discrimination

The general prohibitions against discrimination in the rule are generally based on the prohibitions in existing regulations implementing section 504 and, therefore, are already familiar to State and local entities covered by section 504. In addition, § 35.130

includes a number of provisions derived from title III of the Act that are implicit to a certain degree in the requirements of regulations implementing section 504.

Several commenters suggested that this part should include the section of the proposed title III regulation that implemented section 309 of the Act, which requires that courses and examinations related to applications, licensing, certification, or credentialing be provided in an accessible place and manner or that alternative accessible arrangements be made. The Department has not adopted this suggestion. The requirements of this part, including the general prohibitions of discrimination in this section, the program access requirements of subpart D, and the communications requirements of subpart E, apply to courses and examinations provided by public entities. The Department considers these requirements to be sufficient to ensure that courses and examinations administered by public entities meet the requirements of section 309. For example, a public entity offering an examination must ensure that modifications of policies, practices, or procedures or the provision of auxiliary aids and services furnish the individual with a disability an equal opportunity to demonstrate his or her knowledge or ability. Also, any examination specially designed for individuals with disabilities must be offered as often and in as timely a manner as are other examinations. Further, under this part, courses and examinations must be offered in the most integrated setting appropriate. The analysis of § 35.130(d) is relevant to this determination.

A number of commenters asked that the regulation be amended to require training of law enforcement personnel to recognize the difference between criminal activity and the effects of seizures or other disabilities such as mental retardation, cerebral palsy, traumatic brain injury, mental illness, or deafness. Several disabled commenters gave personal statements about the abuse they had received at the hands of law enforcement personnel. Two organizations that commented cited the Judiciary report at 50 as authority to require law enforcement training.

The Department has not added such a training requirement to the regulation. Discriminatory arrests and brutal treatment are already unlawful police activities. The general regulatory obligation to modify policies, practices, or procedures requires law enforcement to make changes in policies that result in discriminatory arrests or abuse of individuals with disabilities. Under this section law enforcement personnel would be required to make appropriate efforts to determine whether perceived strange or disruptive behavior or unconsciousness is the result of a disability. The Department notes that a number of States have attempted to address the problem of arresting disabled persons for noncriminal conduct resulting from their disability through adoption of the Uniform Duties to Disabled Persons Act, and encourages other jurisdictions to consider that approach.

Paragraph (a) restates the nondiscrimination mandate of section 202 of the ADA. The remaining paragraphs in § 35.130 establish the general principles for analyzing whether any particular action of the public entity violates this mandate.

Paragraph (b) prohibits overt denials of equal treatment of individuals with disabilities. A public entity may not refuse to provide an individual with a disability with an equal opportunity to participate in or benefit from its program simply because the person has a disability.

Paragraph (b)(1)(i) provides that it is discriminatory to deny a person with a disability the right to participate in or benefit from the aid, benefit, or service provided by a public entity. Paragraph (b)(1)(ii) provides that the aids, benefits, and services provided to persons with disabilities must be equal to those provided to others, and paragraph (b)(1)(iii) requires that the aids, benefits, or services provided to individuals with disabilities must be as effective in affording equal opportunity to obtain the same result, to gain the same benefit, or to reach the same level of achievement as those provided to others. These paragraphs are taken from the regulations implementing section 504 and simply restate principles long established under section 504.

Paragraph (b)(1)(iv) permits the public entity to develop separate or different aids, benefits, or services when necessary to provide individuals with disabilities with an equal opportunity to participate in or benefit from the public entity's programs or activities, but only when necessary to ensure that the aids, benefits, or services are as effective as those provided to others. Paragraph (b)(1)(iv) must be read in conjunction with paragraphs (b)(2), (d), and (e). Even when separate or different aids, benefits, or services would be more effective, paragraph (b)(2) provides that a qualified individual with a disability still has the right to choose to participate in the program that is not designed to accommodate individuals with disabilities. Paragraph (d) requires that a public entity administer services, programs, and activities in the most integrated setting appropriate to the needs of qualified individuals with disabilities.

Paragraph (b)(2) specifies that, notwithstanding the existence of separate or different programs or activities provided in accordance with this section, an individual with a disability shall not be denied the opportunity to participate in such programs or activities that are not separate or different. Paragraph (e), which is derived from section 501(d) of the Americans with Disabilities Act, states that nothing in this part shall be construed to require an individual with a disability to accept an accommodation, aid, service, opportunity, or benefit that he or she chooses not to accept.

Taken together, these provisions are intended to prohibit exclusion and segregation of individuals with disabilities and the denial of equal opportunities enjoyed by others, based on, among other things, presumptions, patronizing attitudes, fears, and stereotypes about individuals with disabilities. Consistent with these standards, public entities are required to ensure that their actions are based on facts applicable to individuals and not on presumptions as to what a class of individuals with disabilities can or cannot do.

Integration is fundamental to the purposes of the Americans with Disabilities Act. Provision of segregated accommodations and services relegates persons with disabilities to second-class status. For example, it would be a violation of this provision to require persons with disabilities to eat in the back room of a government cafeteria or to refuse to allow a person with a disability the full use of recreation or exercise facilities because of stereotypes about the person's ability to participate.

Many commenters objected to proposed paragraphs (b)(1)(iv) and (d) as allowing continued segregation of individuals with disabilities. The Department recognizes that promoting integration of individuals with disabilities into the mainstream of society is an important objective of the ADA and agrees that, in most instances, separate programs for individuals with disabilities will not be permitted. Nevertheless, section 504 does permit separate programs in limited circumstances, and Congress clearly intended the regulations issued under title II to adopt the standards of section 504. Furthermore, Congress included authority for separate programs in the specific requirements of title III of the Act. Section 302(b)(1)(A)(iii) of the Act provides for separate benefits in language similar to that in § 35.130(b)(1)(iv), and section 302(b)(1)(B) includes the same requirement for "the most integrated setting appropriate" as in § 35.130(d).

Even when separate programs are permitted, individuals with disabilities cannot be denied the opportunity to participate in programs that are not separate or different. This is an important and overarching principle of the Americans with Disabilities Act. Separate, special, or different programs that are designed to provide a benefit to persons with disabilities cannot be used to restrict the participation of persons with disabilities in general, integrated activities.

For example, a person who is blind may wish to decline participating in a special museum tour that allows persons to touch sculptures in an exhibit and instead tour the exhibit at his or her own pace with the museum's recorded tour. It is not the intent of this section to require the person who is blind to avail himself or herself of the special tour. Modified participation for persons with disabilities must be a choice, not a requirement.

In addition, it would not be a violation of this section for a public entity to offer recreational programs specially designed for children with mobility impairments. However, it would be a violation of this section if the entity then excluded these children from other recreational services for which they are qualified to participate when these services are made available to nondisabled children, or if the entity required children with disabilities to attend only designated programs.

Many commenters asked that the Department clarify a public entity's obligations within the integrated program when it offers a separate program but an individual with a disability chooses not to participate in the separate program. It is impossible to make a blanket statement as to what level of auxiliary aids or modifications would be required in the integrated program. Rather, each situation must be assessed individually. The starting point is to question whether the separate program is in fact necessary or appropriate for the individual. Assuming the separate program would be appropriate for a particular individual, the extent to which that individual must be provided with modifications in the integrated program will depend not only on what the individual needs but also on the limitations and defenses of this part. For example, it may constitute an undue burden for a public accommodation, which provides a full-time interpreter in its special guided tour for individuals with hearing impairments, to hire an additional interpreter for those individuals who choose to attend the integrated program. The Department cannot identify categorically the level of assistance or aid required in the integrated program.

Paragraph (b)(1)(v) provides that a public entity may not aid or perpetuate discrimination against a qualified individual with a disability by providing significant assistance to an agency, organization, or person that discriminates on the basis of disability in providing any aid, benefit, or service to beneficiaries of the public entity's program. This paragraph is taken from the regulations implementing section 504 for federally assisted programs.

Paragraph (b)(1)(vi) prohibits the public entity

from denying a qualified individual with a disability the opportunity to participate as a member of a planning or advisory board.

Paragraph (b)(1)(vii) prohibits the public entity from limiting a qualified individual with a disability in the enjoyment of any right, privilege, advantage, or opportunity enjoyed by others receiving any aid, benefit, or service.

Paragraph (b)(3) prohibits the public entity from utilizing criteria or methods of administration that deny individuals with disabilities access to the public entity's services, programs, and activities or that perpetuate the discrimination of another public entity, if both public entities are subject to common administrative control or are agencies of the same State. The phrase "criteria or methods of administration" refers to official written policies of the public entity and to the actual practices of the public entity. This paragraph prohibits both blatantly exclusionary policies or practices and nonessential policies and practices that are neutral on their face, but deny individuals with disabilities an effective opportunity to participate. This standard is consistent with the interpretation of section 504 by the U.S. Supreme Court in *Alexander v. Choate*, 469 U.S. 287 (1985). The Court in *Choate* explained that members of Congress made numerous statements during passage of section 504 regarding eliminating architectural barriers, providing access to transportation, and eliminating discriminatory effects of job qualification procedures. The Court then noted: "These statements would ring hollow if the resulting legislation could not rectify the harms resulting from action that discriminated by effect as well as by design." *Id.* at 297 (footnote omitted).

Paragraph (b)(4) specifically applies the prohibition enunciated in § 35.130(b)(3) to the process of selecting sites for construction of new facilities or selecting existing facilities to be used by the public entity. Paragraph (b)(4) does not apply to construction of additional buildings at an existing site.

Paragraph (b)(5) prohibits the public entity, in the selection of procurement contractors, from using criteria that subject qualified individuals with disabilities to discrimination on the basis of disability.

Paragraph (b)(6) prohibits the public entity from discriminating against qualified individuals with disabilities on the basis of disability in the granting of licenses or certification. A person is a "qualified individual with a disability" with respect to licensing or certification if he or she can meet the essential eligibility requirements for receiving the license or certification (see § 35.104).

A number of commenters were troubled by the phrase "essential eligibility requirements" as applied to State licensing requirements, especially those for health care professions. Because of the variety of types of programs to which the definition of "qualified individual with a disability" applies, it is not possible to use more specific language in the definition. The phrase "essential eligibility requirements," however, is taken from the definitions in the regulations implementing section 504, so caselaw under section 504 will be applicable to its interpretation. In *Southeastern Community College v. Davis*, 442 U.S. 397, for example, the Supreme Court held that section 504 does not require an institution to "lower or effect substantial modifications of standards to accommodate a handicapped person," 442 U.S. at 413, and that the school had established that the plaintiff was not "qualified" because she was not able to "serve the nursing profession in all customary ways," id. Whether a particular requirement is "essential" will, of course, depend on the facts of the particular case.

In addition, the public entity may not establish requirements for the programs or activities of licensees or certified entities that subject qualified individuals with disabilities to discrimination on the basis of disability. For example, the public entity must comply with this requirement when establishing safety standards for the operations of licensees. In that case the public entity must ensure that standards that it promulgates do not discriminate against the employment of qualified individuals with disabilities in an impermissible manner.

Paragraph (b)(6) does not extend the requirements of the Act or this part directly to the programs or activities of licensees or certified entities themselves. The programs or activities of licensees or certified entities are not themselves programs or activities of the public entity merely by virtue of the license or certificate.

Paragraph (b)(7) is a specific application of the requirement under the general prohibitions of discrimination that public entities make reasonable modifications in policies, practices, or procedures where necessary to avoid discrimination on the basis of disability. Section 302(b)(2)(A)(ii) of the ADA sets out this requirement specifically for public accommodations covered by title III of the Act, and the House Judiciary Committee Report directs the Attorney General to include those specific requirements in the title II regulation to the extent that they do not conflict with the regulations implementing section 504. Judiciary report at 52.

Paragraph (b)(8), a new paragraph not contained in the proposed rule, prohibits the imposition or application of eligibility criteria that screen out or tend to screen out an individual with a disability or any class of individuals with disabilities from fully and equally enjoying any service, program, or activity, unless such criteria can be shown to be necessary for the provision of the service, program, or activity being offered. This prohibition is also a specific application of the general prohibitions of discrimination and is based on section 302(b)(2)(A)(i) of the ADA. It prohibits overt denials of equal treatment of individuals with disabilities, or establishment of exclusive or segregative criteria that would bar individuals with disabilities from participation in services, benefits, or activities.

Paragraph (b)(8) also prohibits policies that unnecessarily impose requirements or burdens on individuals with disabilities that are not placed on others. For example, public entities may not require that a qualified individual with a disability be accompanied by an attendant. A public entity is not, however, required to provide attendant care, or assistance in toileting, eating, or dressing to individuals with disabilities, except in special circumstances, such as where the individual is an inmate of a custodial or correctional institution.

In addition, paragraph (b)(8) prohibits the imposition of criteria that "tend to" screen out an individual with a disability. This concept, which is derived from current regulations under section 504 (see, e.g., 45 CFR 84.13), makes it discriminatory to impose policies or criteria that, while not creating a direct bar to individuals with disabilities, indirectly prevent or limit their ability to participate. For example, requiring presentation of a driver's license as the sole means of identification for purposes of paying by check would violate this section in situations where, for example, individuals with severe vision impairments or developmental disabilities or epilepsy are ineligible to receive a driver's license and the use of an alternative means of identification, such as another photo I.D. or credit card, is feasible.

A public entity may, however, impose neutral rules and criteria that screen out, or tend to screen out, individuals with disabilities if the criteria are necessary for the safe operation of the program in question. Examples of safety qualifications that would be justifiable in appropriate circumstances would include eligibility requirements for drivers' licenses, or a requirement that all participants in a recreational rafting expedition be able to meet a necessary level of swimming proficiency. Safety requirements must be based on actual risks and not on speculation, stereotypes, or generalizations about individuals with disabilities.

Paragraph (c) provides that nothing in this part prohibits a public entity from providing benefits, services, or advantages to individuals with disabilities, or to a particular class of individuals with disabilities, beyond those required by this part. It is derived from a provision in the section 504 regulations that permits programs conducted pursuant to Federal statute or Executive order that are designed to benefit only individuals with disabilities or a given class of individuals with disabilities to be limited to those individuals with disabilities. Section 504 ensures that federally assisted programs are made available to all individuals, without regard to disabilities, unless the Federal program under which the assistance is provided is specifically limited to individuals with disabilities or a particular class of individuals with disabilities. Because coverage under this part is not limited to federally assisted programs, paragraph (c) has been revised to clarify that State and local governments may provide special benefits, beyond those required by the nondiscrimination requirements of this part, that are limited to individuals with disabilities or a particular class of individuals with disabilities, without thereby incurring additional obligations to persons without disabilities or to other classes of individuals with disabilities.

Paragraphs (d) and (e), previously referred to in the discussion of paragraph (b)(1)(iv), provide that the public entity must administer services, programs, and activities in the most integrated setting appropriate to the needs of qualified individuals with disabilities, i.e., in a setting that enables individuals with disabilities to interact with nondisabled persons to the fullest extent possible, and that persons with disabilities must be provided the option of declining to accept a particular accommodation.

Some commenters expressed concern that § 35.130(e), which states that nothing in the rule requires an individual with a disability to accept special accommodations and services provided under the ADA, could be interpreted to allow guardians of infants or older people with disabilities to refuse medical treatment for their wards. Section 35.130(e) has been revised to make it clear that paragraph (e) is inapplicable to the concern of the commenters. A new paragraph (e)(2) has been added stating that nothing in the regulation authorizes the representative or guardian of an individual with a disability to decline food, water, medical treatment, or medical services for that individual. New paragraph (e) clarifies that neither the ADA nor the regulation alters current Federal law ensuring the rights of incompetent individuals with disabilities to receive food, water, and medical treatment. See, e.g., Child Abuse Amendments of 1984 (42 U.S.C. 5106a(b)(10), 5106g(10)); Rehabilitation Act of 1973, as amended (29 U.S.C. 794); the Developmentally Disabled Assistance and Bill of

Rights Act (42 U.S.C. 6042).

Sections 35.130(e) (1) and (2) are based on section 501(d) of the ADA. Section 501(d) was designed to clarify that nothing in the ADA requires individuals with disabilities to accept special accommodations and services for individuals with disabilities that may segregate them:

The Committee added this section [501(d)] to clarify that nothing in the ADA is intended to permit discriminatory treatment on the basis of disability, even when such treatment is rendered under the guise of providing an accommodation, service, aid or benefit to the individual with disability. For example, a blind individual may choose not to avail himself or herself of the right to go to the front of a line, even if a particular public accommodation has chosen to offer such a modification of a policy for blind individuals. Or, a blind individual may choose to decline to participate in a special museum tour that allows persons to touch sculptures in an exhibit and instead tour the exhibits at his or her own pace with the museum's recorded tour.

Judiciary report at 71-72. The Act is not to be construed to mean that an individual with disabilities must accept special accommodations and services for individuals with disabilities when that individual can participate in the regular services already offered. Because medical treatment, including treatment for particular conditions, is not a special accommodation or service for individuals with disabilities under section 501(d), neither the Act nor this part provides affirmative authority to suspend such treatment. Section 501(d) is intended to clarify that the Act is not designed to foster discrimination through mandatory acceptance of special services when other alternatives are provided; this concern does not reach to the provision of medical treatment for the disabling condition itself.

Paragraph (f) provides that a public entity may not place a surcharge on a particular individual with a disability, or any group of individuals with disabilities, to cover any costs of measures required to provide that individual or group with the nondiscriminatory treatment required by the Act or this part. Such measures may include the provision of auxiliary aids or of modifications required to provide program accessibility.

Several commenters asked for clarification that the costs of interpreter services may not be assessed as an element of "court costs." The Department has already recognized that imposition of the cost of courtroom interpreter services is impermissible under section 504. The preamble to the Department's section 504 regulation for its federally assisted programs states that where a court system has an obligation to provide qualified interpreters, "it has the corresponding responsibility to pay for the services of the interpreters." (45 FR 37630 (June 3, 1980)). Accordingly, recouping the costs of interpreter services by assessing them as part of court costs would also be prohibited.

Paragraph (g), which prohibits discrimination on the basis of an individual's or entity's known relationship or association with an individual with a disability, is based on sections 102(b)(4) and 302(b)(1)(E) of the ADA. This paragraph was not contained in the proposed rule. The individuals covered under this paragraph are any individuals who are discriminated against because of their known association with an individual with a disability. For example, it would be a violation of this paragraph for a local government to refuse to allow a theater company to use a school auditorium on the grounds that the company had recently performed for an audience of individuals with HIV disease.

This protection is not limited to those who have a familial relationship with the individual who has a disability. Congress considered, and rejected, amendments that would have limited the scope of this provision to specific associations and relationships. Therefore, if a public entity refuses admission to a person with cerebral palsy and his or her companions, the companions have an independent right of action under the ADA and this section.

During the legislative process, the term "entity" was added to section 302(b)(1)(E) to clarify that the scope of the provision is intended to encompass not only persons who have a known association with a person with a disability, but also entities that provide services to or are otherwise associated with such individuals. This provision was intended to ensure that entities such as health care providers, employees of social service agencies, and others who provide professional services to persons with disabilities are not subjected to discrimination because of their professional association with persons with disabilities.

Section 35.131 Illegal Use of Drugs

Section 35.131 effectuates section 510 of the ADA, which clarifies the Act's application to people who use drugs illegally. Paragraph (a) provides that this part does not prohibit discrimination based on an individual's current illegal use of drugs.

The Act and the regulation distinguish between illegal use of drugs and the legal use of substances, whether or not those substances are "controlled substances," as defined in the Controlled Substances Act

(21 U.S.C. 812). Some controlled substances are prescription drugs that have legitimate medical uses. Section 35.131 does not affect use of controlled substances pursuant to a valid prescription under supervision by a licensed health care professional, or other use that is authorized by the Controlled Substances Act or any other provision of Federal law. It does apply to illegal use of those substances, as well as to illegal use of controlled substances that are not prescription drugs. The key question is whether the individual's use of the substance is illegal, not whether the substance has recognized legal uses. Alcohol is not a controlled substance, so use of alcohol is not addressed by § 35.131 (although alcoholics are individuals with disabilities, subject to the protections of the statute).

A distinction is also made between the use of a substance and the status of being addicted to that substance. Addiction is a disability, and addicts are individuals with disabilities protected by the Act. The protection, however, does not extend to actions based on the illegal use of the substance. In other words, an addict cannot use the fact of his or her addiction as a defense to an action based on illegal use of drugs. This distinction is not artificial. Congress intended to deny protection to people who engage in the illegal use of drugs, whether or not they are addicted, but to provide protection to addicts so long as they are not currently using drugs.

A third distinction is the difficult one between current use and former use. The definition of "current illegal use of drugs" in § 35.104, which is based on the report of the Conference Committee, H.R. Conf. Rep. No. 596, 101st Cong., 2d Sess. 64 (1990) (hereinafter "Conference report"), is "illegal use of drugs that occurred recently enough to justify a reasonable belief that a person's drug use is current or that continuing use is a real and ongoing problem."

Paragraph (a)(2)(i) specifies that an individual who has successfully completed a supervised drug rehabilitation program or has otherwise been rehabilitated successfully and who is not engaging in current illegal use of drugs is protected. Paragraph (a)(2)(ii) clarifies that an individual who is currently participating in a supervised rehabilitation program and is not engaging in current illegal use of drugs is protected. Paragraph (a)(2)(iii) provides that a person who is erroneously regarded as engaging in current illegal use of drugs, but who is not engaging in such use, is protected.

Paragraph (b) provides a limited exception to the exclusion of current illegal users of drugs from the protections of the Act. It prohibits denial of health services, or services provided in connection with drug rehabilitation to an individual on the basis of current illegal use of drugs, if the individual is otherwise entitled to such services. A health care facility, such as a hospital or clinic, may not refuse treatment to an individual in need of the services it provides on the grounds that the individual is illegally using drugs, but it is not required by this section to provide services that it does not ordinarily provide. For example, a health care facility that specializes in a particular type of treatment, such as care of burn victims, is not required to provide drug rehabilitation services, but it cannot refuse to treat a individual's burns on the grounds that the individual is illegally using drugs.

Some commenters pointed out that abstention from the use of drugs is an essential condition of participation in some drug rehabilitation programs, and may be a necessary requirement in inpatient or residential settings. The Department believes that this comment is well-founded. Congress clearly intended to prohibit exclusion from drug treatment programs of the very individuals who need such programs because of their use of drugs, but, once an individual has been admitted to a program, abstention may be a necessary and appropriate condition to continued participation. The final rule therefore provides that a drug rehabilitation or treatment program may prohibit illegal use of drugs by individuals while they are participating in the program.

Paragraph (c) expresses Congress' intention that the Act be neutral with respect to testing for illegal use of drugs. This paragraph implements the provision in section 510(b) of the Act that allows entities "to adopt or administer reasonable policies or procedures, including but not limited to drug testing," that ensure that an individual who is participating in a supervised rehabilitation program, or who has completed such a program or otherwise been rehabilitated successfully is no longer engaging in the illegal use of drugs. The section is not to be "construed to encourage, prohibit, restrict, or authorize the conducting of testing for the illegal use of drugs."

Paragraph 35.131(c) clarifies that it is not a violation of this part to adopt or administer reasonable policies or procedures to ensure that an individual who formerly engaged in the illegal use of drugs is not currently engaging in illegal use of drugs. Any such policies or procedures must, of course, be reasonable, and must be designed to identify accurately the illegal use of drugs. This paragraph does not authorize inquiries, tests, or other procedures that would disclose use of substances that are not controlled substances or are taken under supervision by a licensed health care professional, or other uses authorized by the Controlled Substances Act or other provisions of Federal law, because such uses are not included in the definition of "illegal use of drugs." A commenter argued that the rule should permit testing for lawful use of prescription drugs, but most commenters preferred that tests must be limited to unlawful use in order to avoid revealing the lawful use of prescription medicine used to treat disabilities.

Section 35.132 Smoking

Section 35.132 restates the clarification in section 501(b) of the Act that the Act does not preclude the prohibition of, or imposition of restrictions on, smoking in transportation covered by title II. Some commenters argued that this section is too limited in scope, and that the regulation should prohibit smoking in all facilities used by public entities. The reference to smoking in section 501, however, merely clarifies that the Act does not require public entities to accommodate smokers by permitting them to smoke in transportation facilities.

35.133 Maintenance of Accessible Features

Section 35.133 provides that a public entity shall maintain in operable working condition those features of facilities and equipment that are required to be readily accessible to and usable by persons with disabilities by the Act or this part. The Act requires that, to the maximum extent feasible, facilities must be accessible to, and usable by, individuals with disabilities. This section recognizes that it is not sufficient to provide features such as accessible routes, elevators, or ramps, if those features are not maintained in a manner that enables individuals with disabilities to use them. Inoperable elevators, locked accessible doors, or "accessible" routes that are obstructed by furniture, filing cabinets, or potted plants are neither "accessible to" nor "usable by" individuals with disabilities.

Some commenters objected that this section appeared to establish an absolute requirement and suggested that language from the preamble be included in the text of the regulation. It is, of course, impossible to guarantee that mechanical devices will never fail to operate. Paragraph (b) of the final regulation provides that this section does not prohibit isolated or temporary interruptions in service or access due to maintenance or repairs. This paragraph is intended to clarify that temporary obstructions or isolated instances of mechanical failure would not be considered violations of the Act or this part. However, allowing obstructions or "out of service" equipment to persist beyond a reasonable period of time would violate this part, as would repeated mechanical failures due to improper or inadequate maintenance. Failure of the public entity to ensure that accessible routes are properly maintained and free of obstructions, or failure to arrange prompt repair of inoperable elevators or other equipment intended to provide access would also violate this part.

Other commenters requested that this section be expanded to include specific requirements for inspection and maintenance of equipment, for training staff in the proper operation of equipment, and for maintenance of specific items. The Department believes that this section properly establishes the general requirement for maintaining access and that further details are not necessary.

Section 35.134 Retaliation or Coercion

Section 35.134 implements section 503 of the ADA, which prohibits retaliation against any individual who exercises his or her rights under the Act. This section is unchanged from the proposed rule. Paragraph (a) of § 35.134 provides that no private or public entity shall discriminate against any individual because that individual has exercised his or her right to oppose any act or practice made unlawful by this part, or because that individual made a charge, testified, assisted, or participated in any manner in an investigation, proceeding, or hearing under the Act or this part.

Paragraph (b) provides that no private or public entity shall coerce, intimidate, threaten, or interfere with any individual in the exercise of his or her rights under this part or because that individual aided or encouraged any other individual in the exercise or enjoyment of any right granted or protected by the Act or this part. This section protects not only individuals who allege a violation of the Act or this part, but also any individuals who support or assist them. This section applies to all investigations or proceedings initiated under the Act or this part without regard to the ultimate resolution of the underlying allegations. Because this section prohibits any act of retaliation or coercion in response to an individual's effort to exercise rights established by the Act and this part (or to support the efforts of another individual), the section applies not only to public entities subject to this part, but also to persons acting in an individual capacity or to private entities. For example, it would be a violation of the Act and this part for a private individual to harass or intimidate an individual with a disability in an effort to prevent that individual from attending a concert in a State-owned park. It would, likewise, be a violation of the Act and this part for a private entity to take adverse action against an employee who appeared as a witness on behalf of an individual who sought to enforce the Act.

Section 35.135 Personal Devices and Services

The final rule includes a new § 35.135, entitles "Personal devices and services," which states that the provision of personal devices and services is not required by title II. This new section, which serves as a limitation on all of the requirements of the regulation, replaces § 35.160(b)(2) of the proposed rule, which addressed the issue of personal devices and services explicitly only in the context of communications. The personal devices and services limitation was intended to have general application in the proposed rule in all contexts where it was relevant. The final rule, therefore, clarifies this point by including a general provision that will explicitly apply not only to auxiliary aids and services but across-the-board to include other relevant areas such as, for example, modifications in policies, practices, and procedures (§ 35.130(b)(7)). The language of § 35.135 parallels an analogous provision in the Department's title III regulations (28 CFR 36.306) but preserves the explicit reference to "readers for personal use or study" in § 35.160(b)(2) of the proposed rule. This section does not preclude the short-term loan of personal receivers that are part of an assistive listening system.

Subpart C—Employment

Section 35.140

Employment Discrimination Prohibited

Title II of the ADA applies to all activities of public entities, including their employment practices. The proposed rule cross-referenced the definitions, requirements, and procedures of title I of the ADA, as established by the Equal Employment Opportunity Commission in 29 CFR part 1630. This proposal would have resulted in use, under § 35.140, of the title I definition of "employer," so that a public entity with 25 or more employees would have become subject to the requirements of § 35.140 on July 26, 1992, one with 15 to 24 employees on July 26, 1994, and one with fewer than 15 employees would have been excluded completely.

The Department received comments objecting to this approach. The commenters asserted that Congress intended to establish nondiscrimination requirements for employment by all public entities, including those that employ fewer than 15 employees; and that Congress intended the employment requirements of title II to become effective at the same time that the other requirements of this regulation become effective, January 26, 1992. The Department has reexamined the statutory language and legislative history of the ADA on this issue and has concluded that Congress intended to cover the employment practices of all public entities and that the applicable effective date is that of title II.

The statutory language of section 204(b) of the ADA requires the Department to issue a regulation that is consistent with the ADA and the Department's coordination regulation under section 504, 28 CFR part 41. The coordination regulation specifically requires nondiscrimination in employment, 28 CFR 41.52-41.55, and does not limit coverage based on size of employer. Moreover, under all section 504 implementing regulations issued in accordance with the Department's coordination regulation, employment coverage under section 504 extends to all employers with federally assisted programs or activities, regardless of size, and the effective date for those employment requirements has always been the same as the effective date for nonemployment requirements established in the same regulations. The Department therefore concludes that § 35.140 must apply to all public entities upon the effective date of this regulation.

In the proposed regulation the Department cross-referenced the regulations implementing title I of the ADA, issued by the Equal Employment Opportunity Commission at 29 CFR part 1630, as a compliance standard for § 35.140 because, as proposed, the scope of coverage and effective date of coverage under title II would have been coextensive with title I. In the final regulation this language is modified slightly. Subparagraph (1) of new paragraph (b) makes it clear that the standards established by the Equal Employment Opportunity Commission in 29 CFR part 1630 will be the applicable compliance standards if the public entity is subject to title I. If the public entity is not covered by title I, or until it is covered by title I, subparagraph (b)(2) cross-references section 504 standards for what constitutes employment discrimination, as established by the Department of Justice in 28 CFR part 41. Standards for title I of the ADA and section 504 of the Rehabilitation Act are for the most part identical because title I of the ADA was based on requirements set forth in regulations implementing section 504.

The Department, together with the other Federal agencies responsible for the enforcement of Federal laws prohibiting employment discrimination on the basis of disability, recognizes the potential for jurisdictional overlap that exists with respect to coverage of public entities and the need to avoid problems related to overlapping coverage. The other Federal agencies include the Equal Employment Opportunity Commission, which is the agency primarily responsible for enforcement of title I of the ADA, the Department of Labor, which is the agency responsible for enforcement of section 503 of the Rehabilitation Act of 1973, and 26 Federal agencies with programs of Federal financial assistance, which are responsible for enforcing section 504 in those programs. Section 107 of the ADA requires that coordination mechanisms be developed in connection with the administrative enforcement of complaints alleging discrimination under title I and complaints alleging discrimination in employment in violation of the Rehabilitation Act. Although the ADA does not specifically require inclusion of employment complaints under title II in the coordinating mechanisms required by title I, Federal investigations of title II employment complaints will be coordinated on a government-wide basis also. The Department is currently working with the EEOC and other affected Federal agencies to develop effective coordinating mechanisms, and final regulations on this issue will be issued on or before January 26, 1992.

Subpart D—Program Accessibility

Section 35.149 Discrimination Prohibited

Section 35.149 states the general nondiscrimination principle underlying the program accessibility requirements of ss 35.150 and 35.151.

Section 35.150 Existing Facilities

Consistent with section 204(b) of the Act, this regulation adopts the program accessibility concept found in the section 504 regulations for federally conducted programs or activities (e.g., 28 CFR part 39). The concept of "program accessibility" was first used in the section 504 regulation adopted by the Department of Health, Education, and Welfare for its federally assisted programs and activities in 1977. It allowed recipients to make their federally assisted programs and activities available to individuals with disabilities without extensive retrofitting of their existing buildings and facilities, by offering those programs through alternative methods. Program accessibility has proven to be a useful approach and was adopted in the regulations issued for programs and activities conducted by Federal Executive agencies. The Act provides that the concept of program access will continue to apply with respect to facilities now in existence, because the cost of retrofitting existing facilities is often prohibitive.

Section 35.150 requires that each service, program, or activity conducted by a public entity, when viewed in its entirety, be readily accessible to and usable by individuals with disabilities. The regulation makes clear, however, that a public entity is not required to make each of its existing facilities accessible (s 35.150(a)(1)). Unlike title III of the Act, which requires public accommodations to remove architectural barriers where such removal is "readily achievable," or to provide goods and services through alternative methods, where those methods are "readily achievable," title II requires a public entity to make its programs accessible in all cases, except where to do so would result in a fundamental alteration in the nature of the program or in undue financial and administrative burdens. Congress intended the "undue burden" standard in title II to be significantly higher than the "readily achievable" standard in title III. Thus, although title II may not require removal of barriers in some cases where removal would be required under title III, the program access requirement of title II should enable individuals with disabilities to participate in and benefit from the services, programs, or activities of public entities in all but the most unusual cases.

Paragraph (a)(2), which establishes a special limitation on the obligation to ensure program accessibility in historic preservation programs, is discussed below in connection with paragraph (b).

Paragraph (a)(3), which is taken from the section 504 regulations for federally conducted programs, generally codifies case law that defines the scope of the public entity's obligation to ensure program accessibility. This paragraph provides that, in meeting the program accessibility requirement, a public entity is not required to take any action that would result in a fundamental alteration in the nature of its service, program, or activity or in undue financial and administrative burdens. A similar limitation is provided in § 35.164.

This paragraph does not establish an absolute defense; it does not relieve a public entity of all obligations to individuals with disabilities. Although a public entity is not required to take actions that would result in a fundamental alteration in the nature of a service, program, or activity or in undue financial and administrative burdens, it nevertheless must take any other steps necessary to ensure that individuals with disabilities receive the benefits or services provided by the public entity.

It is the Department's view that compliance with § 35.150(a), like compliance with the corresponding provisions of the section 504 regulations for federally conducted programs, would in most cases not result in undue financial and administrative burdens on a public entity. In determining whether financial and administrative burdens are undue, all public entity resources available for use in the funding and operation of the service, program, or activity should be considered. The burden of proving that compliance with paragraph (a) of § 35.150 would fundamentally alter the nature of a service, program, or activity or would result in undue financial and administrative burdens rests with the public entity.

The decision that compliance would result in such alteration or burdens must be made by the head of the public entity or his or her designee and must be accompanied by a written statement of the reasons for reaching that conclusion. The Department recognizes the difficulty of identifying the official responsible for this determination, given the variety of organizational forms that may be taken by public entities and their components. The intention of this paragraph is that the determination must be made by a high level official, no lower than a Department head, having budgetary authority and responsibility for making spending decisions.

Any person who believes that he or she or any specific class of persons has been injured by the public entity head's decision or failure to make a decision may file a complaint under the compliance procedures established in subpart F.

Paragraph (b)(1) sets forth a number of means by which program accessibility may be achieved, including redesign of equipment, reassignment of services to accessible buildings, and provision of aides.

The Department wishes to clarify that, consistent with longstanding interpretation of section 504, carrying an individual with a disability is considered an ineffective and therefore an unacceptable method for achieving program accessibility. Department of Health, Education, and Welfare, Office of Civil Rights, Policy Interpretation No. 4, 43 FR 36035 (August 14, 1978). Carrying will be permitted only in manifestly exceptional cases, and only if all personnel who are permitted to participate in carrying an individual with a disability are formally instructed on the safest and least humiliating means of carrying. "Manifestly exceptional" cases in which carrying would be permitted might include, for example, programs conducted in unique facilities, such as an oceanographic vessel, for which structural changes and devices necessary to adapt the facility for use by individuals with mobility impairments are unavailable or prohibitively expensive. Carrying is not permitted as an alternative to structural modifications such as installation of a ramp or a chairlift.

In choosing among methods, the public entity shall give priority consideration to those that will be consistent with provision of services in the most integrated setting appropriate to the needs of individuals with disabilities. Structural changes in existing facilities are required only when there is no other feasible way to make the public entity's program accessible. (It should be noted that "structural changes" include all physical changes to a facility; the term does not refer only to changes to structural features, such as removal of or alteration to a load-bearing structural member.) The requirements of § 35.151 for alterations apply to structural changes undertaken to comply with this section. The public entity may comply with the program accessibility requirement by delivering services at alternate accessible sites or making home visits as appropriate.

Section 35.151 New Construction and Alterations

Section 35.151 provides that those buildings that are constructed or altered by, on behalf of, or for the use of a public entity shall be designed, constructed, or altered to be readily accessible to and usable by individuals with disabilities if the construction was commenced after the effective date of this part. Facilities under design on that date will be governed by this section if the date that bids were invited falls after the effective date. This interpretation is consistent with Federal practice under section 504.

Section 35.151(c) establishes two standards for accessible new construction and alteration. Under paragraph (c), design, construction, or alteration of facilities in conformance with the Uniform Federal Accessibility Standards (UFAS) or with the Americans with Disabilities Act Accessibility Guidelines for Buildings and Facilities (hereinafter ADAAG) shall be deemed to comply with the requirements of this section with respect to those facilities except that, if ADAAG is chosen, the elevator exemption contained at ss 36.401(d) and 36.404 does not apply. ADAAG is the standard for private buildings and was issued as guidelines by the Architectural and Transportation Barriers Compliance Board (ATBCB) under title III of the ADA. It has been adopted by the Department of Justice and is published as appendix A to the Department's title III rule in today's Federal Register. Departures from particular requirements of these standards by the use of other methods shall be permitted when it is clearly evident that equivalent access to the facility or part of the facility is thereby provided. Use of two standards is a departure from the proposed rule.

The proposed rule adopted UFAS as the only interim accessibility standard because that standard was referenced by the regulations implementing section 504 of the Rehabilitation Act promulgated by most Federal funding agencies. It is, therefore, familiar to many State and local government entities subject to this rule. The Department, however, received many comments objecting to the adoption of UFAS. Commenters pointed out that, except for the elevator exemption, UFAS is not as stringent as ADAAG. Others suggested that the standard should be the same to lessen confusion.

Section 204(b) of the Act states that title II regulations must be consistent not only with section 504 regulations but also with "this Act." Based on this provision, the Department has determined that a public entity should be entitled to choose to comply either with ADAAG or UFAS.

Public entities who choose to follow ADAAG, however, are not entitled to the elevator exemption contained in title III of the Act and implemented in the title III regulation at § 36.401(d) for new construction and § 36.404 for alterations. Section 303(b) of title III states that, with some exceptions, elevators are not required in facilities that are less than three stories or have less than 3000 square feet per story. The section 504 standard, UFAS, contains no such exemption. Section 501 of the ADA makes clear that nothing in the Act may be construed to apply a lesser standard to public entities than the standards applied under section 504. Because permitting the elevator exemption would clearly result in application of a lesser standard than that applied under section 504, paragraph (c) states that the elevator exemption does not apply when public entities choose to follow ADAAG. Thus, a two-story courthouse, whether built according to UFAS or ADAAG, must be constructed with an elevator. It should be noted that Congress did not include an elevator exemption for public transit facilities covered by subtitle B of title II, which covers public transportation provided by public entities, providing further evidence that Congress intended that public buildings have elevators.

Section 504 of the ADA requires the ATBCB to issue supplemental Minimum Guidelines and Requirements for Accessible Design of buildings and facilities subject to the Act, including title II. Section 204(c) of the ADA provides that the Attorney General shall promulgate regulations implementing title II that are consistent with the ATBCB's ADA guidelines. The ATBCB has announced its intention to issue title II guidelines in the future. The Department anticipates that, after the ATBCB's title II guidelines have been published, this rule will be amended to adopt new accessibility standards consistent with the ATBCB's rulemaking. Until that time, however, public entities will have a choice of following UFAS or ADAAG, without the elevator exemption.

Existing buildings leased by the public entity after the effective date of this part are not required by the regulation to meet accessibility standards simply by virtue of being leased. They are subject, however, to the program accessibility standard for existing facilities in § 35.150. To the extent the buildings are newly constructed or altered, they must also meet the new construction and alteration requirements of § 35.151.

The Department received many comments urging that the Department require that public entities lease only accessible buildings. Federal practice under section 504 has always treated newly leased buildings as subject to the existing facility program accessibility standard. Section 204(b) of the Act states that, in the area of "program accessibility, existing facilities," the title II regulations must be consistent with section 504 regulations. Thus, the Department has adopted the section 504 principles for these types of leased buildings. Unlike the construction of new buildings where architectural barriers can be avoided at little or no cost, the application of new construction standards to an existing building being leased raises the same prospect of retrofitting buildings as the use of an existing Federal facility, and the same program accessibility standard should apply to both owned and leased existing buildings. Similarly, requiring that public entities only lease accessible space would significantly restrict the options of State and local governments in seeking leased space, which would be particularly burdensome in rural or sparsely populated areas.

On the other hand, the more accessible the leased space is, the fewer structural modifications will be required in the future for particular employees whose disabilities may necessitate barrier removal as a reasonable accommodation. Pursuant to the requirements for leased buildings contained in the Minimum Guidelines and Requirements for Accessible Design published under the Architectural Barriers Act by the ATBCB, 36 CFR 1190.34, the Federal Government may not lease a building unless it contains (1) One accessible route from an accessible entrance to those areas in which the principal activities for which the building is leased are conducted, (2) accessible toilet facilities, and (3) accessible parking facilities, if a parking area is included within the lease (36 CFR 1190.34). Although these requirements are not applicable to buildings leased by public entities covered by this regulation, such entities are encouraged to look for the most accessible space available to lease and to attempt to find space complying at least with these minimum Federal requirements.

Section 35.151(d) gives effect to the intent of Congress, expressed in section 504(c) of the Act, that this part recognize the national interest in preserving significant historic structures. Commenters criticized the Department's use of descriptive terms in the proposed rule that are different from those used in the ADA to describe eligible historic properties. In addition, some commenters criticized the Department's decision to use the concept of "substantially impairing" the historic features of a property, which is a concept employed in regulations implementing section 504 of the Rehabilitation Act of 1973. Those commenters recommended that the Department adopt the criteria of "adverse effect" published by the Advisory Council on Historic Preservation under the National Historic Preservation Act, 36 CFR 800.9, as the standard for determining whether an historic property may be altered.

The Department agrees with these comments to the extent that they suggest that the language of the rule should conform to the language employed by Congress in the ADA. A definition of "historic property," drawn from section 504 of the ADA, has been added to § 35.104 to clarify that the term applies to those properties listed or eligible for listing in the National Register of Historic Places, or properties designated as historic under State or local law.

The Department intends that the exception created by this section be applied only in those very rare situations in which it is not possible to provide access to an historic property using the special access provisions established by UFAS and ADAAG. Therefore, paragraph (d)(1) of § 35.151 has been revised to clearly state that alterations to historic properties shall comply, to the maximum extent feasible, with section 4.1.7 of UFAS or section 4.1.7 of ADAAG. Paragraph (d)(2) has been revised to provide that, if it has been determined under the procedures established in UFAS and ADAAG that it is not feasible to provide physical access to an historic property in a manner that will not threaten or destroy the historic significance of the property, alternative methods of access shall be provided pursuant to the requirements of § 35.150.

In response to comments, the Department has added to the final rule a new paragraph (e) setting out the requirements of § 36.151 as applied to curb ramps.

Paragraph (e) is taken from the statement contained in the preamble to the proposed rule that all newly constructed or altered streets, roads, and highways must contain curb ramps at any intersection having curbs or other barriers to entry from a street level pedestrian walkway, and that all newly constructed or altered street level pedestrian walkways must have curb ramps at intersections to streets, roads, or highways.

Section 35.178 State Immunity

Section 35.178 restates the provision of section 502 of the Act that a State is not immune under the eleventh amendment to the Constitution of the United States from an action in Federal or State court for violations of the Act, and that the same remedies are available for any such violations as are available in an action against an entity other than a State.

ADA TITLE III

PUBLIC ACCOMMODATIONS AND SERVICES OPERATED BY PRIVATE ENTITIES

42 U.S.C. §

12181	Definitions
12182	Prohibition of discrimination by public accommodations
12183	New construction and alterations in public accommodations and commercial facilities
12184	Prohibition of discrimination in specified public transportation services provided by private entities
12185	Study
12186	Regulations
12187	Exemptions for private clubs and religious organizations
12188	Enforcement
12189	Examinations and courses

ADA TITLE III

PUBLIC ACCOMMODATIONS AND SERVICES OPERATED BY PRIVATE ENTITIES

§ 12181. Definitions

As used in this subchapter:

(1) Commerce

The term "commerce" means travel, trade, traffic, commerce, transportation, or communication—

(A) among the several States;

(B) between any foreign country or any territory or possession and any State; or

(C) between points in the same State but through another State or foreign country.

(2) Commercial facilities

The term "commercial facilities" means facilities—

(A) that are intended for nonresidential use; and

(B) whose operations will affect commerce.

Such term shall not include railroad locomotives, railroad freight cars, railroad cabooses, railroad cars described in section 242 or covered under this subchapter, railroad rights-of-way, or facilities that are covered or expressly exempted from coverage under the Fair Housing Act of 1968 (42 U.S.C. 3601 et seq.).

(3) Demand responsive system

The term "demand responsive system" means any system of providing transportation of individuals by a vehicle, other than a system which is a fixed route system.

(4) Fixed route system

The term "fixed route system" means a system of providing transportation of individuals (other than by aircraft) on which a vehicle is operated along a prescribed route according to a fixed schedule.

(5) Over-the-road bus

The term "over-the-road bus" means a bus characterized by an elevated passenger deck located over a baggage compartment.

(6) Private entity

The term "private entity" means any entity other than a public entity (as defined in section 12131(1) of this title).

(7) Public accommodation

The following private entities are considered public accommodations for purposes of this subchapter, if the operations of such entities affect commerce

(A) an inn, hotel, motel, or other place of lodging, except for an establishment located within a building that contains not more than five rooms for rent or hire and that is actually occupied by the proprietor of such establishment as the residence of such proprietor;

(B) a restaurant, bar, or other establishment serving food or drink;

(C) a motion picture house, theater, concert hall, stadium, or other place of exhibition or entertainment;

(D) an auditorium, convention center, lecture hall, or other place of public gathering;

(E) a bakery, grocery store, clothing store, hardware store, shopping center, or other sales or rental establishment;

(F) a laundromat, dry-cleaner, bank, barber shop, beauty shop, travel service, shoe repair service, funeral parlor, gas station, office of an accountant or lawyer, pharmacy, insurance office, professional office of a health care provider, hospital, or other service establishment;

(G) a terminal, depot, or other station used for specified public transportation;

(H) a museum, library, gallery, or other place of public display or collection;

(I) a park, zoo, amusement park, or other place of recreation;

(J) a nursery, elementary, secondary, undergraduate, or postgraduate private school, or other place of education;

(K) a day care center, senior citizen center, homeless shelter, food bank, adoption agency, or other social service center establishment; and

(L) a gymnasium, health spa, bowling alley, golf course, or other place of exercise or recreation.

(8) Rail and railroad

The terms "rail" and "railroad" have the meaning given the term "railroad" in section 431(e) of Title 45.

(9) Readily achievable

The term "readily achievable" means easily accomplishable and able to be carried out without much difficulty or expense. In determining whether an action is readily achievable, factors to be considered include—

(A) the nature and cost of the action needed under this chapter;

(B) the overall financial resources of the facility or facilities involved in the action; the number of persons employed at such facility; the effect on expenses and resources, or the impact otherwise of such action upon the operation of the facility;

(C) the overall financial resources of the covered entity; the overall size of the business of a covered entity with respect to the number of its employees; the number, type, and location of its facilities; and

(D) the type of operation or operations of the covered entity, including the composition, structure, and functions of the work force of such entity; the geographic separateness, administrative or fiscal relationship of the facility or facilities in question to the covered entity.

(10) Specified public transportation

The term "specified public transportation" means transportation by bus, rail, or any other conveyance (other than by aircraft) that provides the general public with general or special service (including charter service) on a regular and continuing basis.

(11) Vehicle

The term "vehicle" does not include a rail passenger car, railroad locomotive, railroad freight car, railroad caboose, or a railroad car described in section 12162 of this title or covered under this subchapter.

§ 12182. Prohibition of discrimination by public accommodations

(a) General rule

No individual shall be discriminated against on the basis of disability in the full and equal enjoyment of the goods, services, facilities, privileges, advantages, or accommodations of any place of public accommodation by any person who owns, leases (or leases to), or operates a place of public accommodation.

(b) Construction

(1) General prohibition

(A) Activities

(i) Denial of participation

It shall be discriminatory to subject an individual or class of individuals on the basis of a disability or disabilities of such individual or class, directly, or through contractual, licensing, or other arrangements, to a denial of the opportunity of the individual or class to participate in or benefit from the goods, services, facilities, privileges, advantages, or accommodations of an entity.

(ii) Participation in unequal benefit

It shall be discriminatory to afford an individual or class of individuals, on the basis of a disability or disabilities of such individual or class, directly, or through contractual, licensing, or other arrangements with the opportunity to participate in or benefit from a good, service, facility, privilege, advantage, or accommodation that is not equal to that afforded to other individuals.

(iii) Separate benefit

It shall be discriminatory to provide an individual or class of individuals, on the basis of a disability or disabilities of such individual or class, directly, or through contractual, licensing, or other arrangements with a good, service, facility, privilege, advantage, or accommodation that is different or separate from that provided to other individuals, unless such action is necessary to provide the individual or class of individuals with a good, service, facility, privilege, advantage, or accommodation, or other opportunity that is as effective as that provided to others.

(iv) Individual or class of individuals

For purposes of clauses (i) through (iii) of this subparagraph, the term "individual or class of individuals" refers to the clients or customers of the covered public accommodation that enters into the contractual, licensing or other arrangement.

(B) Integrated settings

Goods, services, facilities, privileges, advantages, and accommodations shall be afforded to an individual with a disability in the most integrated setting appropriate to the needs of the individual.

(C) Opportunity to participate

Notwithstanding the existence of separate or different programs or activities provided in accordance with this section, an individual with a disability shall not be denied the opportunity to participate in such programs or activities that are not separate or different.

(D) Administrative methods

An individual or entity shall not, directly or through contractual or other arrangements, utilize standards or criteria or methods of administration—

(i) that have the effect of discriminating on the basis of disability; or

(ii) that perpetuate the discrimination of others who are subject to common administrative control.

(E) Association

It shall be discriminatory to exclude or otherwise deny equal goods, services, facilities, privileges, advantages, accommodations, or other opportunities to an individual or entity because of the known disability of an individual with whom the individual or entity is known to have a relationship or association.

(2) Specific prohibitions

(A) Discrimination

For purposes of subsection (a) of this section, discrimination includes—

(i) the imposition or application of eligibility criteria that screen out or tend to screen out an individual with a disability or any class of individuals with disabilities from fully and equally enjoying any goods, services, facilities, privileges, advantages, or accommodations, unless such criteria can be shown to be necessary for the provision of the goods, services, facilities, privileges, advantages, or accommodations being offered;

(ii) a failure to make reasonable modifications in policies, practices, or procedures, when such modifications are necessary to afford such goods, services, facilities, privileges, advantages, or accommodations to individuals with disabilities, unless the entity can demonstrate that making such modifications would fundamentally alter the nature of such goods, services, facilities, privileges, advantages, or accommodations;

(iii) a failure to take such steps as may be necessary to ensure that no individual with a disability is excluded, denied services, segregated or otherwise treated differently than other individuals because of the absence of auxiliary aids and services, unless the entity can demonstrate that taking such steps would fundamentally alter the nature of the good, service, facility, privilege, advantage, or accommodation being offered or would result in an undue burden;

(iv) a failure to remove architectural barriers, and communication barriers that are structural in nature, in existing facilities, and transportation barriers in existing vehicles and rail passenger cars used by an establishment for transporting individuals (not including barriers that can only be removed through the retrofitting of vehicles or rail passenger cars by the installation of a hydraulic or other lift), where such removal is readily achievable; and

(v) where an entity can demonstrate that the removal of a barrier under clause (iv) is not readily achievable, a failure to make such goods, services, facilities, privileges, advantages, or accommodations available through alternative methods if such methods are readily achievable.

(B) Fixed route system

(i) Accessibility

It shall be considered discrimination for a private entity which operates a fixed route system and which is not subject to section 12184 of this title to purchase or lease a vehicle with a seating capacity in excess of 16 passengers (including the driver) for use on such system, for which a solicitation is made after the 30th day following the effective date of this subparagraph, that is not readily accessible to and usable by individuals with disabilities, including individuals who use wheelchairs.

(ii) Equivalent service

If a private entity which operates a fixed route system and which is not subject to section 12184 of this title purchases or leases a vehicle with a seating capacity of 16 passengers or less (including the driver) for use on such system after the effective date of this subparagraph that is not readily accessible to or usable by individuals with disabilities, it shall be considered discrimination for such entity to fail to operate such system so that, when viewed in its entirety, such system ensures a level of service to individuals with disabilities, including individuals who use wheelchairs, equivalent to the level of service provided to individuals without disabilities.

(C) Demand responsive system

For purposes of subsection (a) of this section, discrimination includes—

(i) a failure of a private entity which operates a demand responsive system and which is not subject to section 12184 of this title to operate such system so that, when viewed in its entirety, such system ensures a level of service to individuals with disabilities, including individuals who use wheelchairs, equivalent to the level of service provided to individuals without disabilities; and

(ii) the purchase or lease by such entity for use on such system of a vehicle with a seating capacity in excess of 16 passengers (including the driver), for which solicitations are made after the 30th day following the effective date of this subparagraph, that is not readily accessible to and usable by individuals with disabilities (including individuals who use wheelchairs) unless such entity can demonstrate that such system, when viewed in its entirety, provides a level of service to individuals with disabilities equivalent to that provided to individuals without disabilities.

(D) Over-the-road buses

(i) Limitation on applicability

Subparagraphs (B) and (C) do not apply to over-the-road buses.

(ii) Accessibility requirements

For purposes of subsection (a) of this section, discrimination includes (I) the purchase or lease of an over-the-road bus which does not comply with the regulations issued under section 12186(a)(2) of this title by a private entity which provides transportation of individuals and which is not primarily engaged in the business of transporting people, and (II) any other failure of such entity to comply with such regulations.

(3) Specific construction

Nothing in this subchapter shall require an entity to permit an individual to participate in or benefit from the goods, services, facilities, privileges, advantages and accommodations of such entity where such individual poses a direct threat to the health or safety of others. The term "direct threat" means a significant risk to the health or safety of others that cannot be eliminated by a modification of policies, practices, or procedures or by the provision of auxiliary aids or services.

§ 12183. New construction and alterations in public accommodations and commercial facilities

(a) Application of term

Except as provided in subsection (b) of this section, as applied to public accommodations and commercial facilities, discrimination for purposes of section 12182(a) of this title includes—

(1) a failure to design and construct facilities for first occupancy later than 30 months after July 26, 1990, that are readily accessible to and usable by individuals with disabilities, except where an entity can demonstrate that it is structurally impracticable to meet the requirements of such subsection in accordance with standards set forth or incorporated by reference in regulations issued under this subchapter; and

(2) with respect to a facility or part thereof that is altered by, on behalf of, or for the use of an establishment in a manner that affects or could affect the usability of the facility or part thereof, a failure to make alterations in such a manner that, to the maximum extent feasible, the altered portions of the facility are readily accessible to and usable by individuals with disabilities, including individuals who use wheelchairs. Where the entity is undertaking an alteration that affects or could affect usability of or access to an area of the facility containing a primary function, the entity shall also make the alterations in such a manner that, to the maximum extent feasible, the path of travel to the altered area and the bathrooms, telephones, and drinking fountains serving the altered area, are readily accessible to and usable by individuals with disabilities where such alterations to the path of travel or the bathrooms, telephones, and drinking fountains serving the altered area are not disproportionate to the overall alterations in terms of cost and scope (as determined under criteria established by the Attorney General).

(b) Elevator

Subsection (a) of this section shall not be construed to require the installation of an elevator for facilities that are less than three stories or have less than 3,000 square feet per story unless the building is a shopping center, a shopping mall, or the professional office of a health care provider or unless the Attorney General determines that a particular category of such facilities requires the installation of elevators based on the usage of such facilities.

§ 12184. Prohibition of discrimination in specified public transportation services provided by private entities

(a) General rule. No individual shall be discriminated against on the basis of disability in the full and equal enjoyment of specified public transportation services provided by a private entity that is primarily engaged in the business of transporting people and whose operations affect commerce.

(b) Construction. For purposes of subsection (a), discrimination includes—

(1) the imposition or application by a entity described in subsection (a) of eligibility criteria that screen out or tend to screen out an individual with a disability or any class of individuals with disabilities from fully enjoying the specified public transportation services provided by the entity, unless such criteria can be shown to be necessary for the provision of the services being offered;

(2) the failure of such entity to—

(A) make reasonable modifications consistent with those required under section 302(b)(2)(A)(ii) [42 USCS § 12182(b)(2)(A)(ii)];

(B) provide auxiliary aids and services consistent with the requirements of section 302(b)(2)(A)(iii) [42 USCS § 12182(b)(2)(A)(iii)]; and

(C) remove barriers consistent with the requirements of section 302(b)(2)(A) [42 USCS § 12182(b)(2)(A)]and with the requirements of section 303(a)(2) [42 USCS § 12183(a)(2)];

(3) the purchase or lease by such entity of a new vehicle (other than an automobile, a van with a seating capacity of less than 8 passengers, including the driver, or an over-the-road bus) which is to be used to provide specified public transportation and for which a solici-

tation is made after the 30th day following the effective date of this section, that is not readily accessible to and usable by individuals with disabilities, including individuals who use wheelchairs; except that the new vehicle need not be readily accessible to and usable by such individuals if the new vehicle is to be used solely in a demand responsive system and if the entity can demonstrate that such system, when viewed in its entirety, provides a level of service to such individuals equivalent to the level of service provided to the general public;

(4)(A) the purchase or lease by such entity of an over-the-road bus which does not comply with the regulations issued under section 306(a)(2) [42 USCS § 12186(a)(2)]; and

(B) any other failure of such entity to comply with such regulations; and

(5) the purchase or lease by such entity of a new van with a seating capacity of less than 8 passengers, including the driver, which is to be used to provide specified public transportation and for which a solicitation is made after the 30th day following the effective date of this section that is not readily accessible to or usable by individuals with disabilities, including individuals who use wheelchairs; except that the new van need not be readily accessible to and usable by such individuals if the entity can demonstrate that the system for which the van is being purchased or leased, when viewed in its entirety, provides a level of service to such individuals equivalent to the level of service provided to the general public;

(6) the purchase or lease by such entity of a new rail passenger car that is to be used to provide specified public transportation, and for which a solicitation is made later than 30 days after the effective date of this paragraph, that is not readily accessible to and usable by individuals with disabilities, including individuals who use wheelchairs; and

(7) the remanufacture by such entity of a rail passenger car that is to be used to provide specified public transportation so as to extend its usable life for 10 years or more, or the purchase or lease by such entity of such a rail car, unless the rail car, to the maximum extent feasible, is made readily accessible to and usable by individuals with disabilities, including individuals who use wheelchairs.

(c) Historical or antiquated cars.

(1) Exception. To the extent that compliance with subsection (b)(2)(C) or (b)(7) would significantly alter the historic or antiquated character of a historical or antiquated rail passenger car, or a rail station served exclusively by such cars, or would result in violation of any rule, regulation, standard, or order issued by the Secretary of Transportation under the Federal Railroad Safety Act of 1970 [45 USCS §§ 431 et seq.], such compliance shall not be required.

(2) Definition. As used in this subsection, the term "historical or antiquated rail passenger car" means a rail passenger car—

(A) which is not less than 30 years old at the time of its use for transporting individuals;

(B) the manufacturer of which is no longer in the business of manufacturing rail passenger cars; and

(C) which—

(i) has a consequential association with events or persons significant to the past; or

(ii) embodies, or is being restored to embody, the distinctive characteristics of a type of rail passenger car used in the past, or to represent a time period which has passed.

§ 12185. Study

(a) Purposes. The Office of Technology Assessment shall undertake a study to determine—

(1) the access needs of individuals with disabilities to over-the-road buses and over-the-road bus service; and

(2) the most cost-effective methods for providing access to over-the-road buses and over-the-road bus service to individuals with disabilities, particularly individuals who use wheelchairs, through all forms of boarding options.

(b) Contents. The study shall include, at a minimum, an analysis of the following:

(1) The anticipated demand by individuals with disabilities for accessible over-the-road buses and over-the-road bus service.

(2) The degree to which such buses and service, including any service required under sections 304(b)(4) and 306(a)(2) [42 USCS §§ 12184(b)(4), 12186(a)(2)], are readily accessible to and usable by individuals with disabilities.

(3) The effectiveness of various methods of providing accessibility to such buses and service to individuals with disabilities.

(4) The cost of providing accessible over-the-road buses and bus service to individuals with disabilities, including consideration of recent technological and cost saving developments in equipment and devices.

(5) Possible design changes in over-the-road buses that could enhance accessibility, including the installation of accessible restrooms which do not result in a loss of seating capacity.

(6) The impact of accessibility requirements on the continuation of over-the-road bus service, with particular consideration of the impact of such requirements on such service to rural communities.

(c) Advisory committee. In conducting the study required by subsection (a), the Office of Technology Assessment shall establish an advisory committee, which shall consist of—

(1) members selected from among private operators and manufacturers of over-the-road buses;

(2) members selected from among individuals with disabilities, particularly individuals who use wheelchairs, who are potential riders of such buses; and

(3) members selected for their technical expertise on issues included in the study, including manufacturers of boarding assistance equipment and devices. The number of members selected under each of paragraphs (1) and (2) shall be equal, and the total number of members selected under paragraphs (1) and (2) shall exceed the number of members selected under paragraph (3).

(d) Deadline. The study required by subsection (a), along with recommendations by the Office of Technology Assessment, including any policy options for legislative action, shall be submitted to the President and Congress within 36 months after the date of the enactment of this Act [enacted July 26, 1990]. If the President determines that compliance with the regulations issued pursuant to section 306(a)(2)(B) [42 USCS § 12186(a)(2)(B)]on or before the applicable deadlines specified in section 306(a)(2)(B) [42 USCS § 12186(a)(2)(B)] will result in a significant reduction in intercity over-the-road bus service, the President shall extend each such deadline by 1 year.

(e) Review. In developing the study required by subsection (a), the Office of Technology Assessment shall provide a preliminary draft of such study to the Architectural and Transportation Barriers Compliance Board established under section 502 of the Rehabilitation Act of 1973 (29 U.S.C. 792). The Board shall have an opportunity to comment on such draft study, and any such comments by the Board made in writing within 120 days after the Board's receipt of the draft study shall be incorporated as part of the final study required to be submitted under subsection (d).

§ 12186. Regulations

(a) Transportation provisions.

(1) General rule. Not later than 1 year after the date of the enactment of this Act [enacted July 26, 1990], the Secretary of Transportation shall issue regulations in an accessible format to carry out sections 302(b)(2)(B) and (C) [42 USCS § 12182(b)(2)(B), (C)] and to carry out section 304 [42 USCS § 12184] (other than subsection (b)(4)).

(2) Special rules for providing access to over-the-road buses.

(A) Interim requirements.

(i) Issuance. Not later than 1 year after the date of the enactment of this Act [enacted July 26, 1990], the Secretary of Transportation shall issue regulations in an accessible format to carry out sections 304(b)(4) and 302(b)(2)(D)(ii) [42 USCS §§ 12184(b)(4), 12182(b)(2)(D)(ii)] that require each private entity which uses an over-the-road bus to provide transportation of individuals to provide accessibility to such bus; except that such regulations shall not require any structural changes in over-the-road buses in order to provide access to individuals who use wheelchairs during the effective period of such regulations and shall not require the purchase of boarding assistance devices to provide access to such individuals.

(ii) Effective period. The regulations issued pursuant to this subparagraph shall be effective until the effective date of the regulations issued under subparagraph (B).

(B) Final requirement.

(i) Review of study and interim requirements. The Secretary shall review the study submitted under section 305 [42 USCS § 12185] and the regulations issued pursuant to subparagraph (A).

(ii) Issuance. Not later than 1 year after the date of the submission of the study under section 305 [42 USCS § 12185], the Secretary shall issue in an accessible format new regulations to carry out sections 304(b)(4) and 302(b)(2)(D)(ii) [42 USCS §§ 12184(b)(4), 12182(b)(2)(D)(ii)] that require, taking into account the purposes of the study under section 305 [42 USCS § 12185] and any recommendations resulting from such study, each private entity which uses an over-the-road bus to provide transportation to individuals to provide accessibility to such bus to individuals with disabilities, including individuals who use wheelchairs.

(iii) Effective period. Subject to section 305(d) [42 USCS § 12185(d)], the regulations issued pursuant to this subparagraph shall take effect—

(I) with respect to small providers of transportation (as defined by the Secretary), 3 years after the date of issuance of final regulations under clause (ii) [October 29, 2001]; and

(II) with respect to other providers of transportation, 2 years after the date of issuance of such final regulations [October 30, 2000].

(C) Limitation on requiring installation of accessible restrooms. The regulations issued pursuant to this paragraph shall not require the installation of accessible restrooms in over-the-road buses if such installation would result in a loss of seating capacity.

(3) Standards. The regulations issued pursuant to this subsection shall include standards applicable to facilities and vehicles covered by sections 302(b)(2) and 304 [42 USCS §§ 12182(b)(2), 12184].

(b) Other provisions. Not later than 1 year after the date of the enactment of this Act [enacted July 26, 1990], the Attorney General shall issue regulations in an accessible format to carry out the provisions of this title not referred to in subsection (a) that include standards applicable to facilities and vehicles covered under section 302 [42 USCS § 12182].

(c) Consistency with ATBCB guidelines. Standards included in regulations issued under subsections (a) and (b) shall be consistent with the minimum guidelines and requirements issued by the Architectural and Transportation Barriers Compliance Board in accordance with section 504 of this Act [42 USCS § 12204].

(d) Interim accessibility standards.

(1) Facilities. If final regulations have not been issued pursuant to this section, for new construction or alterations for which a valid and appropriate State or local building permit is obtained prior to the issuance of final regulations under this section, and for which the construction or alteration authorized by such permit begins within one year of the receipt of such permit and is completed under the terms of such permit, compliance with the Uniform Federal Accessibility Standards in effect at the time the building permit is issued shall suffice to satisfy the requirement that facilities be readily accessible to and usable by persons with disabilities as required under section 303 [42 USCS § 12183], except that, if such final regulations have not been issued one year after the Architectural and Transportation Barriers Compliance Board has issued the supplemental minimum guidelines required under section 504(a) of this Act [42 USCS § 12204(a)], compliance with such supplemental minimum guidelines shall be necessary to satisfy the requirement that facilities be readily accessible to and usable by persons with disabilities prior to issuance of the final regulations.

(2) Vehicles and rail passenger cars. If final regulations have not been issued pursuant to this section, a private entity shall be considered to have complied with the requirements of this title, if any, that a vehicle or rail passenger car be readily accessible to and usable by individuals with disabilities, if the design for such vehicle or car complies with the laws and regulations (including the Minimum Guidelines and Requirements for Accessible Design and such supplemental minimum guidelines as are issued under section 504(a) of this Act [42 USCS § 12204(a)] governing accessibility of such vehicles or cars, to the extent that such laws and regulations are not inconsistent with this title and are in effect at the time such design is substantially completed.

§ 12187. Exemptions for private clubs and religious organizations

The provisions of this subchapter shall not apply to private clubs or establishments exempted from coverage under title II of the Civil Rights Act of 1964 (42 U.S.C. 2000-a(e)) [FN1PP] or to religious organizations or entities controlled by religious organizations, including places of worship.

§ 12188. Enforcement

(a) In general

(1) Availability of remedies and procedures

The remedies and procedures set forth in section 2000a-3(a) of this title are the remedies and procedures this subchapter provides to any person who is being subjected to discrimination on the basis of disability in violation of this subchapter or who has reasonable grounds for believing that such person is about to be subjected to discrimination in violation of section 12183 of this title. Nothing in this section shall require a person with a disability to engage in a futile gesture if such person has actual notice that a person or organization covered by this subchapter does not intend to comply with its provisions.

(2) Injunctive relief

In the case of violations of sections 12182(b)(2)(A)(iv) of this title and section 12183(a) of this title, injunctive relief shall include an order to alter facilities to make such facilities readily accessible to and usable by individuals with disabilities to the extent required by this subchapter. Where appropriate, injunctive relief shall also include requiring the provision of an auxiliary aid or service, modification of a policy, or provision of alternative methods, to the extent required by this subchapter.

(b) Enforcement by the Attorney General

(1) Denial of rights

(A) Duty to investigate

(i) In general

The Attorney General shall investigate alleged violations of this subchapter, and shall undertake periodic reviews of compliance of covered entities under this subchapter.

(ii) Attorney General certification

On the application of a State or local government, the Attorney General may, in consultation with the Architectural and Transportation Barriers Compliance Board, and after prior notice and a public hearing at which persons, including individuals with disabilities, are provided an opportunity to testify against such certification, certify that a State law or local building code or similar ordinance that establishes accessibility requirements meets or exceeds the minimum requirements of this chapter for the accessibility and usability of covered facilities under this subchapter. At any enforcement proceeding under this section, such certification by the Attorney General shall be rebuttable evidence that such State law or local ordinance does meet or exceed the minimum requirements of this chapter.

(B) Potential violation

If the Attorney General has reasonable cause to believe that—

(i) any person or group of persons is engaged in a pattern or practice of discrimination under this subchapter; or

(ii) any person or group of persons has been discriminated against under this subchapter and such discrimination raises an issue of general public importance, the Attorney General may commence a civil action in any appropriate United States district court.

(2) Authority of court

In a civil action under paragraph (1)(B), the court—

(A) may grant any equitable relief that such court considers to be appropriate, including, to the extent required by this subchapter—

(i) granting temporary, preliminary, or permanent relief;

(ii) providing an auxiliary aid or service, modification of policy, practice, or procedure, or alternative method; and

(iii) making facilities readily accessible to and usable by individuals with disabilities;

(B) may award such other relief as the court considers to be appropriate, including monetary damages to persons aggrieved when requested by the Attorney General; and

(C) may, to vindicate the public interest, assess a civil penalty against the entity in an amount—

(i) not exceeding $50,000 for a first violation; and

(ii) not exceeding $100,000 for any subsequent violation.

(3) Single violation

For purposes of paragraph (2)(C), in determining whether a first or subsequent violation has occurred, a determination in a single action, by judgment or settlement, that the covered entity has engaged in more than one discriminatory act shall be counted as a single violation.

(4) Punitive damages

For purposes of subsection (b)(2)(B) of this section, the term "monetary damages" and "such other relief" does not include punitive damages.

(5) Judicial consideration

In a civil action under paragraph (1)(B), the court, when considering what amount of civil penalty, if any, is appropriate, shall give consideration to any good faith effort or attempt to comply with this chapter by the entity. In evaluating good faith, the court shall consider, among other factors it deems relevant, whether the entity could have reasonably anticipated the need for an appropriate type of auxiliary aid needed to accommodate the unique needs of a particular individual with a disability.

§ 12189. Examinations and courses

Any person that offers examinations or courses related to applications, licensing, certification, or credentialing for secondary or post-secondary education, professional, or trade purposes shall offer such examinations or courses in a place and manner accessible to persons with disabilities or offer alternative accessible arrangements for such individuals.

ADA TITLE III
DOJ REGULATIONS

28 C.F.R. §

Subpart A—General

36.104 Definitions

Subpart B—General Requirements

36.201 General
36.202 Activities
36.203 Integrated settings
36.204 Administrative methods
36.205 Association
36.206 Retaliation or coercion
36.207 Places of public accommodation located in private residences
36.208 Direct threat
36.209 Illegal use of drugs
36.210 Smoking
36.211 Maintenance of accessible features
36.212 Insurance

Subpart C—Specific Requirements

36.301 Eligibility criteria
36.302 Modification in policies, practices, or procedures
36.303 Auxilliary aids and services
36.304 Removal of barriers
36.305 Alternatives to barrier removal
36.306 Personal devices and services
36.307 Accessible or special goods
36.308 Seating in assembly areas
36.309 Examinations and courses

Subpart D—New Construction and Alterations

36.401 New construction
36.402 Alterations
36.403 Alterations: Path of travel
36.404 Alterations: Elevator exemption
36.405 Alterations: Historic preservation
36.406 Standards for new construction and alterations

Subpart E—Enforcement

36.501 Private suits
36.502 Investigations and compliance reviews
36.503 Suit by the Attorney General
36.504 Relief
36.505 Attorney fees

ADA TITLE III DOJ REGULATIONS

Subpart A—General

§ 36.104 Definitions.

For purposes of this part, the term—

Act means the Americans with Disabilities Act of 1990 (Pub. L. 101-336, 104 Stat. 327, 42 U.S.C. 12101-12213 and 47 U.S.C. 225 and 611).

Commerce means travel, trade, traffic, commerce, transportation, or communication—

(1) Among the several States;

(2) Between any foreign country or any territory or possession and any State; or

(3) Between points in the same State but through another State or foreign country.

Commercial facilities means facilities—

(1) Whose operations will affect commerce;

(2) That are intended for nonresidential use by a private entity; and

(3) That are not—

(i) Facilities that are covered or expressly exempted from coverage under the Fair Housing Act of 1968, as amended (42 U.S.C. 3601-3631);

(ii) Aircraft; or

(iii) Railroad locomotives, railroad freight cars, railroad cabooses, commuter or intercity passenger rail cars (including coaches, dining cars, sleeping cars, lounge cars, and food service cars), any other railroad cars described in section 242 of the Act or covered under title II of the Act, or railroad rights-of-way. For purposes of this definition, "rail" and "railroad" have the meaning given the term "railroad" in section 202(e) of the Federal Railroad Safety Act of 1970 (45 U.S.C. 431(e)).

Current illegal use of drugs means illegal use of drugs that occurred recently enough to justify a reasonable belief that a person's drug use is current or that continuing use is a real and ongoing problem.

Disability means, with respect to an individual, a physical or mental impairment that substantially limits one or more of the major life activities of such individual; a record of such an impairment; or being regarded as having such an impairment.

(1) The phrase physical or mental impairment means—

(i) Any physiological disorder or condition, cosmetic disfigurement, or anatomical loss affecting one or more of the following body systems: neurological; musculoskeletal; special sense organs; respiratory, including speech organs; cardiovascular; reproductive; digestive; genitourinary; hemic and lymphatic; skin;

and endocrine;

(ii) Any mental or psychological disorder such as mental retardation, organic brain syndrome, emotional or mental illness, and specific learning disabilities;

(iii) The phrase physical or mental impairment includes, but is not limited to, such contagious and noncontagious diseases and conditions as orthopedic, visual, speech, and hearing impairments, cerebral palsy, epilepsy, muscular dystrophy, multiple sclerosis, cancer, heart disease, diabetes, mental retardation, emotional illness, specific learning disabilities, HIV disease (whether symptomatic or asymptomatic), tuberculosis, drug addiction, and alcoholism;

(iv) The phrase physical or mental impairment does not include homosexuality or bisexuality.

(2) The phrase major life activities means functions such as caring for one's self, performing manual tasks, walking, seeing, hearing, speaking, breathing, learning, and working.

(3) The phrase has a record of such an impairment means has a history of, or has been misclassified as having, a mental or physical impairment that substantially limits one or more major life activities.

(4) The phrase is regarded as having an impairment means—

(i) Has a physical or mental impairment that does not substantially limit major life activities but that is treated by a private entity as constituting such a limitation;

(ii) Has a physical or mental impairment that substantially limits major life activities only as a result of the attitudes of others toward such impairment; or

(iii) Has none of the impairments defined in paragraph (1) of this definition but is treated by a private entity as having such an impairment.

(5) The term disability does not include—

(i) Transvestism, transsexualism, pedophilia, exhibitionism, voyeurism, gender identity disorders not resulting from physical impairments, or other sexual behavior disorders;

(ii) Compulsive gambling, kleptomania, or pyromania; or

(iii) Psychoactive substance use disorders resulting from current illegal use of drugs.

Drug means a controlled substance, as defined in schedules I through V of section 202 of the Controlled Substances Act (21 U.S.C. 812).

Facility means all or any portion of buildings, structures, sites, complexes, equipment, rolling stock or other conveyances, roads, walks, passageways, parking lots, or other real or personal property, including the site where the building, property, structure, or equipment is located.

Illegal use of drugs means the use of one or more drugs, the possession or distribution of which is unlawful under the Controlled Substances Act (21 U.S.C. 812). The term "illegal use of drugs" does not include the use of a drug taken under supervision by a licensed health care professional, or other uses authorized by the Controlled Substances Act or other provisions of Federal law.

Individual with a disability means a person who has a disability. The term "individual with a disability" does not include an individual who is currently engaging in the illegal use of drugs, when the private entity acts on the basis of such use.

Place of public accommodation means a facility, operated by a private entity, whose operations affect commerce and fall within at least one of the following categories—

(1) An inn, hotel, motel, or other place of lodging, except for an establishment located within a building that contains not more than five rooms for rent or hire and that is actually occupied by the proprietor of the establishment as the residence of the proprietor;

(2) A restaurant, bar, or other establishment serving food or drink;

(3) A motion picture house, theater, concert hall, stadium, or other place of exhibition or entertainment;

(4) An auditorium, convention center, lecture hall, or other place of public gathering;

(5) A bakery, grocery store, clothing store, hardware store, shopping center, or other sales or rental establishment;

(6) A laundromat, dry-cleaner, bank, barber shop, beauty shop, travel service, shoe repair service, funeral parlor, gas station, office of an accountant or lawyer, pharmacy, insurance office, professional office of a health care provider, hospital, or other service establishment;

(7) A terminal, depot, or other station used for specified public transportation;

(8) A museum, library, gallery, or other place of public display or collection;

(9) A park, zoo, amusement park, or other place of recreation;

(10) A nursery, elementary, secondary, undergraduate, or postgraduate private school, or other place of education;

(11) A day care center, senior citizen center, homeless shelter, food bank, adoption agency, or other social service center establishment; and

(12) A gymnasium, health spa, bowling alley, golf course, or other place of exercise or recreation.

Private club means a private club or establishment

exempted from coverage under title II of the Civil Rights Act of 1964 (42 U.S.C. 2000a(e)).

Private entity means a person or entity other than a public entity.

Public accommodation means a private entity that owns, leases (or leases to), or operates a place of public accommodation.

Public entity means—

(1) Any State or local government;

(2) Any department, agency, special purpose district, or other instrumentality of a State or States or local government; and

(3) The National Railroad Passenger Corporation, and any commuter authority (as defined in section 103(8) of the Rail Passenger Service Act). (45 U.S.C. 541)

Qualified interpreter means an interpreter who is able to interpret effectively, accurately and impartially both receptively and expressively, using any necessary specialized vocabulary.

Readily achievable means easily accomplishable and able to be carried out without much difficulty or expense. In determining whether an action is readily achievable factors to be considered include—

(1) The nature and cost of the action needed under this part;

(2) The overall financial resources of the site or sites involved in the action; the number of persons employed at the site; the effect on expenses and resources; legitimate safety requirements that are necessary for safe operation, including crime prevention measures; or the impact otherwise of the action upon the operation of the site;

(3) The geographic separateness, and the administrative or fiscal relationship of the site or sites in question to any parent corporation or entity;

(4) If applicable, the overall financial resources of any parent corporation or entity; the overall size of the parent corporation or entity with respect to the number of its employees; the number, type, and location of its facilities; and

(5) If applicable, the type of operation or operations of any parent corporation or entity, including the composition, structure, and functions of the work force of the parent corporation or entity.

Religious entity means a religious organization, including a place of worship.

Service animal means any guide dog, signal dog, or other animal individually trained to do work or perform tasks for the benefit of an individual with a disability, including, but not limited to, guiding individuals with impaired vision, alerting individuals with impaired hearing to intruders or sounds, providing minimal protection or rescue work, pulling a wheelchair, or fetching dropped items.

Specified public transportation means transportation by bus, rail, or any other conveyance (other than by aircraft) that provides the general public with general or special service (including charter service) on a regular and continuing basis.

State means each of the several States, the District of Columbia, the Commonwealth of Puerto Rico, Guam, American Samoa, the Virgin Islands, the Trust Territory of the Pacific Islands, and the Commonwealth of the Northern Mariana Islands.

Undue burden means significant difficulty or expense. In determining whether an action would result in an undue burden, factors to be considered include—

(1) The nature and cost of the action needed under this part;

(2) The overall financial resources of the site or sites involved in the action; the number of persons employed at the site; the effect on expenses and resources; legitimate safety requirements that are necessary for safe operation, including crime prevention measures; or the impact otherwise of the action upon the operation of the site;

(3) The geographic separateness, and the administrative or fiscal relationship of the site or sites in question to any parent corporation or entity;

(4) If applicable, the overall financial resources of any parent corporation or entity; the overall size of the parent corporation or entity with respect to the number of its employees; the number, type, and location of its facilities; and

(5) If applicable, the type of operation or operations of any parent corporation or entity, including the composition, structure, and functions of the work force of the parent corporation or entity.

Subpart B—General Requirements

§ 36.201 General.

(a) *Prohibition of discrimination.* No individual shall be discriminated against on the basis of disability in the full and equal enjoyment of the goods, services, facilities, privileges, advantages, or accommodations of any place of public accommodation by any private entity who owns, leases (or leases to), or operates a place of public accommodation.

(b) *Landlord and tenant responsibilities.* Both the landlord who owns the building that houses a place of public accommodation and the tenant who owns or operates the place of public accommodation are public accommodations subject to the requirements of this part. As between the parties, allocation of responsibility for complying with the obligations of this part may be determined by lease or other contract.

§ 36.202 Activities.

(a) Denial of participation. A public accommodation shall not subject an individual or class of individuals on the basis of a disability or disabilities of such individual or class, directly, or through contractual, licensing, or other arrangements, to a denial of the opportunity of the individual or class to participate in or benefit from the goods, services, facilities, privileges, advantages, or accommodations of a place of public accommodation.

(b) Participation in unequal benefit. A public accommodation shall not afford an individual or class of individuals, on the basis of a disability or disabilities of such individual or class, directly, or through contractual, licensing, or other arrangements, with the opportunity to participate in or benefit from a good, service, facility, privilege, advantage, or accommodation that is not equal to that afforded to other individuals.

(c) Separate benefit. A public accommodation shall not provide an individual or class of individuals, on the basis of a disability or disabilities of such individual or class, directly, or through contractual, licensing, or other arrangements with a good, service, facility, privilege, advantage, or accommodation that is different or separate from that provided to other individuals, unless such action is necessary to provide the individual or class of individuals with a good, service, facility, privilege, advantage, or accommodation, or other opportunity that is as effective as that provided to others.

(d) Individual or class of individuals. For purposes of paragraphs (a) through (c) of this section, the term "individual or class of individuals" refers to the clients or customers of the public accommodation that enters into the contractual, licensing, or other arrangement.

§ 36.203 Integrated settings.

(a) General. A public accommodation shall afford goods, services, facilities, privileges, advantages, and accommodations to an individual with a disability in the most integrated setting appropriate to the needs of the individual.

(b) Opportunity to participate. Notwithstanding the existence of separate or different programs or activities provided in accordance with this subpart, a public accommodation shall not deny an individual with a disability an opportunity to participate in such programs or activities that are not separate or different.

(c) Accommodations and services.

(1) Nothing in this part shall be construed to require an individual with a disability to accept an accommodation, aid, service, opportunity, or benefit available under this part that such individual chooses not to accept.

(2) Nothing in the Act or this part authorizes the representative or guardian of an individual with a disability to decline food, water, medical treatment, or medical services for that individual.

§ 36.204 Administrative methods.

A public accommodation shall not, directly or through contractual or other arrangements, utilize standards or criteria or methods of administration that have the effect of discriminating on the basis of disability, or that perpetuate the discrimination of others who are subject to common administrative control.

§ 36.205 Association.

A public accommodation shall not exclude or otherwise deny equal goods, services, facilities, privileges, advantages, accommodations, or other opportunities to an individual or entity because of the known disability of an individual with whom the individual or entity is known to have a relationship or association.

§ 36.206 Retaliation or coercion.

(a) No private or public entity shall discriminate against any individual because that individual has opposed any act or practice made unlawful by this part, or because that individual made a charge, testified, assisted, or participated in any manner in an investigation, proceeding, or hearing under the Act or this part.

(b) No private or public entity shall coerce, intimidate, threaten, or interfere with any individual in the exercise or enjoyment of, or on account of his or her having exercised or enjoyed, or on account of his or her having aided or encouraged any other individual in the exercise or enjoyment of, any right granted or protected by the Act or this part.

(c) Illustrations of conduct prohibited by this section include, but are not limited to:

(1) Coercing an individual to deny or limit the benefits, services, or advantages to which he or she is entitled under the Act or this part;

(2) Threatening, intimidating, or interfering with an individual with a disability who is seeking to

obtain or use the goods, services, facilities, privileges, advantages, or accommodations of a public accommodation;

(3) Intimidating or threatening any person because that person is assisting or encouraging an individual or group entitled to claim the rights granted or protected by the Act or this part to exercise those rights; or

(4) Retaliating against any person because that person has participated in any investigation or action to enforce the Act or this part.

§ 36.207 Places of public accommodation located in private residences.

(a) When a place of public accommodation is located in a private residence, the portion of the residence used exclusively as a residence is not covered by this part, but that portion used exclusively in the operation of the place of public accommodation or that portion used both for the place of public accommodation and for residential purposes is covered by this part.

(b) The portion of the residence covered under paragraph (a) of this section extends to those elements used to enter the place of public accommodation, including the homeowner's front sidewalk, if any, the door or entryway, and hallways; and those portions of the residence, interior or exterior, available to or used by customers or clients, including restrooms.

§ 36.208 Direct threat.

(a) This part does not require a public accommodation to permit an individual to participate in or benefit from the goods, services, facilities, privileges, advantages and accommodations of that public accommodation when that individual poses a direct threat to the health or safety of others.

(b) Direct threat means a significant risk to the health or safety of others that cannot be eliminated by a modification of policies, practices, or procedures, or by the provision of auxiliary aids or services.

(c) In determining whether an individual poses a direct threat to the health or safety of others, a public accommodation must make an individualized assessment, based on reasonable judgment that relies on current medical knowledge or on the best available objective evidence, to ascertain: the nature, duration, and severity of the risk; the probability that the potential injury will actually occur; and whether reasonable modifications of policies, practices, or procedures will mitigate the risk.

§ 36.209 Illegal use of drugs.

(a) General.

(1) Except as provided in paragraph (b) of this section, this part does not prohibit discrimination against an individual based on that individual's current illegal use of drugs.

(2) A public accommodation shall not discriminate on the basis of illegal use of drugs against an individual who is not engaging in current illegal use of drugs and who—

(i) Has successfully completed a supervised drug rehabilitation program or has otherwise been rehabilitated successfully;

(ii) Is participating in a supervised rehabilitation program; or

(iii) Is erroneously regarded as engaging in such use.

(b) Health and drug rehabilitation services.

(1) A public accommodation shall not deny health services, or services provided in connection with drug rehabilitation, to an individual on the basis of that individual's current illegal use of drugs, if the individual is otherwise entitled to such services.

(2) A drug rehabilitation or treatment program may deny participation to individuals who engage in illegal use of drugs while they are in the program.

(c) Drug testing.

(1) This part does not prohibit a public accommodation from adopting or administering reasonable policies or procedures, including but not limited to drug testing, designed to ensure that an individual who formerly engaged in the illegal use of drugs is not now engaging in current illegal use of drugs.

(2) Nothing in this paragraph (c) shall be construed to encourage, prohibit, restrict, or authorize the conducting of testing for the illegal use of drugs.

§ 36.210 Smoking.

This part does not preclude the prohibition of, or the imposition of restrictions on, smoking in places of public accommodation.

§ 36.211 Maintenance of accessible features.

(a) A public accommodation shall maintain in operable working condition those features of facilities and equipment that are required to be readily accessible to and usable by persons with disabilities by the Act or this part.

(b) This section does not prohibit isolated or temporary interruptions in service or access due to maintenance or repairs.

§ 36.212 Insurance.

(a) This part shall not be construed to prohibit or restrict—

(1) An insurer, hospital or medical service company, health maintenance organization, or any agent, or entity that administers benefit plans, or similar organizations from underwriting risks, classifying risks, or administering such risks that are based on or not inconsistent with State law; or

(2) A person or organization covered by this part from establishing, sponsoring, observing or administering the terms of a bona fide benefit plan that are based on underwriting risks, classifying risks, or administering such risks that are based on or not inconsistent with State law; or

(3) A person or organization covered by this part from establishing, sponsoring, observing or administering the terms of a bona fide benefit plan that is not subject to State laws that regulate insurance.

(b) Paragraphs (a) (1), (2), and (3) of this section shall not be used as a subterfuge to evade the purposes of the Act or this part.

(c) A public accommodation shall not refuse to serve an individual with a disability because its insurance company conditions coverage or rates on the absence of individuals with disabilities.

Subpart C—Specific Requirements

§ 36.301 Eligibility criteria.

(a) General. A public accommodation shall not impose or apply eligibility criteria that screen out or tend to screen out an individual with a disability or any class of individuals with disabilities from fully and equally enjoying any goods, services, facilities, privileges, advantages, or accommodations, unless such criteria can be shown to be necessary for the provision of the goods, services, facilities, privileges, advantages, or accommodations being offered.

(b) Safety. A public accommodation may impose legitimate safety requirements that are necessary for safe operation. Safety requirements must be based on actual risks and not on mere speculation, stereotypes, or generalizations about individuals with disabilities.

(c) Charges. A public accommodation may not impose a surcharge on a particular individual with a disability or any group of individuals with disabilities to cover the costs of measures, such as the provision of auxiliary aids, barrier removal, alternatives to barrier removal, and reasonable modifications in policies, practices, or procedures, that are required to provide that individual or group with the nondiscriminatory treatment required by the Act or this part.

§ 36.302 Modifications in policies, practices, or procedures.

(a) General. A public accommodation shall make reasonable modifications in policies, practices, or procedures, when the modifications are necessary to afford goods, services, facilities, privileges, advantages, or accommodations to individuals with disabilities, unless the public accommodation can demonstrate that making the modifications would fundamentally alter the nature of the goods, services, facilities, privileges, advantages, or accommodations.

(b) Specialties—

(1) General. A public accommodation may refer an individual with a disability to another public accommodation, if that individual is seeking, or requires, treatment or services outside of the referring public accommodation's area of specialization, and if, in the normal course of its operations, the referring public accommodation would make a similar referral for an individual without a disability who seeks or requires the same treatment or services.

(2) Illustration—medical specialties. A health care provider may refer an individual with a disability to another provider, if that individual is seeking, or requires, treatment or services outside of the referring provider's area of specialization, and if the referring provider would make a similar referral for an individual without a disability who seeks or requires the same treatment or services. A physician who specializes in treating only a particular condition cannot refuse to treat an individual with a disability for that condition, but is not required to treat the individual for a different condition.

(c) Service animals—

(1) General. Generally, a public accommodation shall modify policies, practices, or procedures to permit the use of a service animal by an individual with a disability.

(2) Care or supervision of service animals. Nothing in this part requires a public accommodation to supervise or care for a service animal.

(d) Check-out aisles. A store with check-out aisles shall ensure that an adequate number of accessible check-out aisles are kept open during store hours, or shall otherwise modify its policies and practices, in order to ensure that an equivalent level of convenient service is provided to individuals with disabilities as is provided to others. If only one check-out aisle is accessible, and it is generally used for express service, one way of providing equivalent service is to allow persons with mobility impairments to make all their purchases at that aisle.

§ 36.303 Auxiliary aids and services.

(a) General. A public accommodation shall take those steps that may be necessary to ensure that no individual with a disability is excluded, denied services, segregated or otherwise treated differently than other individuals because of the absence of auxiliary aids and services, unless the public accommodation can demonstrate that taking those steps would fundamentally alter the nature of the goods, services, facilities, privileges, advantages, or accommodations being offered or would result in an undue burden, i.e., significant difficulty or expense.

(b) Examples. The term "auxiliary aids and services" includes—

(1) Qualified interpreters, notetakers, computer-aided transcription services, written materials, telephone handset amplifiers, assistive listening devices, assistive listening systems, telephones compatible with hearing aids, closed caption decoders, open and closed captioning, telecommunications devices for deaf persons (TDD's), videotext displays, or other effective methods of making aurally delivered materials available to individuals with hearing impairments;

(2) Qualified readers, taped texts, audio recordings, Brailled materials, large print materials, or other effective methods of making visually delivered materials available to individuals with visual impairments;

(3) Acquisition or modification of equipment or devices; and

(4) Other similar services and actions.

(c) Effective communication. A public accommodation shall furnish appropriate auxiliary aids and services where necessary to ensure effective communication with individuals with disabilities.

(d) Telecommunication devices for the deaf (TDD's).

(1) A public accommodation that offers a customer, client, patient, or participant the opportunity to make outgoing telephone calls on more than an incidental convenience basis shall make available, upon request, a TDD for the use of an individual who has impaired hearing or a communication disorder.

(2) This part does not require a public accommodation to use a TDD for receiving or making telephone calls incident to its operations.

(e) Closed caption decoders. Places of lodging that provide televisions in five or more guest rooms and hospitals that provide televisions for patient use shall provide, upon request, a means for decoding captions for use by an individual with impaired hearing.

(f) Alternatives. If provision of a particular auxiliary aid or service by a public accommodation would result in a fundamental alteration in the nature of the goods, services, facilities, privileges, advantages, or accommodations being offered or in an undue burden, i.e., significant difficulty or expense, the public accommodation shall provide an alternative auxiliary aid or service, if one exists, that would not result in an alteration or such burden but would nevertheless ensure that, to the maximum extent possible, individuals with disabilities receive the goods, services, facilities, privileges, advantages, or accommodations offered by the public accommodation.

§ 36.304 Removal of barriers.

(a) General. A public accommodation shall remove architectural barriers in existing facilities, including communication barriers that are structural in nature, where such removal is readily achievable, i.e., easily accomplishable and able to be carried out without much difficulty or expense.

(b) Examples. Examples of steps to remove barriers include, but are not limited to, the following actions—

(1) Installing ramps;

(2) Making curb cuts in sidewalks and entrances;

(3) Repositioning shelves;

(4) Rearranging tables, chairs, vending machines, display racks, and other furniture;

(5) Repositioning telephones;

(6) Adding raised markings on elevator control buttons;

(7) Installing flashing alarm lights;

(8) Widening doors;

(9) Installing offset hinges to widen doorways;

(10) Eliminating a turnstile or providing an alternative accessible path;

(11) Installing accessible door hardware;

(12) Installing grab bars in toilet stalls;

(13) Rearranging toilet partitions to increase maneuvering space;

(14) Insulating lavatory pipes under sinks to prevent burns;

(15) Installing a raised toilet seat;

(16) Installing a full-length bathroom mirror;

(17) Repositioning the paper towel dispenser in a bathroom;

(18) Creating designated accessible parking spaces;

(19) Installing an accessible paper cup dispenser at an existing inaccessible water fountain;

(20) Removing high pile, low density carpeting; or

(21) Installing vehicle hand controls.

(c) Priorities. A public accommodation is urged to take measures to comply with the barrier removal requirements of this section in accordance with the following order of priorities.

(1) First, a public accommodation should take measures to provide access to a place of public accommodation from public sidewalks, parking, or public transportation. These measures include, for example, installing an entrance ramp, widening entrances, and providing accessible parking spaces.

(2) Second, a public accommodation should take measures to provide access to those areas of a place of public accommodation where goods and services are made available to the public. These measures include, for example, adjusting the layout of display racks, rearranging tables, providing Brailled and raised character signage, widening doors, providing visual alarms, and installing ramps.

(3) Third, a public accommodation should take measures to provide access to restroom facilities. These measures include, for example, removal of obstructing furniture or vending machines, widening of doors, installation of ramps, providing accessible signage, widening of toilet stalls, and installation of grab bars.

(4) Fourth, a public accommodation should take any other measures necessary to provide access to the goods, services, facilities, privileges, advantages, or accommodations of a place of public accommodation.

(d) Relationship to alterations requirements of subpart D of this part.

(1) Except as provided in paragraph (d)(2) of this section, measures taken to comply with the barrier removal requirements of this section shall comply with the applicable requirements for alterations in § 36.402 and ss 36.404-36.406 of this part for the element being altered. The path of travel requirements of § 36.403 shall not apply to measures taken solely to comply with the barrier removal requirements of this section.

(2) If, as a result of compliance with the alterations requirements specified in paragraph (d)(1) of this section, the measures required to remove a barrier would not be readily achievable, a public accommodation may take other readily achievable measures to remove the barrier that do not fully comply with the specified requirements. Such measures include, for example, providing a ramp with a steeper slope or widening a doorway to a narrower width than that mandated by the alterations requirements. No measure shall be taken, however, that poses a significant risk to the health or safety of individuals with disabilities or others.

(e) Portable ramps. Portable ramps should be used to comply with this section only when installation of a permanent ramp is not readily achievable. In order to avoid any significant risk to the health or safety of individuals with disabilities or others in using portable ramps, due consideration shall be given to safety features such as nonslip surfaces, railings, anchoring, and strength of materials.

(f) Selling or serving space. The rearrangement of temporary or movable structures, such as furniture, equipment, and display racks is not readily achievable to the extent that it results in a significant loss of selling or serving space.

(g) Limitation on barrier removal obligations.

(1) The requirements for barrier removal under § 36.304 shall not be interpreted to exceed the standards for alterations in subpart D of this part.

(2) To the extent that relevant standards for alterations are not provided in subpart D of this part, then the requirements of § 36.304 shall not be interpreted to exceed the standards for new construction in subpart D of this part.

(3) This section does not apply to rolling stock and other conveyances to the extent that § 36.310 applies to rolling stock and other conveyances.

§ 36.305 Alternatives to barrier removal.

(a) General. Where a public accommodation can demonstrate that barrier removal is not readily achievable, the public accommodation shall not fail to make its goods, services, facilities, privileges, advantages, or accommodations available through alternative methods, if those methods are readily achievable.

(b) Examples. Examples of alternatives to barrier removal include, but are not limited to, the following actions—

(1) Providing curb service or home delivery;

(2) Retrieving merchandise from inaccessible shelves or racks;

(3) Relocating activities to accessible locations;

(c) Multiscreen cinemas. If it is not readily achievable to remove barriers to provide access by persons with mobility impairments to all of the theaters of a multiscreen cinema, the cinema shall establish a film rotation schedule that provides reasonable access for individuals who use wheelchairs to all films. Reasonable notice shall be provided to the public as to the location and time of accessible showings.

§ 36.306 Personal devices and services.

This part does not require a public accommodation to provide its customers, clients, or participants with personal devices, such as wheelchairs; individually prescribed devices, such as prescription eyeglasses or hearing aids; or services of a personal nature including assistance in eating, toileting, or dressing.

§ 36.307 Accessible or special goods.

(a) This part does not require a public accommodation to alter its inventory to include accessible or special goods that are designed for, or facilitate use by, individuals with disabilities.

(b) A public accommodation shall order accessible or special goods at the request of an individual with disabilities, if, in the normal course of its operation, it makes special orders on request for unstocked goods, and if the accessible or special goods can be obtained from a supplier with whom the public accommodation customarily does business.

(c) Examples of accessible or special goods include items such as Brailled versions of books, books on audio cassettes, closed-captioned video tapes, special sizes or lines of clothing, and special foods to meet particular dietary needs.

§ 36.308 Seating in assembly areas.

(a) Existing facilities.

(1) To the extent that it is readily achievable, a public accommodation in assembly areas shall—

(i) Provide a reasonable number of wheelchair seating spaces and seats with removable aisle-side arm rests; and

(ii) Locate the wheelchair seating spaces so that they—

(A) Are dispersed throughout the seating area;

(B) Provide lines of sight and choice of admission prices comparable to those for members of the general public;

(C) Adjoin an accessible route that also serves as a means of egress in case of emergency; and

(D) Permit individuals who use wheelchairs to sit with family members or other companions.

(2) If removal of seats is not readily achievable, a public accommodation shall provide, to the extent that it is readily achievable to do so, a portable chair or other means to permit a family member or other companion to sit with an individual who uses a wheelchair.

(3) The requirements of paragraph (a) of this section shall not be interpreted to exceed the standards for alterations in subpart D of this part.

(b) New construction and alterations. The provision and location of wheelchair seating spaces in newly constructed or altered assembly areas shall be governed by the standards for new construction and alterations in subpart D of this part.

§ 36.309 Examinations and courses.

(a) General. Any private entity that offers examinations or courses related to applications, licensing, certification, or credentialing for secondary or postsecondary education, professional, or trade purposes shall offer such examinations or courses in a place and manner accessible to persons with disabilities or offer alternative accessible arrangements for such individuals.

(b) Examinations.

(1) Any private entity offering an examination covered by this section must assure that—

(i) The examination is selected and administered so as to best ensure that, when the examination is administered to an individual with a disability that impairs sensory, manual, or speaking skills, the examination results accurately reflect the individual's aptitude or achievement level or whatever other factor the examination purports to measure, rather than reflecting the individual's impaired sensory, manual, or speaking skills (except where those skills are the factors that the examination purports to measure);

(ii) An examination that is designed for individuals with impaired sensory, manual, or speaking skills is offered at equally convenient locations, as often, and in as timely a manner as are other examinations; and

(iii) The examination is administered in facilities that are accessible to individuals with disabilities or alternative accessible arrangements are made.

(2) Required modifications to an examination may include changes in the length of time permitted for completion of the examination and adaptation of the manner in which the examination is given.

(3) A private entity offering an examination covered by this section shall provide appropriate auxiliary aids for persons with impaired sensory, manual, or speaking skills, unless that private entity can demonstrate that offering a particular auxiliary aid would fundamentally alter the measurement of the skills or knowledge the examination is intended to test

or would result in an undue burden. Auxiliary aids and services required by this section may include taped examinations, interpreters or other effective methods of making orally delivered materials available to individuals with hearing impairments, Brailled or large print examinations and answer sheets or qualified readers for individuals with visual impairments or learning disabilities, transcribers for individuals with manual impairments, and other similar services and actions.

(4) Alternative accessible arrangements may include, for example, provision of an examination at an individual's home with a proctor if accessible facilities or equipment are unavailable. Alternative arrangements must provide comparable conditions to those provided for nondisabled individuals.

(c) Courses.

(1) Any private entity that offers a course covered by this section must make such modifications to that course as are necessary to ensure that the place and manner in which the course is given are accessible to individuals with disabilities.

(2) Required modifications may include changes in the length of time permitted for the completion of the course, substitution of specific requirements, or adaptation of the manner in which the course is conducted or course materials are distributed.

(3) A private entity that offers a course covered by this section shall provide appropriate auxiliary aids and services for persons with impaired sensory, manual, or speaking skills, unless the private entity can demonstrate that offering a particular auxiliary aid or service would fundamentally alter the course or would result in an undue burden. Auxiliary aids and services required by this section may include taped texts, interpreters or other effective methods of making orally delivered materials available to individuals with hearing impairments, Brailled or large print texts or qualified readers for individuals with visual impairments and learning disabilities, classroom equipment adapted for use by individuals with manual impairments, and other similar services and actions.

(4) Courses must be administered in facilities that are accessible to individuals with disabilities or alternative accessible arrangements must be made.

(5) Alternative accessible arrangements may include, for example, provision of the course through videotape, cassettes, or prepared notes. Alternative arrangements must provide comparable conditions to those provided for nondisabled individuals.

Subpart D—New Construction and Alterations

§ 36.401 New construction.

(a) General.

(1) Except as provided in paragraphs (b) and (c) of this section, discrimination for purposes of this part includes a failure to design and construct facilities for first occupancy after January 26, 1993, that are readily accessible to and usable by individuals with disabilities.

(2) For purposes of this section, a facility is designed and constructed for first occupancy after January 26, 1993, only—

(i) If the last application for a building permit or permit extension for the facility is certified to be complete, by a State, County, or local government after January 26, 1992 (or, in those jurisdictions where the government does not certify completion of applications, if the last application for a building permit or permit extension for the facility is received by the State, County, or local government after January 26, 1992); and

(ii) If the first certificate of occupancy for the facility is issued after January 26, 1993.

(b) Commercial facilities located in private residences.

(1) When a commercial facility is located in a private residence, the portion of the residence used exclusively as a residence is not covered by this subpart, but that portion used exclusively in the operation of the commercial facility or that portion used both for the commercial facility and for residential purposes is covered by the new construction and alterations requirements of this subpart.

(2) The portion of the residence covered under paragraph (b)(1) of this section extends to those elements used to enter the commercial facility, including the homeowner's front sidewalk, if any, the door or entryway, and hallways; and those portions of the residence, interior or exterior, available to or used by employees or visitors of the commercial facility, including restrooms.

(c) Exception for structural impracticability.

(1) Full compliance with the requirements of this section is not required where an entity can demonstrate that it is structurally impracticable to meet the requirements. Full compliance will be considered structurally impracticable only in those rare circumstances when the unique characteristics of terrain prevent the incorporation of accessibility features.

(2) If full compliance with this section would be structurally impracticable, compliance with this sec-

tion is required to the extent that it is not structurally impracticable. In that case, any portion of the facility that can be made accessible shall be made accessible to the extent that it is not structurally impracticable.

(3) If providing accessibility in conformance with this section to individuals with certain disabilities (e.g., those who use wheelchairs) would be structurally impracticable, accessibility shall nonetheless be ensured to persons with other types of disabilities (e.g., those who use crutches or who have sight, hearing, or mental impairments) in accordance with this section.

(d) Elevator exemption.

(1) For purposes of this paragraph (d)—

(i) Professional office of a health care provider means a location where a person or entity regulated by a State to provide professional services related to the physical or mental health of an individual makes such services available to the public. The facility housing the "professional office of a health care provider" only includes floor levels housing at least one health care provider, or any floor level designed or intended for use by at least one health care provider.

(ii) Shopping center or shopping mall means—

(A) A building housing five or more sales or rental establishments; or

(B) A series of buildings on a common site, either under common ownership or common control or developed either as one project or as a series of related projects, housing five or more sales or rental establishments. For purposes of this section, places of public accommodation of the types listed in paragraph (5) of the definition of "place of public accommodation" in section § 36.104 are considered sales or rental establishments. The facility housing a "shopping center or shopping mall" only includes floor levels housing at least one sales or rental establishment, or any floor level designed or intended for use by at least one sales or rental establishment.

(2) This section does not require the installation of an elevator in a facility that is less than three stories or has less than 3000 square feet per story, except with respect to any facility that houses one or more of the following:

(i) A shopping center or shopping mall, or a professional office of a health care provider.

(ii) A terminal, depot, or other station used for specified public transportation, or an airport passenger terminal. In such a facility, any area housing passenger services, including boarding and debarking, loading and unloading, baggage claim, dining facilities, and other common areas open to the public, must be on an accessible route from an accessible entrance.

(3) The elevator exemption set forth in this paragraph (d) does not obviate or limit, in any way the obligation to comply with the other accessibility requirements established in paragraph (a) of this section. For example, in a facility that houses a shopping center or shopping mall, or a professional office of a health care provider, the floors that are above or below an accessible ground floor and that do not house sales or rental establishments or a professional office of a health care provider, must meet the requirements of this section but for the elevator.

§ 36.402 Alterations.

(a) General.

(1) Any alteration to a place of public accommodation or a commercial facility, after January 26, 1992, shall be made so as to ensure that, to the maximum extent feasible, the altered portions of the facility are readily accessible to and usable by individuals with disabilities, including individuals who use wheelchairs.

(2) An alteration is deemed to be undertaken after January 26, 1992, if the physical alteration of the property begins after that date.

(b) Alteration. For the purposes of this part, an alteration is a change to a place of public accommodation or a commercial facility that affects or could affect the usability of the building or facility or any part thereof.

(1) Alterations include, but are not limited to, remodeling, renovation, rehabilitation, reconstruction, historic restoration, changes or rearrangement in structural parts or elements, and changes or rearrangement in the plan configuration of walls and full-height partitions. Normal maintenance, reroofing, painting or wallpapering, asbestos removal, or changes to mechanical and electrical systems are not alterations unless they affect the usability of the building or facility.

(2) If existing elements, spaces, or common areas are altered, then each such altered element, space, or area shall comply with the applicable provisions of appendix A to this part.

(c) To the maximum extent feasible. The phrase "to the maximum extent feasible," as used in this section, applies to the occasional case where the nature of an existing facility makes it virtually impossible to comply fully with applicable accessibility standards through a planned alteration. In these circumstances, the alteration shall provide the maximum physical accessibility feasible. Any altered features of the facility that can be made accessible shall be made accessible. If providing accessibility in conformance with this section to individuals with certain disabilities (e.g., those who use wheelchairs) would not be feasible, the facility shall be made accessible to persons with other types of disabilities (e.g., those who use crutches, those who have impaired vision or hearing, or those who have other impairments).

§ 36.403 Alterations: Path of travel.

(a) General. An alteration that affects or could affect the usability of or access to an area of a facility that contains a primary function shall be made so as to ensure that, to the maximum extent feasible, the path of travel to the altered area and the restrooms, telephones, and drinking fountains serving the altered area, are readily accessible to and usable by individuals with disabilities, including individuals who use wheelchairs, unless the cost and scope of such alterations is disproportionate to the cost of the overall alteration.

(b) Primary function. A "primary function" is a major activity for which the facility is intended. Areas that contain a primary function include, but are not limited to, the customer services lobby of a bank, the dining area of a cafeteria, the meeting rooms in a conference center, as well as offices and other work areas in which the activities of the public accommodation or other private entity using the facility are carried out. Mechanical rooms, boiler rooms, supply storage rooms, employee lounges or locker rooms, janitorial closets, entrances, corridors, and restrooms are not areas containing a primary function.

(c) Alterations to an area containing a primary function.

(1) Alterations that affect the usability of or access to an area containing a primary function include, but are not limited to—

(i) Remodeling merchandise display areas or employee work areas in a department store;

(ii) Replacing an inaccessible floor surface in the customer service or employee work areas of a bank;

(iii) Redesigning the assembly line area of a factory; or

(iv) Installing a computer center in an accounting firm.

(2) For the purposes of this section, alterations to windows, hardware, controls, electrical outlets, and signage shall not be deemed to be alterations that affect the usability of or access to an area containing a primary function.

(d) Landlord/tenant: If a tenant is making alterations as defined in § 36.402 that would trigger the requirements of this section, those alterations by the tenant in areas that only the tenant occupies do not trigger a path of travel obligation upon the landlord with respect to areas of the facility under the landlord's authority, if those areas are not otherwise being altered.

(e) Path of travel.

(1) A "path of travel" includes a continuous, unobstructed way of pedestrian passage by means of which the altered area may be approached, entered, and exited, and which connects the altered area with an exterior approach (including sidewalks, streets, and parking areas), an entrance to the facility, and other parts of the facility.

(2) An accessible path of travel may consist of walks and sidewalks, curb ramps and other interior or exterior pedestrian ramps; clear floor paths through lobbies, corridors, rooms, and other improved areas; parking access aisles; elevators and lifts; or a combination of these elements.

(3) For the purposes of this part, the term "path of travel" also includes the restrooms, telephones, and drinking fountains serving the altered area.

(f) Disproportionality.

(1) Alterations made to provide an accessible path of travel to the altered area will be deemed disproportionate to the overall alteration when the cost exceeds 20% of the cost of the alteration to the primary function area.

(2) Costs that may be counted as expenditures required to provide an accessible path of travel may include:

(i) Costs associated with providing an accessible entrance and an accessible route to the altered area, for example, the cost of widening doorways or installing ramps;

(ii) Costs associated with making restrooms accessible, such as installing grab bars, enlarging toilet stalls, insulating pipes, or installing accessible faucet controls;

(iii) Costs associated with providing accessible telephones, such as relocating the telephone to an accessible height, installing amplification devices, or installing a telecommunications device for deaf persons (TDD);

(iv) Costs associated with relocating an inaccessible drinking fountain.

(g) Duty to provide accessible features in the event of disproportionality.

(1) When the cost of alterations necessary to make the path of travel to the altered area fully acces-

sible is disproportionate to the cost of the overall alteration, the path of travel shall be made accessible to the extent that it can be made accessible without incurring disproportionate costs.

(2) In choosing which accessible elements to provide, priority should be given to those elements that will provide the greatest access, in the following order:

(i) An accessible entrance;

(ii) An accessible route to the altered area;

(iii) At least one accessible restroom for each sex or a single unisex restroom;

(iv) Accessible telephones;

(v) Accessible drinking fountains; and

(vi) When possible, additional accessible elements such as parking, storage, and alarms.

(h) Series of smaller alterations.

(1) The obligation to provide an accessible path of travel may not be evaded by performing a series of small alterations to the area served by a single path of travel if those alterations could have been performed as a single undertaking.

(2)(i) If an area containing a primary function has been altered without providing an accessible path of travel to that area, and subsequent alterations of that area, or a different area on the same path of travel, are undertaken within three years of the original alteration, the total cost of alterations to the primary function areas on that path of travel during the preceding three year period shall be considered in determining whether the cost of making that path of travel accessible is disproportionate.

(ii) Only alterations undertaken after January 26, 1992, shall be considered in determining if the cost of providing an accessible path of travel is disproportionate to the overall cost of the alterations.

§ 36.404 Alterations: Elevator exemption.

(a) This section does not require the installation of an elevator in an altered facility that is less than three stories or has less than 3,000 square feet per story, except with respect to any facility that houses a shopping center, a shopping mall, the professional office of a health care provider, a terminal, depot, or other station used for specified public transportation, or an airport passenger terminal.

(1) For the purposes of this section, "professional office of a health care provider" means a location where a person or entity regulated by a State to provide professional services related to the physical or mental health of an individual makes such services available to the public. The facility that houses a "professional office of a health care provider" only includes floor levels housing by at least one health care provider, or any floor level designed or intended for use by at least one health care provider.

(2) For the purposes of this section, shopping center or shopping mall means—

(i) A building housing five or more sales or rental establishments; or

(ii) A series of buildings on a common site, connected by a common pedestrian access route above or below the ground floor, that is either under common ownership or common control or developed either as one project or as a series of related projects, housing five or more sales or rental establishments. For purposes of this section, places of public accommodation of the types listed in paragraph (5) of the definition of "place of public accommodation" in § 36.104 are considered sales or rental establishments. The facility housing a "shopping center or shopping mall" only includes floor levels housing at least one sales or rental establishment, or any floor level designed or intended for use by at least one sales or rental establishment.

(b) The exemption provided in paragraph (a) of this section does not obviate or limit in any way the obligation to comply with the other accessibility requirements established in this subpart. For example, alterations to floors above or below the accessible ground floor must be accessible regardless of whether the altered facility has an elevator.

§ 36.405 Alterations: Historic preservation.

(a) Alterations to buildings or facilities that are eligible for listing in the National Register of Historic Places under the National Historic Preservation Act (16 U.S.C. 470 et seq.), or are designated as historic under State or local law, shall comply to the maximum extent feasible with section 4.1.7 of appendix A to this part.

(b) If it is determined under the procedures set out in section 4.1.7 of appendix A that it is not feasible to provide physical access to an historic property that is a place of public accommodation in a manner that will not threaten or destroy the historic significance of the building or facility, alternative methods of access shall be provided pursuant to the requirements of subpart C of this part.

§ 36.406 Standards for new construction and alterations.

(a) New construction and alterations subject to this part shall comply with the standards for accessible design published as appendix A to this part (ADAAG).

(b) The chart in the appendix to this section provides guidance to the user in reading appendix A to this part (ADAAG) together with subparts A through D of this part, when determining requirements for a particular facility.

Subpart E—Enforcement

§ 36.501 Private suits.

(a) General. Any person who is being subjected to discrimination on the basis of disability in violation of the Act or this part or who has reasonable grounds for believing that such person is about to be subjected to discrimination in violation of section 303 of the Act or subpart D of this part may institute a civil action for preventive relief, including an application for a permanent or temporary injunction, restraining order, or other order. Upon timely application, the court may, in its discretion, permit the Attorney General to intervene in the civil action if the Attorney General or his or her designee certifies that the case is of general public importance. Upon application by the complainant and in such circumstances as the court may deem just, the court may appoint an attorney for such complainant and may authorize the commencement of the civil action without the payment of fees, costs, or security. Nothing in this section shall require a person with a disability to engage in a futile gesture if the person has actual notice that a person or organization covered by title III of the Act or this part does not intend to comply with its provisions.

(b) Injunctive relief. In the case of violations of § 36.304, § 36.308, § 36.310(b), § 36.401, § 36.402, § 36.403, and § 36.405 of this part, injunctive relief shall include an order to alter facilities to make such facilities readily accessible to and usable by individuals with disabilities to the extent required by the Act or this part. Where appropriate, injunctive relief shall also include requiring the provision of an auxiliary aid or service, modification of a policy, or provision of alternative methods, to the extent required by the Act or this part.

§ 36.502 Investigations and compliance reviews.

(a) The Attorney General shall investigate alleged violations of the Act or this part.

(b) Any individual who believes that he or she or a specific class of persons has been subjected to discrimination prohibited by the Act or this part may request the Department to institute an investigation.

(c) Where the Attorney General has reason to believe that there may be a violation of this part, he or she may initiate a compliance review.

§ 36.503 Suit by the Attorney General.

Following a compliance review or investigation under § 36.502, or at any other time in his or her discretion, the Attorney General may commence a civil action in any appropriate United States district court if the Attorney General has reasonable cause to believe that—

(a) Any person or group of persons is engaged in a pattern or practice of discrimination in violation of the Act or this part; or

(b) Any person or group of persons has been discriminated against in violation of the Act or this part and the discrimination raises an issue of general public importance.

§ 36.504 Relief.

(a) Authority of court. In a civil action under § 36.503, the court—

(1) May grant any equitable relief that such court considers to be appropriate, including, to the extent required by the Act or this part—

(i) Granting temporary, preliminary, or permanent relief;

(ii) Providing an auxiliary aid or service, modification of policy, practice, or procedure, or alternative method; and

(iii) Making facilities readily accessible to and usable by individuals with disabilities;

(2) May award other relief as the court considers to be appropriate, including monetary damages to persons aggrieved when requested by the Attorney General; and

(3) May, to vindicate the public interest, assess a civil penalty against the entity in an amount

(i) Not exceeding $50,000 for a first violation occurring before September 29, 1999, and not exceeding $55,000 for a first violation occurring on or after September 29, 1999; and

(ii) Not exceeding $100,000 for any subsequent violation occurring before September 29, 1999, and not exceeding $110,000 for any subsequent violation occurring on or after September 29, 1999.

(b) Single violation. For purposes of paragraph (a)(3) of this section, in determining whether a first or subsequent violation has occurred, a determination in a single action, by judgment or settlement, that the covered entity has engaged in more than one discriminatory act shall be counted as a single violation.

(c) Punitive damages. For purposes of paragraph (a)(2) of this section, the terms "monetary damages" and "such other relief" do not include punitive damages.

(d) Judicial consideration. In a civil action under § 36.503, the court, when considering what amount of civil penalty, if any, is appropriate, shall give consideration to any good faith effort or attempt to comply with this part by the entity. In evaluating good faith, the court shall consider, among other factors it deems relevant, whether the entity could have reasonably anticipated the need for an appropriate type of auxiliary aid needed to accommodate the unique needs of a particular individual with a disability.

§ 36.505 Attorneys fees.

In any action or administrative proceeding commenced pursuant to the Act or this part, the court or agency, in its discretion, may allow the prevailing party, other than the United States, a reasonable attorney's fee, including litigation expenses, and costs, and the United States shall be liable for the foregoing the same as a private individual.

ADA TITLE III DOJ INTERPRETIVE GUIDANCE

CODE OF FEDERAL REGULATIONS TITLE 28—JUDICIAL ADMINISTRATION CHAPTER I—DEPARTMENT OF JUSTICE PART 36—NONDISCRIMINATION ON THE BASIS OF DISABILITY BY PUBLIC ACCOMMODATIONS AND IN COMMERCIAL FACILITIES

Current through June 2, 1998; 63 FR 29958

Appendix B to Part 36—Preamble to Regulation on Nondiscrimination on the Basis of Disability by Public Accommodations and in Commercial Facilities (Published July 26, 1991)

Note: For the convenience of the reader, this appendix contains the text of the preamble to the final regulation on nondiscrimination on the basis of disability by public accommodations and in commercial facilities beginning at the heading "Section-by-Section Analysis and Response to Comments" and ending before "List of Subjects in 28 CFR part 36" (56 FR July 26, 1991).

Section-By-Section Analysis and Response to Comments

Subpart A—General

Section 36.101 Purpose

Section 36.101 states the purpose of the rule, which is to effectuate title III of the Americans with Disabilities Act of 1990. This title prohibits discrimination on the basis of disability by public accommodations, requires places of public accommodation and commercial facilities to be designed, constructed, and altered in compliance with the accessibility standards established by this part, and requires that examinations or courses related to licensing or certification for professional or trade purposes be accessible to persons with disabilities.

Section 36.102 Application

Section 36.102 specifies the range of entities and facilities that have obligations under the final rule. The rule applies to any public accommodation or commercial facility as those terms are defined in § 36.104. It also applies, in accordance with section 309 of the ADA, to private entities that offer examinations or courses related to applications, licensing, certification, or credentialing for secondary or postsecondary education, professional, or trade purposes. Except as provided in § 36.206, "Retaliation or coercion," this part does not apply to individuals other than public accommodations or to public entities. Coverage of private individuals and public entities is discussed in the preamble to § 36.206.

As defined in § 36.104, a public accommodation is a private entity that owns, leases or leases to, or operates a place of public accommodation. Section 36.102(b)(2) emphasizes that the general and specific public accommodations requirements of subparts B and C obligate a public accommodation only with respect to the operations of a place of public accommodation. This distinction is drawn in recognition of the fact that a private entity that meets the regulatory definition of public accommodation could also own, lease or lease to, or operate facilities that are not places of public accommodation. The rule would exceed the reach of the ADA if it were to apply the public accommodations requirements of subparts B and C to the operations of a private entity that do not involve a place of public accommodation. Similarly, § 36.102(b)(3) provides that the new construction and alterations requirements of subpart D obligate a public accommodation only with respect to facilities used as, or designed or constructed for use as, places of public accommodation or commercial facilities.

On the other hand, as mandated by the ADA and reflected in § 36.102(c), the new construction and alterations requirements of subpart D apply to a commercial facility whether or not the facility is a place of public accommodation, or is owned, leased, leased to, or operated by a public accommodation.

Section 36.102(e) states that the rule does not apply to any private club, religious entity, or public entity. Each of these terms is defined in § 36.104. The exclusion of private clubs and religious entities is derived from section 307 of the ADA; and the exclusion of public entities is based on the statutory definition of public accommodation in section 301(7) of the ADA, which excludes entities other than private entities from coverage under title III of the ADA.

Section 36.103 Relationship to Other Laws

Section 36.103 is derived from sections 501 (a) and (b) of the ADA. Paragraph (a) provides that, except as otherwise specifically provided by this part, the ADA is not intended to apply lesser standards than are required under title V of the Rehabilitation Act of 1973, as amended (29 U.S.C. 790-794), or the regulations implementing that title. The standards of title V of the Rehabilitation Act apply for purposes of the ADA to the extent that the ADA has not explicitly adopted a different standard from title V. Where the ADA explicitly provides a different standard from section 504, the ADA standard applies to the ADA, but not to section 504. For example, section 504 requires that all federally assisted programs and activities be readily accessible to and usable by individuals with handicaps, even if major structural alterations are necessary to make a program accessible. Title III of the ADA, in contrast, only requires alterations to existing facilities if the modifications are "readily achievable," that is, able to be accomplished easily and without much difficulty or expense. A public accommodation that is covered under both section 504 and the ADA is still required to meet the "program accessibility" standard in order to comply with section 504, but would not be in violation of the ADA unless it failed to make "readily achievable" modifications. On the other hand, an entity covered by the ADA is required to make "readily achievable" modifications, even if the program can be made accessible without any architectural modifications. Thus, an entity covered by both section 504 and title III of the ADA must meet both the "program accessibility" requirement and the "readily achievable" requirement.

Paragraph (b) makes explicit that the rule does not affect the obligation of recipients of Federal financial assistance to comply with the requirements imposed under section 504 of the Rehabilitation Act of 1973.

Paragraph (c) makes clear that Congress did not intend to displace any of the rights or remedies provided by other Federal laws or other State or local laws (including State common law) that provide greater or equal protection to individuals with disabilities. A plaintiff may choose to pursue claims under a State law that does not confer greater substantive rights, or even confers fewer substantive rights, if the alleged violation is protected under the alternative law and the remedies are greater. For example, assume that a person with a physical disability seeks damages under a State law that allows compensatory and punitive damages for discrimination on the basis of physical disability, but does not allow them on the basis of mental disability. In that situation, the State law would provide narrower coverage, by excluding mental disabilities, but broader remedies, and an individual covered by both laws could choose to bring an action under both laws. Moreover, State tort claims confer greater remedies and are not preempted by the ADA. A plaintiff may join a State tort claim to a case brought under the ADA. In such a case, the plaintiff must, of course, prove all the elements of the State tort claim in order to prevail under that cause of action.

A commenter had concerns about privacy requirements for banking transactions using telephone relay services. Title IV of the Act provides adequate protections for ensuring the confidentiality of communications using the relay services. This issue is more appropriately addressed by the Federal Communications Commission in its regulation implementing title IV of the Act.

Section 36.104 Definitions

"Act." The word "Act" is used in the regulation to refer to the Americans with Disabilities Act of 1990, Pub.L. 101-336, which is also referred to as the "ADA."

"Commerce." The definition of "commerce" is identical to the statutory definition provided in section 301(l) of the ADA. It means travel, trade, traffic, commerce, transportation, or communication among the several States, between any foreign country or any territory or possession and any State, or between points in the same State but through another State or foreign country. Commerce is defined in the same manner as in title II of the Civil Rights Act of 1964, which prohibits racial discrimination in public accommodations.

The term "commerce" is used in the definition of "place of public accommodation." According to that definition, one of the criteria that an entity must meet before it can be considered a place of public accommodation is that its operations affect commerce. The term "commerce" is similarly used in the definition of "commercial facility."

The use of the phrase "operations affect commerce" applies the full scope of coverage of the Commerce Clause of the Constitution in enforcing the ADA. The Constitution gives Congress broad authority to regulate interstate commerce, including the activities of local business enterprises (e.g., a physician's office, a neighborhood restaurant, a laundromat, or a bakery) that affect interstate commerce through the purchase or sale of products manufactured in other States, or by providing services to individuals from other States. Because of the integrated nature of the national economy, the ADA and this final rule will have extremely broad application.

"Commercial facilities" are those facilities that are intended for nonresidential use by a private entity and whose operations affect commerce. As explained under § 36.401, "New construction," the new construction and alteration requirements of subpart D of the rule apply to all commercial facilities, whether or not they are places of public accommodation. Those commercial facilities that are not places of public accommodation are not subject to the requirements of subparts B and C (e.g., those requirements concerning auxiliary aids and general nondiscrimination provisions).

Congress recognized that the employees within commercial facilities would generally be protected under title I (employment) of the Act. However, as the House Committee on Education and Labor pointed out, "[t]o the extent that new facilities are built in a manner that make[s] them accessible to all individuals, including potential employees, there will be less of a need for individual employers to engage in reasonable accommodations for particular employees." H.R. Rep. No. 485, 101st Cong., 2d Sess., pt. 2, at 117 (1990) [hereinafter "Education and Labor report"]. While employers of fewer than 15 employees are not covered by title I's employment discrimination provisions, there is no such limitation with respect to new construction covered under title III. Congress chose not to so limit the new construction provisions because of its desire for a uniform requirement of accessibility in new construction, because accessibility can be accomplished easily in the design and construction stage, and because future expansion of a business or sale or lease of the property to a larger employer or to a business that is a place of public accommodation is always a possibility.

The term "commercial facilities" is not intended to be defined by dictionary or common industry definitions. Included in this category are factories, warehouses, office buildings, and other buildings in which employment may occur. The phrase, "whose operations affect commerce," is to be read broadly, to include all types of activities reached under the commerce clause of the Constitution.

Privately operated airports are also included in the category of commercial facilities. They are not, however, places of public accommodation because they are not terminals used for "specified public transportation." (Transportation by aircraft is specifically excluded from the statutory definition of "specified public transportation.") Thus, privately operated airports are subject to the new construction and alteration requirements of this rule (subpart D) but not to subparts B and C. (Airports operated by public entities are covered by title II of the Act.) Places of public accommodation located within airports, such as restaurants, shops, lounges, or conference centers, however, are covered by subparts B and C of this part.

The statute's definition of "commercial facilities" specifically includes only facilities "that are intended for nonresidential use" and specifically exempts those facilities that are covered or expressly exempted from coverage under the Fair Housing Act of 1968, as amended (42 U.S.C. 3601-3631). The interplay between the Fair Housing Act and the ADA with respect to those facilities that are "places of public accommodation" was the subject of many comments and is addressed in the preamble discussion of the definition of "place of public accommodation."

"Current illegal use of drugs." The phrase "current illegal use of drugs" is used in § 36.209. Its meaning is discussed in the preamble for that section.

"Disability." The definition of the term "disability" is comparable to the definition of the term "individual with handicaps" in section 7(8)(B) of the Rehabilitation Act and section 802(h) of the Fair Housing Act. The Education and Labor Committee report makes clear that the analysis of the term "individual with handicaps" by the Department of Health, Education, and Welfare in its regulations implementing section 504 (42 FR 22685 (May 4, 1977)) and the analysis by the Department of Housing and Urban Development in its regulation implementing the Fair Housing Amendments Act of 1988 (54 FR 3232 (Jan. 23, 1989)) should also apply fully to the term "disability" (Education and Labor report at 50).

The use of the term "disability" instead of "handicap" and the term "individual with a disability" instead of "individual with handicaps" represents an effort by the Congress to make use of up-to-date, currently accepted terminology. The terminology applied to individuals with disabilities is a very significant and sensitive issue. As with racial and ethnic terms, the choice of words to describe a person with a disability is overlaid with stereotypes, patronizing attitudes, and other emotional connotations. Many individuals with disabilities, and organizations representing such individuals, object to the use of such terms as "handicapped person" or "the handicapped." In other recent legislation, Congress also recognized this shift in terminology, e.g., by changing the name of the National Council on the Handicapped to the National Council on Disability (Pub.L. 100-630).

In enacting the Americans with Disabilities Act, Congress concluded that it was important for the current legislation to use terminology most in line with the sensibilities of most Americans with disabilities. No change in definition or substance is intended nor should be attributed to this change in phraseology.

The term "disability" means, with respect to an individual—

(A) A physical or mental impairment that substantially limits one or more of the major life activities of such individual;

(B) A record of such an impairment; or

(C) Being regarded as having such an impairment.

If an individual meets any one of these three tests, he or she is considered to be an individual with a disability for purposes of coverage under the Americans with Disabilities Act.

Congress adopted this same basic definition of "disability," first used in the Rehabilitation Act of 1973 and in the Fair Housing Amendments Act of 1988, for a number of reasons. It has worked well since it was adopted in 1974. There is a substantial body of administrative interpretation and judicial precedent on this definition. Finally, it would not be possible to guarantee comprehensiveness by providing a list of specific disabilities, especially because new disorders may be recognized in the future, as they have since the definition was first established in 1974.

Test A—A Physical or Mental Impairment That Substantially Limits One or More of the Major Life Activities of Such Individual

Physical or mental impairment. Under the first test, an individual must have a physical or mental impairment. As explained in paragraph (1)(i) of the definition, "impairment" means any physiological disorder or condition, cosmetic disfigurement, or anatomical loss affecting one or more of the following body systems: Neurological; musculoskeletal; special sense organs (including speech organs that are not respiratory, such as vocal cords, soft palate, and tongue); respiratory, including speech organs; cardiovascular; reproductive; digestive; genitourinary; hemic and lymphatic; skin; and endocrine. It also means any mental or psychological disorder, such as mental retardation, organic brain syndrome, emotional or mental illness, and specific learning disabilities. This list closely tracks the one used in the regulations for section 504 of the Rehabilitation Act of 1973 (see, e.g., 45 CFR 84.3(j)(2)(i)).

Many commenters asked that "traumatic brain injury" be added to the list in paragraph (1)(i). Traumatic brain injury is already included because it is a physiological condition affecting one of the listed body systems, i.e., "neurological." Therefore, it was unnecessary for the Department to add the term to the regulation.

It is not possible to include a list of all the specific conditions, contagious and noncontagious diseases, or infections that would constitute physical or mental impairments because of the difficulty of ensuring the comprehensiveness of such a list, particularly in light of the fact that other conditions or disorders may be identified in the future. However, the list of examples in paragraph (1)(iii) of the definition includes: Orthopedic, visual, speech and hearing impairments; cerebral palsy; epilepsy, muscular dystrophy, multiple sclerosis, cancer, heart disease, diabetes, mental retardation, emotional illness, specific learning disabilities, HIV disease (symptomatic or asymptomatic), tuberculosis, drug addiction, and alcoholism.

The examples of "physical or mental impairments" in paragraph (1)(iii) are the same as those contained in many section 504 regulations, except for the addition of the phrase "contagious and noncontagious" to describe the types of diseases and conditions included, and the addition of "HIV disease (symptomatic or asymptomatic)" and "tuberculosis" to the list of examples. These additions are based on the ADA committee reports, caselaw, and official legal opinions interpreting section 504. In *School Board of Nassau County v. Arline*, 480 U.S. 273 (1987), a case involving an individual with tuberculosis, the Supreme Court held that people with contagious diseases are entitled to the protections afforded by section 504. Following the *Arline* decision, this Department's Office of Legal Counsel issued a legal opinion that concluded that symptomatic HIV disease is an impairment that substantially limits a major life activity; therefore it has been included in the definition of disability under this part. The opinion also concluded that asymptomatic HIV disease is an impairment that substantially limits a major life activity, either because of its actual effect on the individual with HIV disease or because the reactions of other people to individuals with HIV disease cause such individuals to be treated as though they are disabled. See Memorandum from Douglas W. Kmiec, Acting Assistant Attorney General, Office of Legal Counsel, Department of Justice, to Arthur B. Culvahouse, Jr., Counsel to the President (Sept. 27, 1988), reprinted in Hearings on S. 933, the Americans with Disabilities Act, Before the Subcomm. on the Handicapped of the Senate Comm. on Labor and Human Resources, 101st Cong., 1st Sess. 346 (1989). The phrase "symptomatic or asymptomatic" was inserted in the final rule after "HIV disease" in response to commenters who suggested that the clarification was necessary to give full meaning to the Department's opinion.

Paragraph (1)(iv) of the definition states that the phrase "physical or mental impairment" does not include homosexuality or bisexuality. These conditions were never considered impairments under other Federal disability laws. Section 511(a) of the statute makes clear that they are likewise not to be considered impairments under the Americans with Disabilities

Act.

Physical or mental impairment does not include simple physical characteristics, such as blue eyes or black hair. Nor does it include environmental, cultural, economic, or other disadvantages, such as having a prison record, or being poor. Nor is age a disability. Similarly, the definition does not include common personality traits such as poor judgment or a quick temper where these are not symptoms of a mental or psychological disorder. However, a person who has these characteristics and also has a physical or mental impairment may be considered as having a disability for purposes of the Americans with Disabilities Act based on the impairment.

Substantial limitation of a major life activity. Under Test A, the impairment must be one that "substantially limits a major life activity." Major life activities include such things as caring for one's self, performing manual tasks, walking, seeing, hearing, speaking, breathing, learning, and working. For example, a person who is paraplegic is substantially limited in the major life activity of walking, a person who is blind is substantially limited in the major life activity of seeing, and a person who is mentally retarded is substantially limited in the major life activity of learning. A person with traumatic brain injury is substantially limited in the major life activities of caring for one's self, learning, and working because of memory deficit, confusion, contextual difficulties, and inability to reason appropriately.

A person is considered an individual with a disability for purposes of Test A, the first prong of the definition, when the individual's important life activities are restricted as to the conditions, manner, or duration under which they can be performed in comparison to most people. A person with a minor, trivial impairment, such as a simple infected finger, is not impaired in a major life activity. A person who can walk for 10 miles continuously is not substantially limited in walking merely because, on the eleventh mile, he or she begins to experience pain, because most people would not be able to walk eleven miles without experiencing some discomfort.

The Department received many comments on the proposed rule's inclusion of the word "temporary" in the definition of "disability." The preamble indicated that impairments are not necessarily excluded from the definition of "disability" simply because they are temporary, but that the duration, or expected duration, of an impairment is one factor that may properly be considered in determining whether the impairment substantially limits a major life activity. The preamble recognized, however, that temporary impairments, such as a broken leg, are not commonly regarded as disabilities, and only in rare circumstances would the degree of the limitation and its expected duration be substantial: Nevertheless, many commenters objected to inclusion of the word "temporary" both because it is not in the statute and because it is not contained in the definition of "disability" set forth in the title I regulations of the Equal Employment Opportunity Commission (EEOC). The word "temporary" has been deleted from the final rule to conform with the statutory language. The question of whether a temporary impairment is a disability must be resolved on a case-by-case basis, taking into consideration both the duration (or expected duration) of the impairment and the extent to which it actually limits a major life activity of the affected individual.

The question of whether a person has a disability should be assessed without regard to the availability of mitigating measures, such as reasonable modifications or auxiliary aids and services. For example, a person with hearing loss is substantially limited in the major life activity of hearing, even though the loss may be improved through the use of a hearing aid. Likewise, persons with impairments, such as epilepsy or diabetes, that substantially limit a major life activity, are covered under the first prong of the definition of disability, even if the effects of the impairment are controlled by medication.

Many commenters asked that environmental illness (also known as multiple chemical sensitivity) as well as allergy to cigarette smoke be recognized as disabilities. The Department, however, declines to state categorically that these types of allergies or sensitivities are disabilities, because the determination as to whether an impairment is a disability depends on whether, given the particular circumstances at issue, the impairment substantially limits one or more major life activities (or has a history of, or is regarded as having such an effect).

Sometimes respiratory or neurological functioning is so severely affected that an individual will satisfy the requirements to be considered disabled under the regulation. Such an individual would be entitled to all of the protections afforded by the Act and this part. In other cases, individuals may be sensitive to environmental elements or to smoke but their sensitivity will not rise to the level needed to constitute a disability. For example, their major life activity of breathing may be somewhat, but not substantially, impaired. In such circumstances, the individuals are not disabled and are not entitled to the protections of the statute despite their sensitivity to environmental agents.

In sum, the determination as to whether allergies to

cigarette smoke, or allergies or sensitivities characterized by the commenters as environmental illness are disabilities covered by the regulation must be made using the same case-by-case analysis that is applied to all other physical or mental impairments. Moreover, the addition of specific regulatory provisions relating to environmental illness in the final rule would be inappropriate at this time pending future consideration of the issue by the Architectural and Transportation Barriers Compliance Board, the Environmental Protection Agency, and the Occupational Safety and Health Administration of the Department of Labor.

Test B—A Record of Such an Impairment

This test is intended to cover those who have a record of an impairment. As explained in paragraph (3) of the rule's definition of disability, this includes a person who has a history of an impairment that substantially limited a major life activity, such as someone who has recovered from an impairment. It also includes persons who have been misclassified as having an impairment.

This provision is included in the definition in part to protect individuals who have recovered from a physical or mental impairment that previously substantially limited them in a major life activity. Discrimination on the basis of such a past impairment is prohibited. Frequently occurring examples of the first group (those who have a history of an impairment) are persons with histories of mental or emotional illness, heart disease, or cancer; examples of the second group (those who have been misclassified as having an impairment) are persons who have been misclassified as having mental retardation or mental illness.

Test C—Being Regarded as Having Such an Impairment

This test, as contained in paragraph (4) of the definition, is intended to cover persons who are treated by a private entity or public accommodation as having a physical or mental impairment that substantially limits a major life activity. It applies when a person is treated as if he or she has an impairment that substantially limits a major life activity, regardless of whether that person has an impairment.

The Americans with Disabilities Act uses the same "regarded as" test set forth in the regulations implementing section 504 of the Rehabilitation Act. See, e.g., 28 CFR 42.540(k)(2)(iv), which provides:

(iv) "Is regarded as having an impairment" means (A) Has a physical or mental impairment that does not substantially limit major life activities but that is treated by a recipient as constituting such a limitation; (B) Has a physical or mental impairment that substantially limits major life activities only as a result of the attitudes of others toward such impairment; or (C) Has none of the impairments defined in paragraph (k)(2)(i) of this section but is treated by a recipient as having such an impairment.

The perception of the private entity or public accommodation is a key element of this test. A person who perceives himself or herself to have an impairment, but does not have an impairment, and is not treated as if he or she has an impairment, is not protected under this test. A person would be covered under this test if a restaurant refused to serve that person because of a fear of "negative reactions" of others to that person. A person would also be covered if a public accommodation refused to serve a patron because it perceived that the patron had an impairment that limited his or her enjoyment of the goods or services being offered.

For example, persons with severe burns often encounter discrimination in community activities, resulting in substantial limitation of major life activities. These persons would be covered under this test based on the attitudes of others towards the impairment, even if they did not view themselves as "impaired."

The rationale for this third test, as used in the Rehabilitation Act of 1973, was articulated by the Supreme Court in *Arline*, 480 U.S. 273 (1987). The Court noted that, although an individual may have an impairment that does not in fact substantially limit a major life activity, the reaction of others may prove just as disabling. "Such an impairment might not diminish a person's physical or mental capabilities, but could nevertheless substantially limit that person's ability to work as a result of the negative reactions of others to the impairment." *Id.* at 283. The Court concluded that, by including this test in the Rehabilitation Act's definition, "Congress acknowledged that society's accumulated myths and fears about disability and disease are as handicapping as are the physical limitations that flow from actual impairment." *Id.* at 284.

Thus, a person who is not allowed into a public accommodation because of the myths, fears, and stereotypes associated with disabilities would be covered under this third test whether or not the person's physical or mental condition would be considered a disability under the first or second test in the definition.

If a person is refused admittance on the basis of an

actual or perceived physical or mental condition, and the public accommodation can articulate no legitimate reason for the refusal (such as failure to meet eligibility criteria), a perceived concern about admitting persons with disabilities could be inferred and the individual would qualify for coverage under the "regarded as" test. A person who is covered because of being regarded as having an impairment is not required to show that the public accommodation's perception is inaccurate (e.g., that he will be accepted by others, or that insurance rates will not increase) in order to be admitted to the public accommodation.

Paragraph (5) of the definition lists certain conditions that are not included within the definition of "disability." The excluded conditions are: transvestism, transsexualism, pedophilia, exhibitionism, voyeurism, gender identity disorders not resulting from physical impairments, other sexual behavior disorders, compulsive gambling, kleptomania, pyromania, and psychoactive substance use disorders resulting from current illegal use of drugs. Unlike homosexuality and bisexuality, which are not considered impairments under either the Americans with Disabilities Act (see the definition of "disability," paragraph (1)(iv)) or section 504, the conditions listed in paragraph (5), except for transvestism, are not necessarily excluded as impairments under section 504. (Transvestism was excluded from the definition of disability for section 504 by the Fair Housing Amendments Act of 1988, Pub.L. 100-430, § 6(b).) The phrase "current illegal use of drugs" used in this definition is explained in the preamble to § 36.209.

"Drug." The definition of the term "drug" is taken from section 510(d)(2) of the ADA.

"Facility." "Facility" means all or any portion of buildings, structures, sites, complexes, equipment, rolling stock or other conveyances, roads, walks, passageways, parking lots, or other real or personal property, including the site where the building, property, structure, or equipment is located. Committee reports made clear that the definition of facility was drawn from the definition of facility in current Federal regulations (see, e.g., Education and Labor report at 114). It includes both indoor and outdoor areas where human-constructed improvements, structures, equipment, or property have been added to the natural environment.

The term "rolling stock or other conveyances" was not included in the definition of facility in the proposed rule. However, commenters raised questions about the applicability of this part to places of public accommodation operated in mobile facilities (such as cruise ships, floating restaurants, or mobile health units). Those places of public accommodation are covered under this part, and would be included in the definition of "facility." Thus the requirements of subparts B and C would apply to those places of public accommodation. For example, a covered entity could not discriminate on the basis of disability in the full and equal enjoyment of the facilities (§ 36.201). Similarly, a cruise line could not apply eligibility criteria to potential passengers in a manner that would screen out individuals with disabilities, unless the criteria are "necessary," as provided in § 36.301.

However, standards for new construction and alterations of such facilities are not yet included in the Americans with Disabilities Act Accessibility Guidelines for Buildings and Facilities (ADAAG) adopted by § 36.406 and incorporated in Appendix A. The Department therefore will not interpret the new construction and alterations provisions of subpart D to apply to the types of facilities discussed here, pending further development of specific requirements.

Requirements pertaining to accessible transportation services provided by public accommodations are included in § 36.310 of this part; standards pertaining to accessible vehicles will be issued by the Secretary of Transportation pursuant to section 306 of the Act, and will be codified at 49 CFR part 37.

A public accommodation has obligations under this rule with respect to a cruise ship to the extent that its operations are subject to the laws of the United States.

The definition of "facility" only includes the site over which the private entity may exercise control or on which a place of public accommodation or a commercial facility is located. It does not include, for example, adjacent roads or walks controlled by a public entity that is not subject to this part. Public entities are subject to the requirements of title II of the Act. The Department's regulation implementing title II, which will be codified at 28 CFR part 35, addresses the obligations of public entities to ensure accessibility by providing curb ramps at pedestrian walkways.

"Illegal use of drugs." The definition of "illegal use of drugs" is taken from section 510(d)(1) of the Act and clarifies that the term includes the illegal use of one or more drugs.

"Individual with a disability" means a person who has a disability but does not include an individual who is currently illegally using drugs, when the public accommodation acts on the basis of such use. The phrase "current illegal use of drugs" is explained in the preamble to § 36.209.

"Place of public accommodation." The term "place of public accommodation" is an adaptation of the statutory definition of "public accommodation" in section 301(7) of the ADA and appears as an element of the regulatory definition of public accommodation. The final rule defines "place of public accommodation" as a facility, operated by a private entity, whose operations affect commerce and fall within at least one of 12 specified categories. The term "public accommodation," on the other hand, is reserved by the final rule for the private entity that owns, leases (or leases to), or operates a place of public accommodation. It is the public accommodation, and not the place of public accommodation, that is subject to the regulation's nondiscrimination requirements. Placing the obligation not to discriminate on the public accommodation, as defined in the rule, is consistent with section 302(a) of the ADA, which places the obligation not to discriminate on any person who owns, leases (or leases to), or operates a place of public accommodation.

Facilities operated by government agencies or other public entities as defined in this section do not qualify as places of public accommodation. The actions of public entities are governed by title II of the ADA and will be subject to regulations issued by the Department of Justice under that title. The receipt of government assistance by a private entity does not by itself preclude a facility from being considered as a place of public accommodation.

The definition of place of public accommodation incorporates the 12 categories of facilities represented in the statutory definition of public accommodation in section 301(7) of the ADA:

1. Places of lodging.
2. Establishments serving food or drink.
3. Places of exhibition or entertainment.
4. Places of public gathering.
5. Sales or rental establishments.
6. Service establishments.
7. Stations used for specified public transportation.
8. Places of public display or collection.
9. Places of recreation.
10. Places of education.
11. Social service center establishments.
12. Places of exercise or recreation.

In order to be a place of public accommodation, a facility must be operated by a private entity, its operations must affect commerce, and it must fall within one of these 12 categories. While the list of categories is exhaustive, the representative examples of facilities within each category are not. Within each category only a few examples are given. The category of social service center establishments would include not only the types of establishments listed, day care centers, senior citizen centers, homeless shelters, food banks, adoption agencies, but also establishments such as substance abuse treatment centers, rape crisis centers, and halfway houses. As another example, the category of sales or rental establishments would include an innumerable array of facilities that would sweep far beyond the few examples given in the regulation. For example, other retail or wholesale establishments selling or renting items, such as bookstores, videotape rental stores, car rental establishment, pet stores, and jewelry stores would also be covered under this category, even though they are not specifically listed.

Several commenters requested clarification as to the coverage of wholesale establishments under the category of "sales or rental establishments." The Department intends for wholesale establishments to be covered under this category as places of public accommodation except in cases where they sell exclusively to other businesses and not to individuals. For example, a company that grows food produce and supplies its crops exclusively to food processing corporations on a wholesale basis does not become a public accommodation because of these transactions. If this company operates a road side stand where its crops are sold to the public, the road side stand would be a sales establishment covered by the ADA. Conversely, a sales establishment that markets its goods as "wholesale to the public" and sells to individuals would not be exempt from ADA coverage despite its use of the word "wholesale" as a marketing technique.

Of course, a company that operates a place of public accommodation is subject to this part only in the operation of that place of public accommodation. In the example given above, the wholesale produce company that operates a road side stand would be a public accommodation only for the purposes of the operation of that stand. The company would be prohibited from discriminating on the basis of disability in the operation of the road side stand, and it would be required to remove barriers to physical access to the extent that it is readily achievable to do so (see § 36.304); however, in the event that it is not readily achievable to remove barriers, for example, by replacing a gravel surface or regrading the area around the stand to permit access by persons with mobility impairments, the company could meet its obligations through alternative methods of making its goods available, such as delivering produce to a customer in his or her car (see § 36.305). The concepts of readily achievable barrier removal and alternatives to barrier removal are discussed further in the preamble discussion of §§ 36.304 and 36.305.

Even if a facility does not fall within one of the 12 categories, and therefore does not qualify as a place of public accommodation, it still may be a commercial facility as defined in § 36.104 and be subject to the new construction and alterations requirements of subpart D.

A number of commenters questioned the treatment of residential hotels and other residential facilities in the Department's proposed rule. These commenters were essentially seeking resolution of the relationship between the Fair Housing Act and the ADA concerning facilities that are both residential in nature and engage in activities that would cause them to be classified as "places of public accommodation" under the ADA. The ADA's express exemption relating to the Fair Housing Act applies only to "commercial facilities" and not to "places of public accommodation."

A facility whose operations affect interstate commerce is a place of public accommodation for purposes of the ADA to the extent that its operations include those types of activities engaged in or services provided by the facilities contained on the list of 12 categories in section 301(7) of the ADA. Thus, a facility that provides social services would be considered a "social service center establishment." Similarly, the category "places of lodging" would exclude solely residential facilities because the nature of a place of lodging contemplates the use of the facility for short-term stays.

Many facilities, however, are mixed use facilities. For example, in a large hotel that has a separate residential apartment wing, the residential wing would not be covered by the ADA because of the nature of the occupancy of that part of the facility. This residential wing would, however, be covered by the Fair Housing Act. The separate nonresidential accommodations in the rest of the hotel would be a place of lodging, and thus a public accommodation subject to the requirements of this final rule. If a hotel allows both residential and short-term stays, but does not allocate space for these different uses in separate, discrete units, both the ADA and the Fair Housing Act may apply to the facility. Such determinations will need to be made on a case-by-case basis. Any place of lodging of the type described in paragraph (1) of the definition of place of public accommodation and that is an establishment located within a building that contains not more than five rooms for rent or hire and is actually occupied by the proprietor of the establishment as his or her residence is not covered by the ADA. (This exclusion from coverage does not apply to other categories of public accommodations, for example, professional offices or homeless shelters, that are located in a building that is also occupied as a private residence.)

A number of commenters noted that the term "residential hotel" may also apply to a type of hotel commonly known as a "single room occupancy hotel." Although such hotels or portions of such hotels may fall under the Fair Housing Act when operated or used as long-term residences, they are also considered "places of lodging" under the ADA when guests of such hotels are free to use them on a short-term basis. In addition, "single room occupancy hotels" may provide social services to their guests, often through the operation of Federal or State grant programs. In such a situation, the facility would be considered a "social service center establishment" and thus covered by the ADA as a place of public accommodation, regardless of the length of stay of the occupants.

A similar analysis would also be applied to other residential facilities that provide social services, including homeless shelters, shelters for people seeking refuge from domestic violence, nursing homes, residential care facilities, and other facilities where persons may reside for varying lengths of time. Such facilities should be analyzed under the Fair Housing Act to determine the application of that statute. The ADA, however, requires a separate and independent analysis. For example, if the facility, or a portion of the facility, is intended for or permits short-term stays, or if it can appropriately be categorized as a service establishment or as a social service establishment, then the facility or that portion of the facility used for the covered purpose is a place of public accommodation under the ADA. For example, a homeless shelter that is intended and used only for long-term residential stays and that does not provide social services to its residents would not be covered as a place of public accommodation. However, if this facility permitted short-term stays or provided social services to its residents, it would be covered under the ADA either as a "place of lodging" or as a "social service center establishment," or as both.

A private home, by itself, does not fall within any of the 12 categories. However, it can be covered as a place of public accommodation to the extent that it is used as a facility that would fall within one of the 12 categories. For example, if a professional office of a dentist, doctor, or psychologist is located in a private home, the portion of the home dedicated to office use (including areas used both for the residence and the office, e.g., the entrance to the home that is also used as the entrance to the professional office) would be considered a place of public accommodation. Places of public accommodation located in residential facilities are specifically addressed in § 36.207.

If a tour of a commercial facility that is not otherwise a place of public accommodation, such as, for example, a factory or a movie studio production set, is open to the general public, the route followed by the tour is a place of public accommodation and the tour must be operated in accordance with the rule's requirements for public accommodations. The place of public accommodation defined by the tour does not include those portions of the commercial facility that are merely viewed from the tour route. Hence, the barrier removal requirements of § 36.304 only apply to the physical route followed by the tour participants and not to work stations or other areas that are merely adjacent to, or within view of, the tour route. If the tour is not open to the general public, but rather is conducted, for example, for selected business colleagues, partners, customers, or consultants, the tour route is not a place of public accommodation and the tour is not subject to the requirements for public accommodations.

Public accommodations that receive Federal financial assistance are subject to the requirements of section 504 of the Rehabilitation Act as well as the requirements of the ADA.

Private schools, including elementary and secondary schools, are covered by the rule as places of public accommodation. The rule itself, however, does not require a private school to provide a free appropriate education or develop an individualized education program in accordance with regulations of the Department of Education implementing section 504 of the Rehabilitation Act of 1973, as amended (34 CFR part 104), and regulations implementing the Individuals with Disabilities Education Act (34 CFR part 300). The receipt of Federal assistance by a private school, however, would trigger application of the Department of Education's regulations to the extent mandated by the particular type of assistance received.

"Private club." The term "private club" is defined in accordance with section 307 of the ADA as a private club or establishment exempted from coverage under title II of the Civil Rights Act of 1964. Title II of the 1964 Act exempts any "private club or other establishment not in fact open to the public, except to the extent that the facilities of such establishment are made available to the customers or patrons of [a place of public accommodation as defined in title II]." The rule, therefore, as reflected in § 36.102(e) of the application section, limits the coverage of private clubs accordingly. The obligations of a private club that rents space to any other private entity for the operation of a place of public accommodation are discussed further in connection with § 36.201.

In determining whether a private entity qualifies as a private club under title II, courts have considered such factors as the degree of member control of club operations, the selectivity of the membership selection process, whether substantial membership fees are charged, whether the entity is operated on a nonprofit basis, the extent to which the facilities are open to the public, the degree of public funding, and whether the club was created specifically to avoid compliance with the Civil Rights Act. See e.g., *Tillman v. Wheaton-Haven Recreation Ass'n*, 410 U.S. 431 (1973); *Daniel v. Paul*, 395 U.S. 298 (1969); *Olzman v. Lake Hills Swim Club, Inc.*, 495 F.2d 1333 (2d Cir. 1974); *Anderson v. Pass Christian Isles Golf Club, Inc.*, 488 F.2d 855 (5th Cir. 1974); *Smith v. YMCA*, 462 F.2d 634 (5th Cir. 1972); *Stout v. YMCA*, 404 F.2d 687 (5th Cir. 1968); *United States v. Richberg*, 398 F.2d 523 (5th Cir. 1968); *Nesmith v. YMCA*, 397 F.2d 96 (4th Cir. 1968); *United States v. Lansdowne Swim Club*, 713 F. Supp. 785 (E.D. Pa. 1989); *Durham v. Red Lake Fishing and Hunting Club, Inc.*, 666 F. Supp. 954 (W.D. Tex. 1987); *New York v. Ocean Club, Inc.*, 602 F. Supp. 489 (E.D.N.Y. 1984); *Brown v. Loudoun Golf and Country Club, Inc.*, 573 F. Supp. 399 (E.D. Va. 1983); *United States v. Trustees of Fraternal Order of Eagles*, 472 F. Supp. 1174 (E.D. Wis. 1979); *Cornelius v. Benevolent Protective Order of Elks*, 382 F. Supp. 1182 (D. Conn. 1974).

"Private entity." The term "private entity" is defined as any individual or entity other than a public entity. It is used as part of the definition of "public accommodation" in this section.

The definition adds "individual" to the statutory definition of private entity (see section 301(6) of the ADA). This addition clarifies that an individual may be a private entity and, therefore, may be considered a public accommodation if he or she owns, leases (or leases to), or operates a place of public accommodation. The explicit inclusion of individuals under the definition of private entity is consistent with section 302(a) of the ADA, which broadly prohibits discrimination on the basis of disability by any person who owns, leases (or leases to), or operates a place of public accommodation.

"Public accommodation." The term "public accommodation" means a private entity that owns, leases (or leases to), or operates a place of public accommodation. The regulatory term, "public accommodation," corresponds to the statutory term, "person," in section 302(a) of the ADA. The ADA prohibits discrimination "by any person who owns, leases (or leases to), or operates a place of public accommodation." The text of the regulation consequently places the ADA's nondiscrimination obligations on "public accommodations" rather than on "persons" or on "places of public accommodation."

As stated in § 36.102(b)(2), the requirements of subparts B and C obligate a public accommodation only with respect to the operations of a place of public accommodation. A public accommodation must also meet the requirements of subpart D with respect to facilities used as, or designed or constructed for use as, places of public accommodation or commercial facilities.

"Public entity." The term "public entity" is defined in accordance with section 201(1) of the ADA as any State or local government; any department, agency, special purpose district, or other instrumentality of a State or States or local government; and the National Railroad Passenger Corporation, and any commuter authority (as defined in section 103(8) of the Rail Passenger Service Act). It is used in the definition of "private entity" in § 36.104. Public entities are excluded from the definition of private entity and therefore cannot qualify as public accommodations under this regulation. However, the actions of public entities are covered by title II of the ADA and by the Department's title II regulations codified at 28 CFR part 35.

"Qualified interpreter." The Department received substantial comment regarding the lack of a definition of "qualified interpreter." The proposed rule defined auxiliary aids and services to include the statutory term, "qualified interpreters" (§ 36.303(b)), but did not define that term. Section 36.303 requires the use of a qualified interpreter where necessary to achieve effective communication, unless an undue burden or fundamental alteration would result. Commenters stated that a lack of guidance on what the term means would create confusion among those trying to secure interpreting services and often result in less than effective communication.

Many commenters were concerned that, without clear guidance on the issue of "qualified" interpreter, the rule would be interpreted to mean "available, rather than qualified" interpreters. Some claimed that few public accommodations would understand the difference between a qualified interpreter and a person who simply knows a few signs or how to fingerspell.

In order to clarify what is meant by "qualified interpreter" the Department has added a definition of the term to the final rule. A qualified interpreter means an interpreter who is able to interpret effectively, accurately, and impartially both receptively and expressively, using any necessary specialized vocabulary. This definition focuses on the actual ability of the interpreter in a particular interpreting context to facilitate effective communication between the public accommodation and the individual with disabilities.

Public comment also revealed that public accommodations have at times asked persons who are deaf to provide family members or friends to interpret. In certain circumstances, notwithstanding that the family member or friend is able to interpret or is a certified interpreter, the family member or friend may not be qualified to render the necessary interpretation because of factors such as emotional or personal involvement or considerations of confidentiality that may adversely affect the ability to interpret "effectively, accurately, and impartially."

"Readily achievable." The definition of "readily achievable" follows the statutory definition of that term in section 301(9) of the ADA. Readily achievable means easily accomplishable and able to be carried out without much difficulty or expense. The term is used as a limitation on the obligation to remove barriers under §§ 36.304(a), 36.305(a), 36.308(a), and 36.310(b). Further discussion of the meaning and application of the term "readily achievable" may be found in the preamble section for § 36.304.

The definition lists factors to be considered in determining whether barrier removal is readily achievable in any particular circumstance. A significant number of commenters objected to § 36.306 of the proposed rule, which listed identical factors to be considered for determining "readily achievable" and "undue burden" together in one section. They asserted that providing a consolidated section blurred the distinction between the level of effort required by a public accommodation under the two standards. The readily achievable standard is a "lower" standard than the "undue burden" standard in terms of the level of effort required, but the factors used in determining whether an action is readily achievable or would result in an undue burden are identical (See Education and Labor report at 109). Although the preamble to the proposed rule clearly delineated the relationship between the two standards, to eliminate any confusion the Department has deleted § 36.306 of the proposed rule. That section, in any event, as other commenters noted, had merely repeated the lists of factors contained in the definitions of readily achievable and undue burden.

The list of factors included in the definition is derived from section 301(9) of the ADA. It reflects the congressional intention that a wide range of factors be considered in determining whether an action is readily achievable. It also takes into account that many local facilities are owned or operated by parent corporations or entities that conduct operations at many different sites. This section makes clear that, in some instances, resources beyond those of the local facility where the barrier must be removed may be relevant in determining whether an action is readily achievable. One must also evaluate the degree to which any parent entity has resources that may be allocated to the local facility.

The statutory list of factors in section 301(9) of the Act uses the term "covered entity" to refer to the larger entity of which a particular facility may be a part. "Covered entity" is not a defined term in the ADA and is not used consistently throughout the Act. The definition, therefore, substitutes the term "parent entity" in place of "covered entity" in paragraphs (3), (4), and (5) when referring to the larger private entity whose overall resources may be taken into account. This usage is consistent with the House Judiciary Committee's use of the term "parent company" to describe the larger entity of which the local facility is a part (H.R. Rep. No. 485, 101st Cong., 2d Sess., pt. 3, at 40-41, 54-55 (1990) (hereinafter "Judiciary report")).

A number of commenters asked for more specific guidance as to when and how the resources of a parent corporation or entity are to be taken into account in determining what is readily achievable. The Department believes that this complex issue is most appropriately resolved on a case-by-case basis. As the comments reflect, there is a wide variety of possible relationships between the site in question and any parent corporation or other entity. It would be unwise to posit legal ramifications under the ADA of even generic relationships (e.g., banks involved in foreclosures or insurance companies operating as trustees or in other similar fiduciary relationships), because any analysis will depend so completely on the detailed fact situations and the exact nature of the legal relationships involved. The final rule does, however, reorder the factors to be considered. This shift and the addition of the phrase "if applicable" make clear that the line of inquiry concerning factors will start at the site involved in the action itself. This change emphasizes that the overall resources, size, and operations of the parent corporation or entity should be considered to the extent appropriate in light of "the geographic separateness, and the administrative or fiscal relationship of the site or sites in question to any parent corporation or entity."

Although some commenters sought more specific numerical guidance on the definition of readily achievable, the Department has declined to establish in the final rule any kind of numerical formula for determining whether an action is readily achievable. It would be difficult to devise a specific ceiling on compliance costs that would take into account the vast diversity of enterprises covered by the ADA's public accommodations requirements and the economic situation that any particular entity would find itself in at any moment. The final rule, therefore, implements the flexible case-by-case approach chosen by Congress.

A number of commenters requested that security considerations be explicitly recognized as a factor in determining whether a barrier removal action is readily achievable. The Department believes that legitimate safety requirements, including crime prevention measures, may be taken into account so long as they are based on actual risks and are necessary for safe operation of the public accommodation. This point has been included in the definition.

Some commenters urged the Department not to consider acts of barrier removal in complete isolation from each other in determining whether they are readily achievable. The Department believes that it is appropriate to consider the cost of other barrier removal actions as one factor in determining whether a measure is readily achievable.

"Religious entity." The term "religious entity" is defined in accordance with section 307 of the ADA as a religious organization or entity controlled by a religious organization, including a place of worship. Section 36.102(e) of the rule states that the rule does not apply to any religious entity.

The ADA's exemption of religious organizations and religious entities controlled by religious organizations is very broad, encompassing a wide variety of situations. Religious organizations and entities controlled by religious organizations have no obligations under the ADA. Even when a religious organization carries out activities that would otherwise make it a public accommodation, the religious organization is exempt from ADA coverage. Thus, if a church itself operates a day care center, a nursing home, a private school, or a diocesan school system, the operations of the center, home, school, or schools would not be subject to the requirements of the ADA or this part. The religious entity would not lose its exemption merely because the services provided were open to the general public. The test is whether the church or other religious organization operates the public accommodation, not which individuals receive the public accommodation's services.

Religious entities that are controlled by religious organizations are also exempt from the ADA's requirements. Many religious organizations in the United States use lay boards and other secular or corporate mechanisms to operate schools and an array of social services. The use of a lay board or other mechanism does not itself remove the ADA's religious exemption. Thus, a parochial school, having religious doctrine in its curriculum and sponsored by a religious order, could be exempt either as a religious organization or as an entity controlled by a religious organization, even if it has a lay board. The test remains a factual one—whether the church or other religious organization controls the operations of the school or of the service or whether the school or service is itself a religious organization.

Although a religious organization or a religious entity that is controlled by a religious organization has no obligations under the rule, a public accommodation that is not itself a religious organization, but that operates a place of public accommodation in leased space on the property of a religious entity, which is not a place of worship, is subject to the rule's requirements if it is not under control of a religious organization. When a church rents meeting space, which is not a place of worship, to a local community group or to a private, independent day care center, the ADA applies to the activities of the local community group and day care center if a lease exists and consideration is paid.

"Service animal." The term "service animal" encompasses any guide dog, signal dog, or other animal individually trained to provide assistance to an individual with a disability. The term is used in § 36.302(c), which requires public accommodations generally to modify policies, practices, and procedures to accommodate the use of service animals in places of public accommodation.

"Specified public transportation." The definition of "specified public transportation" is identical to the statutory definition in section 301(10) of the ADA. The term means transportation by bus, rail, or any other conveyance (other than by aircraft) that provides the general public with general or special service (including charter service) on a regular and continuing basis. It is used in category (7) of the definition of "place of public accommodation," which includes stations used for specified public transportation.

The effect of this definition, which excludes transportation by aircraft, is that it excludes privately operated airports from coverage as places of public accommodation. However, places of public accommodation located within airports would be covered by this part. Airports that are operated by public entities are covered by title II of the ADA and, if they are operated as part of a program receiving Federal financial assistance, by section 504 of the Rehabilitation Act. Privately operated airports are similarly covered by section 504 if they are operated as part of a program receiving Federal financial assistance. The operations of any portion of any airport that are under the control of an air carrier are covered by the Air Carrier Access Act. In addition, airports are covered as commercial facilities under this rule.

"State." The definition of "State" is identical to the statutory definition in section 3(3) of the ADA. The term is used in the definitions of "commerce" and "public entity" in § 36.104.

"Undue burden." The definition of "undue burden" is analogous to the statutory definition of "undue hardship" in employment under section 101(10) of the ADA. The term undue burden means "significant difficulty or expense" and serves as a limitation on the obligation to provide auxiliary aids and services under § 36.303 and §§ 36.309 (b)(3) and (c)(3). Further discussion of the meaning and application of the term undue burden may be found in the preamble discussion of § 36.303.

The definition lists factors considered in determining whether provision of an auxiliary aid or service in any particular circumstance would result in an undue burden. The factors to be considered in determining whether an action would result in an undue burden are identical to those to be considered in determining whether an action is readily achievable. However, "readily achievable" is a lower standard than "undue burden" in that it requires a lower level of effort on the part of the public accommodation (see Education and Labor report at 109).

Further analysis of the factors to be considered in determining undue burden may be found in the preamble discussion of the definition of the term "readily achievable."

Subpart B—General Requirements

Subpart B includes general prohibitions restricting a public accommodation from discriminating against people with disabilities by denying them the opportunity to benefit from goods or services, by giving them unequal goods or services, or by giving them different or separate goods or services. These general prohibitions are patterned after the basic, general prohibitions that exist in other civil rights laws that prohibit discrimination on the basis of race, sex, color, religion, or national origin.

Section 36.201 General

Section 36.201(a) contains the general rule that prohibits discrimination on the basis of disability in the full and equal enjoyment of goods, services, facilities, privileges, advantages, and accommodations of any place of public accommodation.

Full and equal enjoyment means the right to participate and to have an equal opportunity to obtain the same results as others to the extent possible with such accommodations as may be required by the Act and these regulations. It does not mean that an individual with a disability must achieve an identical result or level of achievement as persons without a disability. For example, an exercise class cannot exclude a person who uses a wheelchair because he or she cannot do all of the exercises and derive the same result from the class as persons without a disability.

Section 302(a) of the ADA states that the prohibition against discrimination applies to "any person who owns, leases (or leases to), or operates a place of public accommodation," and this language is reflected in § 36.201(a). The coverage is quite extensive and would include sublessees, management companies, and any other entity that owns, leases, leases to, or operates a place of public accommodation, even if the operation is only for a short time.

The first sentence of paragraph (b) of § 36.201 reiterates the general principle that both the landlord that owns the building that houses the place of public accommodation, as well as the tenant that owns or operates the place of public accommodation, are public accommodations subject to the requirements of this part. Although the statutory language could be interpreted as placing equal responsibility on all private entities, whether lessor, lessee, or operator of a public accommodation, the committee reports suggest that liability may be allocated. Section 36.201(b) of that section of the proposed rule attempted to allocate liability in the regulation itself. Paragraph (b)(2) of that section made a specific allocation of liability for the obligation to take readily achievable measures to remove barriers, and paragraph (b)(3) made a specific allocation for the obligation to provide auxiliary aids.

Numerous commenters pointed out that these allocations would not apply in all situations. Some asserted that paragraph (b)(2) of the proposed rule only addressed the situation when a lease gave the tenant the right to make alterations with permission of the landlord, but failed to address other types of leases, e.g., those that are silent on the right to make alterations, or those in which the landlord is not permitted to enter a tenant's premises to make alterations. Several commenters noted that many leases contain other clauses more relevant to the ADA than the alterations clause. For example, many leases contain a "compliance clause," a clause which allocates responsibility to a particular party for compliance with all relevant Federal, State, and local laws. Many commenters pointed out various types of relationships that were left unaddressed by the regulation, e.g., sale and leaseback arrangements where the landlord is a financial institution with no control or responsibility for the building; franchises; subleases; and management companies which, at least in the hotel industry, often have control over operations but are unable to make modifications to the premises.

Some commenters raised specific questions as to how the barrier removal allocation would work as a practical matter. Paragraph (b)(2) of the proposed rule provided that the burden of making readily achievable modifications within the tenant's place of public accommodation would shift to the landlord when the modifications were not readily achievable for the tenant or when the landlord denied a tenant's request for permission to make such modifications. Commenters noted that the rule did not specify exactly when the burden would actually shift from tenant to landlord and whether the landlord would have to accept a tenant's word that a particular action is not readily achievable. Others questioned if the tenant should be obligated to use alternative methods of barrier removal before the burden shifts. In light of the fact that readily achievable removal of barriers can include such actions as moving of racks and displays, some commenters doubted the appropriateness of requiring a landlord to become involved in day-to-day operations of its tenants' businesses.

The Department received widely differing comments in response to the preamble question asking whether landlord and tenant obligations should vary depending on the length of time remaining on an existing lease. Many suggested that tenants should have no responsibilities in "shorter leases," which commenters defined as ranging anywhere from 90 days to three years. Other commenters pointed out that the time remaining on the lease should not be a factor in the rule's allocation of responsibilities, but is relevant in determining what is readily achievable for the tenant. The Department agrees with this latter approach and will interpret the rule in that manner.

In recognition of the somewhat limited applicability of the allocation scheme contained in the proposed rule, paragraphs (b)(2) and (b)(3) have been deleted from the final rule. The Department has substituted instead a statement that allocation of responsibility as between the parties for taking readily achievable measures to remove barriers and to provide auxiliary aids and services both in common areas and within places of public accommodation may be determined by the lease or other contractual relationships between the parties. The ADA was not intended to change existing landlord/tenant responsibilities as set forth in the lease. By deleting specific provisions from the rule, the Department gives full recognition to this principle. As between the landlord and tenant, the extent of responsibility for particular obligations may be, and in many cases probably will be, determined by contract.

The suggested allocation of responsibilities contained in the proposed rule may be used if appropriate in a particular situation. Thus, the landlord would generally be held responsible for making readily achievable changes and providing auxiliary aids and services in common areas and for modifying policies, practices, or procedures applicable to all tenants, and the tenant would generally be responsible for readily achievable changes, provision of auxiliary aids, and modification of policies within its own place of public accommodation.

Many commenters objected to the proposed rule's allocation of responsibility for providing auxiliary aids and services solely to the tenant, pointing out that this exclusive allocation may not be appropriate in the case of larger public accommodations that operate their businesses by renting space out to smaller public accommodations. For example, large theaters often rent to smaller traveling companies and hospitals often rely on independent contractors to provide childbirth classes. Groups representing persons with disabilities objected to the proposed rule because, in their view, it permitted the large theater or hospital to evade ADA responsibilities by leasing to independent smaller entities. They suggested that these types of public accommodations are not really landlords because they are in the business of providing a service, rather than renting space, as in the case of a shopping center or office building landlord. These commenters believed that responsibility for providing auxiliary aids should shift to the landlord, if the landlord relies on a smaller public accommodation or independent contractor to provide services closely related to those of the larger public accommodation, and if the needed auxiliary aids prove to be an undue burden for the smaller public accommodation. The final rule no longer lists specific allocations to specific parties but, rather, leaves allocation of responsibilities to the lease negotiations. Parties are, therefore, free to allocate the responsibility for auxiliary aids.

Section 36.201(b)(4) of the proposed rule, which provided that alterations by a tenant on its own premises do not trigger a path of travel obligation on the landlord, has been moved to § 36.403(d) of the final rule.

An entity that is not in and of itself a public accommodation, such as a trade association or performing artist, may become a public accommodation when it leases space for a conference or performance at a hotel, convention center, or stadium. For an entity to become a public accommodation when it is the lessee of space, however, the Department believes that consideration in some form must be given. Thus, a Boy Scout troop that accepts donated space does not become a public accommodation because the troop has not "leased" space, as required by the ADA.

As a public accommodation, the trade association or performing artist will be responsible for compliance with this part. Specific responsibilities should be allocated by contract, but, generally, the lessee should be responsible for providing auxiliary aids and services (which could include interpreters, Braille programs, etc.) for the participants in its conference or performance as well as for assuring that displays are accessible to individuals with disabilities.

Some commenters suggested that the rule should allocate responsibilities for areas other than removal of barriers and auxiliary aids. The final rule leaves allocation of all areas to the lease negotiations. However, in general landlords should not be given responsibility for policies a tenant applies in operating its business, if such policies are solely those of the tenant. Thus, if a restaurant tenant discriminates by refusing to seat a patron, it would be the tenant, and not the landlord, who would be responsible, because the discriminatory policy is imposed solely by the tenant and not by the landlord. If, however, a tenant refuses to modify a "no pets" rule to allow service animals in its restaurant because the landlord mandates such a rule, then both the landlord and the tenant would be liable for violation of the ADA when a person with a service dog is refused entrance. The Department wishes to emphasize, however, that the parties are free to allocate responsibilities in any way they choose.

Private clubs are also exempt from the ADA. However, consistent with title II of the Civil Rights Act (42 U.S.C. 2000a(e), a private club is considered a public accommodation to the extent that "the facilities of such establishment are made available to the customers or patrons" of a place of public accommodation. Thus, if a private club runs a day care center that is open exclusively to its own members, the club, like the church in the example above, would have no responsibility for compliance with the ADA. Nor would the day care center have any responsibilities because it is part of the private club exempt from the ADA.

On the other hand, if the private club rents to a day care center that is open to the public, then the private club would have the same obligations as any other public accommodation that functions as a landlord with respect to compliance with title III within the day care center. In such a situation, both the private club that "leases to" a public accommodation and the public accommodation lessee (the day care center) would be subject to the ADA. This same principle would apply if the private club were to rent to, for example, a bar association, which is not generally a public accommodation but which, as explained above, becomes a public accommodation when it leases space for a conference.

Section 36.202 Activities

Section 36.202 sets out the general forms of discrimination prohibited by title III of the ADA. These general prohibitions are further refined by the specific prohibitions in subpart C. Section 36.213 makes clear that the limitations on the ADA's requirements contained in subpart C, such as "necessity" (§ 36.301(a)) and "safety" (§ 36.301(b)), are applicable to the prohibitions in § 36.202. Thus, it is unnecessary to add these limitations to § 36.202 as has been requested by some commenters. In addition, the language of § 36.202 very closely tracks the language of section 302(b)(1)(A) of the Act, and that statutory provision does not expressly contain these limitations.

Deny participation—Section 36.202(a) provides that it is discriminatory to deny a person with a disability the right to participate in or benefit from the goods, services, facilities, privileges, advantages, or accommodations of a place of public accommodation.

A public accommodation may not exclude persons with disabilities on the basis of disability for reasons other than those specifically set forth in this part. For example, a public accommodation cannot refuse to serve a person with a disability because its insurance company conditions coverage or rates on the absence of persons with disabilities. This is a frequent basis of exclusion from a variety of community activities and is prohibited by this part.

Unequal benefit—Section 36.202(b) prohibits services or accommodations that are not equal to those provided others. For example, persons with disabilities must not be limited to certain performances at a theater.

Separate benefit—Section 36.202(c) permits different or separate benefits or services only when necessary to provide persons with disabilities opportunities as effective as those provided others. This paragraph permitting separate benefits "when necessary" should be read together with § 36.203(a), which requires integration in "the most integrated setting appropriate to the needs of the individual." The preamble to that section provides further guidance on separate programs. Thus, this section would not prohibit the designation of parking spaces for persons with disabilities.

Each of the three paragraphs (a)-(c) prohibits discrimination against an individual or class of individuals "either directly or through contractual, licensing, or other arrangements." The intent of the contractual prohibitions of these paragraphs is to prohibit a public accommodation from doing indirectly, through a contractual relationship, what it may not do directly. Thus, the "individual or class of individuals" referenced in the three paragraphs is intended to refer to the clients and customers of the public accommodation that entered into a contractual arrangement. It is not intended to encompass the clients or customers of other entities. A public accommodation, therefore, is not liable under this provision for discrimination that may be practiced by those with whom it has a contractual relationship, when that discrimination is not directed against its own clients or customers. For example, if an amusement park contracts with a food service company to operate its restaurants at the park, the amusement park is not responsible for other operations of the food service company that do not involve clients or customers of the amusement park. Section 36.202(d) makes this clear by providing that the term "individual or class of individuals" refers to the clients or customers of the public accommodation that enters into the contractual, licensing, or other arrangement.

Section 36.203 Integrated Settings

Section 36.203 addresses the integration of persons with disabilities. The ADA recognizes that the provision of goods and services in an integrated manner is a fundamental tenet of nondiscrimination on the basis of disability. Providing segregated accommodations and services relegates persons with disabilities to the status of second-class citizens. For example, it would be a violation of this provision to require persons with mental disabilities to eat in the back room of a restaurant or to refuse to allow a person with a disability the full use of a health spa because of stereotypes about the person's ability to participate. Section 36.203(a) states that a public accommodation shall afford goods, services, facilities, privileges, advantages, and accommodations to an individual with a disability in the most integrated setting appropriate to the needs of the individual. Section 36.203(b) specifies that, notwithstanding the existence of separate or different programs or activities provided in accordance with this section, an individual with a disability shall not be denied the opportunity to participate in such programs or activities that are not separate or different. Section

306.203(c), which is derived from section 501(d) of the Americans with Disabilities Act, states that nothing in this part shall be construed to require an individual with a disability to accept an accommodation, aid, service, opportunity, or benefit that he or she chooses not to accept.

Taken together, these provisions are intended to prohibit exclusion and segregation of individuals with disabilities and the denial of equal opportunities enjoyed by others, based on, among other things, presumptions, patronizing attitudes, fears, and stereotypes about individuals with disabilities. Consistent with these standards, public accommodations are required to make decisions based on facts applicable to individuals and not on the basis of presumptions as to what a class of individuals with disabilities can or cannot do.

Sections 36.203 (b) and (c) make clear that individuals with disabilities cannot be denied the opportunity to participate in programs that are not separate or different. This is an important and overarching principle of the Americans with Disabilities Act. Separate, special, or different programs that are designed to provide a benefit to persons with disabilities cannot be used to restrict the participation of persons with disabilities in general, integrated activities.

For example, a person who is blind may wish to decline participating in a special museum tour that allows persons to touch sculptures in an exhibit and instead tour the exhibit at his or her own pace with the museum's recorded tour. It is not the intent of this section to require the person who is blind to avail himself or herself of the special tour. Modified participation for persons with disabilities must be a choice, not a requirement.

Further, it would not be a violation of this section for an establishment to offer recreational programs specially designed for children with mobility impairments in those limited circumstances. However, it would be a violation of this section if the entity then excluded these children from other recreational services made available to nondisabled children, or required children with disabilities to attend only designated programs.

Many commenters asked that the Department clarify a public accommodation's obligations within the integrated program when it offers a separate program, but an individual with a disability chooses not to participate in the separate program. It is impossible to make a blanket statement as to what level of auxiliary aids or modifications are required in the integrated program. Rather, each situation must be assessed individually. Assuming the integrated program would be appropriate for a particular individual, the extent to which that individual must be provided with modifications will depend not only on what the individual needs but also on the limitations set forth in subpart C. For example, it may constitute an undue burden for a particular public accommodation, which provides a full-time interpreter in its special guided tour for individuals with hearing impairments, to hire an additional interpreter for those individuals who choose to attend the integrated program. The Department cannot identify categorically the level of assistance or aid required in the integrated program.

The preamble to the proposed rule contained a statement that some interpreted as encouraging the continuation of separate schools, sheltered workshops, special recreational programs, and other similar programs. It is important to emphasize that § 36.202(c) only calls for separate programs when such programs are "necessary" to provide as effective an opportunity to individuals with disabilities as to other individuals. Likewise, § 36.203(a) only permits separate programs when a more integrated setting would not be "appropriate." Separate programs are permitted, then, in only limited circumstances. The sentence at issue has been deleted from the preamble because it was too broadly stated and had been erroneously interpreted as Departmental encouragement of separate programs without qualification.

The proposed rule's reference in § 36.203(b) to separate programs or activities provided in accordance with "this section" has been changed to "this subpart" in recognition of the fact that separate programs or activities may, in some limited circumstances, be permitted not only by § 36.203(a) but also by § 36.202(c).

In addition, some commenters suggested that the individual with the disability is the only one who can decide whether a setting is "appropriate" and what the "needs" are. Others suggested that only the public accommodation can make these determinations. The regulation does not give exclusive responsibility to either party. Rather, the determinations are to be made based on an objective view, presumably one which would take into account views of both parties.

Some commenters expressed concern that § 36.203(c), which states that nothing in the rule requires an individual with a disability to accept special accommodations and services provided under the ADA, could be interpreted to allow guardians of infants or older people with disabilities to refuse medical treatment for their wards. Section 36.203(c) has been revised to make it clear that paragraph (c) is inapplicable to the concern of the commenters. A new paragraph (c)(2) has been added stating that nothing in the regulation authorizes the representative or guardian of an individual with a disability to decline food, water, medical treatment, or medical services for that individual. New paragraph (c) clarifies that neither the ADA nor the regulation alters current Federal law ensuring the rights of incompetent individuals with disabilities to receive food, water, and medical treatment. See, e.g., Child Abuse Amendments of 1984 (42 U.S.C. 5106a(b)(10), 5106g(10)); Rehabilitation Act of 1973, as amended (29 U.S.C 794); Developmentally Disabled Assistance and Bill of Rights Act (42 U.S.C. 6042).

Sections 36.203(c) (1) and (2) are based on section 501(d) of the ADA. Section § 501(d) was designed to clarify that nothing in the ADA requires individuals with disabilities to accept special accommodations and services for individuals with disabilities that may segregate them:

> The Committee added this section (501(d)) to clarify that nothing in the ADA is intended to permit discriminatory treatment on the basis of disability, even when such treatment is rendered under the guise of providing an accommodation, service, aid or benefit to the individual with disability. For example, a blind individual may choose not to avail himself or herself of the right to go to the front of a line, even if a particular public accommodation has chosen to offer such a modification of a policy for blind individuals. Or, a blind individual may choose to decline to participate in a special museum tour that allows persons to touch sculptures in an exhibit and instead tour the exhibits at his or her own pace with the museum's recorded tour.

(Judiciary report at 71-72.) The Act is not to be construed to mean that an individual with disabilities must accept special accommodations and services for individuals with disabilities when that individual chooses to participate in the regular services already offered. Because medical treatment, including treatment for particular conditions, is not a special accommodation or service for individuals with disabilities under section 501(d), neither the Act nor this part provides affirmative authority to suspend such treatment. Section 501(d) is intended to clarify that the Act is not designed to foster discrimination through mandatory acceptance of special services when other alternatives are provided; this concern does not reach to the provision of medical treatment for the disabling condition itself.

Section 36.213 makes clear that the limitations contained in subpart C are to be read into subpart B. Thus, the integration requirement is subject to the various defenses contained in subpart C, such as safety, if eligibility criteria are at issue (§ 36.301(b)), or fundamental alteration and undue burden, if the concern is provision of auxiliary aids (§ 36.303(a)).

Section 36.204 Administrative Methods

Section 36.204 specifies that an individual or entity shall not, directly, or through contractual or other arrangements, utilize standards or criteria or methods of administration that have the effect of discriminating on the basis of disability or that perpetuate the discrimination of others who are subject to common administrative control. The preamble discussion of § 36.301 addresses eligibility criteria in detail.

Section 36.204 is derived from section 302(b)(1)(D) of the Americans with Disabilities Act, and it uses the same language used in the employment section of the ADA (section 102(b)(3)). Both sections incorporate a disparate impact standard to ensure the effectiveness of the legislative mandate to end discrimination. This standard is consistent with the interpretation of section 504 by the U.S. Supreme Court in *Alexander v. Choate*, 469 U.S. 287 (1985). The Court in *Choate* explained that members of Congress made numerous statements during passage of section 504 regarding eliminating architectural barriers, providing access to transportation, and eliminating discriminatory effects of job qualification procedures. The Court then noted: "These statements would ring hollow if the resulting legislation could not rectify the harms resulting from action that discriminated by effect as well as by design." *Id* at 297 (footnote omitted).

Of course, § 36.204 is subject to the various limitations contained in subpart C including, for example, necessity (§ 36.301(a)), safety (§ 36.301(b)), fundamental alteration (§ 36.302(a)), readily achievable (§ 36.304(a)), and undue burden (§ 36.303(a)).

Section 36.205 Association

Section 36.205 implements section 302(b)(1)(E) of the Act, which provides that a public accommodation shall not exclude or otherwise deny equal goods, services, facilities, privileges, advantages, accommodations, or other opportunities to an individual or entity because of the known disability of an individual with whom the individual or entity is known to have a relationship or association. This section is unchanged from the proposed rule.

The individuals covered under this section include any individuals who are discriminated against because of their known association with an individual with a disability. For example, it would be a violation of this part for a day care center to refuse admission to a child because his or her brother has HIV disease.

This protection is not limited to those who have a familial relationship with the individual who has a disability. If a place of public accommodation refuses admission to a person with cerebral palsy and his or her companions, the companions have an independent right of action under the ADA and this section.

During the legislative process, the term "entity" was added to section 302(b)(1)(E) to clarify that the scope of the provision is intended to encompass not only persons who have a known association with a person with a disability, but also entities that provide services to or are otherwise associated with such individuals. This provision was intended to ensure that entities such as health care providers, employees of social service agencies, and others who provide professional services to persons with disabilities are not subjected to discrimination because of their professional association with persons with disabilities. For example, it would be a violation of this section to terminate the lease of a entity operating an independent living center for persons with disabilities, or to seek to evict a health care provider because that individual or entity provides services to persons with mental impairments.

Section 36.206 Retaliation or Coercion

Section 36.206 implements section 503 of the ADA, which prohibits retaliation against any individual who exercises his or her rights under the Act. This section is unchanged from the proposed rule. Paragraph (a) of § 36.206 provides that no private entity or public entity shall discriminate against any individual because that individual has exercised his or her right to oppose any act or practice made unlawful by this part, or because that individual made a charge, testified, assisted, or participated in any manner in an investigation, proceeding, or hearing under the Act or this part.

Paragraph (b) provides that no private entity or public entity shall coerce, intimidate, threaten, or interfere with any individual in the exercise of his or her rights under this part or because that individual aided or encouraged any other individual in the exercise or enjoyment of any right granted or protected by the Act or this part.

Illustrations of practices prohibited by this section are contained in paragraph (c), which is modeled on a similar provision in the regulations issued by the Department of Housing and Urban Development to implement the Fair Housing Act (see 24 CFR 100.400(c)(l)). Prohibited actions may include:

(1) Coercing an individual to deny or limit the benefits, services, or advantages to which he or she is entitled under the Act or this part;

(2) Threatening, intimidating, or interfering with an individual who is seeking to obtain or use the goods, services, facilities, privileges, advantages, or accommodations of a public accommodation;

(3) Intimidating or threatening any person because that person is assisting or encouraging an individual or group entitled to claim the rights granted or protected by the Act or this part to exercise those rights; or

(4) Retaliating against any person because that person has participated in any investigation or action to enforce the Act or this part.

This section protects not only individuals who allege a violation of the Act or this part, but also any individuals who support or assist them. This section applies to all investigations or proceedings initiated under the Act or this part without regard to the ultimate resolution of the underlying allegations. Because this section prohibits any act of retaliation or coercion in response to an individual's effort to exercise rights established by the Act and this part (or to support the efforts of another individual), the section applies not only to public accommodations that are otherwise subject to this part, but also to individuals other than public accommodations or to public entities. For example, it would be a violation of the Act and this part for a private individual, e.g., a restaurant customer, to harass or intimidate an individual with a disability in an effort to prevent that individual from patronizing the restaurant. It would, likewise, be a violation of the Act and this part for a public entity to take adverse action against an employee who appeared as a witness on behalf of an individual who sought to enforce the Act.

Section 36.207 Places of Public Accommodation Located in Private Residences

A private home used exclusively as a residence is not covered by title III because it is neither a "commercial facility" nor a "place of public accommodation." In some situations, however, a private home is not used exclusively as a residence, but houses a place of public accommodation in all or part of a home (e.g., an accountant who meets with his or her clients at his or her residence). Section 36.207(a) provides that those portions of the private residence used in the operation of the place of public accommodation are covered by this part.

For instance, a home or a portion of a home may be

used as a day care center during the day and a residence at night. If all parts of the house are used for the day care center, then the entire residence is a place of public accommodation because no part of the house is used exclusively as a residence. If an accountant uses one room in the house solely as his or her professional office, then a portion of the house is used exclusively as a place of public accommodation and a portion is used exclusively as a residence. Section 36.207 provides that when a portion of a residence is used exclusively as a residence, that portion is not covered by this part. Thus, the portions of the accountant's house, other than the professional office and areas and spaces leading to it, are not covered by this part. All of the requirements of this rule apply to the covered portions, including requirements to make reasonable modifications in policies, eliminate discriminatory eligibility criteria, take readily achievable measures to remove barriers or provide readily achievable alternatives (e.g., making house calls), provide auxiliary aids and services and undertake only accessible new construction and alterations.

Paragraph (b) was added in response to comments that sought clarification on the extent of coverage of the private residence used as the place of public accommodation. The final rule makes clear that the place of accommodation extends to all areas of the home used by clients and customers of the place of public accommodation. Thus, the ADA would apply to any door or entry way, hallways, a restroom, if used by customers and clients; and any other portion of the residence, interior or exterior, used by customers or clients of the public accommodation. This interpretation is simply an application of the general rule for all public accommodations, which extends statutory requirements to all portions of the facility used by customers and clients, including, if applicable, restrooms, hallways, and approaches to the public accommodation. As with other public accommodations, barriers at the entrance and on the sidewalk leading up to the public accommodation, if the sidewalk is under the control of the public accommodation, must be removed if doing so is readily achievable.

The Department recognizes that many businesses that operate out of personal residences are quite small, often employing only the homeowner and having limited total revenues. In these circumstances the effect of ADA coverage would likely be quite minimal. For example, because the obligation to remove existing architectural barriers is limited to those that are easily accomplishable without much difficulty or expense (see § 36.304), the range of required actions would be quite modest. It might not be readily achievable for such a place of public accommodation to remove any existing barriers. If it is not readily achievable to remove existing architectural barriers, a public accommodation located in a private residence may meet its obligations under the Act and this part by providing its goods or services to clients or customers with disabilities through the use of alternative measures, including delivery of goods or services in the home of the customer or client, to the extent that such alternative measures are readily achievable (See § 36.305).

Some commenters asked for clarification as to how the new construction and alteration standards of subpart D will apply to residences. The new construction standards only apply to the extent that the residence or portion of the residence was designed or intended for use as a public accommodation. Thus, for example, if a portion of a home is designed or constructed for use exclusively as a lawyer's office or for use both as a lawyer's office and for residential purposes, then it must be designed in accordance with the new construction standards in the appendix. Likewise, if a homeowner is undertaking alterations to convert all or part of his residence to a place of public accommodation, that work must be done in compliance with the alterations standards in the appendix.

The preamble to the proposed rule addressed the applicable requirements when a commercial facility is located in a private residence. That situation is now addressed in § 36.401(b) of subpart D.

Section 36.208 Direct Threat

Section 36.208(a) implements section 302(b)(3) of the Act by providing that this part does not require a public accommodation to permit an individual to participate in or benefit from the goods, services, facilities, privileges, advantages and accommodations of the public accommodation, if that individual poses a direct threat to the health or safety of others. This section is unchanged from the proposed rule.

The Department received a significant number of comments on this section. Commenters representing individuals with disabilities generally supported this provision, but suggested revisions to further limit its application. Commenters representing public accommodations generally endorsed modifications that would permit a public accommodation to exercise its own judgment in determining whether an individual poses a direct threat.

The inclusion of this provision is not intended to imply that persons with disabilities pose risks to others. It is intended to address concerns that may arise in this area. It establishes a strict standard that must be met before denying service to an individual with a disability or excluding that individual from participation.

Paragraph (b) of this section explains that a "direct threat" is a significant risk to the health or safety of others that cannot be eliminated by a modification of policies, practices, or procedures, or by the provision of auxiliary aids and services. This paragraph codifies the standard first applied by the Supreme Court in *School Board of Nassau County v. Arline,* 480 U.S. 273 (1987), in which the Court held that an individual with a contagious disease may be an "individual with handicaps" under section 504 of the Rehabilitation Act. In *Arline,* the Supreme Court recognized that there is a need to balance the interests of people with disabilities against legitimate concerns for public safety. Although persons with disabilities are generally entitled to the protection of this part, a person who poses a significant risk to others may be excluded if reasonable modifications to the public accommodation's policies, practices, or procedures will not eliminate that risk. The determination that a person poses a direct threat to the health or safety of others may not be based on generalizations or stereotypes about the effects of a particular disability; it must be based on an individual assessment that conforms to the requirements of paragraph (c) of this section.

Paragraph (c) establishes the test to use in determining whether an individual poses a direct threat to the health or safety of others. A public accommodation is required to make an individualized assessment, based on reasonable judgment that relies on current medical evidence or on the best available objective evidence, to determine: The nature, duration, and severity of the risk; the probability that the potential injury will actually occur; and whether reasonable modifications of policies, practices, or procedures will mitigate the risk. This is the test established by the Supreme Court in *Arline.* Such an inquiry is essential if the law is to achieve its goal of protecting disabled individuals from discrimination based on prejudice, stereotypes, or unfounded fear, while giving appropriate weight to legitimate concerns, such as the need to avoid exposing others to significant health and safety risks. Making this assessment will not usually require the services of a physician. Sources for medical knowledge include guidance from public health authorities, such as the U.S. Public Health Service, the Centers for Disease Control, and the National Institutes of Health, including the National Institute of Mental Health.

Many of the commenters sought clarification of the inquiry requirement. Some suggested that public accommodations should be prohibited from making any inquiries to determine if an individual with a disability would pose a direct threat to other persons. The Department believes that to preclude all such inquiries would be inappropriate. Under § 36.301 of this part, a public accommodation is permitted to establish eligibility criteria necessary for the safe operation of the place of public accommodation. Implicit in that right is the right to ask if an individual meets the criteria. However, any eligibility or safety standard established by a public accommodation must be based on actual risk, not on speculation or stereotypes; it must be applied to all clients or customers of the place of public accommodation; and inquiries must be limited to matters necessary to the application of the standard.

Some commenters suggested that the test established in the *Arline* decision, which was developed in the context of an employment case, is too stringent to apply in a public accommodations context where interaction between the public accommodation and its client or customer is often very brief. One suggested alternative was to permit public accommodations to exercise "good faith" judgment in determining whether an individual poses a direct threat, particularly when a public accommodation is dealing with a client or customer engaged in disorderly or disruptive behavior.

The Department believes that the ADA clearly requires that any determination to exclude an individual from participation must be based on an objective standard. A public accommodation may establish neutral eligibility criteria as a condition of receiving its goods or services. As long as these criteria are necessary for the safe provision of the public accommodation's goods and services and applied neutrally to all clients or customers, regardless of whether they are individuals with disabilities, a person who is unable to meet the criteria may be excluded from participation without inquiry into the underlying reason for the inability to comply. In places of public accommodation such as restaurants, theaters, or hotels, where the contact between the public accommodation and its clients is transitory, the uniform application of an eligibility standard precluding violent or disruptive behavior by any client or customer should be sufficient to enable a public accommodation to conduct its business in an orderly manner.

Some other commenters asked for clarification of the application of this provision to persons, particularly children, who have short-term, contagious illnesses, such as fevers, influenza, or the common cold. It is common practice in schools and day care settings to exclude persons with such illnesses until the symptoms subside. The Department believes that these commenters misunderstand the scope of this rule. The ADA only prohibits discrimination against an individual with a disability. Under the ADA and this part, a "disability" is defined as a physical or mental impairment that substantially limits one or more major life activities. Common, short-term illnesses that predictably resolve themselves within a matter of days do not "substantially limit" a major life activity; therefore, it is not a violation of this part to exclude an individual from receiving the services of a public accommodation because of such transitory illness. However, this part does apply to persons who have long-term illnesses. Any determination with respect to a person who has a chronic or long-term illness must be made in compliance with the requirements of this section.

Section 36.209 Illegal Use of Drugs

Section 36.209 effectuates section 510 of the ADA, which clarifies the Act's application to people who use drugs illegally. Paragraph (a) provides that this part does not prohibit discrimination based on an individual's current illegal use of drugs.

The Act and the regulation distinguish between illegal use of drugs and the legal use of substances, whether or not those substances are "controlled substances," as defined in the Controlled Substances Act (21 U.S.C. 812). Some controlled substances are prescription drugs that have legitimate medical uses. Section 36.209 does not affect use of controlled substances pursuant to a valid prescription, under supervision by a licensed health care professional, or other use that is authorized by the Controlled Substances Act or any other provision of Federal law. It does apply to illegal use of those substances, as well as to illegal use of controlled substances that are not prescription drugs. The key question is whether the individual's use of the substance is illegal, not whether the substance has recognized legal uses. Alcohol is not a controlled substance, so use of alcohol is not addressed by § 36.209. Alcoholics are individuals with disabilities, subject to the protections of the statute.

A distinction is also made between the use of a substance and the status of being addicted to that substance. Addiction is a disability, and addicts are individuals with disabilities protected by the Act. The protection, however, does not extend to actions based on the illegal use of the substance. In other words, an addict cannot use the fact of his or her addiction as a defense to an action based on illegal use of drugs. This distinction is not artificial. Congress intended to deny protection to people who engage in the illegal use of drugs, whether or not they are addicted, but to provide protection to addicts so long as they are not currently using drugs.

A third distinction is the difficult one between current use and former use. The definition of "current illegal use of drugs" in § 36.104, which is based on the report of the Conference Committee, H.R. Conf. Rep. No. 596, 101st Cong., 2d Sess. 64 (1990), is "illegal use of drugs that occurred recently enough to justify a reasonable belief that a person's drug use is current or that continuing use is a real and ongoing problem."

Paragraph (a)(2)(i) specifies that an individual who has successfully completed a supervised drug rehabilitation program or has otherwise been rehabilitated successfully and who is not engaging in current illegal use of drugs is protected. Paragraph (a)(2)(ii) clarifies that an individual who is currently participating in a supervised rehabilitation program and is not engaging in current illegal use of drugs is protected. Paragraph (a)(2)(iii) provides that a person who is erroneously regarded as engaging in current illegal use of drugs, but who is not engaging in such use, is protected.

Paragraph (b) provides a limited exception to the exclusion of current illegal users of drugs from the protections of the Act. It prohibits denial of health services, or services provided in connection with drug rehabilitation, to an individual on the basis of current illegal use of drugs, if the individual is otherwise entitled to such services. As explained further in the discussion of § 36.302, a health care facility that specializes in a particular type of treatment, such as care of burn victims, is not required to provide drug rehabilitation services, but it cannot refuse to treat an individual's burns on the grounds that the individual is illegally using drugs.

A commenter argued that health care providers should be permitted to use their medical judgment to postpone discretionary medical treatment of individuals under the influence of alcohol or drugs. The regulation permits a medical practitioner to take into account an individual's use of drugs in determining appropriate medical treatment. Section 36.209 provides that the prohibitions on discrimination in this part do not apply when the public accommodation acts on the basis of current illegal use of drugs. Although those prohibitions do apply under paragraph (b), the limitations established under this part also apply. Thus, under § 36.208, a health care provider or other public accommodation covered under § 36.209(b) may exclude an individual whose current illegal use of drugs poses a direct threat to the health or safety of others, and, under § 36.301, a public accommodation may impose or apply eligibility criteria that are necessary for the provision of the services being offered, and may impose legitimate safety requirements that are necessary for safe operation. These same limitations also apply to individuals with disabilities who use alcohol or prescription drugs. The Department believes that these provisions address this commenter's concerns.

Other commenters pointed out that abstention from the use of drugs is an essential condition for participation in some drug rehabilitation programs, and may be a necessary requirement in inpatient or residential settings. The Department believes that this comment is well-founded. Congress clearly did not intend to exclude from drug treatment programs the very individuals who need such programs because of their use of drugs. In such a situation, however, once an individual has been admitted to a program, abstention may be a necessary and appropriate condition to continued participation. The final rule therefore provides that a drug rehabilitation or treatment program may deny participation to individuals who use drugs while they are in the program.

Paragraph (c) expresses Congress' intention that the Act be neutral with respect to testing for illegal use of drugs. This paragraph implements the provision in section 510(b) of the Act that allows entities "to adopt or administer reasonable policies or procedures, including but not limited to drug testing," that ensure an individual who is participating in a supervised rehabilitation program, or who has completed such a program or otherwise been rehabilitated successfully, is no longer engaging in the illegal use of drugs. Paragraph (c) is not to be construed to encourage, prohibit, restrict, or authorize the conducting of testing for the illegal use of drugs.

Paragraph (c) of § 36.209 clarifies that it is not a violation of this part to adopt or administer reasonable policies or procedures to ensure that an individual who formerly engaged in the illegal use of drugs is not currently engaging in illegal use of drugs. Any such policies or procedures must, of course, be reasonable, and must be designed to identify accurately the illegal use of drugs. This paragraph does not authorize inquiries, tests, or other procedures that would disclose use of substances that are not controlled substances or are taken under supervision by a licensed health care professional, or other uses authorized by the Controlled Substances Act or other provisions of Federal law, because such uses are not included in the definition of "illegal use of drugs."

One commenter argued that the rule should permit testing for lawful use of prescription drugs, but most favored the explanation that tests must be limited to unlawful use in order to avoid revealing the use of prescription medicine used to treat disabilities. Tests revealing legal use of prescription drugs might violate the prohibition in § 36.301 of attempts to unnecessarily identify the existence of a disability.

Section 36.210 Smoking

Section 36.210 restates the clarification in section 501(b) of the Act that the Act does not preclude the prohibition of, or imposition of restrictions on, smoking. Some commenters argued that § 36.210 does not go far enough, and that the regulation should prohibit smoking in all places of public accommodation. The reference to smoking in section 501 merely clarifies that the Act does not require public accommodations to accommodate smokers by permitting them to smoke in places of public accommodations.

Section 36.211 Maintenance of Accessible Features

Section 36.211 provides that a public accommodation shall maintain in operable working condition those features of facilities and equipment that are required to be readily accessible to and usable by persons with disabilities by the Act or this part. The Act requires that, to the maximum extent feasible, facilities must be accessible to, and usable by, individuals with disabilities. This section recognizes that it is not sufficient to provide features such as accessible routes, elevators, or ramps, if those features are not maintained in a manner that enables individuals with disabilities to use them. Inoperable elevators, locked accessible doors, or "accessible" routes that are obstructed by furniture, filing cabinets, or potted plants are neither "accessible to" nor "usable by" individuals with disabilities.

Some commenters objected that this section appeared to establish an absolute requirement and suggested that language from the preamble be included in the text of the regulation. It is, of course, impossible to guarantee that mechanical devices will never fail to operate. Paragraph (b) of the final regulation provides that this section does not prohibit isolated or temporary interruptions in service or access due to maintenance or repairs. This paragraph is intended to clarify that temporary obstructions or isolated instances of mechanical failure would not be considered violations of the Act or this part. However, allowing obstructions or "out of service" equipment to persist beyond a reasonable period of time would violate this part, as would repeated mechanical failures due to improper or inadequate maintenance. Failure of the public accommodation to ensure that accessible routes are properly maintained and free of obstructions, or failure to arrange prompt repair of inoperable elevators or other equipment intended to provide access, would also violate this part.

Other commenters requested that this section be expanded to include specific requirements for inspection and maintenance of equipment, for training staff in the proper operation of equipment, and for maintenance of specific items. The Department believes that this section properly establishes the general requirement for maintaining access and that further, more detailed requirements are not necessary.

Section 36.212 Insurance

The Department received numerous comments on proposed § 36.212. Most supported the proposed regulation but felt that it did not go far enough in protecting individuals with disabilities and persons associated with them from discrimination. Many commenters argued that language from the preamble to the proposed regulation should be included in the text of the final regulation. Other commenters argued that even that language was not strong enough, and that more stringent standards should be established. Only a few commenters argued that the Act does not apply to insurance underwriting practices or the terms of insurance contracts. These commenters cited language from the Senate committee report (S. Rep. No. 116, 101st Cong., 1st Sess., at 84-86 (1989) (hereinafter "Senate report")), indicating that Congress did not intend to affect existing insurance practices.

The Department has decided to adopt the language of the proposed rule without change. Sections 36.212 (a) and (b) restate section 501(c) of the Act, which provides that the Act shall not be construed to restrict certain insurance practices on the part of insurance companies and employers, as long as such practices are not used to evade the purposes of the Act. Section 36.212(c) is a specific application of § 36.202(a), which prohibits denial of participation on the basis of disability. It provides that a public accommodation may not refuse to serve an individual with a disability because of limitations on coverage or rates in its insurance policies (see Judiciary report at 56).

Many commenters supported the requirements of § 36.212(c) in the proposed rule because it addressed an important reason for denial of services by public accommodations. One commenter argued that services could be denied if the insurance coverage required exclusion of people whose disabilities were reasonably related to the risks involved in that particular place of public accommodation. Sections 36.208 and 36.301 establish criteria for denial of participation on the basis of legitimate safety concerns. This paragraph does not prohibit consideration of such concerns in insurance policies, but provides that any exclusion on the basis of disability must be based on the permissible criteria, rather than on the terms of the insurance contract.

Language in the committee reports indicates that Congress intended to reach insurance practices by prohibiting differential treatment of individuals with disabilities in insurance offered by public accommodations unless the differences are justified. "Under the ADA, a person with a disability cannot be denied insurance or be subject to different terms or conditions of insurance based on disability alone, if the disability does not pose increased risks" (Senate report at 84; Education and Labor report at 136). Section 501(c)(1) of the Act was intended to emphasize that "insurers may continue to sell to and underwrite individuals applying for life, health, or other insurance on an individually underwritten basis, or to service such insurance products, so long as the standards used are based on sound actuarial data and not on speculation" (Judiciary report at 70 (emphasis added); see also Senate report at 85; Education and Labor report at 137).

The committee reports indicate that underwriting and classification of risks must be "based on sound actuarial principles or be related to actual or reasonably anticipated experience" (see, e.g., Judiciary report at 71). Moreover, "while a plan which limits certain kinds of coverage based on classification of risk would be allowed * * *, the plan may not refuse to insure, or refuse to continue to insure, or limit the amount, extent, or kind of coverage available to an individual, or charge a different rate for the same coverage solely because of a physical or mental impairment, except where the refusal, limitation, or rate differential is based on sound actuarial principles or is related to actual or reasonably anticipated experience" (Senate report at 85; Education and Labor report at 136-37; Judiciary report at 71). The ADA, therefore, does not prohibit use of legitimate actuarial considerations to justify differential treatment of individuals with disabilities in insurance.

The committee reports provide some guidance on how nondiscrimination principles in the disability rights area relate to insurance practices. For example, a person who is blind may not be denied coverage based on blindness independent of actuarial risk classification. With respect to group health insurance coverage, an individual with a pre-existing condition may be denied coverage for that condition for the period specified in the policy, but cannot be denied coverage for illness or injuries unrelated to the pre-existing condition. Also, a public accommodation may offer insurance policies that limit coverage for certain procedures or treatments, but may not entirely deny coverage to a person with a disability.

The Department requested comment on the extent to which data that would establish statistically sound correlations are available. Numerous commenters cited pervasive problems in the availability and cost of insurance for individuals with disabilities and parents of children with disabilities. No commenters cited specific data, or sources of data, to support specific exclusionary practices. Several commenters reported that, even when statistics are available, they are often outdated and do not reflect current medical technology and treatment methods. Concern was expressed that adequate efforts are not made to distinguish those individuals who are high users of health care from individuals in the same diagnostic groups who may be low users of health care. One insurer reported that "hard data and actuarial statistics are not available to provide precise numerical justifications for every underwriting determination," but argued that decisions may be based on "logical principles generally accepted by actuarial science and fully consistent with state insurance laws." The commenter urged that the Department recognize the validity of information other than statistical data as a basis for insurance determinations.

The most frequent comment was a recommendation that the final regulation should require the insurance company to provide a copy of the actuarial data on which its actions are based when requested by the applicant. Such a requirement would be beyond anything contemplated by the Act or by Congress and has therefore not been included in the Department's final rule. Because the legislative history of the ADA clarifies that different treatment of individuals with disabilities in insurance may be justified by sound actuarial data, such actuarial data will be critical to any potential litigation on this issue. This information would presumably be obtainable in a court proceeding where the insurer's actuarial data was the basis for different treatment of persons with disabilities. In addition, under some State regulatory schemes, insurers may have to file such actuarial information with the State regulatory agency and this information may be obtainable at the State level.

A few commenters representing the insurance industry conceded that underwriting practices in life and health insurance are clearly covered, but argued that property and casualty insurance are not covered.

The Department sees no reason for this distinction. Although life and health insurance are the areas where the regulation will have its greatest application, the Act applies equally to unjustified discrimination in all types of insurance provided by public accommodations. A number of commenters, for example, reported difficulties in obtaining automobile insurance because of their disabilities, despite their having good driving records.

Section 36.213 Relationship of Subpart B to Subparts C and D

This section explains that subpart B sets forth the general principles of nondiscrimination applicable to all entities subject to this regulation, while subparts C and D provide guidance on the application of this part to specific situations. The specific provisions in subparts C and D, including the limitations on those provisions, control over the general provisions in circumstances where both specific and general provisions apply. Resort to the general provisions of subpart B is only appropriate where there are no applicable specific rules of guidance in subparts C or D. This interaction between the specific requirements and the general requirements operates with regard to contractual obligations as well.

One illustration of this principle is its application to the obligation of a public accommodation to provide access to services by removal of architectural barriers or by alternatives to barrier removal. The general requirement, established in subpart B by § 36.203, is that a public accommodation must provide its services to individuals with disabilities in the most integrated setting appropriate. This general requirement would appear to categorically prohibit "segregated" seating for persons in wheelchairs. Section 36.304, however, only requires removal of architectural barriers to the extent that removal is "readily achievable." If providing access to all areas of a restaurant, for example, would not be "readily achievable," a public accommodation may provide access to selected areas only. Also, § 36.305 provides that, where barrier removal is not readily achievable, a public accommodation may use alternative, readily achievable methods of making services available, such as curbside service or home delivery. Thus, in this manner, the specific requirements of §§ 36.304 and 36.305 control over the general requirement of § 36.203.

Subpart C—Specific Requirements

In general, subpart C implements the "specific prohibitions" that comprise section 302(b)(2) of the ADA. It also addresses the requirements of section 309 of the ADA regarding examinations and courses.

Section 36.301 Eligibility Criteria

Section 36.301 of the rule prohibits the imposition or application of eligibility criteria that screen out or tend to screen out an individual with a disability or any class of individuals with disabilities from fully and equally enjoying any goods, services, facilities, privileges, advantages, and accommodations, unless such criteria can be shown to be necessary for the provision of the goods, services, facilities, privileges, advantages, or accommodations being offered. This prohibition is based on section 302(b)(2)(A)(i) of the ADA.

It would violate this section to establish exclusive or segregative eligibility criteria that would bar, for example, all persons who are deaf from playing on a golf course or all individuals with cerebral palsy from attending a movie theater, or limit the seating of individuals with Down's syndrome to only particular areas of a restaurant. The wishes, tastes, or preferences of other customers may not be asserted to justify criteria that would exclude or segregate individuals with disabilities.

Section 36.301 also prohibits attempts by a public accommodation to unnecessarily identify the existence of a disability; for example, it would be a violation of this section for a retail store to require an individual to state on a credit application whether the applicant has epilepsy, mental illness, or any other disability, or to inquire unnecessarily whether an individual has HIV disease.

Section 36.301 also prohibits policies that unnecessarily impose requirements or burdens on individuals with disabilities that are not placed on others. For example, public accommodations may not require that an individual with a disability be accompanied by an attendant. As provided by § 36.306, however, a public accommodation is not required to provide services of a personal nature including assistance in toileting, eating, or dressing.

Paragraph (c) of § 36.301 provides that public accommodations may not place a surcharge on a particular individual with a disability or any group of individuals with disabilities to cover the costs of measures, such as the provision of auxiliary aids and services, barrier removal, alternatives to barrier removal, and reasonable modifications in policies, practices, and procedures, that are required to provide that individual or group with the nondiscriminatory treatment required by the Act or this part.

A number of commenters inquired as to whether deposits required for the use of auxiliary aids, such as assistive listening devices, are prohibited surcharges. It is the Department's view that reasonable, completely refundable, deposits are not to be considered surcharges prohibited by this section. Requiring deposits is an important means of ensuring the availability of equipment necessary to ensure compliance with the ADA.

Other commenters sought clarification as to whether § 36.301(c) prohibits professionals from charging for the additional time that it may take in certain cases to provide services to an individual with disabilities. The Department does not intend § 36.301(c) to prohibit professionals who bill on the basis of time from charging individuals with disabilities on that basis. However, fees may not be charged for the provision of auxiliary aids and services, barrier removal, alternatives to barrier removal, reasonable modifications in policies, practices, and procedures, or any other measures necessary to ensure compliance with the ADA.

Other commenters inquired as to whether day care centers may charge for extra services provided to individuals with disabilities. As stated above, § 36.302(c) is intended only to prohibit charges for measures necessary to achieve compliance with the ADA.

Another commenter asserted that charges may be assessed for home delivery provided as an alternative to barrier removal under § 36.305, when home delivery is provided to all customers for a fee. Charges for home delivery are permissible if home delivery is not considered an alternative to barrier removal. If the public accommodation offers an alternative, such as curb, carry-out, or sidewalk service for which no surcharge is assessed, then it may charge for home delivery in accordance with its standard pricing for home delivery.

In addition, § 36.301 prohibits the imposition of criteria that "tend to" screen out an individual with a disability. This concept, which is derived from current regulations under section 504 (see, e.g., 45 CFR 84.13), makes it discriminatory to impose policies or criteria that, while not creating a direct bar to individuals with disabilities, indirectly prevent or limit their ability to participate. For example, requiring presentation of a driver's license as the sole means of identification for purposes of paying by check would violate this section in situations where, for example, individuals with severe vision impairments or developmental disabilities or epilepsy are ineligible to receive a driver's license and the use of an alternative means of identification, such as another photo I.D. or credit card, is feasible.

A public accommodation may, however, impose neutral rules and criteria that screen out, or tend to screen out, individuals with disabilities, if the criteria are necessary for the safe operation of the public accommodation. Examples of safety qualifications that would be justifiable in appropriate circumstances would include height requirements for certain amusement park rides or a requirement that all participants in a recreational rafting expedition be able to meet a necessary level of swimming proficiency. Safety requirements must be based on actual risks and not on speculation, stereotypes, or generalizations about individuals with disabilities.

Section 36.302 Modifications in Policies, Practices, or Procedures

Section 36.302 of the rule prohibits the failure to make reasonable modifications in policies, practices, and procedures when such modifications may be necessary to afford any goods, services, facilities, privileges, advantages, or accommodations, unless the entity can demonstrate that making such modifications would fundamentally alter the nature of such goods, services, facilities, privileges, advantages, or accommodations. This prohibition is based on section 302(b)(2)(A)(ii) of the ADA.

For example, a parking facility would be required to modify a rule barring all vans or all vans with raised roofs, if an individual who uses a wheelchair-accessible van wishes to park in that facility, and if overhead structures are high enough to accommodate the height of the van. A department store may need to modify a policy of only permitting one person at a time in a dressing room, if an individual with mental retardation needs and requests assistance in dressing from a companion. Public accommodations may need to revise operational policies to ensure that services are available to individuals with disabilities. For instance, a hotel may need to adopt a policy of keeping an accessible room unoccupied until an individual with a disability arrives at the hotel, assuming the individual has properly reserved the room.

One example of application of this principle is specifically included in a new § 36.302(d) on check-out aisles. That paragraph provides that a store with check-out aisles must ensure that an adequate number of accessible check-out aisles is kept open during store hours, or must otherwise modify its policies and practices, in order to ensure that an equivalent level of convenient service is provided to individuals with disabilities as is provided to others. For example, if only one check-out aisle is accessible, and it is generally used for express service, one way of providing equivalent service is to allow persons with mobility impairments to make all of their purchases at that aisle. This principle also applies with respect to other accessible elements and services. For example, a particular bank may be in compliance with the accessibility guidelines for new construction incorporated in appendix A with respect to automated teller machines (ATM) at a new branch office by providing one accessible walk-up machine at that location, even though an adjacent walk-up ATM is not accessible and the drive-up ATM is not accessible. However, the bank would be in violation of this section if the accessible ATM was located in a lobby that was locked during evening hours while the drive-up ATM was available to customers without disabilities during those same hours. The bank would need to ensure that the accessible ATM was available to customers during the hours that any of the other ATM's was available.

A number of commenters inquired as to the relationship between this section and § 36.307, "Accessible or special goods." Under § 36.307, a public accommodation is not required to alter its inventory to include accessible or special goods that are designed for, or facilitate use by, individuals with disabilities. The rule enunciated in § 36.307 is consistent with the "fundamental alteration" defense to the reasonable modifications requirement of § 36.302. Therefore, § 36.302 would not require the inventory of goods provided by a public accommodation to be altered to include goods with accessibility features. For example, § 36.302 would not require a bookstore to stock Brailled books or order Brailled books, if it does not do so in the normal course of its business.

The rule does not require modifications to the legitimate areas of specialization of service providers. Section 36.302(b) provides that a public accommodation may refer an individual with a disability to another public accommodation, if that individual is seeking, or requires, treatment or services outside of the referring public accommodation's area of specialization, and if, in the normal course of its operations, the referring public accommodation would make a similar referral for an individual without a disability who seeks or requires the same treatment or services.

For example, it would not be discriminatory for a physician who specializes only in burn treatment to refer an individual who is deaf to another physician for treatment of an injury other than a burn injury. To require a physician to accept patients outside of his or her specialty would fundamentally alter the nature of the medical practice and, therefore, not be required by this section.

A clinic specializing exclusively in drug rehabilitation could similarly refuse to treat a person who is not a drug addict, but could not refuse to treat a person who is a drug addict simply because the patient tests positive for HIV. Conversely, a clinic that specializes in the treatment of individuals with HIV could refuse to treat an individual that does not have HIV, but could not refuse to treat a person for HIV infection simply because that person is also a drug addict.

Some commenters requested clarification as to how this provision would apply to situations where manifestations of the disability in question, itself, would raise complications requiring the expertise of a different practitioner. It is not the Department's intention in § 36.302(b) to prohibit a physician from referring an individual with a disability to another physician, if the disability itself creates specialized complications for the patient's health that the physician lacks the experience or knowledge to address (see Education and Labor report at 106).

Section 36.302(c)(1) requires that a public accommodation modify its policies, practices, or procedures to permit the use of a service animal by an individual with a disability in any area open to the general public. The term "service animal" is defined in § 36.104 to include guide dogs, signal dogs, or any other animal individually trained to provide assistance to an individual with a disability.

A number of commenters pointed to the difficulty of making the distinction required by the proposed rule between areas open to the general public and those that are not. The ambiguity and uncertainty surrounding these provisions has led the Department to adopt a single standard for all public accommodations.

Section 36.302(c)(1) of the final rule now provides that "[g]enerally, a public accommodation shall modify policies, practices, and procedures to permit the use of a service animal by an individual with a disability." This formulation reflects the general intent of Congress that public accommodations take the necessary steps to accommodate service animals and to ensure that individuals with disabilities are not separated from their service animals. It is intended that the broadest feasible access be provided to service animals in all places of public accommodation, including movie theaters, restaurants, hotels, retail stores, hospitals, and nursing homes (see Education and Labor report at 106; Judiciary report at 59). The section also acknowledges, however, that, in rare circumstances, accommodation of service animals may not be required because a fundamental alteration would result in the nature of the goods, services, facilities, privileges, or accommodations offered or provided, or the safe operation of the public accommodation would be jeopardized.

As specified in § 36.302(c)(2), the rule does not require a public accommodation to supervise or care for any service animal. If a service animal must be separated from an individual with a disability in order to avoid a fundamental alteration or a threat to safety, it is the responsibility of the individual with the disability to arrange for the care and supervision of the animal during the period of separation.

A museum would not be required by § 36.302 to modify a policy barring the touching of delicate works of art in order to enhance the participation of individuals who are blind, if the touching threatened the integrity of the work. Damage to a museum piece would clearly be a fundamental alteration that is not required by this section.

Section 36.303 Auxiliary Aids and Services.

Section 36.303 of the final rule requires a public accommodation to take such steps as may be necessary to ensure that no individual with a disability is excluded, denied services, segregated or otherwise treated differently than other individuals because of the absence of auxiliary aids and services, unless the public accommodation can demonstrate that taking such steps would fundamentally alter the nature of the goods, services, facilities, advantages, or accommodations being offered or would result in an undue burden. This requirement is based on section 302(b)(2)(A)(iii) of the ADA.

Implicit in this duty to provide auxiliary aids and services is the underlying obligation of a public accommodation to communicate effectively with its customers, clients, patients, or participants who have disabilities affecting hearing, vision, or speech. To give emphasis to this underlying obligation, § 36.303(c) of the rule incorporates language derived from section 504 regulations for federally conducted programs (see e.g., 28 CFR 39.160(a)) that requires that appropriate auxiliary aids and services be furnished to ensure that communication with persons with disabilities is as effective as communication with others.

Auxiliary aids and services include a wide range of services and devices for ensuring effective communication. Use of the most advanced technology is not required so long as effective communication is ensured. The Department's proposed § 36.303(b) provided a list of examples of auxiliary aids and services that was taken from the definition of auxiliary aids and services in section 3(1) of the ADA and was supplemented by examples from regulations implementing section 504 in federally conducted programs (see e.g., 28 CFR 39.103). A substantial number of commenters suggested that additional examples be added to this list. The Department has added several items to this list but wishes to clarify that the list is not an all-inclusive or exhaustive catalogue of possible or available auxiliary aids or services. It is not possible to provide an exhaustive list, and such an attempt would omit new devices that will become available with emerging technology.

The Department has added videotext displays, computer-aided transcription services, and open and closed captioning to the list of examples. Videotext displays have become an important means of accessing auditory communications through a public address system. Transcription services are used to relay aurally delivered material almost simultaneously in written form to persons who are deaf or hard of hearing. This technology is often used at conferences, conventions, and hearings. While the proposed rule expressly included television decoder equipment as an auxiliary aid or service, it did not mention captioning itself. The final rule rectifies this omission by mentioning both closed and open captioning.

In this section, the Department has changed the proposed rule's phrase, "orally delivered materials," to the phrase, "aurally delivered materials." This new phrase tracks the language in the definition of "auxiliary aids and services" in section 3 of the ADA and is meant to include nonverbal sounds and alarms and computer-generated speech.

Several persons and organizations requested that the Department replace the term "telecommunications devices for deaf persons" or "TDD's" with the term "text telephone." The Department has declined to do so. The Department is aware that the Architectural and Transportation Barriers Compliance Board has used the phrase "text telephone" in lieu of the statutory term "TDD" in its final accessibility guidelines. Title IV of the ADA, however, uses the term "Telecommunications Device for the Deaf," and the Department believes it would be inappropriate to abandon this statutory term at this time.

Paragraph (b)(2) lists examples of aids and services for making visually delivered materials accessible to persons with visual impairments. Many commenters proposed additional examples such as signage or mapping, audio description services, secondary auditory programs (SAP), telebraillers, and reading machines. While the Department declines to add these items to the list in the regulation, they may be considered appropriate auxiliary aids and services.

Paragraph (b)(3) refers to the acquisition or modification of equipment or devices. For example, tape players used for an audio-guided tour of a museum exhibit may require the addition of Brailled adhesive labels to the buttons on a reasonable number of the tape players to facilitate their use by individuals who are blind. Similarly, permanent or portable assistive listening systems for persons with hearing impairments may be required at a hotel conference center.

Several commenters suggested the addition of current technological innovations in microelectronics and computerized control systems (e.g., voice recognition systems, automatic dialing telephones, and infrared elevator and light control systems) to the list of auxiliary aids and services. The Department interprets auxiliary aids and services as those aids and services designed to provide effective communications, i.e., making aurally and visually delivered information available to persons with hearing, speech, and vision impairments. Methods of making services, programs, or activities accessible to, or usable by, individuals with mobility or manual dexterity impairments are addressed by other sections of this part, including the requirements for modifications in policies, practices, or procedures (§ 36.302), the elimination of existing architectural barriers (§ 36.304), and the provision of alternatives to barriers removal (§ 36.305).

Paragraph (b)(4) refers to other similar services and actions. Several commenters asked for clarification that "similar services and actions" include retrieving items from shelves, assistance in reaching a marginally accessible seat, pushing a barrier aside in order to provide an accessible route, or assistance in removing a sweater or coat. While retrieving an item from a shelf might be an "auxiliary aid or service" for a blind person who could not locate the item without assistance, it might be a readily achievable alternative to barrier removal for a person using a wheelchair who could not reach the shelf, or a reasonable modification to a self-service policy for an individual who lacked the ability to grasp the item. (Of course, a store would not be required to provide a personal shopper.) As explained above, auxiliary aids and services are those aids and services required to provide effective communications. Other forms of assistance are more appropriately addressed by other provisions of the final rule.

The auxiliary aid requirement is a flexible one. A public accommodation can choose among various alternatives as long as the result is effective communication. For example, a restaurant would not be required to provide menus in Braille for patrons who are blind, if the waiters in the restaurant are made available to read the menu. Similarly, a clothing boutique would not be required to have Brailled price tags if sales personnel provide price information orally upon request; and a bookstore would not be required to make available a sign language interpreter, because effective communication can be conducted by notepad.

A critical determination is what constitutes an effective auxiliary aid or service. The Department's proposed rule recommended that, in determining what auxiliary aid to use, the public accommodation consult with an individual before providing him or her with a particular auxiliary aid or service. This suggestion sparked a significant volume of public comment. Many persons with disabilities, particularly persons who are deaf or hard of hearing, recommended that the rule should require that public accommodations give "primary consideration" to the "expressed choice" of an individual with a disability. These commenters asserted that the proposed rule was inconsistent with congressional intent of the ADA, with the Department's proposed rule implementing title II of the ADA, and with longstanding interpretations of section 504 of the Rehabilitation Act.

Based upon a careful review of the ADA legislative history, the Department believes that Congress did not intend under title III to impose upon a public accommodation the requirement that it give primary consideration to the request of the individual with a disability. To the contrary, the legislative history demonstrates congressional intent to strongly encourage consulting with persons with disabilities. In its analysis of the ADA's auxiliary aids requirement for public accommodations, the House Education and Labor Committee stated that it "expects" that "public accommodation(s) will consult with the individual with a disability before providing a particular auxiliary aid or service" (Education and Labor report at 107). Some commenters also cited a different committee statement that used mandatory language as evidence of legislative intent to require primary consideration. However, this statement was made in the context of reasonable accommodations required by title I with respect to employment (Education and Labor report at 67). Thus, the Department finds that strongly encouraging consultation with persons with disabilities, in lieu of mandating primary consideration of their expressed choice, is consistent with congressional intent.

The Department wishes to emphasize that public accommodations must take steps necessary to ensure that an individual with a disability will not be excluded, denied services, segregated or otherwise treated differently from other individuals because of the use of inappropriate or ineffective auxiliary aids. In those situations requiring an interpreter, the public accommodations must secure the services of a qualified interpreter, unless an undue burden would result.

In the analysis of § 36.303(c) in the proposed rule, the Department gave as an example the situation where a note pad and written materials were insufficient to permit effective communication in a doctor's office when the matter to be decided was whether major surgery was necessary. Many commenters objected to this statement, asserting that it gave the impression that only decisions about major surgery would merit the provision of a sign language interpreter. The statement would, as the commenters also claimed, convey the impression to other public accommodations that written communications would meet the regulatory requirements in all but the most extreme situations. The Department, when using the example of major surgery, did not intend to limit the provision of interpreter services to the most extreme situations.

Other situations may also require the use of interpreters to ensure effective communication depending on the facts of the particular case. It is not difficult to imagine a wide range of communications involving areas such as health, legal matters, and finances that would be sufficiently lengthy or complex to require an interpreter for effective communication. In some situations, an effective alternative to use of a notepad or an interpreter may be the use of a computer terminal upon which the representative of the public accommodation and the customer or client can exchange typewritten messages.

Section 36.303(d) specifically addresses requirements for TDD's. Partly because of the availability of telecommunications relay services to be established under title IV of the ADA, § 36.303(d)(2) provides that a public accommodation is not required to use a telecommunication device for the deaf (TDD) in receiving or making telephone calls incident to its operations. Several commenters were concerned that relay services would not be sufficient to provide effective access in a number of situations. Commenters argued that relay systems (1) do not provide effective access to the automated systems that require the caller to respond by pushing a button on a touch tone phone, (2) cannot operate fast enough to convey messages on answering machines, or to permit a TDD user to leave a recorded message, and (3) are not appropriate for calling crisis lines relating to such matters as rape, domestic violence, child abuse, and drugs where confidentiality is a concern. The Department believes that it is more appropriate for the Federal Communications Commission to address these issues in its rulemaking under title IV.

A public accommodation is, however, required to make a TDD available to an individual with impaired hearing or speech, if it customarily offers telephone service to its customers, clients, patients, or participants on more than an incidental convenience basis. Where entry to a place of public accommodation requires use of a security entrance telephone, a TDD or other effective means of communication must be provided for use by an individual with impaired hearing or speech.

In other words, individual retail stores, doctors' offices, restaurants, or similar establishments are not required by this section to have TDD's, because TDD users will be able to make inquiries, appointments, or reservations with such establishments through the relay system established under title IV of the ADA. The public accommodation will likewise be able to contact TDD users through the relay system. On the other hand, hotels, hospitals, and other similar establishments that offer nondisabled individuals the opportunity to make outgoing telephone calls on more than an incidental convenience basis must provide a TDD on request.

Section 36.303(e) requires places of lodging that provide televisions in five or more guest rooms and hospitals to provide, upon request, a means for decoding closed captions for use by an individual with impaired hearing. Hotels should also provide a TDD or similar device at the front desk in order to take calls from guests who use TDD's in their rooms. In this way guests with hearing impairments can avail themselves of such hotel services as making inquiries of the front desk and ordering room service. The term "hospital" is used in its general sense and should be interpreted broadly.

Movie theaters are not required by § 36.303 to present open-captioned films. However, other public accommodations that impart verbal information through soundtracks on films, video tapes, or slide shows are required to make such information accessible to persons with hearing impairments. Captioning is one means to make the information accessible to individuals with disabilities.

The rule specifies that auxiliary aids and services include the acquisition or modification of equipment or devices. For example, tape players used for an audio-guided tour of a museum exhibit may require the addition of Brailled adhesive labels to the buttons on a reasonable number of the tape players to facilitate their use by individuals who are blind. Similarly, a hotel conference center may need to provide permanent or portable assistive listening systems for persons with hearing impairments.

As provided in § 36.303(f), a public accommodation is not required to provide any particular aid or service that would result either in a fundamental alteration in the nature of the goods, services, facilities, privileges, advantages, or accommodations offered or in an undue burden. Both of these statutory limitations are derived from existing regulations and caselaw under section 504 and are to be applied on a case-by-case basis (see, e.g., 28 CFR 39.160(d) and *Southeastern Community College v. Davis*, 442 U.S. 397 (1979)). Congress intended that "undue burden" under § 36.303 and "undue hardship," which is used in the employment provisions of title I of the ADA, should be determined on a case-by-case basis under the same standards and in light of the same factors (Judiciary report at 59). The rule, therefore, in accordance with the definition of undue hardship in section 101(10) of the ADA, defines undue burden as "significant difficulty or expense" (see §§ 36.104 and 36.303(a)) and requires that undue burden be determined in light of the factors listed in the definition in 36.104.

Consistent with regulations implementing section 504 in federally conducted programs (see, e.g., 28 CFR 39.160(d)), § 36.303(f) provides that the fact that the provision of a particular auxiliary aid or service would result in an undue burden does not relieve a public accommodation from the duty to furnish an alternative auxiliary aid or service, if available, that would not result in such a burden.

Section 36.303(g) of the proposed rule has been deleted from this section and included in a new § 36.306. That new section continues to make clear that the auxiliary aids requirement does not mandate the provision of individually prescribed devices, such as prescription eyeglasses or hearing aids.

The costs of compliance with the requirements of this section may not be financed by surcharges limited to particular individuals with disabilities or any group of individuals with disabilities (§ 36.301(c)).

Section 36.304 Removal of Barriers

Section 36.304 requires the removal of architectural barriers and communication barriers that are structural in nature in existing facilities, where such removal is readily achievable, i.e., easily accomplishable and able to be carried out without much difficulty or expense. This requirement is based on section

302(b)(2)(A)(iv) of the ADA.

A number of commenters interpreted the phrase "communication barriers that are structural in nature" broadly to encompass the provision of communications devices such as TDD's, telephone handset amplifiers, assistive listening devices, and digital check-out displays. The statute, however, as read by the Department, limits the application of the phrase "communications barriers that are structural in nature" to those barriers that are an integral part of the physical structure of a facility. In addition to the communications barriers posed by permanent signage and alarm systems noted by Congress (see Education and Labor report at 110), the Department would also include among the communications barriers covered by § 36.304 the failure to provide adequate sound buffers, and the presence of physical partitions that hamper the passage of sound waves between employees and customers. Given that § 36.304's proper focus is on the removal of physical barriers, the Department believes that the obligation to provide communications equipment and devices such as TDD's, telephone handset amplifiers, assistive listening devices, and digital check-out displays is more appropriately determined by the requirements for auxiliary aids and services under § 36.303 (see Education and Labor report at 107-108). The obligation to remove communications barriers that are structural in nature under § 36.304, of course, is independent of any obligation to provide auxiliary aids and services under § 36.303.

The statutory provision also requires the readily achievable removal of certain barriers in existing vehicles and rail passenger cars. This transportation requirement is not included in § 36.304, but rather in § 36.310(b) of the rule.

In striking a balance between guaranteeing access to individuals with disabilities and recognizing the legitimate cost concerns of businesses and other private entities, the ADA establishes different standards for existing facilities and new construction. In existing facilities, which are the subject of § 36.304, where retrofitting may prove costly, a less rigorous degree of accessibility is required than in the case of new construction and alterations (see §§ 36.401-36.406) where accessibility can be more conveniently and economically incorporated in the initial stages of design and construction.

For example, a bank with existing automatic teller machines (ATM's) would have to remove barriers to the use of the ATM's, if it is readily achievable to do so. Whether or not it is necessary to take actions such as ramping a few steps or raising or lowering an ATM would be determined by whether the actions can be accomplished easily and without much difficulty or expense.

On the other hand, a newly constructed bank with ATM's would be required by § 36.401 to have an ATM that is "readily accessible to and usable by" persons with disabilities in accordance with accessibility guidelines incorporated under § 36.406.

The requirement to remove architectural barriers includes the removal of physical barriers of any kind. For example, § 36.304 requires the removal, when readily achievable, of barriers caused by the location of temporary or movable structures, such as furniture, equipment, and display racks. In order to provide access to individuals who use wheelchairs, for example, restaurants may need to rearrange tables and chairs, and department stores may need to reconfigure display racks and shelves. As stated in § 36.304(f), such actions are not readily achievable to the extent that they would result in a significant loss of selling or serving space. If the widening of all aisles in selling or serving areas is not readily achievable, then selected widening should be undertaken to maximize the amount of merchandise or the number of tables accessible to individuals who use wheelchairs. Access to goods and services provided in any remaining inaccessible areas must be made available through alternative methods to barrier removal, as required by § 36.305.

Because the purpose of title III of the ADA is to ensure that public accommodations are accessible to their customers, clients, or patrons (as opposed to their employees, who are the focus of title I), the obligation to remove barriers under § 36.304 does not extend to areas of a facility that are used exclusively as employee work areas.

Section 36.304(b) provides a wide-ranging list of the types of modest measures that may be taken to remove barriers and that are likely to be readily achievable. The list includes examples of measures, such as adding raised letter markings on elevator control buttons and installing flashing alarm lights, that would be used to remove communications barriers that are structural in nature. It is not an exhaustive list, but merely an illustrative one. Moreover, the inclusion of a measure on this list does not mean that it is readily achievable in all cases. Whether or not any of these measures is readily achievable is to be determined on a case-by-case basis in light of the particular circumstances presented and the factors listed in the definition of readily achievable (§ 36.104).

A public accommodation generally would not be required to remove a barrier to physical access posed by a flight of steps, if removal would require extensive ramping or an elevator. Ramping a single step, however, will likely be readily achievable, and ramping several steps will in many circumstances also be readily achievable. The readily achievable standard does not require barrier removal that requires extensive restructuring or burdensome expense. Thus, where it is not readily achievable to do, the ADA would not require a restaurant to provide access to a restroom reachable only by a flight of stairs.

Like § 36.405, this section permits deference to the national interest in preserving significant historic structures. Barrier removal would not be considered "readily achievable" if it would threaten or destroy the historic significance of a building or facility that is eligible for listing in the National Register of Historic Places under the National Historic Preservation Act (16 U.S.C. 470, et seq.), or is designated as historic under State or local law.

The readily achievable defense requires a less demanding level of exertion by a public accommodation than does the undue burden defense to the auxiliary aids requirements of § 36.303. In that sense, it can be characterized as a "lower" standard than the undue burden standard. The readily achievable defense is also less demanding than the undue hardship defense in section 102(b)(5) of the ADA, which limits the obligation to make reasonable accommodation in employment. Barrier removal measures that are not easily accomplishable and are not able to be carried out without much difficulty or expense are not required under the readily achievable standard, even if they do not impose an undue burden or an undue hardship.

Section 36.304(f)(1) of the proposed rule, which stated that "barrier removal is not readily achievable if it would result in significant loss of profit or significant loss of efficiency of operation," has been deleted from the final rule. Many commenters objected to this provision because it impermissibly introduced the notion of profit into a statutory standard that did not include it. Concern was expressed that, in order for an action not to be considered readily achievable, a public accommodation would inappropriately have to show, for example, not only that the action could not be done without "much difficulty or expense", but that a significant loss of profit would result as well. In addition, some commenters asserted use of the word "significant," which is used in the definition of undue hardship under title I (the standard for interpreting the meaning of undue burden as a defense to title III's auxiliary aids requirements) (see §§ 36.104, 36.303(f)), blurs the fact that the readily achievable standard requires a lower level of effort on the part of a public accommodation than does the undue burden standard.

The obligation to engage in readily achievable barrier removal is a continuing one. Over time, barrier removal that initially was not readily achievable may later be required because of changed circumstances. Many commenters expressed support for the Department's position that the obligation to comply with § 36.304 is continuing in nature. Some urged that the rule require public accommodations to assess their compliance on at least an annual basis in light of changes in resources and other factors that would be relevant to determining what barrier removal measures would be readily achievable.

Although the obligation to engage in readily achievable barrier removal is clearly a continuing duty, the Department has declined to establish any independent requirement for an annual assessment or self-evaluation. It is best left to the public accommodations subject to § 36.304 to establish policies to assess compliance that are appropriate to the particular circumstances faced by the wide range of public accommodations covered by the ADA. However, even in the absence of an explicit regulatory requirement for periodic self-evaluations, the Department still urges public accommodations to establish procedures for an ongoing assessment of their compliance with the ADA's barrier removal requirements. The Department recommends that this process include appropriate consultation with individuals with disabilities or organizations representing them. A serious effort at self-assessment and consultation can diminish the threat of litigation and save resources by identifying the most efficient means of providing required access.

The Department has been asked for guidance on the best means for public accommodations to comply voluntarily with this section. Such information is more appropriately part of the Department's technical assistance effort and will be forthcoming over the next several months. The Department recommends, however, the development of an implementation plan designed to achieve compliance with the ADA's barrier removal requirements before they become effective on January 26, 1992. Such a plan, if appropriately designed and diligently executed, could serve as evidence of a good faith effort to comply with the requirements of § 36.104. In developing an implementation plan for readily achievable barrier removal, a public accommodation should consult with local organizations representing persons with disabilities and solicit their suggestions for cost-effective means of making individual places of public accommodation accessible. Such organizations may also be helpful in allocating scarce resources and establishing priorities. Local associations of businesses may want to encourage this process and serve as the forum for discussions on the local level between disability rights organizations and local businesses.

Section 36.304(c) recommends priorities for public accommodations in removing barriers in existing facilities. Because the resources available for barrier removal may not be adequate to remove all existing barriers at any given time, § 36.304(c) suggests priorities for determining which types of barriers should be mitigated or eliminated first. The purpose of these priorities is to facilitate long-term business planning and to maximize, in light of limited resources, the degree of effective access that will result from any given level of expenditure.

Although many commenters expressed support for the concept of establishing priorities, a significant number objected to their mandatory nature in the proposed rule. The Department shares the concern of these commenters that mandatory priorities would increase the likelihood of litigation and inappropriately reduce the discretion of public accommodations to determine the most effective mix of barrier removal measures to undertake in particular circumstances. Therefore, in the final rule the priorities are no longer mandatory.

In response to comments that the priorities failed to address communications issues, the Department wishes to emphasize that the priorities encompass the removal of communications barriers that are structural in nature. It would be counter to the ADA's carefully wrought statutory scheme to include in this provision the wide range of communication devices that are required by the ADA's provisions on auxiliary aids and services. The final rule explicitly includes Brailled and raised letter signage and visual alarms among the examples of steps to remove barriers provided in § 36.304(c)(2).

Section 36.304(c)(1) places the highest priority on measures that will enable individuals with disabilities to physically enter a place of public accommodation. This priority on "getting through the door" recognizes that providing actual physical access to a facility from public sidewalks, public transportation, or parking is generally preferable to any alternative arrangements in terms of both business efficiency and the dignity of individuals with disabilities.

The next priority, which is established in § 36.304(c)(2), is for measures that provide access to those areas of a place of public accommodation where goods and services are made available to the public. For example, in a hardware store, to the extent that it is readily achievable to do so, individuals with disabilities should be given access not only to assistance at the front desk, but also access, like that available to other customers, to the retail display areas of the store.

The Department agrees with those commenters who argued that access to the areas where goods and services are provided is generally more important than the provision of restrooms. Therefore, the final rule reverses priorities two and three of the proposed rule in order to give lower priority to accessible restrooms. Consequently, the third priority in the final rule (§ 36.304(c)(3)) is for measures to provide access to restroom facilities and the last priority is placed on any remaining measures required to remove barriers.

Section 36.304(d) requires that measures taken to remove barriers under § 36.304 be subject to subpart D's requirements for alterations (except for the path of travel requirements in § 36.403). It only permits deviations from the subpart D requirements when compliance with those requirements is not readily achievable. In such cases, § 36.304(d) permits measures to be taken that do not fully comply with the subpart D requirements, so long as the measures do not pose a significant risk to the health or safety of individuals with disabilities or others.

This approach represents a change from the proposed rule which stated that "readily achievable" measures taken solely to remove barriers under § 36.304 are exempt from the alterations requirements of subpart D. The intent of the proposed rule was to maximize the flexibility of public accommodations in undertaking barrier removal by allowing deviations from the technical standards of subpart D. It was thought that allowing slight deviations would provide access and release additional resources for expanding the amount of barrier removal that could be obtained under the readily achievable standard.

Many commenters, however, representing both businesses and individuals with disabilities, questioned this approach because of the likelihood that unsafe or ineffective measures would be taken in the absence of the subpart D standards for alterations as a reference point. Some advocated a rule requiring strict compliance with the subpart D standard.

The Department in the final rule has adopted the view of many commenters that (1) public accommodations should in the first instance be required to comply with the subpart D standards for alterations where it is readily achievable to do so and (2) safe, readily achievable measures must be taken when compliance with the subpart D standards is not readily achievable. Reference to the subpart D standards in this manner will promote certainty and good design at the same time that permitting slight deviations will expand the amount of barrier removal that may be achieved under

§ 36.304.

Because of the inconvenience to individuals with disabilities and the safety problems involved in the use of portable ramps, § 36.304(e) permits the use of a portable ramp to comply with § 36.304(a) only when installation of a permanent ramp is not readily achievable. In order to promote safety, § 36.304(e) requires that due consideration be given to the incorporation of features such as nonslip surfaces, railings, anchoring, and strength of materials in any portable ramp that is used.

Temporary facilities brought in for use at the site of a natural disaster are subject to the barrier removal requirements of § 36.304.

A number of commenters requested clarification regarding how to determine when a public accommodation has discharged its obligation to remove barriers in existing facilities. For example, is a hotel required by § 36.304 to remove barriers in all of its guest rooms? Or is some lesser percentage adequate? A new paragraph (g) has been added to § 36.304 to address this issue. The Department believes that the degree of barrier removal required under § 36.304 may be less, but certainly would not be required to exceed, the standards for alterations under the ADA Accessibility Guidelines incorporated by subpart D of this part (ADAAG). The ADA's requirements for readily achievable barrier removal in existing facilities are intended to be substantially less rigorous than those for new construction and alterations. It, therefore, would be obviously inappropriate to require actions under § 36.304 that would exceed the ADAAG requirements. Hotels, then, in order to satisfy the requirements of § 36.304, would not be required to remove barriers in a higher percentage of rooms than required by ADAAG. If relevant standards for alterations are not provided in ADAAG, then reference should be made to the standards for new construction.

Section 36.305 Alternatives to Barrier Removal

Section 36.305 specifies that where a public accommodation can demonstrate that removal of a barrier is not readily achievable, the public accommodation must make its goods, services, facilities, privileges, advantages, or accommodations available through alternative methods, if such methods are readily achievable. This requirement is based on section 302(b)(2)(A)(v) of the ADA.

For example, if it is not readily achievable for a retail store to raise, lower, or remove shelves or to rearrange display racks to provide accessible aisles, the store must, if readily achievable, provide a clerk or take other alternative measures to retrieve inaccessible merchandise. Similarly, if it is not readily achievable to ramp a long flight of stairs leading to the front door of a restaurant or a pharmacy, the restaurant or the pharmacy must take alternative measures, if readily achievable, such as providing curb service or home delivery. If, within a restaurant, it is not readily achievable to remove physical barriers to a certain section of a restaurant, the restaurant must, where it is readily achievable to do so, offer the same menu in an accessible area of the restaurant.

Where alternative methods are used to provide access, a public accommodation may not charge an individual with a disability for the costs associated with the alternative method (see § 36.301(c)). Further analysis of the issue of charging for alternative measures may be found in the preamble discussion of § 36.301(c).

In some circumstances, because of security considerations, some alternative methods may not be readily achievable. The rule does not require a cashier to leave his or her post to retrieve items for individuals with disabilities, if there are no other employees on duty.

Section 36.305(c) of the proposed rule has been deleted and the requirements have been included in a new § 36.306. That section makes clear that the alternative methods requirement does not mandate the provision of personal devices, such as wheelchairs, or services of a personal nature.

In the final rule, § 36.305(c) provides specific requirements regarding alternatives to barrier removal in multiscreen cinemas. In some situations, it may not be readily achievable to remove enough barriers to provide access to all of the theaters of a multiscreen cinema. If that is the case, § 36.305(c) requires the cinema to establish a film rotation schedule that provides reasonable access for individuals who use wheelchairs to films being presented by the cinema. It further requires that reasonable notice be provided to the public as to the location and time of accessible showings. Methods for providing notice include appropriate use of the international accessibility symbol in a cinema's print advertising and the addition of accessibility information to a cinema's recorded telephone information line.

Section 36.306 Personal Devices and Services

The final rule includes a new § 36.306, entitled "Personal devices and services." Section 36.306 of the proposed rule, "Readily achievable and undue burden: Factors to be considered," was deleted for the reasons described in the preamble discussion of the definition of the term "readily achievable" in § 36.104. In place of §§ 36.303(g) and 36.305(c) of the proposed rule, which addressed the issue of personal devices and services in the contexts of auxiliary aids and alternatives to barrier removal, § 36.306 provides a general statement that the regulation does not require the provision of personal devices and services. This section states that a public accommodation is not required to provide its customers, clients, or participants with personal devices, such as wheelchairs; individually prescribed devices, such as prescription eyeglasses or hearing aids; or services of a personal nature including assistance in eating, toileting, or dressing.

This statement serves as a limitation on all the requirements of the regulation. The personal devices and services limitation was intended to have general application in the proposed rule in all contexts where it was relevant. The final rule, therefore, clarifies this point by including a general provision that will explicitly apply not just to auxiliary aids and services and alternatives to barrier removal, but across-the-board to include such relevant areas as modifications in policies, practices, and procedures (§ 36.302) and examinations and courses (§ 36.309), as well.

The Department wishes to clarify that measures taken as alternatives to barrier removal, such as retrieving items from shelves or providing curb service or home delivery, are not to be considered personal services. Similarly, minimal actions that may be required as modifications in policies, practices, or procedures under § 36.302, such as a waiter's removing the cover from a customer's straw, a kitchen's cutting up food into smaller pieces, or a bank's filling out a deposit slip, are not services of a personal nature within the meaning of § 36.306. (Of course, such modifications may be required under § 36.302 only if they are "reasonable.") Similarly, this section does not preclude the short-term loan of personal receivers that are part of an assistive listening system.

Of course, if personal services are customarily provided to the customers or clients of a public accommodation, e.g., in a hospital or senior citizen center, then these personal services should also be provided to persons with disabilities using the public accommodation.

Section 36.307 Accessible or Special Goods.

Section 36.307 establishes that the rule does not require a public accommodation to alter its inventory to include accessible or special goods with accessibility features that are designed for, or facilitate use by, individuals with disabilities. As specified in § 36.307(c), accessible or special goods include such items as Brailled versions of books, books on audio-cassettes, closed captioned video tapes, special sizes or lines of clothing, and special foods to meet particular dietary needs.

The purpose of the ADA's public accommodations requirements is to ensure accessibility to the goods offered by a public accommodation, not to alter the nature or mix of goods that the public accommodation has typically provided. In other words, a bookstore, for example, must make its facilities and sales operations accessible to individuals with disabilities, but is not required to stock Brailled or large print books. Similarly, a video store must make its facilities and rental operations accessible, but is not required to stock closed-captioned video tapes. The Department has been made aware, however, that the most recent titles in video-tape rental establishments are, in fact, closed captioned.

Although a public accommodation is not required by § 36.307(a) to modify its inventory, it is required by § 36.307(b), at the request of an individual with disabilities, to order accessible or special goods that it does not customarily maintain in stock if, in the normal course of its operation, it makes special orders for unstocked goods, and if the accessible or special goods can be obtained from a supplier with whom the public accommodation customarily does business. For example, a clothing store would be required to order specially-sized clothing at the request of an individual with a disability, if it customarily makes special orders for clothing that it does not keep in stock, and if the clothing can be obtained from one of the store's customary suppliers.

One commenter asserted that the proposed rule could be interpreted to require a store to special order accessible or special goods of all types, even if only one type is specially ordered in the normal course of its business. The Department, however, intends for § 36.307(b) to require special orders only of those particular types of goods for which a public accommodation normally makes special orders. For example, a book and recording store would not have to specially order Brailled books if, in the normal course of its business, it only specially orders recordings and not books.

Section 36.308 Seating in Assembly Areas.

Section 36.308 establishes specific requirements for removing barriers to physical access in assembly areas, which include such facilities as theaters, concert halls, auditoriums, lecture halls, and conference rooms. This section does not address the provision of auxiliary aids or the removal of communications barriers that are structural in nature. These communications requirements are the focus of other provisions of the regulation (see §§ 36.303-36.304).

Individuals who use wheelchairs historically have been relegated to inferior seating in the back of assembly areas separate from accompanying family members and friends. The provisions of § 36.308 are intended to promote integration and equality in seating.

In some instances it may not be readily achievable for auditoriums or theaters to remove seats to allow individuals with wheelchairs to sit next to accompanying family members or friends. In these situations, the final rule retains the requirement that the public accommodation provide portable chairs or other means to allow the accompanying individuals to sit with the persons in wheelchairs. Persons in wheelchairs should have the same opportunity to enjoy movies, plays, and similar events with their families and friends, just as other patrons do. The final rule specifies that portable chairs or other means to permit family members or companions to sit with individuals who use wheelchairs must be provided only when it is readily achievable to do so.

In order to facilitate seating of wheelchair users who wish to transfer to existing seating, paragraph (a)(1) of the final rule adds a requirement that, to the extent readily achievable, a reasonable number of seats with removable aisle-side armrests must be provided. Many persons in wheelchairs are able to transfer to existing seating with this relatively minor modification. This solution avoids the potential safety hazard created by the use of portable chairs and fosters integration. The final ADA Accessibility Guidelines incorporated by subpart D (ADAAG) also add a requirement regarding aisle seating that was not in the proposed guidelines. In situations when a person in a wheelchair transfers to existing seating, the public accommodation shall provide assistance in handling the wheelchair of the patron with the disability.

Likewise, consistent with ADAAG, the final rule adds in § 36.308(a)(1)(ii)(B) a requirement that, to the extent readily achievable, wheelchair seating provide lines of sight and choice of admission prices comparable to those for members of the general public.

Finally, because Congress intended that the requirements for barrier removal in existing facilities be substantially less rigorous than those required for new construction and alterations, the final rule clarifies in § 36.308(a)(3) that in no event can the requirements for existing facilities be interpreted to exceed the standards for alterations under ADAAG. For example, § 4.33 of ADAAG only requires wheelchair spaces to be provided in more than one location when the seating capacity of the assembly area exceeds 300. Therefore, paragraph (a) of § 36.308 may not be interpreted to require readily achievable dispersal of wheelchair seating in assembly areas with 300 or fewer seats. Similarly, § 4.1.3(19) of ADAAG requires six accessible wheelchair locations in an assembly area with 301 to 500 seats. The reasonable number of wheelchair locations required by paragraph (a), therefore, may be less than six, but may not be interpreted to exceed six.

Proposed Section 36.309
Purchase of Furniture and Equipment

Section 36.309 of the proposed rule would have required that newly purchased furniture or equipment made available for use at a place of public accommodation be accessible, to the extent such furniture or equipment is available, unless this requirement would fundamentally alter the goods, services, facilities, privileges, advantages, or accommodations offered, or would not be readily achievable. Proposed § 36.309 has been omitted from the final rule because the Department has determined that its requirements are more properly addressed under other sections, and because there are currently no appropriate accessibility standards addressing many types of furniture and equipment.

Some types of equipment will be required to meet the accessibility requirements of subpart D. For example, ADAAG establishes technical and scoping requirements in new construction and alterations for automated teller machines and telephones. Purchase or modification of equipment is required in certain instances by the provisions in §§ 36.201 and 36.202. For example, an arcade may need to provide accessible video machines in order to ensure full and equal enjoyment of the facilities and to provide an opportunity to participate in the services and facilities it provides. The barrier removal requirements of § 36.304 will apply as well to furniture and equipment (lowering shelves, rearranging furniture, adding Braille labels to a vending machine).

Section 36.309 Examinations and Courses

Section 36.309(a) sets forth the general rule that any private entity that offers examinations or courses related to applications, licensing, certification, or credentialing for secondary or postsecondary education, professional, or trade purposes shall offer such examinations or courses in a place and manner accessible to persons with disabilities or offer alternative accessible arrangements for such individuals.

Paragraph (a) restates section 309 of the Americans with Disabilities Act. Section 309 is intended to fill the gap that is created when licensing, certification, and other testing authorities are not covered by section 504 of the Rehabilitation Act or title II of the ADA. Any such authority that is covered by section 504, because of the receipt of Federal money, or by title II, because it is a function of a State or local government, must make all of its programs accessible to persons with disabilities, which includes physical access as well as modifications in the way the test is administered, e.g., extended time, written instructions, or assistance of a reader.

Many licensing, certification, and testing authorities are not covered by section 504, because no Federal money is received; nor are they covered by title II of the ADA because they are not State or local agencies. However, States often require the licenses provided by such authorities in order for an individual to practice a particular profession or trade. Thus, the provision was included in the ADA in order to assure that persons with disabilities are not foreclosed from educational, professional, or trade opportunities because an examination or course is conducted in an inaccessible site or without needed modifications.

As indicated in the "Application" section of this part (§ 36.102), § 36.309 applies to any private entity that offers the specified types of examinations or courses. This is consistent with section 309 of the Americans with Disabilities Act, which states that the requirements apply to "any person" offering examinations or courses.

The Department received a large number of comments on this section, reflecting the importance of ensuring that the key gateways to education and employment are open to individuals with disabilities. The most frequent comments were objections to the fundamental alteration and undue burden provisions in §§ 36.309 (b)(3) and (c)(3) and to allowing courses and examinations to be provided through alternative accessible arrangements, rather than in an integrated setting.

Although section 309 of the Act does not refer to a fundamental alteration or undue burden limitation, those limitations do appear in section 302(b)(2)(A)(iii) of the Act, which establishes the obligation of public accommodations to provide auxiliary aids and services. The Department, therefore, included it in the paragraphs of § 36.309 requiring the provision of auxiliary aids. One commenter argued that similar limitations should apply to all of the requirements of § 36.309, but the Department did not consider this extension appropriate.

Commenters who objected to permitting "alternative accessible arrangements" argued that such arrangements allow segregation and should not be permitted, unless they are the least restrictive available alternative, for example, for someone who cannot leave home. Some commenters made a distinction between courses, where interaction is an important part of the educational experience, and examinations, where it may be less important. Because the statute specifically authorizes alternative accessible arrangements as a method of meeting the requirements of section 309, the Department has not adopted this suggestion. The Department notes, however, that, while examinations of the type covered by § 36.309 may not be covered elsewhere in the regulation, courses will generally be offered in a "place of education," which is included in the definition of "place of public accommodation" in § 36.104, and, therefore, will be subject to the integrated setting requirement of § 36.203.

Section 36.309(b) sets forth specific requirements for examinations. Examinations covered by this section would include a bar exam or the Scholastic Aptitude Test prepared by the Educational Testing Service. Paragraph (b)(1) is adopted from the Department of Education's section 504 regulation on admission tests to postsecondary educational programs (34 CFR 104.42(b)(3)). Paragraph (b)(1)(i) requires that a private entity offering an examination covered by the section must assure that the examination is selected and administered so as to best ensure that the examination accurately reflects an individual's aptitude or achievement level or other factor the examination purports to measure, rather than reflecting the individual's impaired sensory, manual, or speaking skills (except where those skills are the factors that the examination purports to measure).

Paragraph (b)(1)(ii) requires that any examination specially designed for individuals with disabilities be offered as often and in as timely a manner as other examinations. Some commenters noted that persons with disabilities may be required to travel long distances when the locations for examinations for individuals with disabilities are limited, for example, to only one city in a State instead of a variety of cities. The Department has therefore revised this paragraph to add a requirement that such examinations be offered at locations that are as convenient as the location of other examinations.

Commenters representing organizations that

administer tests wanted to be able to require individuals with disabilities to provide advance notice and appropriate documentation, at the applicants' expense, of their disabilities and of any modifications or aids that would be required. The Department agrees that such requirements are permissible, provided that they are not unreasonable and that the deadline for such notice is no earlier than the deadline for others applying to take the examination. Requiring individuals with disabilities to file earlier applications would violate the requirement that examinations designed for individuals with disabilities be offered in as timely a manner as other examinations.

Examiners may require evidence that an applicant is entitled to modifications or aids as required by this section, but requests for documentation must be reasonable and must be limited to the need for the modification or aid requested. Appropriate documentation might include a letter from a physician or other professional, or evidence of a prior diagnosis or accommodation, such as eligibility for a special education program. The applicant may be required to bear the cost of providing such documentation, but the entity administering the examination cannot charge the applicant for the cost of any modifications or auxiliary aids, such as interpreters, provided for the examination.

Paragraph (b)(1)(iii) requires that examinations be administered in facilities that are accessible to individuals with disabilities or alternative accessible arrangements are made.

Paragraph (b)(2) gives examples of modifications to examinations that may be necessary in order to comply with this section. These may include providing more time for completion of the examination or a change in the manner of giving the examination, e.g., reading the examination to the individual.

Paragraph (b)(3) requires the provision of auxiliary aids and services, unless the private entity offering the examination can demonstrate that offering a particular auxiliary aid would fundamentally alter the examination or result in an undue burden. Examples of auxiliary aids include taped examinations, interpreters or other effective methods of making aurally delivered materials available to individuals with hearing impairments, readers for individuals with visual impairments or learning disabilities, and other similar services and actions. The suggestion that individuals with learning disabilities may need readers is included, although it does not appear in the Department of Education regulation, because, in fact, some individuals with learning disabilities have visual perception problems and would benefit from a reader.

Many commenters pointed out the importance of ensuring that modifications provide the individual with a disability an equal opportunity to demonstrate his or her knowledge or ability. For example, a reader who is unskilled or lacks knowledge of specific terminology used in the examination may be unable to convey the information in the questions or to follow the applicant's instructions effectively. Commenters pointed out that, for persons with visual impairments who read Braille, Braille provides the closest functional equivalent to a printed test. The Department has, therefore, added Brailled examinations to the examples of auxiliary aids and services that may be required. For similar reasons, the Department also added to the list of examples of auxiliary aids and services large print examinations and answer sheets; "qualified" readers; and transcribers to write answers.

A commenter suggested that the phrase "fundamentally alter the examination" in this paragraph of the proposed rule be revised to more accurately reflect the function affected. In the final rule the Department has substituted the phrase "fundamentally alter the measurement of the skills or knowledge the examination is intended to test."

Paragraph (b)(4) gives examples of alternative accessible arrangements. For instance, the private entity might be required to provide the examination at an individual's home with a proctor. Alternative arrangements must provide conditions for individuals with disabilities that are comparable to the conditions under which other individuals take the examinations. In other words, an examination cannot be offered to an individual with a disability in a cold, poorly lit basement, if other individuals are given the examination in a warm, well lit classroom.

Some commenters who provide examinations for licensing or certification for particular occupations or professions urged that they be permitted to refuse to provide modifications or aids for persons seeking to take the examinations if those individuals, because of their disabilities, would be unable to perform the essential functions of the profession or occupation for which the examination is given, or unless the disability is reasonably determined in advance as not being an obstacle to certification. The Department has not changed its rule based on this comment. An examination is one stage of a licensing or certification process. An individual should not be barred from attempting to pass that stage of the process merely because he or she might be unable to meet other requirements of the process. If the examination is not the first stage of the qualification process, an applicant may be required to complete the earlier stages prior to being admitted to the examination. On the other hand, the applicant may not be denied admission to the examination on the basis of doubts about his or her abilities to meet requirements that the examination is not designed to test.

Paragraph (c) sets forth specific requirements for courses. Paragraph (c)(1) contains the general rule that any course covered by this section must be modified to ensure that the place and manner in which the course is given is accessible. Paragraph (c)(2) gives examples of possible modifications that might be required, including extending the time permitted for completion of the course, permitting oral rather than written delivery of an assignment by a person with a visual impairment, or adapting the manner in which the course is conducted (i.e., providing cassettes of class handouts to an individual with a visual impairment). In response to comments, the Department has added to the examples in paragraph (c)(2) specific reference to distribution of course materials. If course materials are published and available from other sources, the entity offering the course may give advance notice of what materials will be used so as to allow an individual to obtain them in Braille or on tape but materials provided by the course offerer must be made available in alternative formats for individuals with disabilities.

In language similar to that of paragraph (b), paragraph (c)(3) requires auxiliary aids and services, unless a fundamental alteration or undue burden would result, and paragraph (c)(4) requires that courses be administered in accessible facilities. Paragraph (c)(5) gives examples of alternative accessible arrangements. These may include provision of the course through videotape, cassettes, or prepared notes. Alternative arrangements must provide comparable conditions to those provided to others, including similar lighting, room temperature, and the like. An entity offering a variety of courses, to fulfill continuing education requirements for a profession, for example, may not limit the selection or choice of courses available to individuals with disabilities.

Section 36.310 Transportation Provided by Public Accommodations

Section 36.310 contains specific provisions relating to public accommodations that provide transportation to their clients or customers. This section has been substantially revised in order to coordinate the requirements of this section with the requirements applicable to these transportation systems that will be contained in the regulations issued by the Secretary of Transportation pursuant to section 306 of the ADA, to be codified at 49 CFR part 37. The Department notes that, although the responsibility for issuing regulations applicable to transportation systems operated by public accommodations is divided between this Department and the Department of Transportation, enforcement authority is assigned only to the Department of Justice.

The Department received relatively few comments on this section of the proposed rule. Most of the comments addressed issues that are not specifically addressed in this part, such as the standards for accessible vehicles and the procedure for determining whether equivalent service is provided. Those standards will be contained in the regulation issued by the Department of Transportation. Other commenters raised questions about the types of transportation that will be subject to this section. In response to these inquiries, the Department has revised the list of examples contained in the regulation.

Paragraph (a)(1) states the general rule that covered public accommodations are subject to all of the specific provisions of subparts B, C, and D, except as provided in § 36.310. Examples of operations covered by the requirements are listed in paragraph (a)(2). The stated examples include hotel and motel airport shuttle services, customer shuttle bus services operated by private companies and shopping centers, student transportation, and shuttle operations of recreational facilities such as stadiums, zoos, amusement parks, and ski resorts. This brief list is not exhaustive. The section applies to any fixed route or demand responsive transportation system operated by a public accommodation for the benefit of its clients or customers. The section does not apply to transportation services provided only to employees. Employee transportation will be subject to the regulations issued by the Equal Employment Opportunity Commission to implement title I of the Act. However, if employees and customers or clients are served by the same transportation system, the provisions of this section will apply.

Paragraph (b) specifically provides that a public accommodation shall remove transportation barriers in existing vehicles to the extent that it is readily achievable to do so, but that the installation of hydraulic or other lifts is not required.

Paragraph (c) provides that public accommodations subject to this section shall comply with the requirements for transportation vehicles and systems contained in the regulations issued by the Secretary of Transportation.

Subpart D—New Construction and Alterations

Subpart D implements section 303 of the Act, which requires that newly constructed or altered places of public accommodation or commercial facilities be readily accessible to and usable by individuals with disabilities. This requirement contemplates a high degree of convenient access. It is intended to ensure that patrons and employees of places of public accommodation and employees of commercial facilities are able to get to, enter, and use the facility.

Potential patrons of places of public accommodation, such as retail establishments, should be able to get to a store, get into the store, and get to the areas where goods are being provided. Employees should have the same types of access, although those individuals require access to and around the employment area as well as to the area in which goods and services are provided.

The ADA is geared to the future—its goal being that, over time, access will be the rule, rather than the exception. Thus, the Act only requires modest expenditures, of the type addressed in § 36.304 of this part, to provide access to existing facilities not otherwise being altered, but requires all new construction and alterations to be accessible.

The Act does not require new construction or alterations; it simply requires that, when a public accommodation or other private entity undertakes the construction or alteration of a facility subject to the Act, the newly constructed or altered facility must be made accessible. This subpart establishes the requirements for new construction and alterations.

As explained under the discussion of the definition of "facility," § 36.104, pending development of specific requirements, the Department will not apply this subpart to places of public accommodation located in mobile units, boats, or other conveyances.

Section 36.401 New Construction

General

Section 36.401 implements the new construction requirements of the ADA. Section 303 (a)(1) of the Act provides that discrimination for purposes of section 302(a) of the Act includes a failure to design and construct facilities for first occupancy later than 30 months after the date of enactment (i.e., after January 26, 1993) that are readily accessible to and usable by individuals with disabilities.

Paragraph 36.401(a)(1) restates the general requirement for accessible new construction. The proposed rule stated that "any public accommodation or other private entity responsible for design and construction" must ensure that facilities conform to this requirement. Various commenters suggested that the proposed language was not consistent with the statute because it substituted "private entity responsible for design and construction" for the statutory language; because it did not address liability on the part of architects, contractors, developers, tenants, owners, and other entities; and because it limited the liability of entities responsible for commercial facilities. In response, the Department has revised this paragraph to repeat the language of section 303(a) of the ADA. The Department will interpret this section in a manner consistent with the intent of the statute and with the nature of the responsibilities of the various entities for design, for construction, or for both.

Designed and Constructed for First Occupancy

According to paragraph (a)(2), a facility is subject to the new construction requirements only if a completed application for a building permit or permit extension is filed after January 26, 1992, and the facility is occupied after January 26, 1993.

The proposed rule set forth for comment two alternative ways by which to determine what facilities are subject to the Act and what standards apply. Paragraph (a)(2) of the final rule is a slight variation on Option One in the proposed rule. The reasons for the Department's choice of Option One are discussed later in this section.

Paragraph (a)(2) acknowledges that Congress did not contemplate having actual occupancy be the sole trigger for the accessibility requirements, because the statute prohibits a failure to "design and construct for first occupancy," rather than requiring accessibility in facilities actually occupied after a particular date.

The commenters overwhelmingly agreed with the Department's proposal to use a date certain; many cited the reasons given in the preamble to the proposed rule. First, it is helpful for designers and builders to have a fixed date for accessible design, so that they can determine accessibility requirements early in the planning and design stage. It is difficult to determine accessibility requirements in anticipation of the actual date of first occupancy because of unpredictable and uncontrollable events (e.g., strikes affecting suppliers or labor, or natural disasters) that may delay occupancy. To redesign or reconstruct portions of a facility if it begins to appear that occupancy will be later than anticipated would be quite costly. A fixed date also assists those responsible for enforcing, or monitoring compliance with, the statute, and those protected by it.

The Department considered using as a trigger date for application of the accessibility standards the date on which a permit is granted. The Department chose instead the date on which a complete permit application is certified as received by the appropriate government entity. Almost all commenters agreed with this choice of a trigger date. This decision is based partly on information that several months or even years can pass between application for a permit and receipt of a permit. Design is virtually complete at the time an application is complete (i.e., certified to contain all the information required by the State, county, or local government). After an application is filed, delays may occur before the permit is granted due to numerous factors (not necessarily relating to accessibility): for example, hazardous waste discovered on the property, flood plain requirements, zoning disputes, or opposition to the project from various groups. These factors should not require redesign for accessibility if the application was completed before January 26, 1992. However, if the facility must be redesigned for other reasons, such as a change in density or environmental preservation, and the final permit is based on a new application, the rule would require accessibility if that application was certified complete after January 26, 1992.

The certification of receipt of a complete application for a building permit is an appropriate point in the process because certifications are issued in writing by governmental authorities. In addition, this approach presents a clear and objective standard.

However, a few commenters pointed out that in some jurisdictions it is not possible to receive a "certification" that an application is complete, and suggested that in those cases the fixed date should be the date on which an application for a permit is received by the government agency. The Department has included such a provision in § 36.401(a)(2)(i).

The date of January 26, 1992, is relevant only with respect to the last application for a permit or permit extension for a facility. Thus, if an entity has applied for only a "foundation" permit, the date of that permit application has no effect, because the entity must also apply for and receive a permit at a later date for the actual superstructure. In this case, it is the date of the later application that would control, unless construction is not completed within the time allowed by the permit, in which case a third permit would be issued and the date of the application for that permit would be determinative for purposes of the rule.

Choice of Option One for Defining "Designed and Constructed for First Occupancy"

Under the option the Department has chosen for determining applicability of the new construction standards, a building would be considered to be "for first occupancy" after January 26, 1993, only (1) if the last application for a building permit or permit extension for the facility is certified to be complete (or, in some jurisdictions, received) by a State, county, or local government after January 26, 1992, and (2) if the first certificate of occupancy is issued after January 26, 1993. The Department also asked for comment on an Option Two, which would have imposed new construction requirements if a completed application for a building permit or permit extension was filed after the enactment of the ADA (July 26, 1990), and the facility was occupied after January 26, 1993.

The request for comment on this issue drew a large number of comments expressing a wide range of views. Most business groups and some disability rights groups favored Option One, and some business groups and most disability rights groups favored Option Two. Individuals and government entities were equally divided; several commenters proposed other options.

Those favoring Option One pointed out that it is more reasonable in that it allows time for those subject to the new construction requirements to anticipate those requirements and to receive technical assistance pursuant to the Act. Numerous commenters said that time frames for designing and constructing some types of facilities (for example, health care facilities) can range from two to four years or more. They expressed concerns that Option Two, which would apply to some facilities already under design or construction as of the date the Act was signed, and to some on which construction began shortly after enactment, could result in costly redesign or reconstruction of those facilities. In the same vein, some Option One supporters found Option Two objectionable on due process grounds. In their view, Option Two would mean that in July 1991 (upon issuance of the final DOJ rule) the responsible entities would learn that ADA standards had been in effect since July 26, 1990, and this would amount to retroactive application of standards. Numerous commenters characterized Option Two as having no support in the statute and Option One as being more consistent with congressional intent.

Those who favored Option Two pointed out that it would include more facilities within the coverage of the new construction standards. They argued that because similar accessibility requirements are in effect under State laws, no hardship would be imposed by this option. Numerous commenters said that hardship would also be eliminated in light of their view that the ADA requires compliance with the Uniform Federal Accessibility Standards (UFAS) until issuance of DOJ standards. Those supporting Option Two claimed that it was more consistent with the statute and its legislative history.

The Department has chosen Option One rather than Option Two, primarily on the basis of the language of three relevant sections of the statute. First, section 303(a) requires compliance with accessibility standards set forth, or incorporated by reference in, regulations to be issued by the Department of Justice. Standing alone, this section cannot be read to require compliance with the Department's standards before those standards are issued (through this rulemaking). Second, according to section 310 of the statute, section 303 becomes effective on January 26, 1992. Thus, section 303 cannot impose requirements on the design of buildings before that date. Third, while section 306(d) of the Act requires compliance with UFAS if final regulations have not been issued, that provision cannot reasonably be read to take effect until July 26, 1991, the date by which the Department of Justice must issue final regulations under title III.

Option Two was based on the premise that the interim standards in section 306(d) take effect as of the ADA's enactment (July 26, 1990), rather than on the date by which the Department of Justice regulations are due to be issued (July 26, 1991). The initial clause of section 306(d)(1) itself is silent on this question:

If final regulations have not been issued pursuant to this section, for new construction for which a * * * building permit is obtained prior to the issuance of final regulations * * * (interim standards apply).

The approach in Option Two relies partly on the language of section 310 of the Act, which provides that section 306, the interim standards provision, takes effect on the date of enactment. Under this interpretation the interim standards provision would prevail over the operative provision, section 303, which requires that new construction be accessible and which becomes effective January 26, 1992. This approach would also require construing the language of section 306(d)(1) to take effect before the Department's standards are due to be issued. The preferred reading of section 306 is that it would require that, if the Department's final standards had not been issued by July 26, 1991, UFAS would apply to certain buildings until such time as the Department's standards were issued.

General Substantive Requirements of the New Construction Provisions

The rule requires, as does the statute, that covered newly constructed facilities be readily accessible to and usable by individuals with disabilities. The phrase "readily accessible to and usable by individuals with disabilities" is a term that, in slightly varied formulations, has been used in the Architectural Barriers Act of 1968, the Fair Housing Act, the regulations implementing section 504 of the Rehabilitation Act of 1973, and current accessibility standards. It means, with respect to a facility or a portion of a facility, that it can be approached, entered, and used by individuals with disabilities (including mobility, sensory, and cognitive impairments) easily and conveniently. A facility that is constructed to meet the requirements of the rule's accessibility standards will be considered readily accessible and usable with respect to construction. To the extent that a particular type or element of a facility is not specifically addressed by the standards, the language of this section is the safest guide.

A private entity that renders an "accessible" building inaccessible in its operation, through policies or practices, may be in violation of section 302 of the Act. For example, a private entity can render an entrance to a facility inaccessible by keeping an accessible entrance open only during certain hours (whereas the facility is available to others for a greater length of time). A facility could similarly be rendered inaccessible if a person with disabilities is significantly limited in her or his choice of a range of accommodations.

Ensuring access to a newly constructed facility will include providing access to the facility from the street or parking lot, to the extent the responsible entity has control over the route from those locations. In some cases, the private entity will have no control over access at the point where streets, curbs, or sidewalks already exist, and in those instances the entity is encouraged to request modifications to a sidewalk, including installation of curb cuts, from a public entity responsible for them. However, as some commenters pointed out, there is no obligation for a private entity subject to title III of the ADA to seek or ensure compliance by a public entity with title II. Thus, although a locality may have an obligation under title II of the Act to install curb cuts at a particular location, that responsibility is separate from the private entity's title III obligation, and any involvement by a private entity in seeking cooperation from a public entity is purely voluntary in this context.

Work Areas

Proposed paragraph 36.401(b) addressed access to employment areas, rather than to the areas where goods or services are being provided. The preamble noted that the proposed paragraph provided guidance for new construction and alterations until more specific guidance was issued by the ATBCB and reflected in this Department's regulation. The entire paragraph has been deleted from this section in the final rule. The concepts of paragraphs (b) (1), (2), and (5) of the proposed rule are included, with modifications and expansion, in ADAAG. Paragraphs (3) and (4) of the proposed rule, concerning fixtures and equipment, are not included in the rule or in ADAAG.

Some commenters asserted that questions relating to new construction and alterations of work areas should be addressed by the EEOC under title I, as employment concerns. However, the legislative history of the statute clearly indicates that the new construction and alterations requirements of title III were intended to ensure accessibility of new facilities to all individuals, including employees. The language of section 303 sweeps broadly in its application to all public accommodations and commercial facilities. EEOC's title I regulations will address accessibility requirements that come into play when "reasonable accommodation" to individual employees or applicants with disabilities is mandated under title I.

The issues dealt with in proposed § 36.401(b) (1) and (2) are now addressed in ADAAG section 4.1.1(3). The Department's proposed paragraphs would have required that areas that will be used only by employees as work stations be constructed so that individuals with disabilities could approach, enter, and exit the areas. They would not have required that all individual work stations be constructed or equipped (for example, with shelves that are accessible or adaptable) to be accessible. This approach was based on the theory that, as long as an employee with disabilities could enter the building and get to and around the employment area, modifications in a particular work station could be instituted as a "reasonable accommodation" to that employee if the modifications were necessary and they did not constitute an undue hardship.

Almost all of the commenters agreed with the proposal to require access to a work area but not to require accessibility of each individual work station. This principle is included in ADAAG 4.1.1(3). Several of the comments related to the requirements of the proposed ADAAG and have been addressed in the accessibility standards.

Proposed paragraphs (b) (3) and (4) would have required that consideration be given to placing fixtures and equipment at accessible heights in the first instance, and to purchasing new equipment and fixtures that are adjustable. These paragraphs have not been included in the final rule because the rule in most instances does not establish accessibility standards for purchased equipment. (See discussion elsewhere in the preamble of proposed § 36.309.) While the Department encourages entities to consider providing accessible or adjustable fixtures and equipment for employees, this rule does not require them to do so.

Paragraph (b)(5) of proposed § 36.401 clarified that proposed paragraph (b) did not limit the requirement that employee areas other than individual work stations must be accessible. For example, areas that are employee "common use" areas and are not solely used as work stations (e.g., employee lounges, cafeterias, health units, exercise facilities) are treated no differently under this regulation than other parts of a building; they must be constructed or altered in compliance with the accessibility standards. This principle is not stated in § 36.401 but is implicit in the requirements of this section and ADAAG.

Commercial Facilities in Private Residences

Section 36.401(b) of the final rule is a new provision relating to commercial facilities located in private residences. The proposed rule addressed these requirements in the preamble to § 36.207, "Places of public accommodation located in private residences." The preamble stated that the approach for commercial facilities would be the same as that for places of public accommodation, i.e., those portions used exclusively as a commercial facility or used as both a commercial facility and for residential purposes would be covered. Because commercial facilities are only subject to new construction and alterations requirements, however, the covered portions would only be subject to subpart D. This approach is reflected in § 36.401(b)(1).

The Department is aware that the statutory definition of "commercial facility" excludes private residences because they are "expressly exempted from coverage under the Fair Housing Act of 1968, as amended." However, the Department interprets that exemption as applying only to facilities that are exclusively residential. When a facility is used as both a residence and a commercial facility, the exemption does not apply.

Paragraph (b)(2) is similar to the new paragraph (b) under § 36.207, "Places of public accommodation located in private residences." The paragraph clarifies that the covered portion includes not only the space used as a commercial facility, but also the elements used to enter the commercial facility, e.g., the homeowner's front sidewalk, if any; the doorway; the hallways; the restroom, if used by employees or visitors of the commercial facility; and any other portion of the residence, interior or exterior, used by employees or visitors of the commercial facility.

As in the case of public accommodations located in private residences, the new construction standards only apply to the extent that a portion of the residence is designed or intended for use as a commercial facility. Likewise, if a homeowner alters a portion of his home to convert it to a commercial facility, that work must be done in compliance with the alterations standards in appendix A.

Structural Impracticability

Proposed § 36.401(c) is included in the final rule with minor changes. It details a statutory exception to the new construction requirement: the requirement that new construction be accessible does not apply where an entity can demonstrate that it is structurally impracticable to meet the requirements of the regulation. This provision is also included in ADAAG, at section 4.1.1(5)(a).

Consistent with the legislative history of the ADA, this narrow exception will apply only in rare and unusual circumstances where unique characteristics of terrain make accessibility unusually difficult. Such limitations for topographical problems are analogous to an acknowledged limitation in the application of the accessibility requirements of the Fair Housing Amendments Act (FHAA) of 1988.

Almost all commenters supported this interpretation. Two commenters argued that the DOJ requirement is too limiting and would not exempt some buildings that should be exempted because of soil conditions, terrain, and other unusual site conditions. These commenters suggested consistency with HUD's Fair Housing Accessibility Guidelines (56 FR 9472 (1991)), which generally would allow exceptions from accessibility requirements, or allow compliance with less stringent requirements, on sites with slopes exceeding 10%.

The Department is aware of the provisions in HUD's guidelines, which were issued on March 6, 1991, after passage of the ADA and publication of the Department's proposed rule. The approach taken in these guidelines, which apply to different types of construction and implement different statutory requirements for new construction, does not bind this Department in regulating under the ADA. The Department has included in the final rule the substance of the proposed provision, which is faithful to the intent of the statute, as expressed in the legislative history. (See Senate report at 70-71; Education and Labor report at 120.)

The limited structural impracticability exception means that it is acceptable to deviate from accessibility requirements only where unique characteristics of terrain prevent the incorporation of accessibility features and where providing accessibility would destroy the physical integrity of a facility. A situation in which a building must be built on stilts because of its location in marshlands or over water is an example of one of the few situations in which the exception for structural impracticability would apply.

This exception to accessibility requirements should not be applied to situations in which a facility is located in "hilly" terrain or on a plot of land upon which there are steep grades. In such circumstances, accessibility can be achieved without destroying the physical integrity of a structure, and is required in the construction of new facilities.

Some commenters asked for clarification concerning when and how to apply the ADA rules or the Fair Housing Accessibility Guidelines, especially when a facility may be subject to both because of mixed use. Guidance on this question is provided in the discussion of the definitions of place of public accommodation and commercial facility. With respect to the structural impracticability exception, a mixed-use facility could not take advantage of the Fair Housing exemption, to the extent that it is less stringent than the ADA exemption, except for those portions of the facility that are subject only to the Fair Housing Act.

As explained in the preamble to the proposed rule, in those rare circumstances in which it is structurally impracticable to achieve full compliance with accessibility retirements under the ADA, places of public accommodation and commercial facilities should still be designed and constructed to incorporate accessibility features to the extent that the features are structurally practicable. The accessibility requirements should not be viewed as an all-or-nothing proposition in such circumstances.

If it is structurally impracticable for a facility in its entirety to be readily accessible to and usable by people with disabilities, then those portions that can be made accessible should be made accessible. If a building cannot be constructed in compliance with the full range of accessibility requirements because of structural impracticability, then it should still incorporate those features that are structurally practicable. If it is structurally impracticable to make a particular facility accessible to persons who have particular types of disabilities, it is still appropriate to require it to be made accessible to persons with other types of disabilities. For example, a facility that is of necessity built on stilts and cannot be made accessible to persons who use wheelchairs because it is structurally impracticable to do so, must be made accessible for individuals with vision or hearing impairments or other kinds of disabilities.

Elevator Exemption

Section 36.401(d) implements the "elevator exemption" for new construction in section 303(b) of the ADA. The elevator exemption is an exception to the general requirement that new facilities be readily accessible to and usable by individuals with disabilities. Generally, an elevator is the most common way to provide individuals who use wheelchairs "ready access" to floor levels above or below the ground floor of a multi-story building. Congress, however, chose not to require elevators in new small buildings, that is, those with less than three stories or less than 3,000 square feet per story. In buildings eligible for the exemption, therefore, "ready access" from the building entrance to a floor above or below the ground floor is not required, because the statute does not require that an elevator be installed in such buildings. The elevator exemption does not apply, however, to a facility housing a shopping center, a shopping mall, or the professional office of a health care provider, or other categories of facilities as determined by the Attorney General. For example, a new office building that will have only two stories, with no elevator planned, will not be required to have an elevator, even if each story has 20,000 square feet. In other words, having either less than 3000 square feet per story or less than three stories qualifies a facility for the exemption; it need not qualify for the exemption on both counts. Similarly, a facility that has five stories of 2800 square feet each qualifies for the exemption. If a facility has three or more stories at any point, it is not eligible for the elevator exemption unless all the stories are less than 3000 square feet.

The terms "shopping center or shopping mall" and "professional office of a health care provider" are defined in this section. They are substantively identical to the definitions included in the proposed rule in § 36.104, "Definitions." They have been moved to this section because, as commenters pointed out, they are relevant only for the purposes of the elevator exemption, and inclusion in the general definitions section could give the incorrect impression that an office of a health care provider is not covered as a place of public accommodation under other sections of the rule, unless the office falls within the definition.

For purposes of § 36.401, a "shopping center or shopping mall" is (1) a building housing five or more sales or rental establishments, or (2) a series of buildings on a common site, either under common ownership or common control or developed either as one project or as a series of related projects, housing five or more sales or rental establishments. The term "shopping center or shopping mall" only includes floor levels containing at least one sales or rental establishment, or any floor level that was designed or intended for use by at least one sales or rental establishment.

Any sales or rental establishment of the type that is included in paragraph (5) of the definition of "place of public accommodation" (for example, a bakery, grocery store, clothing store, or hardware store) is considered a sales or rental establishment for purposes of this definition; the other types of public accommodations (e.g., restaurants, laundromats, banks, travel services, health spas) are not.

In the preamble to the proposed rule, the Department sought comment on whether the definition of "shopping center or mall" should be expanded to include any of these other types of public accommodations. The Department also sought comment on whether a series of buildings should fall within the definition only if they are physically connected.

Most of those responding to the first question (overwhelmingly groups representing people with disabilities, or individual commenters) urged that the definition encompass more places of public accommodation, such as restaurants, motion picture houses, laundromats, dry cleaners, and banks. They pointed out that often it is not known what types of establishments will be tenants in a new facility. In addition, they noted that malls are advertised as entities, that their appeal is in the "package" of services offered to the public, and that this package often includes the additional types of establishments mentioned.

Commenters representing business groups sought to exempt banks, travel services, grocery stores, drug stores, and freestanding retail stores from the elevator requirement. They based this request on the desire to continue the practice in some locations of incorporating mezzanines housing administrative offices, raised pharmacist areas, and raised areas in the front of supermarkets that house safes and are used by managers to oversee operations of check-out aisles and other functions. Many of these concerns are adequately addressed by ADAAG. Apart from those addressed by

ADAAG, the Department sees no reason to treat a particular type of sales or rental establishment differently from any other. Although banks and travel services are not included as "sales or rental establishments," because they do not fall under paragraph (5) of the definition of place of public accommodation, grocery stores and drug stores are included.

The Department has declined to include places of public accommodation other than sales or rental establishments in the definition. The statutory definition of "public accommodation" (section 301(7)) lists 12 types of establishments that are considered public accommodations. Category (E) includes "a bakery, grocery store, clothing store, hardware store, shopping center, or other sales or rental establishment." This arrangement suggests that it is only these types of establishments that would make up a shopping center for purposes of the statute. To include all types of places of public accommodation, or those from 6 or 7 of the categories, as commenters suggest, would overly limit the elevator exemption; the universe of facilities covered by the definition of "shopping center" could well exceed the number of multitenant facilities not covered, which would render the exemption almost meaningless.

For similar reasons, the Department is retaining the requirement that a building or series of buildings must house five or more sales or rental establishments before it falls within the definition of "shopping center." Numerous commenters objected to the number and requested that the number be lowered from five to three or four. Lowering the number in this manner would include an inordinately large number of two-story multitenant buildings within the category of those required to have elevators.

The responses to the question concerning whether a series of buildings should be connected in order to be covered were varied. Generally, disability rights groups and some government agencies said a series of buildings should not have to be connected, and pointed to a trend in some areas to build shopping centers in a garden or village setting. The Department agrees that this design choice should not negate the elevator requirement for new construction. Some business groups answered the question in the affirmative, and some suggested a different definition of shopping center. For example, one commenter recommended the addition of a requirement that the five or more establishments be physically connected on the non-ground floors by a common pedestrian walkway or pathway, because otherwise a series of stand-alone facilities would have to comply with the elevator requirement, which would be unduly burdensome and perhaps infeasible. Another suggested use of what it characterized as the standard industry definition: "A group of retail stores and related business facilities, the whole planned, developed, operated and managed as a unit." While the rule's definition would reach a series of related projects that are under common control but were not developed as a single project, the Department considers such a facility to be a shopping center within the meaning of the statute. However, in light of the hardship that could confront a series of existing small stand-alone buildings if elevators were required in alterations, the Department has included a common access route in the definition of shopping center or shopping mall for purposes of § 36.404.

Some commenters suggested that access to restrooms and other shared facilities open to the public should be required even if those facilities were not on a shopping floor. Such a provision with respect to toilet or bathing facilities is included in the elevator exception in final ADAAG 4.1.3(5).

For purposes of this subpart, the rule does not distinguish between a "shopping mall" (usually a building with a roofed-over common pedestrian area serving more than one tenant in which a majority of the tenants have a main entrance from the common pedestrian area) and a "shopping center" (e.g., a "shopping strip"). Any facility housing five or more of the types of sales or rental establishments described, regardless of the number of other types of places of public accommodation housed there (e.g., offices, movie theatres, restaurants), is a shopping center or shopping mall.

For example, a two-story facility built for mixed-use occupancy on both floors (e.g., by sales and rental establishments, a movie theater, restaurants, and general office space) is a shopping center or shopping mall if it houses five or more sales or rental establishments. If none of these establishments is located on the second floor, then only the ground floor, which contains the sales or rental establishments, would be a "shopping center or shopping mall," unless the second floor was designed or intended for use by at least one sales or rental establishment. In determining whether a floor was intended for such use, factors to be considered include the types of establishments that first occupied the floor, the nature of the developer's marketing strategy, i.e., what types of establishments were sought, and inclusion of any design features particular to rental and sales establishments.

A "professional office of a health care provider" is defined as a location where a person or entity regulated by a State to provide professional services related to the physical or mental health of an individual makes such services available to the public. In a two-story development that houses health care providers only on the ground floor, the "professional office of a health care provider" is limited to the ground floor unless the second floor was designed or intended for use by a health care provider. In determining if a floor was intended for such use, factors to be considered include whether the facility was constructed with special plumbing, electrical, or other features needed by health care providers, whether the developer marketed the facility as a medical office center, and whether any of the establishments that first occupied the floor was, in fact, a health care provider.

In addition to requiring that a building that is a shopping center, shopping mall, or the professional office of a health care provider have an elevator regardless of square footage or number of floors, the ADA (section 303(b)) provides that the Attorney General may determine that a particular category of facilities requires the installation of elevators based on the usage of the facilities. The Department, as it proposed to do, has added to the nonexempt categories terminals, depots, or other stations used for specified public transportation, and airport passenger terminals. Numerous commenters in all categories endorsed this proposal; none opposed it. It is not uncommon for an airport passenger terminal or train station, for example, to have only two floors, with gates on both floors. Because of the significance of transportation, because a person with disabilities could be arriving or departing at any gate, and because inaccessible facilities could result in a total denial of transportation services, it is reasonable to require that newly constructed transit facilities be accessible, regardless of square footage or number of floors. One comment suggested an amendment that would treat terminals and stations similarly to shopping centers, by requiring an accessible route only to those areas used for passenger loading and unloading and for other passenger services. Paragraph (d)(2)(ii) has been modified accordingly.

Some commenters suggested that other types of facilities (e.g., educational facilities, libraries, museums, commercial facilities, and social service facilities) should be included in the category of nonexempt facilities. The Department has not found adequate justification for including any other types of facilities in the nonexempt category at this time.

Section 36.401(d)(2) establishes the operative requirements concerning the elevator exemption and its application to shopping centers and malls, professional offices of health care providers, transit stations, and airport passenger terminals. Under the rule's framework, it is necessary first to determine if a new facility (including one or more buildings) houses places of public accommodation or commercial facilities that are in the categories for which elevators are required. If so, and the facility is a shopping center or shopping mall, or a professional office of a health care provider, then any area housing such an office or a sales or rental establishment or the professional office of a health care provider is not entitled to the elevator exemption.

The following examples illustrate the application of these principles:

1. A shopping mall has an upper and a lower level. There are two "anchor stores" (in this case, major department stores at either end of the mall, both with exterior entrances and an entrance on each level from the common area). In addition, there are 30 stores (sales or rental establishments) on the upper level, all of which have entrances from a common central area. There are 30 stores on the lower level, all of which have entrances from a common central area. According to the rule, elevator access must be provided to each store and to each level of the anchor stores. This requirement could be satisfied with respect to the 60 stores through elevators connecting the two pedestrian levels, provided that an individual could travel from the elevator to any other point on that level (i.e., into any store through a common pedestrian area) on an accessible path.

2. A commercial (nonresidential) "townhouse" development is composed of 20 two-story attached buildings. The facility is developed as one project, with common ownership, and the space will be leased to retailers. Each building has one accessible entrance from a pedestrian walk to the first floor. From that point, one can enter a store on the first floor, or walk up a flight of stairs to a store on the second floor. All 40 stores must be accessible at ground floor level or by accessible vertical access from that level. This does not mean, however, that 20 elevators must be installed. Access could be provided to the second floor by an elevator from the pedestrian area on the lower level to an upper walkway connecting all the areas on the second floor.

3. In the same type of development, it is planned that retail stores will be housed exclusively on the ground floor, with only office space (not professional offices of health care providers) on the second. Elevator access need not be provided to the second floor because all the sales or rental establishments (the entities that make the facility a shopping center) are located on an accessible ground floor.

4. In the same type of development, the space is

designed and marketed as medical or office suites, or as a medical office facility. Accessible vertical access must be provided to all areas, as described in example 2.

Some commenters suggested that building owners who knowingly lease or rent space to nonexempt places of public accommodation would violate § 36.401. However, the Department does not consider leasing or renting inaccessible space in itself to constitute a violation of this part. Nor does a change in use of a facility, with no accompanying alterations (e.g., if a psychiatrist replaces an attorney as a tenant in a second-floor office, but no alterations are made to the office) trigger accessibility requirements.

Entities cannot evade the requirements of this section by constructing facilities in such a way that no story is intended to constitute a "ground floor." For example, if a private entity constructs a building whose main entrance leads only to stairways or escalators that connect with upper or lower floors, the Department would consider at least one level of the facility a ground story.

The rule requires in § 36.401(d)(3), consistent with the proposed rule, that, even if a building falls within the elevator exemption, the floor or floors other than the ground floor must nonetheless be accessible, except for elevator access, to individuals with disabilities, including people who use wheelchairs. This requirement applies to buildings that do not house sales or rental establishments or the professional offices of a health care provider as well as to those in which such establishments or offices are all located on the ground floor. In such a situation, little added cost is entailed in making the second floor accessible, because it is similar in structure and floor plan to the ground floor.

There are several reasons for this provision. First, some individuals who are mobility impaired may work on a building's second floor, which they can reach by stairs and the use of crutches; however, the same individuals, once they reach the second floor, may then use a wheelchair that is kept in the office. Secondly, because the first floor will be accessible, there will be little additional cost entailed in making the second floor, with the same structure and generally the same floor plan, accessible. In addition, the second floor must be accessible to those persons with disabilities who do not need elevators for level changes (for example, persons with sight or hearing impairments and those with certain mobility impairments). Finally, if an elevator is installed in the future for any reason, full access to the floor will be facilitated.

One commenter asserted that this provision goes beyond the Department's authority under the Act, and disagreed with the Department's claim that little additional cost would be entailed in compliance. However, the provision is taken directly from the legislative history (see Education and Labor report at 114).

One commenter said that where an elevator is not required, platform lifts should be required. Two commenters pointed out that the elevator exemption is really an exemption from the requirement for providing an accessible route to a second floor not served by an elevator. The Department agrees with the latter comment. Lifts to provide access between floors are not required in buildings that are not required to have elevators. This point is specifically addressed in the appendix to ADAAG (§ 4.1.3(5)). ADAAG also addresses in detail the situations in which lifts are permitted or required.

Section 36.402 Alterations

Sections 36.402-36.405 implement section 303(a)(2) of the Act, which requires that alterations to existing facilities be made in a way that ensures that the altered portion is readily accessible to and usable by individuals with disabilities. This part does not require alterations; it simply provides that when alterations are undertaken, they must be made in a manner that provides access.

Section 36.402(a)(1) provides that any alteration to a place of public accommodation or a commercial facility, after January 26, 1992, shall be made so as to ensure that, to the maximum extent feasible, the altered portions of the facility are readily accessible to and usable by individuals with disabilities, including individuals who use wheelchairs.

The proposed rule provided that an alteration would be deemed to be undertaken after January 26, 1992, if the physical alteration of the property is in progress after that date. Commenters pointed out that this provision would, in some cases, produce an unjust result by requiring the redesign or retrofitting of projects initiated before this part established the ADA accessibility standards. The Department agrees that the proposed rule would, in some instances, unfairly penalize projects that were substantially completed before the effective date. Therefore, paragraph (a)(2) has been revised to specify that an alteration will be deemed to be undertaken after January 26, 1992, if the physical alteration of the property begins after that date. As a matter of interpretation, the Department will construe this provision to apply to alterations that require a permit from a State, County or local government, if physical alterations pursuant to the terms of the permit begin after January 26, 1992. The Department recognizes that this application of the effective date may require redesign of some facilities that were planned prior to the publication of this part, but no retrofitting will be required of facilities on which the physical alterations were initiated prior to the effective date of the Act. Of course, nothing in this section in any way alters the obligation of any facility to remove architectural barriers in existing facilities to the extent that such barrier removal is readily achievable.

Paragraph (b) provides that, for the purposes of this part, an "alteration" is a change to a place of public accommodation or a commercial facility that affects or could affect the usability of the building or facility or any part thereof. One commenter suggested that the concept of usability should apply only to those changes that affect access by persons with disabilities. The Department remains convinced that the Act requires the concept of "usability" to be read broadly to include any change that affects the usability of the facility, not simply changes that relate directly to access by individuals with disabilities.

The Department received a significant number of comments on the examples provided in paragraphs (b)(1) and (b)(2) of the proposed rule. Some commenters urged the Department to limit the application of this provision to major structural modifications, while others asserted that it should be expanded to include cosmetic changes such as painting and wallpapering. The Department believes that neither approach is consistent with the legislative history, which requires this Department's regulation to be consistent with the accessibility guidelines (ADAAG) developed by the Architectural and Transportation Barriers Compliance Board (ATBCB). Although the legislative history contemplates that, in some instances, the ADA accessibility standards will exceed the current MGRAD requirements, it also clearly indicates the view of the drafters that "minor changes such as painting or papering walls * * * do not affect usability" (Education and Labor report at 111, Judiciary report at 64), and, therefore, are not alterations. The proposed rule was based on the existing MGRAD definition of "alteration." The language of the final rule has been revised to be consistent with ADAAG, incorporated as appendix A to this part.

Some commenters sought clarification of the intended scope of this section. The proposed rule contained illustrations of changes that affect usability and those that do not. The intent of the illustrations was to explain the scope of the alterations requirement; the effect was to obscure it. As a result of the illustrations, some commenters concluded that any alteration to a facility, even a minor alteration such as relocating an electrical outlet, would trigger an extensive obligation to provide access throughout an entire facility. That result was never contemplated.

Therefore, in this final rule paragraph (b)(1) has been revised to include the major provisions of paragraphs (b)(1) and (b)(2) of the proposed rule. The examples in the proposed rule have been deleted. Paragraph (b)(1) now provides that alterations include, but are not limited to, remodeling, renovation, rehabilitation, reconstruction, historic restoration, changes or rearrangement in structural parts or elements, and changes or rearrangement in the plan configuration of walls and full-height partitions. Normal maintenance, reroofing, painting or wallpapering, asbestos removal, or changes to mechanical and electrical systems are not alterations unless they affect the usability of building or facility.

Paragraph (b)(2) of this final rule was added to clarify the scope of the alterations requirement. Paragraph (b)(2) provides that if existing elements, spaces, or common areas are altered, then each such altered element, space, or area shall comply with the applicable provisions of appendix A (ADAAG). As provided in § 36.403, if an altered space or area is an area of the facility that contains a primary function, then the requirements of that section apply.

Therefore, when an entity undertakes a minor alteration to a place of public accommodation or commercial facility, such as moving an electrical outlet, the new outlet must be installed in compliance with ADAAG. (Alteration of the elements listed in § 36.403(c)(2) cannot trigger a path of travel obligation.) If the alteration is to an area, such as an employee lounge or locker room, that is not an area of the facility that contains a primary function, that area must comply with ADAAG. It is only when an alteration affects access to or usability of an area containing a primary function, as opposed to other areas or the elements listed in § 36.403(c)(2), that the path of travel to the altered area must be made accessible.

The Department received relatively few comments on paragraph (c), which explains the statutory phrase "to the maximum extent feasible." Some commenters suggested that the regulation should specify that cost is a factor in determining whether it is feasible to make an altered area accessible. The legislative history of the ADA indicates that the concept of feasibility only reaches the question of whether it is possible to make the alteration accessible in compliance with this part. Costs are to be considered only when an alteration to an area containing a primary function triggers an additional requirement to make the path of travel to the altered area accessible.

Section 36.402(c) is, therefore, essentially unchanged from the proposed rule. At the recommendation of a commenter, the Department has inserted the word "virtually" to modify "impossible" to conform to the language of the legislative history. It explains that the phrase "to the maximum extent feasible" as used in this section applies to the occasional case where the nature of an existing facility makes it virtually impossible to comply fully with applicable accessibility standards through a planned alteration. In the occasional cases in which full compliance is impossible, alterations shall provide the maximum physical accessibility feasible. Any features of the facility that are being altered shall be made accessible unless it is technically infeasible to do so. If providing accessibility in conformance with this section to individuals with certain disabilities (e.g., those who use wheelchairs) would not be feasible, the facility shall be made accessible to persons with other types of disabilities (e.g., those who use crutches or who have impaired vision or hearing, or those who have other types of impairments).

Section 36.403 Alterations: Path of Travel

Section 36.403 implements the statutory requirement that any alteration that affects or could affect the usability of or access to an area of a facility that contains a primary function shall be made so as to ensure that, to the maximum extent feasible, the path of travel to the altered area, and the restrooms, telephones, and drinking fountains serving the altered area, are readily accessible to and usable by individuals with disabilities, including individuals who use wheelchairs, unless the cost and scope of such alterations is disproportionate to the cost of the overall alteration. Paragraph (a) restates this statutory requirement.

Paragraph (b) defines a "primary function" as a major activity for which the facility is intended. This paragraph is unchanged from the proposed rule. Areas that contain a primary function include, but are not limited to, the customer services lobby of a bank, the dining area of a cafeteria, the meeting rooms in a conference center, as well as offices and all other work areas in which the activities of the public accommodation or other private entities using the facility are carried out. The concept of "areas containing a primary function" is analogous to the concept of "functional spaces" in § 3.5 of the existing Uniform Federal Accessibility Standards, which defines "functional spaces" as "[t]he rooms and spaces in a building or facility that house the major activities for which the building or facility is intended."

Paragraph (b) provides that areas such as mechanical rooms, boiler rooms, supply storage rooms, employee lounges and locker rooms, janitorial closets, entrances, corridors, and restrooms are not areas containing a primary function. There may be exceptions to this general rule. For example, the availability of public restrooms at a place of public accommodation at a roadside rest stop may be a major factor affecting customers' decisions to patronize the public accommodation. In that case, a restroom would be considered to be an "area containing a primary function" of the facility.

Most of the commenters who addressed this issue supported the approach taken by the Department; but a few commenters suggested that areas not open to the general public or those used exclusively by employees should be excluded from the definition of primary function. The preamble to the proposed rule noted that the Department considered an alternative approach to the definition of "primary function," under which a primary function of a commercial facility would be defined as a major activity for which the facility was intended, while a primary function of a place of public accommodation would be defined as an activity which involves providing significant goods, services, facilities, privileges, advantages, or accommodations. However, the Department concluded that, although portions of the legislative history of the ADA support this alternative, the better view is that the language now contained in § 36.403(b) most accurately reflects congressional intent. No commenter made a persuasive argument that the Department's interpretation of the legislative history is incorrect.

When the ADA was introduced, the requirement to make alterations accessible was included in section 302 of the Act, which identifies the practices that constitute discrimination by a public accommodation. Because section 302 applies only to the operation of a place of public accommodation, the alterations requirement was intended only to provide access to clients and customers of a public accommodation. It was anticipated that access would be provided to employees with disabilities under the "reasonable accommodation" requirements of title I. However, during its consideration of the ADA, the House Judiciary Committee amended the bill to move the alterations provision from section 302 to section 303, which applies to commercial facilities as well as public accommodations. The Committee report accompanying the bill explains that:

New construction and alterations of both public accommodations and commercial facilities must be made readily accessible to and usable by individuals with disabilities * * *. Essentially, [this requirement] is designed to ensure that patrons and employees of public accommodations and commercial facilities are able to get to, enter and use the facility * * *. The rationale for making new construction accessible applies with equal force to alterations.

Judiciary report at 62-63 (emphasis added).

The ADA, as enacted, contains the language of section 303 as it was reported out of the Judiciary Committee. Therefore, the Department has concluded that the concept of "primary function" should be applied in the same manner to places of public accommodation and to commercial facilities, thereby including employee work areas in places of public accommodation within the scope of this section.

Paragraph (c) provides examples of alterations that affect the usability of or access to an area containing a primary function. The examples include: Remodeling a merchandise display area or employee work areas in a department store; installing a new floor surface to replace an inaccessible surface in the customer service area or employee work areas of a bank; redesigning the assembly line area of a factory; and installing a computer center in an accounting firm. This list is illustrative, not exhaustive. Any change that affects the usability of or access to an area containing a primary function triggers the statutory obligation to make the path of travel to the altered area accessible.

When the proposed rule was drafted, the Department believed that the rule made it clear that the ADA would require alterations to the path of travel only when such alterations are not disproportionate to the alteration to the primary function area. However, the comments that the Department received indicated that many commenters believe that even minor alterations to individual elements would require additional alterations to the path of travel. To address the concern of these commenters, a new paragraph (c)(2) has been added to the final rule to provide that alterations to such elements as windows, hardware, controls (e.g. light switches or thermostats), electrical outlets, or signage will not be deemed to be alterations that affect the usability of or access to an area containing a primary function. Of course, each element that is altered must comply with ADAAG (appendix A). The cost of alterations to individual elements would be included in the overall cost of an alteration for purposes of determining disproportionality and would be counted when determining the aggregate cost of a series of small alterations in accordance with § 36.401(h) if the area is altered in a manner that affects access to or usability of an area containing a primary function.

Paragraph (d) concerns the respective obligations of landlords and tenants in the cases of alterations that trigger the path of travel requirement under § 36.403. This paragraph was contained in the landlord/tenant section of the proposed rule, § 36.201(b). If a tenant is making alterations upon its premises pursuant to terms of a lease that grant it the authority to do so (even if they constitute alterations that trigger the path of travel requirement), and the landlord is not making alterations to other parts of the facility, then the alterations by the tenant on its own premises do not trigger a path of travel obligation upon the landlord in areas of the facility under the landlord's authority that are not otherwise being altered. The legislative history makes clear that the path of travel requirement applies only to the entity that is already making the alteration, and thus the Department has not changed the final rule despite numerous comments suggesting that the tenant be required to provide a path of travel.

Paragraph (e) defines a "path of travel" as a continuous, unobstructed way of pedestrian passage by means of which an altered area may be approached, entered, and exited; and which connects the altered area with an exterior approach (including sidewalks, streets, and parking areas), an entrance to the facility, and other parts of the facility. This concept of an accessible path of travel is analogous to the concepts of "accessible route" and "circulation path" contained in section 3.5 of the current UFAS. Some commenters suggested that this paragraph should address emergency egress. The Department disagrees. "Path of travel" as it is used in this section is a term of art under the ADA that relates only to the obligation of the public accommodation or commercial facility to provide additional accessible elements when an area containing a primary function is altered. The Department recognizes that emergency egress is an important issue, but believes that it is appropriately addressed in ADAAG (appendix A), not in this paragraph. Furthermore, ADAAG does not require changes to emergency egress areas in alterations.

Paragraph (e)(2) is drawn from section 3.5 of UFAS. It provides that an accessible path of travel may consist of walks and sidewalks, curb ramps and other interior or exterior pedestrian ramps; clear floor paths through lobbies, corridors, rooms, and other improved areas; parking access aisles; elevators and lifts; or a combination of such elements. Paragraph (e)(3) provides that, for the purposes of this part, the term "path of travel" also includes the restrooms, telephones, and drinking fountains serving an altered area.

Although the Act establishes an expectation that an accessible path of travel should generally be included when alterations are made to an area containing a primary function, Congress recognized that, in some circumstances, providing an accessible path of travel to an altered area may be sufficiently burdensome in comparison to the alteration being undertaken to the area containing a primary function as to render this requirement unreasonable. Therefore, Congress provided, in section 303(a)(2) of the Act, that alterations to the path of travel that are disproportionate in cost and scope to the overall alteration are not required.

The Act requires the Attorney General to determine at what point the cost of providing an accessible path of travel becomes disproportionate. The proposed rule provided three options for making this determination.

Two committees of Congress specifically addressed this issue: the House Committee on Education and Labor and the House Committee on the Judiciary. The reports issued by each committee suggested that accessibility alterations to a path of travel might be "disproportionate" if they exceed 30% of the alteration costs (Education and Labor report at 113; Judiciary report at 64). Because the Department believed that smaller percentage rates might be appropriate, the proposed rule sought comments on three options: 10%, 20%, or 30%.

The Department received a significant number of comments on this section. Commenters representing individuals with disabilities generally supported the use of 30% (or more); commenters representing covered entities supported a figure of 10% (or less). The Department believes that alterations made to provide an accessible path of travel to the altered area should be deemed disproportionate to the overall alteration when the cost exceeds 20% of the cost of the alteration to the primary function area. This approach appropriately reflects the intent of Congress to provide access for individuals with disabilities without causing economic hardship for the covered public accommodations and commercial facilities.

The Department has determined that the basis for this cost calculation shall be the cost of the alterations to the area containing the primary function. This approach will enable the public accommodation or other private entity that is making the alteration to calculate its obligation as a percentage of a clearly ascertainable base cost, rather than as a percentage of the "total" cost, an amount that will change as accessibility alterations to the path of travel are made.

Paragraph (f)(2) (paragraph (e)(2) in the proposed rule) is unchanged. It provides examples of costs that may be counted as expenditures required to provide an accessible path of travel. They include:

• Costs associated with providing an accessible entrance and an accessible route to the altered area, for example, the cost of widening doorways or installing ramps;

• Costs associated with making restrooms accessible, such as installing grab bars, enlarging toilet stalls, insulating pipes, or installing accessible faucet controls;

• Costs associated with providing accessible telephones, such as relocating telephones to an accessible height, installing amplification devices, or installing telecommunications devices for deaf persons (TDD's);

• Costs associated with relocating an inaccessible drinking fountain.

Paragraph (f)(1) of the proposed rule provided that when the cost of alterations necessary to make the path of travel serving an altered area fully accessible is disproportionate to the cost of the overall alteration, the path of travel shall be made accessible to the maximum extent feasible. In response to the suggestion of a commenter, the Department has made an editorial change in the final rule (paragraph (g)(1)) to clarify that if the cost of providing a fully accessible path of travel is disproportionate, the path of travel shall be made accessible "to the extent that it can be made accessible without incurring disproportionate costs."

Paragraph (g)(2) (paragraph (f)(2) in the NPRM) establishes that priority should be given to those elements that will provide the greatest access, in the following order: An accessible entrance; an accessible route to the altered area; at least one accessible restroom for each sex or a single unisex restroom; accessible telephones; accessible drinking fountains; and, whenever possible, additional accessible elements such as parking, storage, and alarms. This paragraph is unchanged from the proposed rule.

Paragraph (h) (paragraph (g) in the proposed rule) provides that the obligation to provide an accessible path of travel may not be evaded by performing a series of small alterations to the area served by a single path of travel if those alterations could have been performed as a single undertaking. If an area containing a primary function has been altered without providing an accessible path of travel to serve that area, and subsequent alterations of that area, or a different area on the same path of travel, are undertaken within three years of the original alteration, the total cost of alterations to primary function areas on that path of travel during the preceding three year period shall be considered in determining whether the cost of making the path of travel serving that area accessible is disproportionate. Only alterations undertaken after January 26, 1992, shall be considered in determining if the cost of providing accessible features is disproportionate to the overall cost of the alterations.

Section 36.404 Alterations: Elevator Exemption

Section 36.404 implements the elevator exemption in section 303(b) of the Act as it applies to altered facilities. The provisions of section 303(b) are discussed in the preamble to § 36.401(d) above. The statute applies the same exemption to both new construction and alterations. The principal difference between the requirements of § 36.401(d) and § 36.404 is that, in altering an existing facility that is not eligible for the statutory exemption, the public accommodation or other private entity responsible for the alteration is not required to install an elevator if the installation of an elevator would be disproportionate in cost and scope to the cost of the overall alteration as provided in § 36.403(f)(1). In addition, the standards referenced in § 36.406 (ADAAG) provide that installation of an elevator in an altered facility is not required if it is "technically infeasible."

This section has been revised to define the terms "professional office of a health care provider" and "shopping center or shopping mall" for the purposes of this section. The definition of "professional office of a health care provider" is identical to the definition included in § 36.401(d).

It has been brought to the attention of the Department that there is some misunderstanding about the scope of the elevator exemption as it applies to the professional office of a health care provider. A public accommodation, such as the professional office of a health care provider, is required to remove architectural barriers to its facility to the extent that such barrier removal is readily achievable (see § 36.304), but it is not otherwise required by this part to undertake new construction or alterations. This part does not require that an existing two story building that houses the professional office of a health care provider be altered for the purpose of providing elevator access. If, however, alterations to the area housing the office of the health care provider are undertaken for other purposes, the installation of an elevator might be required, but only if the cost of the elevator is not disproportionate to the cost of the overall alteration. Neither the Act nor this part prohibits a health care provider from locating his or her professional office in an existing facility that does not have an elevator.

Because of the unique challenges presented in altering existing facilities, the Department has adopted a definition of "shopping center or shopping mall" for the purposes of this section that is slightly different from the definition adopted under § 36.401(d). For the purposes of this section, a "shopping center or shopping mall" is (1) a building housing five or more sales or rental establishments, or (2) a series of buildings on a common site, connected by a common pedestrian access route above or below the ground floor, either under common ownership or common control or developed either as one project or as a series of related projects, housing five or more sales or rental establishments. As is the case with new construction, the term "shopping center or shopping mall" only includes floor levels housing at least one sales or rental establishment, or any floor level that was designed or intended for use by at least one sales or rental establishment.

The Department believes that it is appropriate to use a different definition of "shopping center or shopping mall" for this section than for § 36.401, in order to make it clear that a series of existing buildings on a common site that is altered for the use of sales or rental establishments does not become a "shopping center or shopping mall" required to install an elevator, unless there is a common means of pedestrian access above or below the ground floor. Without this exemption, separate, but adjacent, buildings that were initially designed and constructed independently of each other could be required to be retrofitted with elevators, if they were later renovated for a purpose not contemplated at the time of construction.

Like § 36.401(d), § 36.404 provides that the exemptions in this paragraph do not obviate or limit in any way the obligation to comply with the other accessibility requirements established in this subpart. For example, alterations to floors above or below the ground floor must be accessible regardless of whether the altered facility has an elevator. If a facility that is not required to install an elevator nonetheless has an elevator, that elevator shall meet, to the maximum extent feasible, the accessibility requirements of this section.

Section 36.405 Alterations: Historic Preservation

Section 36.405 gives effect to the intent of Congress, expressed in section 504(c) of the Act, that this part recognize the national interest in preserving significant historic structures. Commenters criticized the Department's use of descriptive terms in the proposed rule that are different from those used in the ADA to describe eligible historic properties. In addition, some commenters criticized the Department's decision to use the concept of "substantially impairing" the historic features of a property, which is a concept employed in regulations implementing section 504 of the Rehabilitation Act of 1973. Those commenters recommended that the Department adopt the criteria of "adverse effect" published by the Advisory Council on Historic Preservation under the National Historic Preservation Act (36 CFR 800.9) as the standard for determining whether an historic property may be altered.

The Department agrees with these comments to the extent that they suggest that the language of the rule should conform to the language employed by Congress in the ADA. Therefore, the language of this section has been revised to make it clear that this provision applies to buildings or facilities that are eligible for listing in the National Register of Historic Places under the National Historic Preservation Act (16 U.S.C. 470 et seq.) and to buildings or facilities that are designated as historic under State or local law. The Department believes, however, that the criteria of adverse effect employed under the National Historic Preservation Act are inappropriate for this rule because section 504(c) of the ADA specifies that special alterations provisions shall apply only when an alteration would "threaten or destroy the historic significance of qualified historic buildings and facilities."

The Department intends that the exception created by this section be applied only in those very rare situations in which it is not possible to provide access to an historic property using the special access provisions in ADAAG. Therefore, paragraph (a) of § 36.405 has been revised to provide that alterations to historic properties shall comply, to the maximum extent feasible, with section 4.1.7 of ADAAG. Paragraph (b) of this section has been revised to provide that if it has been determined, under the procedures established in ADAAG, that it is not feasible to provide physical access to an historic property that is a place of public accommodation in a manner that will not threaten or destroy the historic significance of the property, alternative methods of access shall be provided pursuant to the requirements of Subpart C.

Section 36.406 Standards for New Construction and Alterations

Section 36.406 implements the requirements of sections 306(b) and 306(c) of the Act, which require the Attorney General to promulgate standards for accessible design for buildings and facilities subject to the Act and this part that are consistent with the supplemental minimum guidelines and requirements for accessible design published by the Architectural and Transportation Barriers Compliance Board (ATBCB or Board) pursuant to section 504 of the Act. This section of the rule provides that new construction and alterations subject to this part shall comply with the standards for accessible design published as appendix A to this part.

Appendix A contains the Americans with Disabilities Act Accessibility Guidelines for Buildings and Facilities (ADAAG) which is being published by the ATBCB as a final rule elsewhere in this issue of the Federal Register. As proposed in this Department's proposed rule, § 36.406(a) adopts ADAAG as the accessibility standard applicable under this rule.

Paragraph (b) was not included in the proposed rule. It provides, in chart form, guidance for using ADAAG together with subparts A through D of this part when determining requirements for a particular facility. This chart is intended solely as guidance for the user; it has no effect for purposes of compliance or enforcement. It does not necessarily provide complete or mandatory information.

Proposed § 36.406(b) is not included in the final rule. That provision, which would have taken effect only if the final rule had followed the proposed Option Two for § 36.401(a), is unnecessary because the Department has chosen Option One, as explained in the preamble for that section.

Section 504(a) of the ADA requires the ATBCB to issue minimum guidelines to supplement the existing Minimum Guidelines and Requirements for Accessible Design (MGRAD) (36 CFR part 1190) for purposes of title III. According to section 504(b) of the Act, the guidelines are to establish additional requirements, consistent with the Act, "to ensure that buildings and facilities are accessible, in terms of architecture and design, . . . and communication, to individuals with disabilities." Section 306(c) of the Act requires that the accessibility standards included in the Department's regulations be consistent with the minimum guidelines, in this case ADAAG.

As explained in the ATBCB's preamble to ADAAG, the substance and form of the guidelines are drawn from several sources. They use as their model the 1984 Uniform Federal Accessibility Standards (UFAS) (41 CFR part 101, subpart 101-19.6, appendix), which are the standards implementing the Architectural Barriers Act. UFAS is based on the Board's 1982 MGRAD. ADAAG follows the numbering system and format of the private sector American National Standard Institute's ANSI A117.1 standards. (American National Specifications for Making

Buildings and Facilities Accessible to and Usable by Physically Handicapped People (ANSI A117-1980) and American National Standard for Buildings and Facilities—Providing Accessibility and Usability for Physically Handicapped People (ANSI A117.1-1986).) ADAAG supplements MGRAD. In developing ADAAG, the Board made every effort to be consistent with MGRAD and the current and proposed ANSI Standards, to the extent consistent with the ADA.

ADAAG consists of nine main sections and a separate appendix. Sections 1 through 3 contain general provisions and definitions. Section 4 contains scoping provisions and technical specifications applicable to all covered buildings and facilities. The scoping provisions are listed separately for new construction of sites and exterior facilities; new construction of buildings; additions; alterations; and alterations to historic properties. The technical specifications generally reprint the text and illustrations of the ANSI A117.1 standard, except where differences are noted by italics. Sections 5 through 9 of the guidelines are special application sections and contain additional requirements for restaurants and cafeterias, medical care facilities, business and mercantile facilities, libraries, and transient lodging. The appendix to the guidelines contains additional information to aid in understanding the technical specifications. The section numbers in the appendix correspond to the sections of the guidelines to which they relate. An asterisk after a section number indicates that additional information appears in the appendix.

ADAAG's provisions are further explained under Summary of ADAAG below.

General Comments

One commenter urged the Department to move all or portions of subpart D, New Construction and Alterations, to the appendix (ADAAG) or to duplicate portions of subpart D in the appendix. The commenter correctly pointed out that subpart D is inherently linked to ADAAG, and that a self-contained set of rules would be helpful to users. The Department has attempted to simplify use of the two documents by deleting some paragraphs from subpart D (e.g., those relating to work areas), because they are included in ADAAG. However, the Department has retained in subpart D those sections that are taken directly from the statute or that give meaning to specific statutory concepts (e.g., structural impracticability, path of travel). While some of the subpart D provisions are duplicated in ADAAG, others are not. For example, issues relating to path of travel and disproportionality in alterations are not addressed in detail in ADAAG. (The structure and contents of the two documents are addressed below under Summary of ADAAG.) While the Department agrees that it would be useful to have one self-contained document, the different focuses of this rule and ADAAG do not permit this result at this time. However, the chart included in § 36.406(b) should assist users in applying the provisions of subparts A through D, and ADAAG together.

Numerous business groups have urged the Department not to adopt the proposed ADAAG as the accessibility standards, because the requirements established are too high, reflect the "state of the art," and are inflexible, rigid, and impractical. Many of these objections have been lodged on the basis that ADAAG exceeds the statutory mandate to establish "minimum" guidelines. In the view of the Department, these commenters have misconstrued the meaning of the term "minimum guidelines." The statute clearly contemplates that the guidelines establish a level of access—a minimum—that the standards must meet or exceed. The guidelines are not to be "minimal" in the sense that they would provide for a low level of access. To the contrary, Congress emphasized that the ADA requires a "high degree of convenient access." Education and Labor report at 117-18. The legislative history explains that the guidelines may not "reduce, weaken, narrow or set less accessibility standards than those included in existing MGRAD" and should provide greater guidance in communication accessibility for individuals with hearing and vision impairments. Id. at 139. Nor did Congress contemplate a set of guidelines less detailed than ADAAG; the statute requires that the ADA guidelines supplement the existing MGRAD. When it established the statutory scheme, Congress was aware of the content and purpose of the 1982 MGRAD; as ADAAG does with respect to ADA, MGRAD establishes a minimum level of access that the Architectural Barriers Act standards (i.e., UFAS) must meet or exceed, and includes a high level of detail.

Many of the same commenters urged the Department to incorporate as its accessibility standards the ANSI standard's technical provisions and to adopt the proposed scoping provisions under development by the Council of American Building Officials' Board for the Coordination of Model Codes (BCMC). They contended that the ANSI standard is familiar to and accepted by professionals, and that both documents are developed through consensus. They suggested that ADAAG will not stay current, because it does not follow an established cyclical review process, and that it is not likely to be adopted by nonfederal jurisdictions in State and local codes. They urged the Department and the Board to coordinate the ADAAG provisions and any substantive changes to them with the ANSI A117 committee in order to maintain a consistent and uniform set of accessibility standards that can be efficiently and effectively implemented at the State and local level through the existing building regulatory processes.

The Department shares the commenters' goal of coordination between the private sector and Federal standards, to the extent that coordination can lead to substantive requirements consistent with the ADA. A single accessibility standard, or consistent accessibility standards, that can be used for ADA purposes and that can be incorporated or referenced by State and local governments, would help to ensure that the ADA requirements are routinely implemented at the design stage. The Department plans to work toward this goal.

The Department, however, must comply with the requirements of the ADA, the Federal Advisory Committee Act (5 U.S.C app. 1 et seq.) and the Administrative Procedure Act (5 U.S.C 551 et seq.). Neither the Department nor the Board can adopt private requirements wholesale. Furthermore, neither the 1991 ANSI A117 Standard revision nor the BCMC process is complete. Although the ANSI and BCMC provisions are not final, the Board has carefully considered both the draft BCMC scoping provisions and draft ANSI technical standards and included their language in ADAAG wherever consistent with the ADA.

Some commenters requested that, if the Department did not adopt ANSI by reference, the Department declare compliance with ANSI/BCMC to constitute equivalency with the ADA standards. The Department has not adopted this recommendation but has instead worked as a member of the ATBCB to ensure that its accessibility standards are practical and usable. In addition, as explained under subpart F, Certification of State Laws or Local Building Codes, the proper forum for further evaluation of this suggested approach would be in conjunction with the certification process.

Some commenters urged the Department to allow an additional comment period after the Board published its guidelines in final form, for purposes of affording the public a further opportunity to evaluate the appropriateness of including them as the Departments accessibility standards. Such an additional comment period is unnecessary and would unduly delay the issuance of final regulations. The Department put the public on notice, through the proposed rule, of its intention to adopt the proposed ADAAG, with any changes made by the Board, as the accessibility standards. As a member of the Board and of its ADA Task Force, the Department participated actively in the public hearings held on the proposed guidelines and in preparation of both the proposed and final versions of ADAAG. Many individuals and groups commented directly to the Department's docket, or at its public hearings, about ADAAG. The comments received on ADAAG, whether by the Board or by this Department, were thoroughly analyzed and considered by the Department in the context of whether the proposed ADAAG was consistent with the ADA and suitable for adoption as both guidelines and standards. The Department is convinced that ADAAG as adopted in its final form is appropriate for these purposes. The final guidelines, adopted here as standards, will ensure the high level of access contemplated by Congress, consistent with the ADA's balance between the interests of people with disabilities and the business community.

A few commenters, citing the Senate report (at 70) and the Education and Labor report (at 119), asked the Department to include in the regulations a provision stating that departures from particular technical and scoping requirements of the accessibility standards will be permitted so long as the alternative methods used will provide substantially equivalent or greater access to and utilization of the facility. Such a provision is found in ADAAG 2.2 and by virtue of that fact is included in these regulations.

Comments on specific provisions of proposed ADAAG

During the course of accepting comments on its proposed rule, the Department received numerous comments on ADAAG. Those areas that elicited the heaviest response included assistive listening systems, automated teller machines, work areas, parking, areas of refuge, telephones (scoping for TDD's and volume controls) and visual alarms. Strenuous objections were raised by some business commenters to the proposed provisions of the guidelines concerning check-out aisles, counters, and scoping for hotels and nursing facilities. All these comments were considered in the same manner as other comments on the Department's proposed rule and, in the Department's view, have been addressed adequately in the final ADAAG.

Largely in response to comments, the Board made numerous changes from its proposal, including the following:

- Generally, at least 50% of public entrances to new buildings must be accessible, rather than all entrances, as would often have resulted from the proposed approach.
- Not all check-out aisles are required to be accessible.
- The final guidelines provide greater flexibility in providing access to sales counters, and no longer require a portion of every counter to be accessible.
- Scoping for TDD's or text telephones was increased. One TDD or text telephone, for speech and hearing impaired persons, must be provided at locations with 4, rather than 6, pay phones, and in hospitals and shopping malls. Use of portable (less expensive) TDD's is allowed.
- Dispersal of wheelchair seating areas in theaters will be required only where there are more than 300 seats, rather than in all cases. Seats with removable armrests (i.e., seats into which persons with mobility impairments can transfer) will also be required.
- Areas of refuge (areas with direct access to a stairway, and where people who cannot use stairs may await assistance during a emergency evacuation) will be required, as proposed, but the final provisions are based on the Uniform Building Code. Such areas are not required in alterations.
- Rather than requiring 5% of new hotel rooms to be accessible to people with mobility impairments, between 2 and 4% accessibility (depending on total number of rooms) is required. In addition, 1% of the rooms must have roll-in showers.
- The proposed rule reserved the provisions on alterations to homeless shelters. The final guidelines apply alterations requirements to homeless shelters, but the requirements are less stringent than those applied to other types of facilities.
- Parking spaces that can be used by people in vans (with lifts) will be required.
- As mandated by the ADA, the Board has established a procedure to be followed with respect to alterations to historic facilities.

Summary of ADAAG

This section of the preamble summarizes the structure of ADAAG, and highlights the more important portions.

Sections 1 Through 3

Sections 1 through 3 contain general requirements, including definitions.

Section 4.1.1, Application

Section 4 contains scoping requirements. Section 4.1.1, Application, provides that all areas of newly designed or newly constructed buildings and facilities and altered portions of existing buildings and facilities required to be accessible by § 4.1.6 must comply with the guidelines unless otherwise provided in § 4.1.1 or a special application section. It addresses areas used only by employees as work areas, temporary structures, and general exceptions.

Section 4.1.1(3) preserves the basic principle of the proposed rule: Areas that may be used by employees with disabilities shall be designed and constructed so that an individual with a disability can approach, enter, and exit the area. The language has been clarified to provide that it applies to any area used only as a work area (not just to areas "that may be used by employees with disabilities"), and that the guidelines do not require that any area used as an individual work station be designed with maneuvering space or equipped to be accessible. The appendix to ADAAG explains that work areas must meet the guidelines' requirements for doors and accessible routes, and recommends, but does not require, that 5% of individual work stations be designed to permit a person using a wheelchair to maneuver within the space.

Further discussion of work areas is found in the preamble concerning proposed § 36.401(b).

Section 4.1.1(5)(a) includes an exception for structural impracticability that corresponds to the one found in § 36.401(c) and discussed in that portion of the preamble.

Section 4.1.2, Accessible Sites and Exterior Facilities: New Construction

This section addresses exterior features, elements, or spaces such as parking, portable toilets, and exterior signage, in new construction. Interior elements and spaces are covered by § 4.1.3.

The final rule retains the UFAS scoping for parking but also requires that at least one of every eight accessible parking spaces be designed with adequate adjacent space to deploy a lift used with a van. These spaces must have a sign indicating that they are van-accessible, but they are not to be reserved exclusively for van users.

Section 4.1.3, Accessible Buildings: New Construction

This section establishes scoping requirements for new construction of buildings and facilities.

Sections 4.1.3 (1) through (4) cover accessible

routes, protruding objects, ground and floor surfaces, and stairs.

Section 4.1.3(5) generally requires elevators to serve each level in a newly constructed building, with four exceptions included in the subsection. Exception 1 is the "elevator exception" established in § 36.401(d), which must be read with this section. Exception 4 allows the use of platform lifts under certain conditions.

Section 4.1.3(6), Windows, is reserved. Section 4.1.3(7) applies to doors.

Under § 4.1.3(8), at least 50% of all public entrances must be accessible. In addition, if a building is designed to provide access to enclosed parking, pedestrian tunnels, or elevated walkways, at least one entrance that serves each such function must be accessible. Each tenancy in a building must be served by an accessible entrance. Where local regulations (e.g., fire codes) require that a minimum number of exits be provided, an equivalent number of accessible entrances must be provided. (The latter provision does not require a greater number of entrances than otherwise planned.)

ADAAG Section 4.1.3(9), with accompanying technical requirements in Section 4.3, requires an area of rescue assistance (i.e., an area with direct access to an exit stairway and where people who are unable to use stairs may await assistance during an emergency evacuation) to be established on each floor of a multi-story building. This was one of the most controversial provisions in the guidelines. The final ADAAG is based on current Uniform Building Code requirements and retains the requirement that areas of refuge (renamed "areas of rescue assistance") be provided, but specifies that this requirement does not apply to buildings that have a supervised automatic sprinkler system. Areas of refuge are not required in alterations.

The next seven subsections deal with drinking fountains (§ 4.1.3(10)); toilet facilities (§ 4.1.3(11)); storage, shelving, and display units (§ 4.1.3(12)), controls and operating mechanisms (§ 4.1.3(13)), emergency warning systems (§ 4.1.3(14)), detectable warnings (§ 4.1.3(15)), and building signage (§ 4.1.3(16)). Paragraph 11 requires that toilet facilities comply with § 4.22, which requires one accessible toilet stall (60" x 60") in each newly constructed restroom. In response to public comments, the final rule requires that a second accessible stall (36" x 60") be provided in restrooms that have six or more stalls.

ADAAG Section 4.1.3(17) establishes requirements for accessibility of pay phones to persons with mobility impairments, hearing impairments (requiring some phones with volume controls), and those who cannot use voice telephones. It requires one interior "text telephone" to be provided at any facility that has a total of four or more public pay phones. (The term "text telephone" has been adopted to reflect current terminology and changes in technology.) In addition, text telephones will be required in specific locations, such as covered shopping malls, hospitals (in emergency rooms, waiting rooms, and recovery areas), and convention centers.

Paragraph 18 of Section 4.1.3 generally requires that at least five percent of fixed or built-in seating or tables be accessible.

Paragraph 19, covering assembly areas, specifies the number of wheelchair seating spaces and types and numbers of assistive listening systems required. It requires dispersal of wheelchair seating locations in facilities where there are more than 300 seats. The guidelines also require that at least one percent of all fixed seats be aisle seats without armrests (or with moveable armrests) on the aisle side to increase accessibility for persons with mobility impairments who prefer to transfer from their wheelchairs to fixed seating. In addition, the final ADAAG requires that fixed seating for a companion be located adjacent to each wheelchair location.

Paragraph 20 requires that where automated teller machines are provided, at least one must comply with section 4.34, which, among other things, requires accessible controls, and instructions and other information that are accessible to persons with sight impairments.

Under paragraph 21, where dressing rooms are provided, five percent or at least one must comply with section 4.35.

Section 4.1.5, Additions

Each addition to an existing building or facility is regarded as an alteration subject to §§ 36.402 through 36.406 of subpart D, including the date established in § 36.402(a). But additions also have attributes of new construction, and to the extent that a space or element in the addition is newly constructed, each new space or element must comply with the applicable scoping provisions of sections 4.1.1 to 4.1.3 for new construction, the applicable technical specifications of sections 4.2 through 4.34, and any applicable special provisions in sections 5 through 10. For instance, if a restroom is provided in the addition, it must comply with the requirements for new construction. Construction of an addition does not, however, create an obligation to retrofit the entire existing building or facility to meet requirements for new construction. Rather, the addition is to be regarded as an alteration and to the extent that it affects or could affect the usability of or access to an area containing a primary function, the requirements in section 4.1.6(2) are triggered with respect to providing an accessible path of travel to the altered area and making the restrooms, telephones, and drinking fountains serving the altered area accessible. For example, if a museum adds a new wing that does not have a separate entrance as part of the addition, an accessible path of travel would have to be provided through the existing building or facility unless it is disproportionate to the overall cost and scope of the addition as established in § 36.403(f).

Section 4.1.6, Alterations

An alteration is a change to a building or facility that affects or could affect the usability of or access to the building or facility or any part thereof. There are three general principles for alterations. First, if any existing element or space is altered, the altered element or space must meet new construction requirements (section 4.1.6(1)(b)). Second, if alterations to the elements in a space when considered together amount to an alteration of the space, the entire space must meet new construction requirements (section 4.1.6(1)(c)). Third, if the alteration affects or could affect the usability of or access to an area containing a primary function, the path of travel to the altered area and the restrooms, drinking fountains, and telephones serving the altered area must be made accessible unless it is disproportionate to the overall alterations in terms of cost and scope as determined under criteria established by the Attorney General (§ 4.1.6(2)).

Section 4.1.6 should be read with §§ 36.402 through 36.405. Requirements concerning alterations to an area serving a primary function are addressed with greater detail in the latter sections than in section 4.1.6(2). Section 4.1.6(1)(j) deals with technical infeasibility. Section 4.1.6(3) contains special technical provisions for alterations to existing buildings and facilities.

Section 4.1.7, Historic Preservation

This section contains scoping provisions and alternative requirements for alterations to qualified historic buildings and facilities. It clarifies the procedures under the National Historic Preservation Act and their application to alterations covered by the ADA. An individual seeking to alter a facility that is subject to the ADA guidelines and to State or local historic preservation statutes shall consult with the State Historic Preservation Officer to determine if the planned alteration would threaten or destroy the historic significance of the facility.

Sections 4.2 Through 4.35

Sections 4.2 through 4.35 contain the technical specifications for elements and spaces required to be accessible by the scoping provisions (sections 4.1 through 4.1.7) and special application sections (sections 5 through 10). The technical specifications are the same as the 1980 version of ANSI A117.1 standard, except as noted in the text by italics.

Sections 5 Through 9

These are special application sections and contain additional requirements for restaurants and cafeterias, medical care facilities, business and mercantile facilities, libraries, and transient lodging. For example, at least 5 percent, but not less than one, of the fixed tables in a restaurant must be accessible.

In section 7, Business and Mercantile, paragraph 7.2 (Sales and Service Counters, Teller Windows, Information Counters) has been revised to provide greater flexibility in new construction than did the proposed rule. At least one of each type of sales or service counter where a cash register is located shall be made accessible. Accessible counters shall be dispersed throughout the facility. At counters such as bank teller windows or ticketing counters, alternative methods of compliance are permitted. A public accommodation may lower a portion of the counter, provide an auxiliary counter, or provide equivalent facilitation through such means as installing a folding shelf on the front of the counter at an accessible height to provide a work surface for a person using a wheelchair.

Section 7.3., Check-out Aisles, provides that, in new construction, a certain number of each design of check-out aisle, as listed in a chart based on the total number of check-out aisles of each design, shall be accessible. The percentage of check-outs required to be accessible generally ranges from 20% to 40%. In a newly constructed or altered facility with less than 5,000 square feet of selling space, at least one of each type of check-out aisle must be accessible. In altered facilities with 5,000 or more square feet of selling space, at least one of each design of check-out aisle must be made accessible when altered, until the number of accessible aisles of each design equals the number that would be required for new construction.

Section 9, Accessible Transient Lodging

Section 9 addresses two types of transient lodging: hotels, motels, inns, boarding houses, dormitories, resorts, and other similar places (sections 9.1 through 9.4); and homeless shelters, halfway houses, transient group homes, and other social service establishments (section 9.5). The interplay of the ADA and Fair Housing Act with respect to such facilities is addressed in the preamble discussion of the definition of "place of public accommodation" in § 36.104.

The final rule establishes scoping requirements for accessibility of newly constructed hotels. Four percent of the first hundred rooms, and roughly two percent of rooms in excess of 100, must meet certain requirements for accessibility to persons with mobility or hearing impairments, and an additional identical percentage must be accessible to persons with hearing impairments. An additional 1% of the available rooms must be equipped with roll-in showers, raising the actual scoping for rooms accessible to persons with mobility impairments to 5% of the first hundred rooms and 3% thereafter. The final ADAAG also provides that when a hotel is being altered, one fully accessible room and one room equipped with visual alarms, notification devices, and amplified telephones shall be provided for each 25 rooms being altered until the number of accessible rooms equals that required under the new construction standard. Accessible rooms must be dispersed in a manner that will provide persons with disabilities with a choice of single or multiple-bed accommodations.

In new construction, homeless shelters and other social service entities must comply with ADAAG; at least one type of amenity in each common area must be accessible. In a facility that is not required to have an elevator, it is not necessary to provide accessible amenities on the inaccessible floors if at least one of each type of amenity is provided in accessible common areas. The percentage of accessible sleeping accommodations required is the same as that required for other places of transient lodging. Requirements for facilities altered for use as a homeless shelter parallel the current MGRAD accessibility requirements for leased buildings. A shelter located in an altered facility must have at least one accessible entrance, accessible sleeping accommodations in a number equivalent to that established for new construction, at least one accessible toilet and bath, at least one accessible common area, and an accessible route connecting all accessible areas. All accessible areas in a homeless shelter in an altered facility may be located on one level.

Section 10, Transportation Facilities

Section 10 of ADAAG is reserved. On March 20, 1991, the ATBCB published a supplemental notice of proposed rulemaking (56 FR 11874) to establish special access requirements for transportation facilities. The Department anticipates that when the ATBCB issues final guidelines for transportation facilities, this part will be amended to include those provisions.

Subpart E—Enforcement

Because the Department of Justice does not have authority to establish procedures for judicial review and enforcement, subpart E generally restates the statutory procedures for enforcement.

Section 36.501 describes the procedures for private suits by individuals and the judicial remedies available. In addition to the language in section 308(a)(1) of the Act, § 36.501(a) of this part includes the language from section 204(a) of the Civil Rights Act of 1964 (42 U.S.C. 2000a-3(a)) which is incorporated by reference in the ADA. A commenter noted that the proposed rule did not include the provision in section 204(a) allowing the court to appoint an attorney for the complainant and authorize the commencement of the civil action without the payment of fees, costs, or security. That provision has been included in the final rule.

Section 308(a)(1) of the ADA permits a private suit by an individual who has reasonable grounds for believing that he or she is "about to be" subjected to discrimination in violation of section 303 of the Act (subpart D of this part), which requires that new construction and alterations be readily accessible to and usable by individuals with disabilities. Authorizing suits to prevent construction of facilities with architectural barriers will avoid the necessity of costly retrofitting that might be required if suits were not permitted until after the facilities were completed. To avoid unnecessary suits, this section requires that the individual bringing the suit have "reasonable grounds" for believing that a violation is about to occur, but does not require the individual to engage in a futile gesture if he or she has notice that a person or organization covered by title III of the Act does not intend to comply with its provisions.

Section 36.501(b) restates the provisions of section 308(a)(2) of the Act, which states that injunctive relief for the failure to remove architectural barriers in existing facilities or the failure to make new construction and alterations accessible "shall include" an order to alter these facilities to make them readily accessible to and usable by persons with disabilities to the extent required by title III. The Report of the Energy and Commerce Committee notes that "an order to make a facility readily accessible to and usable by individuals with disabilities is mandatory" under this standard. H.R. Rep. No. 485, 101st Cong., 2d Sess, pt 4, at 64 (1990). Also, injunctive relief shall include, where appropriate, requiring the provision of an auxiliary aid or service, modification of a policy, or provision of alternative methods, to the extent required by title III of the Act and this part.

Section 36.502 is based on section 308(b)(1)(A)(i) of the Act, which provides that the Attorney General shall investigate alleged violations of title III and undertake periodic reviews of compliance of covered entities. Although the Act does not establish a comprehensive administrative enforcement mechanism for investigation and resolution of all complaints received, the legislative history notes that investigation of alleged violations and periodic compliance reviews are essential to effective enforcement of title III, and that the Attorney General is expected to engage in active enforcement and to allocate sufficient resources to carry out this responsibility. Judiciary Report at 67.

Many commenters argued for inclusion of more specific provisions for administrative resolution of disputes arising under the Act and this part in order to promote voluntary compliance and avoid the need for litigation. Administrative resolution is far more efficient and economical than litigation, particularly in the early stages of implementation of complex legislation when the specific requirements of the statute are not widely understood. The Department has added a new paragraph (c) to this section authorizing the Attorney General to initiate a compliance review where he or she has reason to believe there may be a violation of this rule.

Section 36.503 describes the procedures for suits by the Attorney General set out in section 308(b)(1)(B) of the Act. If the Department has reasonable cause to believe that any person or group of persons is engaged in a pattern or practice of resistance to the full enjoyment of any of the rights granted by title III or that any person or group of persons has been denied any of the rights granted by title III and such denial raises an issue of general public importance, the Attorney General may commence a civil action in any appropriate United States district court. The proposed rule provided for suit by the Attorney General "or his or her designee." The reference to a "designee" has been omitted in the final rule because it is unnecessary. The Attorney General has delegated enforcement authority under the ADA to the Assistant Attorney General for Civil Rights. 55 FR 40653 (October 4, 1990) (to be codified at 28 CFR 0.50(l).)

Section 36.504 describes the relief that may be granted in a suit by the Attorney General under section 308(b)(2) of the Act. In such an action, the court may grant any equitable relief it considers to be appropriate, including granting temporary, preliminary, or permanent relief, providing an auxiliary aid or service, modification of policy or alternative method, or making facilities readily accessible to and usable by individuals with disabilities, to the extent required by title III. In addition, a court may award such other relief as the court considers to be appropriate, including monetary damages to persons aggrieved, when requested by the Attorney General.

Furthermore, the court may vindicate the public interest by assessing a civil penalty against the covered entity in an amount not exceeding $50,000 for a first violation and not exceeding $100,000 for any subsequent violation. Section 36.504(b) of the rule adopts the standard of section 308(b)(3) of the Act. This section makes it clear that, in counting the number of previous determinations of violations for determining whether a "first" or "subsequent" violation has occurred, determinations in the same action that the entity has engaged in more than one discriminatory act are to be counted as a single violation. A "second violation" would not accrue to that entity until the Attorney General brought another suit against the entity and the entity was again held in violation. Again, all of the violations found in the second suit would be cumulatively considered as a "subsequent violation."

Section 36.504(c) clarifies that the terms "monetary damages" and "other relief" do not include punitive damages. They do include, however, all forms of compensatory damages, including out-of-pocket expenses and damages for pain and suffering.

Section 36.504(a)(3) is based on section 308(b)(2)(C) of the Act, which provides that, "to vindicate the public interest," a court may assess a civil penalty against the entity that has been found to be in violation of the Act in suits brought by the Attorney General. In addition, § 36.504(d), which is taken from section 308(b)(5) of the Act, further provides that, in considering what amount of civil penalty, if any, is appropriate, the court shall give consideration to "any good faith effort or attempt to comply with this part." In evaluating such good faith, the court shall consider "among other factors it deems relevant, whether the entity could have reasonably anticipated the need for an appropriate type of auxiliary aid needed to accommodate the unique needs of a particular individual with a disability."

The "good faith" standard referred to in this section is not intended to imply a willful or intentional standard—that is, an entity cannot demonstrate good faith simply by showing that it did not willfully, intentionally, or recklessly disregard the law. At the same time, the absence of such a course of conduct would be a factor a court should weigh in determining the existence of good faith.

Section 36.505 states that courts are authorized to

award attorneys fees, including litigation expenses and costs, as provided in section 505 of the Act. Litigation expenses include items such as expert witness fees, travel expenses, etc. The Judiciary Committee Report specifies that such items are included under the rubric of "attorneys fees" and not "costs" so that such expenses will be assessed against a plaintiff only under the standard set forth in *Christiansburg Garment Co. v. Equal Employment Opportunity Commission*, 434 U.S. 412 (1978). (Judiciary report at 73.)

Section 36.506 restates section 513 of the Act, which encourages use of alternative means of dispute resolution. Section 36.507 explains that, as provided in section 506(e) of the Act, a public accommodation or other private entity is not excused from compliance with the requirements of this part because of any failure to receive technical assistance.

Section 36.305 Effective Date

In general, title III is effective 18 months after enactment of the Americans with Disabilities Act, i.e., January 26, 1992. However, there are several exceptions to this general rule contained throughout title III. Section 36.508 sets forth all of these exceptions in one place.

Paragraph (b) contains the rule on civil actions. It states that, except with respect to new construction and alterations, no civil action shall be brought for a violation of this part that occurs before July 26, 1992, against businesses with 25 or fewer employees and gross receipts of $1,000,000 or less; and before January 26, 1993, against businesses with 10 or fewer employees and gross receipts of $500,000 or less. In determining what constitutes gross receipts, it is appropriate to exclude amounts collected for sales taxes.

Paragraph (c) concerns transportation services provided by public accommodations not primarily engaged in the business of transporting people. The 18-month effective date applies to all of the transportation provisions except those requiring newly purchased or leased vehicles to be accessible. Vehicles subject to that requirement must be accessible to and usable by individuals with disabilities if the solicitation for the vehicle is made on or after August 26, 1990.

Subpart F—Certification of State Laws or Local Building Codes

Subpart F establishes procedures to implement section 308(b)(1)(A)(ii) of the Act, which provides that, on the application of a State or local government, the Attorney General may certify that a State law or local building code or similar ordinance meets or exceeds the minimum accessibility requirements of the Act. In enforcement proceedings, this certification will constitute rebuttable evidence that the law or code meets or exceeds the ADA's requirements.

Three significant changes, further explained below, were made from the proposed subpart, in response to comments. First, the State or local jurisdiction is required to hold a public hearing on its proposed request for certification and to submit to the Department, as part of the information and materials in support of a request for certification, a transcript of the hearing. Second, the time allowed for interested persons and organizations to comment on the request filed with the Department (§ 36.605(a)(1)) has been changed from 30 to 60 days. Finally, a new § 36.608, Guidance concerning model codes, has been added.

Section 36.601 establishes the definitions to be used for purposes of this subpart. Two of the definitions have been modified, and a definition of "model code" has been added. First, in response to a comment, a reference to a code "or part thereof" has been added to the definition of "code." The purpose of this addition is to clarify that an entire code need not be submitted if only part of it is relevant to accessibility, or if the jurisdiction seeks certification of only some of the portions that concern accessibility. The Department does not intend to encourage "piecemeal" requests for certification by a single jurisdiction. In fact, the Department expects that in some cases, rather than certifying portions of a particular code and refusing to certify others, it may notify a submitting jurisdiction of deficiencies and encourage a reapplication that cures those deficiencies, so that the entire code can be certified eventually. Second, the definition of "submitting official" has been modified. The proposed rule defined the submitting official to be the State or local official who has principal responsibility for administration of a code. Commenters pointed out that in some cases more than one code within the same jurisdiction is relevant for purposes of certification. It was also suggested that the Department allow a State to submit a single application on behalf of the State, as well as on behalf of any local jurisdictions required to follow the State accessibility requirements. Consistent with these comments, the Department has added to the definition language clarifying that the official can be one authorized to submit a code on behalf of a jurisdiction.

A definition of "model code" has been added in light of new § 36.608.

Most commenters generally approved of the proposed certification process. Some approved of what they saw as the Department's attempt to bring State and local codes into alignment with the ADA. A State agency said that this section will be the backbone of the intergovernmental cooperation essential if the accessibility provisions of the ADA are to be effective.

Some comments disapproved of the proposed process as time-consuming and laborious for the Department, although some of these comments pointed out that, if the Attorney General certified model codes on which State and local codes are based, many perceived problems would be alleviated. (This point is further addressed by new § 36.608.)

Many of the comments received from business organizations, as well as those from some individuals and disability rights groups, addressed the relationship of the ADA requirements and their enforcement, to existing State and local codes and code enforcement systems. These commenters urged the Department to use existing code-making bodies for interpretations of the ADA, and to actively participate in the integration of the ADA into the text of the national model codes that are adopted by State and local enforcement agencies. These issues are discussed in preamble section 36.406 under General comments.

Many commenters urged the Department to evaluate or certify the entire code enforcement system (including any process for hearing appeals from builders of denials by the building code official of requests for variances, waivers, or modifications). Some urged that certification not be allowed in jurisdictions where waivers can be granted, unless there is a clearly identified decision- making process, with written rulings and notice to affected parties of any waiver or modification request. One commenter urged establishment of a dispute resolution mechanism, providing for interpretation (usually through a building official) and an administrative appeals mechanism (generally called Boards of Appeal, Boards of Construction Appeals, or Boards of Review), before certification could be granted.

The Department thoroughly considered these proposals but has declined to provide for certification of processes of enforcement or administration of State and local codes. The statute clearly authorizes the Department to certify the codes themselves for equivalency with the statute; it would be ill-advised for the Department at this point to inquire beyond the face of the code and written interpretations of it. It would be inappropriate to require those jurisdictions that grant waivers or modifications to establish certain procedures before they can apply for certification, or to insist that no deviations can be permitted. In fact, the Department expects that many jurisdictions will allow slight variations from a particular code, consistent with ADAAG itself. ADAAG includes in § 2.2 a statement allowing departures from particular requirements where substantially equivalent or greater access and usability is provided. Several sections specifically allow for alternative methods providing equivalent facilitation and, in some cases, provide examples. (See, e.g., section 4.31.9, Text Telephones; section 7.2(2) (iii), Sales and Service Counters.) Section 4.1.6 includes less stringent requirements that are permitted in alterations, in certain circumstances.

However, in an attempt to ensure that it does not certify a code that in practice has been or will be applied in a manner that defeats its equivalency with the ADA, the Department will require that the submitting official include, with the application for certification, any relevant manuals, guides, or any other interpretive information issued that pertain to the code. (§ 36.603(c)(1).) The requirement that this information be provided is in addition to the NPRM's requirement that the official provide any pertinent formal opinions of the State Attorney General or the chief legal officer of the jurisdiction.

The first step in the certification process is a request for certification, filed by a "submitting official" (§ 36.603). The Department will not accept requests for certification until after January 26, 1992, the effective date of this part. The Department received numerous comments from individuals and organizations representing a variety of interests, urging that the hearing required to be held by the Assistant Attorney General in Washington, DC, after a preliminary determination of equivalency (§ 36.605(a)(2)), be held within the State or locality requesting certification, in order to facilitate greater participation by all interested parties. While the Department has not modified the requirement that it hold a hearing in Washington, it has added a new subparagraph 36.603(b)(3) requiring a hearing within the State or locality before a request for certification is filed. The hearing must be held after adequate notice to the public and must be on the record; a transcript must be provided with the request for certification. This procedure will insure input from the public at the State or local level and will also insure a Washington, DC, hearing as mentioned in the legislative history.

The request for certification, along with supporting documents (§ 36.603(c)), must be filed in duplicate with the office of the Assistant Attorney General for Civil Rights. The Assistant Attorney General may request further information. The request and supporting materials will be available for public examination at the office of the Assistant Attorney General and at the office of the State or local agency charged with administration and enforcement of the code. The submitting official must publish public notice of the request for certification.

Next, under § 36.604, the Assistant Attorney General's office will consult with the ATBCB and make a preliminary determination to either (1) find that the code is equivalent (make a "preliminary determination of equivalency") or (2) deny certification. The next step depends on which of these preliminary determinations is made.

If the preliminary determination is to find equivalency, the Assistant Attorney General, under § 36.605, will inform the submitting official in writing of the preliminary determination and publish a notice in the Federal Register informing the public of the preliminary determination and inviting comment for 60 days. (This time period has been increased from 30 days in light of public comment pointing out the need for more time within which to evaluate the code.) After considering the information received in response to the comments, the Department will hold an hearing in Washington. This hearing will not be subject to the formal requirements of the Administrative Procedure Act. In fact, this requirement could be satisfied by a meeting with interested parties. After the hearing, the Assistant Attorney General's office will consult again with the ATBCB and make a final determination of equivalency or a final determination to deny the request for certification, with a notice of the determination published in the Federal Register.

If the preliminary determination is to deny certification, there will be no hearing (§ 36.606). The Department will notify the submitting official of the preliminary determination, and may specify how the code could be modified in order to receive a preliminary determination of equivalency. The Department will allow at least 15 days for the submitting official to submit relevant material in opposition to the preliminary denial. If none is received, no further action will be taken. If more information is received, the Department will consider it and make either a final decision to deny certification or a preliminary determination of equivalency. If at that stage the Assistant Attorney General makes a preliminary determination of equivalency, the hearing procedures set out in § 36.605 will be followed.

Section 36.607 addresses the effect of certification. First, certification will only be effective concerning those features or elements that are both (1) covered by the certified code and (2) addressed by the regulations against which they are being certified. For example, if children's facilities are not addressed by the Department's standards, and the building in question is a private elementary school, certification will not be effective for those features of the building to be used by children. And if the Department's regulations addressed equipment but the local code did not, a building's equipment would not be covered by the certification.

In addition, certification will be effective only for the particular edition of the code that is certified. Amendments will not automatically be considered certified, and a submitting official will need to reapply for certification of the changed or additional provisions.

Certification will not be effective in those situations where a State or local building code official allows a facility to be constructed or altered in a manner that does not follow the technical or scoping provisions of the certified code. Thus, if an official either waives an accessible element or feature or allows a change that does not provide equivalent facilitation, the fact that the Department has certified the code itself will not stand as evidence that the facility has been constructed or altered in accordance with the minimum accessibility requirements of the ADA. The Department's certification of a code is effective only with respect to the standards in the code; it is not to be interpreted to apply to a State or local government's application of the code. The fact that the Department has certified a code with provisions concerning waivers, variances, or equivalent facilitation shall not be interpreted as an endorsement of actions taken pursuant to those provisions.

The final rule includes a new § 36.608 concerning model codes. It was drafted in response to concerns raised by numerous commenters, many of which have been discussed under General comments (§ 36.406). It is intended to assist in alleviating the difficulties posed by attempting to certify possibly tens of thousands of codes. It is included in recognition of the fact that many codes are based on, or incorporate, model or consensus standards developed by nationally recognized organizations (e.g., the American National Standards Institute (ANSI); Building Officials and Code Administrators (BOCA) International; Council of American Building Officials (CABO) and its Board for the Coordination of Model Codes (BCMC); Southern Building Code Congress International (SBCCI). While the Department will not certify or "precertify" model codes, as urged by some commenters, it does wish to encourage the continued viability of the consensus and model code process consistent with the purposes of the ADA.

The new section therefore allows an authorized

representative of a private entity responsible for developing a model code to apply to the Assistant Attorney General for review of the code. The review process will be informal and will not be subject to the procedures of §§ 36.602 through 36.607. The result of the review will take the form of guidance from the Assistant Attorney General as to whether and in what respects the model code is consistent with the ADA's requirements. The guidance will not be binding on any entity or on the Department; it will assist in evaluations of individual State or local codes and may serve as a basis for establishing priorities for consideration of individual codes. The Department anticipates that this approach will foster further cooperation among various government levels, the private entities developing standards, and individuals with disabilities.

ADA TITLE IV

47 U.S.C. § 225. Telecommunications services for hearing-impaired and speech-impaired individuals

(a) Definitions

As used in this section—

(1) Common carrier or carrier

The term "common carrier" or "carrier" includes any common carrier engaged in interstate communication by wire or radio as defined in section 153 of this title and any common carrier engaged in intrastate communication by wire or radio, notwithstanding sections 152(b) and 221(b) of this title.

(2) TDD

The term "TDD" means a Telecommunications Device for the Deaf, which is a machine that employs graphic communication in the transmission of coded signals through a wire or radio communication system.

(3) Telecommunications relay services

The term "telecommunications relay services" means telephone transmission services that provide the ability for an individual who has a hearing impairment or speech impairment to engage in communication by wire or radio with a hearing individual in a manner that is functionally equivalent to the ability of an individual who does not have a hearing impairment or speech impairment to communicate using voice communication services by wire or radio. Such term includes services that enable two-way communication between an individual who uses a TDD or other non-voice terminal device and an individual who does not use such a device.

(b) Availability of telecommunications relay services

(1) In general

In order to carry out the purposes established under section 151 of this title, to make available to all individuals in the United States a rapid, efficient nationwide communication service, and to increase the utility of the telephone system of the Nation, the Commission shall ensure that interstate and intrastate telecommunications relay services are available, to the extent possible and in the most efficient manner, to hearing-impaired and speech- impaired individuals in the United States.

(2) Use of general authority and remedies

For the purposes of administering and enforcing the provisions of this section and the regulations prescribed thereunder, the Commission shall have the same authority, power, and functions with respect to common carriers engaged in intrastate communication as the Commission has in administering and enforcing the provisions of this title with respect to any common carrier engaged in interstate communication. Any violation of this section by any common carrier engaged in intrastate communication shall be subject to the same remedies, penalties, and procedures as are applicable to a violation of this chapter by a common carrier engaged in interstate communication.

(c) Provision of services

Each common carrier providing telephone voice transmission services shall, not later than 3 years after July 26, 1990, provide in compliance with the regulations prescribed under this section, throughout the area in which it offers service, telecommunications relay services, individually, through designees, through a competitively selected vendor, or in concert with other carriers. A common carrier shall be considered to be in compliance with such regulations—

(1) with respect to intrastate telecommunications relay services in any State that does not have a certified program under subsection (f) of this section and with respect to interstate telecommunications relay services, if such common carrier (or other entity through which the carrier is providing such relay services) is in compliance with the Commission's regulations under subsection (d) of this section; or

(2) with respect to intrastate telecommunications relay services in any State that has a certified program under subsection (f) of this section for such State, if such common carrier (or other entity through which the carrier is providing such relay services) is in compliance with the program certified under subsection (f) of this section for such State.

(d) Regulations

(1) In general

The Commission shall, not later than 1 year after July 26, 1990, prescribe regulations to implement this section, including regulations that—

(A) establish functional requirements, guidelines, and operations procedures for telecommunications relay services;

(B) establish minimum standards that shall be met in carrying out subsection (c) of this section;

(C) require that telecommunications relay services operate every day for 24 hours per day;

(D) require that users of telecommunications relay services pay rates no greater than the rates paid for functionally equivalent voice communication services with respect to such factors as the duration of the call, the time of day, and the distance from point of origination to point of termination;

(E) prohibit relay operators from failing to fulfill the obligations of common carriers by refusing calls or limiting the length of calls that use telecommunications relay services;

(F) prohibit relay operators from disclosing the content of any relayed conversation and from keeping records of the content of any such conversation beyond the duration of the call; and

(G) prohibit relay operators from intentionally altering a relayed conversation.

(2) Technology

The Commission shall ensure that regulations prescribed to implement this section encourage, consistent with section 157(a) of this title, the use of existing technology and do not discourage or impair the development of improved technology.

(3) Jurisdictional separation of costs

(A) In general

Consistent with the provisions of section 410 of this title, the Commission shall prescribe regulations governing the jurisdictional separation of costs for the services provided pursuant to this section.

(B) Recovering costs

Such regulations shall generally provide that costs caused by interstate telecommunications relay services shall be recovered from all subscribers for every interstate service and costs caused by intrastate telecommunications relay services shall be recovered from the intrastate jurisdiction. In a State that has a certified program under subsection (f) of this section, a State commission shall permit a common carrier to recover the costs incurred in providing intrastate telecommunications relay services by a method consistent with the requirements of this section.

(e) Enforcement

(1) In general

Subject to subsections (f) and (g) of this section, the Commission shall enforce this section.

(2) Complaint

The Commission shall resolve, by final order, a complaint alleging a violation of this section within 180 days after the date such complaint is filed.

(f) Certification

(1) State documentation

Any State desiring to establish a State program under this section shall submit documentation to the Commission that describes the program of such State for implementing intrastate telecommunications relay services and the procedures and remedies available for enforcing any requirements imposed by the State program.

(2) Requirements for certification

After review of such documentation, the Commission shall certify the State program if the Commission determines that—

(A) the program makes available to hearing-impaired and speech-impaired individuals, either directly, through designees, through a competitively selected vendor, or through regulation of intrastate common carriers, intrastate telecommunications relay services in such State in a manner that meets or exceeds the requirements of regulations prescribed by the Commission under subsection (d) of this section; and

(B) the program makes available adequate procedures and remedies for enforcing the requirements of the State program.

(3) Method of funding

Except as provided in subsection (d) of this section, the Commission shall not refuse to certify a State program based solely on the method such State will implement for funding intrastate telecommunication relay services.

(4) Suspension or revocation of certification

The Commission may suspend or revoke such certification if, after notice and opportunity for hearing, the Commission determines that such certification is no longer warranted. In a State whose program has been suspended or revoked, the Commission shall take such steps as may be necessary, consistent with this section, to ensure continuity of telecommunications relay services.

(g) Complaint

(1) Referral of complaint

If a complaint to the Commission alleges a violation of this section with respect to intrastate telecommunications relay services within a State and certification of the program of such State under subsection (f) of this section is in effect, the Commission shall refer such complaint to such State.

(2) Jurisdiction of Commission

After referring a complaint to a State under paragraph (1), the Commission shall exercise jurisdiction over such complaint only if—

(A) final action under such State program has not been taken on such complaint by such State—

(i) within 180 days after the complaint is filed with such State; or

(ii) within a shorter period as prescribed by the regulations of such State; or

(B) the Commission determines that such State program is no longer qualified for certification under subsection (f) of this section.

ADA TITLE V

MISCELLANEOUS PROVISIONS

42 U.S.C. §

- 12201 Construction
- 12202 State immunity
- 12203 Prohibition against retaliation and coercion
- 12204 Regulations by the Architectural and Transportation Barriers Compliance Board
- 12205 Attorney's fees
- 12206 Technical assistance
- 12207 Federal wilderness areas
- 12208 Transvestites
- 12209 Coverage of Congress and the agencies of the legislative branch
- 12210 Illegal use of drugs
- 12211 Definitions
- 12212 Alternative means of dispute resolution
- 12213 Severability

ADA TITLE V

MISCELLANEOUS PROVISIONS

§ 12201 Construction

(a) In general

Except as otherwise provided in this chapter, nothing in this chapter shall be construed to apply a lesser standard than the standards applied under title V of the Rehabilitation Act of 1973 (29 U.S.C. 790 et seq.) or the regulations issued by Federal agencies pursuant to such title.

(b) Relationship to other laws

Nothing in this chapter shall be construed to invalidate or limit the remedies, rights, and procedures of any Federal law or law of any State or political subdivision of any State or jurisdiction that provides greater or equal protection for the rights of individuals with disabilities than are afforded by this chapter. Nothing in this chapter shall be construed to preclude the prohibition of, or the imposition of restrictions on, smoking in places of employment covered by subchapter I of this chapter, in transportation covered by subchapter II or III of this chapter, or in places of public accommodation covered by subchapter III of this chapter.

(c) Insurance

Subchapters I through III of this chapter and title IV of this Act shall not be construed to prohibit or restrict—

(1) an insurer, hospital or medical service company, health maintenance organization, or any agent, or entity that administers benefit plans, or similar organizations from underwriting risks, classifying risks, or administering such risks that are based on or not inconsistent with State law; or

(2) a person or organization covered by this chapter from establishing, sponsoring, observing or administering the terms of a bona fide benefit plan that are based on underwriting risks, classifying risks, or administering such risks that are based on or not inconsistent with State law; or

(3) a person or organization covered by this chapter from establishing, sponsoring, observing or administering the terms of a bona fide benefit plan that is not subject to State laws that regulate insurance.

Paragraphs (1), (2), and (3) shall not be used as a subterfuge to evade the purposes of subchapters I and III of this chapter.

(d) Accommodations and services

Nothing in this chapter shall be construed to require an individual with a disability to accept an accommodation, aid, service, opportunity, or benefit which such individual chooses not to accept.

§ 12202 State immunity

A State shall not be immune under the eleventh amendment to the Constitution of the United States from an action in Federal or State court of competent jurisdiction for a violation of this chapter. In any action against a State for a violation of the requirements of this chapter, remedies (including remedies both at law and in equity) are available for such a violation to the same extent as such remedies are available for such a violation in an action against any public or private entity other than a State.

§ 12203 Prohibition against retaliation and coercion

(a) Retaliation

No person shall discriminate against any individual because such individual has opposed any act or practice made unlawful by this chapter or because such individual made a charge, testified, assisted, or participated in any manner in an investigation, proceeding, or hearing under this chapter.

(b) Interference, coercion, or intimidation

It shall be unlawful to coerce, intimidate, threaten, or interfere with any individual in the exercise or enjoyment of, or on account of his or her having exercised or enjoyed, or on account of his or her having aided or encouraged any other individual in the exercise or enjoyment of, any right granted or protected by this chapter.

(c) Remedies and procedures

The remedies and procedures available under sections 12117, 12133, and 12188 of this title shall be available to aggrieved persons for violations of subsections (a) and (b) of this section, with respect to subchapter I, subchapter II and subchapter III, respectively, of this chapter.

§ 12204 Regulations by the Architectural and Transportation Barriers Compliance Board

(a) Issuance of guidelines. Not later than 9 months after the date of enactment of this Act [enacted July 26, 1990], the Architectural and Transportation Barriers Compliance Board shall issue minimum guidelines that shall supplement the existing Minimum Guidelines and Requirements for Accessible Design for purposes of titles II and III of this Act [42 USCS §§ 12131 et seq., 12181 et seq.].

(b) Contents of guidelines. The supplemental guidelines issued under subsection (a) shall establish additional requirements, consistent with this Act, to ensure that buildings, facilities, rail passenger cars, and vehicles are accessible, in terms of architecture and design, transportation, and communication, to individuals with disabilities.

(c) Qualified historic properties.

(1) In general. The supplemental guidelines issued under subsection (a) shall include procedures and requirements for alterations that will threaten or destroy the historic significance of qualified historic buildings and facilities as defined in 4.1.7(1)(a) of the Uniform Federal Accessibility Standards.

(2) Sites eligible for listing in National Register. With respect to alterations of buildings or facilities that are eligible for listing in the National Register of Historic Places under the National Historic Preservation Act (16 U.S.C. 470 et seq.), the guidelines described in paragraph (1) shall, at a minimum, maintain the procedures and requirements established in 4.1.7 (1) and (2) of the Uniform Federal Accessibility Standards.

(3) Other sites. With respect to alterations of buildings or facilities designated as historic under State or local law, the guidelines described in paragraph (1) shall establish procedures equivalent to those established by 4.1.7(1)(b) and (c) of the Uniform Federal Accessibility Standards, and shall require, at a minimum, compliance with the requirements established in 4.1.7(2) of such standards.

§ 12205 Attorney's fees

In any action or administrative proceeding commenced pursuant to this Act, the court or agency, in its discretion, may allow the prevailing party, other than the United States, a reasonable attorney's fee, including litigation expenses, and costs, and the United States shall be liable for the foregoing the same as a private individual.

§ 12206 Technical assistance

(a) Plan for assistance.

(1) In general. Not later than 180 days after the date of enactment of this Act [enacted July 26, 1990], the Attorney General, in consultation with the Chair of the Equal Employment Opportunity Commission, the Secretary of Transportation, the Chair of the Architectural and Transportation Barriers Compliance Board, and the Chairman of the Federal Communications Commission, shall develop a plan to assist entities covered under this Act, and other Federal agencies, in understanding the responsibility of such entities and agencies under this Act.

(2) Publication of plan. The Attorney General shall publish the plan referred to in paragraph (1) for public comment in accordance with subchapter II of chapter 5 of title 5, United States Code [5 USCS §§ 551 et seq.] (commonly known as the Administrative Procedure Act).

(b) Agency and public assistance. The Attorney General may obtain the assistance of other Federal agencies in carrying out subsection (a), including the National Council on Disability, the President's Committee on Employment of People with Disabilities, the Small Business Administration, and the Department of Commerce.

(c) Implementation.

(1) Rendering assistance. Each Federal agency that has responsibility under paragraph (2) for implementing this Act may render technical assistance to individuals and institutions that have rights or duties under the respective title or titles for which such agency has responsibility.

(2) Implementation of Titles.

(A) Title I. The Equal Employment Opportunity Commission and the Attorney General shall implement the plan for assistance developed under subsection (a), for title I [42 USCS §§ 12111 et seq.].

(B) Title II.

(i) Subtitle A. The Attorney General shall implement such plan for assistance for subtitle A of title II [42 USCS §§ 12131 et seq.].

(ii) Subtitle B. The Secretary of Transportation shall implement such plan for assistance for subtitle B of title II [42 USCS §§ 12141 et seq.].

(C) Title III. The Attorney General, in coordination with the Secretary of Transportation and the Chair of the Architectural Transportation Barriers Compliance Board, shall implement such plan for assistance for title III [42 USCS §§ 12181 et seq.], except for section 304 [42 USCS § 12184], the plan for assistance for which shall be implemented by the Secretary of Transportation.

(D) Title IV. The Chairman of the Federal Communications Commission, in coordination with the Attorney General, shall implement such plan for assistance for title IV.

(3) Technical assistance manuals. Each Federal agency that has responsibility under paragraph (2) for implementing this Act shall, as part of its implementation responsibilities, ensure the availability and provision of appropriate technical assistance manuals to individuals or entities with rights or duties under this Act no later than six months after applicable final regulations are published under titles I, II, III, and IV.

(d) Grants and contracts.

(1) In general. Each Federal agency that has responsibility under subsection (c)(2) for implementing this Act may make grants or award contracts to effectuate the purposes of this section, subject to the availability of appropriations. Such grants and contracts may be awarded to individuals, institutions not organized for profit and no part of the net earnings of which inures to the benefit of any private shareholder or individual (including educational institutions), and associations representing individuals who have rights or duties under this Act. Contracts may be awarded to entities organized for profit, but such entities may not be the recipients or grants described in this paragraph.

(2) Dissemination of information. Such grants and contracts, among other uses, may be designed to ensure wide dissemination of information about the rights and duties established by this Act and to provide information and technical assistance about techniques for effective compliance with this Act.

(e) Failure to receive assistance. An employer, public accommodation, or other entity covered under this Act shall not be excused from compliance with the requirements of this Act because of any failure to receive technical assistance under this section, including any failure in the development or dissemination of any technical assistance manual authorized by this section.

§ 12207 Federal wilderness areas

(a) Study. The National Council on Disability shall conduct a study and report on the effect that wilderness designations and wilderness land management practices have on the ability of individuals with disabilities to use and enjoy the National Wilderness Preservation System as established under the Wilderness Act (16 U.S.C. 1131 et seq.).

(b) Submission of report. Not later than 1 year after the enactment of this Act [enacted July 26, 1990], the National Council on Disability shall submit the report required under subsection (a) to Congress.

(c) Specific wilderness access.

(1) In general. Congress reaffirms that nothing in the Wilderness Act is to be construed as prohibiting the use of a wheelchair in a wilderness area by an individual whose disability requires use of a wheelchair, and consistent with the Wilderness Act no agency is required to provide any form of special treatment or accommodation, or to construct any facilities or modify any conditions of lands within a wilderness area in order to facilitate such use.

(2) Definition. For purposes of paragraph (1), the term "wheelchair" means a device designed solely for use by a mobility-impaired person for locomotion, that is suitable for use in an indoor pedestrian area.

§ 12208 Transvestites

For the purposes of this Act, the term "disabled" or "disability" shall not apply to an individual solely because that individual is a transvestite.

§ 12209. Instrumentalities of the Congress

The General Accounting Office, the Government Printing Office, and the Library of Congress shall be covered as follows:

(1) In general

The rights and protections under this chapter shall, subject to paragraph (2), apply with respect to the conduct of each instrumentality of the Congress.

(2) Establishment of remedies and procedures by instrumentalities

The chief official of each instrumentality of the Congress shall establish remedies and procedures to be utilized with respect to the rights and protections provided pursuant to paragraph (1).

(3) Report to Congress

The chief official of each instrumentality of the Congress shall, after establishing remedies and procedures for purposes of paragraph (2), submit to the Congress a report describing the remedies and procedures.

(4) Definition of instrumentality

For purposes of this section, the term "instrumentality of the Congress" means the following: the General Accounting Office, the Government Printing Office, and the Library of Congress.

(5) Enforcement of employment rights

The remedies and procedures set forth in section 2000e-16 of this title shall be available to any employee of an instrumentality of the Congress who alleges a violation of the rights and protections under sections 12112 through 12114 of this title that are made applicable by this section, except that the authorities of the Equal Employment Opportunity Commission shall be exercised by the chief official of the instrumentality of the Congress.

(6) Enforcement of rights to public services and accommodations

The remedies and procedures set forth in section 2000e-16 of this title shall be available to any qualified person with a disability who is a visitor, guest, or patron of an instrumentality of Congress and who alleges a violation of the rights and protections under sections 12131 through 12150 or section 12182 or 12183 of this title that are made applicable by this section, except that the authorities of the Equal Employment Opportunity Commission shall be exercised by the chief official of the instrumentality of the Congress.

(7) Construction

Nothing in this section shall alter the enforcement procedures for individuals with disabilities provided in the General Accounting Office Personnel Act of 1980 and regulations promulgated pursuant to that Act.

§ 12210 Illegal use of drugs

(a) In general

For purposes of this chapter, the term "individual with a disability" does not include an individual who is currently engaging in the illegal use of drugs, when the covered entity acts on the basis of such use.

(b) Rules of construction

Nothing in subsection (a) of this section shall be construed to exclude as an individual with a disability an individual who—

(1) has successfully completed a supervised drug rehabilitation program and is no longer engaging in the illegal use of drugs, or has otherwise been rehabilitated successfully and is no longer engaging in such use;

(2) is participating in a supervised rehabilitation program and is no longer engaging in such use; or

(3) is erroneously regarded as engaging in such use, but is not engaging in such use;

except that it shall not be a violation of this chapter for a covered entity to adopt or administer reasonable policies or procedures, including but not limited to drug testing, designed to ensure that an individual described in paragraph (1) or (2) is no longer engaging in the illegal use of drugs; however, nothing in this section shall be construed to encourage, prohibit, restrict, or authorize the conducting of testing for the illegal use of drugs.

(c) Health and other services

Notwithstanding subsection (a) of this section and section 12211(b)(3) of this title, an individual shall not be denied health services, or services provided in connection with drug rehabilitation, on the basis of the current illegal use of drugs if the individual is otherwise entitled to such services.

(d) Definition of illegal use of drugs

(1) In general

The term "illegal use of drugs" means the use of drugs, the possession or distribution of which is unlawful under the Controlled Substances Act (21 U.S.C. 812). Such term does not include the use of a drug taken under supervision by a licensed health care professional, or other uses authorized by the Controlled Substances Act [21 U.S.C.A. § 801 et seq.] or other provisions of Federal law.

(2) Drugs

The term "drug" means a controlled substance, as defined in schedules I through V of section 202 of the Controlled Substances Act [21 U.S.C.A. § 812].

§ 12211 Definitions

(a) Homosexuality and bisexuality

For purposes of the definition of "disability" in section 12102(2) of this title, homosexuality and bisexuality are not impairments and as such are not disabilities under this chapter.

(b) Certain conditions

Under this chapter, the term "disability" shall not include—

(1) transvestism, transsexualism, pedophilia, exhibitionism, voyeurism, gender identity disorders not resulting from physical impairments, or other sexual behavior disorders;

(2) compulsive gambling, kleptomania, or pyromania; or

(3) psychoactive substance use disorders resulting from current illegal use of drugs.

§ 12212 Alternative means of dispute resolution

Where appropriate and to the extent authorized by law, the use of alternative means of dispute resolution, including settlement negotiations, conciliation, facilitation, mediation, factfinding, minitrials, and arbitration, is encouraged to resolve disputes arising under this chapter.

§ 12213 Severability

Should any provision in this chapter be found to be unconstitutional by a court of law, such provision shall be severed from the remainder of this chapter and such action shall not affect the enforceability of the remaining provisions of this chapter.

REHABILITATION ACT

SECTIONS 501, 503, AND 504 OF THE REHABILITATION ACT OF 1973

29 U.S.C. §
- 705 Definitions
- 791 Employment of Individuals with Disabilities
- 793 Employment under Federal Contracts
- 794 Nondiscrimination under federal grants and programs
- 794a Remedies and attorney fees

SECTION 504 OF THE REHABILITATION ACT OF 1973

GENERAL PROVISIONS

§ 705 Definitions

For the purposes of this chapter [29 USCS §§ 701 et seq.]:

(1) Administrative costs

The term "administrative costs" means expenditures incurred in the performance of administrative functions under the vocational rehabilitation program carried out under subchapter I of this chapter [29 USCS § 720 et seq.], including expenses related to program planning, development, monitoring, and evaluation, including expenses for—

(A) quality assurance;

(B) budgeting, accounting, financial management, information systems, and related data processing;

(C) providing information about the program to the public;

(D) technical assistance and support services to other State agencies, private nonprofit organizations, and businesses and industries, except for technical assistance and support services described in section 723(b)(5) of this title;

(E) the State Rehabilitation Council and other advisory committees;

(F) professional organization membership dues for designated State unit employees;

(G) the removal of architectural barriers in State vocational rehabilitation agency offices and State operated rehabilitation facilities;

(H) operating and maintaining designated State unit facilities, equipment, and grounds;

(I) supplies;

(J) administration of the comprehensive system of personnel development described in section 721(a)(7) of this title, including personnel administration, administration of affirmative action plans, and training and staff development;

(K) administrative salaries, including clerical and other support staff salaries, in support of these administrative functions;

(L) travel costs related to carrying out the program, other than travel costs related to the provision of services;

(M) costs incurred in conducting reviews of rehabilitation counselor or coordinator determinations under section 722(c) of this title; and

(N) legal expenses required in the administration of the program.

(2) Assessment for determining eligibility and vocational rehabilitation needs

The term "assessment for determining eligibility and vocational rehabilitation needs" means, as appropriate in each case—

(A)(i) a review of existing data—

(I) to determine whether an individual is eligible for vocational rehabilitation services; and

(II) to assign priority for an order of selection described in section 721(a)(5)(A) of this title in the States that use an order of selection pursuant to section 721(a)(5)(A) of this title; and

(ii) to the extent necessary, the provision of appropriate assessment activities to obtain necessary additional data to make such determination and assignment;

(B) to the extent additional data is necessary to make a determination of the employment outcomes, and the nature and scope of vocational rehabilitation services, to be included in the individualized plan for employment of an eligible individual, a comprehensive assessment to determine the unique strengths, resources, priorities, concerns, abilities, capabilities, interests, and informed choice, including the need for supported employment, of the eligible individual, which comprehensive assessment—

(i) is limited to information that is necessary to identify the rehabilitation needs of the individual and to develop the individualized plan for employment of the eligible individual;

(ii) uses, as a primary source of such information, to the maximum extent possible and appropriate and in accordance with confidentiality requirements—

(I) existing information obtained for the purposes of determining the eligibility of the individual and assigning priority for an order of selection described in section 721(a)(5)(A) of this title for the individual; and

(II) such information as can be provided by

the individual and, where appropriate, by the family of the individual;

(iii) may include, to the degree needed to make such a determination, an assessment of the personality, interests, interpersonal skills, intelligence and related functional capacities, educational achievements, work experience, vocational aptitudes, personal and social adjustments, and employment opportunities of the individual, and the medical, psychiatric, psychological, and other pertinent vocational, educational, cultural, social, recreational, and environmental factors, that affect the employment and rehabilitation needs of the individual; and

(iv) may include, to the degree needed, an appraisal of the patterns of work behavior of the individual and services needed for the individual to acquire occupational skills, and to develop work attitudes, work habits, work tolerance, and social and behavior patterns necessary for successful job performance, including the utilization of work in real job situations to assess and develop the capacities of the individual to perform adequately in a work environment;

(C) referral, for the provision of rehabilitation technology services to the individual, to assess and develop the capacities of the individual to perform in a work environment; and

(D) an exploration of the individual's abilities, capabilities, and capacity to perform in work situations, which shall be assessed periodically during trial work experiences, including experiences in which the individual is provided appropriate supports and training.

(3) Assistive technology device

The term "assistive technology device" has the meaning given such term in section 3002 of this title, except that the reference in such section to the term "individuals with disabilities" shall be deemed to mean more than one individual with a disability as defined in paragraph (20)(A).

(4) Assistive technology service

The term "assistive technology service" has the meaning given such term in section 3002 of this title, except that the reference in such section—

(A) to the term "individual with a disability" shall be deemed to mean an individual with a disability, as defined in paragraph (20)(A); and

(B) to the term "individuals with disabilities" shall be deemed to mean more than one such individual.

(5) Community rehabilitation program

The term "community rehabilitation program" means a program that provides directly or facilitates the provision of vocational rehabilitation services to individuals with disabilities, and that provides, singly or in combination, for an individual with a disability to enable the individual to maximize opportunities for employment, including career advancement—

(A) medical, psychiatric, psychological, social, and vocational services that are provided under one management;

(B) testing, fitting, or training in the use of prosthetic and orthotic devices;

(C) recreational therapy;

(D) physical and occupational therapy;

(E) speech, language, and hearing therapy;

(F) psychiatric, psychological, and social services, including positive behavior management;

(G) assessment for determining eligibility and vocational rehabilitation needs;

(H) rehabilitation technology;

(I) job development, placement, and retention services;

(J) evaluation or control of specific disabilities;

(K) orientation and mobility services for individuals who are blind;

(L) extended employment;

(M) psychosocial rehabilitation services;

(N) supported employment services and extended services;

(O) services to family members when necessary to the vocational rehabilitation of the individual;

(P) personal assistance services; or

(Q) services similar to the services described in one of subparagraphs (A) through (P).

(6) Construction; cost of construction—

(A) Construction

The term "construction" means—

(i) the construction of new buildings;

(ii) the acquisition, expansion, remodeling, alteration, and renovation of existing buildings; and

(iii) initial equipment of buildings described in clauses (i) and (ii).

(B) Cost of construction

The term "cost of construction" includes architects' fees and the cost of acquisition of land in connection with construction but does not include the cost of off-site improvements.

(7) Repealed. 105-277, Div. A, § 101(f) [Title VIII, § 402(c)(1)(B)], Oct. 21, 1998, 112 Stat. 2681-415

(8) Designated State agency; designated State unit—

(A) Designated State agency

The term "designated State agency" means an agency designated under section 721(a)(2)(A) of this title.

(B) Designated State unit

The term "designated State unit" means—

(i) any State agency unit required under section 721(a)(2)(B)(ii) of this title; or

(ii) in cases in which no such unit is so required, the State agency described in section 721(a)(2)(B)(i) of this title.

(9) Disability

The term "disability" means—

(A) except as otherwise provided in subparagraph (B), a physical or mental impairment that constitutes or results in a substantial impediment to employment; or

(B) for purposes of sections 701, 711, and 712 of this title and subchapters II, IV, V, and VII of this chapter [29 USCS §§ 760 et seq., 780 et seq., 790 et seq., and 796 et seq.], a physical or mental impairment that substantially limits one or more major life activities.

(10) Drug and illegal use of drugs

(A) Drug

The term "drug" means a controlled substance, as defined in schedules I through V of section 202 of the Controlled Substances Act (21 U.S.C. 812).

(B) Illegal use of drugs

The term "illegal use of drugs" means the use of drugs, the possession or distribution of which is unlawful under the Controlled Substances Act. Such term does not include the use of a drug taken under supervision by a licensed health care professional, or other uses authorized by the Controlled Substances Act or other provisions of Federal law.

(11) Employment outcome

The term "employment outcome" means, with respect to an individual—

(A) entering or retaining full-time or, if appropriate, part-time competitive employment in the integrated labor market;

(B) satisfying the vocational outcome of supported employment; or

(C) satisfying any other vocational outcome the Secretary may determine to be appropriate (including satisfying the vocational outcome of self-employment, telecommuting, or business ownership), in a manner consistent with this chapter [29 USCS § 701 et seq.].

(12) Establishment of a community rehabilitation program

The term "establishment of a community rehabilitation program" includes the acquisition, expansion, remodeling, or alteration of existing buildings necessary to adapt them to community rehabilitation program purposes or to increase their effectiveness for such purposes (subject, however, to such limitations as the Secretary may determine, in accordance with regulations the Secretary shall prescribe, in order to prevent impairment of the objectives of, or duplication of, other Federal laws providing Federal assistance in the construction of facilities for community rehabilitation programs), and may include such additional equipment and staffing as the Commissioner considers appropriate.

(13) Extended services

The term "extended services" means ongoing support services and other appropriate services, needed to support and maintain an individual with a most significant disability in supported employment, that—

(A) are provided singly or in combination and are organized and made available in such a way as to assist an eligible individual in maintaining supported employment;

(B) are based on a determination of the needs of an eligible individual, as specified in an individualized plan for employment; and

(C) are provided by a State agency, a nonprofit private organization, employer, or any other appropriate resource, after an individual has made the transition from support provided by the designated State unit.

(14) Federal share

(A) In general

Subject to subparagraph (B), the term "Federal share" means 78.7 percent.

(B) Exception

The term "Federal share" means the share specifically set forth in section 731(a)(3) of this title, except that with respect to payments pursuant to part B of subchapter I of this chapter [29 USCS § 730 et seq.] to any State that are used to meet the costs of construction of those rehabilitation facilities identified in section 723(b)(2) of this title in such State, the Federal share shall be the percentages determined in accordance with the provisions of section 731(a)(3) of this title applicable with respect to the State.

(C) Relationship to expenditures by a political subdivision

For the purpose of determining the non-Federal share with respect to a State, expenditures by a political subdivision thereof or by a local agency shall be regarded as expenditures by such State, subject to such limitations and conditions as the Secretary shall by regulation prescribe.

(15) Governor

The term "Governor" means a chief executive officer of a State.

(16) Impartial hearing officer

(A) In general

The term "impartial hearing officer" means an individual—

(i) who is not an employee of a public agency (other than an administrative law judge, hearing examiner, or employee of an institution of higher education);

(ii) who is not a member of the State Rehabilitation Council described in section 725 of this title;

(iii) who has not been involved previously in the vocational rehabilitation of the applicant or eligible individual;

(iv) who has knowledge of the delivery of vocational rehabilitation services, the State plan under section 721 of this title, and the Federal and State rules governing the provision of such services and training with respect to the performance of official duties; and

(v) who has no personal or financial interest that would be in conflict with the objectivity of the individual.

(B) Construction

An individual shall not be considered to be an employee of a public agency for purposes of subparagraph (A)(i) solely because the individual is paid by the agency to serve as a hearing officer.

(17) Independent living core services

The term "independent living core services" means—

(A) information and referral services;

(B) independent living skills training;

(C) peer counseling (including cross-disability peer counseling); and

(D) individual and systems advocacy.

(18) Independent living services

The term "independent living services" includes—

(A) independent living core services; and

(B)(i) counseling services, including psychological, psychotherapeutic, and related services;

(ii) services related to securing housing or shelter, including services related to community group living, and supportive of the purposes of this chapter [29 USCS § 701 et seq.] and of the subchapters of this chapter, and adaptive housing services (including appropriate accommodations to and modifications of any space used to serve, or occupied by, individuals with disabilities);

(iii) rehabilitation technology;

(iv) mobility training;

(v) services and training for individuals with cognitive and sensory disabilities, including life skills training, and interpreter and reader services;

(vi) personal assistance services, including attendant care and the training of personnel providing such services;

(vii) surveys, directories, and other activities to identify appropriate housing, recreation opportunities, and accessible transportation, and other support services;

(viii) consumer information programs on rehabilitation and independent living services available under this chapter [29 USCS § 701 et seq.], especially for minorities and other individuals with disabilities who have traditionally been unserved or underserved by programs under this chapter;

(ix) education and training necessary for living in a community and participating in community activities;

(x) supported living;

(xi) transportation, including referral and assistance for such transportation and training in the use of public transportation vehicles and systems;

(xii) physical rehabilitation;

(xiii) therapeutic treatment;

(xiv) provision of needed prostheses and other appliances and devices;

(xv) individual and group social and recreational services;

(xvi) training to develop skills specifically designed for youths who are individuals with disabilities to promote self-awareness and esteem, develop advocacy and self-empowerment skills, and explore career options;

(xvii) services for children;

(xviii) services under other Federal, State, or local programs designed to provide resources, training, counseling, or other assistance, of substantial benefit in enhancing the independence, productivity, and quality of life of individuals with disabilities;

(xix) appropriate preventive services to decrease the need of individuals assisted under this chapter for similar services in the future;

(xx) community awareness programs to enhance the understanding and integration into society of individuals with disabilities; and

(xxi) such other services as may be necessary and not inconsistent with the provisions of this chapter.

(19) Indian; American Indian; Indian American; Indian tribe—

(A) In general

The terms "Indian", "American Indian", and "Indian American" mean an individual who is a member of an Indian tribe.

(B) Indian tribe

The term "Indian tribe" means any Federal or State Indian tribe, band, rancheria, pueblo, colony, or community, including any Alaskan native village or regional village corporation (as defined in or established pursuant to the Alaska Native Claims Settlement Act).

(20) Individual with a disability

(A) In general

Except as otherwise provided in subparagraph (B), the term "individual with a disability" means any individual who—

(i) has a physical or mental impairment which for such individual constitutes or results in a substantial impediment to employment; and

(ii) can benefit in terms of an employment outcome from vocational rehabilitation services provided pursuant to subchapter I, III, or VI of this chapter [29 USCS § 720 et seq., 771 et seq., or 795 et seq.].

(B) Certain programs; limitations on major life activities

Subject to subparagraphs (C), (D), (E), and (F), the term "individual with a disability" means, for purposes of sections 701, 711, and 712 of this title and subchapters II, IV, V, and VII of this chapter [29 USCS §§ 760 et seq., 780 et seq., 790 et seq., and 796 et seq.], any person who—

(i) has a physical or mental impairment which substantially limits one or more of such person's major life activities;

(ii) has a record of such an impairment; or

(iii) is regarded as having such an impairment.

(C) Rights and advocacy provision.

(i) In general; exclusion of individuals engaging in drug use

For purposes of subchapter V of this chapter [29 USCS § 790 et seq.], the term "individual with a disability" does not include an individual who is currently engaging in the illegal use of drugs, when a covered entity acts on the basis of such use.

(ii) Exception for individuals no longer engaging in drug use

Nothing in clause (i) shall be construed to exclude as an individual with a disability an individual who—

(I) has successfully completed a supervised drug rehabilitation program and is no longer engaging in the illegal use of drugs, or has otherwise been rehabilitated successfully and is no longer engaging in such use;

(II) is participating in a supervised rehabilitation program and is no longer engaging in such use; or

(III) is erroneously regarded as engaging in such use, but is not engaging in such use; except that it shall not be a violation of this chapter [29 USCS § 701 et seq.] for a covered entity to adopt or administer reasonable policies or procedures, including but not limited to drug testing, designed to ensure that an individual described in subclause (I) or (II) is no longer engaging in the illegal use of drugs.

(iii) Exclusion for certain services

Notwithstanding clause (i), for purposes of programs and activities providing health services and services provided under subchapters I, II, and III of this chapter [29 USCS §§ 720 et seq., 760 et seq., and 771 et seq.], an individual shall not be excluded from the benefits of such programs or activities on the basis of his or her current illegal use of drugs if he or she is otherwise entitled to such services.

(iv) Disciplinary action

For purposes of programs and activities providing educational services, local educational agencies may take disciplinary action pertaining to the use or possession of illegal drugs or alcohol against any student who is an individual with a disability and who currently is engaging in the illegal use of drugs or in the use of alcohol to the same extent that such disciplinary action is taken against students who are not individuals with disabilities. Furthermore, the due process procedures at section 104.36 of title 34, Code of Federal Regulations (or any corresponding similar regulation or ruling) shall not apply to such disciplinary actions.

(v) Employment; exclusion of alcoholics

For purposes of sections 793 and 794 of this title as such sections relate to employment, the term "individual with a disability" does not include any individual who is an alcoholic whose current use of alcohol prevents such individual from performing the duties of the job in question or whose employment, by reason of such current alcohol abuse, would constitute a direct threat to property or the safety of others.

(D) Employment; exclusion of individuals with certain diseases or infections

For the purposes of sections 793 and 794 of this title, as such sections relate to employment, such term does not include an individual who has a currently contagious disease or infection and who, by reason of such disease or infection, would constitute a direct threat to the health or safety of other individuals or who, by reason of the currently contagious disease or infection, is unable to perform the duties of the job.

(E) Rights provisions; exclusion of individuals on basis of homosexuality or bisexuality

For the purposes of sections 791, 793, and 794 of this title—

(i) for purposes of the application of subparagraph (B) to such sections, the term "impairment" does not include homosexuality or bisexuality; and

(ii) therefore the term "individual with a disability" does not include an individual on the basis of homosexuality or bisexuality.

(F) Rights provisions; exclusion of individuals on basis of certain disorders

For the purposes of sections 791, 793, and 794 of

this title, the term "individual with a disability" does not include an individual on the basis of—

(i) transvestism, transsexualism, pedophilia, exhibitionism, voyeurism, gender identity disorders not resulting from physical impairments, or other sexual behavior disorders;

(ii) compulsive gambling, kleptomania, or pyromania; or

(iii) psychoactive substance use disorders resulting from current illegal use of drugs.

(G) Individuals with disabilities

The term "individuals with disabilities" means more than one individual with a disability.

(21) Individual with a significant disability

(A) In general

Except as provided in subparagraph (B) or (C), the term "individual with a significant disability" means an individual with a disability—

(i) who has a severe physical or mental impairment which seriously limits one or more functional capacities (such as mobility, communication, self-care, self-direction, interpersonal skills, work tolerance, or work skills) in terms of an employment outcome;

(ii) whose vocational rehabilitation can be expected to require multiple vocational rehabilitation services over an extended period of time; and

(iii) who has one or more physical or mental disabilities resulting from amputation, arthritis, autism, blindness, burn injury, cancer, cerebral palsy, cystic fibrosis, deafness, head injury, heart disease, hemiplegia, hemophilia, respiratory or pulmonary dysfunction, mental retardation, mental illness, multiple sclerosis, muscular dystrophy, musculo-skeletal disorders, neurological disorders (including stroke and epilepsy), paraplegia, quadriplegia, and other spinal cord conditions, sickle cell anemia, specific learning disability, end-stage renal disease, or another disability or combination of disabilities determined on the basis of an assessment for determining eligibility and vocational rehabilitation needs described in subparagraphs (A) and (B) of paragraph (2) to cause comparable substantial functional limitation.

(B) Independent living services and centers for independent living

For purposes of subchapter VII of this chapter [29 USCS § 796 et seq.], the term "individual with a significant disability" means an individual with a severe physical or mental impairment whose ability to function independently in the family or community or whose ability to obtain, maintain, or advance in employment is substantially limited and for whom the delivery of independent living services will improve the ability to function, continue functioning, or move toward functioning independently in the family or community or to continue in employment, respectively.

(C) Research and training

For purposes of subchapter II of this chapter [29 USCS § 760 et seq.], the term "individual with a significant disability" includes an individual described in subparagraph (A) or (B).

(D) Individuals with significant disabilities

The term "individuals with significant disabilities" means more than one individual with a significant disability.

(E) Individual with a most significant disability

(i) In general

The term "individual with a most significant disability", used with respect to an individual in a State, means an individual with a significant disability who meets criteria established by the State under section 721(a)(5)(C) of this title.

(ii) Individuals with the most significant disabilities

The term "individuals with the most significant disabilities" means more than one individual with a most significant disability.

(22) Individual's representative; applicant's representative

The terms "individual's representative" and "applicant's representative" mean a parent, a family member, a guardian, an advocate, or an authorized representative of an individual or applicant, respectively.

(23) Institution of higher education

The term "institution of higher education" has the meaning given the term in section 1.01 of this title.

(24) Local agency

The term "local agency" means an agency of a unit of general local government or of an Indian tribe (or combination of such units or tribes) which has an agreement with the designated State agency to conduct a vocational rehabilitation program under the supervision of such State agency in accordance with the State plan approved under section 721 of this title. Nothing in the preceding sentence of this paragraph or in section 721 of this title shall be construed to prevent the local agency from arranging to utilize another local public or nonprofit agency to provide vocational rehabilitation services if such an arrangement is made part of the agreement specified in this paragraph.

(25) Local workforce investment board

The term "local workforce investment board" means a local workforce investment board established under section 117 of the Workforce Investment Act of 1998 [29 USCS § 2832].

(26) Nonprofit

The term "nonprofit', when used with respect to a community rehabilitation program, means a community rehabilitation program carried out by a corporation or association, no part of the net earnings of which inures, or may lawfully inure, to the benefit of any private shareholder or individual and the income of which is exempt from taxation under section 501(c)(3) of Title 26.

(27) Ongoing support services

The term "ongoing support services" means services—

(A) provided to individuals with the most significant disabilities;

(B) provided, at a minimum, twice monthly—

(i) to make an assessment, regarding the employment situation, at the worksite of each such individual in supported employment, or, under special circumstances, especially at the request of the client, off site; and

(ii) based on the assessment, to provide for the coordination or provision of specific intensive services, at or away from the worksite, that are needed to maintain employment stability; and

(C) consisting of—

(i) a particularized assessment supplementary to the comprehensive assessment described in paragraph (2)(B);

(ii) the provision of skilled job trainers who accompany the individual for intensive job skill training at the worksite;

(iii) job development, job retention, and placement services;

(iv) social skills training;

(v) regular observation or supervision of the individual;

(vi) followup services such as regular contact with the employers, the individuals, the individuals' representatives, and other appropriate individuals, in order to reinforce and stabilize the job placement;

(vii) facilitation of natural supports at the worksite;

(viii) any other service identified in section 723 of this title; or

(ix) a service similar to another service described in this subparagraph.

(28) Personal assistance services

The term "personal assistance services" means a range of services, provided by one or more persons, designed to assist an individual with a disability to perform daily living activities on or off the job that the individual would typically perform if the individual did not have a disability. Such services shall be designed to increase the individual's control in life and ability to perform everyday activities on or off the job.

(29) Public or nonprofit

The term "public or nonprofit", used with respect to an agency or organization, includes an Indian tribe.

(30) Rehabilitation technology

The term "rehabilitation technology" means the systematic application of technologies, engineering methodologies, or scientific principles to meet the needs of and address the barriers confronted by individuals with disabilities in areas which include education, rehabilitation, employment, transportation, independent living, and recreation. The term includes rehabilitation engineering, assistive technology devices, and assistive technology services.

(31) Secretary

The term "Secretary", except when the context otherwise requires, means the Secretary of Education.

(32) State

The term "State" includes, in addition to each of the several States of the United States, the District of Columbia, the Commonwealth of Puerto Rico, the United States Virgin Islands, Guam, American Samoa, and the Commonwealth of the Northern Mariana Islands.

(33) State workforce investment board

The term "State workforce investment board" means a State workforce investment board established under section 111 of the Workforce Investment Act of 1998 [29 USCS § 2821].

(34) Statewide workforce investment system

The term "statewide workforce investment system" means a system described in section 111(d)(2) of the Workforce Investment Act of 1998 [29 USCS § 2821(d)(2)].

(35) Supported employment

(A) In general

The term "supported employment" means competitive work in integrated work settings, or employment in integrated work settings in which individuals are working toward competitive work, consistent with the strengths, resources, priorities, concerns, abilities, capabilities, interests, and informed choice of the individuals, for individuals with the most significant disabilities—

(i)(I) for whom competitive employment has not traditionally occurred; or

(II) for whom competitive employment has been interrupted or intermittent as a result of a significant disability; and

(ii) who, because of the nature and severity of their disability, need intensive supported employment services for the period, and any extension, described in paragraph (36)(C) and extended services after the transition described in paragraph (13)(C) in order to perform such work.

(B) Certain transitional employment

Such term includes transitional employment for persons who are individuals with the most significant disabilities due to mental illness.

(36) Supported employment services

The term "supported employment services" means ongoing support services and other appropriate services needed to support and maintain an individual with a most significant disability in supported employment, that—

(A) are provided singly or in combination and are organized and made available in such a way as to assist an eligible individual to achieve competitive employment;

(B) are based on a determination of the needs of an eligible individual, as specified in an individualized plan for employment; and

(C) are provided by the designated State unit for a period of time not to extend beyond 18 months, unless under special circumstances the eligible individual and the rehabilitation counselor or coordinator involved jointly agree to extend the time in order to achieve the employment outcome identified in the individualized plan for employment.

(37) Transition services

The term "transition services" means a coordinated set of activities for a student, designed within an outcome-oriented process, that promotes movement from school to post school activities, including postsecondary education, vocational training, integrated employment (including supported employment), continuing and adult education, adult services, independent living, or community participation. The coordinated set of activities shall be based upon the individual student's needs, taking into account the student's preferences and interests, and shall include instruction, community experiences, the development of employment and other post school adult living objectives, and, when appropriate, acquisition of daily living skills and functional vocational evaluation.

(38) Vocational rehabilitation services

The term "vocational rehabilitation services" means those services identified in section 723 of this title which are provided to individuals with disabilities under this chapter [29 USCS § 701 et seq.].

(39) Workforce investment activities

The term "workforce investment activities" means workforce investment activities, as defined in section 101 of the Workforce Investment Act of 1998, that are carried out under that Act.

§ 791. Employment of individuals with disabilities

(a) Interagency Committee on Employees who are Individuals with Disabilities; establishment; membership; co-chairmen; availability of other Committee resources; purpose and functions

There is established within the Federal Government an Interagency Committee on Employees who are Individuals with Disabilities (hereinafter in this section referred to as the "Committee"), comprised of such members as the President may select, including the following (or their designees whose positions are Executive Level IV or higher): the Chairman of the Equal Employment Opportunity Commission (hereafter in this section referred to as the "Commission"), the Director of the Office of Personnel Management, the Secretary of Veterans Affairs, the Secretary of Labor, the Secretary of Education, and the Secretary of Health and Human Services. Either the Director of the Office of Personnel Management and the Chairman of the Commission shall serve as co-chairpersons of the Committee or the Director or Chairman shall serve as the sole chairperson of the Committee, as the Director and Chairman jointly determine, from time to time, to be appropriate. The resources of the President's Committees on Employment of People With Disabilities and on Mental Retardation shall be made fully available to the Committee. It shall be the purpose and function of the Committee (1) to provide a focus for Federal and other employment of individuals with disabilities, and to review, on a periodic basis, in cooperation with the Commission, the adequacy of hiring, placement, and advancement practices with respect to individuals with disabilities, by each department, agency, and instrumentality in the executive branch of Government and the Smithsonian Institution, and to insure that the special needs of such individuals are being met; and (2) to consult with the Commission to assist the Commission to carry out its responsibilities under subsections (b), (c), and (d) of this section. On the basis of such review and consultation, the Committee shall periodically make to the Commission such recommendations for legislative and administrative changes as it deems necessary or desirable. The Commission shall timely transmit to the appropriate committees of Congress any such recommendations.

(b) Federal agencies; affirmative action program plans

Each department, agency, and instrumentality (including the United States Postal Service and the Postal Regulatory Commission) in the executive branch and the Smithsonian Institution shall, within one hundred and eighty days after September 26,

1973, submit to the Commission and to the Committee an affirmative action program plan for the hiring, placement, and advancement of individuals with disabilities in such department, agency, instrumentality, or Institution. Such plan shall include a description of the extent to which and methods whereby the special needs of employees who are individuals with disabilities are being met. Such plan shall be updated annually, and shall be reviewed annually and approved by the Commission, if the Commission determines, after consultation with the Committee, that such plan provides sufficient assurances, procedures and commitments to provide adequate hiring, placement, and advancement opportunities for individuals with disabilities.

(c) State agencies; rehabilitated individuals, employment

The Commission, after consultation with the Committee, shall develop and recommend to the Secretary for referral to the appropriate State agencies, policies and procedures which will facilitate the hiring, placement, and advancement in employment of individuals who have received rehabilitation services under State vocational rehabilitation programs, veterans' programs, or any other program for individuals with disabilities, including the promotion of job opportunities for such individuals. The Secretary shall encourage such State agencies to adopt and implement such policies and procedures.

(d) Report to Congressional committees

The Commission, after consultation with the Committee, shall, on June 30, 1974, and at the end of each subsequent fiscal year, make a complete report to the appropriate committees of the Congress with respect to the practices of and achievements in hiring, placement, and advancement of individuals with disabilities by each department, agency, and instrumentality and the Smithsonian Institution and the effectiveness of the affirmative action programs required by subsection (b) of this section, together with recommendations as to legislation which have been submitted to the Commission under subsection (a) of this section, or other appropriate action to insure the adequacy of such practices. Such report shall also include an evaluation by the Committee of the effectiveness of the activities of the Commission under subsections (b) and (c) of this section.

(e) Federal work experience without pay; non-Federal status

An individual who, as a part of an individualized plan for employment under a State plan approved under this chapter, participates in a program of unpaid work experience in a Federal agency, shall not, by reason thereof, be considered to be a Federal employee or to be subject to the provisions of law relating to Federal employment, including those relating to hours of work, rates of compensation, leave, unemployment compensation, and Federal employee benefits.

(f) Federal agency cooperation; special consideration for positions on President's Committee on Employment of People With Disabilities

(1) The Secretary of Labor and the Secretary of Education are authorized and directed to cooperate with the President's Committee on Employment of People With Disabilities in carrying out its functions.

(2) In selecting personnel to fill all positions on the President's Committee on Employment of People With Disabilities, special consideration shall be given to qualified individuals with disabilities.

(g) Standards used in determining violation of section

The standards used to determine whether this section has been violated in a complaint alleging nonaffirmative action employment discrimination under this section shall be the standards applied under title I of the Americans with Disabilities Act of 1990 (42 U.S.C. 12111 et seq.) and the provisions of sections 501 through 504, and 510, of the Americans with Disabilities Act of 1990 (42 U.S.C. 12201-12204 and 12210), as such sections relate to employment.

§ 793. Employment under Federal contracts

(a) Amount of contracts or subcontracts; provision for employment and advancement of qualified individuals with disabilities; regulations

Any contract in excess of $10,000 entered into by any Federal department or agency for the procurement of personal property and nonpersonal services (including construction) for the United States shall contain a provision requiring that the party contracting with the United States shall take affirmative action to employ and advance in employment qualified individuals with disabilities. The provisions of this section shall apply to any subcontract in excess of $10,000 entered into by a prime contractor in carrying out any contract for the procurement of personal property and nonpersonal services (including construction) for the United States. The President shall implement the provisions of this section by promulgating regulations within ninety days after September 26, 1973.

(b) Administrative enforcement; complaints; investigations; departmental action

If any individual with a disability believes any contractor has failed or refused to comply with the provisions of a contract with the United States, relating to employment of individuals with disabilities, such individual may file a complaint with the Department of

Labor. The Department shall promptly investigate such complaint and shall take such action thereon as the facts and circumstances warrant, consistent with the terms of such contract and the laws and regulations applicable thereto.

(c) Waiver by President; national interest special circumstances for waiver of particular agreements; waiver by Secretary of Labor of affirmative action requirements

(1) The requirements of this section may be waived, in whole or in part, by the President with respect to a particular contract or subcontract, in accordance with guidelines set forth in regulations which the President shall prescribe, when the President determines that special circumstances in the national interest so require and states in writing the reasons for such determination.

(2)(A) The Secretary of Labor may waive the requirements of the affirmative action clause required by regulations promulgated under subsection (a) of this section with respect to any of a prime contractor's or subcontractor's facilities that are found to be in all respects separate and distinct from activities of the prime contractor or subcontractor related to the performance of the contract or subcontract, if the Secretary of Labor also finds that such a waiver will not interfere with or impede the effectuation of this chapter.

(B) Such waivers shall be considered only upon the request of the contractor or subcontractor. The Secretary of Labor shall promulgate regulations that set forth the standards used for granting such a waiver.

(d) Standards used in determining violation of section

The standards used to determine whether this section has been violated in a complaint alleging nonaffirmative action employment discrimination under this section shall be the standards applied under title I of the Americans with Disabilities Act of 1990 (42 U.S.C. 12111 et seq.) and the provisions of sections 501 through 504, and 510, of the Americans with Disabilities Act of 1990 (42 U.S.C. 12201-12204 and 12210), as such sections relate to employment.

(e) Avoidance of duplicative efforts and inconsistencies

The Secretary shall develop procedures to ensure that administrative complaints filed under this section and under the Americans with Disabilities Act of 1990 [42 U.S.C.A. § 12101 et seq.] are dealt with in a manner that avoids duplication of effort and prevents imposition of inconsistent or conflicting standards for the same requirements under this section and the Americans with Disabilities Act of 1990 [42 U.S.C.A. § 12101 et seq.].

§ 794 Nondiscrimination under federal grants and programs

(a) Promulgation of rules and regulations

No otherwise qualified individual with a disability in the United States, as defined in section 705(20) of this title, shall, solely by reason of her or his disability, be excluded from the participation in, be denied the benefits of, or be subjected to discrimination under any program or activity receiving Federal financial assistance or under any program or activity conducted by any Executive agency or by the United States Postal Service. The head of each such agency shall promulgate such regulations as may be necessary to carry out the amendments to this section made by the Rehabilitation, Comprehensive Services, and Developmental Disabilities Act of 1978. Copies of any proposed regulation shall be submitted to appropriate authorizing committees of the Congress, and such regulation may take effect no earlier than the thirtieth day after the date on which such regulation is so submitted to such committees.

(b) "Program or activity" defined

For the purposes of this section, the term "program or activity" means all of the operations of—

(1)(A) a department, agency, special purpose district, or other instrumentality of a State or of a local government; or

(B) the entity of such State or local government that distributes such assistance and each such department or agency (and each other State or local government entity) to which the assistance is extended, in the case of assistance to a State or local government;

(2)(A) a college, university, or other post-secondary institution, or a public system of higher education; or

(B) a local educational agency (as defined in section 7801 of Title 20) system of vocational education, or other school system;

(3)(A) an entire corporation, partnership, or other private organization, or an entire sole proprietorship—

(i) if assistance is extended to such corporation, partnership, private organization, or sole proprietorship as a whole; or

(ii) which is principally engaged in the business of providing education, health care, housing, social services, or parks and recreation; or

(B) the entire plant or other comparable, geographically separate facility to which Federal financial assistance is extended, in the case of any other corporation, partnership, private organization, or sole proprietorship; or

(4) any other entity which is established by two or

more of the entities described in paragraph (1), (2), or (3); any part of which is extended Federal financial assistance.

(c) Significant structural alterations by small providers; exception

Small providers are not required by subsection (a) of this section to make significant structural alterations to their existing facilities for the purpose of assuring program accessibility, if alternative means of providing the services are available. The terms used in this subsection shall be construed with reference to the regulations existing on March 22, 1988.

(d) Standards used in determining violation of section

The standards used to determine whether this section has been violated in a complaint alleging employment discrimination under this section shall be the standards applied under title I of the Americans with Disabilities Act of 1990 (42 U.S.C. 12111 et seq.) and the provisions of sections 501 through 504, and 510, of the Americans with Disabilities Act of 1990 (42 U.S.C. 12201-12204 and 12210), as such sections relate to employment.

§ 794a Remedies and attorney fees

(a)(1) The remedies, procedures, and rights set forth in section 717 of the Civil Rights Act of 1964 (42 U.S.C. 2000e-16), including the application of sections 706(f) through 706(k) (42 U.S.C. 2000e-5(f) through (k)), shall be available, with respect to any complaint under section 791 of this title, to any employee or applicant for employment aggrieved by the final disposition of such complaint, or by the failure to take final action on such complaint. In fashioning an equitable or affirmative action remedy under such section, a court may take into account the reasonableness of the cost of any necessary work place accommodation, and the availability of alternatives therefor or other appropriate relief in order to achieve an equitable and appropriate remedy.

(2) The remedies, procedures, and rights set forth in title VI of the Civil Rights Act of 1964 [42 U.S.C.A. § 2000d et seq.] shall be available to any person aggrieved by any act or failure to act by any recipient of Federal assistance or Federal provider of such assistance under section 794 of this title.

(b) In any action or proceeding to enforce or charge a violation of a provision of this subchapter, the court, in its discretion, may allow the prevailing party, other than the United States, a reasonable attorney's fee as part of the costs.

REHABILITATION ACT DEPARTMENT OF LABOR REGULATIONS

29 C.F.R. §

Subpart A—General Provisions

32.1 Purpose.
32.2 Application.
32.3 Definitions.
32.4 Discrimination prohibited.
32.5 Assurances required.
32.6 Remedial action, voluntary action, and self-evaluation.
32.7 Designation of responsible employee.
32.8 Notice.
32.9 Administrative requirements for small recipients.
32.10 Effect of State or local law or other requirements and effect of employment opportunities.

Subpart B—Employment Practices and Employment Related Training Program Participation

32.12 Discrimination prohibited.
32.13 Reasonable accommodation.
32.14 Job qualifications.
32.15 Preemployment inquiries.
32.16 Listing of employment openings.
32.17 Labor unions and recruiting and training agencies.

Subpart C—Program Accessibility

32.26 Discrimination prohibited.
32.27 Access to programs.
32.28 Architectural standards.

REHABILITATION ACT REGULATIONS
Subpart A—General Provisions

§ 32.1 Purpose.

Section 504 of the Rehabilitation Act of 1973 prohibits discrimination on the basis of handicap in any program or activity receiving Federal financial assistance. The purpose of this part is to implement section 504 with respect to programs or activities receiving or benefiting from Federal financial assistance from the Department of Labor.

§ 32.2 Application.

(a) This part applies to each recipient of Federal financial assistance from the Department of Labor, and to every program or activity that receives such assistance.

(b) A government contractor covered by the provisions of section 503 of the Act shall be deemed in compliance with the employment provisions of these regulations if it is in compliance with 41 CFR Part 60-741 (as amended after publication of these regulations) with respect to Federal financial assistance from the Department of Labor.

§ 32.3 Definitions.

As used in this part, the term:

The Act means the Rehabilitation Act of 1973, Pub.L. 93-112, as amended by the Rehabilitation Act Amendments of 1974, Pub.L. 93-516, and by the Rehabilitation, Comprehensive Services, and Developmental Disabilities Amendments of 1978, Pub.L. 95-602.

Assistant Secretary means the Assistant Secretary for Employment and Training Administration or his or her designee.

Applicant for assistance means one who submits an application, request, or plan required to be approved by a Department official or by a recipient as a condition to becoming a recipient.

Department means the Department of Labor.

Facility means all or any portion of the buildings, structures, equipment, roads, walks, parking lots or other real or personal property or interest in such property which are utilized in the execution of the program or activity for which Federal financial assistance is received.

Federal financial assistance means any grant, loan, contract (other than a procurement contract or a contract of insurance or guarantee), or any other arrangement by which the Department provides or otherwise makes available assistance in the form of:

(a) Funds;
(b) Services of Federal personnel; or
(c) Real and personal property or any interest in or use of such property, including:

(1) Transfers or leases of such property for less than fair market value or for reduced consideration; and

(2) Proceeds from a subsequent transfer or lease of such property if the Federal share of its fair market value is not returned to the Federal Government.

Government means the Government of the United States of America.

Handicap means any condition or characteristic that renders a person a handicapped individual as defined in this section.

Handicapped individual

(a) Handicapped individual means any person

who—

(1) Has a physical or mental impairment which substantially limits one or more major life activities;

(2) Has a record of such an impairment; or

(3) Is regarded as having such an impairment.

(b) As used in the proceeding paragraph of this section, the phrase:

(1) Physical or mental impairment means—

(i) Any physiological disorder or condition, cosmetic disfigurement, or anatomical loss affecting one or more of the following body systems: neurological; musculoskeletal; special sense organs; respiratory, including speech organs; cardiovascular; reproductive; digestive; genito-urinary; hemic and lymphatic; skin; and endocrine;

(ii) Any mental or psychological disorder, such as mental retardation, organic brain syndrome, emotional or mental illness, and specific learning disabilities.

(iii) The term physical or mental impairment includes but is not limited to such diseases and conditions as orthopedic, visual, speech and hearing impairments, cerebral palsy, epilepsy, muscular dystrophy, multiple sclerosis, cancer, heart disease, diabetes, mental retardation, emotional illness, and drug addiction and alcoholism.

(2) Substantially limits means the degree that the impairment affects an individual becoming a beneficiary of a program or activity receiving Federal financial assistance or affects an individual's employability. A handicapped individual who is likely to experience difficulty in securing or retaining benefits or in securing, or retaining, or advancing in employment would be considered substantially limited.

(3) Major life activities means functions such as caring for one's self, performing manual tasks, walking, seeing, hearing, speaking, breathing, learning, working, and receiving education or vocational training.

(4) Has a record of such an impairment means that the individual has a history of, or has been misclassified as having, a mental or physical impairment that substantially limits one or more life activity.

(5) Is regarded as having such an impairment means that the individual—

(i) Has a physical or mental impairment that does not substantially limit major life activities but that is treated by a recipient as constituting such a limitation;

(ii) Has a physical or mental impairment that substantially limits major life activities only as a result of the attitudes of others toward such impairment; or

(iii) Has none of the impairments defined in paragraph (b)(1) of this section but is treated by a recipient as having such an impairment.

Program or activity means all of the operations of any entity described in paragraphs (1) through (4) of this definition, any part of which is extended Federal financial assistance:

(1)(i) A department, agency, special purpose district, or other instrumentality of a State or of a local government; or

(ii) The entity of such State or local government that distributes such assistance and each such department or agency (and each other State or local government entity) to which the assistance is extended, in the case of assistance to a State or local government;

(2)(i) A college, university, or other postsecondary institution, or a public system of higher education; or

(ii) A local educational agency (as defined in 20 U.S.C. 7801), system of vocational education, or other school system;

(3)(i) An entire corporation, partnership, or other private organization, or an entire sole proprietorship—

(A) If assistance is extended to such corporation, partnership, private organization, or sole proprietorship as a whole; or

(B) Which is principally engaged in the business of providing education, health care, housing, social services, or parks and recreation; or

(ii) The entire plant or other comparable, geographically separate facility to which Federal financial assistance is extended, in the case of any other corporation, partnership, private organization, or sole proprietorship; or

(4) Any other entity which is established by two or more of the entities described in paragraph (1), (2), or (3) of this definition.

Qualified handicapped individual means:

(a) With respect to employment, an individual with a handicap who is capable of performing the essential functions of the job or jobs for which he or she is being considered with reasonable accommodation to his or her handicap;

(b) With respect to services, a handicapped individual who meets eligibility requirements relevant to the receipt of services provided in the program or activity;

(c) With respect to employment and to employment related training, a handicapped individual who meets both the eligibility requirements for participation in the program or activity and valid job or training qualifications with reasonable accommodation.

Reasonable accommodation means the changes and modifications which can be made in the structure of a job or employment and training, or in the manner in which a job is performed or employment and training program is conducted, unless it would impose an undue hardship on the operation of the recipient's program or activity. Reasonable accommodation may include:

(a) Making the facilities used by the employees or participants in the area where the program or activity is conducted, including common areas used by all employees or participants such as hallways, restrooms, cafeterias and lounges, readily accessible to and usable by handicapped persons, and

(b) Job restructuring, part-time or modified work schedules, acquisition or modification of equipment or devices, the provision of readers or interpreters, and other similar actions.

Recipient means any state or its political subdivisions, any instrumentality of a State or its political subdivisions, any public or private agency, institution, organization, or other entity, or any person to which Federal financial assistance is extended directly or through another recipient, including any successor, assignee, or transferee of a recipient, but excluding the ultimate beneficiary of the assistance.

Secretary means the Secretary of Labor, U.S. Department of Labor, or his or her designee.Section 504 means section 504 of the Act.

Small recipient means a recipient who serves fewer than 15 beneficiaries, and employs fewer than 15 employees at all times during a grant year.

United States means the several States, the District of Columbia, the Virgin Islands, the Commonwealth of Puerto Rico, Guam, American Samoa and the Trust Territory of the Pacific Islands.

§ 32.4 Discrimination prohibited.

(a) General. No qualified handicapped individual shall, on the basis of handicap, be excluded from participation in, be denied the benefits of, or otherwise be subjected to discrimination under any program or activity which receives Federal financial assistance.

(b) Discriminatory actions prohibited.

(1) A recipient, in providing any aid, benefit, service or training, may not, directly or through contractual, licensing, or other arrangements, on the basis of handicap:

(i) Deny a qualified handicapped individual the opportunity to participate in or benefit from the aid, benefit, service or training;

(ii) Afford a qualified handicapped individual an opportunity to participate in or benefit from the aid, benefit, service or training that is not equal to that afforded others;

(iii) Provide a qualified handicapped individual with any aid, benefit, service or training that is not as effective as that provided to others;

(iv) Provide different or separate aid, benefits, or services to handicapped individuals or to any class of handicapped individuals unless such action is necessary to provide qualified handicapped individuals with aid, benefits, services or training that are as effective as those provided to others;

(v) Aid or perpetuate discrimination against a qualified handicapped individual by providing significant assistance to an agency, organization, or person that discriminates on the basis of handicap in providing any aid, benefit, service or training to beneficiaries of the recipient's program or activity;

(vi) Deny a qualified handicapped individual the opportunity to participate as a member of planning or advisory boards; or

(vii) Otherwise limit a qualified handicapped individual in enjoyment of any right, privilege, advantage, or opportunity enjoyed by others receiving any aid, benefit, service or training.

(2) For purposes of this part, aid, benefits, services or training, to be equally effective, are not required to produce the identical result or level of achievement for handicapped and nonhandicapped individuals, but must afford handicapped individuals equal opportunity to obtain the same result, to gain the same benefit, or to reach the same level of achievement, in the most integrated setting appropriate to the person's needs.

(3) A recipient may not deny a qualified handicapped individual the opportunity to participate in its regular aid, benefits, services, or training, despite the existence of separate or different aid, benefits, services, or training for the handicapped which are established in accordance with this Part.

(4) A recipient may not, directly or through contractual or other arrangements, utilize criteria or methods of administration:

(i) That have the effect of subjecting qualified handicapped individuals to discrimination on the basis of handicap;

(ii) That have the purpose or effect of defeating or substantially impairing accomplishment of the objectives of the recipient's program or activity with respect to handicapped individuals; or

(iii) That perpetuate the discrimination of another recipient if both recipients are subject to common administrative control or are agencies of the same State.

(5) In determining the site or location of a facility, an applicant for assistance or a recipient may not make selections:

(i) That have the effect of excluding handicapped individuals from, denying them the benefits of, or otherwise subjecting them to discrimination under any program or activity that receives Federal financial assistance; or

(ii) That have the purpose or effect of defeating or substantially impairing the accomplishment of the objectives of the program or activity with respect to handicapped individuals.

(6) As used in this section, the aid, benefit, service or training provided under a program or activity receiving Federal financial assistance includes any aid, benefit, service or training provided in or through a facility that has been constructed, expanded, altered, leased, rented, or otherwise acquired, in whole or in part, with Federal financial assistance.

(7)(i) In providing services receiving Federal financial assistance, except for employment-related training, a recipient to which this subpart applies, except small recipients, shall ensure that no handicapped participant is denied the benefits of, excluded from participation in, or otherwise subjected to discrimination under the program or activity operated by the recipient because of the absence of auxiliary aids for participants with impaired sensory, manual or speaking skills. In employment and employment-related training, this paragraph shall apply only to the intake, assessment and referral services. A recipient shall operate each program or activity to which this subpart applies so that, when viewed in its entirety, auxiliary aids are readily available.

(ii) Auxiliary aids may include brailled and taped written materials, interpreters or other effective methods of making orally delivered information available to persons with hearing impairments, readers for persons with visual impairments, equipment adapted for use by persons with manual impairments, and other similar services and actions. Recipients need not provide attendants, individually prescribed devices, readers for personal use or study, or other devices or services of a personal nature.

(c) Aid, benefits, services, or training limited by Federal law. The exclusion of nonhandicapped persons from aid, benefits, program services, or training limited by Federal statute or Executive Order to handicapped individuals or the exclusion of a specific class of handicapped individuals from aid, benefits, services, or training limited by Federal statute or Executive Order to a different class of handicapped individuals is not prohibited by this part.

(d) Integrated setting. Recipients shall administer programs or activities in the most integrated setting appropriate to the needs of qualified handicapped individuals.

(e) Communications with individuals with impaired vision and hearing. Recipients shall take appropriate steps to ensure that communications with their applicants, employees, and beneficiaries are available to persons with impaired vision and hearing.

§ 32.5 Assurances required.

(a) Assurances. An applicant for Federal financial assistance for a program or activity to which this part applies shall submit an assurance, on a form specified by the Assistant Secretary, that the program will be operated in compliance with this part. An applicant may incorporate these assurances by reference in subsequent applications to the Department.

(b) Duration of obligation.

(1) In the case of Federal financial assistance extended in the form of real property or structures on the property, the assurance will obligate the recipient or, in the case of a subsequent transfer, the transferee, for the period during which the real property or structures are used for the purpose involving the provision of similar services or benefits.

(2) In the case of Federal financial assistance extended to provide personal property, the assurance will obligate the recipient for the period during which it retains ownership or possession of the property.

(3) In all other cases the assurance will obligate the recipient for the period during which Federal financial assistance is extended or the federally-funded program is operated, whichever is longer.

(c) Covenants.

(1) Where Federal financial assistance is provided in the form of real property or interest in the property from the Department, the instrument effecting or recording this transfer shall contain a covenant running with the land to assure nondiscrimination for the period during which the real property is used for a purpose for which the Federal financial assistance is extended or for another purpose involving the provision of similar services or benefits.

(2) Where no Federal transfer of property is involved but property is purchased or improved with Federal financial assistance, the recipient shall agree to include the covenant described in paragraph (c)(1) of this section in the instrument effecting or recording any subsequent transfer of the property.

(3) Where Federal financial assistance is provided in the form of real property or interest in the property from the Department, the covenant shall also include a condition coupled with a right to be reserved by the Department to revert title to the property in the event of a breach of the covenant. If a transferee of real prop-

erty proposes to mortgage or otherwise encumber the real property as security to finance construction of new, or improvement of existing, facilities on the property for the purposes for which the property was transferred, the Assistant Secretary may agree to forbear the exercise of such right to revert title for so long as the lien of such mortgage or other encumbrance remains effective. Such an agreement by the Assistant Secretary may be entered into only upon the request of the transferee (recipient) if it is necessary to accomplish such financing and upon such terms and conditions as the Assistant Secretary deems appropriate.

(d) *Interagency agreements.* Where funds are granted by the Department to another Federal agency to carry out a program under a law administered by the Department, and where the grant obligates the recipient agency to comply with the rules and regulations of the Department applicable to that grant the provisions of this part shall apply to programs or activities operated with such funds.

§ 32.6 Remedial action, voluntary action, and self-evaluation.

(a) *Remedial action.*

(1) If the Assistant Secretary finds that a recipient has discriminated against persons on the basis of handicap in violation of section 504 [or] this part, the recipient shall take such remedial action as the Assistant Secretary deems necessary to overcome the effects of the discrimination.

(2) Where a recipient is found to have discriminated against persons on the basis of handicap in violation of section 504 or this part and where another recipient exercises control over the recipient that has discriminated, the Assistant Secretary, where appropriate, may require either or both recipients to take remedial action.

(3) The Assistant Secretary may, where necessary to overcome the effects of discrimination in violation of section 504 or this part, require a recipient to take remedial action:

(i) With respect to handicapped individuals who would have been participants in the program had the discrimination not occurred; and

(ii) With respect to handicapped persons who are no longer participants in the recipient's program but who were participants in the program when the discrimination occurred; and

(iii) With respect to employees and applicants for employment.

(b) *Voluntary action.* A recipient may take steps, in addition to any action that is required by this part, to overcome the effects of conditions that resulted in limited participation in the recipient's program or activity by qualified handicapped individuals.

(c) *Self-evaluation.*

(1) A recipient shall, within one year of the effective date of this part:

(i) Evaluate, with the assistance of interested persons who are selected by the recipient, including handicapped individuals or organizations representing handicapped individuals, its current policies and practices and the effects thereof that do not or may not meet the requirements of this part;

(ii) Modify, after consultation with interested persons who are selected by the recipient, including handicapped individuals or organizations representing handicapped individuals, any policies and practices that do not meet the requirements of this part; and

(iii) Take, after consultation with interested persons who are selected by the recipient, including handicapped individuals or organizations representing handicapped individuals, appropriate remedial steps to eliminate the effects of any discrimination that resulted from adherence to these policies and practices.

(2) A recipient, other than a small recipient, shall for at least three years following completion of the evaluation required under paragraph (c)(1) of this section, maintain on file, make available for public inspection, and provide to the Assistant Secretary upon request:

(i) A list of the interested persons consulted;

(ii) A description of areas examined and any problems identified; and

(iii) A description of any modifications made and of any remedial steps taken.

§ 32.7 Designation of responsible employee.

A recipient, other than a small recipient, shall designate at least one person to coordinate its efforts to comply with this part.

§ 32.8 Notice.

(a) A recipient, other than a small recipient, shall take appropriate initial and continuing steps to notify participants, beneficiaries, referral sources, applicants, and employees, including those with impaired vision or hearing, and unions or professional organizations which have collective bargaining or professional agreements with the recipient, that it does not discriminate on the basis of handicap in violation of section 504 and of this part. The notification shall state, where appropriate, that the recipient does not discriminate in the admission or access to, or treatment or employment in, its programs and activities. The notification shall also include an identification of the responsible employee designated pursuant to Sec. 32.7. A recipient shall make the initial notifications required by this paragraph within 90 days of the effective date of this part. Methods of initial and continuing notification may include the posting of notices, publication in newspapers and magazines, placement of notices in recipient's publications, and distribution of memoranda or other written communications.

(b) If a recipient publishes or uses recruitment materials or publications containing general information that it makes available to participants, beneficiaries, applicants, or employees, it shall include in those materials or publications a statement of the policy described in paragraph (a) of this section. A recipient may meet the requirement of this paragraph either by including appropriate inserts in existing materials and publications or by revising and reprinting the materials and publications.

§ 32.9 Administrative requirements for small recipients.

The Assistant Secretary may require any recipient that provides services to fewer than 15 beneficiaries or with fewer than 15 employees, or any class of such recipients, to comply with Secs. 32.7 and 32.8, in whole or in part, when the Assistant Secretary finds a violation of this part or finds that such compliance will not significantly impair the ability of the recipient or class of recipients to provide benefits or services.

§ 32.10 Effect of State or local law or other requirements and effect of employment opportunities.

(a) The obligation to comply with this part is not obviated or alleviated by the existence of any State or local law or other requirement that, on the basis of handicap, imposes prohibitions or limits upon the eligibility of qualified handicapped individuals to receive services, participate in programs or practice any occupation or profession.

(b) The obligation to comply with this part is not obviated or alleviated because employment opportunities in any occupation or profession are or may be more limited for handicapped individuals than for non-handicapped persons.

Subpart B—Employment Practices and Employment Related Training Program Participation

§ 32.12 Discrimination prohibited.

(a) General.

(1) No qualified handicapped individual shall, on the basis of handicap, be subjected to discrimination in employment under any program or activity to which this part applies. This subpart is applicable to employees and applicants for employment with all recipients and to participants in employment and training programs financed in whole or in part by Federal financial assistance.

(2) A recipient shall make all decisions concerning employment or training under any program or activity to which this subpart applies in a manner which ensures that discrimination on the basis of handicap does not occur and may not limit, segregate, or classify applicants or employees or participants in any way that adversely affects their opportunities or status because of handicap.

(3) A recipient may not participate in a contractual or other relationship that has the effect of subjecting qualified handicapped applicants, employees or participants to discrimination prohibited by this subpart. The relationships referred to in this subparagraph include relationships with employment and referral agencies, with labor unions, with organizations providing or administering fringe benefits to employees of the recipient, and with organizations providing training and apprenticeship programs.

(b) Specific activities. The provisions of this subpart apply to:

(1) Recruitment advertising, and the processing of applicants for employment;

(2) Hiring, upgrading, promotion, award of tenure, demotion, transfer, layoff, termination, right of return from layoff and rehiring;

(3) Rates of pay or any other form of compensation and changes in compensation;

(4) Job assignments, job classifications, organizational structures, position descriptions, lines of progression, and seniority lists;

(5) Leaves of absence, sick leave, or any other leave;

(6) Fringe benefits available by virtue of employment, whether or not administered by the recipient;

(7) Selection and financial support for training, including apprenticeship, professional meetings, conferences, and other related activities, and selection for leaves of absence to pursue training;

(8) Employer-sponsored activities, including social or recreational programs; and

(9) Any other term, condition, or privilege of employment.

(c) Collective bargaining agreements. Whenever a recipient's obligation to comply with this subpart and to correct discriminatory practices impacts on and/or necessitates changes in a term of a collective bargaining agreement(s) to which the recipient is a party, the recipient shall attempt to achieve compliance consistent with the provisions of Sec. 32.17(a). However a recipient's obligation to comply with this subpart is not relieved by a term of any such collective bargaining agreement(s).

(d) Compensation. In offering employment or promotions to handicapped individuals, the recipient shall not reduce the amount of compensation offered because of any disability income, pension or other benefit the applicant or employee receives from other source.

32.13 Reasonable accommodation.

(a) A recipient shall make reasonable accommodation to the known physical or mental limitations of an otherwise qualified handicapped applicant, employee or participant unless the recipient can demonstrate that the accommodation would impose an undue hardship on the operation of its program.

(b) In determining pursuant to paragraph (a) of this section whether an accommodation would impose an undue hardship on the operation of a recipient's program, factors to be considered include;

(1) The overall size of the recipient's program with respect to number of employees, number of participants, number and type of facilities, and size of budget;

(2) The type of the recipient's operation, including the composition and structure of the recipient's workforce, and duration and type of training program; and

(3) The nature and cost of the accommodation needed.

(c) A recipient may not deny any employment or training opportunity to a qualified handicapped employee, applicant or participant if the basis for the denial is the need to make reasonable accommodation to the physical or mental limitations of the employee, applicant or participant.

(d) Nothing in this paragraph shall relieve a recipient of its obligation to make its program accessible as required in subpart C of this part, or to provide auxiliary aids, as required by Sec. 32.4(b)(7).

§ 32.14 Job qualifications.

(a) The recipient shall provide for, and shall adhere to, a schedule for the review of the appropriateness of all job qualifications to ensure that to the extent job qualifications tend to exclude handicapped individuals because of their handicap, they are related to the performance of the job and are consistent with business necessity and safe performance.

(b) Whenever a recipient applies job qualifications in the selection of applicants, employees or participants for employment or training or other change in employment status such as promotion, demotion or training, which would tend to exclude handicapped individuals because of their handicap, the qualifications shall be related to the specific job or jobs for which the individual is being considered and shall be consistent with business necessity and safe performance. The recipient shall have the burden to demonstrate that it has complied with the requirements of this paragraph.

§ 32.15 Preemployment inquiries.

(a) Except as provided in paragraphs (b) and (c) of this section, a recipient may not conduct preemployment medical examinations or make preemployment inquiry of an applicant for employment or training as to whether the applicant is a handicapped person or as to the nature or the severity of a handicap. A recipient may, however, make preemployment inquiry into an applicant's ability to perform job-related functions.

(b) When a recipient is taking remedial action to correct the effects of past discrimination, when a recipient is taking voluntary action to overcome the effects of conditions that resulted in limited participation in its federally-assisted program or activity, or when a recipient is taking affirmative action pursuant to section 503 of the Act, the recipient may invite applicants for employment or training to indicate whether and to what extent they are handicapped if:

(1) The recipient states clearly on any written questionnaire used for this purpose or makes clear orally, if no written questionnaire is used, that the information requested is intended for use solely in connection with its remedial action obligations or its voluntary or affirmative action efforts.

(2) The recipient states clearly that the information is being requested on a voluntary basis, that it will be kept confidential as provided in paragraph (d) of this section, that refusal to provide it will not subject the applicant, employee or participant to any adverse treatment, and that it will be used only in accordance with this part.

(c) An employer who routinely requires medical examinations as part of the employment selection process must demonstrate that each of the requirements of this subsection are met:

(1) The medical examination shall be performed by a physician qualified to make functional assessments of individuals in a form which will express residual capacity for work or training. Such an assessment does not require clinical determinations of disease or disability, but shall provide selecting or referring officials sufficient information regarding any functional limita-

tions relevant to proper job placement or referral to appropriate training programs. Factors which may be assessed may include, for example, use of limbs and extremities, mobility and posture, endurance and energy expenditure, ability to withstand various working conditions and environments, use of senses and mental capacity;

(2) The results of the medical examination shall be specific and objective so as to be susceptible to review by independent medical evaluators and shall be transmitted to the applicant or employee at the same time as the employing official;

(3) The results of the medical examination shall not be used to screen out qualified applicants and employees but to determine proper placement and reasonable accommodation. The employing official using physical or mental information obtained pursuant to this section should be familiar with physical or mental activities involved in performing the job, and the working conditions and environment in which it is carried out. If the applicant is being considered for a variety of jobs having different requirements or skills, the employing official should make a functional assessment of the physical or mental demands of the jobs in order to match the applicant with the most suitable vacancy;

(4) All of potential employees for the jobs are subjected to the medical examination;

(5) The procedures for using medical examinations or the medical information shall be constructed in such a manner that:

(i) A conditional job offer was made or the individual was conditionally placed in a job pool or conditionally placed on an eligibility list prior to the medical examination being performed; or

(ii) The results of the medical examination were considered by the employing official only after a conditional decision to make a job offer or the individual had been placed conditionally in a job pool or conditionally placed on an eligibility list; that is the medical results were the last factor evaluated by the employing officials before a final decision to make an offer of employment was made.

(6) Unless a conditional job offer is made prior to the medical examination, all potential employees for the job shall be informed at the time of the medical examination that:

(i) The results of the medical examination are the last factor evaluated by the employing official before a final decision to make an offer of employment is made, and

(ii) The medical examination results shall be transmitted to the employing official and the applicant only after a conditional decision to make a job offer has been made.

(d) Information obtained in accordance with this section as to the medical condition or history of the applicant shall be collected and maintained on separate forms that shall be accorded confidentiality as medical records, except that:

(1) Employing officials may obtain the information after making a conditional decision to make a job offer to the applicant or the applicant was placed conditionally in a job pool or placed conditionally on an eligibility list;

(2) Supervisors and managers may be informed regarding restrictions on the work or duties of qualified handicapped persons and regarding necessary accommodations;

(3) First aid and safety personnel may be informed, where appropriate, if the condition might require emergency treatment; and

(4) Government officials investigating compliance with the Act shall be provided information upon request.

§ 32.16 Listing of employment openings.

Recipients should request State employment security agencies to refer qualified handicapped individuals for consideration for employment.

§ 32.17 Labor unions and recruiting and training agencies.

The performance of a recipient's obligations under the nondiscrimination provisions of these regulations may necessitate a revision in a collective bargaining agreement(s). The policy of the Department of Labor is to use its best efforts, directly or through the recipients, subgrantees, local officials, vocational rehabilitation facilities, and other available instrumentalities, to cause any labor union, recruiting and training agency or other representative or workers who are or may be engaged in work under programs of Federal financial assistance to cooperate with, and to comply in the implementation of section 504.

(b) To effectuate the purposes of paragraph (a) of this section, the Assistant Secretary may hold hearings, public or private, with respect to the practices and policies of any such labor union or recruiting and training agency.

(c) Whenever compliance with section 504 necessitates a revision of a collective bargaining agreement or otherwise significantly affects a substantial number of employees represented by the union, the collective bargaining representatives shall be given an opportunity to present their views to the Assistant Secretary.

(d) The Assistant Secretary may notify any Federal, State, or local agency of his/her conclusions and recommendations with respect to any such labor organization or recruiting and training agency which in his/her judgment has failed to cooperate with the Department of Labor, recipients, subgrantees or applicants in carrying out the purposes of section 504. The Assistant Secretary also may notify other appropriate Federal agencies when there is reason to believe that the practices of any such labor organization or agency violates other provisions of Federal law.

Subpart C—Program Accessibility

§ 32.26 Discrimination prohibited.

No qualified handicapped individual shall, because a recipient's facilities are inaccessible to or unusable by handicapped individuals, be denied the benefits of, be excluded from participation in, or otherwise be subjected to discrimination under any program or activity to which this part applies.

§ 32.27 Access to programs.

(a) Purpose. A recipient shall operate each program or activity to which this part applies so that the program or activity, when viewed in its entirety, is readily accessible to qualified handicapped individuals. This paragraph does not require a recipient to make each of its existing facilities or every part of a facility accessible to and usable by qualified handicapped individuals. However, if a particular program is available in only one location, that site must be made accessible or the program must be made available at an alternative accessible site or sites. Program accessibility requires nonpersonal aids to make the program accessible to mobility impaired persons. Reasonable accommodations, as defined in Sec. 32.3, are required for particular handicapped individuals in response to the specific limitations of their handicaps.

(b) Scope and application.

(1) For the purpose of this subpart, prime sponsors under the Comprehensive Employment and Training Act and any other individual or organization which receives a grant directly from the Department to establish or operate any program or activity shall assure that the program or activity, including Public Service Employment, Work Experience, Classroom Training and On-the-Job-Training, when viewed in its entirety, is readily accessible to qualified handicapped individuals.

(2) Job Corps. All agencies, grantees, or contractors which screen or recruit applicants for the Job Corps shall comply with the nondiscrimination provisions of this part. Each regional office of the Department of Labor's Employment and Training Administration which makes the decision on the assignment of a Job Corps applicant to a particular center may, where it finds, after consultation with the qualified handicapped person seeking Job Corps services, that there is no method of complying with Sec. 32.27(a) at a particular Job Corps Center, other than by making a significant alteration in its existing facilities or in its training programs, assign that individual to another Job Corps Center which is accessible in accordance with this section and which is offering comparable training. The Job Corps, and each regional office of the Employment and Training Administration, shall assure that the Job Corps Program, when viewed in its entirety, is readily accessible to qualified handicapped individuals and that all future construction, including improvements to existing Centers, be made accessible to the handicapped.

(3) If a small recipient finds, after consultation with a qualified handicapped person seeking its services, that there is no method of complying with Sec. 32.27(a) other than making a significant alteration in its existing facilities or facility the recipient may, as an alternative, refer the qualified handicapped person to other providers of those services that are accessible.

(c) Methods. A recipient may comply with the requirement of Sec. 32.27(a) through such means as redesign of equipment, reassignment of classes or other services to accessible buildings, assignment of aides to beneficiaries, home visits, delivery of services at alternate accessible sites, alteration of existing facilities and construction of new facilities in conformance with the requirements of Sec. 32.28, or any other method that results in making its program or activity accessible to handicapped individuals. A recipient is not required to make structural changes in existing facilities where other methods are effective in achieving compliance with Sec. 32.27(a). In choosing among available methods for meeting the requirement of Sec. 32.27(a), a recipient shall give priority to those methods that offer programs and activities to handicapped persons in the most integrated setting appropriate.

(d) Time period. A recipient shall comply with the requirements of Sec. 32.27(a) within 60 days of the effective date of this part except that where structural changes in facilities are necessary, such changes shall be made within three years of the effective date of this part, but in any even as expeditiously as possible.

(e) Transition plan. In the event that structural changes to facilities are necessary to meet the requirement of Sec. 32.27(a), a recipient shall develop, within six months of the effective date of this part, a transition plan setting forth the steps necessary to complete such changes. The plan shall be developed with the assistance of interested persons, including qualified handicapped individuals. A copy of the transition plan shall be made available for public inspection. The plan shall, at a minimum:

(1) Identify physical obstacles in the recipient's facilities that limit the accessibility of its program or activity to qualified handicapped individuals;

(2) Describe in detail the methods that will be used to make the facilities accessible;

(3) Specify the schedule for taking the steps necessary to achieve full program accessibility and, if the time period of the transition plan is longer than one year, identify steps that will be taken during each year of the transition period; and

(4) Indicate the person responsible for implementation of the plan.

(f) Notice. The recipient shall adopt and implement procedures to ensure that interested persons, including persons with impaired vision or hearing, can obtain information as to the existence and location of services, activities, and facilities that are accessible to and usable by qualified handicapped individuals.

§ 32.28 Architectural standards.

(a) Design and construction. Each facility or part of a facility constructed by, on behalf of, or for the use of a recipient shall be designed and constructed in such manner that the facility or part of the facility is readily accessible to and usable by qualified handicapped individuals, if the construction was commenced after the effective date of this part.

(b) Alteration. Each facility or part of a facility which is altered by, on behalf of, or for the use of a recipient after the effective date of this part in a manner that affects or could affect the usability of the facility or part of the facility shall, to the maximum extent feasible, be altered in such manner that the altered portion of the facility is readily accessible to and usable by qualified handicapped individuals.

(c) Standards for architectural accessibility. Design, construction, or alteration of facilities under this subpart shall meet the most current standards for physical accessibility prescribed by the General Services Administration under the Architectural Barriers Act at 41 CFR 101-19.6. Alternative standards may be adopted when it is clearly evident that equivalent or greater access to the facility or part of the facility is thereby provided.

FAIR HOUSING

FAIR HOUSING ACT AMENDMENTS OF 1988

42 U.S.C. §
- 3601 Declaration of policy
- 3602 Definitions
- 3603 Effective dates of certain prohibitions
- 3604 Discrimination in the sale or rental of housing and other prohibited practices
- 3605 Discrimination in residential real estate-related transactions
- 3606 Discrimination in provision of brokerage services
- 3607 Exemption

FAIR HOUSING ACT AMENDMENTS OF 1988

§ 3601. Declaration of policy

It is the policy of the United States to provide, within constitutional limitations, for fair housing throughout the United States.

§ 3602. Definitions

As used in this subchapter—

(a) "Secretary" means the Secretary of Housing and Urban Development.

(b) "Dwelling" means any building, structure, or portion thereof which is occupied as, or designed or intended for occupancy as, a residence by one or more families, and any vacant land which is offered for sale or lease for the construction or location thereon of any such building, structure, or portion thereof.

(c) "Family" includes a single individual.

(d) "Person" includes one or more individuals, corporations, partnerships, associations, labor organizations, legal representatives, mutual companies, joint-stock companies, trusts, unincorporated organizations, trustees, trustees in cases under Title 11, receivers, and fiduciaries.

(e) "To rent" includes to lease, to sublease, to let and otherwise to grant for a consideration the right to occupy premises not owned by the occupant.

(f) "Discriminatory housing practice" means an act that is unlawful under section 3604, 3605, 3606, or 3617 of this title.

(g) "State" means any of the several States, the District of Columbia, the Commonwealth of Puerto Rico, or any of the territories and possessions of the United States.

(h) "Handicap" means, with respect to a person—

(1) a physical or mental impairment which substantially limits one or more of such person's major life activities,

(2) a record of having such an impairment, or

(3) being regarded as having such an impairment,

but such term does not include current, illegal use of or addiction to a controlled substance as defined in section 802 of Title 21.

(i) "Aggrieved person" includes any person who—

(1) claims to have been injured by a discriminatory housing practice; or

(2) believes that such person will be injured by a discriminatory housing practice that is about to occur.

(j) "Complainant" means the person (including the Secretary) who files a complaint under section 3610 of this title.

(k) "Familial status" means one or more individuals (who have not attained the age of 18 years) being domiciled with—

(1) a parent or another person having legal custody of such individual or individuals; or

(2) the designee of such parent or other person having such custody, with the written permission of such parent or other person.

The protections afforded against discrimination on the basis of familial status shall apply to any person who is pregnant or is in the process of securing legal custody of any individual who has not attained the age of 18 years.

(l) "Conciliation" means the attempted resolution of issues raised by a complaint, or by the investigation of such complaint, through informal negotiations involving the aggrieved person, the respondent, and the Secretary.

(m) "Conciliation agreement" means a written agreement setting forth the resolution of the issues in conciliation.

(n) "Respondent" means—

(1) the person or other entity accused in a complaint of an unfair housing practice; and

(2) any other person or entity identified in the course of investigation and notified as required with respect to respondents so identified under section 3610(a) of this title.

(o) "Prevailing party" has the same meaning as such term has in section 1988 of this title.

§ 3603. Effective dates of certain prohibitions

(a) Application to certain described dwellings

Subject to the provisions of subsection (b) of this section and section 3607 of this title, the prohibitions against discrimination in the sale or rental of housing set forth in section 3604 of this title shall apply:

(1) Upon enactment of this subchapter, to—

(A) dwellings owned or operated by the Federal Government;

(B) dwellings provided in whole or in part with the aid of loans, advances, grants, or contributions made by the Federal Government, under agreements entered into after November 20, 1962, unless payment due thereon has been made in full prior to April 11, 1968;

(C) dwellings provided in whole or in part by loans insured, guaranteed, or otherwise secured by the credit of the Federal Government, under agreements entered into after November 20, 1962, unless payment thereon has been made in full prior to April 11, 1968: Provided, That nothing contained in subparagraphs (B) and (C) of this subsection shall be applicable to dwellings solely by virtue of the fact that they are subject to mortgages held by an FDIC or FSLIC institution; and

(D) dwellings provided by the development or the redevelopment of real property purchased, rented, or otherwise obtained from a State or local public agency receiving Federal financial assistance for slum clearance or urban renewal with respect to such real property under loan or grant contracts entered into after November 20, 1962.

(2) After December 31, 1968, to all dwellings covered by paragraph (1) and to all other dwellings except as exempted by subsection (b) of this section.

(b) Exemptions

Nothing in section 3604 of this title (other than subsection (c)) shall apply to—

(1) any single-family house sold or rented by an owner: Provided, That such private individual owner does not own more than three such single-family houses at any one time: Provided further, That in the case of the sale of any such single-family house by a private individual owner not residing in such house at the time of such sale or who was not the most recent resident of such house prior to such sale, the exemption granted by this subsection shall apply only with respect to one such sale within any twenty-four month period: Provided further, That such bona fide private individual owner does not own any interest in, nor is there owned or reserved on his behalf, under any express or voluntary agreement, title to or any right to all or a portion of the proceeds from the sale or rental of, more than three such single-family houses at any one time: Provided further, That after December 31, 1969, the sale or rental of any such single-family house shall be excepted from the application of this subchapter only if such house is sold or rented (A) without the use in any manner of the sales or rental facilities or the sales or rental services of any real estate broker, agent, or salesman, or of such facilities or services of any person in the business of selling or renting dwellings, or of any employee or agent of any such broker, agent, salesman, or person and (B) without the publication, posting or mailing, after notice, of any advertisement or written notice in violation of section 3604(c) of this title; but nothing in this proviso shall prohibit the use of attorneys, escrow agents, abstractors, title companies, and other such professional assistance as necessary to perfect or transfer the title, or

(2) rooms or units in dwellings containing living quarters occupied or intended to be occupied by no more than four families living independently of each other, if the owner actually maintains and occupies one of such living quarters as his residence.

(c) Business of selling or renting dwellings defined

For the purposes of subsection (b) of this section, a person shall be deemed to be in the business of selling or renting dwellings if—

(1) he has, within the preceding twelve months, participated as principal in three or more transactions involving the sale or rental of any dwelling or any interest therein, or

(2) he has, within the preceding twelve months, participated as agent, other than in the sale of his own personal residence in providing sales or rental facilities or sales or rental services in two or more transactions involving the sale or rental of any dwelling or any interest therein, or

(3) he is the owner of any dwelling designed or intended for occupancy by, or occupied by, five or more families.

§ 3604. Discrimination in the sale or rental of housing and other prohibited practices

As made applicable by section 3603 of this title and except as exempted by sections 3603(b) and 3607 of this title, it shall be unlawful—

(a) To refuse to sell or rent after the making of a bona fide offer, or to refuse to negotiate for the sale or rental of, or otherwise make unavailable or deny, a dwelling to any person because of race, color, religion, sex, familial status, or national origin.

(b) To discriminate against any person in the terms, conditions, or privileges of sale or rental of a dwelling, or in the provision of services or facilities in connection therewith, because of race, color, religion, sex, familial status, or national origin.

(c) To make, print, or publish, or cause to be made, printed, or published any notice, statement, or advertisement, with respect to the sale or rental of a dwelling that indicates any preference, limitation, or discrimination based on race, color, religion, sex, handicap, familial status, or national origin, or an intention to make any such preference, limitation, or discrimination.

(d) To represent to any person because of race, color, religion, sex, handicap, familial status, or national origin that any dwelling is not available for inspection, sale, or rental when such dwelling is in fact so available.

(e) For profit, to induce or attempt to induce any person to sell or rent any dwelling by representations regarding the entry or prospective entry into the neighborhood of a person or persons of a particular race, color, religion, sex, handicap, familial status, or national origin.

(f)(1) To discriminate in the sale or rental, or to otherwise make unavailable or deny, a dwelling to any buyer or renter because of a handicap of—

(A) that buyer or renter;

(B) a person residing in or intending to reside in that dwelling after it is so sold, rented, or made available; or

(C) any person associated with that buyer or renter.

(2) To discriminate against any person in the terms, conditions, or privileges of sale or rental of a dwelling, or in the provision of services or facilities in connection with such dwelling, because of a handicap of—

(A) that person; or

(B) a person residing in or intending to reside in that dwelling after it is so sold, rented, or made available; or

(C) any person associated with that person.

(3) For purposes of this subsection, discrimination includes—

(A) a refusal to permit, at the expense of the handicapped person, reasonable modifications of existing premises occupied or to be occupied by such person if such modifications may be necessary to afford such person full enjoyment of the premises except that, in the case of a rental, the landlord may where it is reasonable to do so condition permission for a modification on the renter agreeing to restore the interior of the premises to the condition that existed before the modification, reasonable wear and tear excepted;

(B) a refusal to make reasonable accommodations in rules, policies, practices, or services, when such accommodations may be necessary to afford such person equal opportunity to use and enjoy a dwelling; or

(C) in connection with the design and construction of covered multifamily dwellings for first occupancy after the date that is 30 months after September 13, 1988, a failure to design and construct those dwellings in such a manner that—(i) the public use and common use portions of such dwellings are readily accessible to and usable by handicapped persons;

(ii) all the doors designed to allow passage into and within all premises within such dwellings are sufficiently wide to allow passage by handicapped persons in wheelchairs; and

(iii) all premises within such dwellings contain the following features of adaptive design:

(I) an accessible route into and through the dwelling;

(II) light switches, electrical outlets, thermostats, and other environmental controls in accessible locations;

(III) reinforcements in bathroom walls to allow later installation of grab bars; and

(IV) usable kitchens and bathrooms such that an individual in a wheelchair can maneuver about the space.

(4) Compliance with the appropriate requirements of the American National Standard for buildings and facilities providing accessibility and usability for physically handicapped people (commonly cited as "ANSI A117.1") suffices to satisfy the requirements of paragraph (3)(C)(iii).

(5)(A) If a State or unit of general local government has incorporated into its laws the requirements set forth in paragraph (3)(C), compliance with such laws shall be deemed to satisfy the requirements of that paragraph.

(B) A State or unit of general local government may review and approve newly constructed covered multifamily dwellings for the purpose of making determinations as to whether the design and construction requirements of paragraph (3)(C) are met.

(C) The Secretary shall encourage, but may not require, States and units of local government to include in their existing procedures for the review and approval of newly constructed covered multifamily dwellings, determinations as to whether the design and construction of such dwellings are consistent with paragraph (3)(C), and shall provide technical assistance to States and units of local government and other persons to implement the requirements of paragraph (3)(C).

(D) Nothing in this subchapter shall be construed to require the Secretary to review or approve the plans, designs or construction of all covered multifamily dwellings, to determine whether the design and construction of such dwellings are consistent with the requirements of paragraph 3(C).

(6)(A) Nothing in paragraph (5) shall be construed to affect the authority and responsibility of the

Secretary or a State or local public agency certified pursuant to section 3610(f)(3) of this title to receive and process complaints or otherwise engage in enforcement activities under this subchapter.

(B) Determinations by a State or a unit of general local government under paragraphs (5)(A) and (B) shall not be conclusive in enforcement proceedings under this subchapter.

(7) As used in this subsection, the term "covered multifamily dwellings" means—

(A) buildings consisting of 4 or more units if such buildings have one or more elevators; and

(B) ground floor units in other buildings consisting of 4 or more units.

(8) Nothing in this subchapter shall be construed to invalidate or limit any law of a State or political subdivision of a State, or other jurisdiction in which this subchapter shall be effective, that requires dwellings to be designed and constructed in a manner that affords handicapped persons greater access than is required by this subchapter.

(9) Nothing in this subsection requires that a dwelling be made available to an individual whose tenancy would constitute a direct threat to the health or safety of other individuals or whose tenancy would result in substantial physical damage to the property of others.

§ 3605. Discrimination in residential real estate-related transactions

(a) In general

It shall be unlawful for any person or other entity whose business includes engaging in residential real estate-related transactions to discriminate against any person in making available such a transaction, or in the terms or conditions of such a transaction, because of race, color, religion, sex, handicap, familial status, or national origin.

(b) Definition

As used in this section, the term "residential real estate-related transaction" means any of the following:

(1) The making or purchasing of loans or providing other financial assistance—

(A) for purchasing, constructing, improving, repairing, or maintaining a dwelling; or

(B) secured by residential real estate.

(2) The selling, brokering, or appraising of residential real property.

(c) Appraisal exemption

Nothing in this subchapter prohibits a person engaged in the business of furnishing appraisals of real property to take into consideration factors other than race, color, religion, national origin, sex, handicap, or familial status.

§ 3606. Discrimination in provision of brokerage services

After December 31, 1968, it shall be unlawful to deny any person access to or membership or participation in any multiple-listing service, real estate brokers' organization or other service, organization, or facility relating to the business of selling or renting dwellings, or to discriminate against him in the terms or conditions of such access, membership, or participation, on account of race, color, religion, sex, handicap, familial status, or national origin.

§ 3607. Exemption

(a) Religious organizations and private clubs

Nothing in this subchapter shall prohibit a religious organization, association, or society, or any nonprofit institution or organization operated, supervised or controlled by or in conjunction with a religious organization, association, or society, from limiting the sale, rental or occupancy of dwellings which it owns or operates for other than a commercial purpose to persons of the same religion, or from giving preference to such persons, unless membership in such religion is restricted on account of race, color, or national origin. Nor shall anything in this subchapter prohibit a private club not in fact open to the public, which as an incident to its primary purpose or purposes provides lodgings which it owns or operates for other than a commercial purpose, from limiting the rental or occupancy of such lodgings to its members or from giving preference to its members.

(b) Numbers of occupants; housing for older persons; persons convicted of making or distributing controlled substances

(1) Nothing in this subchapter limits the applicability of any reasonable local, State, or Federal restrictions regarding the maximum number of occupants permitted to occupy a dwelling. Nor does any provision in this subchapter regarding familial status apply with respect to housing for older persons.

(2) As used in this section, "housing for older persons" means housing—

(A) provided under any State or Federal program that the Secretary determines is specifically designed and operated to assist elderly persons (as defined in the State or Federal program); or

(B) intended for, and solely occupied by, persons 62 years of age or older; or

(C) intended and operated for occupancy by persons 55 years of age or older, and—

(i) at least 80 percent of the occupied units are occupied by at least one person who is 55 years of age or older;

(ii) the housing facility or community publishes and adheres to policies and procedures that demonstrate the intent required under this subparagraph; and

(iii) the housing facility or community complies with rules issued by the Secretary for verification of occupancy, which shall—

(I) provide for verification by reliable surveys and affidavits; and

(II) include examples of the types of policies and procedures relevant to a determination of compliance with the requirement of clause (ii). Such surveys and affidavits shall be admissible in administrative and judicial proceedings for the purposes of such verification.

(3) Housing shall not fail to meet the requirements for housing for older persons by reason of:

(A) persons residing in such housing as of September 13, 1988, who do not meet the age requirements of subsections (2)(B) or (C): Provided, That new occupants of such housing meet the age requirements of subsection (2)(B) or (C); or

(B) unoccupied units: Provided, That such units are reserved for occupancy by persons who meet the age requirements of subsection (2)(B) or (C).

(4) Nothing in this subchapter prohibits conduct against a person because such person has been convicted by any court of competent jurisdiction of the illegal manufacture or distribution of a controlled substance as defined in section 802 of Title 21.

(5)(A) A person shall not be held personally liable for monetary damages for a violation of this subchapter if such person reasonably relied, in good faith, on the application of the exemption under this subsection relating to housing for older persons.

(B) For the purposes of this paragraph, a person may only show good faith reliance on the application of the exemption by showing that—

(i) such person has no actual knowledge that the facility or community is not, or will not be, eligible for such exemption; and

(ii) the facility or community has stated formally, in writing, that the facility or community complies with the requirements for such exemption.

FAIR HOUSING ACT AMENDMENTS HUD REGULATIONS

24 C.F.R §

Subpart A—General

100.1 Authority
100.5 Scope
100.10 Exemptions
100.20 Definitions

Subpart B—Discriminatory Housing Practices

100.50 Real estate practices prohibited
100.60 Unlawful refusal to sell or rent or to negotiate for the sale or rental
100.65 Discrimination in terms, conditions and privileges and in services and facilities
100.70 Other prohibited sale and rental conduct
100.75 Discriminatory advertisements, statements and notices
100.80 Discriminatory representations on the availability of dwellings
100.85 Blockbusting
100.90 Discrimination in the provision of brokerage services

Subpart C—Discrimination in Residential Real Estate-Related Transactions

100.110 Discriminatory practices in residential real estate-related transactions
100.115 Residential real estate-related transactions
100.120 Discrimination in the making of loans and in the provision of other financial assistance
100.125 Discrimination in the purchasing of loans
100.130 Discrimination in the terms and conditions for making available loans or other financial assistance
100.135 Unlawful practices in the selling, brokering, or appraising of residential real property

Subpart D—Prohibition Against Discrimination Because of Handicap

100.200 Purpose
100.201 Definitions
100.202 General prohibitions against discrimination because of handicap
100.203 Reasonable modifications of existing premises
100.204 Reasonable accommodations
100.205 Design and construction requirements

FAIR HOUSING ACT AMENDMENTS HUD REGULATIONS

Subpart A—General

§ 100.1 Authority.

This regulation is issued under the authority of the Secretary of Housing and Urban Development to administer and enforce Title VIII of the Civil Rights Act of 1968, as amended by the Fair Housing Amendments Act of 1988 (the Fair Housing Act).

§ 100.5 Scope.

(a) It is the policy of the United States to provide, within constitutional limitations, for fair housing throughout the United States. No person shall be subjected to discrimination because of race, color, religion, sex, handicap, familial status, or national origin in the sale, rental, or advertising of dwellings, in the provision of brokerage services, or in the availability of residential real estate-related transactions.

(b) This part provides the Department's interpretation of the coverage of the Fair Housing Act regarding discrimination related to the sale or rental of dwellings, the provision of services in connection therewith, and the availability of residential real estate-related transactions.

(c) Nothing in this part relieves persons participating in a Federal or Federally-assisted program or activity from other requirements applicable to buildings and dwellings.

§ 100.10 Exemptions.

(a) This part does not:
(1) Prohibit a religious organization, association, or society, or any nonprofit institution or organization operated, supervised or controlled by or in conjunction with a religious organization, association, or society, from limiting the sale, rental or occupancy of dwellings which it owns or operates for other than a commercial purpose to persons of the same religion, or from giving preference to such persons, unless membership in such religion is restricted because of race, color, or national origin;
(2) Prohibit a private club, not in fact open to

the public, which, incident to its primary purpose or purposes, provides lodgings which it owns or operates for other than a commercial purpose, from limiting the rental or occupancy of such lodgings to its members or from giving preference to its members;

(3) Limit the applicability of any reasonable local, State or Federal restrictions regarding the maximum number of occupants permitted to occupy a dwelling; or

(4) Prohibit conduct against a person because such person has been convicted by any court of competent jurisdiction of the illegal manufacture or distribution of a controlled substance as defined in Section 102 of the Controlled Substances Act (21 U.S.C. 802).

(b) Nothing in this part regarding discrimination based on familial status applies with respect to housing for older persons as defined in Subpart E of this part.

(c) Nothing in this part, other than the prohibitions against discriminatory advertising, applies to:

(1) The sale or rental of any single family house by an owner, provided the following conditions are met:

(i) The owner does not own or have any interest in more than three single family houses at any one time.

(ii) The house is sold or rented without the use of a real estate broker, agent or salesperson or the facilities of any person in the business of selling or renting dwellings. If the owner selling the house does not reside in it at the time of the sale or was not the most recent resident of the house prior to such sale, the exemption in this paragraph (c)(1) of this section applies to only one such sale in any 24-month period.

(2) Rooms or units in dwellings containing living quarters occupied or intended to be occupied by no more than four families living independently of each other, if the owner actually maintains and occupies one of such living quarters as his or her residence.

§ 100.20 Definitions.

The terms "Department," "Fair Housing Act," and "Secretary" are defined in 24 CFR part 5. As used in this part:

"Aggrieved person" includes any person who—

(a) Claims to have been injured by a discriminatory housing practice; or

(b) Believes that such person will be injured by a discriminatory housing practice that is about to occur.

"Broker" or "Agent" includes any person authorized to perform an action on behalf of another person regarding any matter related to the sale or rental of dwellings, including offers, solicitations or contracts and the administration of matters regarding such offers, solicitations or contracts or any residential real estate-related transactions.

"Discriminatory housing practice" means an act that is unlawful under section 804, 805, 806, or 818 of the Fair Housing Act.

"Dwelling" means any building, structure or portion thereof which is occupied as, or designed or intended for occupancy as, a residence by one or more families, and any vacant land which is offered for sale or lease for the construction or location thereon of any such building, structure or portion thereof.

"Familial status" means one or more individuals (who have not attained the age of 18 years) being domiciled with—

(a) A parent or another person having legal custody of such individual or individuals; or

(b) The designee of such parent or other person having such custody, with the written permission of such parent or other person.

The protections afforded against discrimination on the basis of familial status shall apply to any person who is pregnant or is in the process of securing legal custody of any individual who has not attained the age of 18 years.

"Handicap" is defined in § 100.201.

"Person" includes one or more individuals, corporations, partnerships, associations, labor organizations, legal representatives, mutual companies, joint-stock companies, trusts, unincorporated organizations, trustees, trustees in cases under Title 11 of the United States Code, receivers, and fiduciaries.

"Person in the business of selling or renting dwellings" means any person who:

(a) Within the preceding twelve months, has participated as principal in three or more transactions involving the sale or rental of any dwelling or any interest therein;

(b) Within the preceding twelve months, has participated as agent, other than in the sale of his or her own personal residence, in providing sales or rental facilities or sales or rental services in two or more transactions involving the sale or rental of any dwelling or any interest therein; or

(c) Is the owner of any dwelling designed or intended for occupancy by, or occupied by, five or more families.

"State" means any of the several states, the District of Columbia, the Commonwealth of Puerto Rico, or any of the territories and possessions of the United States.

Subpart B—Discriminatory Housing Practices

§ 100.50 Real estate practices prohibited.

(a) This subpart provides the Department's interpretation of conduct that is unlawful housing discrimination under section 804 and section 806 of the Fair Housing Act. In general the prohibited actions are set forth under sections of this subpart which are most applicable to the discriminatory conduct described. However, an action illustrated in one section can constitute a violation under sections in the subpart. For example, the conduct described in § 100.60(b)(3) and (4) would constitute a violation of § 100.65(a) as well as § 100.60(a).

(b) It shall be unlawful to:

(1) Refuse to sell or rent a dwelling after a bona fide offer has been made, or to refuse to negotiate for the sale or rental of a dwelling because of race, color, religion, sex, familial status, or national origin, or to discriminate in the sale or rental of a dwelling because of handicap.

(2) Discriminate in the terms, conditions or privileges of sale or rental of a dwelling, or in the provision of services or facilities in connection with sales or rentals, because of race, color, religion, sex, handicap, familial status, or national origin.

(3) Engage in any conduct relating to the provision of housing which otherwise makes unavailable or denies dwellings to persons because of race, color, religion, sex, handicap, familial status, or national origin.

(4) Make, print or publish, or cause to be made, printed or published, any notice, statement or advertisement with respect to the sale or rental of a dwelling that indicates any preference, limitation or discrimination because of race, color, religion, sex, handicap, familial status, or national origin, or an intention to make any such preference, limitation or discrimination.

(5) Represent to any person because of race, color, religion, sex, handicap, familial status, or national origin that a dwelling is not available for sale or rental when such dwelling is in fact available.

(6) Engage in blockbusting practices in connection with the sale or rental of dwellings because of race, color, religion, sex, handicap, familial status, or national origin.

(7) Deny access to or membership or participation in, or to discriminate against any person in his or her access to or membership or participation in, any multiple-listing service, real estate brokers' association, or other service organization or facility relating to the business of selling or renting a dwelling or in the terms or conditions or membership or participation, because of race, color, religion, sex, handicap, familial status, or national origin.

(c) The application of the Fair Housing Act with respect to persons with handicaps is discussed in Subpart D of this part.

§ 100.60 Unlawful refusal to sell or rent or to negotiate for the sale or rental.

(a) It shall be unlawful for a person to refuse to sell or rent a dwelling to a person who has made a bona fide offer, because of race, color, religion, sex, familial status, or national origin or to refuse to negotiate with a person for the sale or rental of a dwelling because of race, color, religion, sex, familial status, or national origin, or to discriminate against any person in the sale or rental of a dwelling because of handicap.

(b) Prohibited actions under this section include, but are not limited to:

(1) Failing to accept or consider a bona fide offer because of race, color, religion, sex, handicap, familial status, or national origin.

(2) Refusing to sell or rent a dwelling to, or to negotiate for the sale or rental of a dwelling with, any person because of race, color, religion, sex, handicap, familial status, or national origin.

(3) Imposing different sales prices or rental charges for the sale or rental of a dwelling upon any person because of race, color, religion, sex, handicap, familial status, or national origin.

(4) Using different qualification criteria or applications, or sale or rental standards or procedures, such as income standards, application requirements, application fees, credit analysis or sale or rental approval procedures or other requirements, because of race, color, religion, sex, handicap, familial status, or national origin.

(5) Evicting tenants because of their race, color, religion, sex, handicap, familial status, or national origin or because of the race, color, religion, sex, handicap, familial status, or national origin of a tenant's guest.

§ 100.65 Discrimination in terms, conditions and privileges and in services and facilities.

(a) It shall be unlawful, because of race, color, religion, sex, handicap, familial status, or national origin, to impose different terms, conditions or privileges relating to the sale or rental of a dwelling or to deny or limit services or facilities in connection with the sale or rental of a dwelling.

(b) Prohibited actions under this section include, but are not limited to:

(1) Using different provisions in leases or contracts of sale, such as those relating to rental charges, security deposits and the terms of a lease and those relating to down payment and closing requirements, because of race, color, religion, sex, handicap, familial status, or national origin.

(2) Failing or delaying maintenance or repairs of sale or rental dwellings because of race, color, religion, sex, handicap, familial status, or national origin.

(3) Failing to process an offer for the sale or rental of a dwelling or to communicate an offer accurately because of race, color, religion, sex, handicap, familial status, or national origin.

(4) Limiting the use of privileges, services or facilities associated with a dwelling because of race, color, religion, sex, handicap, familial status, or national origin of an owner, tenant or a person associated with him or her.

(5) Denying or limiting services or facilities in connection with the sale or rental of a dwelling, because a person failed or refused to provide sexual favors.

§ 100.70 Other prohibited sale and rental conduct.

(a) It shall be unlawful, because of race, color, religion, sex, handicap, familial status, or national origin, to restrict or attempt to restrict the choices of a person by word or conduct in connection with seeking, negotiating for, buying or renting a dwelling so as to perpetuate, or tend to perpetuate, segregated housing patterns, or to discourage or obstruct choices in a community, neighborhood or development.

(b) It shall be unlawful, because of race, color, religion, sex, handicap, familial status, or national origin, to engage in any conduct relating to the provision of housing or of services and facilities in connection therewith that otherwise makes unavailable or denies dwellings to persons.

(c) Prohibited actions under paragraph (a) of this section, which are generally referred to as unlawful steering practices, include, but are not limited to:

(1) Discouraging any person from inspecting, purchasing or renting a dwelling because of race, color, religion, sex, handicap, familial status, or national origin, or because of the race, color, religion, sex, handicap, familial status, or national origin of persons in a community, neighborhood or development.

(2) Discouraging the purchase or rental of a dwelling because of race, color, religion, sex, handicap, familial status, or national origin, by exaggerating drawbacks or failing to inform any person of desirable features of a dwelling or of a community, neighborhood, or development.

(3) Communicating to any prospective purchaser that he or she would not be comfortable or compatible with existing residents of a community, neighborhood or development because of race, color, religion, sex, handicap, familial status, or national origin.

(4) Assigning any person to a particular section of a community, neighborhood or development, or to a particular floor of a building, because of race, color, religion, sex, handicap, familial status, or national origin.

(d) Prohibited activities relating to dwellings under paragraph (b) of this section include, but are not limited to:

(1) Discharging or taking other adverse action against an employee, broker or agent because he or she refused to participate in a discriminatory housing practice.

(2) Employing codes or other devices to segregate or reject applicants, purchasers or renters, refusing to take or to show listings of dwellings in certain areas because of race, color, religion, sex, handicap, familial status, or national origin, or refusing to deal with certain brokers or agents because they or one or more of their clients are of a particular race, color, religion, sex, handicap, familial status, or national origin.

(3) Denying or delaying the processing of an application made by a purchaser or renter or refusing to approve such a person for occupancy in a cooperative or condominium dwelling because of race, color, religion, sex, handicap, familial status, or national origin.

(4) Refusing to provide municipal services or property or hazard insurance for dwellings or providing such services or insurance differently because of race, color, religion, sex, handicap, familial status, or national origin.

§ 100.75 Discriminatory advertisements, statements and notices.

(a) It shall be unlawful to make, print or publish, or cause to be made, printed or published, any notice, statement or advertisement with respect to the sale or rental of a dwelling which indicates any preference, limitation or discrimination because of race, color, religion, sex, handicap, familial status, or national origin, or an intention to make any such preference, limitation or discrimination.

(b) The prohibitions in this section shall apply to all

written or oral notices or statements by a person engaged in the sale or rental of a dwelling. Written notices and statements include any applications, flyers, brochures, deeds, signs, banners, posters, billboards or any documents used with respect to the sale or rental of a dwelling.

(c) Discriminatory notices, statements and advertisements include, but are not limited to:

(1) Using words, phrases, photographs, illustrations, symbols or forms which convey that dwellings are available or not available to a particular group of persons because of race, color, religion, sex, handicap, familial status, or national origin.

(2) Expressing to agents, brokers, employees, prospective sellers or renters or any other persons a preference for or limitation on any purchaser or renter because of race, color, religion, sex, handicap, familial status, or national origin of such persons.

(3) Selecting media or locations for advertising the sale or rental of dwellings which deny particular segments of the housing market information about housing opportunities because of race, color, religion, sex, handicap, familial status, or national origin.

(4) Refusing to publish advertising for the sale or rental of dwellings or requiring different charges or terms for such advertising because of race, color, religion, sex, handicap, familial status, or national origin.

(d) 24 CFR Part 109 provides information to assist persons to advertise dwellings in a nondiscriminatory manner and describes the matters the Department will review in evaluating compliance with the Fair Housing Act and in investigating complaints alleging discriminatory housing practices involving advertising.

§ 100.80 Discriminatory representations on the availability of dwellings.

(a) It shall be unlawful, because of race, color, religion, sex, handicap, familial status, or national origin, to provide inaccurate or untrue information about the availability of dwellings for sale or rental.

(b) Prohibited actions under this section include, but are not limited to:

(1) Indicating through words or conduct that a dwelling which is available for inspection, sale, or rental has been sold or rented, because of race, color, religion, sex, handicap, familial status, or national origin.

(2) Representing that covenants or other deed, trust or lease provisions which purport to restrict the sale or rental of dwellings because of race, color, religion, sex, handicap, familial status, or national origin preclude the sale of rental of a dwelling to a person.

(3) Enforcing covenants or other deed, trust, or lease provisions which preclude the sale or rental of a dwelling to any person because of race, color, religion, sex, handicap, familial status, or national origin.

(4) Limiting information, by word or conduct, regarding suitably priced dwellings available for inspection, sale or rental, because of race, color, religion, sex, handicap, familial status, or national origin.

(5) Providing false or inaccurate information regarding the availability of a dwelling for sale or rental to any person, including testers, regardless of whether such person is actually seeking housing, because of race, color, religion, sex, handicap, familial status, or national origin.

§ 100.85 Blockbusting.

(a) It shall be unlawful, for profit, to induce or attempt to induce a person to sell or rent a dwelling by representations regarding the entry or prospective entry into the neighborhood of a person or persons of a particular race, color, religion, sex, familial status, or national origin or with a handicap.

(b) In establishing a discriminatory housing practice under this section it is not necessary that there was in fact profit as long as profit was a factor for engaging in the blockbusting activity.

(c) Prohibited actions under this section include, but are not limited to:

(1) Engaging, for profit, in conduct (including uninvited solicitations for listings) which conveys to a person that a neighborhood is undergoing or is about to undergo a change in the race, color, religion, sex, handicap, familial status, or national origin of persons residing in it, in order to encourage the person to offer a dwelling for sale or rental.

(2) Encouraging, for profit, any person to sell or rent a dwelling through assertions that the entry or prospective entry of persons of a particular race, color, religion, sex, familial status, or national origin, or with handicaps, can or will result in undesirable consequences for the project, neighborhood or community, such as a lowering of property values, an increase in criminal or antisocial behavior, or a decline in the quality of schools or other services or facilities.

§ 100.90 Discrimination in the provision of brokerage services.

(a) It shall be unlawful to deny any person access to or membership or participation in any multiple listing service, real estate brokers' organization or other service, organization, or facility relating to the business of selling or renting dwellings, or to discriminate against any person in the terms or conditions of such access, membership or participation, because of race, color, religion, sex, handicap, familial status, or national origin.

(b) Prohibited actions under this section include, but are not limited to:

(1) Setting different fees for access to or membership in a multiple listing service because of race, color, religion, sex, handicap, familial status, or national origin.

(2) Denying or limiting benefits accruing to members in a real estate brokers' organization because of race, color, religion, sex, handicap, familial status, or national origin.

(3) Imposing different standards or criteria for membership in a real estate sales or rental organization because of race, color, religion, sex, handicap, familial status, or national origin.

(4) Establishing geographic boundaries or office location or residence requirements for access to or membership or participation in any multiple listing service, real estate brokers' organization or other service, organization or facility relating to the business of selling or renting dwellings, because of race, color, religion, sex, handicap, familial status, or national origin.

Subpart C—Discrimination in Residential Real Estate-Related Transactions

§ 100.110 Discriminatory practices in residential real estate-related transactions.

(a) This subpart provides the Department's interpretation of the conduct that is unlawful housing discrimination under section 805 of the Fair Housing Act.

(b) It shall be unlawful for any person or other entity whose business includes engaging in residential real estate-related transactions to discriminate against any person in making available such a transaction, or in the terms or conditions of such a transaction, because of race, color, religion, sex, handicap, familial status, or national origin.

§ 100.115 Residential real estate-related transactions.

The term residential "real estate-related transactions" means:

(a) The making or purchasing of loans or providing other financial assistance—

(1) For purchasing, constructing, improving, repairing or maintaining a dwelling; or

(2) Secured by residential real estate; or

(b) The selling, brokering or appraising of residential real property.

§ 100.120 Discrimination in the making of loans and in the provision of other financial assistance.

(a) It shall be unlawful for any person or entity whose business includes engaging in residential real estate-related transactions to discriminate against any person in making available loans or other financial assistance for a dwelling, or which is or is to be secured by a dwelling, because of race, color, religion, sex, handicap, familial status, or national origin.

(b) Prohibited practices under this section include, but are not limited to, failing or refusing to provide to any person, in connection with a residential real estate-related transaction, information regarding the availability of loans or other financial assistance, application requirements, procedures or standards for the review and approval of loans or financial assistance, or providing information which is inaccurate or different from that provided others, because of race, color, religion, sex, handicap, familial status, or national origin.

§ 100.125 Discrimination in the purchasing of loans.

(a) It shall be unlawful for any person or entity engaged in the purchasing of loans or other debts or securities which support the purchase, construction, improvement, repair or maintenance of a dwelling, or which are secured by residential real estate, to refuse to purchase such loans, debts, or securities, or to impose different terms or conditions for such purchases, because of race, color, religion, sex, handicap, familial status, or national origin.

(b) Unlawful conduct under this section includes, but is not limited to:

(1) Purchasing loans or other debts or securities which relate to, or which are secured by dwellings in certain communities or neighborhoods but not in others because of the race, color, religion, sex, handicap, familial status, or national origin of persons in such neighborhoods or communities.

(2) Pooling or packaging loans or other debts or securities which relate to, or which are secured by, dwellings differently because of race, color, religion, sex, handicap, familial status, or national origin.

(3) Imposing or using different terms or conditions on the marketing or sale of securities issued on the basis of loans or other debts or securities which relate to, or which are secured by, dwellings because

of race, color, religion, sex, handicap, familial status, or national origin.

(c) This section does not prevent consideration, in the purchasing of loans, of factors justified by business necessity, including requirements of Federal law, relating to a transaction's financial security or to protection against default or reduction of the value of the security. Thus, this provision would not preclude considerations employed in normal and prudent transactions, provided that no such factor may in any way relate to race, color, religion, sex, handicap, familial status or national origin.

§ 100.130 Discrimination in the terms and conditions for making available loans or other financial assistance.

(a) It shall be unlawful for any person or entity engaged in the making of loans or in the provision of other financial assistance relating to the purchase, construction, improvement, repair or maintenance of dwellings or which are secured by residential real estate to impose different terms or conditions for the availability of such loans or other financial assistance because of race, color, religion, sex, handicap, familial status, or national origin.

(b) Unlawful conduct under this section includes, but is not limited to:

(1) Using different policies, practices or procedures in evaluating or in determining credit-worthiness of any person in connection with the provision of any loan or other financial assistance for a dwelling or for any loan or other financial assistance which is secured by residential real estate because of race, color, religion, sex, handicap, familial status, or national origin.

(2) Determining the type of loan or other financial assistance to be provided with respect to a dwelling, or fixing the amount, interest rate, duration or other terms for a loan or other financial assistance for a dwelling or which is secured by residential real estate, because of race, color, religion, sex, handicap, familial status, or national origin.

§ 100.135 Unlawful practices in the selling, brokering, or appraising of residential real property.

(a) It shall be unlawful for any person or other entity whose business includes engaging in the selling, brokering or appraising of residential real property to discriminate against any person in making available such services, or in the performance of such services, because of race, color, religion, sex, handicap, familial status, or national origin.

(b) For the purposes of this section, the term appraisal means an estimate or opinion of the value of a specified residential real property made in a business context in connection with the sale, rental, financing or refinancing of a dwelling or in connection with any activity that otherwise affects the availability of a residential real estate-related transaction, whether the appraisal is oral or written, or transmitted formally or informally. The appraisal includes all written comments and other documents submitted as support for the estimate or opinion of value.

(c) Nothing in this section prohibits a person engaged in the business of making or furnishing appraisals of residential real property from taking into consideration factors other than race, color, religion, sex, handicap, familial status, or national origin.

(d) Practices which are unlawful under this section include, but are not limited to, using an appraisal of residential real property in connection with the sale, rental, or financing of any dwelling where the person knows or reasonably should know that the appraisal improperly takes into consideration race, color, religion, sex, handicap, familial status or national origin.

Subpart D—Prohibition Against Discrimination Because of Handicap

§ 100.200 Purpose.

The purpose of this subpart is to effectuate sections 6 (a) and (b) and 15 of the Fair Housing Amendments Act of 1988.

§ 100.201 Definitions.

As used in this subpart:

"Accessible", when used with respect to the public and common use areas of a building containing covered multifamily dwellings, means that the public or common use areas of the building can be approached, entered, and used by individuals with physical handicaps. The phrase "readily accessible to and usable by" is synonymous with accessible. A public or common use area that complies with the appropriate requirements of ANSI A117.1-1986 or a comparable standard is "accessible" within the meaning of this paragraph.

"Accessible route" means a continuous unobstructed path connecting accessible elements and spaces in a building or within a site that can be negotiated by a person with a severe disability using a wheelchair and that is also safe for and usable by people with other disabilities. Interior accessible routes may include corridors, floors, ramps, elevators and lifts. Exterior accessible routes may include parking access aisles, curb ramps, walks, ramps and lifts. A route that complies with the appropriate requirements of ANSI A117.1-1986 or a comparable standard is an "accessible route".

"ANSI A117.1-1986" means the 1986 edition of the American National Standard for buildings and facilities providing accessibility and usability for physically handicapped people. This incorporation by reference was approved by the Director of the Federal Register in accordance with 5 U.S.C. 552(a) and 1 CFR Part 51. Copies may be obtained from American National Standards Institute, Inc., 1430 Broadway, New York, New York 10018. Copies may be inspected at the Department of Housing and Urban Development, 451 Seventh Street, S.W., Room 10276, Washington, D.C., or at the Office of the Federal Register, 1100 L Street, N.W., Room 8401, Washington, D.C.

"Building" means a structure, facility or portion thereof that contains or serves one or more dwelling units.

"Building entrance on an accessible route" means an accessible entrance to a building that is connected by an accessible route to public transportation stops, to accessible parking and passenger loading zones, or to public streets or sidewalks, if available. A building entrance that complies with ANSI A117.1-1986 or a comparable standard complies with the requirements of this paragraph.

"Common use areas" means rooms, spaces or elements inside or outside of a building that are made available for the use of residents of a building or the guests thereof. These areas include hallways, lounges, lobbies, laundry rooms, refuse rooms, mail rooms, recreational areas and passageways among and between buildings.

"Controlled substance" means any drug or other substance, or immediate precursor included in the definition in section 102 of the Controlled Substances Act (21 U.S.C. 802).

"Covered multifamily dwellings" means buildings consisting of 4 or more dwelling units if such buildings have one or more elevators; and ground floor dwelling units in other buildings consisting of 4 or more dwelling units.

"Dwelling unit" means a single unit of residence for a family or one or more persons. Examples of dwelling units include: a single family home; an apartment unit within an apartment building; and in other types of dwellings in which sleeping accommodations are provided but toileting or cooking facilities are shared by occupants of more than one room or portion of the dwelling, rooms in which people sleep. Examples of the latter include dormitory rooms and sleeping accommodations in shelters intended for occupancy as a residence for homeless persons.

"Entrance" means any access point to a building or portion of a building used by residents for the purpose of entering.

"Exterior" means all areas of the premises outside of an individual dwelling unit.

"First occupancy" means a building that has never before been used for any purpose.

"Ground floor" means a floor of a building with a building entrance on an accessible route. A building may have more than one ground floor.

"Handicap" means, with respect to a person, a physical or mental impairment which substantially limits one or more major life activities; a record of such an impairment; or being regarded as having such an impairment. This term does not include current, illegal use of or addiction to a controlled substance. For purposes of this part, an individual shall not be considered to have a handicap solely because that individual is a transvestite. As used in this definition:

(a) "Physical or mental impairment" includes:

(1) Any physiological disorder or condition, cosmetic disfigurement, or anatomical loss affecting one or more of the following body systems: Neurological; musculoskeletal; special sense organs; respiratory, including speech organs; cardiovascular; reproductive; digestive; genito-urinary; hemic and lymphatic; skin; and endocrine; or

(2) Any mental or psychological disorder, such as mental retardation, organic brain syndrome, emotional or mental illness, and specific learning disabilities. The term "physical or mental impairment" includes, but is not limited to, such diseases and conditions as orthopedic, visual, speech and hearing impairments, cerebral palsy, autism, epilepsy, muscular dystrophy, multiple sclerosis, cancer, heart disease, diabetes, Human Immunodeficiency Virus infection, mental retardation, emotional illness, drug addiction (other than addiction caused by current, illegal use of a controlled substance) and alcoholism.

(b) "Major life activities" means functions such as caring for one's self, performing manual tasks, walking, seeing, hearing, speaking, breathing, learning and working.

(c) "Has a record of such an impairment" means has a history of, or has been misclassified as having, a mental or physical impairment that substantially limits one or more major life activities.

(d) "Is regarded as having an impairment" means:

(1) Has a physical or mental impairment that does not substantially limit one or more major life

activities but that is treated by another person as constituting such a limitation;

(2) Has a physical or mental impairment that substantially limits one or more major life activities only as a result of the attitudes of other toward such impairment; or

(3) Has none of the impairments defined in paragraph (a) of this definition but is treated by another person as having such an impairment.

"Interior" means the spaces, parts, components or elements of an individual dwelling unit.

"Modification" means any change to the public or common use areas of a building or any change to a dwelling unit.

"Premises" means the interior or exterior spaces, parts, components or elements of a building, including individual dwelling units and the public and common use areas of a building.

"Public use areas" means interior or exterior rooms or spaces of a building that are made available to the general public. Public use may be provided at a building that is privately or publicly owned.

"Site" means a parcel of land bounded by a property line or a designated portion of a public right or way.

§ 100.202 General prohibitions against discrimination because of handicap.

(a) It shall be unlawful to discriminate in the sale or rental, or to otherwise make unavailable or deny, a dwelling to any buyer or renter because of a handicap of—

(1) That buyer or renter;

(2) A person residing in or intending to reside in that dwelling after it is so sold, rented, or made available; or

(3) Any person associated with that person.

(b) It shall be unlawful to discriminate against any person in the terms, conditions, or privileges of the sale or rental of a dwelling, or in the provision of services or facilities in connection with such dwelling, because of a handicap of—

(1) That buyer or renter;

(2) A person residing in or intending to reside in that dwelling after it is so sold, rented, or made available; or

(3) Any person associated with that person.

(c) It shall be unlawful to make an inquiry to determine whether an applicant for a dwelling, a person intending to reside in that dwelling after it is so sold, rented or made available, or any person associated with that person, has a handicap or to make inquiry as to the nature or severity of a handicap of such a person. However, this paragraph does not prohibit the following inquiries, provided these inquiries are made of all applicants, whether or not they have handicaps:

(1) Inquiry into an applicant's ability to meet the requirements of ownership or tenancy;

(2) Inquiry to determine whether an applicant is qualified for a dwelling available only to persons with handicaps or to persons with a particular type of handicap;

(3) Inquiry to determine whether an applicant for a dwelling is qualified for a priority available to persons with handicaps or to persons with a particular type of handicap;

(4) Inquiring whether an applicant for a dwelling is a current illegal abuser or addict of a controlled substance;

(5) Inquiring whether an applicant has been convicted of the illegal manufacture or distribution of a controlled substance.

(d) Nothing in this subpart requires that a dwelling be made available to an individual whose tenancy would constitute a direct threat to the health or safety of other individuals or whose tenancy would result in substantial physical damage to the property of others.

§ 100.203 Reasonable modifications of existing premises.

(a) It shall be unlawful for any person to refuse to permit, at the expense of a handicapped person, reasonable modifications of existing premises, occupied or to be occupied by a handicapped person, if the proposed modifications may be necessary to afford the handicapped person full enjoyment of the premises of a dwelling. In the case of a rental, the landlord may, where it is reasonable to do so, condition permission for a modification on the renter agreeing to restore the interior of the premises to the condition that existed before the modification, reasonable wear and tear excepted. The landlord may not increase for handicapped persons any customarily required security deposit. However, where it is necessary in order to ensure with reasonable certainty that funds will be available to pay for the restorations at the end of the tenancy, the landlord may negotiate as part of such a restoration agreement a provision requiring that the tenant pay into an interest bearing escrow account, over a reasonable period, a reasonable amount of money not to exceed the cost of the restorations. The interest in any such account shall accrue to the benefit of the tenant.

(b) A landlord may condition permission for a modification on the renter providing a reasonable description of the proposed modifications as well as reasonable assurances that the work will be done in a workmanlike manner and that any required building permits will be obtained.

(c) The application of paragraph (a) of this section may be illustrated by the following examples:

Example (1): A tenant with a handicap asks his or her landlord for permission to install grab bars in the bathroom at his or her own expense. It is necessary to reinforce the walls with blocking between studs in order to affix the grab bars. It is unlawful for the landlord to refuse to permit the tenant, at the tenant's own expense, from making the modifications necessary to add the grab bars. However, the landlord may condition permission for the modification on the tenant agreeing to restore the bathroom to the condition that existed before the modification, reasonable wear and tear excepted. It would be reasonable for the landlord to require the tenant to remove the grab bars at the end of the tenancy. The landlord may also reasonably require that the wall to which the grab bars are to be attached be repaired and restored to its original condition, reasonable wear and tear excepted. However, it would be unreasonable for the landlord to require the tenant to remove the blocking, since the reinforced walls will not interfere in any way with the landlord's or the next tenant's use and enjoyment of the premises and may be needed by some future tenant.

Example (2): An applicant for rental housing has a child who uses a wheelchair. The bathroom door in the dwelling unit is too narrow to permit the wheelchair to pass. The applicant asks the landlord for permission to widen the doorway at the applicant's own expense. It is unlawful for the landlord to refuse to permit the applicant to make the modification. Further, the landlord may not, in usual circumstances, condition permission for the modification on the applicant paying for the doorway to be narrowed at the end of the lease because a wider doorway will not interfere with the landlord's or the next tenant's use and enjoyment of the premises.

§ 100.204 Reasonable accommodations.

(a) It shall be unlawful for any person to refuse to make reasonable accommodations in rules, policies, practices, or services, when such accommodations may be necessary to afford a handicapped person equal opportunity to use and enjoy a dwelling unit, including public and common use areas.

(b) The application of this section may be illustrated by the following examples:

Example (1): A blind applicant for rental housing wants live in a dwelling unit with a seeing eye dog. The building has a "no pets" policy. It is a violation of § 100.204 for the owner or manager of the apartment complex to refuse to permit the applicant to live in the apartment with a seeing eye dog because, without the seeing eye dog, the blind person will not have an equal opportunity to use and enjoy a dwelling.

Example (2): Progress Gardens is a 300 unit apartment complex with 450 parking spaces which are available to tenants and guests of Progress Gardens on a "first come first served" basis. John applies for housing in Progress Gardens. John is mobility impaired and is unable to walk more than a short distance and therefore requests that a parking space near his unit be reserved for him so he will not have to walk very far to get to his apartment. It is a violation of § 100.204 for the owner or manager of Progress Gardens to refuse to make this accommodation. Without a reserved space, John might be unable to live in Progress Gardens at all or, when he has to park in a space far from his unit, might have great difficulty getting from his car to his apartment unit. The accommodation therefore is necessary to afford John an equal opportunity to use and enjoy a dwelling. The accommodation is reasonable because it is feasible and practical under the circumstances.

§ 100.205 Design and construction requirements.

(a) Covered multifamily dwellings for first occupancy after March 13, 1991 shall be designed and constructed to have at least one building entrance on an accessible route unless it is impractical to do so because of the terrain or unusual characteristics of the site. For purposes of this section, a covered multifamily dwelling shall be deemed to be designed and constructed for first occupancy on or before March 13, 1991, if the dwelling is occupied by that date, or if the last building permit or renewal thereof for the dwelling is issued by a State, County or local government on or before June 15, 1990. The burden of establishing impracticality because of terrain or unusual site characteristics is on the person or persons who designed or constructed the housing facility.

(b) The application of paragraph (a) of this section may be illustrated by the following examples:

Example (1): A real estate developer plans to construct six covered multifamily dwelling units on a site with a hilly terrain. Because of the terrain, it will be necessary to climb a long and steep stairway in order to enter the dwellings. Since there is no practical way to provide an accessible route to any of the dwellings, one need not be provided.

Example (2): A real estate developer plans to construct a building consisting of 10 units of multifamily housing on a waterfront site that floods frequently. Because of this unusual characteristic of the site, the builder plans to construct the building on stilts. It is customary for housing in the geographic area where the site is located to be built on stilts. The housing may lawfully be constructed on the proposed site on stilts even though this means that there will be no practical way to provide an accessible route to the building entrance.

Example (3): A real estate developer plans to construct a multifamily housing facility on a particular site. The developer would like the facility to be built on the site to contain as many units as possible. Because of the configuration and terrain of the site, it is possible to construct a building with 105 units on the site provided the site does not have an accessible route leading to the building entrance. It is also possible to construct a building on the site with an accessible route leading to the building entrance. However, such a building would have no more than 100 dwelling units. The building to be constructed on the site must have a building entrance on an accessible route because it is not impractical to provide such an entrance because of the terrain or unusual characteristics of the site.

(c) All covered multifamily dwellings for first occupancy after March 13, 1991 with a building entrance on an accessible route shall be designed and constructed in such a manner that—

(1) The public and common use areas are readily accessible to and usable by handicapped persons;

(2) All the doors designed to allow passage into and within all premises are sufficiently wide to allow passage by handicapped persons in wheelchairs; and

(3) All premises within covered multifamily dwelling units contain the following features of adaptable design:

(i) An accessible route into and through the covered dwelling unit;

(ii) Light switches, electrical outlets, thermostats, and other environmental controls in accessible locations;

(iii) Reinforcements in bathroom walls to allow later installation of grab bars around the toilet, tub, shower, stall and shower seat, where such facilities are provided; and

(iv) Usable kitchens and bathrooms such that an individual in a wheelchair can maneuver about the space.

(d) The application of paragraph (c) of this section may be illustrated by the following examples:

Example (1): A developer plans to construct a 100 unit condominium apartment building with one elevator. In accordance with paragraph (a), the building has at least one accessible route leading to an accessible entrance. All 100 units are covered multifamily dwelling units and they all must be designed and constructed so that they comply with the accessibility requirements of paragraph (c) of this section.

Example (2): A developer plans to construct 30 garden apartments in a three story building. The building will not have an elevator. The building will have one accessible entrance which will be on the first floor. Since the building does not have an elevator, only the "ground floor" units are covered multifamily units. The "ground floor" is the first floor because that is the floor that has an accessible entrance. All of the dwelling units on the first floor must meet the accessibility requirements of paragraph (c) of this section and must have access to at least one of each type of public or common use area available for residents in the building.

(e) Compliance with the appropriate requirements of ANSI A117.1-1986 suffices to satisfy the requirements of paragraph (c)(3) of this section.

(f) Compliance with a duly enacted law of a State or unit of general local government that includes the requirements of paragraphs (a) and (c) of this section satisfies the requirements of paragraphs (a) and (c) of this section.

(g)(1) It is the policy of HUD to encourage States and units of general local government to include, in their existing procedures for the review and approval of newly constructed covered multifamily dwellings, determinations as to whether the design and construction of such dwellings are consistent with paragraphs (a) and (c) of this section.

(2) A State or unit of general local government may review and approve newly constructed multifamily dwellings for the purpose of making determinations as to whether the requirements of paragraphs (a) and (c) of this section are met.

(h) Determinations of compliance or noncompliance by a State or a unit of general local government under paragraph (f) or (g) of this section are not conclusive in enforcement proceedings under the Fair Housing Amendments Act.

(i) This subpart does not invalidate or limit any law of a State or political subdivision of a State that requires dwellings to be designed and constructed in a manner that affords handicapped persons greater access than is required by this subpart.

DAMAGES

CIVIL RIGHTS ACT OF 1991

42 U.S.C. § 1981a. Damages in cases of intentional discrimination in employment

(a) Right of recovery

(1) Civil rights

In an action brought by a complaining party under section 706 or 717 of the Civil Rights Act of 1964 (42 U.S.C. 2000e-5) [42 U.S.C.A. § 2000e-5 or 42 U.S.C.A. § 2000e-16] against a respondent who engaged in unlawful intentional discrimination (not an employment practice that is unlawful because of its disparate impact) prohibited under section 703, 704, or 717 of the Act (42 U.S.C. 2000e-2 or 2000e-3) [42 U.S.C.A. § 2000e-2, 42 U.S.C.A. § 2000e-3, or 42 U.S.C.A. § 2000e-16], and provided that the complaining party cannot recover under section 1981 of this title, the complaining party may recover compensatory and punitive damages as allowed in subsection (b) of this section, in addition to any relief authorized by section 706(g) of the Civil Rights Act of 1964 [42 U.S.C.A. § 2000e-5(g)], from the respondent.

(2) Disability

In an action brought by a complaining party under the powers, remedies, and procedures set forth in section 706 or 717 of the Civil Rights Act of 1964 [42 U.S.C.A. § 2000e-5 or 42 U.S.C.A. § 2000e-16] (as provided in section 107(a) of the Americans with Disabilities Act of 1990 (42 U.S.C. 12117(a)), and section 794a(a)(1) of Title 29, respectively) against a respondent who engaged in unlawful intentional discrimination (not an employment practice that is unlawful because of its disparate impact) under section 791 of Title 29 and the regulations implementing section 791 of Title 29, or who violated the requirements of section 791 of Title 29 or the regulations implementing section 791 of Title 29 concerning the provision of a reasonable accommodation, or section 102 of the Americans with Disabilities Act of 1990 (42 U.S.C. 12112), or committed a violation of section 102(b)(5) of the Act [42 U.S.C.A. § 12112(b)(5)], against an individual, the complaining party may recover compensatory and punitive damages as allowed in subsection (b) of this section, in addition to any relief authorized by section 706(g) of the Civil Rights Act of 1964 [42 U.S.C.A. § 2000e-5(g)], from the respondent.

(3) Reasonable accommodation and good faith effort

In cases where a discriminatory practice involves the provision of a reasonable accommodation pursuant to section 102(b)(5) of the Americans with Disabilities Act of 1990 [42 U.S.C.A. § 12112(b)(5)] or regulations implementing section 791 of Title 29, damages may not be awarded under this section where the covered entity demonstrates good faith efforts, in consultation with the person with the disability who has informed the covered entity that accommodation is needed, to identify and make a reasonable accommodation that would provide such individual with an equally effective opportunity and would not cause an undue hardship on the operation of the business.

(b) Compensatory and punitive damages

(1) Determination of punitive damages

A complaining party may recover punitive damages under this section against a respondent (other than a government, government agency or political subdivision) if the complaining party demonstrates that the respondent engaged in a discriminatory practice or discriminatory practices with malice or with reckless indifference to the federally protected rights of an aggrieved individual.

(2) Exclusions from compensatory damages

Compensatory damages awarded under this section shall not include backpay, interest on backpay, or any other type of relief authorized under section 706(g) of the Civil Rights Act of 1964 [42 U.S.C.A. § 2000e-5(g)].

(3) Limitations

The sum of the amount of compensatory damages awarded under this section for future pecuniary losses, emotional pain, suffering, inconvenience, mental anguish, loss of enjoyment of life, and other nonpecuniary losses, and the amount of punitive damages awarded under this section, shall not exceed, for each complaining party—

(A) in the case of a respondent who has more than 14 and fewer than 101 employees in each of 20 or more calendar weeks in the current or preceding calendar year, $50,000;

(B) in the case of a respondent who has more than 100 and fewer than 201 employees in each of 20 or more calendar weeks in the current or preceding calendar year, $100,000; and

(C) in the case of a respondent who has more than 200 and fewer than 501 employees in each of 20 or more calendar weeks in the current or preceding calendar year, $200,000; and

(D) in the case of a respondent who has more than 500 employees in each of 20 or more calendar weeks in the current or preceding calendar year, $300,000.

(4) Construction

Nothing in this section shall be construed to limit the scope of, or the relief available under, section 1981 of this title.

(c) Jury trial

If a complaining party seeks compensatory or punitive damages under this section—

(1) any party may demand a trial by jury; and

(2) the court shall not inform the jury of the limitations described in subsection (b)(3) of this section.

(d) Definitions

As used in this section:

(1) Complaining party

The term "complaining party" means—

(A) in the case of a person seeking to bring an action under subsection (a)(1) of this section, the Equal Employment Opportunity Commission, the Attorney General, or a person who may bring an action or proceeding under title VII of the Civil Rights Act of 1964 (42 U.S.C. 2000e et seq.); or

(B) in the case of a person seeking to bring an action under subsection (a)(2) of this section, the Equal Employment Opportunity Commission, the Attorney General, a person who may bring an action or proceeding under section 794a(a)(1) of Title 29, or a person who may bring an action or proceeding under title I of the Americans with Disabilities Act of 1990 (42 U.S.C. 12101 et seq.).

(2) Discriminatory practice

The term "discriminatory practice" means the discrimination described in paragraph (1), or the discrimination or the violation described in paragraph (2), of subsection (a) of this section.

IDEA

Part A — General Provisions

20 U.S.C. §
- 1400 Congressional statements and declarations
- 1402 Definitions
- 1402 Office of Special Education Programs
- 1403 Abrogation of State sovereign immunity
- 1404 Acquisition of equipment; construction or alteration of facilities
- 1405 Employment of individuals with disabilities
- 1406 Requirements for prescribing regulations
- 1407 State administration.
- 1408 Paperwork reduction.
- 1409 Freely associated states.

IDEA

Part A — General Provisions

§ 1400. Short title; table of contents; findings; purposes

(a) Short title

This title may be cited as the "Individuals with Disabilities Education Act".

(b) Omitted

(c) Findings

Congress finds the following:

(1) Disability is a natural part of the human experience and in no way diminishes the right of individuals to participate in or contribute to society. Improving educational results for children with disabilities is an essential element of our national policy of ensuring equality of opportunity, full participation, independent living, and economic self-sufficiency for individuals with disabilities.

(2) Before the date of enactment of the Education for All Handicapped Children Act of 1975 (Public Law 94-142), the educational needs of millions of children with disabilities were not being fully met because —

(A) the children did not receive appropriate educational services;

(B) the children were excluded entirely from the public school system and from being educated with their peers;

(C) undiagnosed disabilities prevented the children from having a successful educational experience; or

(D) a lack of adequate resources within the public school system forced families to find services outside the public school system.

(d) Purposes

The purposes of this title are —

(1)(A) to ensure that all children with disabilities have available to them a free appropriate public education that emphasizes special education and related services designed to meet their unique needs and prepare them for further education, employment, and independent living;

(B) to ensure that the rights of children with disabilities and parents of such children are protected; and

(C) to assist States, localities, educational service agencies, and Federal agencies to provide for the education of all children with disabilities;

(2) to assist States in the implementation of a statewide, comprehensive, coordinated, multidisciplinary, interagency system of early intervention services for infants and toddlers with disabilities and their families;

(3) to ensure that educators and parents have the necessary tools to improve educational results for children with disabilities by supporting system improvement activities; coordinated research and personnel preparation; coordinated technical assistance, dissemination, and support; and technology development and media services; and

(4) to assess, and ensure the effectiveness of, efforts to educate children with disabilities.

§ 1401. Definitions

Except as otherwise provided, in this title:

(1) Assistive technology device

(A) In general

The term "assistive technology device" means any item, piece of equipment, or product system, whether acquired commercially off the shelf, modified, or customized, that is used to increase, maintain, or improve functional capabilities of a child with a disability.

(B) Exception

The term does not include a medical device that is surgically implanted, or the replacement of such device.

(2) Assistive technology service

The term "assistive technology service" means any service that directly assists a child with a disability in the selection, acquisition, or use of an assistive technology device. Such term includes —

(A) the evaluation of the needs of such child, including a functional evaluation of the child in the child's customary environment;

(B) purchasing, leasing, or otherwise providing for the acquisition of assistive technology devices by such child;

(C) selecting, designing, fitting, customizing, adapting, applying, maintaining, repairing, or replacing assistive technology devices;

(D) coordinating and using other therapies, interventions, or services with assistive technology devices, such as those associated with existing education and rehabilitation plans and programs;

(E) training or technical assistance for such child, or, where appropriate, the family of such child; and

(F) training or technical assistance for professionals (including individuals providing education and rehabilitation services), employers, or other individuals who provide services to, employ, or are otherwise substantially involved in the major life functions of such child.

(3) Child with a disability

(A) In general

The term "child with a disability" means a child —

(i) with mental retardation, hearing impairments (including deafness), speech or language impairments, visual impairments (including blindness), serious emotional disturbance (referred to in this title as "emotional disturbance"), orthopedic impairments, autism, traumatic brain injury, other health impairments, or specific learning disabilities; and

(ii) who, by reason thereof, needs special education and related services.

(B) Child aged 3 through 9

The term "child with a disability" for a child aged 3 through 9 (or any subset of that age range, including ages 3 through 5), may, at the discretion of the State and the local educational agency, include a child —

(i) experiencing developmental delays, as defined by the State and as measured by appropriate diagnostic instruments and procedures, in 1 or more of the following areas: physical development; cognitive development; communication development; social or emotional development; or adaptive development; and

(ii) who, by reason thereof, needs special education and related services.

(4) Core academic subjects

The term "core academic subjects" has the meaning given the term in section 9101 of the Elementary and Secondary Education Act of 1965.

(5) Educational service agency

The term "educational service agency" —

(A) means a regional public multiservice agency–

(i) authorized by State law to develop, manage, and provide services or programs to local educational agencies; and

(ii) recognized as an administrative agency for purposes of the provision of special education and related services provided within public elementary schools and secondary schools of the State; and

(B) includes any other public institution or agency having administrative control and direction over a public elementary school or secondary school.

(6) Elementary school

The term "elementary school" means a nonprofit institutional day or residential school, including a public elementary charter school, that provides elementary education, as determined under State law.

(7) Equipment

The term "equipment" includes —

(A) machinery, utilities, and built-in equipment, and any necessary enclosures or structures to house such machinery, utilities, or equipment; and

(B) all other items necessary for the functioning of a particular facility as a facility for the provision of educational services, including items such as instructional equipment and necessary furniture; printed, published, and audio-visual instructional materials; telecommunications, sensory, and other technological aids and devices; and books, periodicals, documents, and other related materials.

(8) Excess costs

The term "excess costs" means those costs that are in excess of the average annual per-student expenditure in a local educational agency during the preceding school year for an elementary school or secondary school student, as may be appropriate, and which shall be computed after deducting —

(A) amounts received —

(i) under part B [subchapter II of this chapter];

(ii) under part A of title I of the Elementary and Secondary Education Act of 1965; and

(iii) under parts A and B of title III of that Act; and

(B) any State or local funds expended for programs that would qualify for assistance under any of those parts.

(9) Free appropriate public education

The term "free appropriate public education" means special education and related services that —

(A) have been provided at public expense, under public supervision and direction, and without charge;

(B) meet the standards of the State educational agency;

(C) include an appropriate preschool, elementary school, or secondary school education in the State involved; and

(D) are provided in conformity with the individualized education program required under section 1414(d) of this title.

(10) Highly qualified

(A) In general

For any special education teacher, the term "highly qualified" has the meaning given the term in section 9101 of the Elementary and Secondary Education Act of 1965, except that such term also —

(i) includes the requirements described in subparagraph (B); and

(ii) includes the option for teachers to meet the requirements of section 9101 of such Act by meeting the requirements of subparagraph (C) or (D).

(B) Requirements for special education teachers

When used with respect to any public elementary school or secondary school special education teacher teaching in a State, such term means that —

(i) the teacher has obtained full State certification as a special education teacher (including certification obtained through alternative routes to certification), or passed the State special education teacher licensing examination, and holds a license to teach in the State as a special education teacher, except that when used with respect to any teacher teaching in a public charter school, the term means that the teacher meets the requirements set forth in the State's public charter school law;

(ii) the teacher has not had special education certification or licensure requirements waived on an emergency, temporary, or provisional basis; and

(iii) the teacher holds at least a bachelor's degree.

(C) Special education teachers teaching to alternate achievement standards

When used with respect to a special education teacher who teaches core academic subjects exclusively to children who are assessed against alternate achievement standards established under the regulations promulgated under section 1111(b)(1) of the Elementary and Secondary Education Act of 1965, such term means the teacher, whether new or not new to the profession, may either —

(i) meet the applicable requirements of section 9101 of such Act for any elementary, middle, or secondary school teacher who is new or not new to the profession; or

(ii) meet the requirements of subparagraph (B) or (C) of section 9101(23) of such Act as applied to an elementary school teacher, or, in the case of instruction above the elementary level, has subject matter knowledge appropriate to the level of instruction being provided, as determined by the State, needed to effectively teach to those standards.

(D) Special education teachers teaching multiple subjectsWhen used with respect to a special education teacher who teaches 2 or more core academic subjects exclusively to children with disabilities, such term means that the teacher may either —

    (i) meet the applicable requirements of section 9101 of the Elementary and Secondary Education Act of 1965 for any elementary, middle, or secondary school teacher who is new or not new to the profession;

    (ii) in the case of a teacher who is not new to the profession, demonstrate competence in all the core academic subjects in which the teacher teaches in the same manner as is required for an elementary, middle, or secondary school teacher who is not new to the profession under section 9101(23)(C)(ii) of such Act, which may include a single, high objective uniform State standard of evaluation covering multiple subjects; or

    (iii) in the case of a new special education teacher who teaches multiple subjects and who is highly qualified in mathematics, language arts, or science, demonstrate competence in the other core academic subjects in which the teacher teaches in the same manner as is required for an elementary, middle, or secondary school teacher under section 9101(23)(C)(ii) of such Act, which may include a single, high objective uniform State standard of evaluation covering multiple subjects, not later than 2 years after the date of employment

  (E) Rule of construction

Notwithstanding any other individual right of action that a parent or student may maintain under this subchapter, nothing in this section or subchapter shall be construed to create a right of action on behalf of an individual student or class of students for the failure of a particular State educational agency or local educational agency employee to be highly qualified.

  (F) Definition for purposes of the ESEA

A teacher who is highly qualified under this paragraph shall be considered highly qualified for purposes of the Elementary and Secondary Education Act of 1965

(11) Homeless children

The term "homeless children" has the meaning given the term "homeless children and youths" in section 11434a of Title 42.

(12) Indian

The term "Indian" means an individual who is a member of an Indian tribe.

(13) Indian tribe

The term "Indian tribe" means any Federal or State Indian tribe, band, rancheria, pueblo, colony, or community, including any Alaska Native village or regional village corporation (as defined in or established under the Alaska Native Claims Settlement Act (43 U.S.C. 1601 et seq.)).

(14) Individualized education program; IEP

The term "individualized education program" or "IEP" means a written statement for each child with a disability that is developed, reviewed, and revised in accordance with section 1414(d) of this title.

(15) Individualized family service plan

The term "individualized family service plan" has the meaning given the term in section 1436 of this title.

(16) Infant or toddler with a disability

The term "infant or toddler with a disability" has the meaning given the term in section 1432 of this title.

(17) Institution of higher education

The term "institution of higher education" —

  (A) has the meaning given the term in section 1001 of this title; and

  (B) also includes any community college receiving funding from the Secretary of the Interior under the Tribally Controlled College or University Assistance Act of 1978.

(18) Limited English proficient

The term "limited English proficient" has the meaning given the term in section 9101 of the Elementary and Secondary Education Act of 1965.

(19) Local educational agency

  (A) In general

The term "local educational agency" means a public board of education or other public authority legally constituted within a State for either administrative control or direction of, or to perform a service function for, public elementary schools or secondary schools in a city, county, township, school district, or other political subdivision of a State, or for such combination of school districts or counties as are recognized in a State as an administrative agency for its public elementary schools or secondary schools.

(B) Educational service agencies and other public institutions or agencies

The term includes —

    (i) an educational service agency; and

    (ii) any other public institution or agency having administrative control and direction of a public elementary school or secondary school.

(C) BIA funded schools

The term includes an elementary school or secondary school funded by the Bureau of Indian Affairs, but only to the extent that such inclusion makes the school eligible for programs for which specific eligibility is not provided to the school in another provision of law and the school does not have a student population that is smaller than the student population of the local educational agency receiving assistance under this chapter with the smallest student population, except that the school shall not be subject to the jurisdiction of any State educational agency other than the Bureau of Indian Affairs.

(20) Native language

The term "native language", when used with respect to an individual who is limited English proficient, means the language normally used by the individual or, in the case of a child, the language normally used by the parents of the child.

(21) Nonprofit

The term "nonprofit", as applied to a school, agency, organization, or institution, means a school, agency, organization, or institution owned and operated by 1 or more nonprofit corporations or associations no part of the net earnings of which inures, or may lawfully inure, to the benefit of any private shareholder or individual.

(22) Outlying area

The term "outlying area" means the United States Virgin Islands, Guam, American Samoa, and the Commonwealth of the Northern Mariana Islands.

(23) Parent

The term "parent" means —

    (A) a natural, adoptive, or foster parent of a child (unless a foster parent is prohibited by State law from serving as a parent);

    (B) a guardian (but not the State if the child is a ward of the State);

    (C) an individual acting in the place of a natural or adoptive parent (including a grandparent, stepparent, or other relative) with whom the child lives, or an individual who is legally responsible for the child's welfare; or

    (D) except as used in sections 1415(b)(2) of this title and 1439(a)(5) of this title, an individual assigned under either of those sections to be a surrogate parent.

(24) Parent organization

The term "parent organization" has the meaning given the term in section 1471(g) of this title.

(25) Parent training and information center

The term "parent training and information center" means a center assisted under section 1471 or 1472 of this title.

(26) Related service

(A) In general

The term "related services" means transportation, and such developmental, corrective, and other supportive services (including speech-language pathology and audiology services, interpreting services, psychological services, physical and occupational therapy, recreation, including therapeutic recreation, social work services, school nurse services designed to enable a child with a disability to receive a free appropriate public education as described in the individualized education program of the child, counseling services, including rehabilitation counseling, orientation and mobility services, and medical services, except that such medical services shall be for diagnostic and evaluation purposes only) as may be required to assist a child with a disability to benefit from special education, and includes the early identification and assessment of disabling conditions in children.

(B) Exception

The term does not include a medical device that is surgically implanted, or the replacement of such device.

(27) Secondary school

The term "secondary school" means a nonprofit institutional day or residential school, including a public secondary charter school, that provides secondary education, as determined under State law, except that it does not include any education beyond grade 12.

(28) Secretary
The term "Secretary" means the Secretary of Education.

(29) Special education
The term "special education" means specially designed instruction, at no cost to parents, to meet the unique needs of a child with a disability, including —

    (A) instruction conducted in the classroom, in the home, in hospitals and institutions, and in other settings; and

    (B) instruction in physical education.

(30) Specific learning disability

    (A) In general

    The term "specific learning disability" means a disorder in 1 or more of the basic psychological processes involved in understanding or in using language, spoken or written, which disorder may manifest itself in the imperfect ability to listen, think, speak, read, write, spell, or do mathematical calculations.

    (B) Disorders included

    Such term includes such conditions as perceptual disabilities, brain injury, minimal brain dysfunction, dyslexia, and developmental aphasia

    (C) Disorders not included

    Such term does not include a learning problem that is primarily the result of visual, hearing, or motor disabilities, of mental retardation, of emotional disturbance, or of environmental, cultural, or economic disadvantage.

(31) State
The term "State" means each of the 50 States, the District of Columbia, the Commonwealth of Puerto Rico, and each of the outlying areas.

(32) State educational agency
The term "State educational agency" means the State board of education or other agency or officer primarily responsible for the State supervision of public elementary schools and secondary schools, or, if there is no such officer or agency, an officer or agency designated by the Governor or by State law.

(33) Supplementary aids and services
The term "supplementary aids and services" means aids, services, and other supports that are provided in regular education classes or other education-related settings to enable children with disabilities to be educated with nondisabled children to the maximum extent appropriate in accordance with section 1412(a)(5) of this title.

(34) Transition services
The term "transition services" means a coordinated set of activities for a child with a disability that —

    (A) is designed to be within a results-oriented process, that is focused on improving the academic and functional achievement of the child with a disability to facilitate the child's movement from school to post-school activities, including post-secondary education, vocational education, integrated employment (including supported employment), continuing and adult education, adult services, independent living, or community participation;

    (B) is based on the individual child's needs, taking into account the child's strengths, preferences, and interests; and

    (C) includes instruction, related services, community experiences, the development of employment and other post-school adult living objectives, and, when appropriate, acquisition of daily living skills and functional vocational evaluation.

(35) Universal design
The term "universal design" has the meaning given the term in section 3002 of Title 29.

(36) Ward of the State

    (A) In general

    The term "ward of the State" means a child who, as determined by the State where the child resides, is a foster child, is a ward of the State, or is in the custody of a public child welfare agency.

    (B) Exception

    The term does not include a foster child who has a foster parent who meets the definition of a parent in paragraph (23).

§ 1402. Office of Special Education Programs

(a) Establishment.

There shall be, within the Office of Special Education and Rehabilitative Services in the Department of Education, an Office of Special Education Programs, which shall be the principal agency in the Department for administering and carrying out this title and other programs and activities concerning the education of children with disabilities.

(b) Director.

The Office established under subsection (a) shall be headed by a Director who shall be selected by the Secretary and shall report directly to the Assistant Secretary for Special Education and Rehabilitative Services.

(c) Voluntary and uncompensated services.

Notwithstanding section 1342 of title 31, United States Code, the Secretary is authorized to accept voluntary and uncompensated services in furtherance of the purposes of this title.

§ 1403. Abrogation of State sovereign immunity

(a) In general.

A State shall not be immune under the 11th amendment to the Constitution of the United States from suit in Federal court for a violation of this title.

(b) Remedies.

In a suit against a State for a violation of this title, remedies (including remedies both at law and in equity) are available for such a violation to the same extent as those remedies are available for such a violation in the suit against any public entity other than a State.

(c) Effective date.

Subsections (a) and (b) apply with respect to violations that occur in whole or part after the date of enactment of the Education of the Handicapped Act Amendments of 1990.

§ 1404. Acquisition of equipment; construction or alteration of facilities

(a) In general.

If the Secretary determines that a program authorized under this title will be improved by permitting program funds to be used to acquire appropriate equipment, or to construct new facilities or alter existing facilities, the Secretary is authorized to allow the use of those funds for those purposes.

(b) Compliance with certain regulations.

Any construction of new facilities or alteration of existing facilities under subsection (a) shall comply with the requirements of —

(1) appendix A of part 36 of title 28, Code of Federal Regulations (commonly known as the "Americans with Disabilities Accessibility Guidelines for Buildings and Facilities"); or

(2) appendix A of subpart 101-19.6 of title 41, Code of Federal Regulations (commonly known as the "Uniform Federal Accessibility Standards").

§ 1405. Employment of individuals with disabilities

The Secretary shall ensure that each recipient of assistance under this title makes positive efforts to employ and advance in employment qualified individuals with disabilities in programs assisted under this title.

§ 1406. Requirements for prescribing regulations

(a) In general.

In carrying out the provisions of this title, the Secretary shall issue regulations under this title only to the extent that such regulations are necessary to ensure that there is compliance with the specific requirements of this title.

(b) Protections provided to children.

The Secretary may not implement, or publish in final form, any regulation prescribed pursuant to this title that —

(1) violates or contradicts any provision of this title; or

(2) procedurally or substantively lessens the protections provided to children with disabilities under this title, as embodied in regulations in effect on July 20, 1983 (particularly as such protections related to parental consent to initial evaluation or initial placement in special education, least restrictive environment, related services, timelines, attendance of evaluation personnel at individualized education program meetings, or qualifications of personnel), except to the extent that such regulation reflects the clear and unequivocal intent of Congress in legislation.

(c) Public comment period.

The Secretary shall provide a public comment period of not less than 75 days on any regulation proposed under part B or part C on which an opportunity for public comment is otherwise required by law.

(d) Policy letters and statements.

The Secretary may not issue policy letters or

other statements (including letters or statements regarding issues of national significance) that —

(1) violate or contradict any provision of this title; or

(2) establish a rule that is required for compliance with, and eligibility under, this title without following the requirements of section 553 of title 5, United States Code.

(e) Explanation and assurances.

Any written response by the Secretary under subsection (d) regarding a policy, question, or interpretation under part B shall include an explanation in the written response that —

(1) such response is provided as informal guidance and is not legally binding;

(2) when required, such response is issued in compliance with the requirements of section 553 of title 5, United States Code; and

(3) such response represents the interpretation by the Department of Education of the applicable statutory or regulatory requirements in the context of the specific facts presented.

(f) Correspondence from department of education describing interpretations of this title.

(1) In general.

The Secretary shall, on a quarterly basis, publish in the Federal Register, and widely disseminate to interested entities through various additional forms of communication, a list of correspondence from the Department of Education received by individuals during the previous quarter that describes the interpretations of the Department of Education of this title or the regulations implemented pursuant to this title.

(2) Additional information.

For each item of correspondence published in a list under paragraph (1), the Secretary shall —

(A) identify the topic addressed by the correspondence and shall include such other summary information as the Secretary determines to be appropriate; and

(B) ensure that all such correspondence is issued, where applicable, in compliance with the requirements of section 553 of title 5, United States Code.

§ 1407 State administration

(a) Rulemaking.

Each State that receives funds under this title shall —

(1) ensure that any State rules, regulations, and policies relating to this title conform to the purposes of this title;

(2) identify in writing to local educational agencies located in the State and the Secretary any such rule, regulation, or policy as a State-imposed requirement that is not required by this title and Federal regulations; and

(3) minimize the number of rules, regulations, and policies to which the local educational agencies and schools located in the State are subject under this title.

(b) Support and facilitation

State rules, regulations, and policies under this title shall support and facilitate local educational agency and school-level system improvement designed to enable children with disabilities to meet the challenging State student academic achievement standards.

§ 1408 Paperwork reduction

(a) Pilot program.

(1) Purpose. The purpose of this section is to provide an opportunity for States to identify ways to reduce paperwork burdens and other administrative duties that are directly associated with the requirements of this title, in order to increase the time and resources available for instruction and other activities aimed at improving educational and functional results for children with disabilities.

(2) Authorization.

(A) In general.

In order to carry out the purpose of this section, the Secretary is authorized to grant waivers of statutory requirements of, or regulatory requirements relating to, part B for a period of time not to exceed 4 years with respect to not more than 15 States based on proposals submitted by States to reduce excessive paperwork and noninstructional time burdens that do not assist in improving educational and functional results for children with disabilities.

(B) Exception.

The Secretary shall not waive under this section any statutory requirements of, or regulatory requirements relating to, applicable civil rights requirements.

(C) Rule of construction.

Nothing in this section shall be construed to —

(i) affect the right of a child with a disability to receive a free appropriate public education under part B; and

(ii) permit a State or local educational agency to waive procedural safeguards under section 615.

(3) Proposal.

(A) In general.

A State desiring to participate in the program under this section shall submit a proposal to the Secretary at such time and in such manner as the Secretary may reasonably require.

(B) Content.

The proposal shall include —

(i) a list of any statutory requirements of, or regulatory requirements relating to, part B that the State desires the Secretary to waive, in whole or in part; and

(ii) a list of any State requirements that the State proposes to waive or change, in whole or in part, to carry out a waiver granted to the State by the Secretary.

(4) Termination of waiver.

The Secretary shall terminate a State's waiver under this section if the Secretary determines that the State —

(A) needs assistance under section 616(d)(2)(A)(ii) and that the waiver has contributed to or caused such need for assistance;

(B) needs intervention under section 616(d)(2)(A)(iii) or needs substantial intervention under section 616(d)(2)(A)(iv); or

(C) failed to appropriately implement its waiver.

(b) Report.

Beginning 2 years after the date of enactment of the Individuals with Disabilities Education Improvement Act of 2004, the Secretary shall include in the annual report to Congress submitted pursuant to section 426 of the Department of Education Organization Act information related to the effectiveness of waivers granted under subsection (a), including any specific recommendations for broader implementation of such waivers, in —

(1) reducing —

(A) the paperwork burden on teachers, principals, administrators, and related service providers; and

(B) noninstructional time spent by teachers in complying with part B;

(2) enhancing longer-term educational planning;

(3) improving positive outcomes for children with disabilities;

(4) promoting collaboration between IEP Team members; and

(5) ensuring satisfaction of family members.

§ 1409 Freely associated states

The Republic of the Marshall Islands, the Federated States of Micronesia, and the Republic of Palau shall continue to be eligible for competitive grants administered by the Secretary under this title to the extent that such grants continue to be available to States and local educational agencies under this title.

PART B — ASSISTANCE FOR EDUCATION OF ALL CHILDREN WITH DISABILITIES

20 U.S.C. §
1411 Authorization; allotment; use of funds; authorization of appropriations
1412 State eligibility
1413 Local educational agency eligibility
1414 Evaluations, eligibility determinations, individualized education programs, and educational placements
1415 Procedural safeguards
1416 Withholding and judicial review
1417 Administration
1418 Program information
1419 Preschool grants

PART B — ASSISTANCE FOR EDUCATION OF ALL CHILDREN WITH DISABILITIES

§ 1411. Authorization; allotment; use of funds; authorization of appropriations

(a) Grants to States

(1) Purpose of grants.

The Secretary shall make grants to States, outlying areas, and freely associated States, and provide funds to the Secretary of the Interior, to assist them to provide special education and related services to children with disabilities in accordance with this part.

(2) Maximum amount.

The maximum amount of the grant a State may receive under this section —

(A) for fiscal years 2005 and 2006 is —

(i) the number of children with disabilities in the State who are receiving special education and related services —

(I) aged 3 through 5 if the State is eligible for a grant under section 619; and

(II) aged 6 through 21; multiplied by

(ii) 40 percent of the average per-pupil expenditure in public elementary schools and secondary schools in the United States; and

(B) for fiscal year 2007 and subsequent fiscal years is —

(i) the number of children with disabilities in the 2004-2005 school year in the State who received special education and related services —

(I) aged 3 through 5 if the State is eligible for a grant under section 619; and

(II) aged 6 through 21; multiplied by

(ii) 40 percent of the average per-pupil expenditure in public elementary schools and secondary schools in the United States; adjusted by

(iii) the rate of annual change in the sum of —

(I) 85 percent of such State's population described in subsection (d)(3)(A)(i)(II); and

(II) 15 percent of such State's population described in subsection (d)(3)(A)(i)(III).

(b) Outlying areas and freely associated states; Secretary of the Interior.

(1) Outlying areas and freely associated states.

(A) Funds reserved.

From the amount appropriated for any fiscal year under subsection (i), the Secretary shall reserve not more than 1 percent, which shall be used —

(i) to provide assistance to the outlying areas in accordance with their respective populations of individuals aged 3 through 21; and

(ii) to provide each freely associated State a grant in the amount that such freely associated State received for fiscal year 2003 under this part, but only if the freely associated State meets the applicable requirements of this part, as well as the requirements of section 611(b)(2)(C) as such section was in effect on the day before the date of enactment of the Individuals with Disabilities Education Improvement Act of 2004.

(B) Special rule.

The provisions of Public Law 95-134, permitting the consolidation of grants by the outlying areas, shall not apply to funds provided to the outlying areas or the freely associated States under this section.

(C) Definition.

In this paragraph, the term "freely associated States" means the Republic of the Marshall Islands, the Federated States of

Micronesia, and the Republic of Palau.

(2) Secretary of the Interior.

From the amount appropriated for any fiscal year under subsection (i), the Secretary shall reserve 1.226 percent to provide assistance to the Secretary of the Interior in accordance with subsection (h).

(c) Technical assistance.

(1) In general.

The Secretary may reserve not more than 1/2 of 1 percent of the amounts appropriated under this part for each fiscal year to provide technical assistance activities authorized under section 616(i).

(2) Maximum Amount.

The maximum amount the Secretary may reserve under paragraph (1) for any fiscal year is $25,000,000, cumulatively adjusted by the rate of inflation as measured by the percentage increase, if any, from the preceding fiscal year in the Consumer Price Index For All Urban Consumers, published by the Bureau of Labor Statistics of the Department of Labor.

(d) Allocations to states.

(1) In general.

After reserving funds for technical assistance, and for payments to the outlying areas, the freely associated States, and the Secretary of the Interior under subsections (b) and (c) for a fiscal year, the Secretary shall allocate the remaining amount among the States in accordance with this subsection.

(2) Special rule for use of fiscal year 1999 amount.

If a State received any funds under this section for fiscal year 1999 on the basis of children aged 3 through 5, but does not make a free appropriate public education available to all children with disabilities aged 3 through 5 in the State in any subsequent fiscal year, the Secretary shall compute the State's amount for fiscal year 1999, solely for the purpose of calculating the State's allocation in that subsequent year under paragraph (3) or (4), by subtracting the amount allocated to the State for fiscal year 1999 on the basis of those children.

(3) Increase in funds.

If the amount available for allocations to States under paragraph (1) for a fiscal year is equal to or greater than the amount allocated to the States under this paragraph for the preceding fiscal year, those allocations shall be calculated as follows:

(A) Allocation of increase.

(i) In general.

Except as provided in subparagraph (B), the Secretary shall allocate for the fiscal year —

(I) to each State the amount the State received under this section for fiscal year 1999;

(II) 85 percent of any remaining funds to States on the basis of the States' relative populations of children aged 3 through 21 who are of the same age as children with disabilities for whom the State ensures the availability of a free appropriate public education under this part; and

(III) 15 percent of those remaining funds to States on the basis of the States' relative populations of children described in subclause (II) who are living in poverty.

(ii) Data.

For the purpose of making grants under this paragraph, the Secretary shall use the most recent population data, including data on children living in poverty, that are available and satisfactory to the Secretary.

(B) Limitations.

Notwithstanding subparagraph (A), allocations under this paragraph shall be subject to the following:

(i) Preceding year allocation.

No State's allocation shall be less than its allocation under this section for the preceding fiscal year.

(ii) Minimum.

No State's allocation shall be less than the greatest of —

(I) the sum of —

(aa) the amount the State received under this section for fiscal year 1999; and

(bb) 1/3 of 1 percent of the amount by which the amount appropriated under subsection (i) for the fiscal year exceeds the amount appropriated for this section for fiscal year 1999;

(II) the sum of —

(aa) the amount the State received under this section for the preceding fiscal year; and

(bb) that amount multiplied by

the percentage by which the increase in the funds appropriated for this section from the preceding fiscal year exceeds 1.5 percent; or

(III) the sum of —

(aa) the amount the State received under this section for the preceding fiscal year; and

(bb) that amount multiplied by 90 percent of the percentage increase in the amount appropriated for this section from the preceding fiscal year.

(iii) Maximum.

Notwithstanding clause (ii), no State's allocation under this paragraph shall exceed the sum of —

(I) the amount the State received under this section for the preceding fiscal year; and

(II) that amount multiplied by the sum of 1.5 percent and the percentage increase in the amount appropriated under this section from the preceding fiscal year.

(C) Ratable reduction.

If the amount available for allocations under this paragraph is insufficient to pay those allocations in full, those allocations shall be ratably reduced, subject to subparagraph (B)(i).

(4) Decrease in funds.

If the amount available for allocations to States under paragraph (1) for a fiscal year is less than the amount allocated to the States under this section for the preceding fiscal year, those allocations shall be calculated as follows:

(A) Amounts greater than fiscal year 1999 allocations.

If the amount available for allocations is greater than the amount allocated to the States for fiscal year 1999, each State shall be allocated the sum of —

(i) the amount the State received under this section for fiscal year 1999; and

(ii) an amount that bears the same relation to any remaining funds as the increase the State received under this section for the preceding fiscal year over fiscal year 1999 bears to the total of all such increases for all States.

(B) Amounts equal to or less than fiscal year 1999 allocations.

(i) In general.

If the amount available for allocations under this paragraph is equal to or less than the amount allocated to the States for fiscal year 1999, each State shall be allocated the amount the State received for fiscal year 1999.

(ii) Ratable reduction.

If the amount available for allocations under this paragraph is insufficient to make the allocations described in clause (i), those allocations shall be ratably reduced.

(e) State-level activities.

(1) State Administration.

(A) In general.

For the purpose of administering this part, including paragraph (3), section 619, and the coordination of activities under this part with, and providing technical assistance to, other programs that provide services to children with disabilities —

(i) each State may reserve for each fiscal year not more than the maximum amount the State was eligible to reserve for State administration under this section for fiscal year 2004 or $800,000 (adjusted in accordance with subparagraph (B)), whichever is greater; and

(ii) each outlying area may reserve for each fiscal year not more than 5 percent of the amount the outlying area receives under subsection (b)(1) for the fiscal year or $35,000, whichever is greater.

(B) Cumulative annual adjustments.

For each fiscal year beginning with fiscal year 2005, the Secretary shall cumulatively adjust —

(i) the maximum amount the State was eligible to reserve for State administration under this part for fiscal year 2004; and

(ii) $800,000,

by the rate of inflation as measured by the percentage increase, if any, from the preceding fiscal year in the Consumer Price Index For All Urban Consumers, published by the Bureau of Labor Statistics of the Department of Labor.

(C) Certification.

Prior to expenditure of funds under this paragraph, the State shall certify to the Secretary that the arrangements to establish responsibility for services pursuant to section 612(a)(12)(A) are current.

(D) Part C.

Funds reserved under subparagraph (A) may be used for the administration of part C, if the State educational agency is the lead agency for the State under such part.

(2) Other state-level activities.

(A) State-level activities.

(i) In general.

Except as provided in clause (iii), for the purpose of carrying out State-level activities, each State may reserve for each of the fiscal years 2005 and 2006 not more than 10 percent from the amount of the State's allocation under subsection (d) for each of the fiscal years 2005 and 2006, respectively. For fiscal year 2007 and each subsequent fiscal year, the State may reserve the maximum amount the State was eligible to reserve under the preceding sentence for fiscal year 2006 (cumulatively adjusted by the rate of inflation as measured by the percentage increase, if any, from the preceding fiscal year in the Consumer Price Index For All Urban Consumers, published by the Bureau of Labor Statistics of the Department of Labor).

(ii) Small state adjustment.

Notwithstanding clause (i) and except as provided in clause (iii), in the case of a State for which the maximum amount reserved for State administration is not greater than $850,000, the State may reserve for the purpose of carrying out State-level activities for each of the fiscal years 2005 and 2006, not more than 10.5 percent from the amount of the State"s allocation under subsection (d) for each of the fiscal years 2005 and 2006, respectively. For fiscal year 2007 and each subsequent fiscal year, such State may reserve the maximum amount the State was eligible to reserve under the preceding sentence for fiscal year 2006 (cumulatively adjusted by the rate of inflation as measured by the percentage increase, if any, from the preceding fiscal year in the Consumer Price Index For All Urban Consumers, published by the Bureau of Labor Statistics of the Department of Labor).

(iii) Exception.

If a State does not reserve funds under paragraph (3) for a fiscal year, then —

(I) in the case of a State that is not described in clause (ii), for fiscal year 2005 or 2006, clause (i) shall be applied by substituting "9.0 percent" for "10 percent"; and

(II) in the case of a State that is described in clause (ii), for fiscal year 2005 or 2006, clause (ii) shall be applied by substituting "9.5 percent" for "10.5 percent".

(B) Required activities.

Funds reserved under subparagraph (A) shall be used to carry out the following activities:

(i) For monitoring, enforcement, and complaint investigation.

(ii) To establish and implement the mediation process required by section 615(e), including providing for the cost of mediators and support personnel.

(C) Authorized activities.

Funds reserved under subparagraph (A) may be used to carry out the following activities:

(i) For support and direct services, including technical assistance, personnel preparation, and professional development and training.

(ii) To support paperwork reduction activities, including expanding the use of technology in the IEP process.

(iii) To assist local educational agencies in providing positive behavioral interventions and supports and appropriate mental health services for children with disabilities

(iv) To improve the use of technology in the classroom by children with disabilities to enhance learning.

(v) To support the use of technology, including technology with universal design principles and assistive technology devices, to maximize accessibility to the general education curriculum for children with disabilities.

(vi) Development and implementation of transition programs, including coordination of services with agencies involved in supporting the transition of children with disabilities to postsecondary activities.

(vii) To assist local educational agencies in meeting personnel shortages.

(viii) To support capacity building activities and improve the delivery of services by local educational agencies to improve results for children with disabilities.

(ix) Alternative programming for children with disabilities who have been expelled from school, and services for children with disabilities in correctional facilities, children enrolled in State-operated or State-supported schools, and children with disabilities in charter schools.

(x) To support the development and provision of appropriate accommodations for children with disabilities, or the development and provision of alternate assessments that are valid and reliable for assessing the performance of children with disabilities, in accordance with sections 1111(b) and 6111 of the Elementary and Secondary Education Act of 1965.

(xi) To provide technical assistance to schools and local educational agencies, and direct services, including supplemental educational services as defined in 1116(e) of the Elementary and Secondary Education Act of 1965 to children with disabilities, in schools or local educational agencies identified for improvement under section 1116 of the Elementary and Secondary Education Act of 1965 on the sole basis of the assessment results of the disaggregated subgroup of children with disabilities, including providing professional development to special and regular education teachers, who teach children with disabilities, based on scientifically based research to improve educational instruction, in order to improve academic achievement to meet or exceed the objectives established by the State under section 1111(b)(2)(G) the Elementary and Secondary Education Act of 1965.

(3) Local educational agency risk pool.
(A) In general.
(i) Reservation of funds.

For the purpose of assisting local educational agencies (including a charter school that is a local educational agency or a consortium of local educational agencies) in addressing the needs of high need children with disabilities, each State shall have the option to reserve for each fiscal year 10 percent of the amount of funds the State reserves for State-level activities under paragraph (2)(A) —

(I) to establish and make disbursements from the high cost fund to local educational agencies in accordance with this paragraph during the first and succeeding fiscal years of the high cost fund; and

(II) to support innovative and effective ways of cost sharing by the State, by a local educational agency, or among a consortium of local educational agencies, as determined by the State in coordination with representatives from local educational agencies, subject to subparagraph (B)(ii).

(ii) Definition of local educational agency.

In this paragraph the term "local educational agency" includes a charter school that is a local educational agency, or a consortium of local educational agencies.

(B) Limitation on uses of funds.
(i) Establishment of high cost fund.

A State shall not use any of the funds the State reserves pursuant to subparagraph (A)(i), but may use the funds the State reserves under paragraph (1), to establish and support the high cost fund.

(ii) Innovative and effective cost sharing.

A State shall not use more than 5 percent of the funds the State reserves pursuant to subparagraph (A)(i) for each fiscal year to support innovative and effective ways of cost sharing among consortia of local educational agencies.

(C) State plan for high cost fund.
(i) Definition.

The State educational agency shall establish the State's definition of a high need child with a disability, which definition shall be developed in consultation with local educational agencies.

(ii) State plan.

The State educational agency shall develop, not later than 90 days after the State reserves funds under this paragraph, annually review, and amend as necessary, a State plan for the high cost fund. Such State plan shall —

(I) establish, in coordination with representatives from local educational agencies, a definition of a high need child with a disability that, at a minimum —

(aa) addresses the financial impact a high need child with a disability has on the budget of the child's local educational agency; and

(bb) ensures that the cost of the

high need child with a disability is greater than 3 times the average per pupil expenditure (as defined in section 9101 of the Elementary and Secondary Education Act of 1965) in that State;

(II) establish eligibility criteria for the participation of a local educational agency that, at a minimum, takes into account the number and percentage of high need children with disabilities served by a local educational agency;

(III) develop a funding mechanism that provides distributions each fiscal year to local educational agencies that meet the criteria developed by the State under subclause (II); and

(IV) establish an annual schedule by which the State educational agency shall make its distributions from the high cost fund each fiscal year.

(iii) Public availability.

The State shall make its final State plan publicly available not less than 30 days before the beginning of the school year, including dissemination of such information on the State website.

(D) Disbursements from the high cost fund.

(i) In general.

Each State educational agency shall make all annual disbursements from the high cost fund established under subparagraph (A)(i) in accordance with the State plan published pursuant to subparagraph (C).

(ii) Use of disbursements.

Each State educational agency shall make annual disbursements to eligible local educational agencies in accordance with its State plan under subparagraph (C)(ii).

(iii) Appropriate costs.

The costs associated with educating a high need child with a disability under subparagraph (C)(i) are only those costs associated with providing direct special education and related services to such child that are identified in such child's IEP.

(E) Legal fees.

The disbursements under subparagraph (D) shall not support legal fees, court costs, or other costs associated with a cause of action brought on behalf of a child with a disability to ensure a free appropriate public education for such child.

(F) Assurance of a Free Appropriate Public Education.

Nothing in this paragraph shall be construed

(i) to limit or condition the right of a child with a disability who is assisted under this part to receive a free appropriate public education pursuant to section 612(a)(1) in the least restrictive environment pursuant to section 612(a)(5); or

(ii) to authorize a State educational agency or local educational agency to establish a limit on what may be spent on the education of a child with a disability.

(G) Special rule for risk pool and high need assistance programs in effect as of January 1, 2004.

Notwithstanding the provisions of subparagraphs (A) through (F), a State may use funds reserved pursuant to this paragraph for implementing a placement neutral cost sharing and reimbursement program of high need, low incidence, catastrophic, or extraordinary aid to local educational agencies that provides services to high need students based on eligibility criteria for such programs that were created not later than January 1, 2004, and are currently in operation, if such program serves children that meet the requirement of the definition of a high need child with a disability as described in subparagraph (C)(ii)(I).

(H) Medicaid services not affected.

Disbursements provided under this paragraph shall not be used to pay costs that otherwise would be reimbursed as medical assistance for a child with a disability under the State medicaid program under title XIX of the Social Security Act.

(I) Remaining funds.

Funds reserved under subparagraph (A) in any fiscal year but not expended in that fiscal year pursuant to subparagraph (D) shall be allocated to local educational agencies for the succeeding fiscal year in the same manner as funds are allocated to local educational agencies under subsection (f) for the succeeding fiscal year.

(4) Inapplicability of certain prohibitions.

A State may use funds the State reserves under paragraphs (1) and (2) without regard to —

(A) the prohibition on commingling of funds in section 612(a)(17)(B); and

(B) the prohibition on supplanting other funds in section 612(a)(17)(C).

(5) Report on use of funds.

As part of the information required to be submitted to the Secretary under section 612, each State shall annually describe how amounts under this section —

(A) will be used to meet the requirements of this title; and

(B) will be allocated among the activities described in this section to meet State priorities based on input from local educational agencies.

(6) Special rule for increased funds.

A State may use funds the State reserves under paragraph (1)(A) as a result of inflationary increases under paragraph (1)(B) to carry out activities authorized under clause (i), (iii), (vii), or (viii) of paragraph (2)(C).

(7) Flexibility in using funds for Part C.

Any State eligible to receive a grant under section 619 may use funds made available under paragraph (1)(A), subsection (f)(3), or section 619(f)(5) to develop and implement a State policy jointly with the lead agency under part C and the State educational agency to provide early intervention services (which shall include an educational component that promotes school readiness and incorporates preliteracy, language, and numeracy skills) in accordance with part C to children with disabilities who are eligible for services under section 619 and who previously received services under part C until such children enter, or are eligible under State law to enter, kindergarten, or elementary school as appropriate.

(f) Subgrants to local educational agencies.

(1) Subgrants required.

Each State that receives a grant under this section for any fiscal year shall distribute any funds the State does not reserve under subsection (e) to local educational agencies (including public charter schools that operate as local educational agencies) in the State that have established their eligibility under section 613 for use in accordance with this part.

(2) Procedure for allocations to local educational agencies.

For each fiscal year for which funds are allocated to States under subsection (d), each State shall allocate funds under paragraph (1) as follows:

(A) Base payments.

The State shall first award each local educational agency described in paragraph (1) the amount the local educational agency would have received under this section for fiscal year 1999, if the State had distributed 75 percent of its grant for that year under section 611(d) as section 611(d) was then in effect.

(B) Allocation of remaining funds.

After making allocations under subparagraph (A), the State shall —

(i) allocate 85 percent of any remaining funds to those local educational agencies on the basis of the relative numbers of children enrolled in public and private elementary schools and secondary schools within the local educational agency's jurisdiction; and

(ii) allocate 15 percent of those remaining funds to those local educational agencies in accordance with their relative numbers of children living in poverty, as determined by the State educational agency.

(3) Reallocation of funds.

If a State educational agency determines that a local educational agency is adequately providing a free appropriate public education to all children with disabilities residing in the area served by that local educational agency with State and local funds, the State educational agency may reallocate any portion of the funds under this part that are not needed by that local educational agency to provide a free appropriate public education to other local educational agencies in the State that are not adequately providing special education and related services to all children with disabilities residing in the areas served by those other local educational agencies.

(g) Definitions.

In this section:

(1) Average per-pupil expenditure in public elementary schools and secondary schools in the United States.

The term "average per-pupil expenditure in public elementary schools and secondary schools in the United States" means —

(A) without regard to the source of funds —

(i) the aggregate current expenditures, during the second fiscal year preceding the fiscal year for which the determination is made (or, if satisfactory data for that year are not available, during the most recent preceding fiscal year for which satisfactory data are available) of all local educational agencies in the 50 States and the District of Columbia; plus

(ii) any direct expenditures by the State for the operation of those agencies; divided by

(B) the aggregate number of children in average daily attendance to whom those agencies provided free public education during that preceding year.

(2) State.

The term "State" means each of the 50 States, the District of Columbia, and the Commonwealth of Puerto Rico

(h) Use of amounts by Secretary of the Interior.

(1) Provision of amounts for assistance.

(A) In general.

The Secretary of Education shall provide amounts to the Secretary of the Interior to meet the need for assistance for the education of children with disabilities on reservations aged 5 to 21, inclusive, enrolled in elementary schools and secondary schools for Indian children operated or funded by the Secretary of the Interior. The amount of such payment for any fiscal year shall be equal to 80 percent of the amount allotted under subsection (b)(2) for that fiscal year. Of the amount described in the preceding sentence —

(i) 80 percent shall be allocated to such schools by July 1 of that fiscal year; and

(ii) 20 percent shall be allocated to such schools by September 30 of that fiscal year.

(B) Calculation of number of children.

In the case of Indian students aged 3 to 5, inclusive, who are enrolled in programs affiliated with the Bureau of Indian Affairs (referred to in this subsection as the "BIA") schools and that are required by the States in which such schools are located to attain or maintain State accreditation, and which schools have such accreditation prior to the date of enactment of the Individuals with Disabilities Education Act Amendments of 1991, the school shall be allowed to count those children for the purpose of distribution of the funds provided under this paragraph to the Secretary of the Interior. The Secretary of the Interior shall be responsible for meeting all of the requirements of this part for those children, in accordance with paragraph (2).

(C) Additional requirement.

With respect to all other children aged 3 to 21, inclusive, on reservations, the State educational agency shall be responsible for ensuring that all of the requirements of this part are implemented.

(2) Submission of information.

The Secretary of Education may provide the Secretary of the Interior amounts under paragraph (1) for a fiscal year only if the Secretary of the Interior submits to the Secretary of Education information that —

(A) demonstrates that the Department of the Interior meets the appropriate requirements, as determined by the Secretary of Education, of sections 612 (including monitoring and evaluation activities) and 613;

(B) includes a description of how the Secretary of the Interior will coordinate the provision of services under this part with local educational agencies, tribes and tribal organizations, and other private and Federal service providers;

(C) includes an assurance that there are public hearings, adequate notice of such hearings, and an opportunity for comment afforded to members of tribes, tribal governing bodies, and affected local school boards before the adoption of the policies, programs, and procedures related to the requirements described in subparagraph (A);

(D) includes an assurance that the Secretary of the Interior will provide such information as the Secretary of Education may require to comply with section 618;

(E) includes an assurance that the Secretary of the Interior and the Secretary of Health and Human Services have entered into a memorandum of agreement, to be provided to the Secretary of Education, for the coordination of services, resources, and personnel between their respective Federal, State, and local offices and with State and local educational agencies and other entities to facilitate the provision of services to Indian children with disabilities residing on or near reservations (such agreement shall provide for the apportionment of responsibilities and costs, including child find, evaluation, diagnosis, remediation or therapeutic measures, and (where appropriate) equipment and medical or personal supplies as needed for a child to remain in school or a program); and

(F) includes an assurance that the Department of the Interior will cooperate with the Department of Education in its exercise of monitoring and oversight of this application, and any agreements entered into between the Secretary of the Interior and other entities under this part, and will fulfill its duties under this part.

(3) Applicability.

The Secretary shall withhold payments under this subsection with respect to the information described in paragraph (2) in the same manner as the Secretary withholds payments under section 616(e)(6).

(4) Payments for education and services for Indian children with disabilities aged 3 through 5.

(A) In general.

With funds appropriated under subsection (i), the Secretary of Education shall make payments to the Secretary of the Interior to be distributed to tribes or tribal organizations (as defined under section 4 of the Indian Self-Determination and Education Assistance Act) or consortia of tribes or tribal organizations to provide for the coordination of assistance for special education and related services for children with disabilities aged 3 through 5 on reservations served by elementary schools and secondary schools for Indian children operated or funded by the Department of the Interior. The amount of such payments under subparagraph (B) for any fiscal year shall be equal to 20 percent of the amount allotted under subsection (b)(2).

(B) Distribution of funds.

The Secretary of the Interior shall distribute the total amount of the payment under subparagraph (A) by allocating to each tribe, tribal organization, or consortium an amount based on the number of children with disabilities aged 3 through 5 residing on reservations as reported annually, divided by the total of those children served by all tribes or tribal organizations.

(C) Submission of information.

To receive a payment under this paragraph, the tribe or tribal organization shall submit such figures to the Secretary of the Interior as required to determine the amounts to be allocated under subparagraph (B). This information shall be compiled and submitted to the Secretary of Education.

(D) Use of funds.

The funds received by a tribe or tribal organization shall be used to assist in child find, screening, and other procedures for the early identification of children aged 3 through 5, parent training, and the provision of direct services. These activities may be carried out directly or through contracts or cooperative agreements with the BIA, local educational agencies, and other public or private nonprofit organizations. The tribe or tribal organization is encouraged to involve Indian parents in the development and implementation of these activities. The tribe or tribal organization shall, as appropriate, make referrals to local, State, or Federal entities for the provision of services or further diagnosis.

(E) Biennial report.

To be eligible to receive a grant pursuant to subparagraph (A), the tribe or tribal organization shall provide to the Secretary of the Interior a biennial report of activities undertaken under this paragraph, including the number of contracts and cooperative agreements entered into, the number of children contacted and receiving services for each year, and the estimated number of children needing services during the 2 years following the year in which the report is made. The Secretary of the Interior shall include a summary of this information on a biennial basis in the report to the Secretary of Education required under this subsection. The Secretary of Education may require any additional information from the Secretary of the Interior.

(F) Prohibitions.

None of the funds allocated under this paragraph may be used by the Secretary of the Interior for administrative purposes, including child count and the provision of technical assistance.

(5) Plan for coordination of services.

The Secretary of the Interior shall develop and implement a plan for the coordination of services for all Indian children with disabilities residing on reservations covered under this title. Such plan shall provide for the coordination of services benefiting those children from whatever source, including tribes, the Indian Health Service, other BIA divisions, and other Federal agencies. In developing the plan, the Secretary of the Interior shall consult with all interested and involved parties. The plan shall be based on the needs of the children and the system best suited for meeting those needs, and may involve the establishment of cooperative agreements between the BIA, other Federal agencies, and other entities. The plan shall also be distributed upon request to States, State educational agencies and local educational agencies, and other agencies providing services to infants, toddlers, and children with disabilities, to tribes, and to other interested parties.

(6) Establishment of advisory board.

To meet the requirements of section 612(a)(21), the Secretary of the Interior shall establish, under the BIA, an advisory board composed of individuals involved in or concerned with the education and provision of services to Indian infants, toddlers, children, and youth with disabilities, including Indians with disabilities, Indian parents or guardians of such children, teachers, service providers, State and local educational officials, representatives of tribes or tribal organizations, representatives from State Interagency Coordinating Councils under section 641 in States having reservations, and other members representing the various divisions and entities of the BIA. The chairperson shall be selected by the Secretary of the Interior. The advisory board shall —

(A) assist in the coordination of services within the BIA and with other local, State, and Federal agencies in the provision of education for infants, toddlers, and children with disabilities;

(B) advise and assist the Secretary of the Interior in the performance of the Secretary of the Interior's responsibilities described in this subsection;

(C) develop and recommend policies concerning effective inter- and intra-agency collaboration, including modifications to regulations, and the elimination of barriers to inter- and intra-agency programs and activities;

(D) provide assistance and disseminate information on best practices, effective program coordination strategies, and recommendations for improved early intervention services or educational programming for Indian infants, toddlers, and children with disabilities; and

(E) provide assistance in the preparation of information required under paragraph (2)(D).

(7) Annual reports.

(A) In general.

The advisory board established under paragraph (6) shall prepare and submit to the Secretary of the Interior and to Congress an annual report containing a description of the activities of the advisory board for the preceding year.

(B) Availability.

The Secretary of the Interior shall make available to the Secretary of Education the report described in subparagraph (A).

(i) Authorization of appropriations.

For the purpose of carrying out this part, other than section 619, there are authorized to be appropriated —

(1) $12,358,376,571 for fiscal year 2005;
(2) $14,648,647,143 for fiscal year 2006;
(3) $16,938,917,714 for fiscal year 2007;
(4) $19,229,188,286 for fiscal year 2008;
(5) $21,519,458,857 for fiscal year 2009;
(6) $23,809,729,429 for fiscal year 2010;
(7) $26,100,000,000 for fiscal year 2011; and
(8) such sums as may be necessary for fiscal year 2012 and each succeeding fiscal year.

§ 1412. State eligibility

(a) In general.

A State is eligible for assistance under this part for a fiscal year if the State submits a plan that provides assurances to the Secretary that the State has in effect policies and procedures to ensure that the State meets each of the following conditions:

(1) Free appropriate public education.

(A) In general.

A free appropriate public education is available to all children with disabilities residing in the State between the ages of 3 and 21, inclusive, including children with disabilities who have been suspended or expelled from school.

(B) Limitation.

The obligation to make a free appropriate public education available to all children with disabilities does not apply with respect to children —

(i) aged 3 through 5 and 18 through 21 in a State to the extent that its application to those children would be inconsistent with State law or practice, or the order of any court, respecting the provision of public education to children in those age ranges; and

(ii) aged 18 through 21 to the extent that State law does not require that special education and related services under this part be provided to children with disabilities who, in the educational placement prior to their incarceration in an adult correctional facility —

(I) were not actually identified as being a child with a disability under section 602; or

(II) did not have an individualized education program under this part.

(C) State flexibility.

A State that provides early intervention services in accordance with part C to a child who is eligible for services under section 619, is not required to provide such child with a free appropriate public education.

(2) Full educational opportunity goal.

The State has established a goal of providing full educational opportunity to all children with disabilities and a detailed timetable for accomplishing that goal.

(3) Child find.

(A) In general.

All children with disabilities residing in the State, including children with disabilities who are homeless children or are wards of the State and children with disabilities attending private schools, regardless of the severity of their disabilities, and who are in need of special education and related services, are identified, located, and evaluated and a practical method is developed and implemented to determine which children with disabilities are currently receiving needed special education and related services.

(B) Construction.

Nothing in this title requires that children be classified by their disability so long as each child who has a disability listed in section 602 and who, by reason of that disability, needs special education and related services is regarded as a child with a disability under this part.

(4) Individualized education program.

An individualized education program, or an individualized family service plan that meets the requirements of section 636(d), is developed, reviewed, and revised for each child with a disability in accordance with section 614(d).

(5) Least restrictive environment.

(A) In general.

To the maximum extent appropriate, children with disabilities, including children in public or private institutions or other care facilities, are educated with children who are not disabled, and special classes, separate schooling, or other removal of children with disabilities from the regular educational environment occurs only when the nature or severity of the disability of a child is such that education in regular classes with the use of supplementary aids and services cannot be achieved satisfactorily.

(B) Additional requirement.

(i) In general.

A State funding mechanism shall not result in placements that violate the requirements of subparagraph (A), and a State shall not use a funding mechanism by which the State distributes funds on the basis of the type of setting in which a child is served that will result in the failure to provide a child with a disability a free appropriate public education according to the unique needs of the child as described in the child's IEP.

(ii) Assurance.

If the State does not have policies and procedures to ensure compliance with clause (i), the State shall provide the Secretary an assurance that the State will revise the funding mechanism as soon as feasible to ensure that such mechanism does not result in such placements.

(6) Procedural safeguards.

(A) In general.

Children with disabilities and their parents are afforded the procedural safeguards required by section 615.

(B) Additional procedural safeguards.

Procedures to ensure that testing and evaluation materials and procedures utilized for the purposes of evaluation and placement of children with disabilities for services under this title will be selected and administered so as not to be racially or culturally discriminatory. Such materials or procedures shall be provided and administered in the child's native language or mode of communication, unless it clearly is not feasible to do so, and no single procedure shall be the sole criterion for determining an appropriate educational program for a child.

(7) Evaluation.

Children with disabilities are evaluated in accordance with subsections (a) through (c) of section 614.

(8) Confidentiality.

Agencies in the State comply with section 617(c) (relating to the confidentiality of records and information).

(9) Transition from Part C to preschool programs.

Children participating in early intervention programs assisted under part C, and who will participate in preschool programs assisted under this part, experience a smooth and effective transition to those preschool programs in a manner consistent with section 637(a)(9). By the third birthday of such a child, an individualized education program or, if consistent with sections 614(d)(2)(B) and 636(d), an individualized family service plan, has been developed and is being implemented for the child. The local educational agency will participate in transition planning conferences arranged by the designated lead agency under section 635(a)(10).

(10) Children in private schools.

(A) Children enrolled in private schools by their parents.

(i) In general.

To the extent consistent with the number and location of children with disabilities in the State who are enrolled by their parents in private elementary schools and secondary schools in the school district served by a local educational agency, provision is made for the participation of those children in the program assisted or carried out under this part by providing for such children special education and related services in accordance with the following requirements, unless the Secretary has arranged for services to those children under subsection (f):

(I) Amounts to be expended for the provision of those services (including direct services to parentally placed private school children) by the local educational agency shall be equal to a proportionate amount of Federal funds made available under this part.

(II) In calculating the proportionate amount of Federal funds, the local educational agency, after timely and meaningful consultation with representatives of private schools as described in clause (iii), shall conduct a thorough and complete child find process to determine the number of parentally placed children with disabilities attending private schools located in the local educational agency.

(III) Such services to parentally placed private school children with disabilities may be provided to the children on the premises of private, including religious, schools, to the extent consistent with law.

(IV) State and local funds may supplement and in no case shall supplant the proportionate amount of Federal funds required to be expended under this subparagraph.

(V) Each local educational agency shall maintain in its records and provide to the State educational agency the number of children evaluated under this subparagraph, the number of children determined to be children with disabilities under this paragraph, and the number of children served under this paragraph.

(ii) Child find requirement.
(I) In general.
The requirements of paragraph (3) (relating to child find) shall apply with respect to children with disabilities in the State who are enrolled in private, including religious, elementary schools and secondary schools.
(II) Equitable participation.
The child find process shall be designed to ensure the equitable participation of parentally placed private school children with disabilities and an accurate count of such children.
(III) Activities.
In carrying out this clause, the local educational agency, or where applicable, the State educational agency, shall undertake activities similar to those activities undertaken for the agency's public school children.
(IV) Cost.
The cost of carrying out this clause, including individual evaluations, may not be considered in determining whether a local educational agency has met its obligations under clause (i).
(V) Completion period.
Such child find process shall be completed in a time period comparable to that for other students attending public schools in the local educational agency.
(iii) Consultation.
To ensure timely and meaningful consultation, a local educational agency, or where appropriate, a State educational agency, shall consult with private school representatives and representatives of parents of parentally placed private school children with disabilities during the design and development of special education and related services for the children, including regarding —
(I) the child find process and how parentally placed private school children suspected of having a disability can participate equitably, including how parents, teachers, and private school officials will be informed of the process;
(II) the determination of the proportionate amount of Federal funds available to serve parentally placed private school children with disabilities under this subparagraph, including the determination of how the amount was calculated;
(III) the consultation process among the local educational agency, private school officials, and representatives of parents of parentally placed private school children with disabilities, including how such process will operate throughout the school year to ensure that parentally placed private school children with disabilities identified through the child find process can meaningfully participate in special education and related services;
(IV) how, where, and by whom special education and related services will be provided for parentally placed private school children with disabilities, including a discussion of types of services, including direct services and alternate service delivery mechanisms, how such services will be apportioned if funds are insufficient to serve all children, and how and when these decisions will be made; and
(V) how, if the local educational agency disagrees with the views of the private school officials on the provision of services or the types of services, whether provided directly or through a contract, the local educational agency shall provide to the private school officials a written explanation of the reasons why the local educational agency chose not to provide services directly or through a contract.
(iv) Written affirmation.
When timely and meaningful consultation as required by clause (iii) has occurred, the local educational agency shall obtain a written affirmation signed by the representatives of participating private schools, and if such representatives do not provide such affirmation within a reasonable period of time, the local educational agency shall forward the documentation of the consultation process to the State educational agency.
(v) Compliance.
(I) In general.
A private school official shall have the right to submit a complaint to the State educational agency that the local educational agency did not engage in consultation that was meaningful and timely, or did not give due consideration to the views of the private school official.

(II) Procedure.

If the private school official wishes to submit a complaint, the official shall provide the basis of the noncompliance with this subparagraph by the local educational agency to the State educational agency, and the local educational agency shall forward the appropriate documentation to the State educational agency. If the private school official is dissatisfied with the decision of the State educational agency, such official may submit a complaint to the Secretary by providing the basis of the noncompliance with this subparagraph by the local educational agency to the Secretary, and the State educational agency shall forward the appropriate documentation to the Secretary.

(vi) Provision of equitable services.

(I) Directly or through contracts.

The provision of services pursuant to this subparagraph shall be provided —

(aa) by employees of a public agency; or

(bb) through contract by the public agency with an individual, association, agency, organization, or other entity.

(II) Secular, neutral, nonideological.

Special education and related services provided to parentally placed private school children with disabilities, including materials and equipment, shall be secular, neutral, and nonideological.

(vii) Public control of funds.

The control of funds used to provide special education and related services under this subparagraph, and title to materials, equipment, and property purchased with those funds, shall be in a public agency for the uses and purposes provided in this title, and a public agency shall administer the funds and property.

(B) Children placed in, or referred to, private schools by public agencies.

(i) In general.

Children with disabilities in private schools and facilities are provided special education and related services, in accordance with an individualized education program, at no cost to their parents, if such children are placed in, or referred to, such schools or facilities by the State or appropriate local educational agency as the means of carrying out the requirements of this part or any other applicable law requiring the provision of special education and related services to all children with disabilities within such State.

(ii) Standards.

In all cases described in clause (i), the State educational agency shall determine whether such schools and facilities meet standards that apply to State educational agencies and local educational agencies and that children so served have all the rights the children would have if served by such agencies.

(C) Payment for education of children enrolled in private schools without consent of or referral by the public agency.

(i) In general.

Subject to subparagraph (A), this part does not require a local educational agency to pay for the cost of education, including special education and related services, of a child with a disability at a private school or facility if that agency made a free appropriate public education available to the child and the parents elected to place the child in such private school or facility.

(ii) Reimbursement for private school placement.

If the parents of a child with a disability, who previously received special education and related services under the authority of a public agency, enroll the child in a private elementary school or secondary school without the consent of or referral by the public agency, a court or a hearing officer may require the agency to reimburse the parents for the cost of that enrollment if the court or hearing officer finds that the agency had not made a free appropriate public education available to the child in a timely manner prior to that enrollment.

(iii) Limitation on reimbursement.

The cost of reimbursement described in clause (ii) may be reduced or denied —

(I) if —

(aa) at the most recent IEP meeting that the parents attended prior to removal of the child from the public school, the parents did not inform the IEP Team that they were rejecting the placement proposed by the public agency to provide a free appropriate public education to their child, including stating their concerns and their intent to enroll their child in a private school at public expense; or

(bb) 10 business days (including any holidays that occur on a business day) prior to the removal of the child from the public school, the parents did not give written notice to the public agency of the information described in item (aa);

(II) if, prior to the parents' removal of the child from the public school, the public agency informed the parents, through the notice requirements described in section 615(b)(3), of its intent to evaluate the child (including a statement of the purpose of the evaluation that was appropriate and reasonable), but the parents did not make the child available for such evaluation; or

(III) upon a judicial finding of unreasonableness with respect to actions taken by the parents.

(iv) Exception.

Notwithstanding the notice requirement in clause (iii)(I), the cost of reimbursement —

(I) shall not be reduced or denied for failure to provide such notice if —

(aa) the school prevented the parent from providing such notice;

(bb) the parents had not received notice, pursuant to section 615, of the notice requirement in clause (iii)(I); or

(cc) compliance with clause (iii)(I) would likely result in physical harm to the child; and

(II) may, in the discretion of a court or a hearing officer, not be reduced or denied for failure to provide such notice if —

(aa) the parent is illiterate or cannot write in English; or

(bb) compliance with clause (iii)(I) would likely result in serious emotional harm to the child.

(11) State educational agency responsible for general supervision.

(A) In general.

The State educational agency is responsible for ensuring that —

(i) the requirements of this part are met;

(ii) all educational programs for children with disabilities in the State, including all such programs administered by any other State agency or local agency —

(I) are under the general supervision of individuals in the State who are responsible for educational programs for children with disabilities; and

(II) meet the educational standards of the State educational agency; and

(iii) in carrying out this part with respect to homeless children, the requirements of subtitle B of title VII of the McKinney-Vento Homeless Assistance Act (42 U.S.C. 11431 et seq.) are met.

(B) Limitation.

Subparagraph (A) shall not limit the responsibility of agencies in the State other than the State educational agency to provide, or pay for some or all of the costs of, a free appropriate public education for any child with a disability in the State.

(C) Exception.

Notwithstanding subparagraphs (A) and (B), the Governor (or another individual pursuant to State law), consistent with State law, may assign to any public agency in the State the responsibility of ensuring that the requirements of this part are met with respect to children with disabilities who are convicted as adults under State law and incarcerated in adult prisons.

(12) Obligations related to and methods of ensuring services.

(A) Establishing responsibility for services.

The Chief Executive Officer of a State or designee of the officer shall ensure that an interagency agreement or other mechanism for interagency coordination is in effect between each public agency described in subparagraph (B) and the State educational agency, in order to ensure that all services described in subparagraph (B)(i) that are needed to ensure a free appropriate public education are provided, including the provision of such services during the pendency of any dispute under clause (iii). Such agreement or mechanism shall include the following:

(i) Agency financial responsibility.

An identification of, or a method for defining, the financial responsibility of each agency for providing services described in subparagraph (B)(i) to ensure a free appropriate public education to children with disabilities, provided that the financial responsibility of each public agency described in subparagraph (B), including the State medicaid agency and other public insurers of children with disabilities, shall precede the financial responsibility of the local educational agency (or the State agency responsible for developing the child's IEP).

(ii) Conditions and terms of reimbursement.

The conditions, terms, and procedures under which a local educational agency shall be reimbursed by other agencies.

(iii) Interagency disputes.

Procedures for resolving interagency disputes (including procedures under which local educational agencies may initiate proceedings) under the agreement or other mechanism to secure reimbursement from other agencies or otherwise implement the provisions of the agreement or mechanism.

(iv) Coordination of services procedures.

Policies and procedures for agencies to determine and identify the interagency coordination responsibilities of each agency to promote the coordination and timely and appropriate delivery of services described in subparagraph (B)(i).

(B) Obligation of public agency.

(i) In general.

If any public agency other than an educational agency is otherwise obligated under Federal or State law, or assigned responsibility under State policy pursuant to subparagraph (A), to provide or pay for any services that are also considered special education or related services (such as, but not limited to, services described in section 602(1) relating to assistive technology devices, 602(2) relating to assistive technology services, 602(26) relating to related services, 602(33) relating to supplementary aids and services, and 602(34) relating to transition services) that are necessary for ensuring a free appropriate public education to children with disabilities within the State, such public agency shall fulfill that obligation or responsibility, either directly or through contract or other arrangement pursuant to subparagraph (A) or an agreement pursuant to subparagraph (C).

(ii) Reimbursement for services by public agency.

If a public agency other than an educational agency fails to provide or pay for the special education and related services described in clause (i), the local educational agency (or State agency responsible for developing the child's IEP) shall provide or pay for such services to the child. Such local educational agency or State agency is authorized to claim reimbursement for the services from the public agency that failed to provide or pay for such services and such public agency shall reimburse the local educational agency or State agency pursuant to the terms of the interagency agreement or other mechanism described in subparagraph (A)(i) according to the procedures established in such agreement pursuant to subparagraph (A)(ii).

(C) Special rule.

The requirements of subparagraph (A) may be met through —

(i) State statute or regulation;

(ii) signed agreements between respective agency officials that clearly identify the responsibilities of each agency relating to the provision of services; or

(iii) other appropriate written methods as determined by the Chief Executive Officer of the State or designee of the officer and approved by the Secretary.

(13) Procedural requirements relating to local educational agency eligibility.

The State educational agency will not make a final determination that a local educational agency is not eligible for assistance under this part without first affording that agency reasonable notice and an opportunity for a hearing.

(14) Personnel qualifications.

(A) In general.

The State educational agency has established and maintains qualifications to ensure that personnel necessary to carry out this part are appropriately and adequately prepared and trained, including that those personnel have the content knowledge and skills to serve children with disabilities.

(B) Related services personnel and paraprofessionals.

The qualifications under subparagraph (A) include qualifications for related services personnel and paraprofessionals that —

(i) are consistent with any State-approved or State-recognized certification, licensing, registration, or other comparable requirements that apply to the professional discipline in which those personnel are providing special education or related services;

(ii) ensure that related services personnel who deliver services in their discipline or profession meet the requirements of clause (i) and have not had certification or licensure requirements waived on an emergency, temporary, or provisional basis; and

(iii) allow paraprofessionals and assistants who are appropriately trained and supervised, in accordance with State law, regulation, or written policy, in meeting the requirements of this part to be used to assist in the provision of special education and related services under this part to children with disabilities.

(C) Qualifications for special education teachers.

The qualifications described in subparagraph (A) shall ensure that each person employed as a special education teacher in the State who teaches elementary school, middle school, or secondary school is highly qualified by the deadline established in section 1119(a)(2) of the Elementary and Secondary Education Act of 1965.

(D) Policy.

In implementing this section, a State shall adopt a policy that includes a requirement that local educational agencies in the State take measurable steps to recruit, hire, train, and retain highly qualified personnel to provide special education and related services under this part to children with disabilities.

(E) Rule of construction.

Notwithstanding any other individual right of action that a parent or student may maintain under this part, nothing in this paragraph shall be construed to create a right of action on behalf of an individual student for the failure of a particular State educational agency or local educational agency staff person to be highly qualified, or to prevent a parent from filing a complaint about staff qualifications with the State educational agency as provided for under this part.

(15) Performance goals and indicators.

The State —

(A) has established goals for the performance of children with disabilities in the State that —

(i) promote the purposes of this title, as stated in section 601(d);

(ii) are the same as the State's definition of adequate yearly progress, including the State's objectives for progress by children with disabilities, under section 1111(b)(2)(C) of the Elementary and Secondary Education Act of 1965;

(iii) address graduation rates and dropout rates, as well as such other factors as the State may determine; and

(iv) are consistent, to the extent appropriate, with any other goals and standards for children established by the State;

(B) has established performance indicators the State will use to assess progress toward achieving the goals described in subparagraph (A), including measurable annual objectives for progress by children with disabilities under section 1111(b)(2)(C)(v)(II)(cc) of the Elementary and Secondary Education Act of 1965; and

(C) will annually report to the Secretary and the public on the progress of the State, and of children with disabilities in the State, toward meeting the goals established under subparagraph (A), which may include elements of the reports required under section 1111(h) of the Elementary and Secondary Education Act of 1965.

(16) Participation in assessments.

(A) In general.

All children with disabilities are included in all general State and districtwide assessment programs, including assessments described under section 1111 of the Elementary and Secondary Education Act of 1965, with appropriate accommodations and alternate assessments where necessary and as indicated in their respective individualized education programs.

(B) Accommodation guidelines.

The State (or, in the case of a districtwide assessment, the local educational agency) has developed guidelines for the provision of appropriate accommodations.

(C) Alternate assessments.

(i) In general.

The State (or, in the case of a districtwide assessment, the local educational agency) has developed and implemented guidelines for the participation of children with disabilities in alternate assessments for those children who cannot participate in regular assessments under subparagraph (A) with accommodations as indicated in their respective individualized education programs.

(ii) Requirements for alternate assessments.

The guidelines under clause (i) shall provide for alternate assessments that —

(I) are aligned with the State's challenging academic content standards and challenging student academic achievement standards; and

(II) if the State has adopted alternate academic achievement standards permitted under the regulations promulgated to carry out section 1111(b)(1) of the Elementary and Secondary Education Act of 1965, measure the achievement of children with disabilities against those standards.

(iii) Conduct of alternate assessments.

The State conducts the alternate assessments described in this subparagraph.

(D) Reports.

The State educational agency (or, in the case of a districtwide assessment, the local educational agency) makes available to the public, and reports to the public with the same frequency and in the same detail as it reports on the assessment of nondisabled children, the following:

(i) The number of children with disabilities participating in regular assessments, and the number of those children who were provided accommodations in order to participate in those assessments.

(ii) The number of children with disabilities participating in alternate assessments described in subparagraph (C)(ii)(I).

(iii) The number of children with disabilities participating in alternate assessments described in subparagraph (C)(ii)(II).

(iv) The performance of children with disabilities on regular assessments and on alternate assessments (if the number of children with disabilities participating in those assessments is sufficient to yield statistically reliable information and reporting that information will not reveal personally identifiable information about an individual student), compared with the achievement of all children, including children with disabilities, on those assessments.

(E) Universal design.

The State educational agency (or, in the case of a districtwide assessment, the local educational agency) shall, to the extent feasible, use universal design principles in developing and administering any assessments under this paragraph.

(17) Supplementation of state, local, and other federal funds.

(A) Expenditures.

Funds paid to a State under this part will be expended in accordance with all the provisions of this part.

(B) Prohibition against commingling.

Funds paid to a State under this part will not be commingled with State funds.

(C) Prohibition against supplantation and conditions for waiver by secretary.

Except as provided in section 613, funds paid to a State under this part will be used to supplement the level of Federal, State, and local funds (including funds that are not under the direct control of State or local educational agencies) expended for special education and related services provided to children with disabilities under this part and in no case to supplant such Federal, State, and local funds, except that, where the State provides clear and convincing evidence that all children with disabilities have available to them a free appropriate public education, the Secretary may waive, in whole or in part, the requirements of this subparagraph if the Secretary concurs with the evidence provided by the State.

(18) Maintenance of state financial support.

(A) In general.

The State does not reduce the amount

of State financial support for special education and related services for children with disabilities, or otherwise made available because of the excess costs of educating those children, below the amount of that support for the preceding fiscal year.

(B) Reduction of funds for failure to maintain support.

The Secretary shall reduce the allocation of funds under section 611 for any fiscal year following the fiscal year in which the State fails to comply with the requirement of subparagraph (A) by the same amount by which the State fails to meet the requirement.

(C) Waivers for exceptional or uncontrollable circumstances.

The Secretary may waive the requirement of subparagraph (A) for a State, for 1 fiscal year at a time, if the Secretary determines that —

(i) granting a waiver would be equitable due to exceptional or uncontrollable circumstances such as a natural disaster or a precipitous and unforeseen decline in the financial resources of the State; or

(ii) the State meets the standard in paragraph (17)(C) for a waiver of the requirement to supplement, and not to supplant, funds received under this part.

(D) Subsequent years.

If, for any year, a State fails to meet the requirement of subparagraph (A), including any year for which the State is granted a waiver under subparagraph (C), the financial support required of the State in future years under subparagraph (A) shall be the amount that would have been required in the absence of that failure and not the reduced level of the State's support.

(19) Public participation.

Prior to the adoption of any policies and procedures needed to comply with this section (including any amendments to such policies and procedures), the State ensures that there are public hearings, adequate notice of the hearings, and an opportunity for comment available to the general public, including individuals with disabilities and parents of children with disabilities.

(20) Rule of construction.

In complying with paragraphs (17) and (18), a State may not use funds paid to it under this part to satisfy State-law mandated funding obligations to local educational agencies, including funding based on student attendance or enrollment, or inflation.

(21) State advisory panel.

(A) In general.

The State has established and maintains an advisory panel for the purpose of providing policy guidance with respect to special education and related services for children with disabilities in the State.

(B) Membership.

Such advisory panel shall consist of members appointed by the Governor, or any other official authorized under State law to make such appointments, be representative of the State population, and be composed of individuals involved in, or concerned with, the education of children with disabilities, including —

(i) parents of children with disabilities (ages birth through 26);

(ii) individuals with disabilities;

(iii) teachers;

(iv) representatives of institutions of higher education that prepare special education and related services personnel;

(v) State and local education officials, including officials who carry out activities under subtitle B of title VII of the McKinney-Vento Homeless Assistance Act (42 U.S.C. 11431 et seq.);

(vi) administrators of programs for children with disabilities;

(vii) representatives of other State agencies involved in the financing or delivery of related services to children with disabilities;

(viii) representatives of private schools and public charter schools;

(ix) not less than 1 representative of a vocational, community, or business organization concerned with the provision of transition services to children with disabilities;

(x) a representative from the State child welfare agency responsible for foster care; and

(xi) representatives from the State juvenile and adult corrections agencies.

(C) Special rule.

A majority of the members of the panel shall be individuals with disabilities or parents of children with disabilities (ages birth through 26).

(D) Duties.

The advisory panel shall —

(i) advise the State educational agency of unmet needs within the State in the education of children with disabilities;

(ii) comment publicly on any rules or regulations proposed by the State regarding the education of children with disabilities;

(iii) advise the State educational agency in developing evaluations and reporting on data to the Secretary under section 618;

(iv) advise the State educational agency in developing corrective action plans to address findings identified in Federal monitoring reports under this part; and

(v) advise the State educational agency in developing and implementing policies relating to the coordination of services for children with disabilities.

(22) Suspension and expulsion rates.

(A) In general.

The State educational agency examines data, including data disaggregated by race and ethnicity, to determine if significant discrepancies are occurring in the rate of long-term suspensions and expulsions of children with disabilities —

(i) among local educational agencies in the State; or

(ii) compared to such rates for nondisabled children within such agencies.

(B) Review and revision of policies.

If such discrepancies are occurring, the State educational agency reviews and, if appropriate, revises (or requires the affected State or local educational agency to revise) its policies, procedures, and practices relating to the development and implementation of IEPs, the use of positive behavioral interventions and supports, and procedural safeguards, to ensure that such policies, procedures, and practices comply with this title.

(23) Access to instructional materials.

(A) In general.

The State adopts the National Instructional Materials Accessibility Standard for the purposes of providing instructional materials to blind persons or other persons with print disabilities, in a timely manner after the publication of the National Instructional Materials Accessibility Standard in the Federal Register.

(B) Rights of state educational agency.

Nothing in this paragraph shall be construed to require any State educational agency to coordinate with the National Instructional Materials Access Center. If a State educational agency chooses not to coordinate with the National Instructional Materials Access Center, such agency shall provide an assurance to the Secretary that the agency will provide instructional materials to blind persons or other persons with print disabilities in a timely manner.

(C) Preparation and delivery of files.

If a State educational agency chooses to coordinate with the National Instructional Materials Access Center, not later than 2 years after the date of enactment of the Individuals with Disabilities Education Improvement Act of 2004, the agency, as part of any print instructional materials adoption process, procurement contract, or other practice or instrument used for purchase of print instructional materials, shall enter into a written contract with the publisher of the print instructional materials to —

(i) require the publisher to prepare and, on or before delivery of the print instructional materials, provide to the National Instructional Materials Access Center electronic files containing the contents of the print instructional materials using the National Instructional Materials Accessibility Standard; or

(ii) purchase instructional materials from the publisher that are produced in, or may be rendered in, specialized formats.

(D) Assistive technology.

In carrying out this paragraph, the State educational agency, to the maximum extent possible, shall work collaboratively with the State agency responsible for assistive technology programs.

(E) Definitions.

In this paragraph:

(i) National instructional materials access center.

The term "National Instructional Materials Access Center" means the center established pursuant to section 674(e).

(ii) National instructional materials accessibility standard.

The term "National Instructional Materials Accessibility Standard" has the meaning given the term in section 674(e)(3)(A).

(iii) Specialized formats.

The term "specialized formats" has the meaning given the term in section 674(e)(3)(D).

(24) Overidentification and disproportionality.

The State has in effect, consistent with the purposes of this title and with section 618(d), policies and procedures designed to prevent the inappropriate overidentification or disproportionate representation by race and ethnicity of children as children with disabilities, including children with disabilities with a particular impairment described in section 602.

(25) Prohibition on mandatory medication.

(A) In general.

The State educational agency shall prohibit State and local educational agency personnel from requiring a child to obtain a prescription for a substance covered by the Controlled Substances Act (21 U.S.C. 801 et seq.) as a condition of attending school, receiving an evaluation under subsection (a) or (c) of section 614, or receiving services under this title.

(B) Rule of construction.

Nothing in subparagraph (A) shall be construed to create a Federal prohibition against teachers and other school personnel consulting or sharing classroom-based observations with parents or guardians regarding a student's academic and functional performance, or behavior in the classroom or school, or regarding the need for evaluation for special education or related services under paragraph (3).

(b) State educational agency as provider of free appropriate public education or direct services.

If the State educational agency provides free appropriate public education to children with disabilities, or provides direct services to such children, such agency —

(1) shall comply with any additional requirements of section 613(a), as if such agency were a local educational agency; and

(2) may use amounts that are otherwise available to such agency under this part to serve those children without regard to section 613(a)(2)(A)(i) (relating to excess costs).

(c) Exception for prior state plans.

(1) In general.

If a State has on file with the Secretary policies and procedures that demonstrate that such State meets any requirement of subsection (a), including any policies and procedures filed under this part as in effect before the effective date of the Individuals with Disabilities Education Improvement Act of 2004, the Secretary shall consider such State to have met such requirement for purposes of receiving a grant under this part.

(2) Modifications made by state.

Subject to paragraph (3), an application submitted by a State in accordance with this section shall remain in effect until the State submits to the Secretary such modifications as the State determines necessary. This section shall apply to a modification to an application to the same extent and in the same manner as this section applies to the original plan.

(3) Modifications required by the secretary.

If, after the effective date of the Individuals with Disabilities Education Improvement Act of 2004, the provisions of this title are amended (or the regulations developed to carry out this title are amended), there is a new interpretation of this title by a Federal court or a State's highest court, or there is an official finding of noncompliance with Federal law or regulations, then the Secretary may require a State to modify its application only to the extent necessary to ensure the State's compliance with this part.

(d) Approval by the secretary.

(1) In general.

If the Secretary determines that a State is eligible to receive a grant under this part, the Secretary shall notify the State of that determination.

(2) Notice and hearing.

The Secretary shall not make a final determination that a State is not eligible to receive a grant under this part until after providing the State —

(A) with reasonable notice; and

(B) with an opportunity for a hearing.

(e) Assistance under other federal programs.

Nothing in this title permits a State to reduce medical and other assistance available, or to alter eligibility, under titles V and XIX of the Social Security Act with respect to the provision of a free appropriate public education for children with disabilities in the State.

(f) By-pass for children in private schools.

(1) In general.

If, on the date of enactment of the Education of the Handicapped Act Amendments of 1983, a State educational agency was prohibited by law from providing for the equitable participation in special programs of children with disabilities enrolled in private elementary schools and secondary schools as required by subsection (a)(10)(A), or if the Secretary determines that a State educational agency, local educational agency, or other entity has substantially failed or is unwilling to provide for such equitable participation, then the Secretary shall, notwithstanding such provision of law, arrange for the provision of services to such children through arrangements that shall be subject to the requirements of such subsection.

(2) Payments.

(A) Determination of amounts.

If the Secretary arranges for services pursuant to this subsection, the Secretary, after consultation with the appropriate public and private school officials, shall pay to the provider of such services for a fiscal year an amount per child that does not exceed the amount determined by dividing —

(i) the total amount received by the State under this part for such fiscal year; by

(ii) the number of children with disabilities served in the prior year, as reported to the Secretary by the State under section 618.

(B) Withholding of certain amounts.

Pending final resolution of any investigation or complaint that may result in a determination under this subsection, the Secretary may withhold from the allocation of the affected State educational agency the amount the Secretary estimates will be necessary to pay the cost of services described in subparagraph (A).

(C) Period of payments.

The period under which payments are made under subparagraph (A) shall continue until the Secretary determines that there will no longer be any failure or inability on the part of the State educational agency to meet the requirements of subsection (a)(10)(A).

(3) Notice and hearing.

(A) In general.

The Secretary shall not take any final action under this subsection until the State educational agency affected by such action has had an opportunity, for not less than 45 days after receiving written notice thereof, to submit written objections and to appear before the Secretary or the Secretary's designee to show cause why such action should not be taken.

(B) Review of action.

If a State educational agency is dissatisfied with the Secretary's final action after a proceeding under subparagraph (A), such agency may, not later than 60 days after notice of such action, file with the United States court of appeals for the circuit in which such State is located a petition for review of that action. A copy of the petition shall be forthwith transmitted by the clerk of the court to the Secretary. The Secretary thereupon shall file in the court the record of the proceedings on which the Secretary based the Secretary's action, as provided in section 2112 of title 28, United States Code.

(C) Review of findings of fact.

The findings of fact by the Secretary, if supported by substantial evidence, shall be conclusive, but the court, for good cause shown, may remand the case to the Secretary to take further evidence, and the Secretary may thereupon make new or modified findings of fact and may modify the Secretary's previous action, and shall file in the court the record of the further proceedings. Such new or modified findings of fact shall likewise be conclusive if supported by substantial evidence.

(D) Jurisdiction of court of appeals; review by united states supreme court.

Upon the filing of a petition under subparagraph (B), the United States court of appeals shall have jurisdiction to affirm the action of the Secretary or to set it aside, in whole or in part. The judgment of the court shall be subject to review by the Supreme Court of the United States upon certiorari or certification as provided in section 1254 of title 28, United States Code.

§ 1413. Local educational agency eligibility

(a) In general.

A local educational agency is eligible for assistance under this part for a fiscal year if such agency submits a plan that provides assurances to the State educational agency that the local educational agency meets each of the following conditions:

(1) Consistency with state policies.

The local educational agency, in providing for the education of children with disabilities within its jurisdiction, has in effect policies, procedures, and programs that are consistent with the State policies and procedures established under section 612.

(2) Use of amounts.

(A) In general.

Amounts provided to the local educational agency under this part shall be expended in accordance with the applicable provisions of this part and —

(i) shall be used only to pay the excess costs of providing special education and related services to children with disabilities;

(ii) shall be used to supplement State, local, and other Federal funds and not to supplant such funds; and

(iii) shall not be used, except as provided in subparagraphs (B) and (C), to reduce the level of expenditures for the education of children with disabilities made by the local educational agency from local funds below the level of those expenditures for the preceding fiscal year.

(B) Exception.

Notwithstanding the restriction in subparagraph (A)(iii), a local educational agency may reduce the level of expenditures where such reduction is attributable to —

(i) the voluntary departure, by retirement or otherwise, or departure for just cause, of special education personnel;

(ii) a decrease in the enrollment of children with disabilities;

(iii) the termination of the obligation of the agency, consistent with this part, to provide a program of special education to a particular child with a disability that is an exceptionally costly program, as determined by the State educational agency, because the child —

(I) has left the jurisdiction of the agency;

(II) has reached the age at which the obligation of the agency to provide a free appropriate public education to the child has terminated; or

(III) no longer needs such program of special education; or

(iv) the termination of costly expenditures for long-term purchases, such as the acquisition of equipment or the construction of school facilities.

(C) Adjustment to local fiscal effort in certain fiscal years.

(i) Amounts in excess.

Notwithstanding clauses (ii) and (iii) of subparagraph (A), for any fiscal year for which the allocation received by a local educational agency under section 611(f) exceeds the amount the local educational agency received for the previous fiscal year, the local educational agency may reduce the level of expenditures otherwise required by subparagraph (A)(iii) by not more than 50 percent of the amount of such excess.

(ii) Use of amounts to carry out activities under ESEA.

If a local educational agency exercises the authority under clause (i), the agency shall use an amount of local funds equal to the reduction in expenditures under clause (i) to carry out activities authorized under the Elementary and Secondary Education Act of 1965.

(iii) State prohibition.

Notwithstanding clause (i), if a State educational agency determines that a local educational agency is unable to establish and maintain programs of free appropriate public education that meet the requirements of subsection (a) or the State educational agency has taken action against the local educational agency under section 616, the State educational agency shall prohibit the local educational agency from reducing the level of expenditures under clause (i) for that fiscal year.

(iv) Special rule.

The amount of funds expended by a local educational agency under subsection (f) shall count toward the maximum amount of expenditures such local educational agency may reduce under clause (i).

(D) Schoolwide programs under Title I of the ESEA. —

Notwithstanding subparagraph (A) or any other provision of this part, a local educational agency may use funds received under this part for any fiscal year to carry out a schoolwide program under section 1114 of the Elementary and Secondary Education Act of 1965, except that the amount so used in any such program shall not exceed —

(i) the number of children with disabilities participating in the schoolwide program; multiplied by

(ii)(I) the amount received by the local educational agency under this part for that fiscal year; divided by

(II) the number of children with disabilities in the jurisdiction of that agency.

(3) Personnel development.

The local educational agency shall ensure that all personnel necessary to carry out this part are appropriately and adequately prepared, subject to the requirements of section 612(a)(14) and section 2122 of the Elementary and Secondary Education Act of 1965.

(4) Permissive use of funds.

(A) Uses.

Notwithstanding paragraph (2)(A) or section 612(a)(17)(B) (relating to commingled funds), funds provided to the local educational agency under this part may be used for the following activities:

(i) Services and aids that also benefit nondisabled children.

For the costs of special education and related services, and supplementary aids and services, provided in a regular class or other education-related setting to a child with a disability in accordance with the individualized education program of the child, even if 1 or more nondisabled children benefit from such services.

(ii) Early intervening services.

To develop and implement coordinated, early intervening educational services in accordance with subsection (f).

(iii) High cost education and related services.

To establish and implement cost or risk sharing funds, consortia, or cooperatives for the local educational agency itself, or for local educational agencies working in a consortium of which the local educational agency is a part, to pay for high cost special education and related services.

(B) Administrative case management.

A local educational agency may use funds received under this part to purchase appropriate technology for recordkeeping, data collection, and related case management activities of teachers and related services personnel providing services described in the individualized education program of children with disabilities, that is needed for the implementation of such case management activities.

(5) Treatment of charter schools and their students.

In carrying out this part with respect to charter schools that are public schools of the local educational agency, the local educational agency —

(A) serves children with disabilities attending those charter schools in the same manner as the local educational agency serves children with disabilities in its other schools, including providing supplementary and related services on site at the charter school to the same extent to which the local educational agency has a policy or practice of providing such services on the site to its other public schools; and

(B) provides funds under this part to those charter schools —

(i) on the same basis as the local educational agency provides funds to the local educational agency's other public schools, including proportional distribution based on relative enrollment of children with disabilities; and

(ii) at the same time as the agency distributes other Federal funds to the agency's other public schools, consistent with the State's charter school law.

(6) Purchase of instructional materials.

(A) In general.

Not later than 2 years after the date of enactment of the Individuals with Disabilities Education Improvement Act of 2004, a local educational agency that chooses to coordinate with the National Instructional Materials Access Center, when purchasing print instructional materials, shall acquire the print instructional materials in the same manner and subject to the same conditions as a State educational agency acquires print instructional materials under section 612(a)(23).

(B) Rights of local educational agency.

Nothing in this paragraph shall be construed to require a local educational agency to coordinate with the National Instructional Materials Access Center. If a local educational agency chooses not to coordinate with the National Instructional Materials Access Center, the local educational agency shall provide an assurance to the State educational agency that the local educational agency will provide instructional materials to blind persons or other persons with print disabilities in a timely manner.

(7) Information for state educational agency.

The local educational agency shall provide the State educational agency with information necessary to enable the State educational agency to carry out its duties under this part, including, with respect to paragraphs (15) and (16) of section 612(a), information relating to the performance of children with disabilities participating in programs carried out under this part.

(8) Public information.

The local educational agency shall make available to parents of children with disabilities and to the general public all documents relating to the eligibility of such agency under this part.

(9) Records regarding migratory children with disabilities.

The local educational agency shall cooperate in the Secretary's efforts under section 1308 of the Elementary and Secondary Education Act of 1965 to ensure the linkage of records pertaining to migratory children with a disability for the purpose of electronically exchanging, among the States, health and educational information regarding such children.

(b) Exception for prior local plans.

(1) In general.

If a local educational agency or State agency has on file with the State educational agency policies and procedures that demonstrate that such local educational agency, or such State agency, as the case may be, meets any requirement of subsection (a), including any policies and procedures filed under this part as in effect before the effective date of the Individuals with Disabilities Education Improvement Act of 2004, the State educational agency shall consider such local educational agency or State agency, as the case may be, to have met such requirement for purposes of receiving assistance under this part.

(2) Modification made by local educational agency.

Subject to paragraph (3), an application submitted by a local educational agency in accordance with this section shall remain in effect until the local educational agency submits to the State educational agency such modifications as the local educational agency determines necessary.

(3) Modifications required by state educational agency.

If, after the effective date of the Individuals with Disabilities Education Improvement Act of 2004, the provisions of this title are amended (or the regulations developed to carry out this title are amended), there is a new interpretation of this title by Federal or State courts, or there is an official finding of noncompliance with Federal or State law or regulations, then the State educational agency may require a local educational agency to modify its application only to the extent necessary to ensure the local educational agency's compliance with this part or State law.

(c) Notification of local educational agency or state agency in case of ineligibility.

If the State educational agency determines that a local educational agency or State agency is not eligible under this section, then the State educational agency shall notify the local educational agency or State agency, as the case may be, of that determination and shall provide such local educational agency or State agency with reasonable notice and an opportunity for a hearing.

(d) Local educational agency compliance.

(1) In general.

If the State educational agency, after reasonable notice and an opportunity for a hearing, finds that a local educational agency or State agency that has been determined to be eligible under this section is failing to comply with any requirement described in subsection (a), the State educational agency shall reduce or shall not provide any further payments to the local educational agency or State agency until the State educational agency is satisfied that the local educational agency or State agency, as the case may be, is complying with that requirement.

(2) Additional requirement.

Any State agency or local educational agency in receipt of a notice described in paragraph (1) shall, by means of public notice, take such measures as may be necessary to bring the pendency of an action pursuant to this subsection to the attention of the public within the jurisdiction of such agency.

(3) Consideration.

In carrying out its responsibilities under paragraph (1), the State educational agency shall consider any decision made in a hearing held under section 615 that is adverse to the local educational agency or State agency involved in that decision.

(e) Joint establishment of eligibility.

(1) Joint establishment.

(A) In general.

A State educational agency may require a local educational agency to establish its eligibility jointly with another local educational agency if the State educational agency determines that the local educational agency will be ineligible under this section because the local educational agency will not be able to establish and maintain programs of sufficient size and scope to effectively meet the needs of children with disabilities.

(B) Charter school exception.

A State educational agency may not require a charter school that is a local educational agency to jointly establish its eligibility under subparagraph (A) unless the charter school is explicitly permitted to do so under the State's charter school law.

(2) Amount of payments.

If a State educational agency requires the joint establishment of eligibility under paragraph (1), the total amount of funds made available to the affected local educational agencies shall be equal to the sum of the payments that each such local educational agency would have received under section 611(f) if such agencies were eligible for such payments.

(3) Requirements.

Local educational agencies that establish joint eligibility under this subsection shall —

(A) adopt policies and procedures that are consistent with the State's policies and procedures under section 612(a); and

(B) be jointly responsible for implementing programs that receive assistance under this part.

(4) Requirements for educational service agencies.

(A) In general.

If an educational service agency is required by State law to carry out programs under this part, the joint responsibilities given to local educational agencies under this subsection shall —

(i) not apply to the administration and disbursement of any payments received by that educational service agency; and

(ii) be carried out only by that educational service agency.

(B) Additional requirement.

Notwithstanding any other provision of this subsection, an educational service agency shall provide for the education of children with disabilities in the least restrictive environment, as required by section 612(a)(5).

(f) Early intervening services.

(1) In general.

A local educational agency may not use more than 15 percent of the amount such agency receives under this part for any fiscal year, less any amount reduced by the agency pursuant to subsection (a)(2)(C), if any, in combination with other amounts (which may include amounts other than education funds), to develop and implement coordinated, early intervening services, which may include interagency financing structures, for students in kindergarten through grade 12 (with a particular emphasis on students in kindergarten through grade 3) who have not been identified as needing special education or related services but who need additional academic and behavioral support to succeed in a general education environment.

(2) Activities.

In implementing coordinated, early intervening services under this subsection, a local educational agency may carry out activities that include —

(A) professional development (which may be provided by entities other than local educational agencies) for teachers and other school staff to enable such personnel to deliver scientifically based academic instruction and behavioral interventions, including scientifically based literacy instruction, and, where appropriate, instruction on the use of adaptive and instructional software; and

(B) providing educational and behavioral evaluations, services, and supports, including scientifically based literacy instruction.

(3) Construction.

Nothing in this subsection shall be construed to limit or create a right to a free appropriate public education under this part.

(4) Reporting.

Each local educational agency that develops and maintains coordinated, early intervening services under this subsection shall annually report to the State educational agency on —

(A) the number of students served under this subsection; and

(B) the number of students served under this subsection who subsequently receive special education and related services under this title during the preceding 2-year period.

(5) Coordination with Elementary and Secondary Education Act of 1965.

Funds made available to carry out this subsection may be used to carry out coordinated, early intervening services aligned with activities funded by, and carried out under, the Elementary and Secondary Education Act of 1965 if such funds are used to supplement, and not supplant, funds made available under the Elementary and Secondary Education Act of 1965 for the activities and services assisted under this subsection.

(g) Direct services by the state educational agency.

(1) In general.

A State educational agency shall use the payments that would otherwise have been available to a local educational agency or to a State agency to provide special education and related services directly to children with disabilities residing in the area served by that local educational agency, or for whom that State agency is responsible, if the State educational agency determines that the local educational agency or State agency, as the case may be —

(A) has not provided the information needed to establish the eligibility of such local educational agency or State agency under this section;

(B) is unable to establish and maintain programs of free appropriate public education that meet the requirements of subsection (a);

(C) is unable or unwilling to be consolidated with 1 or more local educational agencies in order to establish and maintain such programs; or

(D) has 1 or more children with disabilities who can best be served by a regional or State program or service delivery system designed to meet the needs of such children.

(2) Manner and location of education and services.

The State educational agency may provide special education and related services under paragraph (1) in such manner and at such locations (including regional or State centers) as the State educational agency considers appropriate. Such education and services shall be provided in accordance with this part.

(h) State agency eligibility.

Any State agency that desires to receive a subgrant for any fiscal year under section 611(f) shall demonstrate to the satisfaction of the State educational agency that —

(1) all children with disabilities who are

participating in programs and projects funded under this part receive a free appropriate public education, and that those children and their parents are provided all the rights and procedural safeguards described in this part; and

(2) the agency meets such other conditions of this section as the Secretary determines to be appropriate.

(i) Disciplinary information.

The State may require that a local educational agency include in the records of a child with a disability a statement of any current or previous disciplinary action that has been taken against the child and transmit such statement to the same extent that such disciplinary information is included in, and transmitted with, the student records of nondisabled children. The statement may include a description of any behavior engaged in by the child that required disciplinary action, a description of the disciplinary action taken, and any other information that is relevant to the safety of the child and other individuals involved with the child. If the State adopts such a policy, and the child transfers from 1 school to another, the transmission of any of the child's records shall include both the child's current individualized education program and any such statement of current or previous disciplinary action that has been taken against the child.

(j) State agency flexibility.

(1) Adjustment to state fiscal effort in certain fiscal years.

For any fiscal year for which the allotment received by a State under section 611 exceeds the amount the State received for the previous fiscal year and if the State in school year 2003-2004 or any subsequent school year pays or reimburses all local educational agencies within the State from State revenue 100 percent of the non-Federal share of the costs of special education and related services, the State educational agency, notwithstanding paragraphs (17) and (18) of section 612(a) and section 612(b), may reduce the level of expenditures from State sources for the education of children with disabilities by not more than 50 percent of the amount of such excess.

(2) Prohibition.

Notwithstanding paragraph (1), if the Secretary determines that a State educational agency is unable to establish, maintain, or oversee programs of free appropriate public education that meet the requirements of this part, or that the State needs assistance, intervention, or substantial intervention under section 616(d)(2)(A), the Secretary shall prohibit the State educational agency from exercising the authority in paragraph (1).

(3) Education activities.

If a State educational agency exercises the authority under paragraph (1), the agency shall use funds from State sources, in an amount equal to the amount of the reduction under paragraph (1), to support activities authorized under the Elementary and Secondary Education Act of 1965 or to support need based student or teacher higher education programs.

(4) Report.

For each fiscal year for which a State educational agency exercises the authority under paragraph (1), the State educational agency shall report to the Secretary the amount of expenditures reduced pursuant to such paragraph and the activities that were funded pursuant to paragraph (3).

(5) Limitation.

Notwithstanding paragraph (1), a State educational agency may not reduce the level of expenditures described in paragraph (1) if any local educational agency in the State would, as a result of such reduction, receive less than 100 percent of the amount necessary to ensure that all children with disabilities served by the local educational agency receive a free appropriate public education from the combination of Federal funds received under this title and State funds received from the State educational agency.

§ 1414. Evaluations, eligibility determinations, individualized education programs, and educational placements

(a) Evaluations and reevaluations

(1) Initial evaluations

(A) In general

A State educational agency, other State agency, or local educational agency shall conduct a full and individual initial evaluation in accordance with this paragraph and subsection (b), before the initial provision of special education and related services to a child with a disability under this part.

(B) Request for initial evaluation.

Consistent with subparagraph (D), either a parent of a child, or a State educational agency, other State agency, or local educational agency may initiate a request for an initial evaluation to determine if the child is a child with a disability.

(C) Procedures.

(i) In general.

Such initial evaluation shall consist of procedures —

(I) to determine whether a child is a child with a disability (as defined in section 602) within 60 days of receiving parental consent for the evaluation, or, if the State establishes a timeframe within which the evaluation must be conducted, within such timeframe; and

(II) to determine the educational needs of such child.

(ii) Exception.

The relevant timeframe in clause (i)(I) shall not apply to a local educational agency if —

(I) a child enrolls in a school served by the local educational agency after the relevant timeframe in clause (i)(I) has begun and prior to a determination by the child's previous local educational agency as to whether the child is a child with a disability (as defined in section 602), but only if the subsequent local educational agency is making sufficient progress to ensure a prompt completion of the evaluation, and the parent and subsequent local educational agency agree to a specific time when the evaluation will be completed; or

(II) the parent of a child repeatedly fails or refuses to produce the child for the evaluation.

(D) Parental consent.

(i) In general.

(I) Consent for initial evaluation.

The agency proposing to conduct an initial evaluation to determine if the child qualifies as a child with a disability as defined in section 602 shall obtain informed consent from the parent of such child before conducting the evaluation. Parental consent for evaluation shall not be construed as consent for placement for receipt of special education and related services.

(II) Consent for services.

An agency that is responsible for making a free appropriate public education available to a child with a disability under this part shall seek to obtain informed consent from the parent of such child before providing special education and related services to the child.

(ii) Absence of consent.

(I) For initial evaluation.

If the parent of such child does not provide consent for an initial evaluation under clause (i)(I), or the parent fails to respond to a request to provide the consent, the local educational agency may pursue the initial evaluation of the child by utilizing the procedures described in section 615, except to the extent inconsistent with State law relating to such parental consent.

(II) For services.

If the parent of such child refuses to consent to services under clause (i)(II), the local educational agency shall not provide special education and related services to the child by utilizing the procedures described in section 615.

(III) Effect on agency obligations.

If the parent of such child refuses to consent to the receipt of special education and related services, or the parent fails to respond to a request to provide such consent —

(aa) the local educational agency shall not be considered to be in violation of the requirement to make available a free appropriate public education to the child for the failure to provide such child with the special education and related services for which the local educational agency requests such consent; and

(bb) the local educational agency shall not be required to convene an IEP meeting or develop an IEP under this section for the child for the special education and related services for which the local educational agency requests such consent.

(iii) Consent for wards of the state.
(I) In general.
If the child is a ward of the State and is not residing with the child's parent, the agency shall make reasonable efforts to obtain the informed consent from the parent (as defined in section 602) of the child for an initial evaluation to determine whether the child is a child with a disability.
(II) Exception.
The agency shall not be required to obtain informed consent from the parent of a child for an initial evaluation to determine whether the child is a child with a disability if —

(aa) despite reasonable efforts to do so, the agency cannot discover the whereabouts of the parent of the child;
(bb) the rights of the parents of the child have been terminated in accordance with State law; or
(cc) the rights of the parent to make educational decisions have been subrogated by a judge in accordance with State law and consent for an initial evaluation has been given by an individual appointed by the judge to represent the child.
(E) Rule of construction.
The screening of a student by a teacher or specialist to determine appropriate instructional strategies for curriculum implementation shall not be considered to be an evaluation for eligibility for special education and related services.
(2) Reevaluations.
(A) In general.
A local educational agency shall ensure that a reevaluation of each child with a disability is conducted in accordance with subsections (b) and (c) —
(i) if the local educational agency determines that the educational or related services needs, including improved academic achievement and functional performance, of the child warrant a reevaluation; or
(ii) if the child's parents or teacher requests a reevaluation.
(B) Limitation.
A reevaluation conducted under subparagraph (A) shall occur —
(i) not more frequently than once a year, unless the parent and the local educational agency agree otherwise; and
(ii) at least once every 3 years, unless the parent and the local educational agency agree that a reevaluation is unnecessary.
(b) Evaluation procedures.
(1) Notice.
The local educational agency shall provide notice to the parents of a child with a disability, in accordance with subsections (b)(3), (b)(4), and (c) of section 615, that describes any evaluation procedures such agency proposes to conduct.
(2) Conduct of evaluation.
In conducting the evaluation, the local educational agency shall —
(A) use a variety of assessment tools and strategies to gather relevant functional, developmental, and academic information, including information provided by the parent, that may assist in determining —
(i) whether the child is a child with a disability; and
(ii) the content of the child's individualized education program, including information related to enabling the child to be involved in and progress in the general education curriculum, or, for preschool children, to participate in appropriate activities;
(B) not use any single measure or assessment as the sole criterion for determining whether a child is a child with a disability or determining an appropriate educational program for the child; and
(C) use technically sound instruments that may assess the relative contribution of cognitive and behavioral factors, in addition to physical or developmental factors.
(3) Additional requirements.
Each local educational agency shall ensure that —
(A) assessments and other evaluation materials used to assess a child under this section —
(i) are selected and administered so as not to be discriminatory on a racial or cultural basis;
(ii) are provided and administered in the language and form most likely to yield accurate information on what the child knows and can do academically, developmentally, and functionally, unless it is not feasible to so provide or administer;

(iii) are used for purposes for which the assessments or measures are valid and reliable;

(iv) are administered by trained and knowledgeable personnel; and

(v) are administered in accordance with any instructions provided by the producer of such assessments;

(B) the child is assessed in all areas of suspected disability;

(C) assessment tools and strategies that provide relevant information that directly assists persons in determining the educational needs of the child are provided; and

(D) assessments of children with disabilities who transfer from 1 school district to another school district in the same academic year are coordinated with such children's prior and subsequent schools, as necessary and as expeditiously as possible, to ensure prompt completion of full evaluations.

(4) Determination of eligibility and educational need.

Upon completion of the administration of assessments and other evaluation measures —

(A) the determination of whether the child is a child with a disability as defined in section 602(3) and the educational needs of the child shall be made by a team of qualified professionals and the parent of the child in accordance with paragraph (5); and

(B) a copy of the evaluation report and the documentation of determination of eligibility shall be given to the parent.

(5) Special rule for eligibility determination.

In making a determination of eligibility under paragraph (4)(A), a child shall not be determined to be a child with a disability if the determinant factor for such determination is —

(A) lack of appropriate instruction in reading, including in the essential components of reading instruction (as defined in section 1208(3) of the Elementary and Secondary Education Act of 1965);

(B) lack of instruction in math; or

(C) limited English proficiency.

(6) Specific learning disabilities.

(A) In general.

Notwithstanding section 607(b), when determining whether a child has a specific learning disability as defined in section 602, a local educational agency shall not be required to take into consideration whether a child has a severe discrepancy between achievement and intellectual ability in oral expression, listening comprehension, written expression, basic reading skill, reading comprehension, mathematical calculation, or mathematical reasoning.

(B) Additional authority.

In determining whether a child has a specific learning disability, a local educational agency may use a process that determines if the child responds to scientific, research-based intervention as a part of the evaluation procedures described in paragraphs (2) and (3).

(c) Additional requirements for evaluation and reevaluations.

(1) Review of existing evaluation data.

As part of an initial evaluation (if appropriate) and as part of any reevaluation under this section, the IEP Team and other qualified professionals, as appropriate, shall —

(A) review existing evaluation data on the child, including —

(i) evaluations and information provided by the parents of the child;

(ii) current classroom-based, local, or State assessments, and classroom-based observations; and

(iii) observations by teachers and related services providers; and

(B) on the basis of that review, and input from the child's parents, identify what additional data, if any, are needed to determine —

(i) whether the child is a child with a disability as defined in section 602(3), and the educational needs of the child, or, in case of a reevaluation of a child, whether the child continues to have such a disability and such educational needs;

(ii) the present levels of academic achievement and related developmental needs of the child;

(iii) whether the child needs special education and related services, or in the case of a reevaluation of a child, whether the child continues to need special education and related services; and

(iv) whether any additions or modifications to the special education and related services are needed to enable the child to meet the measurable annual goals set out in the individualized education program of the child and to participate, as appropriate, in the general education curriculum.

(2) Source of data.

The local educational agency shall administer such assessments and other evaluation measures as may be needed to produce the data identified by the IEP Team under paragraph (1)(B).

(3) Parental consent.

Each local educational agency shall obtain informed parental consent, in accordance with subsection (a)(1)(D), prior to conducting any reevaluation of a child with a disability, except that such informed parental consent need not be obtained if the local educational agency can demonstrate that it had taken reasonable measures to obtain such consent and the child's parent has failed to respond.

(4) Requirements if additional data are not needed.

If the IEP Team and other qualified professionals, as appropriate, determine that no additional data are needed to determine whether the child continues to be a child with a disability and to determine the child's educational needs, the local educational agency —

(A) shall notify the child's parents of —

(i) that determination and the reasons for the determination; and

(ii) the right of such parents to request an assessment to determine whether the child continues to be a child with a disability and to determine the child's educational needs; and

(B) shall not be required to conduct such an assessment unless requested to by the child's parents.

(5) Evaluations before change in eligibility.

(A) In general.

Except as provided in subparagraph (B), a local educational agency shall evaluate a child with a disability in accordance with this section before determining that the child is no longer a child with a disability.

(B) Exception.

(i) In general.

The evaluation described in subparagraph (A) shall not be required before the termination of a child's eligibility under this part due to graduation from secondary school with a regular diploma, or due to exceeding the age eligibility for a free appropriate public education under State law.

(ii) Summary of performance.

For a child whose eligibility under this part terminates under circumstances described in clause (i), a local educational agency shall provide the child with a summary of the child's academic achievement and functional performance, which shall include recommendations on how to assist the child in meeting the child's postsecondary goals.

(d) Individualized education programs.

(1) definitions.

In this title:

(A) Individualized education program.

(i) In general.

The term "individualized education program" or "IEP" means a written statement for each child with a disability that is developed, reviewed, and revised in accordance with this section and that includes —

(I) a statement of the child's present levels of academic achievement and functional performance, including —

(aa) how the child's disability affects the child's involvement and progress in the general education curriculum;

(bb) for preschool children, as appropriate, how the disability affects the child's participation in appropriate activities; and

(cc) for children with disabilities who take alternate assessments aligned to alternate achievement standards, a description of benchmarks or short-term objectives;

(II) a statement of measurable annual goals, including academic and functional goals, designed to —

(aa) meet the child's needs that result from the child's disability to enable the child to be involved in and make progress in the general education curriculum; and

(bb) meet each of the child's other educational needs that result from the child's disability;

(III) a description of how the child's progress toward meeting the annual goals described in subclause (II) will be measured and when periodic reports on the progress the child is making toward meeting the annual goals (such as through the use of quarterly or other periodic reports, concurrent with the issuance of report cards) will be provided;

(IV) a statement of the special education and related services and supplementary aids and services, based on peer-reviewed research to the extent practicable, to be provided to the child, or on behalf of the child, and a statement of the program modifications or supports for school personnel that will be provided for the child —

(aa) to advance appropriately toward attaining the annual goals;

(bb) to be involved in and make progress in the general education curriculum in accordance with subclause (I) and to participate in extracurricular and other nonacademic activities; and

(cc) to be educated and participate with other children with disabilities and nondisabled children in the activities described in this subparagraph;

(V) an explanation of the extent, if any, to which the child will not participate with nondisabled children in the regular class and in the activities described in subclause (IV)(cc);

(VI)(aa) a statement of any individual appropriate accommodations that are necessary to measure the academic achievement and functional performance of the child on State and districtwide assessments consistent with section 612(a)(16)(A); and

(bb) if the IEP Team determines that the child shall take an alternate assessment on a particular State or districtwide assessment of student achievement, a statement of why —

(AA) the child cannot participate in the regular assessment; and

(BB) the particular alternate assessment selected is appropriate for the child;

(VII) the projected date for the beginning of the services and modifications described in subclause (IV), and the anticipated frequency, location, and duration of those services and modifications; and

(VIII) beginning not later than the first IEP to be in effect when the child is 16, and updated annually thereafter —

(aa) appropriate measurable postsecondary goals based upon age appropriate transition assessments related to training, education, employment, and, where appropriate, independent living skills;

(bb) the transition services (including courses of study) needed to assist the child in reaching those goals; and

(cc) beginning not later than 1 year before the child reaches the age of majority under State law, a statement that the child has been informed of the child's rights under this title, if any, that will transfer to the child on reaching the age of majority under section 615(m).

(ii) Rule of construction.

Nothing in this section shall be construed to require —

(I) that additional information be included in a child's IEP beyond what is explicitly required in this section; and

(II) the IEP Team to include information under 1 component of a child's IEP that is already contained under another component of such IEP.

(B) Individualized education program team.

The term "individualized education program team" or "IEP Team" means a group of individuals composed of —

(i) the parents of a child with a disability;

(ii) not less than 1 regular education teacher of such child (if the child is, or may be, participating in the regular education environment);

(iii) not less than 1 special education teacher, or where appropriate, not less than 1 special education provider of such child;

(iv) a representative of the local educational agency who —

(I) is qualified to provide, or supervise the provision of, specially designed instruction to meet the unique needs of children with disabilities;

(II) is knowledgeable about the general education curriculum; and

(III) is knowledgeable about the availability of resources of the local educational agency;

(v) an individual who can interpret the instructional implications of evaluation results, who may be a member of the team described in clauses (ii) through (vi);

(vi) at the discretion of the parent or the agency, other individuals who have knowledge or special expertise regarding the child, including related services personnel as appropriate; and

(vii) whenever appropriate, the child with a disability.

(C) IEP team attendance.

(i) Attendance not necessary.

A member of the IEP Team shall not be required to attend an IEP meeting, in whole or in part, if the parent of a child with a disability and the local educational agency agree that the attendance of such member is not necessary because the member's area of the curriculum or related services is not being modified or discussed in the meeting.

(ii) Excusal.

A member of the IEP Team may be excused from attending an IEP meeting, in whole or in part, when the meeting involves a modification to or discussion of the member's area of the curriculum or related services, if —

(I) the parent and the local educational agency consent to the excusal; and

(II) the member submits, in writing to the parent and the IEP Team, input into the development of the IEP prior to the meeting.

(iii) Written agreement and consent required.

A parent's agreement under clause (i) and consent under clause (ii) shall be in writing.

(D) IEP team transition.

In the case of a child who was previously served under part C, an invitation to the initial IEP meeting shall, at the request of the parent, be sent to the part C service coordinator or other representatives of the part C system to assist with the smooth transition of services.

(2) Requirement that program be in effect—

(A) In general.

At the beginning of each school year, each local educational agency, State educational agency, or other State agency, as the case may be, shall have in effect, for each child with a disability in the agency's jurisdiction, an individualized education program, as defined in paragraph (1)(A).

(B) Program for child aged 3 through 5.

In the case of a child with a disability aged 3 through 5 (or, at the discretion of the State educational agency, a 2-year-old child with a disability who will turn age 3 during the school year), the IEP Team shall consider the individualized family service plan that contains the material described in section 636, and that is developed in accordance with this section, and the individualized family service plan may serve as the IEP of the child if using that plan as the IEP is —

(i) consistent with State policy; and

(ii) agreed to by the agency and the child's parents.

(C) Program for children who transfer school districts.

(i) In general.

(I) Transfer within the same state.

In the case of a child with a disability who transfers school districts within the same academic year, who enrolls in a new school, and who had an IEP that was in effect in the same State, the local educational agency shall provide such child with a free appropriate public education, including services comparable to those described in the previously held IEP, in consultation with the parents until such time as the local educational agency adopts the previously held IEP or develops, adopts, and implements a new IEP that is consistent with Federal and State law.

(II) Transfer outside state.

In the case of a child with a disability who transfers school districts within the same academic year, who enrolls in a new school, and who had an IEP that was in effect in another State, the local educational agency shall provide such child with a free appropriate public education, including services comparable to those described in the previously held IEP, in consultation with the parents until such time as the local educational agency conducts an evaluation pursuant to subsection (a)(1), if determined to be necessary by such agency, and develops a new IEP, if appropriate, that is consistent with Federal and State law.

(ii) Transmittal of records.

To facilitate the transition for a child described in clause (i) —

(I) the new school in which the child enrolls shall take reasonable steps to promptly obtain the child's records, including the IEP and supporting documents and any other records relating to the provision of special education or related services to the child, from the previous school in which the child was enrolled, pursuant to section 99.31(a)(2) of title 34, Code of Federal Regulations; and

(II) the previous school in which the child was enrolled shall take reasonable steps to promptly respond to such request from the new school.

(3) Development of IEP.

(A) In general. — In developing each child's IEP, the IEP Team, subject to subparagraph (C), shall consider —

(i) the strengths of the child;

(ii) the concerns of the parents for enhancing the education of their child;

(iii) the results of the initial evaluation or most recent evaluation of the child; and

(iv) the academic, developmental, and functional needs of the child.

(B) Consideration of special factors.

The IEP Team shall —

(i) in the case of a child whose behavior impedes the child's learning or that of others, consider the use of positive behavioral interventions and supports, and other strategies, to address that behavior;

(ii) in the case of a child with limited English proficiency, consider the language needs of the child as such needs relate to the child's IEP;

(iii) in the case of a child who is blind or visually impaired, provide for instruction in Braille and the use of Braille unless the IEP Team determines, after an evaluation of the child's reading and writing skills, needs, and appropriate reading and writing media (including an evaluation of the child's future needs for instruction in Braille or the use of Braille), that instruction in Braille or the use of Braille is not appropriate for the child;

(iv) consider the communication needs of the child, and in the case of a child who is deaf or hard of hearing, consider the child's language and communication needs, opportunities for direct communications with peers and professional personnel in the child's language and communication mode, academic level, and full range of needs, including opportunities for direct instruction in the child's language and communication mode; and

(v) consider whether the child needs assistive technology devices and services.

(C) Requirement with respect to regular education teacher.

A regular education teacher of the child, as a member of the IEP Team, shall, to the extent appropriate, participate in the development of the IEP of the child, including the determination of appropriate positive behavioral interventions and supports, and other strategies, and the determination of supplementary aids and services, program modifications, and support for school personnel consistent with paragraph (1)(A)(i)(IV).

(D) Agreement.

In making changes to a child's IEP after the annual IEP meeting for a school year, the parent of a child with a disability and the local educational agency may agree not to convene an IEP meeting for the purposes of making such changes, and instead may develop a written document to amend or modify the child's current IEP.

(E) Consolidation of iep team meetings.

To the extent possible, the local educational agency shall encourage the consolidation of reevaluation meetings for the child and other IEP Team meetings for the child.

(F) Amendments.

Changes to the IEP may be made either by the entire IEP Team or, as provided in subparagraph (D), by amending the IEP rather than by redrafting the entire IEP. Upon request, a parent shall be provided with a revised copy of the IEP with the amendments incorporated.

(4) Review and revision of IEP.

(A) In general.

The local educational agency shall

ensure that, subject to subparagraph (B), the IEP Team —

(i) reviews the child's IEP periodically, but not less frequently than annually, to determine whether the annual goals for the child are being achieved; and

(ii) revises the IEP as appropriate to address —

(I) any lack of expected progress toward the annual goals and in the general education curriculum, where appropriate;

(II) the results of any reevaluation conducted under this section;

(III) information about the child provided to, or by, the parents, as described in subsection (c)(1)(B);

(IV) the child's anticipated needs; or

(V) other matters.

(B) Requirement with respect to regular education teacher.

A regular education teacher of the child, as a member of the IEP Team, shall, consistent with paragraph (1)(C), participate in the review and revision of the IEP of the child.

(5) Multi-year IEP demonstration.

(A) Pilot program.

(i) Purpose.

The purpose of this paragraph is to provide an opportunity for States to allow parents and local educational agencies the opportunity for long-term planning by offering the option of developing a comprehensive multi-year IEP, not to exceed 3 years, that is designed to coincide with the natural transition points for the child.

(ii) Authorization.

In order to carry out the purpose of this paragraph, the Secretary is authorized to approve not more than 15 proposals from States to carry out the activity described in clause (I).

(iii) Proposal.

(I) In general.

A State desiring to participate in the program under this paragraph shall submit a proposal to the Secretary at such time and in such manner as the Secretary may reasonably require.

(II) Content.

The proposal shall include —

(aa) assurances that the development of a multi-year IEP under this paragraph is optional for parents;

(bb) assurances that the parent is required to provide informed consent before a comprehensive multi-year IEP is developed;

(cc) a list of required elements for each multi-year IEP, including —

(AA) measurable goals pursuant to paragraph (1)(A)(i)(II), coinciding with natural transition points for the child, that will enable the child to be involved in and make progress in the general education curriculum and that will meet the child's other needs that result from the child's disability; and

(BB) measurable annual goals for determining progress toward meeting the goals described in subitem (AA); and

(dd) a description of the process for the review and revision of each multi-year IEP, including —

(AA) a review by the IEP Team of the child's multi-year IEP at each of the child's natural transition points;

(BB) in years other than a child's natural transition points, an annual review of the child's IEP to determine the child's current levels of progress and whether the annual goals for the child are being achieved, and a requirement to amend the IEP, as appropriate, to enable the child to continue to meet the measurable goals set out in the IEP;

(CC) if the IEP Team determines on the basis of a review that the child is not making sufficient progress toward the goals described in the multi-year IEP, a requirement that the local educational agency shall ensure that the IEP Team carries out a more thorough review of the IEP in accordance with paragraph (4) within 30 calendar days; and

(DD) at the request of the parent, a requirement that the IEP Team shall conduct a review of the child's multi-year IEP rather than or subsequent to an annual review.

(B) Report.

Beginning 2 years after the date of enactment of the Individuals with Disabilities Education Improvement Act of 2004, the

Secretary shall submit an annual report to the Committee on Education and the Workforce of the House of Representatives and the Committee on Health, Education, Labor, and Pensions of the Senate regarding the effectiveness of the program under this paragraph and any specific recommendations for broader implementation of such program, including —

    (i) reducing —

        (I) the paperwork burden on teachers, principals, administrators, and related service providers; and

        (II) noninstructional time spent by teachers in complying with this part;

    (ii) enhancing longer-term educational plannin

    (iii) improving positive outcomes for children with disabilities;

    (iv) promoting collaboration between IEP Team members; and

    (v) ensuring satisfaction of family members.

    (C) Definition.

In this paragraph, the term "natural transition points" means those periods that are close in time to the transition of a child with a disability from preschool to elementary grades, from elementary grades to middle or junior high school grades, from middle or junior high school grades to secondary school grades, and from secondary school grades to post-secondary activities, but in no case a period longer than 3 years.

(6) Failure to meet transition objectives.

If a participating agency, other than the local educational agency, fails to provide the transition services described in the IEP in accordance with paragraph (1)(A)(i)(VIII), the local educational agency shall reconvene the IEP Team to identify alternative strategies to meet the transition objectives for the child set out in the IEP.

(7) Children with disabilities in adult prisons.

    (A) In general.

The following requirements shall not apply to children with disabilities who are convicted as adults under State law and incarcerated in adult prisons:

    (i) The requirements contained in section 612(a)(16) and paragraph (1)(A)(i)(VI) (relating to participation of children with disabilities in general assessments).

    (ii) The requirements of items (aa) and (bb) of paragraph (1)(A)(i)(VIII) (relating to transition planning and transition services), do not apply with respect to such children whose eligibility under this part will end, because of such children's age, before such children will be released from prison.

    (B) Additional requirement.

If a child with a disability is convicted as an adult under State law and incarcerated in an adult prison, the child's IEP Team may modify the child's IEP or placement notwithstanding the requirements of sections 612(a)(5)(A) and paragraph (1)(A) if the State has demonstrated a bona fide security or compelling penological interest that cannot otherwise be accommodated.

(e) Educational placements.

Each local educational agency or State educational agency shall ensure that the parents of each child with a disability are members of any group that makes decisions on the educational placement of their child.

(f) Alternative means of meeting participation.

When conducting IEP team meetings and placement meetings pursuant to this section, section 615(e), and section 615(f)(1)(B), and carrying out administrative matters under section 615 (such as scheduling, exchange of witness lists, and status conferences), the parent of a child with a disability and a local educational agency may agree to use alternative means of meeting participation, such as video conferences and conference calls.

§ 1415. Procedural safeguards

(a) Establishment of procedures

Any State educational agency, State agency, or local educational agency that receives assistance under this part shall establish and maintain procedures in accordance with this section to ensure that children with disabilities and their parents are guaranteed procedural safeguards with respect to the provision of a free appropriate public education by such agencies.

(b) Types of procedures.

The procedures required by this section shall include the following:

(1) An opportunity for the parents of a child with a disability to examine all records relating to such child and to participate in meetings with respect to the identification, evaluation, and educational placement of the child, and the provision of a free appropriate public education to such child, and to obtain an independent educational evaluation of the child.

(2)(A) Procedures to protect the rights of the child whenever the parents of the child are not known, the agency cannot, after reasonable efforts, locate the parents, or the child is a ward of the State, including the assignment of an individual to act as a surrogate for the parents, which surrogate shall not be an employee of the State educational agency, the local educational agency, or any other agency that is involved in the education or care of the child. In the case of —

(i) a child who is a ward of the State, such surrogate may alternatively be appointed by the judge overseeing the child's care provided that the surrogate meets the requirements of this paragraph; and

(ii) an unaccompanied homeless youth as defined in section 725(6) of the McKinney-Vento Homeless Assistance Act (42 U.S.C. 11434a(6)), the local educational agency shall appoint a surrogate in accordance with this paragraph.

(B) The State shall make reasonable efforts to ensure the assignment of a surrogate not more than 30 days after there is a determination by the agency that the child needs a surrogate.

(3) Written prior notice to the parents of the child, in accordance with subsection (c)(1), whenever the local educational agency —

(A) proposes to initiate or change; or

(B) refuses to initiate or change, the identification, evaluation, or educational placement of the child, or the provision of a free appropriate public education to the child.

(4) Procedures designed to ensure that the notice required by paragraph (3) is in the native language of the parents, unless it clearly is not feasible to do so.

(5) An opportunity for mediation, in accordance with subsection (e).

(6) An opportunity for any party to present a complaint —

(A) with respect to any matter relating to the identification, evaluation, or educational placement of the child, or the provision of a free appropriate public education to such child; and

(B) which sets forth an alleged violation that occurred not more than 2 years before the date the parent or public agency knew or should have known about the alleged action that forms the basis of the complaint, or, if the State has an explicit time limitation for presenting such a complaint under this part, in such time as the State law allows, except that the exceptions to the timeline described in subsection (f)(3)(D) shall apply to the timeline described in this subparagraph.

(7)(A) Procedures that require either party, or the attorney representing a party, to provide due process complaint notice in accordance with subsection (c)(2) (which shall remain confidential) —

(i) to the other party, in the complaint filed under paragraph (6), and forward a copy of such notice to the State educational agency; and

(ii) that shall include —

(I) the name of the child, the address of the residence of the child (or available contact information in the case of a homeless child), and the name of the school the child is attending;

(II) in the case of a homeless child or youth (within the meaning of section 725(2) of the McKinney-Vento Homeless Assistance Act (42 U.S.C. 11434a(2)), available contact information for the child and the name of the school the child is attending;

(III) a description of the nature of the problem of the child relating to such proposed initiation or change, including facts relating to such problem; and

(IV) a proposed resolution of the problem to the extent known and available to the party at the time.

(B) A requirement that a party may not have a due process hearing until the party, or the attorney representing the party, files a notice that meets the requirements of subparagraph (A)(ii).

(8) Procedures that require the State educational agency to develop a model form to assist parents in filing a complaint and due process complaint notice in accordance with paragraphs (6) and (7), respectively.

(c) Notification requirements.

(1) Content of prior written notice.

The notice required by subsection (b)(3) shall include —

(A) a description of the action proposed or refused by the agency;

(B) an explanation of why the agency proposes or refuses to take the action and a description of each evaluation procedure, assessment, record, or report the agency used as a basis for the proposed or refused action;

(C) a statement that the parents of a child with a disability have protection under the procedural safeguards of this part and, if this notice is not an initial referral for evaluation, the means by which a copy of a description of the procedural safeguards can be obtained;

(D) sources for parents to contact to obtain assistance in understanding the provisions of this part;

(E) a description of other options considered by the IEP Team and the reason why those options were rejected; and

(F) a description of the factors that are relevant to the agency's proposal or refusal.

(2) Due process complaint notice.

(A) Complaint.

The due process complaint notice required under subsection (b)(7)(A) shall be deemed to be sufficient unless the party receiving the notice notifies the hearing officer and the other party in writing that the receiving party believes the notice has not met the requirements of subsection (b)(7)(A).

(B) Response to complaint.

(i) Local educational agency response.

(I) In general.

If the local educational agency has not sent a prior written notice to the parent regarding the subject matter contained in the parent's due process complaint notice, such local educational agency shall, within 10 days of receiving the complaint, send to the parent a response that shall include —

(aa) an explanation of why the agency proposed or refused to take the action raised in the complaint;

(bb) a description of other options that the IEP Team considered and the reasons why those options were rejected;

(cc) a description of each evaluation procedure, assessment, record, or report the agency used as the basis for the proposed or refused action; and

(dd) a description of the factors that are relevant to the agency's proposal or refusal.

(II) Sufficiency.

A response filed by a local educational agency pursuant to subclause (I) shall not be construed to preclude such local educational agency from asserting that the parent's due process complaint notice was insufficient where appropriate.

(ii) Other party response.

Except as provided in clause (i), the non-complaining party shall, within 10 days of receiving the complaint, send to the complaint a response that specifically addresses the issues raised in the complaint.

(C) Timing.

The party providing a hearing officer notification under subparagraph (A) shall provide the notification within 15 days of receiving the complaint.

(D) Determination.

Within 5 days of receipt of the notification provided under subparagraph (C), the hearing officer shall make a determination on the face of the notice of whether the notification meets the requirements of subsection (b)(7)(A), and shall immediately notify the parties in writing of such determination.

(E) Amended complaint notice.

(i) In general.

A party may amend its due process complaint notice only if —

(I) the other party consents in writing to such amendment and is given the opportunity to resolve the complaint through a meeting held pursuant to subsection (f)(1)(B); or

(II) the hearing officer grants permission, except that the hearing officer may only grant such permission at any time not later than 5 days before a due process hearing occurs.

(ii) Applicable timeline.

The applicable timeline for a due process hearing under this part shall recommence at the time the party files an amended notice, including the timeline under subsection (f)(1)(B).

(d) Procedural safeguards notice.

(1) In general.

(A) Copy to parents.

A copy of the procedural safeguards available to the parents of a child with a disability shall be given to the parents only 1 time a year, except that a copy also shall be given to the parents —

(i) upon initial referral or parental request for evaluation;

(ii) upon the first occurrence of the filing of a complaint under subsection (b)(6); and

(iii) upon request by a parent.

(B) Internet website.

A local educational agency may place a current copy of the procedural safeguards notice on its Internet website if such website exists.

(2) Contents.

The procedural safeguards notice shall include a full explanation of the procedural safeguards, written in the native language of the parents (unless it clearly is not feasible to do so) and written in an easily understandable manner, available under this section and under regulations promulgated by the Secretary relating to —

(A) independent educational evaluation;

(B) prior written notice;

(C) parental consent;

(D) access to educational records;

(E) the opportunity to present and resolve complaints, including —

(i) the time period in which to make a complaint;

(ii) the opportunity for the agency to resolve the complaint; and

(iii) the availability of mediation;

(F) the child's placement during pendency of due process proceedings;

(G) procedures for students who are subject to placement in an interim alternative educational setting;

(H) requirements for unilateral placement by parents of children in private schools at public expense;

(I) due process hearings, including requirements for disclosure of evaluation results and recommendations;

(J) State-level appeals (if applicable in that State);

(K) civil actions, including the time period in which to file such actions; and

(L) attorneys' fees.

(e) Mediation.

(1) In general.

Any State educational agency or local educational agency that receives assistance under this part shall ensure that procedures are established and implemented to allow parties to disputes involving any matter, including matters arising prior to the filing of a complaint pursuant to subsection (b)(6), to resolve such disputes through a mediation process.

(2) Requirements.

Such procedures shall meet the following requirements:

(A) The procedures shall ensure that the mediation process —

(i) is voluntary on the part of the parties;

(ii) is not used to deny or delay a parent's right to a due process hearing under subsection (f), or to deny any other rights afforded under this part; and

(iii) is conducted by a qualified and impartial mediator who is trained in effective mediation techniques.

(B) Opportunity to meet with a disinterested party.

A local educational agency or a State agency may establish procedures to offer to parents and schools that choose not to use the mediation process, an opportunity to meet, at a time and location convenient to the parents, with a disinterested party who is under contract with —

(i) a parent training and information center or community parent resource center in the State established under section 671 or 672; or

(ii) an appropriate alternative dispute resolution entity, to encourage the use, and explain the benefits, of the mediation process to the parents.

(C) List of qualified mediators.

The State shall maintain a list of individuals who are qualified mediators and knowledgeable in laws and regulations relating to the provision of special education and related services.

(D) Costs.

The State shall bear the cost of the mediation process, including the costs of meetings described in subparagraph (B).

(E) Scheduling and location.

Each session in the mediation process shall be scheduled in a timely manner and shall be held in a location that is convenient to the parties to the dispute.

(F) Written agreement.

In the case that a resolution is reached to resolve the complaint through the mediation process, the parties shall execute a legally binding agreement that sets forth such resolution and that —

(i) states that all discussions that occurred during the mediation process shall be confidential and may not be used as evidence in any subsequent due process hearing or civil proceeding;

(ii) is signed by both the parent and a representative of the agency who has the authority to bind such agency; and

(iii) is enforceable in any State court of competent jurisdiction or in a district court of the United States.

(G) Mediation discussions.

Discussions that occur during the mediation process shall be confidential and may not be used as evidence in any subsequent due process hearing or civil proceeding.

(f) Impartial due process hearing.

(1) In general.

(A) Hearing.

Whenever a complaint has been received under subsection (b)(6) or (k), the parents or the local educational agency involved in such complaint shall have an opportunity for an impartial due process hearing, which shall be conducted by the State educational agency or by the local educational agency, as determined by State law or by the State educational agency.

(B) Resolution session.

(i) Preliminary meeting.

Prior to the opportunity for an impartial due process hearing under subparagraph (A), the local educational agency shall convene a meeting with the parents and the relevant member or members of the IEP Team who have specific knowledge of the facts identified in the complaint —

(I) within 15 days of receiving notice of the parents' complaint;

(II) which shall include a representative of the agency who has decisionmaking authority on behalf of such agency;

(III) which may not include an attorney of the local educational agency unless the parent is accompanied by an attorney; and

(IV) where the parents of the child discuss their complaint, and the facts that form the basis of the complaint, and the local educational agency is provided the opportunity to resolve the complaint unless the parents and the local educational agency agree in writing to waive such meeting, or agree to use the mediation process described in subsection (e).

(ii) Hearing.

If the local educational agency has not resolved the complaint to the satisfaction of the parents within 30 days of the receipt of the complaint, the due process hearing may occur, and all of the applicable timelines for a due process hearing under this part shall commence.

(iii) Written settlement agreement.

In the case that a resolution is reached to resolve the complaint at a meeting described in clause (i), the parties shall execute a legally binding agreement that is —

(I) signed by both the parent and a representative of the agency who has the authority to bind such agency; and

(II) enforceable in any State court of competent jurisdiction or in a district court of the United States.

(iv) Review period.

If the parties execute an agreement pursuant to clause (iii), a party may void such agreement within 3 business days of the agreement's execution.

(2) Disclosure of evaluations and recommendations.

(A) In general.

Not less than 5 business days prior to a hearing conducted pursuant to paragraph (1), each party shall disclose to all other parties all evaluations completed by that date, and recommendations based on the offering party's evaluations, that the party intends to use at the hearing.

(B) Failure to disclose.

A hearing officer may bar any party that fails to comply with subparagraph (A) from introducing the relevant evaluation or recommendation at the hearing without the consent of the other party.

(3) Limitations on hearing.

(A) Person conducting hearing.

A hearing officer conducting a hearing pursuant to paragraph (1)(A) shall, at a minimum —

(i) not be —

(I) an employee of the State educational agency or the local educational agency involved in the education or care of the child; or

(II) a person having a personal or professional interest that conflicts with the person's objectivity in the hearing;

(ii) possess knowledge of, and the ability to understand, the provisions of this title, Federal and State regulations pertaining to this title, and legal interpretations of this title by Federal and State courts;

(iii) possess the knowledge and ability to conduct hearings in accordance with appropriate, standard legal practice; and

(iv) possess the knowledge and ability to render and write decisions in accordance with appropriate, standard legal practice.

(B) Subject matter of hearing.

The party requesting the due process hearing shall not be allowed to raise issues at the due process hearing that were not raised in the notice filed under subsection (b)(7), unless the other party agrees otherwise.

(C) Timeline for requesting hearing.

A parent or agency shall request an impartial due process hearing within 2 years of the date the parent or agency knew or should have known about the alleged action that forms the basis of the complaint, or, if the State has an explicit time limitation for requesting such a hearing under this part, in such time as the State law allows.

(D) Exceptions to the timeline.

The timeline described in subparagraph (C) shall not apply to a parent if the parent was prevented from requesting the hearing due to —

(i) specific misrepresentations by the local educational agency that it had resolved the problem forming the basis of the complaint; or

(ii) the local educational agency's withholding of information from the parent that was required under this part to be provided to the parent.

(E) Decision of hearing officer.

(i) In general.

Subject to clause (ii), a decision made by a hearing officer shall be made on substantive grounds based on a determination of whether the child received a free appropriate public education.

(ii) Procedural issues.

In matters alleging a procedural violation, a hearing officer may find that a child did not receive a free appropriate public education only if the procedural inadequacies —

(I) impeded the child's right to a free appropriate public education;

(II) significantly impeded the parents' opportunity to participate in the decisionmaking process regarding the provision of a free appropriate public education to the parents' child; or

(III) caused a deprivation of educational benefits.

(iii) Rule of construction.

Nothing in this subparagraph shall be construed to preclude a hearing officer from ordering a local educational agency to comply with procedural requirements under this section.

(F) Rule of construction.

Nothing in this paragraph shall be construed to affect the right of a parent to file a complaint with the State educational agency.

(g) Appeal.

(1) In general.

If the hearing required by subsection (f) is conducted by a local educational agency, any party aggrieved by the findings and decision rendered in such a hearing may appeal such findings and decision to the State educational agency.

(2) Impartial review and independent decision.

The State educational agency shall conduct an impartial review of the findings and decision appealed under paragraph (1). The officer conducting such review shall make an independent decision upon completion of such review.

(h) Safeguards.

Any party to a hearing conducted pursuant to subsection (f) or (k), or an appeal conducted pursuant to subsection (g), shall be accorded —

(1) the right to be accompanied and advised by counsel and by individuals with special knowledge or training with respect to the problems of children with disabilities;

(2) the right to present evidence and confront, cross-examine, and compel the attendance of witnesses;

(3) the right to a written, or, at the option of the parents, electronic verbatim record of such hearing; and

(4) the right to written, or, at the option of the parents, electronic findings of fact and decisions, which findings and decisions —

(A) shall be made available to the public consistent with the requirements of section 617(b) (relating to the confidentiality of data, information, and records); and

(B) shall be transmitted to the advisory panel established pursuant to section 612(a)(21).

(i) Administrative procedures.

(1) In general.

(A) Decision made in hearing.

A decision made in a hearing conducted pursuant to subsection (f) or (k) shall be final, except that any party involved in such hearing may appeal such decision under the provisions of subsection (g) and paragraph (2).

(B) Decision made at appeal.

A decision made under subsection (g) shall be final, except that any party may bring an action under paragraph (2).

(2) Right to bring civil action.

(A) In general.

Any party aggrieved by the findings and decision made under subsection (f) or (k) who does not have the right to an appeal under subsection (g), and any party aggrieved by the findings and decision made under this subsection, shall have the right to bring a civil action with respect to the complaint presented pursuant to this section, which action may be brought in any State court of competent jurisdiction or in a district court of the United States, without regard to the amount in controversy.

(B) Limitation.

The party bringing the action shall have 90 days from the date of the decision of the hearing officer to bring such an action, or, if the State has an explicit time limitation for bringing such action under this part, in such time as the State law allows.

(C) Additional requirements.

In any action brought under this paragraph, the court —

(i) shall receive the records of the administrative proceedings;

(ii) shall hear additional evidence at the request of a party; and

(iii) basing its decision on the preponderance of the evidence, shall grant such relief as the court determines is appropriate.

(3) Jurisdiction of district courts; attorneys' fees.

(A) In general.

The district courts of the United States shall have jurisdiction of actions brought under this section without regard to the amount in controversy.

(B) Award of attorneys' fees.

(i) In general.

In any action or proceeding brought under this section, the court, in its discretion, may award reasonable attorneys' fees as part of the costs —

(I) to a prevailing party who is the parent of a child with a disability;

(II) to a prevailing party who is a State educational agency or local educational agency against the attorney of a parent who files a complaint or subsequent cause of action that is frivolous, unreasonable, or without foundation, or against the attorney of a parent who continued to litigate after the litigation clearly became frivolous, unreasonable, or without foundation; or

(III) to a prevailing State educational agency or local educational agency against the attorney of a parent, or against the parent, if the parent's complaint or subsequent cause of action was presented for any improper purpose, such as to harass, to cause unnecessary delay, or to needlessly increase the cost of litigation.

(ii) Rule of construction.

Nothing in this subparagraph shall be construed to affect section 327 of the District of Columbia Appropriations Act, 2005.

(C) Determination of amount of attorneys' fees.

Fees awarded under this paragraph shall be based on rates prevailing in the community in which the action or proceeding arose for the kind and quality of services furnished. No bonus or multiplier may be used in calculating the fees awarded under this subsection.

(D) Prohibition of attorneys' fees and related costs for certain services.

(i) In general.

Attorneys' fees may not be awarded and related costs may not be reimbursed in any action or proceeding under this section for services performed subsequent to the time of a written offer of settlement to a parent if —

(I) the offer is made within the time prescribed by Rule 68 of the Federal Rules of Civil Procedure or, in the case of an administrative proceeding, at any time more than 10 days before the proceeding begins;

(II) the offer is not accepted within 10 days; and

(III) the court or administrative hearing officer finds that the relief finally obtained by the parents is not more favorable to the parents than the offer of settlement.

(ii) IEP team meetings.

Attorneys' fees may not be awarded relating to any meeting of the IEP Team unless such meeting is convened as a result of an administrative proceeding or judicial action, or, at the discretion of the State, for a mediation described in subsection (e).

(iii) Opportunity to resolve complaints.

A meeting conducted pursuant to subsection (f)(1)(B)(i) shall not be considered —

(I) a meeting convened as a result of an administrative hearing or judicial action; or

(II) an administrative hearing or judicial action for purposes of this paragraph.

(E) Exception to prohibition on attorneys' fees and related costs.

Notwithstanding subparagraph (D), an award of attorneys' fees and related costs may be made to a parent who is the prevailing party and who was substantially justified in rejecting the settlement offer.

(F) Reduction in amount of attorneys' fees.

Except as provided in subparagraph (G), whenever the court finds that —

(i) the parent, or the parent's attorney, during the course of the action or proceeding, unreasonably protracted the final resolution of the controversy;

(ii) the amount of the attorneys' fees otherwise authorized to be awarded unreasonably exceeds the hourly rate prevailing in the community for similar services by attorneys of reasonably comparable skill, reputation, and experience;

(iii) the time spent and legal services furnished were excessive considering the nature of the action or proceeding; or

(iv) the attorney representing the parent did not provide to the local educational agency the appropriate information in the notice of the complaint described in subsection (b)(7)(A), the court shall reduce, accordingly, the amount of the attorneys' fees awarded under this section.

(G) Exception to reduction in amount of attorneys' fees.

The provisions of subparagraph (F) shall not apply in any action or proceeding if the court finds that the State or local educational agency unreasonably protracted the final resolution of the action or proceeding or there was a violation of this section.

(j) Maintenance of current educational placement.

Except as provided in subsection (k)(4), during the pendency of any proceedings conducted pursuant to this section, unless the State or local educational agency and the parents otherwise agree, the child shall remain in the then-current educational placement of the child, or, if applying for initial admission to a public school, shall, with the consent of the parents, be placed in the public school program until all such proceedings have been completed.

(k) Placement in alternative educational setting.

(1) Authority of school personnel.

(A) Case-by-case determination.

School personnel may consider any unique circumstances on a case-by-case basis when determining whether to order a change in placement for a child with a disability who violates a code of student conduct.

(B) Authority.

School personnel under this subsection may remove a child with a disability who violates a code of student conduct from their current placement to an appropriate interim alternative educational setting, another setting, or suspension, for not more than 10 school days (to the extent such alternatives are applied to children without disabilities).

(C) Additional authority.

If school personnel seek to order a change in placement that would exceed 10 school days and the behavior that gave rise to the violation of the school code is determined not to be a manifestation of the child's disability pursuant to subparagraph (E), the relevant disciplinary procedures applicable to children without disabilities may be applied to the child in the same manner and for the same duration in which the procedures would be applied to children without disabilities, except as provided in section 612(a)(1) although it may be provided in an interim alternative educational setting.

(D) Services.

A child with a disability who is removed from the child's current placement under subparagraph (G) (irrespective of whether the behavior is determined to be a manifestation of the child's disability) or subparagraph (C) shall —

(i) continue to receive educational services, as provided in section 612(a)(1), so as to enable the child to continue to participate in the general education curriculum, although in another setting, and to progress toward meeting the goals set out in the child's IEP; and

(ii) receive, as appropriate, a functional behavioral assessment, behavioral intervention services and modifications, that are designed to address the behavior violation so that it does not recur.

(E) Manifestation determination.

(i) In general.

Except as provided in subparagraph (B), within 10 school days of any decision to change the placement of a child with a disability because of a violation of a code of student conduct, the local educational agency, the parent, and relevant members of the IEP Team (as determined by the parent and the local educational agency) shall review all relevant information in the student's file, including the child's IEP, any teacher observations, and any relevant information provided by the parents to determine —

(I) if the conduct in question was caused by, or had a direct and substantial relationship to, the child's disability; or

(II) if the conduct in question was the direct result of the local educational agency's failure to implement the IEP.

(ii) Manifestation.

If the local educational agency, the parent, and relevant members of the IEP Team determine that either subclause (I) or (II) of clause (i) is applicable for the child, the conduct shall be determined to be a manifestation of the child's disability.

(F) Determination that behavior was a manifestation.

If the local educational agency, the parent, and relevant members of the IEP Team make the determination that the conduct was a manifestation of the child's disability, the IEP Team shall —

(i) conduct a functional behavioral assessment, and implement a behavioral intervention plan for such child, provided that the local educational agency had not conducted such assessment prior to such determination before the behavior that resulted in a change in placement described in subparagraph (C) or (G);

(ii) in the situation where a behavioral intervention plan has been developed, review the behavioral intervention plan if the child already has such a behavioral intervention plan, and modify it, as necessary, to address the behavior; and

(iii) except as provided in subparagraph (G), return the child to the placement from which the child was removed, unless the parent and the local educational agency agree to a change of placement as part of the modification of the behavioral intervention plan.

(G) special circumstances.

School personnel may remove a student to an interim alternative educational setting for not more than 45 school days without regard to whether the behavior is determined to be a manifestation of the child's disability, in cases where a child —

(i) carries or possesses a weapon to or at school, on school premises, or to or at a school function under the jurisdiction of a State or local educational agency;

(ii) knowingly possesses or uses illegal drugs, or sells or solicits the sale of a controlled substance, while at school, on school premises, or at a school function under the jurisdiction of a State or local educational agency; or

(iii) has inflicted serious bodily injury upon another person while at school, on school premises, or at a school function under the jurisdiction of a State or local educational agency.

(H) Notification.

Not later than the date on which the decision to take disciplinary action is made, the local educational agency shall notify the parents of that decision, and of all procedural safeguards accorded under this section.

(2) Determination of setting.

The interim alternative educational setting in subparagraphs (C) and (G) of paragraph (1) shall be determined by the IEP Team.

(3) Appeal.

(A) In general.

The parent of a child with a disability who disagrees with any decision regarding placement, or the manifestation determination under this subsection, or a local educational agency that believes that maintaining the current placement of the child is substantially likely to result in injury to the child or to others, may request a hearing.

(B) Authority of hearing officer.

(i) In general.

A hearing officer shall hear, and make a determination regarding, an appeal requested under subparagraph (A).

(ii) Change of placement order.

In making the determination under clause (i), the hearing officer may order a change in placement of a child with a disability. In such situations, the hearing officer may —

(I) return a child with a disability to the placement from which the child was removed; or

(II) order a change in placement of a child with a disability to an appropriate interim alternative educational setting for not more than 45 school days if the hearing officer determines that maintaining the current placement of such child is substantially likely to result in injury to the child or to others.

(4) Placement during appeals.

When an appeal under paragraph (3) has been requested by either the parent or the local educational agency —

(A) the child shall remain in the interim alternative educational setting pending the decision of the hearing officer or until the expiration of the time period provided for in paragraph (1)(C), whichever occurs first, unless the parent and the State or local educational agency agree otherwise; and

(B) the State or local educational agency shall arrange for an expedited hearing, which shall occur within 20 school days of the date the hearing is requested and shall result in a determination within 10 school days after the hearing.

(5) Protections for children not yet eligible for special education and related services.

(A) In general.

A child who has not been determined to be eligible for special education and related services under this part and who has engaged in behavior that violates a code of student conduct, may assert any of the protections provided for in this part if the local educational agency had knowledge (as determined in accordance with this paragraph) that the child was a child with a disability before the behavior that precipitated the disciplinary action occurred.

(B) Basis of knowledge.

A local educational agency shall be deemed to have knowledge that a child is a child with a disability if, before the behavior that precipitated the disciplinary action occurred —

(i) the parent of the child has expressed concern in writing to supervisory or administrative personnel of the appropriate educational agency, or a teacher of the child, that the child is in need of special education and related services;

(ii) the parent of the child has requested an evaluation of the child pursuant to section 614(a)(1)(B); or

(iii) the teacher of the child, or other personnel of the local educational agency, has expressed specific concerns about a pattern of behavior demonstrated by the child, directly to the director of special education of such agency or to other supervisory personnel of the agency.

(C) Exception.

A local educational agency shall not be deemed to have knowledge that the child is a child with a disability if the parent of the child has not allowed an evaluation of the child pursuant to section 614 or has refused services under this part or the child has been evaluated and it was determined that the child was not a child with a disability under this part.

(D) Conditions that apply if no basis of knowledge.

(i) In general.

If a local educational agency does not have knowledge that a child is a child with a disability (in accordance with subparagraph (B) or (C)) prior to taking disciplinary measures against the child, the child may be subjected to disciplinary measures applied to children without disabilities who engaged in comparable behaviors consistent with clause (ii).

(ii) Limitations.

If a request is made for an evaluation of a child during the time period in which the child is subjected to disciplinary measures under this subsection, the evaluation shall be conducted in an expedited manner. If the child is determined to be a child with a disability, taking into consideration information from the evaluation conducted by the agency and information provided by the parents, the agency shall provide special education and related services in accordance with this part, except that, pending the results of the evaluation, the child shall remain in the educational placement determined by school authorities.

(6) Referral to and action by law enforcement and judicial authorities.

(A) Rule of construction.

Nothing in this part shall be construed to prohibit an agency from reporting a crime committed by a child with a disability to appropriate authorities or to prevent State law enforcement and judicial authorities from exercising their responsibilities with regard to the application of Federal and State law to crimes committed by a child with a disability.

(B) Transmittal of records.

An agency reporting a crime committed by a child with a disability shall ensure that copies of the special education and disciplinary records of the child are transmitted for consideration by the appropriate authorities to whom the agency reports the crime.

(7) Definitions.

In this subsection:

(A) Controlled substance.

The term "controlled substance" means a drug or other substance identified under schedule I, II, III, IV, or V in section 202(c) of the Controlled Substances Act (21 U.S.C. 812(c)).

(B) Illegal drug.

The term "illegal drug" means a controlled substance but does not include a controlled substance that is legally possessed or used under the supervision of a licensed health-care professional or that is legally possessed or used under any other authority under that Act or under any other provision of Federal law.

(C) Weapon.

The term "weapon" has the meaning given the term "dangerous weapon" under section 930(g)(2) of title 18, United States Code.

(D) Serious bodily injury.

The term "serious bodily injury" has

the meaning given the term "serious bodily injury" under paragraph (3) of subsection (h) of section 1365 of title 18, United States Code.

(l) Rule of construction.

Nothing in this title shall be construed to restrict or limit the rights, procedures, and remedies available under the Constitution, the Americans with Disabilities Act of 1990, title V of the Rehabilitation Act of 1973, or other Federal laws protecting the rights of children with disabilities, except that before the filing of a civil action under such laws seeking relief that is also available under this part, the procedures under subsections (f) and (g) shall be exhausted to the same extent as would be required had the action been brought under this part.

(m) Transfer of parental rights at age of majority.

(1) In general.

A State that receives amounts from a grant under this part may provide that, when a child with a disability reaches the age of majority under State law (except for a child with a disability who has been determined to be incompetent under State law) —

(A) the agency shall provide any notice required by this section to both the individual and the parents;

(B) all other rights accorded to parents under this part transfer to the child;

(C) the agency shall notify the individual and the parents of the transfer of rights; and

(D) all rights accorded to parents under this part transfer to children who are incarcerated in an adult or juvenile Federal, State, or local correctional institution.

(2) Special rule.

If, under State law, a child with a disability who has reached the age of majority under State law, who has not been determined to be incompetent, but who is determined not to have the ability to provide informed consent with respect to the educational program of the child, the State shall establish procedures for appointing the parent of the child, or if the parent is not available, another appropriate individual, to represent the educational interests of the child throughout the period of eligibility of the child under this part.

(n) Electronic mail.

A parent of a child with a disability may elect to receive notices required under this section by an electronic mail (e-mail) communication, if the agency makes such option available.

(o) Separate complaint.

Nothing in this section shall be construed to preclude a parent from filing a separate due process complaint on an issue separate from a due process complaint already filed.

§ 1416. Withholding and judicial review

(a) Withholding of payments

(1) In general

The Secretary shall —

(A) monitor implementation of this part through —

(i) oversight of the exercise of general supervision by the States, as required in section 612(a)(11); and

(ii) the State performance plans, described in subsection (b);

(B) enforce this part in accordance with subsection (e); and

(C) require States to —

(i) monitor implementation of this part by local educational agencies; and

(ii) enforce this part in accordance with paragraph (3) and subsection (e).

(2) Focused monitoring.

The primary focus of Federal and State monitoring activities described in paragraph (1) shall be on —

(A) improving educational results and functional outcomes for all children with disabilities; and

(B) ensuring that States meet the program requirements under this part, with a particular emphasis on those requirements that are most closely related to improving educational results for children with disabilities.

(3) Monitoring priorities.

The Secretary shall monitor the States, and shall require each State to monitor the local educational agencies located in the State (except the State exercise of general supervisory responsibility), using quantifiable indicators in each of the following priority areas, and using such qualitative indicators as are needed to adequately measure performance in the following priority areas:

(A) Provision of a free appropriate public education in the least restrictive environment.

(B) State exercise of general supervisory authority, including child find, effective monitoring, the use of resolution sessions, mediation, voluntary binding arbitration, and a system of transition services as defined in sections 602(34) and 637(a)(9).

(C) Disproportionate representation of racial and ethnic groups in special education and related services, to the extent the representation is the result of inappropriate identification.

(4) Permissive areas of review.

The Secretary shall consider other relevant information and data, including data provided by States under section 618.

(b) State performance plans.

(1) Plan.

(A) In general.

Not later than 1 year after the date of enactment of the Individuals with Disabilities Education Improvement Act of 2004, each State shall have in place a performance plan that evaluates that State's efforts to implement the requirements and purposes of this part and describes how the State will improve such implementation.

(B) Submission for approval.

Each State shall submit the State's performance plan to the Secretary for approval in accordance with the approval process described in subsection (c).

(C) Review.

Each State shall review its State performance plan at least once every 6 years and submit any amendments to the Secretary.

(2) Targets.

(A) In general.

As a part of the State performance plan described under paragraph (1), each State shall establish measurable and rigorous targets for the indicators established under the priority areas described in subsection (a)(3).

(B) Data collection.

(i) In general.

Each State shall collect valid and reliable information as needed to report annually to the Secretary on the priority areas described in subsection (a)(3).

(ii) Rule of construction.

Nothing in this title shall be construed to authorize the development of a nationwide database of personally identifiable information on individuals involved in studies or other collections of data under this part.

(C) Public reporting and privacy.

(i) In general.

The State shall use the targets established in the plan and priority areas described in subsection (a)(3) to analyze the performance of each local educational agency in the State in implementing this part.

(ii) Report.

(I) Public report.

The State shall report annually to the public on the performance of each local educational agency located in the State on the targets in the State's performance plan. The State shall make the State's performance plan available through public means, including by posting on the website of the State educational agency, distribution to the media, and distribution through public agencies.

(II) State performance report.

The State shall report annually to the Secretary on the performance of the State under the State's performance plan.

(iii) Privacy.

The State shall not report to the public or the Secretary any information on performance that would result in the disclosure of personally identifiable information about individual children or where the available data is insufficient to yield statistically reliable information.

(c) Approval process.

(1) Deemed approval.

The Secretary shall review (including the specific provisions described in subsection (b)) each performance plan submitted by a State pursuant to subsection (b)(1)(B) and the plan shall be deemed to be approved by the Secretary unless the Secretary makes a written determination, prior to the expiration of the 120-day period beginning on the date on which the Secretary received the plan, that the plan does not meet the requirements of this section, including the specific provisions described in subsection (b).

(2) Disapproval.

The Secretary shall not finally disapprove a performance plan, except after giving the State notice and an opportunity for a hearing.

(3) Notification.

If the Secretary finds that the plan does not meet the requirements, in whole or in part, of this section, the Secretary shall —

(A) give the State notice and an opportunity for a hearing; and

(B) notify the State of the finding, and in such notification shall —

(i) cite the specific provisions in the plan that do not meet the requirements; and

(ii) request additional information, only as to the provisions not meeting the requirements, needed for the plan to meet the requirements of this section.

(4) Response.

If the State responds to the Secretary's notification described in paragraph (3)(B) during the 30-day period beginning on the date on which the State received the notification, and resubmits the plan with the requested information described in paragraph (3)(B)(ii), the Secretary shall approve or disapprove such plan prior to the later of —

(A) the expiration of the 30-day period beginning on the date on which the plan is resubmitted; or

(B) the expiration of the 120-day period described in paragraph (1).

(5) Failure to respond.

If the State does not respond to the Secretary's notification described in paragraph (3)(B) during the 30-day period beginning on the date on which the State received the notification, such plan shall be deemed to be disapproved.

(d) Secretary's review and determination.

(1) Review.

The Secretary shall annually review the State performance report submitted pursuant to subsection (b)(2)(C)(ii)(II) in accordance with this section.

(2) Determination.

(A) In general.

Based on the information provided by the State in the State performance report, information obtained through monitoring visits, and any other public information made available, the Secretary shall determine if the State —

(i) meets the requirements and purposes of this part;

(ii) needs assistance in implementing the requirements of this part;

(iii) needs intervention in implementing the requirements of this part; or

(iv) needs substantial intervention in implementing the requirements of this part.

(B) Notice and opportunity for a hearing.

For determinations made under clause (iii) or (iv) of subparagraph (A), the Secretary shall provide reasonable notice and an opportunity for a hearing on such determination.

(e) Enforcement.

(1) Needs assistance.

If the Secretary determines, for 2 consecutive years, that a State needs assistance under subsection (d)(2)(A)(ii) in implementing the requirements of this part, the Secretary shall take 1 or more of the following actions:

(A) Advise the State of available sources of technical assistance that may help the State address the areas in which the State needs assistance, which may include assistance from the Office of Special Education Programs, other offices of the Department of Education, other Federal agencies, technical assistance providers approved by the Secretary, and other federally funded nonprofit agencies, and require the State to work with appropriate entities. Such technical assistance may include —

(i) the provision of advice by experts to address the areas in which the State needs assistance, including explicit plans for addressing the area for concern within a specified period of time;

(ii) assistance in identifying and implementing professional development, instructional strategies, and methods of instruction that are based on scientifically based research;

(iii) designating and using distinguished superintendents, principals, special education administrators, special education teachers, and other teachers to provide advice, technical assistance, and support; and

(iv) devising additional approaches to providing technical assistance, such as collaborating with institutions of higher education, educational service agencies, national centers of technical assistance supported under part D, and private providers of scientifically based technical assistance.

(B) Direct the use of State-level funds under section 611(e) on the area or areas in which the State needs assistance.

(C) Identify the State as a high-risk grantee and impose special conditions on the State's grant under this part.

(2) Needs intervention.

If the Secretary determines, for 3 or more consecutive years, that a State needs intervention under subsection (d)(2)(A)(iii) in implementing the requirements of this part, the following shall apply:

(A) The Secretary may take any of the actions described in paragraph (1).

(B) The Secretary shall take 1 or more of the following actions:

(i) Require the State to prepare a corrective action plan or improvement plan if the Secretary determines that the State should be able to correct the problem within 1 year.

(ii) Require the State to enter into a compliance agreement under section 457 of the General Education Provisions Act, if the Secretary has reason to believe that the State cannot correct the problem within 1 year.

(iii) For each year of the determination, withhold not less than 20 percent and not more than 50 percent of the State's funds under section 611(e), until the Secretary determines the State has sufficiently addressed the areas in which the State needs intervention.

(iv) Seek to recover funds under section 452 of the General Education Provisions Act.

(v) Withhold, in whole or in part, any further payments to the State under this part pursuant to paragraph (5).

(vi) Refer the matter for appropriate enforcement action, which may include referral to the Department of Justice.

(3) Needs substantial intervention. —

Notwithstanding paragraph (1) or (2), at any time that the Secretary determines that a State needs substantial intervention in implementing the requirements of this part or that there is a substantial failure to comply with any condition of a State educational agency's or local educational agency's eligibility under this part, the Secretary shall take 1 or more of the following actions:

(A) Recover funds under section 452 of the General Education Provisions Act.

(B) Withhold, in whole or in part, any further payments to the State under this part.

(C) Refer the case to the Office of the Inspector General at the Department of Education.

(D) Refer the matter for appropriate enforcement action, which may include referral to the Department of Justice.

(4) Opportunity for hearing.

(A) Withholding funds.

Prior to withholding any funds under this section, the Secretary shall provide reasonable notice and an opportunity for a hearing to the State educational agency involved.

(B) Suspension.

Pending the outcome of any hearing to withhold payments under subsection (b), the Secretary may suspend payments to a recipient, suspend the authority of the recipient to obligate funds under this part, or both, after such recipient has been given reasonable notice and an opportunity to show cause why future payments or authority to obligate funds under this part should not be suspended.

(5) Report to congress.

The Secretary shall report to the Committee on Education and the Workforce of the House of Representatives and the Committee on Health, Education, Labor, and Pensions of the Senate within 30 days of taking enforcement action pursuant to paragraph (1), (2), or (3), on the specific action taken and the reasons why enforcement action was taken.

(6) Nature of withholding.

(A) Limitation.

If the Secretary withholds further payments pursuant to paragraph (2) or (3), the Secretary may determine —

(i) that such withholding will be limited to programs or projects, or portions of programs or projects, that affected the Secretary's determination under subsection (d)(2); or

(ii) that the State educational agency

shall not make further payments under this part to specified State agencies or local educational agencies that caused or were involved in the Secretary's determination under subsection (d)(2).

(B) Withholding until rectified.

Until the Secretary is satisfied that the condition that caused the initial withholding has been substantially rectified —

(i) payments to the State under this part shall be withheld in whole or in part; and

(ii) payments by the State educational agency under this part shall be limited to State agencies and local educational agencies whose actions did not cause or were not involved in the Secretary's determination under subsection (d)(2), as the case may be.

(7) Public attention.

Any State that has received notice under subsection (d)(2) shall, by means of a public notice, take such measures as may be necessary to bring the pendency of an action pursuant to this subsection to the attention of the public within the State.

(8) Judicial review.

(A) In general.

If any State is dissatisfied with the Secretary's action with respect to the eligibility of the State under section 612, such State may, not later than 60 days after notice of such action, file with the United States court of appeals for the circuit in which such State is located a petition for review of that action. A copy of the petition shall be transmitted by the clerk of the court to the Secretary. The Secretary thereupon shall file in the court the record of the proceedings upon which the Secretary's action was based, as provided in section 2112 of title 28, United States Code.

(B) Jurisdiction; review by united states supreme court.

Upon the filing of such petition, the court shall have jurisdiction to affirm the action of the Secretary or to set it aside, in whole or in part. The judgment of the court shall be subject to review by the Supreme Court of the United States upon certiorari or certification as provided in section 1254 of title 28, United States Code.

(C) Standard of review.

The findings of fact by the Secretary, if supported by substantial evidence, shall be conclusive, but the court, for good cause shown, may remand the case to the Secretary to take further evidence, and the Secretary may thereupon make new or modified findings of fact and may modify the Secretary's previous action, and shall file in the court the record of the further proceedings. Such new or modified findings of fact shall be conclusive if supported by substantial evidence.

(f) State enforcement.

If a State educational agency determines that a local educational agency is not meeting the requirements of this part, including the targets in the State's performance plan, the State educational agency shall prohibit the local educational agency from reducing the local educational agency's maintenance of effort under section 613(a)(2)(C) for any fiscal year.

(g) Rule of construction.

Nothing in this section shall be construed to restrict the Secretary from utilizing any authority under the General Education Provisions Act to monitor and enforce the requirements of this title.

(h) Divided state agency responsibility.

For purposes of this section, where responsibility for ensuring that the requirements of this part are met with respect to children with disabilities who are convicted as adults under State law and incarcerated in adult prisons is assigned to a public agency other than the State educational agency pursuant to section 612(a)(11)(C), the Secretary, in instances where the Secretary finds that the failure to comply substantially with the provisions of this part are related to a failure by the public agency, shall take appropriate corrective action to ensure compliance with this part, except that —

(1) any reduction or withholding of payments to the State shall be proportionate to the total funds allotted under section 611 to the State as the number of eligible children with disabilities in adult prisons under the supervision of the other public agency is proportionate to the number of eligible individuals with disabilities in the State under the supervision of the State educational agency; and

(2) any withholding of funds under paragraph (1) shall be limited to the specific

agency responsible for the failure to comply with this part.

(i) Data capacity and technical assistance review.

The Secretary shall —

(1) review the data collection and analysis capacity of States to ensure that data and information determined necessary for implementation of this section is collected, analyzed, and accurately reported to the Secretary; and

(2) provide technical assistance (from funds reserved under section 611(c)), where needed, to improve the capacity of States to meet the data collection requirements.

§ 1417. Administration

(a) Responsibilities of Secretary

In carrying out this subchapter, the Secretary shall —

(1) cooperate with, and (directly or by grant or contract) furnish technical assistance necessary to, a State in matters relating to —

(A) the education of children with disabilities; and

(B) carrying out this part; and

(2) provide short-term training programs and institutes.

(b) Prohibition against federal mandates, direction, or control.

Nothing in this title shall be construed to authorize an officer or employee of the Federal Government to mandate, direct, or control a State, local educational agency, or school's specific instructional content, academic achievement standards and assessments, curriculum, or program of instruction.

(c) Confidentiality.

The Secretary shall take appropriate action, in accordance with section 444 of the General Education Provisions Act, to ensure the protection of the confidentiality of any personally identifiable data, information, and records collected or maintained by the Secretary and by State educational agencies and local educational agencies pursuant to this part.

(d) Personnel.

The Secretary is authorized to hire qualified personnel necessary to carry out the Secretary's duties under subsection (a), under section 618, and under subpart 4 of part D, without regard to the provisions of title 5, United States Code, relating to appointments in the competitive service and without regard to chapter 51 and subchapter III of chapter 53 of such title relating to classification and general schedule pay rates, except that no more than 20 such personnel shall be employed at any time.

(e) Model forms.

Not later than the date that the Secretary publishes final regulations under this title, to implement amendments made by the Individuals with Disabilities Education Improvement Act of 2004, the Secretary shall publish and disseminate widely to States, local educational agencies, and parent and community training and information centers —

(1) a model IEP form;

(2) a model individualized family service plan (IFSP) form;

(3) a model form of the notice of procedural safeguards described in section 615(d); and

(4) a model form of the prior written notice described in subsections (b)(3) and (c)(1) of section 615 that is consistent with the requirements of this part and is sufficient to meet such requirements.

§ 1418. Program information

(a) In general

Each State that receives assistance under this part, and the Secretary of the Interior, shall provide data each year to the Secretary of Education and the public on the following:

(1)(A) The number and percentage of children with disabilities, by race, ethnicity, limited English proficiency status, gender, and disability category, who are in each of the following separate categories:

(i) Receiving a free appropriate public education.

(ii) Participating in regular education.

(iii) In separate classes, separate schools or facilities, or public or private residential facilities.

(iv) For each year of age from age 14 through 21, stopped receiving special education and related services because of program completion (including graduation with a regular secondary school diploma), or other reasons, and the reasons why those children stopped receiving special education and related services.

(v)(I) Removed to an interim alternative educational setting under section 615(k)(1).

(II) The acts or items precipitating those removals.

(III) The number of children with disabilities who are subject to long-term suspensions or expulsions.

(B) The number and percentage of children with disabilities, by race, gender, and ethnicity, who are receiving early intervention services.

(C) The number and percentage of children with disabilities, by race, gender, and ethnicity, who, from birth through age 2, stopped receiving early intervention services because of program completion or for other reasons.

(D) The incidence and duration of disciplinary actions by race, ethnicity, limited English proficiency status, gender, and disability category, of children with disabilities, including suspensions of 1 day or more.

(E) The number and percentage of children with disabilities who are removed to alternative educational settings or expelled as compared to children without disabilities who are removed to alternative educational settings or expelled.

(F) The number of due process complaints filed under section 615 and the number of hearings conducted.

(G) The number of hearings requested under section 615(k) and the number of changes in placements ordered as a result of those hearings.

(H) The number of mediations held and the number of settlement agreements reached through such mediations.

(2) The number and percentage of infants and toddlers, by race, and ethnicity, who are at risk of having substantial developmental delays (as defined in section 632), and who are receiving early intervention services under part C.

(3) Any other information that may be required by the Secretary.

(b) Data reporting.

(1) Protection of identifiable data.

The data described in subsection (a) shall be publicly reported by each State in a manner that does not result in the disclosure of data identifiable to individual children.

(2) Sampling.

The Secretary may permit States and the Secretary of the Interior to obtain the data described in subsection (a) through sampling.

(c) Technical assistance.

The Secretary may provide technical assistance to States to ensure compliance with the data collection and reporting requirements under this title.

(d) Disproportionality.

(1) In general.

Each State that receives assistance under this part, and the Secretary of the Interior, shall provide for the collection and examination of data to determine if significant disproportionality based on race and ethnicity is occurring in the State and the local educational agencies of the State with respect to —

(A) the identification of children as children with disabilities, including the identification of children as children with disabilities in accordance with a particular impairment described in section 602(3);

(B) the placement in particular educational settings of such children; and

(C) the incidence, duration, and type of disciplinary actions, including suspensions and expulsions.

(2) Review and revision of policies, practices, and procedures.

In the case of a determination of significant disproportionality with respect to the identification of children as children with disabilities, or the placement in particular educational settings of such children, in accordance with paragraph (1), the State or the Secretary of the Interior, as the case may be, shall —

(A) provide for the review and, if appropriate, revision of the policies, procedures, and practices used in such identification or placement to ensure that such policies, procedures, and practices comply with the requirements of this title;

(B) require any local educational agency identified under paragraph (1) to reserve the maximum amount of funds under section 613(f) to provide comprehensive coordinated early intervening services to serve children in the local educational agency, particularly children in those groups that were significantly overidentified under paragraph (1); and

(C) require the local educational agency to publicly report on the revision of policies, practices, and procedures described under subparagraph (A).

§ 1419. Preschool grants

(a) In general

The Secretary shall provide grants under this section to assist States to provide special education and related services, in accordance with this part —

(1) to children with disabilities aged 3 through 5, inclusive; and

(2) at the State's discretion, to 2-year-old children with disabilities who will turn 3 during the school year.

(b) Eligibility.

A State shall be eligible for a grant under this section if such State —

(1) is eligible under section 612 to receive a grant under this part; and

(2) makes a free appropriate public education available to all children with disabilities, aged 3 through 5, residing in the State.

(c) Allocations to states.

(1) In general.

The Secretary shall allocate the amount made available to carry out this section for a fiscal year among the States in accordance with paragraph (2) or (3), as the case may be.

(2) Increase in funds.

If the amount available for allocations to States under paragraph (1) for a fiscal year is equal to or greater than the amount allocated to the States under this section for the preceding fiscal year, those allocations shall be calculated as follows:

(A) Allocation.

(i) In general.

Except as provided in subparagraph (B), the Secretary shall —

(I) allocate to each State the amount the State received under this section for fiscal year 1997;

(II) allocate 85 percent of any remaining funds to States on the basis of the States' relative populations of children aged 3 through 5; and

(III) allocate 15 percent of those remaining funds to States on the basis of the States' relative populations of all children aged 3 through 5 who are living in poverty.

(ii) Data.

For the purpose of making grants under this paragraph, the Secretary shall use the most recent population data, including data on children living in poverty, that are available and satisfactory to the Secretary.

(B) Limitations.

Notwithstanding subparagraph (A), allocations under this paragraph shall be subject to the following:

(i) Preceding years.

No State's allocation shall be less than its allocation under this section for the preceding fiscal year.

(ii) Minimum.

No State's allocation shall be less than the greatest of —

(I) the sum of —

(aa) the amount the State received under this section for fiscal year 1997; and

(bb) 1/3 of 1 percent of the amount by which the amount appropriated under subsection (j) for the fiscal year exceeds the amount appropriated for this section for fiscal year 1997;

(II) the sum of —

(aa) the amount the State received under this section for the preceding fiscal year; and

(bb) that amount multiplied by the percentage by which the increase in the funds appropriated under this section from the preceding fiscal year exceeds 1.5 percent; or

(III) the sum of —

(aa) the amount the State received under this section for the preceding fiscal year; and

(bb) that amount multiplied by 90 percent of the percentage increase in the amount appropriated under this section from the preceding fiscal year.

(iii) Maximum.

Notwithstanding clause (ii), no State's allocation under this paragraph shall exceed the sum of —

(I) the amount the State received under this section for the preceding fiscal year; and

(II) that amount multiplied by the sum of 1.5 percent and the percentage increase in the amount appropriated under this section from the preceding fiscal year.

(C) Ratable reductions.

If the amount available for allocations under this paragraph is insufficient to pay those allocations in full, those allocations shall be ratably reduced, subject to subparagraph (B)(I).

(3) Decrease in funds.

If the amount available for allocations to States under paragraph (1) for a fiscal year is less than the amount allocated to the States under this section for the preceding fiscal year, those allocations shall be calculated as follows:

(A) Allocations.

If the amount available for allocations is greater than the amount allocated to the States for fiscal year 1997, each State shall be allocated the sum of —

(i) the amount the State received under this section for fiscal year 1997; and

(ii) an amount that bears the same relation to any remaining funds as the increase the State received under this section for the preceding fiscal year over fiscal year 1997 bears to the total of all such increases for all States.

(B) Ratable reductions.

If the amount available for allocations is equal to or less than the amount allocated to the States for fiscal year 1997, each State shall be allocated the amount the State received for fiscal year 1997, ratably reduced, if necessary.

(d) Reservation for state activities.

(1) In general.

Each State may reserve not more than the amount described in paragraph (2) for administration and other State-level activities in accordance with subsections (e) and (f).

(2) Amount described.

For each fiscal year, the Secretary shall determine and report to the State educational agency an amount that is 25 percent of the amount the State received under this section for fiscal year 1997, cumulatively adjusted by the Secretary for each succeeding fiscal year by the lesser of —

(A) the percentage increase, if any, from the preceding fiscal year in the State's allocation under this section; or

(B) the percentage increase, if any, from the preceding fiscal year in the Consumer Price Index For All Urban Consumers published by the Bureau of Labor Statistics of the Department of Labor.

(e) State administration.

(1) In general.

For the purpose of administering this section (including the coordination of activities under this part with, and providing technical assistance to, other programs that provide services to children with disabilities) a State may use not more than 20 percent of the maximum amount the State may reserve under subsection (d) for any fiscal year.

(2) Administration of part C.

Funds described in paragraph (1) may also be used for the administration of part C.

(f) Other state-level activities.

Each State shall use any funds the State reserves under subsection (d) and does not use for administration under subsection (e) —

(1) for support services (including establishing and implementing the mediation process required by section 615(e)), which may benefit children with disabilities younger than 3 or older than 5 as long as those services also benefit children with disabilities aged 3 through 5;

(2) for direct services for children eligible for services under this section;

(3) for activities at the State and local levels to meet the performance goals established by the State under section 612(a)(15);

(4) to supplement other funds used to develop and implement a statewide coordinated services system designed to improve results for children and families, including children with disabilities and their families, but not more than 1 percent of the amount received by the State under this section for a fiscal year;

(5) to provide early intervention services (which shall include an educational component that promotes school readiness and incor-

porates preliteracy, language, and numeracy skills) in accordance with part C to children with disabilities who are eligible for services under this section and who previously received services under part C until such children enter, or are eligible under State law to enter, kindergarten;

(6) at the State's discretion, to continue service coordination or case management for families who receive services under part C.

(g) Subgrants to local educational agencies.

(1) Subgrants required.

Each State that receives a grant under this section for any fiscal year shall distribute all of the grant funds that the State does not reserve under subsection (d) to local educational agencies in the State that have established their eligibility under section 613, as follows:

(A) Base payments.

The State shall first award each local educational agency described in paragraph (1) the amount that agency would have received under this section for fiscal year 1997 if the State had distributed 75 percent of its grant for that year under section 619(c)(3), as such section was then in effect.

(B) Allocation of remaining funds.

After making allocations under subparagraph (A), the State shall —

(i) allocate 85 percent of any remaining funds to those local educational agencies on the basis of the relative numbers of children enrolled in public and private elementary schools and secondary schools within the local educational agency's jurisdiction; and

(ii) allocate 15 percent of those remaining funds to those local educational agencies in accordance with their relative numbers of children living in poverty, as determined by the State educational agency.

(2) Reallocation of funds.

If a State educational agency determines that a local educational agency is adequately providing a free appropriate public education to all children with disabilities aged 3 through 5 residing in the area served by the local educational agency with State and local funds, the State educational agency may reallocate any portion of the funds under this section that are not needed by that local educational agency to provide a free appropriate public education to other local educational agencies in the State that are not adequately providing special education and related services to all children with disabilities aged 3 through 5 residing in the areas the other local educational agencies serve.

(h) Part C inapplicable.

Part C does not apply to any child with a disability receiving a free appropriate public education, in accordance with this part, with funds received under this section.

(i) State defined.

In this section, the term "State" means each of the 50 States, the District of Columbia, and the Commonwealth of Puerto Rico.

(j) Authorization of appropriations.

There are authorized to be appropriated to carry out this section such sums as may be necessary.

Part C — Infants and Toddlers with Disabilities

20 U.S.C §
1431	Findings and policy
1432	Definitions
1433	General authority
1434	Eligibility
1435	Requirements for statewide system
1436	Individualized family service plan
1437	State application and assurances
1438	Uses of funds
1439	Procedural safeguards
1440	Payor of last resort
1441	State interagency coordinating council
1442	Federal administration
1443	Allocation of funds
1444	Authorization of appropriations

Part C — Infants and Toddlers with Disabilities

§1431. Findings and policy

(a) Findings

The Congress finds that there is an urgent and substantial need —

(1) to enhance the development of infants and toddlers with disabilities, to minimize their potential for developmental delay, and to recognize the significant brain development that occurs during a child's first 3 years of life;

(2) to reduce the educational costs to our society, including our Nation's schools, by minimizing the need for special education and related services after infants and toddlers with disabilities reach school age;

(3) to maximize the potential for individuals with disabilities to live independently in society;

(4) to enhance the capacity of families to meet the special needs of their infants and toddlers with disabilities; and

(5) to enhance the capacity of State and local agencies and service providers to identify, evaluate, and meet the needs of all children, particularly minority, low-income, inner city, and rural children, and infants and toddlers in foster care.

(b) Policy.

It is the policy of the United States to provide financial assistance to States —

(1) to develop and implement a statewide, comprehensive, coordinated, multidisciplinary, interagency system that provides early intervention services for infants and toddlers with disabilities and their families;

(2) to facilitate the coordination of payment for early intervention services from Federal, State, local, and private sources (including public and private insurance coverage);

(3) to enhance State capacity to provide quality early intervention services and expand and improve existing early intervention services being provided to infants and toddlers with disabilities and their families; and

(4) to encourage States to expand opportunities for children under 3 years of age who would be at risk of having substantial developmental delay if they did not receive early intervention services.

§ 1432. Definitions

As used in this subchapter:

(1) At-risk infant or toddler

The term "at-risk infant or toddler" means an individual under 3 years of age who would be at risk of experiencing a substantial developmental delay if early intervention services were not provided to the individual.

(2) Council.

The term "council" means a State interagency coordinating council established under section 641.

(3) Developmental delay.

The term "developmental delay", when used with respect to an individual residing in a State, has the meaning given such term by the State under section 635(a)(1).

(4) Early intervention services.

The term "early intervention services" means developmental services that —

(A) are provided under public supervision;

(B) are provided at no cost except where Federal or State law provides for a system of payments by families, including a schedule of sliding fees;

(C) are designed to meet the developmental needs of an infant or toddler with a disability, as identified by the individualized family service plan team, in any 1 or more of the following areas:

(i) physical development;
(ii) cognitive development;
(iii) communication development;
(iv) social or emotional development; or
(v) adaptive development;

(D) meet the standards of the State in which the services are provided, including the requirements of this part;

(E) include —
(i) family training, counseling, and home visits;
(ii) special instruction;
(iii) speech-language pathology and audiology services, and sign language and cued language services;
(iv) occupational therapy;
(v) physical therapy;
(vi) psychological services;
(vii) service coordination services;
(viii) medical services only for diagnostic or evaluation purposes;
(ix) early identification, screening, and assessment services;
(x) health services necessary to enable the infant or toddler to benefit from the other early intervention services;
(xi) social work services;
(xii) vision services;
(xiii) assistive technology devices and assistive technology services; and
(xiv) transportation and related costs that are necessary to enable an infant or toddler and the infant's or toddler's family to receive another service described in this paragraph;

(F) are provided by qualified personnel, including —
(i) special educators;
(ii) speech-language pathologists and audiologists;
(iii) occupational therapists;
(iv) physical therapists;
(v) psychologists;
(vi) social workers;
(vii) nurses;
(viii) registered dietitians;
(ix) family therapists;
(x) vision specialists, including ophthalmologists and optometrists;
(xi) orientation and mobility specialists; and
(xii) pediatricians and other physicians;

(G) to the maximum extent appropriate, are provided in natural environments, including the home, and community settings in which children without disabilities participate; and

(H) are provided in conformity with an individualized family service plan adopted in accordance with section 636.

(5) Infant or toddler with a disability.

The term "infant or toddler with a disability" —

(A) means an individual under 3 years of age who needs early intervention services because the individual —
(i) is experiencing developmental delays, as measured by appropriate diagnostic instruments and procedures in 1 or more of the areas of cognitive development, physical development, communication development, social or emotional development, and adaptive development; or
(ii) has a diagnosed physical or mental condition that has a high probability of resulting in developmental delay; and

(B) may also include, at a State's discretion —
(i) at-risk infants and toddlers; and
(ii) children with disabilities who are eligible for services under section 619 and who previously received services under this part until such children enter, or are eligible under State law to enter, kindergarten or elementary school, as appropriate, provided that any programs under this part serving such children shall include —
(I) an educational component that promotes school readiness and incorporates pre-literacy, language, and numeracy skills; and
(II) a written notification to parents of their rights and responsibilities in determining whether their child will continue to receive services under this part or participate in preschool programs under section 619.

§ 1433. General authority

The Secretary shall, in accordance with this part, make grants to States (from their allotments under section 643) to assist each State to maintain and implement a statewide, comprehensive, coordinated, multidisciplinary, interagency system to provide early intervention services for infants and toddlers with disabilities and their families.

§ 1434. Eligibility

In order to be eligible for a grant under section 633, a State shall provide assurances to the Secretary that the State —

(1) has adopted a policy that appropriate early intervention services are available to all infants and toddlers with disabilities in the State and their families, including Indian infants and toddlers with disabilities and their families residing on a reservation geographically located in the State, infants and toddlers with disabilities who are homeless children and their families, and infants and toddlers with disabilities who are wards of the State; and

(2) has in effect a statewide system that meets the requirements of section 635

§ 1435. Requirements for statewide system

(a) In general

A statewide system described in section 633 shall include, at a minimum, the following components:

(1) A rigorous definition of the term "developmental delay" that will be used by the State in carrying out programs under this part in order to appropriately identify infants and toddlers with disabilities that are in need of services under this part.

(2) A State policy that is in effect and that ensures that appropriate early intervention services based on scientifically based research, to the extent practicable, are available to all infants and toddlers with disabilities and their families, including Indian infants and toddlers with disabilities and their families residing on a reservation geographically located in the State and infants and toddlers with disabilities who are homeless children and their families.

(3) A timely, comprehensive, multidisciplinary evaluation of the functioning of each infant or toddler with a disability in the State, and a family-directed identification of the needs of each family of such an infant or toddler, to assist appropriately in the development of the infant or toddler.

(4) For each infant or toddler with a disability in the State, an individualized family service plan in accordance with section 636, including service coordination services in accordance with such service plan.

(5) A comprehensive child find system, consistent with part B, including a system for making referrals to service providers that includes timelines and provides for participation by primary referral sources and that ensures rigorous standards for appropriately identifying infants and toddlers with disabilities for services under this part that will reduce the need for future services.

(6) A public awareness program focusing on early identification of infants and toddlers with disabilities, including the preparation and dissemination by the lead agency designated or established under paragraph (10) to all primary referral sources, especially hospitals and physicians, of information to be given to parents, especially to inform parents with premature infants, or infants with other physical risk factors associated with learning or developmental complications, on the availability of early intervention services under this part and of services under section 619, and procedures for assisting such sources in disseminating such information to parents of infants and toddlers with disabilities.

(7) A central directory that includes information on early intervention services, resources, and experts available in the State and research and demonstration projects being conducted in the State.

(8) A comprehensive system of personnel development, including the training of paraprofessionals and the training of primary referral sources with respect to the basic components of early intervention services available in the State that —

(A) shall include —

(i) implementing innovative strategies and activities for the recruitment and retention of early education service providers;

(ii) promoting the preparation of early intervention providers who are fully and appropriately qualified provide early intervention services under this part; and

(iii) training personnel to coordinate transition services for infants and toddlers served under this part from a program providing early intervention services under this part and under part B (other than section 619), to a preschool program receiving funds under section 619, or another appropriate program; and

(B) may include —

(i) training personnel to work in rural and inner-city areas; and

(ii) training personnel in the emotional and social development of young children.

(9) Policies and procedures relating to the establishment and maintenance of qualifications to ensure that personnel necessary to carry out this part are appropriately and adequately prepared and trained, including the establishment and maintenance of qualifications that are consistent with any State-approved or recognized certification, licensing, registration, or other comparable requirements that apply to the area in which such personnel are providing early intervention services, except that nothing in this part (including this paragraph) shall be construed to prohibit the use of paraprofessionals and assistants who are appropriately trained and supervised in accordance with State law, regulation, or written policy, to assist in the provision of early intervention services under this part to infants and toddlers with disabilities.

(10) A single line of responsibility in a lead agency designated or established by the Governor for carrying out —

(A) the general administration and supervision of programs and activities receiving assistance under section 633, and the monitoring of programs and activities used by the State to carry out this part, whether or not such programs or activities are receiving assistance made available under section 633, to ensure that the State complies with this part;

(B) the identification and coordination of all available resources within the State from Federal, State, local, and private sources;

(C) the assignment of financial responsibility in accordance with section 637(a)(2) to the appropriate agencies;

(D) the development of procedures to ensure that services are provided to infants and toddlers with disabilities and their families under this part in a timely manner pending the resolution of any disputes among public agencies or service providers;

(E) the resolution of intra- and interagency disputes; and

(F) the entry into formal interagency agreements that define the financial responsibility of each agency for paying for early intervention services (consistent with State law) and procedures for resolving disputes and that include all additional components necessary to ensure meaningful cooperation and coordination.

(11) A policy pertaining to the contracting or making of other arrangements with service providers to provide early intervention services in the State, consistent with the provisions of this part, including the contents of the application used and the conditions of the contract or other arrangements.

(12) A procedure for securing timely reimbursements of funds used under this part in accordance with section 640(a).

(13) Procedural safeguards with respect to programs under this part, as required by section 639.

(14) A system for compiling data requested by the Secretary under section 618 that relates to this part.

(15) A State interagency coordinating council that meets the requirements of section 641.

(16) Policies and procedures to ensure that, consistent with section 636(d)(5) —

(A) to the maximum extent appropriate, early intervention services are provided in natural environments; and

(B) the provision of early intervention services for any infant or toddler with a disability occurs in a setting other than a natural environment that is most appropriate, as determined by the parent and the individualized family service plan team, only when early intervention cannot be achieved satisfactorily for the infant or toddler in a natural environment.

(b) Policy.

In implementing subsection (a)(9), a State may adopt a policy that includes making ongoing good-faith efforts to recruit and hire appropriately and adequately trained personnel to provide early intervention services to infants and toddlers with disabilities, including, in a geographic area of the State where there is a shortage of such personnel, the most qualified individuals available who are making satisfactory progress toward completing applicable course work necessary to meet the standards described in subsection (a)(9).

(c) Flexibility to serve children 3 years of age until entrance into elementary school.

(1) In general.

A statewide system described in section 633 may include a State policy, developed and implemented jointly by the lead agency and the State educational agency, under which parents of children with disabilities who are eligible for services under section 619 and previously received services under this part, may choose the continuation of early intervention services (which shall include an educational component that promotes school readiness and incorporates preliteracy, language, and numeracy skills) for such children under this part until such children enter, or are eligible under State law to enter, kindergarten.

(2) Requirements.

If a statewide system includes a State policy described in paragraph (1), the statewide system shall ensure that —

(A) parents of children with disabilities served pursuant to this subsection are provided annual notice that contains —

(i) a description of the rights of such parents to elect to receive services pursuant to this subsection or under part B; and

(ii) an explanation of the differences between services provided pursuant to this subsection and services provided under part B, including —

(I) types of services and the locations at which the services are provided;

(II) applicable procedural safeguards; and

(III) possible costs (including any fees to be charged to families as described in section 632(4)(B)), if any, to parents of infants or toddlers with disabilities;

(B) services provided pursuant to this subsection include an educational component that promotes school readiness and incorporates preliteracy, language, and numeracy skills;

(C) the State policy will not affect the right of any child served pursuant to this subsection to instead receive a free appropriate public education under part B;

(D) all early intervention services outlined in the child's individualized family service plan under section 636 are continued while any eligibility determination is being made for services under this subsection;

(E) the parents of infants or toddlers with disabilities (as defined in section 632(5)(A)) provide informed written consent to the State, before such infants or toddlers reach 3 years of age, as to whether such parents intend to choose the continuation of early intervention services pursuant to this subsection for such infants or toddlers;

(F) the requirements under section 637(a)(9) shall not apply with respect to a child who is receiving services in accordance with this subsection until not less than 90 days (and at the discretion of the parties to the conference, not more than 9 months) before the time the child will no longer receive those services; and

(G) there will be a referral for evaluation for early intervention services of a child who experiences a substantiated case of trauma due to exposure to family violence (as defined in section 320 of the Family Violence Prevention and Services Act).

(3) Reporting requirement.

If a statewide system includes a State policy described in paragraph (1), the State shall submit to the Secretary, in the State's report under section 637(b)(4)(A), a report on the number and percentage of children with disabilities who are eligible for services under section 619 but whose parents choose for such children to continue to receive early intervention services under this part.

(4) Available funds.

If a statewide system includes a State policy described in paragraph (1), the policy shall describe the funds (including an identification as Federal, State, or local funds) that will be used to ensure that the option described in paragraph (1) is available to eligible children and families who provide the consent described in paragraph (2)(E), including fees (if any) to be charged to families as described in section 632(4)(B).

(5) Rules of construction.

(A) Services under part B.

If a statewide system includes a State policy described in paragraph (1), a State that provides services in accordance with this subsection to a child with a disability who is eligible for services under section 619 shall not be required to provide the child with a free appropriate public education under part B for the period of time in which the child is receiving services under this part.

(B) Services under this part.

Nothing in this subsection shall be construed to require a provider of services under this part to provide a child served under this part with a free appropriate public education.

§ 1436. Individualized family service plan

(a) Assessment and program development

A statewide system described in section 633 shall provide, at a minimum, for each infant or toddler with a disability, and the infant's or toddler's family, to receive —

(1) a multidisciplinary assessment of the unique strengths and needs of the infant or toddler and the identification of services appropriate to meet such needs;

(2) a family-directed assessment of the resources, priorities, and concerns of the family and the identification of the supports and services necessary to enhance the family's capacity to meet the developmental needs of the infant or toddler; and

(3) a written individualized family service plan developed by a multidisciplinary team, including the parents, as required by subsection (e), including a description of the appropriate transition services for the infant or toddler.

(b) Periodic review.

The individualized family service plan shall be evaluated once a year and the family shall be provided a review of the plan at 6-month intervals (or more often where appropriate based on infant or toddler and family needs).

(c) Promptness after assessment.

The individualized family service plan shall be developed within a reasonable time after the assessment required by subsection (a)(1) is completed. With the parents' consent, early intervention services may commence prior to the completion of the assessment.

(d) Content of plan.

The individualized family service plan shall be in writing and contain —

(1) a statement of the infant's or toddler's present levels of physical development, cognitive development, communication development, social or emotional development, and adaptive development, based on objective criteria;

(2) a statement of the family's resources, priorities, and concerns relating to enancing the development of the family's infant or toddler with a disability;

(3) a statement of the measurable results or outcomes expected to be achieved for the infant or toddler and the family, including pre-literacy and language skills, as developmentally appropriate for the child, and the criteria, procedures, and timelines used to determine the degree to which progress toward achieving the results or outcomes is being made and whether modifications or revisions of the results or outcomes or services are necessary;

(4) a statement of specific early intervention services based on peer-reviewed research, to the extent practicable, necessary to meet the unique needs of the infant or toddler and the family, including the frequency, intensity, and method of delivering services;

(5) a statement of the natural environments in which early intervention services will appropriately be provided, including a justification of the extent, if any, to which the services will not be provided in a natural environment;

(6) the projected dates for initiation of services and the anticipated length, duration, and frequency of the services;

(7) the identification of the service coordinator from the profession most immediately relevant to the infant's or toddler's or family's needs (or who is otherwise qualified to carry out all applicable responsibilities under this part) who will be responsible for the implementation of the plan and coordination with other agencies and persons, including transition services; and

(8) the steps to be taken to support the transition of the toddler with a disability to preschool or other appropriate services.

(e) Parental consent.

The contents of the individualized family service plan shall be fully explained to the parents and informed written consent from the parents shall be obtained prior to the provision of early intervention services described in such plan. If the parents do not provide consent with respect to a particular early intervention service, then only the early intervention services to which consent is obtained shall be provided.

§1437. State application and assurances

(a) Application

A State desiring to receive a grant under section 633 shall submit an application to the Secretary at such time and in such manner as the Secretary may reasonably require. The application shall contain —

(1) a designation of the lead agency in the State that will be responsible for the administration of funds provided under section 633;

(2) a certification to the Secretary that the arrangements to establish financial responsibility for services provided under this part pursuant to section 640(b) are current as of the date of submission of the certification;

(3) information demonstrating eligibility of the State under section 634, including —

(A) information demonstrating to the Secretary's satisfaction that the State has in effect the statewide system required by section 633; and

(B) a description of services to be provided to infants and toddlers with disabilities and their families through the system;

(4) if the State provides services to at-risk infants and toddlers through the statewide system, a description of such services;

(5) a description of the uses for which funds will be expended in accordance with this part;

(6) a description of the State policies and procedures that require the referral for early intervention services under this part of a child under the age of 3 who —

(A) is involved in a substantiated case of child abuse or neglect; or

(B) is identified as affected by illegal substance abuse, or withdrawal symptoms resulting from prenatal drug exposure;

(7) a description of the procedure used to ensure that resources are made available under this part for all geographic areas within the State;

(8) a description of State policies and procedures that ensure that, prior to the adoption by the State of any other policy or procedure necessary to meet the requirements of this part, there are public hearings, adequate notice of the hearings, and an opportunity for comment available to the general public, including individuals with disabilities and parents of infants and toddlers with disabilities;

(9) a description of the policies and procedures to be used —

(A) to ensure a smooth transition for toddlers receiving early intervention services under this part (and children receiving those services under section 635(c)) to preschool, school, other appropriate services, or exiting the program, including a description of how —

(i) the families of such toddlers and children will be included in the transition plans required by subparagraph (C); and

(ii) the lead agency designated or established under section 635(a)(10) will —

(I) notify the local educational agency for the area in which such a child resides that the child will shortly reach the age of eligibility for preschool services under part B, as determined in accordance with State law;

(II) in the case of a child who may be eligible for such preschool services, with the approval of the family of the child, convene a conference among the lead agency, the family, and the local educational agency not less than 90 days (and at the discretion of all such parties, not more than 9 months) before the child is eligible for the preschool services, to discuss any such services that the child may receive; and

(III) in the case of a child who may not be eligible for such preschool services, with the approval of the family, make reasonable efforts to convene a conference among the lead agency, the family, and providers of other appropriate services for children who are not eligible for preschool services under part B, to discuss the appropriate services that the child may receive;

(B) to review the child's program options for the period from the child's third birthday through the remainder of the school year; and

(C) to establish a transition plan, including, as appropriate, steps to exit from the program;

(10) a description of State efforts to promote collaboration among Early Head Start programs under section 645A of the Head Start Act, early education and child care programs, and services under part C; and

(11) such other information and assurances as the Secretary may reasonably require.

(b) Assurances.

The application described in subsection (a) —

(1) shall provide satisfactory assurance that Federal funds made available under section 643 to the State will be expended in accordance with this part;

(2) shall contain an assurance that the State will comply with the requirements of section 640;

(3) shall provide satisfactory assurance that the control of funds provided under section 643, and title to property derived from those funds, will be in a public agency for the uses and purposes provided in this part and that a public agency will administer such funds and property;

(4) shall provide for —

(A) making such reports in such form and containing such information as the Secretary may require to carry out the Secretary's functions under this part; and

(B) keeping such reports and affording such access to the reports as the Secretary may find necessary to ensure the correctness and verification of those reports and proper disbursement of Federal funds under this part;

(5) provide satisfactory assurance that Federal funds made available under section 643 to the State —

(A) will not be commingled with State funds; and

(B) will be used so as to supplement the level of State and local funds expended for infants and toddlers with disabilities and their families and in no case to supplant those State and local funds;

(6) shall provide satisfactory assurance that such fiscal control and fund accounting procedures will be adopted as may be necessary to ensure proper disbursement of, and accounting for, Federal funds paid under section 643 to the State;

(7) shall provide satisfactory assurance that policies and procedures have been adopted to ensure meaningful involvement of underserved groups, including minority, low-income, homeless, and rural families and children with disabilities who are wards of the State, in the planning and implementation of all the requirements of this part; and

(8) shall contain such other information and assurances as the Secretary may reasonably require by regulation.

(c) Standard for disapproval of application.

The Secretary may not disapprove such an application unless the Secretary determines, after notice and opportunity for a hearing, that the application fails to comply with the requirements of this section.

(d) Subsequent state application.

If a State has on file with the Secretary a policy, procedure, or assurance that demonstrates that the State meets a requirement of this section, including any policy or procedure filed under this part (as in effect before the date of enactment of the Individuals with Disabilities Education Improvement Act of 2004), the Secretary shall consider the State to have met the requirement for purposes of receiving a grant under this part.

(e) Modification of application.

An application submitted by a State in accordance with this section shall remain in effect until the State submits to the Secretary such modifications as the State determines necessary. This section shall apply to a modification of an application to the same extent and in the same manner as this section applies to the original application.

(f) Modifications required by the secretary.

The Secretary may require a State to modify its application under this section, but only to the extent necessary to ensure the State's compliance with this part, if —

(1) an amendment is made to this title, or a Federal regulation issued under this title;

(2) a new interpretation of this title is

made by a Federal court or the State's highest court; or

(3) an official finding of noncompliance with Federal law or regulations is made with respect to the State.

§ 1438. Uses of funds

In addition to using funds provided under section 633 to maintain and implement the statewide system required by such section, a State may use such funds —

(1) for direct early intervention services for infants and toddlers with disabilities, and their families, under this part that are not otherwise funded through other public or private sources;

(2) to expand and improve on services for infants and toddlers and their families under this part that are otherwise available;

(3) to provide a free appropriate public education, in accordance with part B, to children with disabilities from their third birthday to the beginning of the following school year;

(4) with the written consent of the parents, to continue to provide early intervention services under this part to children with disabilities from their 3rd birthday until such children enter, or are eligible under State law to enter, kindergarten, in lieu of a free appropriate public education provided in accordance with part B; and

(5) in any State that does not provide services for at-risk infants and toddlers under section 637(a)(4), to strengthen the statewide system by initiating, expanding, or improving collaborative efforts related to at-risk infants and toddlers, including establishing linkages with appropriate public or private community-based organizations, services, and personnel for the purposes of —

(A) identifying and evaluating at-risk infants and toddlers;

(B) making referrals of the infants and toddlers identified and evaluated under subparagraph (A); and

(C) conducting periodic follow-up on each such referral to determine if the status of the infant or toddler involved has changed with respect to the eligibility of the infant or toddler for services under this part.

§ 1439. Procedural safeguards

(a) Minimum procedures

The procedural safeguards required to be included in a statewide system under section 635(a)(13) shall provide, at a minimum, the following:

(1) The timely administrative resolution of complaints by parents. Any party aggrieved by the findings and decision regarding an administrative complaint shall have the right to bring a civil action with respect to the complaint in any State court of competent jurisdiction or in a district court of the United States without regard to the amount in controversy. In any action brought under this paragraph, the court shall receive the records of the administrative proceedings, shall hear additional evidence at the request of a party, and, basing its decision on the preponderance of the evidence, shall grant such relief as the court determines is appropriate.

(2) The right to confidentiality of personally identifiable information, including the right of parents to written notice of and written consent to the exchange of such information among agencies consistent with Federal and State law.

(3) The right of the parents to determine whether they, their infant or toddler, or other family members will accept or decline any early intervention service under this part in accordance with State law without jeopardizing other early intervention services under this part.

(4) The opportunity for parents to examine records relating to assessment, screening, eligibility determinations, and the development and implementation of the individualized family service plan.

(5) Procedures to protect the rights of the infant or toddler whenever the parents of the infant or toddler are not known or cannot be found or the infant or toddler is a ward of the State, including the assignment of an individual (who shall not be an employee of the State lead agency, or other State agency, and who shall not be any person, or any employee of a person, providing early intervention services to the infant or toddler or any family member of the infant or toddler) to act as a surrogate for the parents.

(6) Written prior notice to the parents of

the infant or toddler with a disability whenever the State agency or service provider proposes to initiate or change, or refuses to initiate or change, the identification, evaluation, or placement of the infant or toddler with a disability, or the provision of appropriate early intervention services to the infant or toddler.

(7) Procedures designed to ensure that the notice required by paragraph (6) fully informs the parents, in the parents' native language, unless it clearly is not feasible to do so, of all procedures available pursuant to this section.

(8) The right of parents to use mediation in accordance with section 615, except that —

(A) any reference in the section to a State educational agency shall be considered to be a reference to a State's lead agency established or designated under section 635(a)(10);

(B) any reference in the section to a local educational agency shall be considered to be a reference to a local service provider or the State's lead agency under this part, as the case may be; and

(C) any reference in the section to the provision of a free appropriate public education to children with disabilities shall be considered to be a reference to the provision of appropriate early intervention services to infants and toddlers with disabilities.

(b) Services during pendency of proceedings.

During the pendency of any proceeding or action involving a complaint by the parents of an infant or toddler with a disability, unless the State agency and the parents otherwise agree, the infant or toddler shall continue to receive the appropriate early intervention services currently being provided or, if applying for initial services, shall receive the services not in dispute.

§ 1440. Payor of last resort

(a) Nonsubstitution

Funds provided under section 643 may not be used to satisfy a financial commitment for services that would have been paid for from another public or private source, including any medical program administered by the Secretary of Defense, but for the enactment of this part, except that whenever considered necessary to prevent a delay in the receipt of appropriate early intervention services by an infant, toddler, or family in a timely fashion, funds provided under section 643 may be used to pay the provider of services pending reimbursement from the agency that has ultimate responsibility for the payment.

(b) Obligations related to and methods of ensuring services.

(1) Establishing financial responsibility for services.

(A) In general.

The Chief Executive Officer of a State or designee of the officer shall ensure that an interagency agreement or other mechanism for interagency coordination is in effect between each public agency and the designated lead agency, in order to ensure —

(i) the provision of, and financial responsibility for, services provided under this part; and

(ii) such services are consistent with the requirements of section 635 and the State's application pursuant to section 637, including the provision of such services during the pendency of any such dispute.

(B) Consistency between agreements or mechanisms under part B.

The Chief Executive Officer of a State or designee of the officer shall ensure that the terms and conditions of such agreement or mechanism are consistent with the terms and conditions of the State's agreement or mechanism under section 612(a)(12), where appropriate.

(2) Reimbursement for services by public agency.

(A) In general.

If a public agency other than an educational agency fails to provide or pay for the services pursuant to an agreement required under paragraph (1), the local educational agency or State agency (as determined by the Chief Executive Officer or designee) shall provide or pay for the provision of such services to the child.

(B) Reimbursement.

Such local educational agency or State agency is authorized to claim reimbursement for the services from the public agency that failed to provide or pay for such services and such public agency shall reimburse the local educational agency or State agency pursuant to the terms of the interagency agreement or other mechanism required under paragraph (1).

(3) Special rule.

The requirements of paragraph (1) may be met through —

(A) State statute or regulation;

(B) signed agreements between respective agency officials that clearly identify the responsibilities of each agency relating to the provision of services; or

(C) other appropriate written methods as determined by the Chief Executive Officer of the State or designee of the officer and approved by the Secretary through the review and approval of the State's application pursuant to section 637.

(c) Reduction of other benefits.

Nothing in this part shall be construed to permit the State to reduce medical or other assistance available or to alter eligibility under title V of the Social Security Act (relating to maternal and child health) or title XIX of the Social Security Act (relating to medicaid for infants or toddlers with disabilities) within the State.

§ 1441. State interagency coordinating council

(a) Establishment

(1) In general

A State that desires to receive financial assistance under this part shall establish a State interagency coordinating council.

(2) Appointment.

The council shall be appointed by the Governor. In making appointments to the council, the Governor shall ensure that the membership of the council reasonably represents the population of the State.

(3) Chairperson.

The Governor shall designate a member of the council to serve as the chairperson of the council, or shall require the council to so designate such a member. Any member of the council who is a representative of the lead agency designated under section 635(a)(10) may not serve as the chairperson of the council.

(b) Composition.

(1) In general.

The council shall be composed as follows:

(A) Parents.

Not less than 20 percent of the members shall be parents of infants or toddlers with disabilities or children with disabilities aged 12 or younger, with knowledge of, or experience with, programs for infants and toddlers with disabilities. Not less than 1 such member shall be a parent of an infant or toddler with a disability or a child with a disability aged 6 or younger.

(B) Service providers.

Not less than 20 percent of the members shall be public or private providers of early intervention services.

(C) State legislature.

Not less than 1 member shall be from the State legislature.

(D) Personnel preparation.

Not less than 1 member shall be involved in personnel preparation.

(E) Agency for early intervention services.

Not less than 1 member shall be from each of the State agencies involved in the provision of, or payment for, early intervention services to infants and toddlers with disabilities and their families and shall have sufficient authority to engage in policy planning and implementation on behalf of such agencies.

(F) Agency for preschool services.

Not less than 1 member shall be from the State educational agency responsible for preschool services to children with disabilities and shall have sufficient authority to engage in policy planning and implementation on behalf of such agency.

(G) State medicaid agency.

Not less than 1 member shall be from the agency responsible for the State medicaid program.

(H) Head start agency.

Not less than 1 member shall be a representative from a Head Start agency or program in the State.

(I) Child care agency.

Not less than 1 member shall be a representative from a State agency responsible for child care.

(J) Agency for health insurance.

Not less than 1 member shall be from the agency responsible for the State regulation of health insurance.

(K) Office of the coordinator of education of homeless children and youth.

Not less than 1 member shall be a representative designated by the Office of Coordinator for Education of Homeless Children and Youths.

(L) State foster care representative.

Not less than 1 member shall be a representative from the State child welfare agency responsible for foster care.

(M) Mental health agency.

Not less than 1 member shall be a representative from the State agency responsible for children's mental health.

(2) Other members.

The council may include other members selected by the Governor, including a representative from the Bureau of Indian Affairs (BIA), or where there is no BIA-operated or BIA-funded school, from the Indian Health Service or the tribe or tribal council.

(c) Meetings.

The council shall meet, at a minimum, on a quarterly basis, and in such places as the council determines necessary. The meetings shall be publicly announced, and, to the extent appropriate, open and accessible to the general public.

(d) Management authority.

Subject to the approval of the Governor, the council may prepare and approve a budget using funds under this part to conduct hearings and forums, to reimburse members of the council for reasonable and necessary expenses for attending council meetings and performing council duties (including child care for parent representatives), to pay compensation to a member of the council if the member is not employed or must forfeit wages from other employment when performing official council business, to hire staff, and to obtain the services of such professional, technical, and clerical personnel as may be necessary to carry out its functions under this part.

(e) Functions of council.

(1) Duties.

The council shall —

(A) advise and assist the lead agency designated or established under section 635(a)(10) in the performance of the responsibilities set forth in such section, particularly the identification of the sources of fiscal and other support for services for early intervention programs, assignment of financial responsibility to the appropriate agency, and the promotion of the interagency agreements;

(B) advise and assist the lead agency in the preparation of applications and amendments thereto;

(C) advise and assist the State educational agency regarding the transition of toddlers with disabilities to preschool and other appropriate services; and

(D) prepare and submit an annual report to the Governor and to the Secretary on the status of early intervention programs for infants and toddlers with disabilities and their families operated within the State.

(2) Authorized activity.

The council may advise and assist the lead agency and the State educational agency regarding the provision of appropriate services for children from birth through age 5. The council may advise appropriate agencies in the State with respect to the integration of services for infants and toddlers with disabilities and at-risk infants and toddlers and their families, regardless of whether at-risk infants and toddlers are eligible for early intervention services in the State.

(f) Conflict of interest.

No member of the council shall cast a vote on any matter that is likely to provide a direct financial benefit to that member or otherwise give the appearance of a conflict of interest under State law.

§ 1442. Federal administration

Sections 616, 617, and 618 shall, to the extent not inconsistent with this part, apply to the program authorized by this part, except that —

(1) any reference in such sections to a State educational agency shall be considered to be a reference to a State's lead agency established or designated under section 635(a)(10);

(2) any reference in such sections to a local educational agency, educational service agency, or a State agency shall be considered to be a reference to an early intervention service provider under this part; and

(3) any reference to the education of children with disabilities or the education of all children with disabilities shall be considered to be a reference to the provision of appropriate early intervention services to infants and toddlers with disabilities.

§ 1443. Allocation of funds

(a) Reservation of funds for outlying areas

(1) In general

From the sums appropriated to carry out this part for any fiscal year, the Secretary may reserve not more than 1 percent for payments to Guam, American Samoa, the United States Virgin Islands, and the Commonwealth of the Northern Mariana Islands in accordance with their respective needs for assistance under this part.

(2) Consolidation of funds.

The provisions of Public Law 95-134, permitting the consolidation of grants to the outlying areas, shall not apply to funds those areas receive under this part.

(b) Payments to Indians.

(1) In general.

The Secretary shall, subject to this subsection, make payments to the Secretary of the Interior to be distributed to tribes, tribal organizations (as defined under section 4 of the Indian Self-Determination and Education Assistance Act), or consortia of the above entities for the coordination of assistance in the provision of early intervention services by the States to infants and toddlers with disabilities and their families on reservations served by elementary schools and secondary schools for Indian children operated or funded by the Department of the Interior. The amount of such payment for any fiscal year shall be 1.25 percent of the aggregate of the amount available to all States under this part for such fiscal year.

(2) Allocation.

For each fiscal year, the Secretary of the Interior shall distribute the entire payment received under paragraph (1) by providing to each tribe, tribal organization, or consortium an amount based on the number of infants and toddlers residing on the reservation, as determined annually, divided by the total of such children served by all tribes, tribal organizations, or consortia.

(3) Information.

To receive a payment under this subsection, the tribe, tribal organization, or consortium shall submit such information to the Secretary of the Interior as is needed to determine the amounts to be distributed under paragraph (2).

(4) Use of funds.

The funds received by a tribe, tribal organization, or consortium shall be used to assist States in child find, screening, and other procedures for the early identification of Indian children under 3 years of age and for parent training. Such funds may also be used to provide early intervention services in accordance with this part. Such activities may be carried out directly or through contracts or cooperative agreements with the Bureau of Indian Affairs, local educational agencies, and other public or private nonprofit organizations. The tribe, tribal organization, or consortium is encouraged to involve Indian parents in the development and implementation of these activities. The above entities shall, as appropriate, make referrals to local, State, or Federal entities for the provision of services or further diagnosis.

(5) Reports.

To be eligible to receive a payment under paragraph (2), a tribe, tribal organization, or consortium shall make a biennial report to the Secretary of the Interior of activities undertaken under this subsection, including the number of contracts and cooperative agreements entered into, the number of infants and toddlers contacted and receiving services for each year, and the estimated number of infants and toddlers needing services during the 2 years following the year in which the report is made. The Secretary of the Interior shall include a summary of this information on a biennial basis to the Secretary of Education along with such other information as required under section 611(h)(3)(E). The Secretary of Education may require any additional information from the Secretary of the Interior.

(6) Prohibited uses of funds.

None of the funds under this subsection may be used by the Secretary of the Interior for administrative purposes, including child count, and the provision of technical assistance.

(c) State allotments.

(1) In general.

Except as provided in paragraphs (2) and (3), from the funds remaining for each fiscal year after the reservation and payments under subsections (a), (b), and (e), the Secretary shall first allot to each State an amount that bears the same ratio to the amount of such remainder as the number of infants and toddlers in the State bears to the number of infants and toddlers in all States.

(2) Minimum allotments.

Except as provided in paragraph (3), no State shall receive an amount under this section for any fiscal year that is less than the greater of —

(A) 1/2 of 1 percent of the remaining amount described in paragraph (1); or

(B) $500,000.

(3) Ratable reduction.

(A) In general.

If the sums made available under this part for any fiscal year are insufficient to pay the full amounts that all States are eligible to receive under this subsection for such year, the Secretary shall ratably reduce the allotments to such States for such year.

(B) Additional funds.

If additional funds become available for making payments under this subsection for a fiscal year, allotments that were reduced under subparagraph (A) shall be increased on the same basis the allotments were reduced.

(4) Definitions.

In this subsection —

(A) the terms "infants" and "toddlers" mean children under 3 years of age; and

(B) the term "State" means each of the 50 States, the District of Columbia, and the Commonwealth of Puerto Rico.

(d) Reallotment of funds.

If a State elects not to receive its allotment under subsection (c), the Secretary shall reallot, among the remaining States, amounts from such State in accordance with such subsection.

(e) Reservation for state incentive grants.

(1) In general.

For any fiscal year for which the amount appropriated pursuant to the authorization of appropriations under section 644 exceeds $460,000,000, the Secretary shall reserve 15 percent of such appropriated amount to provide grants to States that are carrying out the policy described in section 635(c) in order to facilitate the implementation of such policy.

(2) Amount of grant.

(A) In general.

Notwithstanding paragraphs (2) and (3) of subsection (c), the Secretary shall provide a grant to each State under paragraph (1) in an amount that bears the same ratio to the amount reserved under such paragraph as the number of infants and toddlers in the State bears to the number of infants and toddlers in all States receiving grants under such paragraph.

(B) Maximum amount.

No State shall receive a grant under paragraph (1) for any fiscal year in an amount that is greater than 20 percent of the amount reserved under such paragraph for the fiscal year.

(3) Carryover of amounts.

(A) First succeeding fiscal year.

Pursuant to section 421(b) of the General Education Provisions Act, amounts under a grant provided under paragraph (1) that are not obligated and expended prior to the beginning of the first fiscal year succeeding the fiscal year for which such amounts were appropriated shall remain available for obligation and expenditure during such first succeeding fiscal year.

(B) Second succeeding fiscal year.

Amounts under a grant provided under paragraph (1) that are not obligated and expended prior to the beginning of the second fiscal year succeeding the fiscal year for which such amounts were appropriated shall be returned to the Secretary and used to make grants to States under section 633 (from their allotments under this section) during such second succeeding fiscal year.

§ 1444. Authorization of appropriations

For the purpose of carrying out this part, there are authorized to be appropriated such sums as may be necessary for each of the fiscal years 2005 through 2010.

Part D — National Activities to Improve Education of Children with Disabilities

20 U.S.C. § 1450 Findings

Part D — National Activities to Improve Education of Children with Disabilities

§ 1450. Findings and purpose

(a) Findings

The Congress finds the following:

(1) The Federal Government has an ongoing obligation to support activities that contribute to positive results for children with disabilities, enabling those children to lead productive and independent adult lives.

(2) Systemic change benefiting all students, including children with disabilities, requires the involvement of States, local educational agencies, parents, individuals with disabilities and their families, teachers and other service providers, and other interested individuals and organizations to develop and implement comprehensive strategies that improve educational results for children with disabilities.

(3) State educational agencies, in partnership with local educational agencies, parents of children with disabilities, and other individuals and organizations, are in the best position to improve education for children with disabilities and to address their special needs.

(4) An effective educational system serving students with disabilities should —

(A) maintain high academic achievement standards and clear performance goals for children with disabilities, consistent with the standards and expectations for all students in the educational system, and provide for appropriate and effective strategies and methods to ensure that all children with disabilities have the opportunity to achieve those standards and goals;

(B) clearly define, in objective, measurable terms, the school and post-school results that children with disabilities are expected to achieve; and

(C) promote transition services and coordinate State and local education, social, health, mental health, and other services, in addressing the full range of student needs, particularly the needs of children with disabilities who need significant levels of support to participate and learn in school and the community.

(5) The availability of an adequate number of qualified personnel is critical —

(A) to serve effectively children with disabilities;

(B) to assume leadership positions in administration and direct services;

(C) to provide teacher training; and

(D) to conduct high quality research to improve special education.

(6) High quality, comprehensive professional development programs are essential to ensure that the persons responsible for the education or transition of children with disabilities possess the skills and knowledge necessary to address the educational and related needs of those children.

(7) Models of professional development should be scientifically based and reflect successful practices, including strategies for recruiting, preparing, and retaining personnel.

(8) Continued support is essential for the development and maintenance of a coordinated and high quality program of research to inform successful teaching practices and model curricula for educating children with disabilities.

(9) Training, technical assistance, support, and dissemination activities are necessary to ensure that parts B and C are fully implemented and achieve high quality early intervention, educational, and transitional results for children with disabilities and their families.

(10) Parents, teachers, administrators, and related services personnel need technical assistance and information in a timely, coordinated, and accessible manner in order to improve early intervention, educational, and transitional services and results at the State and local levels for children with disabilities and their families.

(11) Parent training and information activities assist parents of a child with a disability in dealing with the multiple pressures of parenting such a child and are of particular importance in —

(A) playing a vital role in creating and preserving constructive relationships between parents of children with disabilities and schools by facilitating open communication between the parents and schools; encouraging dispute resolution at the earliest possible point in time; and discouraging the escalation of an adversarial process between the parents and schools;

(B) ensuring the involvement of parents in planning and decisionmaking with respect to early intervention, educational, and transitional services;

(C) achieving high quality early intervention, educational, and transitional results for children with disabilities;

(D) providing such parents information on their rights, protections, and responsibilities under this title to ensure improved early intervention, educational, and transitional results for children with disabilities;

(E) assisting such parents in the development of skills to participate effectively in the education and development of their children and in the transitions described in section 673(b)(6);

(F) supporting the roles of such parents as participants within partnerships seeking to improve early intervention, educational, and transitional services and results for children with disabilities and their families; and

(G) supporting such parents who may have limited access to services and supports, due to economic, cultural, or linguistic barriers.

(12) Support is needed to improve technological resources and integrate technology, including universally designed technologies, into the lives of children with disabilities, parents of children with disabilities, school personnel, and others through curricula, services, and assistive technologies.

SUBPART 1 — STATE PERSONNEL DEVELOPMENT GRANTS

20 U.S.C. §
1451 Purpose; definition of personnel; program authority
1452 Eligibility and collaborative process
1453 Applications
1454 Use of funds
1455 Authorization of appropriations

SUBPART 1 — STATE PERSONNEL DEVELOPMENT GRANTS

§ 1451. Purpose; definition of personnel; program authority

(a) Purpose.

The purpose of this subpart is to assist State educational agencies in reforming and improving their systems for personnel preparation and professional development in early intervention, educational, and transition services in order to improve results for children with disabilities.

(b) Definition of personnel.

In this subpart the term "personnel" means special education teachers, regular education teachers, principals, administrators, related services personnel, paraprofessionals, and early intervention personnel serving infants, toddlers, preschoolers, or children with disabilities, except where a particular category of personnel, such as related services personnel, is identified.

(c) Competitive grants.

(1) In general.

Except as provided in subsection (d), for any fiscal year for which the amount appropriated under section 655, that remains after the Secretary reserves funds under subsection (e) for the fiscal year, is less than $100,000,000, the Secretary shall award grants, on a competitive basis, to State educational agencies to carry out the activities described in the State plan submitted under section 653.

(2) Priority.

In awarding grants under paragraph (1), the Secretary may give priority to State educational agencies that —

(A) are in States with the greatest personnel shortages; or

(B) demonstrate the greatest difficulty meeting the requirements of section 612(a)(14).

(3) Minimum amount.

The Secretary shall make a grant to each State educational agency selected under paragraph (1) in an amount for each fiscal year that is —

(A) not less than $500,000, nor more than $4,000,000, in the case of the 50 States, the District of Columbia, and the Commonwealth of Puerto Rico; and

(B) not less than $80,000 in the case of an outlying area.

(4) Increase in amount.

The Secretary may increase the amounts of grants under paragraph (4) to account for inflation.

(5) Factors.

The Secretary shall determine the amount of a grant under paragraph (1) after considering —

(A) the amount of funds available for making the grants;

(B) the relative population of the State or outlying area;

(C) the types of activities proposed by the State or outlying area;

(D) the alignment of proposed activities with section 612(a)(14);

(E) the alignment of proposed activities with the State plans and applications submitted under sections 1111 and 2112, respectively, of the Elementary and Secondary Education Act of 1965; and

(F) the use, as appropriate, of scientifically based research activities.

(d) Formula grants.

(1) In general.

Except as provided in paragraphs (2) and (3), for the first fiscal year for which the amount appropriated under section 655, that remains after the Secretary reserves funds under subsection (e) for the fiscal year, is equal to or greater than $100,000,000, and for each fiscal year thereafter, the Secretary shall allot to each State educational agency, whose application meets the requirements of this subpart, an amount that bears the same relation to the amount remaining as the amount the State received under section 611(d) for that fiscal year bears to the amount of funds received by all States (whose applications meet the requirements of this subpart) under section 611(d) for that fiscal year.

(2) Minimum allotments for states that received competitive grants.

(A) In general.

The amount allotted under this subsection to any State educational agency that received a competitive multi-year grant under subsection (c) for which the grant period has not expired shall be not less than the amount specified for that fiscal year in the State educational agency's grant award document under that subsection.

(B) Special rule.

Each such State educational agency shall use the minimum amount described in subparagraph (A) for the activities described in the State educational agency's competitive grant award document for that year, unless the Secretary approves a request from the State educational agency to spend the funds on other activities.

(3) Minimum allotment.

The amount of any State educational agency's allotment under this subsection for any fiscal year shall not be less than —

(A) the greater of $500,000 or 1/2 of 1 percent of the total amount available under this subsection for that year, in the case of each of the 50 States, the District of Columbia, and the Commonwealth of Puerto Rico; and

(B) $80,000, in the case of an outlying area.

(4) Direct benefit.

In using grant funds allotted under paragraph (1), a State educational agency shall, through grants, contracts, or cooperative agreements, undertake activities that significantly and directly benefit the local educational agencies in the State.

(e) Continuation awards.

(1) In general.

Notwithstanding any other provision of this subpart, from funds appropriated under section 655 for each fiscal year, the Secretary shall reserve the amount that is necessary to make a continuation award to any State educational agency (at the request of the State educational agency) that received a multi-year award under this part (as this part was in effect on the day before the date of enactment of the Individuals with Disabilities Education Improvement Act of 2004), to enable the State educational agency to carry out activities in accordance with the terms of the multi-year award.

(2) Prohibition.

A State educational agency that receives a continuation award under paragraph (1) for any fiscal year may not receive any other award under this subpart for that fiscal year.

§ 1452. Eligibility and collaborative process

(a) Eligible applicants

A State educational agency may apply for a grant under this subpart for a grant period of not less than 1 year and not more than 5 years.

(b) Partners.

(1) In general.

In order to be considered for a grant under this subpart, a State educational agency shall establish a partnership with local educational agencies and other State agencies involved in, or concerned with, the education of children with disabilities, including —

(A) not less than 1 institution of higher education; and

(B) the State agencies responsible for administering part C, early education, child care, and vocational rehabilitation programs.

(2) Other partners.

In order to be considered for a grant under this subpart, a State educational agency shall work in partnership with other persons and organizations involved in, and concerned with, the education of children with disabilities, which may include —

(A) the Governor;

(B) parents of children with disabilities ages birth through 26;

(C) parents of nondisabled children ages birth through 26;

(D) individuals with disabilities;

(E) parent training and information centers or community parent resource centers funded under sections 671 and 672, respectively;

(F) community based and other non-profit organizations involved in the education and employment of individuals with disabilities;

(G) personnel as defined in section 651(b);

(H) the State advisory panel established under part B;

(I) the State interagency coordinating council established under part C;

(J) individuals knowledgeable about vocational education;

(K) the State agency for higher education;

(L) public agencies with jurisdiction in the areas of health, mental health, social services, and juvenile justice;

(M) other providers of professional development that work with infants, toddlers, preschoolers, and children with disabilities; and

(N) other individuals.

(3) Required partner.

If State law assigns responsibility for teacher preparation and certification to an individual, entity, or agency other than the State educational agency, the State educational agency shall —

(A) include that individual, entity, or agency as a partner in the partnership under this subsection; and

(B) ensure that any activities the State educational agency will carry out under this subpart that are within that partner's jurisdiction (which may include activities described in section 654(b)) are carried out by that partner.

§ 1453. Applications

(a) In general

(1) Submission

A State educational agency that desires to receive a grant under this subpart shall submit to the Secretary an application at such time, in such manner, and including such information as the Secretary may require.

(2) State plan.

The application shall include a plan that identifies and addresses the State and local needs for the personnel preparation and professional development of personnel, as well as individuals who provide direct supplementary aids and services to children with disabilities, and that —

(A) is designed to enable the State to meet the requirements of section 612(a)(14) and section 635(a) (8) and (9);

(B) is based on an assessment of State and local needs that identifies critical aspects and areas in need of improvement related to the preparation, ongoing training, and professional development of personnel who serve infants, toddlers, preschoolers, and children with disabilities within the State, including —

(i) current and anticipated personnel vacancies and shortages; and

(ii) the number of preservice and inservice programs; and

(C) is integrated and aligned, to the maximum extent possible, with State plans and activities under the Elementary and Secondary Education Act of 1965, the Rehabilitation Act of 1973, and the Higher Education Act of 1965.

(3) Requirement.

The State application shall contain an assurance that the State educational agency will carry out each of the strategies described in subsection (b)(4).

(b) Elements of state personnel development plan.

Each State personnel development plan under subsection (a)(2) shall —

(1) describe a partnership agreement that is in effect for the period of the grant, which agreement shall specify —

(A) the nature and extent of the partnership described in section 652(b) and the respective roles of each member of the partnership, including the partner described in section 652(b)(3) if applicable; and

(B) how the State educational agency will work with other persons and organizations involved in, and concerned with, the education of children with disabilities, including the respective roles of each of the persons and organizations;

(2) describe how the strategies and activities described in paragraph (4) will be coordinated with activities supported with other public resources (including part B and part C funds retained for use at the State level for personnel and professional development purposes) and private resources;

(3) describe how the State educational agency will align its personnel development plan under this subpart with the plan and application submitted under sections 1111 and 2112, respectively, of the Elementary and Secondary Education Act of 1965;

(4) describe those strategies the State educational agency will use to address the professional development and personnel needs identified under subsection (a)(2) and how such strategies will be implemented, including —

(A) a description of the programs and activities to be supported under this subpart that will provide personnel with the knowledge and skills to meet the needs of, and improve the performance and achievement of, infants, toddlers, preschoolers, and children with disabilities; and

(B) how such strategies will be integrated, to the maximum extent possible, with other activities supported by grants funded under section 662;

(5) provide an assurance that the State educational agency will provide technical assistance to local educational agencies to improve the quality of professional development available to meet the needs of personnel who serve children with disabilities;

(6) provide an assurance that the State educational agency will provide technical assistance to entities that provide services to infants and toddlers with disabilities to improve the quality of professional development available to meet the needs of personnel serving such children;

(7) describe how the State educational agency will recruit and retain highly qualified teachers and other qualified personnel in geographic areas of greatest need;

(8) describe the steps the State educational agency will take to ensure that poor and minority children are not taught at higher rates by teachers who are not highly qualified; and

(9) describe how the State educational agency will assess, on a regular basis, the extent to which the strategies implemented under this subpart have been effective in meeting the performance goals described in section 612(a)(15).

(c) Peer review.

(1) In general.

The Secretary shall use a panel of experts who are competent, by virtue of their training, expertise, or experience, to evaluate applications for grants under section 651(c)(1).

(2) Composition of panel.

A majority of a panel described in paragraph (1) shall be composed of individuals who are not employees of the Federal Government.

(3) payment of fees and expenses of certain members.

The Secretary may use available funds appropriated to carry out this subpart to pay the expenses and fees of panel members who are not employees of the Federal Government.

(d) Reporting procedures.

Each State educational agency that receives a grant under this subpart shall submit annual performance reports to the Secretary. The reports shall —

(1) describe the progress of the State educational agency in implementing its plan;

(2) analyze the effectiveness of the State educational agency's activities under this subpart and of the State educational agency's strategies for meeting its goals under section 612(a)(15); and

(3) identify changes in the strategies used by the State educational agency and described in subsection (b)(4), if any, to improve the State educational agency's performance.

§ 1454. Use of funds

(a) Professional development activities.

A State educational agency that receives a grant under this subpart shall use the grant funds to support activities in accordance with the State's plan described in section 653, including 1 or more of the following:

(1) Carrying out programs that provide support to both special education and regular education teachers of children with disabilities and principals, such as programs that —

(A) provide teacher mentoring, team teaching, reduced class schedules and case loads, and intensive professional development;

(B) use standards or assessments for guiding beginning teachers that are consistent with challenging State student academic achievement and functional standards and with the requirements for professional development, as defined in section 9101 of the Elementary and Secondary Education Act of 1965; and

(C) encourage collaborative and consultative models of providing early intervention, special education, and related services.

(2) Encouraging and supporting the training of special education and regular education teachers and administrators to effectively use and integrate technology —

(A) into curricula and instruction, including training to improve the ability to collect, manage, and analyze data to improve teaching, decisionmaking, school improvement efforts, and accountability;

(B) to enhance learning by children with disabilities; and

(C) to effectively communicate with parents.

(3) Providing professional development activities that —

(A) improve the knowledge of special education and regular education teachers concerning —

(i) the academic and developmental or functional needs of students with disabilities; or

(ii) effective instructional strategies, methods, and skills, and the use of State academic content standards and student academic achievement and functional standards, and State assessments, to improve teaching practices and student academic achievement;

(B) improve the knowledge of special education and regular education teachers and principals and, in appropriate cases, paraprofessionals, concerning effective instructional practices, and that —

(i) provide training in how to teach and address the needs of children with different learning styles and children who are limited English proficient;

(ii) involve collaborative groups of teachers, administrators, and, in appropriate cases, related services personnel;

(iii) provide training in methods of —

(I) positive behavioral interventions and supports to improve student behavior in the classroom;

(II) scientifically based reading instruction, including early literacy instruction;

(III) early and appropriate interventions to identify and help children with disabilities;

(IV) effective instruction for children with low incidence disabilities;

(V) successful transitioning to postsecondary opportunities; and

(VI) using classroom-based techniques to assist children prior to referral for special education;

(iv) provide training to enable personnel to work with and involve parents in their child's education, including parents of low income and limited English proficient children with disabilities;

(v) provide training for special education personnel and regular education personnel in planning, developing, and implementing effective and appropriate IEPs; and

(vi) provide training to meet the needs of students with significant health, mobility, or behavioral needs prior to serving such students;

(C) train administrators, principals, and other relevant school personnel in conducting effective IEP meetings; and

(D) train early intervention, preschool, and related services providers, and other relevant school personnel, in conducting effective individualized family service plan (IFSP) meetings.

(4) Developing and implementing initiatives to promote the recruitment and retention of highly qualified special education teachers, particularly initiatives that have been proven effective in recruiting and retaining highly qualified teachers, including programs that provide —

(A) teacher mentoring from exemplary special education teachers, principals, or superintendents;

(B) induction and support for special education teachers during their first 3 years of employment as teachers; or

(C) incentives, including financial incentives, to retain special education teachers who have a record of success in helping students with disabilities.

(5) Carrying out programs and activities that are designed to improve the quality of personnel who serve children with disabilities, such as —

(A) innovative professional development programs (which may be provided through partnerships that include institutions of higher education), including programs that train teachers and principals to integrate technology into curricula and instruction to improve teaching, learning, and technology literacy, which professional development shall be consistent with the definition of professional development in section 9101 of the Elementary and Secondary Education Act of 1965; and

(B) the development and use of proven, cost effective strategies for the implementation of professional development activities, such as through the use of technology and distance learning.

(6) Carrying out programs and activities that are designed to improve the quality of early intervention personnel, including paraprofessionals and primary referral sources, such as —

(A) professional development programs to improve the delivery of early intervention services;

(B) initiatives to promote the recruitment and retention of early intervention personnel; and

(C) interagency activities to ensure that early intervention personnel are adequately prepared and trained.

(b) Other activities.

A State educational agency that receives a grant under this subpart shall use the grant funds to support activities in accordance with the State's plan described in section 653, including 1 or more of the following:

(1) Reforming special education and regular education teacher certification (including recertification) or licensing requirements to ensure that —

(A) special education and regular education teachers have —

(i) the training and information necessary to address the full range of needs of children with disabilities across disability categories; and

(ii) the necessary subject matter knowledge and teaching skills in the academic subjects that the teachers teach;

(B) special education and regular education teacher certification (including recertification) or licensing requirements are aligned with challenging State academic content standards; and

(C) special education and regular education teachers have the subject matter knowledge and teaching skills, including technology literacy, necessary to help students with disabilities meet challenging State student academic achievement and functional standards.

(2) Programs that establish, expand, or improve alternative routes for State certification of special education teachers for highly qualified individuals with a baccalaureate or master's degree, including mid-career professionals from other occupations, paraprofessionals, and recent college or university graduates with records of academic distinction who demonstrate the potential to become highly effective special education teachers.

(3) Teacher advancement initiatives for special education teachers that promote professional growth and emphasize multiple career paths (such as paths to becoming a career teacher, mentor teacher, or exemplary teacher) and pay differentiation.

(4) Developing and implementing mechanisms to assist local educational agencies and schools in effectively recruiting and retaining highly qualified special education teachers.

(5) Reforming tenure systems, implementing teacher testing for subject matter knowledge, and implementing teacher testing for State certification or licensing, consistent with title II of the Higher Education Act of 1965.

(6) Funding projects to promote reciprocity of teacher certification or licensing between or among States for special education teachers, except that no reciprocity agreement developed under this paragraph or developed using funds provided under this subpart may lead to the weakening of any State teaching certification or licensing requirement.

(7) Assisting local educational agencies to serve children with disabilities through the development and use of proven, innovative strategies to deliver intensive professional development programs that are both cost effective and easily accessible, such as strategies that involve delivery through the use of technology, peer networks, and distance learning.

(8) Developing, or assisting local educational agencies in developing, merit based performance systems, and strategies that provide differential and bonus pay for special education teachers.

(9) Supporting activities that ensure that teachers are able to use challenging State academic content standards and student academic achievement and functional standards, and State assessments for all children with disabilities, to improve instructional practices and improve the academic achievement of children with disabilities.

(10) When applicable, coordinating with, and expanding centers established under, section 2113(c)(18) of the Elementary and Secondary Education Act of 1965 to benefit special education teachers.

(c) Contracts and subgrants.

A State educational agency that receives a grant under this subpart —

(1) shall award contracts or subgrants to local educational agencies, institutions of higher education, parent training and information centers, or community parent resource centers, as appropriate, to carry out its State plan under this subpart; and

(2) may award contracts and subgrants to other public and private entities, including the lead agency under part C, to carry out the State plan.

(d) Use of funds for professional development.

A State educational agency that receives a grant under this subpart shall use —

(1) not less than 90 percent of the funds the State educational agency receives under the grant for any fiscal year for activities under subsection (a); and

(2) not more than 10 percent of the funds the State educational agency receives under the grant for any fiscal year for activities under subsection (b).

(e) Grants to outlying areas.

Public Law 95-134, permitting the consolidation of grants to the outlying areas, shall not apply to funds received under this subpart.

§ 1455. Authorization of appropriations

There are authorized to be appropriated to carry out this subpart such sums as may be necessary for each of the fiscal years 2005 through 2010.

SUBPART 2 — PERSONNEL PREPARATION, TECHNICAL ASSISTANCE, MODEL DEMONSTRATION PROJECTS, AND DISSEMINATION OF INFORMATION

20 U.S.C. §
1461. Purpose; definition of eligible entity.
1462. Personnel development to improve services and results for children with disabilities.
1463 Technical assistance, demonstration projects, dissemination of information, and implementation of scientifically based research.
1464. Studies and evaluations.
1465. Interim alternative educational settings, behavioral supports, and systemic school interventions.
1466 Authorization of appropriations.

§ 1461. Purpose; definition of eligible entity.

(a) Purpose.

The purpose of this subpart is —

(1) to provide Federal funding for personnel preparation, technical assistance, model demonstration projects, information dissemination, and studies and evaluations, in order to improve early intervention, educational, and transitional results for children with disabilities; and

(2) to assist State educational agencies and local educational agencies in improving their education systems for children with disabilities.

(b) Definition of eligible entity.

(1) In general.

In this subpart, the term "eligible entity" means —

(A) a State educational agency;

(B) a local educational agency;

(C) a public charter school that is a local educational agency under State law;

(D) an institution of higher education;

(E) a public agency not described in subparagraphs (A) through (D);

(F) a private nonprofit organization;

(G) an outlying area;

(H) an Indian tribe or a tribal organization (as defined under section 4 of the Indian Self-Determination and Education Assistance Act); or

(I) a for-profit organization, if the Secretary finds it appropriate in light of the purposes of a particular competition for a grant, contract, or cooperative agreement under this subpart.

(2) Special rule.

The Secretary may limit which eligible entities described in paragraph (1) are eligible for a grant, contract, or cooperative agreement under this subpart to 1 or more of the categories of eligible entities described in paragraph (1).

§ 1462. Personnel development to improve services and results for children with disabilities.

(a) In general.

The Secretary, on a competitive basis, shall award grants to, or enter into contracts or cooperative agreements with, eligible entities to carry out 1 or more of the following objectives:

(1) To help address the needs identified in the State plan described in section 653(a)(2) for highly qualified personnel, as defined in section 651(b), to work with infants or toddlers with disabilities, or children with disabilities, consistent with the qualifications described in section 612(a)(14).

(2) To ensure that those personnel have the necessary skills and knowledge, derived from practices that have been determined, through scientifically based research, to be successful in serving those children.

(3) To encourage increased focus on academics and core content areas in special education personnel preparation programs.

(4) To ensure that regular education teachers have the necessary skills and knowledge to provide instruction to students with disabilities in the regular education classroom.

(5) To ensure that all special education teachers are highly qualified.

(6) To ensure that preservice and in-service personnel preparation programs include training in —

(A) the use of new technologies;

(B) the area of early intervention, educational, and transition services;

(C) effectively involving parents; and

(D) positive behavioral supports.

(7) To provide high-quality professional development for principals, superintendents, and other administrators, including training in —

(A) instructional leadership;

(B) behavioral supports in the school and classroom;

(C) paperwork reduction;

(D) promoting improved collaboration between special education and general education teachers;

(E) assessment and accountability;

(F) ensuring effective learning environments; and

(G) fostering positive relationships with parents.

(b) Personnel development; enhanced support for beginning special educators.

(1) In general.

In carrying out this section, the Secretary shall support activities —

(A) for personnel development, including activities for the preparation of personnel who will serve children with high incidence and low incidence disabilities, to prepare special education and general education teachers, principals, administrators, and related services personnel (and school board members, when appropriate) to meet the diverse and individualized instructional needs of children with disabilities and improve early intervention, educational, and transitional services and results for children with disabilities, consistent with the objectives described in subsection (a); and

(B) for enhanced support for beginning special educators, consistent with the objectives described in subsection (a).

(2) Personnel development.

In carrying out paragraph (1)(A), the Secretary shall support not less than 1 of the following activities:

(A) Assisting effective existing, improving existing, or developing new, collaborative personnel preparation activities undertaken by institutions of higher education, local educational agencies, and other local entities that incorporate best practices and scientifically based research, where applicable, in providing special education and general education teachers, principals, administrators, and related services personnel with the knowledge and skills to effectively support students with disabilities, including —

(i) working collaboratively in regular classroom settings;

(ii) using appropriate supports, accommodations, and curriculum modifications;

(iii) implementing effective teaching strategies, classroom-based techniques, and interventions to ensure appropriate identification of students who may be eligible for special education services, and to prevent the misidentification, inappropriate overidentification, or underidentification of children as having a disability, especially minority and limited English proficient children;

(iv) effectively working with and involving parents in the education of their children;

(v) utilizing strategies, including positive behavioral interventions, for addressing the conduct of children with disabilities that impedes their learning and that of others in the classroom;

(vi) effectively constructing IEPs, participating in IEP meetings, and implementing IEPs;

(vii) preparing children with disabilities to participate in statewide assessments (with or without accommodations) and alternate assessments, as appropriate, and to ensure that all children with disabilities are a part of all accountability systems under the Elementary and Secondary Education Act of 1965; and

(viii) working in high need elementary schools and secondary schools, including urban schools, rural schools, and schools operated by an entity described in section 7113(d)(1)(A)(ii) of the Elementary and Secondary Education Act of 1965, and schools that serve high numbers or percentages of limited English proficient children.

(B) Developing, evaluating, and disseminating innovative models for the recruitment, induction, retention, and assessment of new, highly qualified teachers to reduce teacher shortages, especially from groups that are underrepresented in the teaching profession, including individuals with disabilities.

(C) Providing continuous personnel preparation, training, and professional development designed to provide support and ensure retention of special education and general education teachers and personnel who teach and provide related services to children with disabilities.

(D) Developing and improving programs for paraprofessionals to become special education teachers, related services personnel, and early intervention personnel, including interdisciplinary training to enable the paraprofessionals to improve early intervention, educational, and transitional results for children with disabilities.

(E) In the case of principals and superintendents, providing activities to promote instructional leadership and improved collaboration between general educators, special education teachers, and related services personnel.

(F) Supporting institutions of higher education with minority enrollments of not less than 25 percent for the purpose of preparing personnel to work with children with disabilities.

(G) Developing and improving programs to train special education teachers to develop an expertise in autism spectrum disorders.

(H) Providing continuous personnel preparation, training, and professional development designed to provide support and improve the qualifications of personnel who provide related services to children with disabilities, including to enable such personnel to obtain advanced degrees.

(3) Enhanced support for beginning special educators.

In carrying out paragraph (1)(B), the Secretary shall support not less than 1 of the following activities:

(A) Enhancing and restructuring existing programs or developing preservice teacher education programs to prepare special education teachers, at colleges or departments of education within institutions of higher education, by incorporating an extended (such as an additional 5th year) clinical learning opportunity, field experience, or supervised practicum into such programs.

(B) Creating or supporting teacher-faculty partnerships (such as professional development schools) that —

(i) consist of not less than —

(I) 1 or more institutions of higher education with special education personnel preparation programs;

(II) 1 or more local educational agencies that serve high numbers or percentages of low-income students; or

(III) 1 or more elementary schools or secondary schools, particularly schools that have failed to make adequate yearly progress on the basis, in whole and in part, of the assessment results of the disaggregated subgroup of students with disabilities;

(ii) may include other entities eligible for assistance under this part; and

(iii) provide —

(I) high-quality mentoring and induction opportunities with ongoing support for beginning special education teachers; or

(II) inservice professional development to beginning and veteran special education teachers through the ongoing exchange of information and instructional strategies with faculty.

(c) Low incidence disabilities; authorized activities.

(1) In general.

In carrying out this section, the Secretary shall support activities, consistent with the objectives described in subsection (a), that benefit children with low incidence disabilities.

(2) Authorized activities.

Activities that may be carried out under this subsection include activities such as the following:

(A) Preparing persons who —

(i) have prior training in educational and other related service fields; and

(ii) are studying to obtain degrees, certificates, or licensure that will enable the persons to assist children with low incidence disabilities to achieve the objectives set out in their individualized education programs described in section 614(d), or to assist infants and toddlers with low incidence disabilities to achieve the outcomes described in their individualized family service plans described in section 636.

(B) Providing personnel from various disciplines with interdisciplinary training that will contribute to improvement in early intervention, educational, and transitional results for children with low incidence disabilities.

(C) Preparing personnel in the innovative uses and application of technology, including universally designed technologies, assistive technology devices, and assistive technology services —

(i) to enhance learning by children with low incidence disabilities through early intervention, educational, and transitional services; and

(ii) to improve communication with parents.

(D) Preparing personnel who provide services to visually impaired or blind children to teach and use Braille in the provision of services to such children.

(E) Preparing personnel to be qualified educational interpreters, to assist children with low incidence disabilities, particularly deaf and hard of hearing children in school and school related activities, and deaf and hard of hearing infants and toddlers and preschool children in early intervention and preschool programs.

(F) Preparing personnel who provide services to children with significant cognitive disabilities and children with multiple disabilities.

(G) Preparing personnel who provide services to children with low incidence disabilities and limited English proficient children.

(3) Definition.

In this section, the term "low incidence disability" means —

(A) a visual or hearing impairment, or simultaneous visual and hearing impairments;

(B) a significant cognitive impairment; or

(C) any impairment for which a small number of personnel with highly specialized skills and knowledge are needed in order for children with that impairment to receive early intervention services or a free appropriate public education.

(4) Selection of recipients.

In selecting eligible entities for assistance under this subsection, the Secretary may give preference to eligible entities submitting applications that include 1 or more of the following:

   (A) A proposal to prepare personnel in more than 1 low incidence disability, such as deafness and blindness.

   (B) A demonstration of an effective collaboration between an eligible entity and a local educational agency that promotes recruitment and subsequent retention of highly qualified personnel to serve children with low incidence disabilities.

  (5) Preparation in use of braille.

  The Secretary shall ensure that all recipients of awards under this subsection who will use that assistance to prepare personnel to provide services to visually impaired or blind children that can appropriately be provided in Braille, will prepare those individuals to provide those services in Braille.

(d) Leadership preparation; authorized activities.

  (1) In general.

  In carrying out this section, the Secretary shall support leadership preparation activities that are consistent with the objectives described in subsection (a).

  (2) Authorized activities.

  Activities that may be carried out under this subsection include activities such as the following:

   (A) Preparing personnel at the graduate, doctoral, and postdoctoral levels of training to administer, enhance, or provide services to improve results for children with disabilities.

   (B) Providing interdisciplinary training for various types of leadership personnel, including teacher preparation faculty, related services faculty, administrators, researchers, supervisors, principals, and other persons whose work affects early intervention, educational, and transitional services for children with disabilities, including children with disabilities who are limited English proficient children

(e) Applications.

  (1) In general.

  An eligible entity that wishes to receive a grant, or enter into a contract or cooperative agreement, under this section shall submit an application to the Secretary at such time, in such manner, and containing such information as the Secretary may require.

  (2) Identified state needs.

   (A) Requirement to address identified needs.

   An application for assistance under subsection (b), (c), or (d) shall include information demonstrating to the satisfaction of the Secretary that the activities described in the application will address needs identified by the State or States the eligible entity proposes to serve.

   (B) Cooperation with state educational agencies.

   An eligible entity that is not a local educational agency or a State educational agency shall include in the eligible entity's application information demonstrating to the satisfaction of the Secretary that the eligible entity and 1 or more State educational agencies or local educational agencies will cooperate in carrying out and monitoring the proposed project.

  (3) Acceptance by states of personnel preparation requirements.

  The Secretary may require eligible entities to provide in the eligible entities' applications assurances from 1 or more States that such States intend to accept successful completion of the proposed personnel preparation program as meeting State personnel standards or other requirements in State law or regulation for serving children with disabilities or serving infants and toddlers with disabilities.

(f) Selection of recipients.

  (1) Impact of project.

  In selecting eligible entities for assistance under this section, the Secretary shall consider the impact of the proposed project described in the application in meeting the need for personnel identified by the States.

  (2) Requirement for eligible entities to meet state and professional qualifications.

  The Secretary shall make grants and enter into contracts and cooperative agreements under this section only to eligible entities that meet State and professionally recognized qualifications for the preparation of special education and related services personnel, if the purpose of the project is to assist personnel in obtaining degrees.

(3) Preferences.

In selecting eligible entities for assistance under this section, the Secretary may give preference to eligible entities that are institutions of higher education that are —

(A) educating regular education personnel to meet the needs of children with disabilities in integrated settings;

(B) educating special education personnel to work in collaboration with regular educators in integrated settings; and

(C) successfully recruiting and preparing individuals with disabilities and individuals from groups that are underrepresented in the profession for which the institution of higher education is preparing individuals.

(g) Scholarships.

The Secretary may include funds for scholarships, with necessary stipends and allowances, in awards under subsections (b), (c), and (d).

(h) Service obligation.

(1) In general.

Each application for assistance under subsections (b), (c), and (d) shall include an assurance that the eligible entity will ensure that individuals who receive a scholarship under the proposed project agree to subsequently provide special education and related services to children with disabilities, or in the case of leadership personnel to subsequently work in the appropriate field, for a period of 2 years for every year for which the scholarship was received or repay all or part of the amount of the scholarship, in accordance with regulations issued by the Secretary.

(2) Special rule.

Notwithstanding paragraph (1), the Secretary may reduce or waive the service obligation requirement under paragraph (1) if the Secretary determines that the service obligation is acting as a deterrent to the recruitment of students into special education or a related field.

(3) Secretary's responsibility.

The Secretary —

(A) shall ensure that individuals described in paragraph (1) comply with the requirements of that paragraph; and

(B) may use not more than 0.5 percent of the funds appropriated under subsection (i) for each fiscal year, to carry out subparagraph (A), in addition to any other funds that are available for that purpose.

(i) Authorization of appropriations.

There are authorized to be appropriated to carry out this section such sums as may be necessary for each of the fiscal years 2005 through 2010.

§ 1463 Technical assistance, demonstration projects, dissemination of information, and implementation of scientifically based research.

(a) In general.

The Secretary shall make competitive grants to, or enter into contracts or cooperative agreements with, eligible entities to provide technical assistance, support model demonstration projects, disseminate useful information, and implement activities that are supported by scientifically based research.

(b) Required activities.

Funds received under this section shall be used to support activities to improve services provided under this title, including the practices of professionals and others involved in providing such services to children with disabilities, that promote academic achievement and improve results for children with disabilities through —

(1) implementing effective strategies for addressing inappropriate behavior of students with disabilities in schools, including strategies to prevent children with emotional and behavioral problems from developing emotional disturbances that require the provision of special education and related services;

(2) improving the alignment, compatibility, and development of valid and reliable assessments and alternate assessments for assessing adequate yearly progress, as described under section 1111(b)(2)(B) of the Elementary and Secondary Education Act of 1965;

(3) providing training for both regular education teachers and special education teachers to address the needs of students with different learning styles;

(4) disseminating information about innovative, effective, and efficient curricula designs, instructional approaches, and strate-

gies, and identifying positive academic and social learning opportunities, that —

(A) provide effective transitions between educational settings or from school to post school settings; and

(B) improve educational and transitional results at all levels of the educational system in which the activities are carried out and, in particular, that improve the progress of children with disabilities, as measured by assessments within the general education curriculum involved; and

(5) applying scientifically based findings to facilitate systemic changes, related to the provision of services to children with disabilities, in policy, procedure, practice, and the training and use of personnel.

(c) Authorized activities.

Activities that may be carried out under this section include activities to improve services provided under this title, including the practices of professionals and others involved in providing such services to children with disabilities, that promote academic achievement and improve results for children with disabilities through —

(1) applying and testing research findings in typical settings where children with disabilities receive services to determine the usefulness, effectiveness, and general applicability of such research findings in such areas as improving instructional methods, curricula, and tools, such as textbooks and media;

(2) supporting and promoting the coordination of early intervention and educational services for children with disabilities with services provided by health, rehabilitation, and social service agencies;

(3) promoting improved alignment and compatibility of general and special education reforms concerned with curricular and instructional reform, and evaluation of such reforms;

(4) enabling professionals, parents of children with disabilities, and other persons to learn about, and implement, the findings of scientifically based research, and successful practices developed in model demonstration projects, relating to the provision of services to children with disabilities;

(5) conducting outreach, and disseminating information, relating to successful approaches to overcoming systemic barriers to the effective and efficient delivery of early intervention, educational, and transitional services to personnel who provide services to children with disabilities;

(6) assisting States and local educational agencies with the process of planning systemic changes that will promote improved early intervention, educational, and transitional results for children with disabilities;

(7) promoting change through a multistate or regional framework that benefits States, local educational agencies, and other participants in partnerships that are in the process of achieving systemic-change outcomes;

(8) focusing on the needs and issues that are specific to a population of children with disabilities, such as providing single-State and multi-State technical assistance and in-service training —

(A) to schools and agencies serving deaf-blind children and their families;

(B) to programs and agencies serving other groups of children with low incidence disabilities and their families;

(C) addressing the postsecondary education needs of individuals who are deaf or hard-of-hearing; and

(D) to schools and personnel providing special education and related services for children with autism spectrum disorders;

(9) demonstrating models of personnel preparation to ensure appropriate placements and services for all students and to reduce disproportionality in eligibility, placement, and disciplinary actions for minority and limited English proficient children; and

(10) disseminating information on how to reduce inappropriate racial and ethnic disproportionalities identified under section 618.

(d) Balance among activities and age ranges.

In carrying out this section, the Secretary shall ensure that there is an appropriate balance across all age ranges of children with disabilities.

(e) Linking states to information sources.

In carrying out this section, the Secretary shall support projects that link States to technical assistance resources, including special education and general education resources, and shall make research and related products available through libraries, electronic networks, parent training projects, and other information sources, including through the activities of the National Center for Education Evaluation and Regional Assistance established under part D of the Education Sciences Reform Act of 2002.

(f) Applications.

(1) In general.

An eligible entity that wishes to receive a grant, or enter into a contract or cooperative agreement, under this section shall submit an application to the Secretary at such time, in such manner, and containing such information as the Secretary may require.

(2) Standards.

To the maximum extent feasible, each eligible entity shall demonstrate that the project described in the eligible entity's application is supported by scientifically valid research that has been carried out in accordance with the standards for the conduct and evaluation of all relevant research and development established by the National Center for Education Research.

(3) Priority.

As appropriate, the Secretary shall give priority to applications that propose to serve teachers and school personnel directly in the school environment.

§ 1464. Studies and evaluations.

(a) Studies and evaluations.

(1) Delegation.

The Secretary shall delegate to the Director of the Institute of Education Sciences responsibility to carry out this section, other than subsections (d) and (f).

(2) Assessment.

The Secretary shall, directly or through grants, contracts, or cooperative agreements awarded to eligible entities on a competitive basis, assess the progress in the implementation of this title, including the effectiveness of State and local efforts to provide —

(A) a free appropriate public education to children with disabilities; and

(B) early intervention services to infants and toddlers with disabilities, and infants and toddlers who would be at risk of having substantial developmental delays if early intervention services were not provided to the infants and toddlers.

(b) Assessment of national activities.

(1) In general.

The Secretary shall carry out a national assessment of activities carried out with Federal funds under this title in order —

(A) to determine the effectiveness of this title in achieving the purposes of this title;

(B) to provide timely information to the President, Congress, the States, local educational agencies, and the public on how to implement this title more effectively; and

(C) to provide the President and Congress with information that will be useful in developing legislation to achieve the purposes of this title more effectively.

(2) Scope of assessment.

The national assessment shall assess activities supported under this title, including —

(A) the implementation of programs assisted under this title and the impact of such programs on addressing the developmental needs of, and improving the academic achievement of, children with disabilities to enable the children to reach challenging developmental goals and challenging State academic content standards based on State academic assessments;

(B) the types of programs and services that have demonstrated the greatest likelihood of helping students reach the challenging State academic content standards and developmental goals;

(C) the implementation of the professional development activities assisted under this title and the impact on instruction, student academic achievement, and teacher qualifications to enhance the ability of special education teachers and regular education teachers to improve results for children with disabilities; and

(D) the effectiveness of schools, local educational agencies, States, other recipients of assistance under this title, and the Secretary in achieving the purposes of this title by —

(i) improving the academic achievement of children with disabilities and their performance on regular statewide assessments as compared to nondisabled children, and the performance of children with disabilities on alternate assessments;

(ii) improving the participation of children with disabilities in the general education curriculum;

(iii) improving the transitions of children with disabilities at natural transition points;

(iv) placing and serving children with disabilities, including minority children, in the least restrictive environment appropriate;

(v) preventing children with disabilities, especially children with emotional disturbances and specific learning disabilities, from dropping out of school;

(vi) addressing the reading and literacy needs of children with disabilities;

(vii) reducing the inappropriate overidentification of children, especially minority and limited English proficient children, as having a disability;

(viii) improving the participation of parents of children with disabilities in the education of their children; and

(ix) resolving disagreements between education personnel and parents through alternate dispute resolution activities, including mediation.

(3) Interim and final reports.

The Secretary shall submit to the President and Congress —

(A) an interim report that summarizes the preliminary findings of the assessment not later than 3 years after the date of enactment of the Individuals with Disabilities Education Improvement Act of 2004; and

(B) a final report of the findings of the assessment not later than 5 years after the date of enactment of such Act.

(c) Study on ensuring accountability for students who are held to alternative achievement standards.

The Secretary shall carry out a national study or studies to examine —

(1) the criteria that States use to determine —

(A) eligibility for alternate assessments; and

(B) the number and type of children who take those assessments and are held accountable to alternative achievement standards;

(2) the validity and reliability of alternate assessment instruments and procedures;

(3) the alignment of alternate assessments and alternative achievement standards to State academic content standards in reading, mathematics, and science; and

(4) the use and effectiveness of alternate assessments in appropriately measuring student progress and outcomes specific to individualized instructional need.

(d) Annual report.

The Secretary shall provide an annual report to Congress that —

(1) summarizes the research conducted under part E of the Education Sciences Reform Act of 2002;

(2) analyzes and summarizes the data reported by the States and the Secretary of the Interior under section 618;

(3) summarizes the studies and evaluations conducted under this section and the timeline for their completion;

(4) describes the extent and progress of the assessment of national activities; and

(5) describes the findings and determinations resulting from reviews of State implementation of this title.

(e) Authorized activities.

In carrying out this section, the Secretary may support objective studies, evaluations, and assessments, including studies that —

(1) analyze measurable impact, outcomes, and results achieved by State educational agencies and local educational agencies through their activities to reform policies, procedures, and practices designed to improve educational and transitional services and results for children with disabilities;

(2) analyze State and local needs for professional development, parent training, and other appropriate activities that can reduce the need for disciplinary actions involving children with disabilities;

(3) assess educational and transitional services and results for children with disabilities from minority backgrounds, including —

(A) data on —

(i) the number of minority children who are referred for special education evaluation;

(ii) the number of minority children

who are receiving special education and related services and their educational or other service placement;

      (iii) the number of minority children who graduated from secondary programs with a regular diploma in the standard number of years; and

      (iv) the number of minority children who drop out of the educational system; and

   (B) the performance of children with disabilities from minority backgrounds on State assessments and other performance indicators established for all students;

 (4) measure educational and transitional services and results for children with disabilities served under this title, including longitudinal studies that —

   (A) examine educational and transitional services and results for children with disabilities who are 3 through 17 years of age and are receiving special education and related services under this title, using a national, representative sample of distinct age cohorts and disability categories; and

   (B) examine educational results, transition services, postsecondary placement, and employment status for individuals with disabilities, 18 through 21 years of age, who are receiving or have received special education and related services under this title; and

 (5) identify and report on the placement of children with disabilities by disability category.

(f) Study.

The Secretary shall study, and report to Congress regarding, the extent to which States adopt policies described in section 635(c)(1) and on the effects of those policies.

§ 1465. Interim alternative educational settings, behavioral supports, and systemic school interventions.

(a) Program authorized.

The Secretary may award grants, and enter into contracts and cooperative agreements, to support safe learning environments that support academic achievement for all students by —

 (1) improving the quality of interim alternative educational settings; and

 (2) providing increased behavioral supports and research-based, systemic interventions in schools.

(b) Authorized activities.

In carrying out this section, the Secretary may support activities to —

 (1) establish, expand, or increase the scope of behavioral supports and systemic interventions by providing for effective, research-based practices, including —

   (A) training for school staff on early identification, prereferral, and referral procedures;

   (B) training for administrators, teachers, related services personnel, behavioral specialists, and other school staff in positive behavioral interventions and supports, behavioral intervention planning, and classroom and student management techniques;

   (C) joint training for administrators, parents, teachers, related services personnel, behavioral specialists, and other school staff on effective strategies for positive behavioral interventions and behavior management strategies that focus on the prevention of behavior problems;

   (D) developing or implementing specific curricula, programs, or interventions aimed at addressing behavioral problems;

   (E) stronger linkages between school-based services and community-based resources, such as community mental health and primary care providers; or

   (F) using behavioral specialists, related services personnel, and other staff necessary to implement behavioral supports; or

 (2) improve interim alternative educational settings by —

   (A) improving the training of administrators, teachers, related services personnel, behavioral specialists, and other school staff (including ongoing mentoring of new teachers) in behavioral supports and interventions;

   (B) attracting and retaining a high quality, diverse staff;

   (C) providing for referral to counseling services;

   (D) utilizing research-based interventions, curriculum, and practices;

   (E) allowing students to use instructional technology that provides individualized instruction;

   (F) ensuring that the services are fully

consistent with the goals of the individual student's IEP;

(G) promoting effective case management and collaboration among parents, teachers, physicians, related services personnel, behavioral specialists, principals, administrators, and other school staff;

(H) promoting interagency coordination and coordinated service delivery among schools, juvenile courts, child welfare agencies, community mental health providers, primary care providers, public recreation agencies, and community-based organizations; or

(I) providing for behavioral specialists to help students transitioning from interim alternative educational settings reintegrate into their regular classrooms.

(c) Definition of eligible entity.

In this section, the term "eligible entity" means —

(1) a local educational agency; or

(2) a consortium consisting of a local educational agency and 1 or more of the following entities:

(A) Another local educational agency.

(B) A community-based organization with a demonstrated record of effectiveness in helping children with disabilities who have behavioral challenges succeed.

(C) An institution of higher education.

(D) A community mental health provider.

(E) An educational service agency.

(d) Applications.

Any eligible entity that wishes to receive a grant, or enter into a contract or cooperative agreement, under this section shall —

(1) submit an application to the Secretary at such time, in such manner, and containing such information as the Secretary may require; and

(2) involve parents of participating students in the design and implementation of the activities funded under this section.

(e) Report and evaluation.

Each eligible entity receiving a grant under this section shall prepare and submit annually to the Secretary a report on the outcomes of the activities assisted under the grant.

§ 1466 Authorization of appropriations.

(a) In general.

There are authorized to be appropriated to carry out this subpart (other than section 662) such sums as may be necessary for each of the fiscal years 2005 through 2010.

(b) Reservation.

From amounts appropriated under subsection (a) for fiscal year 2005, the Secretary shall reserve $1,000,000 to carry out the study authorized in section 664(c). From amounts appropriated under subsection (a) for a succeeding fiscal year, the Secretary may reserve an additional amount to carry out such study if the Secretary determines the additional amount is necessary.

SUBPART 3 — SUPPORTS TO IMPROVE RESULTS FOR CHILDREN WITH DISABILITIES

20 U.S.C. §
1470. Purposes.
1471. Parent training and information centers.
1472. Community parent resource centers.
1473. Technical assistance for parent training and information centers.
1474. Technology development, demonstration, and utilization; and media services.
1475. Authorization of appropriations.

SUBPART 3 — SUPPORTS TO IMPROVE RESULTS FOR CHILDREN WITH DISABILITIES

§ 1470. Purposes.

The purposes of this subpart are to ensure that —

(1) children with disabilities and their parents receive training and information designed to assist the children in meeting developmental and functional goals and challenging academic achievement goals, and in preparing to lead productive independent adult lives;

(2) children with disabilities and their parents receive training and information on their rights, responsibilities, and protections under this title, in order to develop the skills necessary to cooperatively and effectively participate in planning and decision making relating

to early intervention, educational, and transitional services;

(3) parents, teachers, administrators, early intervention personnel, related services personnel, and transition personnel receive coordinated and accessible technical assistance and information to assist such personnel in improving early intervention, educational, and transitional services and results for children with disabilities and their families; and

(4) appropriate technology and media are researched, developed, and demonstrated, to improve and implement early intervention, educational, and transitional services and results for children with disabilities and their families.

§ 1471. Parent training and information centers.

(a) Program authorized.

(1) In general.

The Secretary may award grants to, and enter into contracts and cooperative agreements with, parent organizations to support parent training and information centers to carry out activities under this section.

(2) Definition of parent organization.

In this section, the term "parent organization" means a private nonprofit organization (other than an institution of higher education) that —

(A) has a board of directors —

(i) the majority of whom are parents of children with disabilities ages birth through 26;

(ii) that includes —

(I) individuals working in the fields of special education, related services, and early intervention; and

(II) individuals with disabilities; and

(iii) the parent and professional members of which are broadly representative of the population to be served, including low-income parents and parents of limited English proficient children; and

(B) has as its mission serving families of children with disabilities who —

(i) are ages birth through 26; and

(ii) have the full range of disabilities described in section 602(3).

(b) Required activities.

Each parent training and information center that receives assistance under this section shall —

(1) provide training and information that meets the needs of parents of children with disabilities living in the area served by the center, particularly underserved parents and parents of children who may be inappropriately identified, to enable their children with disabilities to —

(A) meet developmental and functional goals, and challenging academic achievement goals that have been established for all children; and

(B) be prepared to lead productive independent adult lives, to the maximum extent possible;

(2) serve the parents of infants, toddlers, and children with the full range of disabilities described in section 602(3);

(3) ensure that the training and information provided meets the needs of low-income parents and parents of limited English proficient children;

(4) assist parents to —

(A) better understand the nature of their children's disabilities and their educational, developmental, and transitional needs;

(B) communicate effectively and work collaboratively with personnel responsible for providing special education, early intervention services, transition services, and related services;

(C) participate in decisionmaking processes and the development of individualized education programs under part B and individualized family service plans under part C;

(D) obtain appropriate information about the range, type, and quality of —

(i) options, programs, services, technologies, practices and interventions based on scientifically based research, to the extent practicable; and

(ii) resources available to assist children with disabilities and their families in school and at home;

(E) understand the provisions of this title for the education of, and the provision of early intervention services to, children with disabilities;

(F) participate in activities at the school level that benefit their children; and

(G) participate in school reform activities;

(5) in States where the State elects to contract with the parent training and information center, contract with State educational agencies to provide, consistent with subparagraphs (B) and (D) of section 615(e)(2), individuals who meet with parents to explain the mediation process to the parents;

(6) assist parents in resolving disputes in the most expeditious and effective way possible, including encouraging the use, and explaining the benefits, of alternative methods of dispute resolution, such as the mediation process described in section 615(e);

(7) assist parents and students with disabilities to understand their rights and responsibilities under this title, including those under section 615(m) upon the student's reaching the age of majority (as appropriate under State law);

(8) assist parents to understand the availability of, and how to effectively use, procedural safeguards under this title, including the resolution session described in section 615(e);

(9) assist parents in understanding, preparing for, and participating in, the process described in section 615(f)(1)(B);

(10) establish cooperative partnerships with community parent resource centers funded under section 672;

(11) network with appropriate clearinghouses, including organizations conducting national dissemination activities under section 663 and the Institute of Education Sciences, and with other national, State, and local organizations and agencies, such as protection and advocacy agencies, that serve parents and families of children with the full range of disabilities described in section 602(3); and

(12) annually report to the Secretary on —

(A) the number and demographics of parents to whom the center provided information and training in the most recently concluded fiscal year;

(B) the effectiveness of strategies used to reach and serve parents, including underserved parents of children with disabilities; and

(C) the number of parents served who have resolved disputes through alternative methods of dispute resolution.

(c) Optional activities.

A parent training and information center that receives assistance under this section may provide information to teachers and other professionals to assist the teachers and professionals in improving results for children with disabilities.

(d) Application requirements.

Each application for assistance under this section shall identify with specificity the special efforts that the parent organization will undertake —

(1) to ensure that the needs for training and information of underserved parents of children with disabilities in the area to be served are effectively met; and

(2) to work with community based organizations, including community based organizations that work with low-income parents and parents of limited English proficient children.

(e) Distribution of funds.

(1) In general.

The Secretary shall —

(A) make not less than 1 award to a parent organization in each State for a parent training and information center that is designated as the statewide parent training and information center; or

(B) in the case of a large State, make awards to multiple parent training and information centers, but only if the centers demonstrate that coordinated services and supports will occur among the multiple centers.

(2) Selection requirement.

The Secretary shall select among applications submitted by parent organizations in a State in a manner that ensures the most effective assistance to parents, including parents in urban and rural areas, in the State.

(f) Quarterly review.

(1) Meetings.

The board of directors of each parent organization that receives an award under this section shall meet not less than once in each calendar quarter to review the activities for which the award was made.

(2) Continuation award.

When a parent organization requests a continuation award under this section, the board of directors shall submit to the Secretary a written review of the parent training and information program conducted by the parent organization during the preceding fiscal year.

§ 1472. Community parent resource centers.

(a) Program authorized.

(1) In general.

The Secretary may award grants to, and enter into contracts and cooperative agreements with, local parent organizations to support community parent resource centers that will help ensure that underserved parents of children with disabilities, including low income parents, parents of limited English proficient children, and parents with disabilities, have the training and information the parents need to enable the parents to participate effectively in helping their children with disabilities —

(A) to meet developmental and functional goals, and challenging academic achievement goals that have been established for all children; and

(B) to be prepared to lead productive independent adult lives, to the maximum extent possible.

(2) Definition of local parent organization.

In this section, the term "local parent organization" means a parent organization, as defined in section 671(a)(2), that —

(A) has a board of directors the majority of whom are parents of children with disabilities ages birth through 26 from the community to be served; and

(B) has as its mission serving parents of children with disabilities who —

(i) are ages birth through 26; and

(ii) have the full range of disabilities described in section 602(3).

(b) Required activities.

Each community parent resource center assisted under this section shall —

(1) provide training and information that meets the training and information needs of parents of children with disabilities proposed to be served by the grant, contract, or cooperative agreement;

(2) carry out the activities required of parent training and information centers under paragraphs (2) through (9) of section 671(b);

(3) establish cooperative partnerships with the parent training and information centers funded under section 671; and

(4) be designed to meet the specific needs of families who experience significant isolation from available sources of information and support.

§ 1473. Technical assistance for parent training and information centers.

(a) Program authorized.

(1) In general.

The Secretary may, directly or through awards to eligible entities, provide technical assistance for developing, assisting, and coordinating parent training and information programs carried out by parent training and information centers receiving assistance under section 671 and community parent resource centers receiving assistance under section 672.

(2) Definition of eligible entity.

In this section, the term "eligible entity" has the meaning given the term in section 661(b).

(b) Authorized activities.

The Secretary may provide technical assistance to a parent training and information center or a community parent resource center under this section in areas such as —

(1) effective coordination of parent training efforts;

(2) dissemination of scientifically based research and information;

(3) promotion of the use of technology, including assistive technology devices and assistive technology services;

(4) reaching underserved populations, including parents of low-income and limited English proficient children with disabilities;

(5) including children with disabilities in general education programs;

(6) facilitation of transitions from —

(A) early intervention services to preschool;

(B) preschool to elementary school;

(C) elementary school to secondary school; and

(D) secondary school to postsecondary environments; and

(7) promotion of alternative methods of dispute resolution, including mediation.

(c) Collaboration with the resource centers.

Each eligible entity receiving an award under subsection (a) shall develop collaborative agreements with the geographically appropriate regional resource center and, as appropriate, the regional educational laboratory supported under section 174 of the Education Sciences Reform Act of 2002, to further parent and professional collaboration.

§ 1474. Technology development, demonstration, and utilization; media services; and instructional materials.

(a) Program authorized.

(1) In general.

The Secretary, on a competitive basis, shall award grants to, and enter into contracts and cooperative agreements with, eligible entities to support activities described in subsections (b) and (c).

(2) Definition of eligible entity.

In this section, the term "eligible entity" has the meaning given the term in section 661(b).

(b) Technology development, demonstration, and use.

(1) In general.

In carrying out this section, the Secretary shall support activities to promote the development, demonstration, and use of technology.

(2) Authorized activities.

The following activities may be carried out under this subsection:

(A) Conducting research on and promoting the demonstration and use of innovative, emerging, and universally designed technologies for children with disabilities, by improving the transfer of technology from research and development to practice.

(B) Supporting research, development, and dissemination of technology with universal design features, so that the technology is accessible to the broadest range of individuals with disabilities without further modification or adaptation.

(C) Demonstrating the use of systems to provide parents and teachers with information and training concerning early diagnosis of, intervention for, and effective teaching strategies for, young children with reading disabilities.

(D) Supporting the use of Internet-based communications for students with cognitive disabilities in order to maximize their academic and functional skills.

(c) Educational media services.

(1) In general.

In carrying out this section, the Secretary shall support —

(A) educational media activities that are designed to be of educational value in the classroom setting to children with disabilities;

(B) providing video description, open captioning, or closed captioning, that is appropriate for use in the classroom setting, of —

(i) television programs;

(ii) videos;

(iii) other materials, including programs and materials associated with new and emerging technologies, such as CDs, DVDs, video streaming, and other forms of multimedia; or

(iv) news (but only until September 30, 2006);

(C) distributing materials described in subparagraphs (A) and (B) through such mechanisms as a loan service; and

(D) providing free educational materials, including textbooks, in accessible media for visually impaired and print disabled students in elementary schools and secondary schools, postsecondary schools, and graduate schools.

(2) Limitation.

The video description, open captioning, or closed captioning described in paragraph (1)(B) shall be provided only when the description or captioning has not been previously provided by the producer or distributor, or has not been fully funded by other sources.

(d) Applications.

(1) In general.

Any eligible entity that wishes to receive a grant, or enter into a contract or cooperative agreement, under subsection (b) or (c) shall submit an application to the Secretary at such time, in such manner, and containing such information as the Secretary may require.

(2) Special rule.

For the purpose of an application for an

award to carry out activities described in subsection (c)(1)(D), such eligible entity shall —

(A) be a national, nonprofit entity with a proven track record of meeting the needs of students with print disabilities through services described in subsection (c)(1)(D);

(B) have the capacity to produce, maintain, and distribute in a timely fashion, up-to-date textbooks in digital audio formats to qualified students; and

(C) have a demonstrated ability to significantly leverage Federal funds through other public and private contributions, as well as through the expansive use of volunteers.

(e) National instructional materials access center.

(1) In general.

The Secretary shall establish and support, through the American Printing House for the Blind, a center to be known as the "National Instructional Materials Access Center" not later than 1 year after the date of enactment of the Individuals with Disabilities Education Improvement Act of 2004.

(2) Duties. The duties of the National Instructional Materials Access Center are the following:

(A) To receive and maintain a catalog of print instructional materials prepared in the National Instructional Materials Accessibility Standard, as established by the Secretary, made available to such center by the textbook publishing industry, State educational agencies, and local educational agencies.

(B) To provide access to print instructional materials, including textbooks, in accessible media, free of charge, to blind or other persons with print disabilities in elementary schools and secondary schools, in accordance with such terms and procedures as the National Instructional Materials Access Center may prescribe.

(C) To develop, adopt and publish procedures to protect against copyright infringement, with respect to the print instructional materials provided under sections 612(a)(23) and 613(a)(6).

(3) Definitions.

In this subsection:

(A) Blind or other persons with print disabilities.

The term "blind or other persons with print disabilities" means children served under this Act and who may qualify in accordance with the Act entitled "An Act to provide books for the adult blind", approved March 3, 1931 (2 U.S.C. 135a; 46 Stat. 1487) to receive books and other publications produced in specialized formats.

(B) National instructional materials accessibility standard.

The term "National Instructional Materials Accessibility Standard" means the standard established by the Secretary to be used in the preparation of electronic files suitable and used solely for efficient conversion into specialized formats.

(C) Print instructional materials.

The term "print instructional materials" means printed textbooks and related printed core materials that are written and published primarily for use in elementary school and secondary school instruction and are required by a State educational agency or local educational agency for use by students in the classroom.

(D) Specialized formats.

The term "specialized formats" has the meaning given the term in section 121(d)(3) of title 17, United States Code.

(4) Applicability.

This subsection shall apply to print instructional materials published after the date on which the final rule establishing the National Instructional Materials Accessibility Standard was published in the Federal Register.

(5) Liability of the secretary.

Nothing in this subsection shall be construed to establish a private right of action against the Secretary for failure to provide instructional materials directly, or for failure by the National Instructional Materials Access Center to perform the duties of such center, or to otherwise authorize a private right of action related to the performance by such center, including through the application of the rights of children and parents established under this Act.

(6) Inapplicability.

Subsections (a) through (d) shall not apply to this subsection.

§ 1475. Authorization of appropriations.

There are authorized to be appropriated to carry out this subpart such sums as may be necessary for each of the fiscal years 2005 through 2010.

SUBPART 4 — GENERAL PROVISIONS

20 U.S.C. §
1481   Comprehensive plan for subparts 2 and 3
1482   Administrative provisions

SUBPART 4 — GENERAL PROVISIONS

§ 1481. Comprehensive plan for subparts 2 and 3.

(a) Comprehensive plan.

(1) In general.

After receiving input from interested individuals with relevant expertise, the Secretary shall develop and implement a comprehensive plan for activities carried out under subparts 2 and 3 in order to enhance the provision of early intervention services, educational services, related services, and transitional services to children with disabilities under parts B and C. To the extent practicable, the plan shall be coordinated with the plan developed pursuant to section 178(c) of the Education Sciences Reform Act of 2002 and shall include mechanisms to address early intervention, educational, related service and transitional needs identified by State educational agencies in applications submitted for State personnel development grants under subpart 1 and for grants under subparts 2 and 3.

(2) Public comment.

The Secretary shall provide a public comment period of not less than 45 days on the plan.

(3) Distribution of funds.

In implementing the plan, the Secretary shall, to the extent appropriate, ensure that funds awarded under subparts 2 and 3 are used to carry out activities that benefit, directly or indirectly, children with the full range of disabilities and of all ages.

(4) Reports to congress.

The Secretary shall annually report to Congress on the Secretary's activities under subparts 2 and 3, including an initial report not later than 12 months after the date of enactment of the Individuals with Disabilities Education Improvement Act of 2004.

(b) Assistance authorized.

The Secretary is authorized to award grants

to, or enter into contracts or cooperative agreements with, eligible entities to enable the eligible entities to carry out the purposes of such subparts in accordance with the comprehensive plan described in subsection (a).

(c) Special populations.

(1) Application requirement.

In making an award of a grant, contract, or cooperative agreement under subpart 2 or 3, the Secretary shall, as appropriate, require an eligible entity to demonstrate how the eligible entity will address the needs of children with disabilities from minority backgrounds.

(2) Required outreach and technical assistance.

Notwithstanding any other provision of this title, the Secretary shall reserve not less than 2 percent of the total amount of funds appropriated to carry out subparts 2 and 3 for either or both of the following activities:

(A) Providing outreach and technical assistance to historically Black colleges and universities, and to institutions of higher education with minority enrollments of not less than 25 percent, to promote the participation of such colleges, universities, and institutions in activities under this subpart.

(B) Enabling historically Black colleges and universities, and the institutions described in subparagraph (A), to assist other colleges, universities, institutions, and agencies in improving educational and transitional results for children with disabilities, if the historically Black colleges and universities and the institutions of higher education described in subparagraph (A) meet the criteria established by the Secretary under this subpart.

(d) Priorities.

The Secretary, in making an award of a grant, contract, or cooperative agreement under subpart 2 or 3, may, without regard to the rulemaking procedures under section 553 of title 5, United States Code, limit competitions to, or otherwise give priority to —

(1) projects that address 1 or more —

(A) age ranges;

(B) disabilities;

(C) school grades;

(D) types of educational placements or early intervention environments;

(E) types of services;

(F) content areas, such as reading; or

(G) effective strategies for helping children with disabilities learn appropriate behavior in the school and other community based educational settings;

(2) projects that address the needs of children based on the severity or incidence of their disability;

(3) projects that address the needs of —

(A) low achieving students;

(B) underserved populations;

(C) children from low income families;

(D) limited English proficient children;

(E) unserved and underserved areas;

(F) rural or urban areas;

(G) children whose behavior interferes with their learning and socialization;

(H) children with reading difficulties;

(I) children in public charter schools;

(J) children who are gifted and talented; or

(K) children with disabilities served by local educational agencies that receive payments under title VIII of the Elementary and Secondary Education Act of 1965;

(4) projects to reduce inappropriate identification of children as children with disabilities, particularly among minority children;

(5) projects that are carried out in particular areas of the country, to ensure broad geographic coverage;

(6) projects that promote the development and use of technologies with universal design, assistive technology devices, and assistive technology services to maximize children with disabilities' access to and participation in the general education curriculum; and

(7) any activity that is authorized in subpart 2 or 3.

(e) Eligibility for financial assistance.

No State or local educational agency, or other public institution or agency, may receive a grant or enter into a contract or cooperative agreement under subpart 2 or 3 that relates exclusively to programs, projects, and activities pertaining to children aged 3 through 5, inclusive, unless the State is eligible to receive a grant under section 619(b).

§ 1482. Administrative provisions.

(a) Applicant and recipient responsibilities.

(1) Development and assessment of projects.

The Secretary shall require that an applicant for, and a recipient of, a grant, contract, or cooperative agreement for a project under subpart 2 or 3 —

(A) involve individuals with disabilities or parents of individuals with disabilities ages birth through 26 in planning, implementing, and evaluating the project; and

(B) where appropriate, determine whether the project has any potential for replication and adoption by other entities.

(2) Additional responsibilities.

The Secretary may require a recipient of a grant, contract, or cooperative agreement under subpart 2 or 3 to —

(A) share in the cost of the project;

(B) prepare any findings and products from the project in formats that are useful for specific audiences, including parents, administrators, teachers, early intervention personnel, related services personnel, and individuals with disabilities;

(C) disseminate such findings and products; and

(D) collaborate with other such recipients in carrying out subparagraphs (B) and (C).

(b) Application management.

(1) Standing panel.

(A) In general.

The Secretary shall establish and use a standing panel of experts who are qualified, by virtue of their training, expertise, or experience, to evaluate each application under subpart 2 or 3 that requests more than $75,000 per year in Federal financial assistance.

(B) Membership.

The standing panel shall include, at a minimum —

(i) individuals who are representatives of institutions of higher education that plan, develop, and carry out high quality programs of personnel preparation;

(ii) individuals who design and carry out scientifically based research targeted to the improvement of special education programs and services;

(iii) individuals who have recognized experience and knowledge necessary to integrate and apply scientifically based research findings to improve educational and transitional results for children with disabilities;

(iv) individuals who administer programs at the State or local level in which children with disabilities participate;

(v) individuals who prepare parents of children with disabilities to participate in making decisions about the education of their children;

(vi) individuals who establish policies that affect the delivery of services to children with disabilities;

(vii) individuals who are parents of children with disabilities ages birth through 26 who are benefiting, or have benefited, from coordinated research, personnel preparation, and technical assistance; and

(viii) individuals with disabilities.

(C) Term.

No individual shall serve on the standing panel for more than 3 consecutive years.

(2) Peer-review panels for particular competitions.

(A) Composition.

The Secretary shall ensure that each subpanel selected from the standing panel that reviews an application under subpart 2 or 3 includes —

(i) individuals with knowledge and expertise on the issues addressed by the activities described in the application; and

(ii) to the extent practicable, parents of children with disabilities ages birth through 26, individuals with disabilities, and persons from diverse backgrounds.

(B) Federal employment limitation.

A majority of the individuals on each subpanel that reviews an application under subpart 2 or 3 shall be individuals who are not employees of the Federal Government.

(3) Use of discretionary funds for administrative purposes.

(A) Expenses and fees of non-federal panel members.

The Secretary may use funds available under subpart 2 or 3 to pay the expenses and fees of the panel members who are not officers or employees of the Federal Government.

(B) Administrative support.

The Secretary may use not more than 1 percent of the funds appropriated to carry out subpart 2 or 3 to pay non-Federal entities for administrative support related to management of applications submitted under subpart 2 or 3, respectively.

(c) Program evaluation.

The Secretary may use funds made available to carry out subpart 2 or 3 to evaluate activities carried out under subpart 2 or 3, respectively.

(d) Minimum funding required.

(1) In general.

Subject to paragraph (2), the Secretary shall ensure that, for each fiscal year, not less than the following amounts are provided under subparts 2 and 3 to address the following needs:

(A) $12,832,000 to address the educational, related services, transitional, and early intervention needs of children with deaf-blindness.

(B) $4,000,000 to address the postsecondary, vocational, technical, continuing, and adult education needs of individuals with deafness.

(C) $4,000,000 to address the educational, related services, and transitional needs of children with an emotional disturbance and those who are at risk of developing an emotional disturbance.

(2) Ratable reduction.

If the sum of the amount appropriated to carry out subparts 2 and 3, and part E of the Education Sciences Reform Act of 2002 for any fiscal year is less than $130,000,000, the amounts listed in paragraph (1) shall be ratably reduced for the fiscal year.

IDEA DEPARTMENT OF EDUCATION REGULATIONS

United States Department of Education Individuals with Disabilities Education Act Regulations (Selected Regulations)

34 CFR § 300.1 Purposes.

The purposes of this part are—

(a) To ensure that all children with disabilities have available to them a free appropriate public education that emphasizes special education and related services designed to meet their unique needs and prepare them for further education, employment, and independent living;

(b) To ensure that the rights of children with disabilities and their parents are protected;

(c) To assist States, localities, educational service agencies, and Federal agencies to provide for the education of all children with disabilities; and

(d) To assess and ensure the effectiveness of efforts to educate children with disabilities.

§ 300.2 Applicability of this part to State and local agencies.

(a) *States.* This part applies to each State that receives payments under Part B of the Act, as defined in § 300.4.

(b) *Public agencies within the State.* The provisions of this part—

(1) Apply to all political subdivisions of the State that are involved in the education of children with disabilities, including:

(i) The State educational agency (SEA).

(ii) Local educational agencies (LEAs), educational service agencies (ESAs), and public charter schools that are not otherwise included as LEAs or ESAs and are not a school of an LEA or ESA.

(iii) Other State agencies and schools (such as Departments of Mental Health and Welfare and State schools for children with deafness or children with blindness).

(iv) State and local juvenile and adult correctional facilities; and

(2) Are binding on each public agency in the State that provides special education and related services to children with disabilities, regardless of whether that agency is receiving funds under Part B of the Act.

(c) *Private schools and facilities.* Each public agency in the State is responsible for ensuring that the rights and protections under Part B of the Act are given to children with disabilities—

(1) Referred to or placed in private schools and facilities by that public agency; or

(2) Placed in private schools by their parents under the provisions of § 300.148.

Definitions Used in This Part

§ 300.4 Act.

Act means the Individuals with Disabilities Education Act, as amended.

§ 300.5 Assistive technology device.

Assistive technology device means any item, piece of equipment, or product system, whether acquired commercially off the shelf, modified, or customized, that is used to increase, maintain, or improve the functional capabilities of a child with a disability. The term does not include a medical device that is surgically implanted, or the replacement of such device.

§ 300.6 Assistive technology service.

Assistive technology service means any service that directly assists a child with a disability in the selection, acquisition, or use of an assistive technology device. The term includes—

(a) The evaluation of the needs of a child with a disability, including a functional evaluation of the child in the child's customary environment;

(b) Purchasing, leasing, or otherwise providing for the acquisition of assistive technology devices by children with disabilities;

(c) Selecting, designing, fitting, customizing, adapting, applying, maintaining, repairing, or replacing assistive technology devices;

(d) Coordinating and using other therapies, interventions, or services with assistive technology devices, such as those associated with existing education and rehabilitation plans and programs;

(e) Training or technical assistance for a child with a disability or, if appropriate, that child's family; and

(f) Training or technical assistance for professionals (including individuals providing education or rehabilitation services), employers, or other individuals who provide services to, employ, or are otherwise substantially involved in the major life functions of that child.

§ 300.7 Charter school.

Charter school has the meaning given the term in section 5210(1) of the Elementary and Secondary Education Act of 1965, as amended, 20 U.S.C. 6301 et seq. (ESEA).

§ 300.8 Child with a disability.

(a) General.

(1) Child with a disability means a child evaluated in accordance with §§ 300.304 through 300.311 as having mental retardation, a hearing impairment (including deafness), a speech or language impairment, a visual impairment (including blindness), a serious emotional disturbance (referred to in this part as "emotional disturbance"), an orthopedic impairment, autism, traumatic brain injury, an other health impairment, a specific learning disability, deaf-blindness, or multiple disabilities, and who, by reason thereof, needs special education and related services.

(2)(i) Subject to paragraph (a)(2)(ii) of this section, if it is determined, through an appropriate evaluation under §§ 300.304 through 300.311, that a child has one of the disabilities identified in paragraph (a)(1) of this section, but only needs a related service and not special education, the child is not a child with a disability under this part.

(ii) If, consistent with § 300.39(a)(2), the related service required by the child is considered special education rather than a related service under State standards, the child would be determined to be a child with a disability under paragraph (a)(1) of this section.

(b) Children aged three through nine experiencing developmental delays. Child with a disability for children aged three through nine (or any subset of that age range, including ages three through five), may, subject to the conditions described in § 300.111(b), include a child—

(1) Who is experiencing developmental delays, as defined by the State and as measured by appropriate diagnostic instruments and procedures, in one or more of the following areas: Physical development, cognitive development, communication development, social or emotional development, or adaptive development; and

(2) Who, by reason thereof, needs special education and related services.

(c) Definitions of disability terms. The terms used in this definition of a child with a disability are defined as follows:

(1)(i) Autism means a developmental disability significantly affecting verbal and nonverbal communication and social interaction, generally evident before age three, that adversely affects a child's educational performance. Other characteristics often associated with autism are engagement in repetitive activities and stereotyped movements, resistance to environmental change or change in daily routines, and unusual responses to sensory experiences.

(ii) Autism does not apply if a child's educational performance is adversely affected primarily because the child has an emotional disturbance, as defined in paragraph (c)(4) of this section.

(iii) A child who manifests the characteristics of autism after age three could be identified as having autism if the criteria in paragraph (c)(1)(i) of this section are satisfied.

(2) Deaf-blindness means concomitant hearing and visual impairments, the combination of which causes such severe communication and other developmental and educational needs that they cannot be accommodated in special education programs solely for children with deafness or children with blindness.

(3) Deafness means a hearing impairment that is so severe that the child is impaired in processing linguistic information through hearing, with or without amplification that adversely affects a child's educational performance.

(4)(i) Emotional disturbance means a condition exhibiting one or more of the following characteristics over a long period of time and to a marked degree that adversely affects a child's educational performance:

(A) An inability to learn that cannot be explained by intellectual, sensory, or health factors.

(B) An inability to build or maintain satisfactory interpersonal relationships with peers and teachers.

(C) Inappropriate types of behavior or feelings under normal circumstances.

(D) A general pervasive mood of unhappiness or depression.

(E) A tendency to develop physical symptoms or fears associated with personal or school problems.

(ii) Emotional disturbance includes schizophrenia. The term does not apply to children who are socially maladjusted, unless it is determined that they have an emotional disturbance under paragraph (c)(4)(i) of this section.

(5) Hearing impairment means an impairment in hearing, whether permanent or fluctuating, that adversely affects a child's educational performance but that is not included under the definition of deafness in this section.

(6) Mental retardation means significantly subaverage general intellectual functioning, existing concurrently with deficits in adaptive behavior and manifested during the developmental period, that adversely affects a child's educational performance.

(7) Multiple disabilities means concomitant impairments (such as mental retardation-blindness or mental retardation-orthopedic impairment), the combination of which causes such severe educational needs that they cannot be accommodated in special education programs solely for one of the impairments. Multiple disabilities does not include deaf-blindness.

(8) Orthopedic impairment means a severe orthopedic impairment that adversely affects a child's educational performance. The term includes impairments caused by a congenital anomaly, impairments caused by disease (e.g., poliomyelitis, bone tuberculosis), and impairments from other causes (e.g., cerebral palsy, amputations, and fractures or burns that cause contractures).

(9) Other health impairment means having limited strength, vitality, or alertness, including a heightened alertness to environmental stimuli, that results in limited alertness with respect to the educational environment, that—

(i) Is due to chronic or acute health problems such as asthma, attention deficit disorder or attention deficit hyperactivity disorder, diabetes, epilepsy, a heart condition, hemophilia, lead poisoning, leukemia, nephritis, rheumatic fever, sickle cell anemia, and Tourette syndrome; and

(ii) Adversely affects a child's educational performance.

(10) Specific learning disability—

(i) General. Specific learning disability means a disorder in one or more of the basic psychological processes involved in understanding or in using language, spoken or written, that may manifest itself in the imperfect ability to listen, think, speak, read, write, spell, or to do mathematical calculations, including conditions such as perceptual disabilities, brain injury, minimal brain dysfunction, dyslexia, and developmental aphasia.

(ii) Disorders not included. Specific learning disability does not include learning problems that are primarily the result of visual, hearing, or motor disabilities, of mental retardation, of emotional disturbance, or of environmental, cultural, or economic disadvantage.

(11) Speech or language impairment means a communication disorder, such as stuttering, impaired articulation, a language impairment, or a voice impairment, that adversely affects a child's educational performance.

(12) Traumatic brain injury means an acquired injury to the brain caused by an external physical force, resulting in total or partial functional disability or psychosocial impairment, or both, that adversely affects a child's educational performance. Traumatic brain injury applies to open or closed head injuries resulting in impairments in one or more areas, such as cognition; language; memory; attention; reasoning; abstract thinking; judgment; problem-solving; sensory, perceptual, and motor abilities; psychosocial behavior; physical functions; information processing; and speech. Traumatic brain injury does not apply to brain injuries that are con-

genital or degenerative, or to brain injuries induced by birth trauma.

(13) Visual impairment including blindness means an impairment in vision that, even with correction, adversely affects a child's educational performance. The term includes both partial sight and blindness.

§ 300.9 Consent.

Consent means that—

(a) The parent has been fully informed of all information relevant to the activity for which consent is sought, in his or her native language, or other mode of communication;

(b) The parent understands and agrees in writing to the carrying out of the activity for which his or her consent is sought, and the consent describes that activity and lists the records (if any) that will be released and to whom; and

(c)(1) The parent understands that the granting of consent is voluntary on the part of the parent and may be revoked at anytime.

(2) If a parent revokes consent, that revocation is not retroactive (i.e., it does not negate an action that has occurred after the consent was given and before the consent was revoked).

§ 300.10 Core academic subjects.

Core academic subjects means English, reading or language arts, mathematics, science, foreign languages, civics and government, economics, arts, history, and geography.

§ 300.11 Day; business day; school day.

(a) Day means calendar day unless otherwise indicated as business day or school day.

(b) Business day means Monday through Friday, except for Federal and State holidays (unless holidays are specifically included in the designation of business day, as in § 300.148(d)(1)(ii)).

(c)(1) School day means any day, including a partial day that children are in attendance at school for instructional purposes.

(2) School day has the same meaning for all children in school, including children with and without disabilities.

§ 300.12 Educational service agency.

Educational service agency means—

(a) A regional public multiservice agency—

(1) Authorized by State law to develop, manage, and provide services or programs to LEAs;

(2) Recognized as an administrative agency for purposes of the provision of special education and related services provided within public elementary schools and secondary schools of the State;

(b) Includes any other public institution or agency having administrative control and direction over a public elementary school or secondary school; and

(c) Includes entities that meet the definition of intermediate educational unit in section 602(23) of the Act as in effect prior to June 4, 1997.

§ 300.13 Elementary school.

Elementary school means a nonprofit institutional day or residential school, including a public elementary charter school, that provides elementary education, as determined under State law.

§ 300.14 Equipment.

Equipment means—

(a) Machinery, utilities, and built-in equipment, and any necessary enclosures or structures to house the machinery, utilities, or equipment; and

(b) All other items necessary for the functioning of a particular facility as a facility for the provision of educational services, including items such as instructional equipment and necessary furniture; printed, published and audio-visual instructional materials; telecommunications, sensory, and other technological aids and devices; and books, periodicals, documents, and other related materials.

§ 300.15 Evaluation.

Evaluation means procedures used in accordance with §§ 300.304 through 300.311 to determine whether a child has a disability and the nature and extent of the special education and related services that the child needs.

§ 300.16 Excess costs.

Excess costs means those costs that are in excess of the average annual per-student expenditure in an LEA during the preceding school year for an elementary school or secondary school student, as may be appropriate, and that must be computed after deducting—

(a) Amounts received—

(1) Under Part B of the Act;

(2) Under Part A of title I of the ESEA; and

(3) Under Parts A and B of title III of the ESEA and;

(b) Any State or local funds expended for programs that would qualify for assistance under any of the parts described in paragraph (a) of this section, but excluding any amounts for capital outlay or debt service. (See Appendix A to part 300 for an example of how excess costs must be calculated.)

§ 300.17 Free appropriate public education.

Free appropriate public education or FAPE means special education and related services that—

(a) Are provided at public expense, under public supervision and direction, and without charge;

(b) Meet the standards of the SEA, including the requirements of this part;

(c) Include an appropriate preschool, elementary school, or secondary school education in the State involved; and

(d) Are provided in conformity with an individualized education program (IEP) that meets the requirements of §§ 300.320 through 300.324.

§ 300.18 Highly qualified special education teachers.

(a) *Requirements for special education teachers teaching core academic subjects.* For any public elementary or secondary school special education teacher teaching core academic subjects, the term highly qualified has the meaning given the term in section 9101 of the ESEA and 34 CFR 200.56, except that the requirements for highly qualified also—

(1) Include the requirements described in paragraph (b) of this section; and

(2) Include the option for teachers to meet the requirements of section 9101 of the ESEA by meeting the requirements of paragraphs (c) and (d) of this section.

(b) *Requirements for special education teachers in general.*

(1) When used with respect to any public elementary school or secondary school special education teacher teaching in a State, highly qualified requires that—

(i) The teacher has obtained full State certification as a special education teacher (including certification obtained through alternative routes to certification), or passed the State special education teacher licensing examination, and holds a license to teach in the State as a special education teacher, except that when used with respect to any teacher teaching in a public charter school, highly qualified means that the teacher meets the certification or licensing requirements, if any, set forth in the State's public charter school law;

(ii) The teacher has not had special education certification or licensure requirements waived on an emergency, temporary, or provisional basis; and

(iii) The teacher holds at least a bachelor's degree.

(2) A teacher will be considered to meet the standard in paragraph (b)(1)(i) of this section if that teacher is participating in an alternative route to special education certification program under which—

(i) The teacher—

(A) Receives high-quality professional development that is sustained, intensive, and classroom-focused in order to have a positive and lasting impact on classroom instruction, before and while teaching;

(B) Participates in a program of intensive supervision that consists of structured guidance and regular ongoing support for teachers or a teacher mentoring program;

(C) Assumes functions as a teacher only for a specified period of time not to exceed three years; and

(D) Demonstrates satisfactory progress toward full certification as prescribed by the State; and

(ii) The State ensures, through its certification and licensure process, that the provisions in paragraph (b)(2)(i) of this section are met.

(3) Any public elementary school or secondary school special education teacher teaching in a State, who is not teaching a core academic subject, is highly qualified if the teacher meets the requirements in paragraph (b)(1) or the requirements in (b)(1)(iii) and (b)(2) of this section.

(c) Requirements for special education teachers teaching to alternate achievement standards. When used with respect to a special education teacher who teaches core academic subjects exclusively to children who are assessed against alternate achievement standards established under 34 CFR 200.1(d), highly qualified means the teacher, whether new or not new to the profession, may either—

(1) Meet the applicable requirements of section 9101 of the ESEA and 34 CFR 200.56 for any elementary, middle, or secondary school teacher who is new or not new to the profession; or

(2) Meet the requirements of paragraph (B) or (C) of section 9101(23) of the ESEA as applied to an elementary school teacher, or, in the case of instruction above the elementary level, meet the requirements of paragraph (B) or (C) of section 9101(23) of the ESEA as applied to an elementary school teacher and have subject matter knowledge appropriate to the level of instruction being provided and needed to effectively teach to those standards, as determined by the State.

(d) Requirements for special education teachers teaching multiple subjects. Subject to paragraph (e) of this section, when used with respect to a special education teacher who teaches two or more core academic subjects exclusively to children with disabilities, highly qualified means that the teacher may either—

(1) Meet the applicable requirements of section 9101 of the ESEA and 34 CFR 200.56(b) or (c);

(2) In the case of a teacher who is not new to the profession, demonstrate competence in all the core academic subjects in which the teacher teaches in the same manner as is required for an elementary, middle, or secondary school teacher who is not new to the profession under 34 CFR 200.56(c) which may include a single, high objective uniform State standard of evaluation (HOUSSE) covering multiple subjects; or

(3) In the case of a new special education teacher who teaches multiple subjects and who is highly qualified in mathematics, language arts, or science, demonstrate, not later than two years after the date of employment, competence in the other core academic subjects in which the teacher teaches in the same manner as is required for an elementary, middle, or secondary school teacher under 34 CFR 200.56(c), which may include a single HOUSSE covering multiple subjects.

(e) Separate HOUSSE standards for special education teachers. Provided that any adaptations of the State's HOUSSE would not establish a lower standard for the content knowledge requirements for special education teachers and meets all the requirements for a HOUSSE for regular education teachers—

(1) A State may develop a separate HOUSSE for special education teachers; and

(2) The standards described in paragraph (e)(1) of this section may include single HOUSSE evaluations that cover multiple subjects.

(f) Rule of construction. Notwithstanding any other individual right of action that a parent or student may maintain under this part, nothing in this part shall be construed to create a right of action on behalf of an individual student or class of students for the failure of a particular SEA or LEA employee to be highly qualified, or to prevent a parent from filing a complaint under §§ 300.151 through 300.153 about staff qualifications with the SEA as provided for under this part.

(g) Applicability of definition to ESEA; and clarification of new special education teacher.

(1) A teacher who is highly qualified under this section is considered highly qualified for purposes of the ESEA.

(2) For purposes of § 300.18(d)(3), a fully certified regular education teacher who subsequently becomes fully certified or licensed as a special education teacher is a new special education teacher when first hired as a special education teacher.

(h) Private school teachers not covered. The requirements in this section do not apply to teachers hired by private elementary schools and secondary schools including private school teachers hired or contracted by LEAs to provide equitable services to parentally-placed private school children with disabilities under § 300.138.

§ 300.19 Homeless children.

Homeless children has the meaning given the term homeless children and youths in section 725 (42 U.S.C. 11434a) of the McKinney-Vento Homeless Assistance Act, as amended, 42 U.S.C. 11431 et seq.

§ 300.20 Include.

Include means that the items named are not all of the possible items that are covered, whether like or unlike the ones named.

§ 300.21 Indian and Indian tribe.

(a) Indian means an individual who is a member of an Indian tribe.

(b) Indian tribe means any Federal or State Indian tribe, band, rancheria, pueblo, colony, or community, including any Alaska Native village or regional village corporation (as defined in or established under the Alaska Native Claims Settlement Act, 43 U.S.C. 1601 et seq.).

(c) Nothing in this definition is intended to indicate that the Secretary of the Interior is required to provide services or funding to a State Indian tribe that is not listed in the Federal Register list of Indian entities recognized as eligible to receive services from the United States, published pursuant to Section 104 of the Federally Recognized Indian Tribe List Act of 1994, 25 U.S.C. 479a-1.

§ 300.22 Individualized education program.

Individualized education program or IEP means a written statement for a child with a disability that is developed, reviewed, and revised in accordance with §§ 300.320 through 300.324.

§ 300.23 Individualized education program team.

Individualized education program team or IEP Team means a group of individuals described in § 300.321 that is responsible for developing, reviewing, or revising an IEP for a child with a disability.

§ 300.24 Individualized family service plan.

Individualized family service plan or IFSP has the meaning given the term in section 636 of the Act.

§ 300.25 Infant or toddler with a disability.

Infant or toddler with a disability—

(a) Means an individual under three years of age who needs early intervention services because the individual—

(1) Is experiencing developmental delays, as measured by appropriate diagnostic instruments and procedures in one or more of the areas of cognitive development, physical development, communication development, social or emotional development, and adaptive development; or

(2) Has a diagnosed physical or mental condition that has a high probability of resulting in developmental delay; and

(b) May also include, at a State's discretion—

(1) At-risk infants and toddlers; and

(2) Children with disabilities who are eligible for services under section 619 and who previously received services under Part C of the Act until such children enter, or are eligible under State law to enter, kindergarten or elementary school, as appropriate, provided that any programs under Part C of the Act serving such children shall include—

(i) An educational component that promotes school readiness and incorporates pre-literacy, language, and numeracy skills; and

(ii) A written notification to parents of their rights and responsibilities in determining whether their child will continue to receive services under Part C of the Act or participate in preschool programs under section 619.

§ 300.26 Institution of higher education.

Institution of higher education—

(a) Has the meaning given the term in section 101 of the Higher Education Act of 1965, as amended, 20 U.S.C. 1021 et seq. (HEA); and

(b) Also includes any community college receiving funds from the Secretary of the Interior under the Tribally Controlled Community College or University Assistance Act of 1978, 25 U.S.C. 1801, et seq.

§ 300.27 Limited English proficient.

Limited English proficient has the meaning given the term in section 9101(25) of the ESEA.

§ 300.28 Local educational agency.

(a) General. Local educational agency or LEA means a public board of education or other public authority legally constituted within a State for either administrative control or direction of, or to perform a service function for, public elementary or secondary schools in a city, county, township, school district, or other political subdivision of a State, or for a combination of school districts or counties as are recognized in a State as an administrative agency for its public elementary schools or secondary schools.

(b) Educational service agencies and other public institutions or agencies. The term includes—

(1) An educational service agency, as defined in § 300.12; and

(2) Any other public institution or agency having administrative control and direction of a public elementary school or secondary school, including a public nonprofit charter school that is established as an LEA under State law.

(c) BIA funded schools. The term includes an elementary school or secondary school funded by the Bureau of Indian Affairs, and not subject to the jurisdiction of any SEA other than the Bureau of Indian Affairs, but only to the extent that the inclusion makes the school eligible for programs for which specific eligibility is not provided to the school in another provision of law and the school does not have a student population that is smaller than the student population of the LEA receiving assistance under the Act with the smallest student population.

§ 300.29 Native language.

(a) Native language, when used with respect to an individual who is limited English proficient, means the following:

(1) The language normally used by that individual, or, in the case of a child, the language normally used by the parents of the child, except as provided in paragraph (a)(2) of this section.

(2) In all direct contact with a child (including evaluation of the child), the language normally used by the child in the home or learning environment.

(b) For an individual with deafness or blindness, or for an individual with no written language, the mode of communication is that normally used by the individual (such as sign language, Braille, or oral communication).

§ 300.30 Parent.

(a) Parent means—

(1) A biological or adoptive parent of a child;

(2) A foster parent, unless State law, regulations, or contractual obligations with a State or local entity prohibit a foster parent from acting as a parent;

(3) A guardian generally authorized to act as the child's parent, or authorized to make educational decisions for the child (but not the State if the child is a ward of the State);

(4) An individual acting in the place of a biological or adoptive parent (including a grandparent, stepparent, or other relative) with whom the child lives, or an individual who is legally responsible for the child's welfare; or

(5) A surrogate parent who has been appointed in accordance with § 300.519 or section 639(a)(5) of the Act.

(b)(1) Except as provided in paragraph (b)(2) of this section, the biological or adoptive parent, when attempting to act as the parent under this part and when more than one party is qualified under paragraph (a) of this section to act as a parent, must be presumed to be the parent for purposes of this section unless the biological or adoptive parent does not have legal authority to make educational decisions for the child.

(2) If a judicial decree or order identifies a specific person or persons under paragraphs (a)(1) through (4) of this section to act as the "parent" of a child or to make educational decisions on behalf of a child, then such person or persons shall be determined to be the "parent" for purposes of this section.

§ 300.31 Parent training and information center.

Parent training and information center means a center assisted under sections 671 or 672 of the Act.

§ 300.32 Personally identifiable.

Personally identifiable means information that contains—

(a) The name of the child, the child's parent, or other family member;

(b) The address of the child;

(c) A personal identifier, such as the child's social security number or student number; or

(d) A list of personal characteristics or other information that would make it possible to identify the child with reasonable certainty.

§ 300.33 Public agency.

Public agency includes the SEA, LEAs, ESAs, nonprofit public charter schools that are not otherwise included as LEAs or ESAs and are not a school of an LEA or ESA, and any other political subdivisions of the State that are responsible for providing education to children with disabilities.

§ 300.34 Related services.

(a) General. Related services means transportation and such developmental, corrective, and other supportive services as are required to assist a child with a disability to benefit from special education, and includes speech-language pathology and audiology services, interpreting services, psychological services, physical and occupational therapy, recreation, including therapeutic recreation, early identification and assessment of disabilities in children, counseling services, including rehabilitation counseling, orientation and mobility services, and medical services for diagnostic or evaluation purposes. Related services also include school health services and school nurse services, social work services in schools, and parent counseling and training.

(b) Exception; services that apply to children with surgically implanted devices, including cochlear implants.

(1) Related services do not include a medical device that is surgically implanted, the optimization of that device's functioning (e.g., mapping), maintenance of that device, or the replacement of that device.

(2) Nothing in paragraph (b)(1) of this section—

(i) Limits the right of a child with a surgically implanted device (e.g., cochlear implant) to receive related services (as listed in paragraph (a) of this section) that are determined by the IEP Team to be necessary for the child to receive FAPE.

(ii) Limits the responsibility of a public agency to appropriately monitor and maintain medical devices that are needed to maintain the health and safety of the child, including breathing, nutrition, or operation of other bodily functions, while the child is transported to and from school or is at school; or

(iii) Prevents the routine checking of an external component of a surgically implanted device to make sure it is functioning properly, as required in § 300.113(b).

(c) Individual related services terms defined. The terms used in this definition are defined as follows:

(1) Audiology includes—

(i) Identification of children with hearing loss;

(ii) Determination of the range, nature, and degree of hearing loss, including referral for medical or other professional attention for the habilitation of hearing;

(iii) Provision of habilitative activities, such as language habilitation, auditory training, speech reading (lip-reading), hearing evaluation, and speech conservation;

(iv) Creation and administration of programs for prevention of hearing loss;

(v) Counseling and guidance of children, parents, and teachers regarding hearing loss; and

(vi) Determination of children's needs for group and individual amplification, selecting and fitting an appropriate aid, and evaluating the effectiveness of amplification.

(2) Counseling services means services provided by qualified social workers, psychologists, guidance counselors, or other qualified personnel.

(3) Early identification and assessment of disabilities in children means the implementation of a formal plan for identifying a disability as early as possible in a child's life.

(4) Interpreting services includes—

(i) The following, when used with respect to children who are deaf or hard of hearing: Oral transliteration services, cued language transliteration services, sign language transliteration and interpreting services, and transcription services, such as communication access real-time translation (CART), C-Print, and TypeWell; and

(ii) Special interpreting services for children who are deaf-blind.

(5) Medical services means services provided by a licensed physician to determine a child's medically related disability that results in the child's need for special education and related services.

(6) Occupational therapy—

(i) Means services provided by a qualified occupational therapist; and

(ii) Includes—

(A) Improving, developing, or restoring functions impaired or lost through illness, injury, or deprivation;

(B) Improving ability to perform tasks for independent functioning if functions are impaired or lost; and

(C) Preventing, through early intervention, initial or further impairment or loss of function.

(7) Orientation and mobility services—

(i) Means services provided to blind or visually impaired children by qualified personnel to enable those students to attain systematic orientation to and safe movement within their environments in school, home, and community; and

(ii) Includes teaching children the following, as appropriate:

(A) Spatial and environmental concepts and use of information received by the senses (such as sound, temperature and vibrations) to establish, maintain, or regain orientation and line of travel (e.g., using sound at a traffic light to cross the street);

(B) To use the long cane or a service animal to supplement visual travel skills or as a tool for safely negotiating the environment for children with no available travel vision;

(C) To understand and use remaining vision and distance low vision aids; and

(D) Other concepts, techniques, and tools.

(8)(i) Parent counseling and training means assisting parents in understanding the special needs of their child;

(ii) Providing parents with information about child development; and

(iii) Helping parents to acquire the necessary skills that will allow them to support the implementation of their child's IEP or IFSP.

(9) Physical therapy means services provided by a qualified physical therapist.

(10) Psychological services includes—

(i) Administering psychological and educational tests, and other assessment procedures;

(ii) Interpreting assessment results;

(iii) Obtaining, integrating, and interpreting information about child behavior and conditions relating to learning;

(iv) Consulting with other staff members in planning school programs to meet the special educational needs of children as indicated by psychological tests, interviews, direct observation, and behavioral evaluations;

(v) Planning and managing a program of psychological services, including psychological counseling for children and parents; and

(vi) Assisting in developing positive behavioral intervention strategies.

(11) Recreation includes—

(i) Assessment of leisure function;

(ii) Therapeutic recreation services;

(iii) Recreation programs in schools and community agencies; and

(iv) Leisure education.

(12) Rehabilitation counseling services means services provided by qualified personnel in individual or group sessions that focus specifically on career development, employment preparation, achieving independence, and integration in the workplace and community of a student with a disability. The term also includes vocational rehabilitation services provided to a student with a disability by vocational rehabilitation programs funded under the Rehabilitation Act of 1973, as amended, 29 U.S.C. 701 et seq.

(13) School health services and school nurse services means health services that are designed to enable a child with a disability to receive FAPE as described in the child's IEP. School nurse services are services provided by a qualified school nurse. School health services are services that may be provided by either a qualified school nurse or other qualified person.

(14) Social work services in schools includes—

(i) Preparing a social or developmental history on a child with a disability;

(ii) Group and individual counseling with the child and family;

(iii) Working in partnership with parents and others on those problems in a child's living situation (home, school, and community) that affect the child's adjustment in school;

(iv) Mobilizing school and community resources to enable the child to learn as effectively as possible in his or her educational program; and

(v) Assisting in developing positive behavioral intervention strategies.

(15) Speech-language pathology services includes—

(i) Identification of children with speech or language impairments;

(ii) Diagnosis and appraisal of specific speech or language impairments;

(iii) Referral for medical or other professional attention necessary for the habilitation of speech or language impairments;

(iv) Provision of speech and language services for the habilitation or prevention of communicative impairments; and

(v) Counseling and guidance of parents, children, and teachers regarding speech and language impairments.

(16) Transportation includes—

(i) Travel to and from school and between schools;

(ii) Travel in and around school buildings; and

(iii) Specialized equipment (such as special or adapted buses, lifts, and ramps), if required to provide special transportation for a child with a disability.

§ 300.35 Scientifically based research.

Scientifically based research has the meaning given the term in section 9101(37) of the ESEA.

§ 300.36 Secondary school.

Secondary school means a nonprofit institutional day or residential school, including a public secondary charter school that provides secondary education, as determined under State law, except that it does not include any education beyond grade 12.

§ 300.37 Services plan.

Services plan means a written statement that describes the special education and related services the LEA will provide to a parentally-placed child with a disability enrolled in a private school who has been designated to receive services, including the location of the services and any transportation necessary, consistent with § 300.132, and is developed and implemented in accordance with §§ 300.137 through 300.139.

§ 300.38 Secretary.

Secretary means the Secretary of Education.

§ 300.39 Special education.

(a) General.

(1) Special education means specially designed instruction, at no cost to the parents, to meet the unique needs of a child with a disability, including—

(i) Instruction conducted in the classroom, in the home, in hospitals and institutions, and in other settings; and

(ii) Instruction in physical education.

(2) Special education includes each of the following, if the services otherwise meet the requirements of paragraph (a)(1) of this section—

(i) Speech-language pathology services, or any other related service, if the service is considered special education rather than a related service under State standards;

(ii) Travel training; and

(iii) Vocational education.

(b) Individual special education terms defined. The terms in this definition are defined as follows:

(1) At no cost means that all specially-designed instruction is provided without charge, but does not preclude incidental fees that are normally charged to nondisabled students or their parents as a part of the regular education program.

(2) Physical education means—

(i) The development of—

(A) Physical and motor fitness;

(B) Fundamental motor skills and patterns; and

(C) Skills in aquatics, dance, and individual and group games and sports (including intramural and lifetime sports); and

(ii) Includes special physical education, adapted physical education, movement education, and motor development.

(3) Specially designed instruction means adapting, as appropriate to the needs of an eligible child under this part, the content, methodology, or delivery of instruction—

(i) To address the unique needs of the child that result from the child's disability; and

(ii) To ensure access of the child to the general curriculum, so that the child can meet the educational standards within the jurisdiction of the public agency that apply to all children.

(4) Travel training means providing instruction, as appropriate, to children with significant cognitive disabilities, and any other children with disabilities who require this instruction, to enable them to—

(i) Develop an awareness of the environment in which they live; and

(ii) Learn the skills necessary to move effectively and safely from place to place within that environment (e.g., in school, in the home, at work, and in the community).

(5) Vocational education means organized educational programs that are directly related to the preparation of individuals for paid or unpaid employment, or for additional preparation for a career not requiring a baccalaureate or advanced degree.

§ 300.40 State.

State means each of the 50 States, the District of Columbia, the Commonwealth of Puerto Rico, and each of the outlying areas.

§ 300.41 State educational agency.

State educational agency or SEA means the State board of education or other agency or officer primarily responsible for the State supervision of public elementary schools and secondary schools, or, if there is no such officer or agency, an officer or agency designated by the Governor or by State law.

§ 300.42 Supplementary aids and services.

Supplementary aids and services means aids, services, and other supports that are provided in regular education classes, other education-related settings, and in extracurricular and nonacademic settings, to enable children with disabilities to be educated with nondisabled children to the maximum extent appropriate in accordance with §§ 300.114 through 300.116.

§ 300.43 Transition services.

(a) Transition services means a coordinated set of activities for a child with a disability that—

(1) Is designed to be within a results-oriented process, that is focused on improving the academic and functional achievement of the child with a disability to facilitate the child's movement from school to post-school activities, including postsecondary education, vocational education, integrated employment (including supported employment), continuing and adult education, adult services, independent living, or community participation;

(2) Is based on the individual child's needs, taking into account the child's strengths, preferences, and interests; and includes—

(i) Instruction;

(ii) Related services;

(iii) Community experiences;

(iv) The development of employment and other post-school adult living objectives; and

(v) If appropriate, acquisition of daily living skills and provision of a functional vocational evaluation.

(b) Transition services for children with disabilities may be special education, if provided as specially designed instruction, or a related service, if required to assist a child with a disability to benefit from special education.

§ 300.44 Universal design.

Universal design has the meaning given the term in section 3 of the Assistive Technology Act of 1998, as amended, 29 U.S.C. 3002.

§ 300.45 Ward of the State.

(a) General. Subject to paragraph (b) of this section, ward of the State means a child who, as determined by the State where the child resides, is—

(1) A foster child;

(2) A ward of the State; or

(3) In the custody of a public child welfare agency.

(b) Exception. Ward of the State does not include a foster child who has a foster parent who meets the definition of a parent in § 300.30.

§ 300.100 Eligibility for assistance.

A State is eligible for assistance under Part B of the Act for a fiscal year if the State submits a plan that provides assurances to the Secretary that the State has in effect policies and procedures to ensure that the State meets the conditions in §§ 300.101 through 300.176.

FAPE Requirements
§ 300.101 Free appropriate public education (FAPE).

(a) *General.* A free appropriate public education must be available to all children residing in the State between the ages of 3 and 21, inclusive, including children with disabilities who have been suspended or expelled from school, as provided for in § 300.530(d).

(b) *FAPE for children beginning at age 3.*

(1) Each State must ensure that—

(i) The obligation to make FAPE available to each eligible child residing in the State begins no later than the child's third birthday; and

(ii) An IEP or an IFSP is in effect for the child by that date, in accordance with § 300.323(b).

(2) If a child's third birthday occurs during the summer, the child's IEP Team shall determine the date when services under the IEP or IFSP will begin.

(c) *Children advancing from grade to grade.*

(1) Each State must ensure that FAPE is available to any individual child with a disability who needs special education and related services, even though the child has not failed or been retained in a course or grade, and is advancing from grade to grade.

(2) The determination that a child described in paragraph (a) of this section is eligible under this part, must be made on an individual basis by the group responsible within the child's LEA for making eligibility determinations.

§ 300.102 Limitation—exception to FAPE for certain ages.

(a) *General.* The obligation to make FAPE available to all children with disabilities does not apply with respect to the following:

(1) Children aged 3, 4, 5, 18, 19, 20, or 21 in a State to the extent that its application to those children would be inconsistent with State law or practice, or the order of any court, respecting the provision of public education to children of those ages.

(2)(i) Children aged 18 through 21 to the extent that State law does not require that special education and related services under Part B of the Act be provided to students with disabilities who, in the last educational placement prior to their incarceration in an adult correctional facility—

(A) Were not actually identified as being a child with a disability under § 300.8; and

(B) Did not have an IEP under Part B of the Act.

(ii) The exception in paragraph (a)(2)(i) of this section does not apply to children with disabilities, aged 18 through 21, who—

(A) Had been identified as a child with a disability under § 300.8 and had received services in accordance with an IEP, but who left school prior to their incarceration; or

(B) Did not have an IEP in their last educational setting, but who had actually been identified as a child with a disability under § 300.8.

(3)(i) Children with disabilities who have graduated from high school with a regular high school diploma.

(ii) The exception in paragraph (a)(3)(i) of this section does not apply to children who have graduated from high school but have not been awarded a regular high school diploma.

(iii) Graduation from high school with a regular high school diploma constitutes a change in placement, requiring written prior notice in accordance with § 300.503.

(iv) As used in paragraphs (a)(3)(i) through (a)(3)(iii) of this section, the term regular high school diploma does not include an alternative degree that is not fully aligned with the State's academic standards, such as a certificate or a general educational development credential (GED).

(4) Children with disabilities who are eligible under subpart H of this part, but who receive early intervention services under Part C of the Act.

(b) *Documents relating to exceptions.* The State must assure that the information it has provided to the Secretary regarding the exceptions in paragraph (a) of this section, as required by § 300.700 (for purposes of making grants to States under this part), is current and accurate.

Other FAPE Requirements
§ 300.103 FAPE—methods and payments.

(a) Each State may use whatever State, local, Federal, and private sources of support are available in the State to meet the requirements of this part. For example, if it is necessary to place a child with a disability in a residential facility, a State could use joint agreements between the agencies involved for sharing the cost of that placement.

(b) Nothing in this part relieves an insurer or similar third party from an otherwise valid obligation to provide or to pay for services provided to a child with a disability.

(c) Consistent with § 300.323(c), the State must ensure that there is no delay in implementing a child's IEP, including any case in which the payment source for providing or paying for special education and related services to the child is being determined.

§ 300.104 Residential placement

If placement in a public or private residential program is necessary to provide special education and related services to a child with a disability, the program, including non-medical care and room and board, must be at no cost to the parents of the child.

§ 300.105 Assistive technology.

(a) Each public agency must ensure that assistive technology devices or assistive technology services, or both, as those terms are defined in §§ 300.5 and 300.6, respectively, are made available to a child with a disability if required as a part of the child's—

(1) Special education under § 300.36;

(2) Related services under § 300.34; or

(3) Supplementary aids and services under §§ 300.38 and 300.114(a)(2)(ii).

(b) On a case-by-case basis, the use of school-purchased assistive technology devices in a child's home or in other settings is required if the child's IEP Team determines that the child needs access to those devices in order to receive FAPE.

§ 300.106 Extended school year services.

(a) General.

(1) Each public agency must ensure that extended school year services are available as necessary to provide FAPE, consistent with paragraph (a)(2) of this section.

(2) Extended school year services must be provided only if a child's IEP Team determines, on an individual basis, in accordance with §§ 300.320 through 300.324, that the services are necessary for the provision of FAPE to the child.

(3) In implementing the requirements of this section, a public agency may not—

(i) Limit extended school year services to particular categories of disability; or

(ii) Unilaterally limit the type, amount, or duration of those services.

(b) Definition. As used in this section, the term extended school year services means special education and related services that—

(1) Are provided to a child with a disability—

(i) Beyond the normal school year of the public agency;

(ii) In accordance with the child's IEP; and

(iii) At no cost to the parents of the child; and

(2) Meet the standards of the SEA.

§ 300.107 Nonacademic services.

The State must ensure the following:

(a) Each public agency must take steps, including the provision of supplementary aids and services determined appropriate and necessary by the child's IEP Team, to provide nonacademic and extracurricular services and activities in the manner necessary to afford children with disabilities an equal opportunity for participation in those services and activities.

(b) Nonacademic and extracurricular services and activities may include counseling services, athletics, transportation, health services, recreational activities, special interest groups or clubs sponsored by the public agency, referrals to agencies that provide assistance to individuals with disabilities, and employment of students, including both employment by the public agency and assistance in making outside employment available.

§ 300.108 Physical education.

The State must ensure that public agencies in the State comply with the following:

(a) General. Physical education services, specially designed if necessary, must be made available to every child with a disability receiving FAPE, unless the public agency enrolls children without disabilities and does not provide physical education to children without disabilities in the same grades.

(b) Regular physical education. Each child with a disability must be afforded the opportunity to participate in the regular physical education program available to nondisabled children unless—

(1) The child is enrolled full time in a separate facility; or

(2) The child needs specially designed physical education, as prescribed in the child's IEP.

(c) Special physical education. If specially designed physical education is prescribed in a child's IEP, the public agency responsible for the education of that child must provide the services directly or make arrangements for those services to be provided through other public or private programs.

(d) Education in separate facilities. The public agency responsible for the education of a child with a disability who is enrolled in a separate facility must ensure that the child receives appropriate physical education services in compliance with this section.

§ 300.109 Full educational opportunity goal (FEOG).

The State must have in effect policies and procedures to demonstrate that the State has established a goal of providing full educational opportunity to all children with disabilities, aged birth through 21, and a detailed timetable for accomplishing that goal.

§ 300.110 Program options.

The State must ensure that each public agency takes steps to ensure that its children with disabilities have available to them the variety of educational programs and services available to nondisabled children in the area served by the agency, including art, music, industrial arts, consumer and homemaking education, and vocational education.

§ 300.111 Child find.

(a) General.

(1) The State must have in effect policies and procedures to ensure that—

(i) All children with disabilities residing in the State, including children with disabilities who are homeless children or are wards of the State, and children with disabilities attending private schools, regardless of the severity of their disability, and who are in need of special education and related services, are identified, located, and evaluated; and

(ii) A practical method is developed and implemented to determine which children are currently receiving needed special education and related services.

(b) Use of term developmental delay. The following provisions apply with respect to implementing the child find requirements of this section:

(1) A State that adopts a definition of developmental delay under § 300.8(b) determines whether the term applies to children aged three through nine, or to a subset of that age range (e.g., ages three through five).

(2) A State may not require an LEA to adopt and use the term developmental delay for any children within its jurisdiction.

(3) If an LEA uses the term developmental delay for children described in § 300.8(b), the LEA must conform to both the State's definition of that term and to the age range that has been adopted by the State.

(4) If a State does not adopt the term developmental delay, an LEA may not independently use that term as a basis for establishing a child's eligibility under this part.

(c) Other children in child find. Child find also must include—

(1) Children who are suspected of being a child with a disability under § 300.8 and in need of special education, even though they are advancing from grade to grade; and

(2) Highly mobile children, including migrant children.

(d) Construction. Nothing in the Act requires that children be classified by their disability so long as each child who has a disability that is listed in § 300.8 and who, by reason of that disability, needs special education and related services is regarded as a child with a disability under Part B of the Act.

§ 300.112 Individualized education programs (IEP).

The State must ensure that an IEP, or an IFSP that meets the requirements of section 636(d) of the Act, is developed, reviewed, and revised for each child with a disability in accordance with §§ 300.320 through 300.324, except as provided in § 300.300(b)(3)(ii).

§ 300.113 Routine checking of hearing aids and external components of surgically implanted medical devices.

(a) Hearing aids. Each public agency must ensure that hearing aids worn in school by children with hearing impairments, including deafness, are functioning properly.

(b) External components of surgically implanted medical devices.

(1) Subject to paragraph (b)(2) of this section, each public agency must ensure that the external components of surgically implanted medical devices are functioning properly.

(2) For a child with a surgically implanted medical device who is receiving special education and related services under this part, a public agency is not responsible for the post-surgical maintenance, programming, or replacement of the medical device that has been surgically implanted (or of an external component of the surgically implanted medical device).

Least Restrictive Environment (Lre)
§ 300.114 LRE requirements.

(a) General.

(1) Except as provided in § 300.324(d)(2) (regarding children with disabilities in adult prisons), the State must have in effect policies and procedures to ensure that public agencies in the State meet the LRE requirements of this section and §§ 300.115 through 300.120.

(2) Each public agency must ensure that—

(i) To the maximum extent appropriate, children with disabilities, including children in public or private institutions or other care facilities, are educated with children who are nondisabled; and

(ii) Special classes, separate schooling, or other removal of children with disabilities from the regular educational environment occurs only if the nature or severity of the disability is such that education in regular classes with the use of supplementary aids and services cannot be achieved satisfactorily.

(b) Additional requirement—State funding mechanism—

(1) General.

(i) A State funding mechanism must not result in placements that violate the requirements of paragraph (a) of this section; and

(ii) A State must not use a funding mechanism by which the State distributes funds on the basis of the type of setting in which a child is served that will result in the failure to provide a child with a disability FAPE according to the unique needs of the child, as described in the child's IEP.

(2) Assurance. If the State does not have policies and procedures to ensure compliance with paragraph (b)(1) of this section, the State must provide the Secretary an assurance that the State will revise the funding mechanism as soon as feasible to ensure that the mechanism does not result in placements that violate that paragraph.

§ 300.115 Continuum of alternative placements.

(a) Each public agency must ensure that a continuum of alternative placements is available to meet the needs of children with disabilities for special education and related services.

(b) The continuum required in paragraph (a) of this section must—

(1) Include the alternative placements listed in the definition of special education under § 300.38 (instruction in regular classes, special classes, special schools, home instruction, and instruction in hospitals and institutions); and

(2) Make provision for supplementary services (such as resource room or itinerant instruction) to be provided in conjunction with regular class placement.

§ 300.116 Placements.

In determining the educational placement of a child with a disability, including a preschool child with a disability, each public agency must ensure that—

(a) The placement decision—

(1) Is made by a group of persons, including the parents, and other persons knowledgeable about the child, the meaning of the evaluation data, and the placement options; and

(2) Is made in conformity with the LRE provisions of this subpart, including §§ 300.114 through 300.118;

(b) The child's placement—

(1) Is determined at least annually;

(2) Is based on the child's IEP; and

(3) Is as close as possible to the child's home;

(c) Unless the IEP of a child with a disability requires some other arrangement, the child is educated in the school that he or she would attend if nondisabled;

(d) In selecting the LRE, consideration is given to any potential harmful effect on the child or on the quality of services that he or she needs; and

(e) A child with a disability is not removed from education in age-appropriate regular classrooms solely because of needed modifications in the general education curriculum.

§ 300.117 Nonacademic settings.

In providing or arranging for the provision of nonacademic and extracurricular services and activities, including meals, recess periods, and the services and activities set forth in § 300.107, each public agency must ensure that each child with a disability participates with nondisabled children in the extracurricular services and activities to the maximum extent appropriate to the needs of that child. The public agency must ensure that each child with a disability has the supplementary aids and services determined by the child's IEP Team to be appropriate and necessary for the child to participate in nonacademic settings.

§ 300.118 Children in public or private institutions.

Except as provided in § 300.149(d) (regarding agency responsibility for general supervision for some individuals in adult prisons), an SEA must ensure that § 300.114 is effectively implemented, including, if necessary, making arrangements with public and private institutions (such as a memorandum of agreement or special implementation procedures).

§ 300.119 Technical assistance and training activities.

Each SEA must carry out activities to ensure that teachers and administrators in all public agencies—

(a) Are fully informed about their responsibilities for implementing § 300.114; and

(b) Are provided with technical assistance and training necessary to assist them in this effort.

§ 300.120 Monitoring activities.

(a) The SEA must carry out activities to ensure that § 300.114 is implemented by each public agency.

(b) If there is evidence that a public agency makes placements that are inconsistent with § 300.114, the SEA must—

(1) Review the public agency's justification for its actions; and

(2) Assist in planning and implementing any necessary corrective action.

Additional Eligibility Requirements

§ 300.121 Procedural safeguards.

(a) General. The State must have procedural safeguards in effect to ensure that each public agency in the State meets the requirements of §§ 300.500 through 300.536.

(b) Procedural safeguards identified. Children with disabilities and their parents must be afforded the procedural safeguards identified in paragraph (a) of this section.

§ 300.122 Evaluation.

Children with disabilities must be evaluated in accordance with §§ 300.300 through 300.311 of subpart D of this part.

§ 300.123 Confidentiality of personally identifiable information.

The State must have policies and procedures in effect to ensure that public agencies in the State comply with §§ 300.610 through 300.626 related to protecting the confidentiality of any personally identifiable information collected, used, or maintained under Part B of the Act.

§ 300.124 Transition of children from the Part C program to preschool programs.

The State must have in effect policies and procedures to ensure that—

(a) Children participating in early intervention programs assisted under Part C of the Act, and who will participate in preschool programs assisted under Part B of the Act, experience a smooth and effective transition to those preschool programs in a manner consistent with section 637(a)(9) of the Act;

(b) By the third birthday of a child described in paragraph (a) of this section, an IEP or, if consistent with § 300.323(b) and section 636(d) of the Act, an IFSP, has been developed and is being implemented for the child consistent with § 300.101(b); and

(c) Each affected LEA will participate in transition planning conferences arranged by the designated lead agency under section 635(a)(10) of the Act.

§§ 300.125 to 300.128 [Reserved]
§§ 300.125 to 300.128 [Reserved]

Children in Private Schools

§ 300.129 State responsibility regarding children in private schools.

The State must have in effect policies and procedures that ensure that LEAs, and, if applicable, the SEA, meet the private school requirements in §§ 300.130 through 300.148.

Children with Disabilities Enrolled by Their Parents in Private Schools

§ 300.130 Definition of parentally-placed private school children with disabilities.

Parentally-placed private school children with disabilities means children with disabilities enrolled by their parents in private, including religious, schools or facilities that meet the definition of elementary school in § 300.13 or secondary school in § 300.36, other than children with disabilities covered under §§ 300.145 through 300.147.

§ 300.131 Child find for parentally-placed private school children with disabilities.

(a) General. Each LEA must locate, identify, and evaluate all children with disabilities who are enrolled by their parents in private, including religious, elementary schools and secondary schools located in the school district served by the LEA, in accordance with paragraphs (b) through (e) of this section, and §§ 300.111 and 300.201.

(b) Child find design. The child find process must be designed to ensure—

(1) The equitable participation of parentally-placed private school children; and

(2) An accurate count of those children.

(c) Activities. In carrying out the requirements of this section, the LEA, or, if applicable, the SEA, must undertake activities similar to the activities undertaken for the agency's public school children.

(d) Cost. The cost of carrying out the child find requirements in this section, including individual evaluations, may not be considered in determining if an LEA has met its obligation under § 300.133.

(e) Completion period. The child find process must be completed in a time period comparable to that for students attending public schools in the LEA consistent with § 300.301.

(f) Out-of-State children. Each LEA in which private, including religious, elementary schools and secondary schools are located must, in carrying out the child find requirements in this section, include parentally-placed private school children who reside in a State other than the State in which the private schools that they attend are located.

§ 300.132 Provision of services for parentally-placed private school children with disabilities—basic requirement.

(a) General. To the extent consistent with the number and location of children with disabilities who are enrolled by their parents in private, including religious, elementary schools and secondary schools located in the school district served by the LEA, provision is made for the participation of those children in the program assisted or carried out under Part B of the Act by providing them with special education and related services, including direct services determined in accordance with § 300.137, unless the Secretary has arranged for services to those children under the by-pass provisions in §§ 300.190 through 300.198.

(b) Services plan for parentally-placed private school children with disabilities. In accordance with paragraph (a) of this section and §§ 300.137 through 300.139, a services plan must be developed and implemented for each private school child with a disability who has been designated by the LEA in which the private school is located to receive special education and related services under this part.

(c) Record keeping. Each LEA must maintain in its records, and provide to the SEA, the following information related to parentally-placed private school children covered under §§ 300.130 through 300.144:

(1) The number of children evaluated;

(2) The number of children determined to be children with disabilities; and

(3) The number of children served.

§ 300.133 Expenditures.

(a) Formula. To meet the requirement of § 300.132(a), each LEA must spend the following on providing special education and related services (including direct services) to parentally-placed private school children with disabilities:

(1) For children aged 3 through 21, an amount that is the same proportion of the

LEA's total subgrant under section 611(f) of the Act as the number of private school children with disabilities aged 3 through 21 who are enrolled by their parents in private, including religious, elementary schools and secondary schools located in the school district served by the LEA, is to the total number of children with disabilities in its jurisdiction aged 3 through 21.

(2)(i) For children aged three through five, an amount that is the same proportion of the LEA's total subgrant under section 619(g) of the Act as the number of parentally-placed private school children with disabilities aged three through five who are enrolled by their parents in a private, including religious, elementary school located in the school district served by the LEA, is to the total number of children with disabilities in its jurisdiction aged three through five.

(ii) As described in paragraph (a)(2)(i) of this section, children aged three through five are considered to be parentally-placed private school children with disabilities enrolled by their parents in private, including religious, elementary schools, if they are enrolled in a private school that meets the definition of elementary school in § 300.13.

(3) If an LEA has not expended for equitable services all of the funds described in paragraphs (a)(1) and (a)(2) of this section by the end of the fiscal year for which Congress appropriated the funds, the LEA must obligate the remaining funds for special education and related services (including direct services) to parentally-placed private school children with disabilities during a carry-over period of one additional year.

(b) Calculating proportionate amount. In calculating the proportionate amount of Federal funds to be provided for parentally-placed private school children with disabilities, the LEA, after timely and meaningful consultation with representatives of private schools under § 300.134, must conduct a thorough and complete child find process to determine the number of parentally-placed children with disabilities attending private schools located in the LEA. (See Appendix B for an example of how proportionate share is calculated).

(c) Annual count of the number of parentally-placed private school children with disabilities.

(1) Each LEA must—

(i) After timely and meaningful consultation with representatives of parentally-placed private school children with disabilities (consistent with § 300.134), determine the number of parentally-placed private school children with disabilities attending private schools located in the LEA; and

(ii) Ensure that the count is conducted on any date between October 1 and December 1, inclusive, of each year.

(2) The count must be used to determine the amount that the LEA must spend on providing special education and related services to parentally-placed private school children with disabilities in the next subsequent fiscal year.

(d) Supplement, not supplant. State and local funds may supplement and in no case supplant the proportionate amount of Federal funds required to be expended for parentally-placed private school children with disabilities under this part.

§ 300.134 Consultation.

To ensure timely and meaningful consultation, an LEA, or, if appropriate, an SEA, must consult with private school representatives and representatives of parents of parentally-placed private school children with disabilities during the design and development of special education and related services for the children regarding the following:

(a) Child find. The child find process, including—

(1) How parentally-placed private school children suspected of having a disability can participate equitably; and

(2) How parents, teachers, and private school officials will be informed of the process.

(b) Proportionate share of funds. The determination of the proportionate share of Federal funds available to serve parentally-placed private school children with disabilities under § 300.133(b), including the determination of how the proportionate share of those funds was calculated.

(c) *Consultation process.* The consultation process among the LEA, private school officials, and representatives of parents of parentally-placed private school children with disabilities, including how the process will operate throughout the school year to ensure that parentally-placed children with disabilities identified through the child find process can meaningfully participate in special education and related services.

(d) *Provision of special education and related services.* How, where, and by whom special education and related services will be provided for parentally-placed private school children with disabilities, including a discussion of—

(1) The types of services, including direct services and alternate service delivery mechanisms; and

(2) How special education and related services will be apportioned if funds are insufficient to serve all parentally-placed private school children; and

(3) How and when those decisions will be made;

(e) *Written explanation by LEA regarding services.* How, if the LEA disagrees with the views of the private school officials on the provision of services or the types of services (whether provided directly or through a contract), the LEA will provide to the private school officials a written explanation of the reasons why the LEA chose not to provide services directly or through a contract.

§ 300.135 Written affirmation.

(a) When timely and meaningful consultation, as required by § 300.134, has occurred, the LEA must obtain a written affirmation signed by the representatives of participating private schools.

(b) If the representatives do not provide the affirmation within a reasonable period of time, the LEA must forward the documentation of the consultation process to the SEA.

§ 300.136 Compliance.

(a) *General.* A private school official has the right to submit a complaint to the SEA that the LEA—

(1) Did not engage in consultation that was meaningful and timely; or

(2) Did not give due consideration to the views of the private school official.

(b) *Procedure.*

(1) If the private school official wishes to submit a complaint, the official must provide to the SEA the basis of the noncompliance by the LEA with the applicable private school provisions in this part; and

(2) The LEA must forward the appropriate documentation to the SEA.

(3)(i) If the private school official is dissatisfied with the decision of the SEA, the official may submit a complaint to the Secretary by providing the information on noncompliance described in paragraph (b)(1) of this section; and

(ii) The SEA must forward the appropriate documentation to the Secretary.

§ 300.137 Equitable services determined.

(a) *No individual right to special education and related services.* No parentally-placed private school child with a disability has an individual right to receive some or all of the special education and related services that the child would receive if enrolled in a public school.

(b) *Decisions.*

(1) Decisions about the services that will be provided to parentally-placed private school children with disabilities under §§ 300.130 through 300.144 must be made in accordance with paragraph (c) of this section and § 300.134(c).

(2) The LEA must make the final decisions with respect to the services to be provided to eligible parentally-placed private school children with disabilities.

(c) *Services plan for each child served under §§ 300.130 through 300.144.* If a child with a disability is enrolled in a religious or other private school by the child's parents and will receive special education or related services from an LEA, the LEA must—

(1) Initiate and conduct meetings to develop, review, and revise a services plan for the child, in accordance with § 300.138(b); and

(2) Ensure that a representative of the religious or other private school attends each meeting. If the representative cannot attend, the LEA shall use other methods to ensure participation by the religious or other private

school, including individual or conference telephone calls.

§ 300.138 Equitable services provided.

(a) General.

(1) The services provided to parentally-placed private school children with disabilities must be provided by personnel meeting the same standards as personnel providing services in the public schools, except that private elementary school and secondary school teachers who are providing equitable services to parentally-placed private school children with disabilities do not have to meet the highly qualified special education teacher requirements of § 300.18.

(2) Parentally-placed private school children with disabilities may receive a different amount of services than children with disabilities in public schools.

(b) Services provided in accordance with a services plan.

(1) Each parentally-placed private school child with a disability who has been designated to receive services under § 300.132 must have a services plan that describes the specific special education and related services that the LEA will provide to the child in light of the services that the LEA has determined, through the process described in §§ 300.134 and 300.137, it will make available to parentally-placed private school children with disabilities.

(2) The services plan must, to the extent appropriate—

(i) Meet the requirements of § 300.320, or for a child ages three through five, meet the requirements of § 300.323(b) with respect to the services provided; and

(ii) Be developed, reviewed, and revised consistent with §§ 300.321 through 300.324.

(c) Provision of equitable services.

(1) The provision of services pursuant to this section and §§ 300.139 through 300.143 must be provided:

(i) By employees of a public agency; or

(ii) Through contract by the public agency with an individual, association, agency, organization, or other entity.

(2) Special education and related services provided to parentally-placed private school children with disabilities, including materials and equipment, must be secular, neutral, and nonideological.

§ 300.139 Location of services and transportation.

(a) Services on private school premises. Services to parentally-placed private school children with disabilities may be provided on the premises of private, including religious, schools, to the extent consistent with law.

(b) Transportation—

(1) General.

(i) If necessary for the child to benefit from or participate in the services provided under this part, a parentally-placed private school child with a disability must be provided transportation—

(A) From the child's school or the child's home to a site other than the private school; and

(B) From the service site to the private school, or to the child's home, depending on the timing of the services.

(ii) LEAs are not required to provide transportation from the child's home to the private school.

(2) Cost of transportation. The cost of the transportation described in paragraph (b)(1)(i) of this section may be included in calculating whether the LEA has met the requirement of § 300.133.

§ 300.140 Due process complaints and State complaints.

(a) Due process not applicable, except for child find.

(1) Except as provided in paragraph (b) of this section, the procedures in §§ 300.504 through 300.519 do not apply to complaints that an LEA has failed to meet the requirements of §§ 300.132 through 300.139, including the provision of services indicated on the child's services plan.

(b) Child find complaints—to be filed with the LEA in which the private school is located.

(1) The procedures in §§ 300.504 through 300.519 apply to complaints that an LEA has failed to meet the child find requirements in § 300.131, including the requirements in §§ 300.300 through 300.311.

(2) Any due process complaint regarding the child find requirements (as described in paragraph (b)(1) of this section) must be filed with the LEA in which the private school is located and a copy must be forwarded to the SEA.

(c) State complaints.

(1) Any complaint that an SEA or LEA has failed to meet the requirements in §§ 300.132 through 300.135 and 300.137 through 300.144 must be filed in accordance with the procedures described in §§ 300.151 through 300.153.

(2) A complaint filed by a private school official under § 300.136(a) must be filed with the SEA in accordance with the procedures in § 300.136(b).

§ 300.141 Requirement that funds not benefit a private school.

(a) An LEA may not use funds provided under section 611 or 619 of the Act to finance the existing level of instruction in a private school or to otherwise benefit the private school.

(b) The LEA must use funds provided under Part B of the Act to meet the special education and related services needs of parentally-placed private school children with disabilities, but not for meeting—

(1) The needs of a private school; or

(2) The general needs of the students enrolled in the private school.

§ 300.142 Use of personnel.

(a) Use of public school personnel. An LEA may use funds available under sections 611 and 619 of the Act to make public school personnel available in other than public facilities—

(1) To the extent necessary to provide services under §§ 300.130 through 300.144 for parentally-placed private school children with disabilities; and

(2) If those services are not normally provided by the private school.

(b) Use of private school personnel. An LEA may use funds available under sections 611 and 619 of the Act to pay for the services of an employee of a private school to provide services under §§ 300.130 through 300.144 if—

(1) The employee performs the services outside of his or her regular hours of duty; and

(2) The employee performs the services under public supervision and control.

§ 300.143 Separate classes prohibited.

An LEA may not use funds available under section 611 or 619 of the Act for classes that are organized separately on the basis of school enrollment or religion of the children if—'

(a) The classes are at the same site; and

(b) The classes include children enrolled in public schools and children enrolled in private schools.

§ 300.144 Property, equipment, and supplies.

(a) A public agency must control and administer the funds used to provide special education and related services under §§ 300.137 through 300.139, and hold title to and administer materials, equipment, and property purchased with those funds for the uses and purposes provided in the Act.

(b) The public agency may place equipment and supplies in a private school for the period of time needed for the Part B program.

(c) The public agency must ensure that the equipment and supplies placed in a private school—

(1) Are used only for Part B purposes; and

(2) Can be removed from the private school without remodeling the private school facility.

(d) The public agency must remove equipment and supplies from a private school if—

(1) The equipment and supplies are no longer needed for Part B purposes; or

(2) Removal is necessary to avoid unauthorized use of the equipment and supplies for other than Part B purposes.

(e) No funds under Part B of the Act may be used for repairs, minor remodeling, or construction of private school facilities.

Children with Disabilities in Private Schools Placed or Referred by Public Agencies

§ 300.145 Applicability of §§ 300.146 through 300.147.

Sections 300.146 through 300.147 apply only to children with disabilities who are or have been placed in or referred to a private school or facility by a public agency as a means of providing special education and related services.

§ 300.146 Responsibility of SEA.

Each SEA must ensure that a child with a disability who is placed in or referred to a private school or facility by a public agency—

(a) Is provided special education and related services—

(1) In conformance with an IEP that meets the requirements of §§ 300.320 through 300.325; and

(2) At no cost to the parents;

(b) Is provided an education that meets the standards that apply to education provided by the SEA and LEAs including the requirements of this part, except for § 300.18 and § 300.156(c); and

(c) Has all of the rights of a child with a disability who is served by a public agency.

§ 300.147 Implementation by SEA.

In implementing § 300.146, the SEA must—

(a) Monitor compliance through procedures such as written reports, on-site visits, and parent questionnaires;

(b) Disseminate copies of applicable standards to each private school and facility to which a public agency has referred or placed a child with a disability; and

(c) Provide an opportunity for those private schools and facilities to participate in the development and revision of State standards that apply to them.

Children with Disabilities Enrolled by Their Parents in Private Schools When FAPE is at Issue

§ 300.148 Placement of children by parents when FAPE is at issue.

(a) General. This part does not require an LEA to pay for the cost of education, including special education and related services, of a child with a disability at a private school or facility if that agency made FAPE available to the child and the parents elected to place the child in a private school or facility. However, the public agency must include that child in the population whose needs are addressed consistent with §§ 300.131 through 300.144.

(b) Disagreements about FAPE. Disagreements between the parents and a public agency regarding the availability of a program appropriate for the child, and the question of financial reimbursement, are subject to the due process procedures in §§ 300.504 through 300.520.

(c) Reimbursement for private school placement. If the parents of a child with a disability, who previously received special education and related services under the authority of a public agency, enroll the child in a private preschool, elementary school, or secondary school without the consent of or referral by the public agency, a court or a hearing officer may require the agency to reimburse the parents for the cost of that enrollment if the court or hearing officer finds that the agency had not made FAPE available to the child in a timely manner prior to that enrollment and that the private placement is appropriate. A parental placement may be found to be appropriate by a hearing officer or a court even if it does not meet the State standards that apply to education provided by the SEA and LEAs.

(d) Limitation on reimbursement. The cost of reimbursement described in paragraph (c) of this section may be reduced or denied—

(1) If—

(i) At the most recent IEP Team meeting that the parents attended prior to removal of the child from the public school, the parents did not inform the IEP Team that they were rejecting the placement proposed by the public agency to provide FAPE to their child, including stating their concerns and their intent to enroll their child in a private school at public expense; or

(ii) At least ten (10) business days (including any holidays that occur on a business day) prior to the removal of the child from the public school, the parents did not give written notice to the public agency of the information described in paragraph (d)(1)(i) of this section;

(2) If, prior to the parents' removal of the child from the public school, the public agency informed the parents, through the notice requirements described in § 300.503(a)(1), of its intent to evaluate the child (including a statement of the purpose of the evaluation that was appropriate and reasonable), but the parents did not make the child available for the evaluation; or

(3) Upon a judicial finding of unreasonableness with respect to actions taken by the parents.

(e) Exception. Notwithstanding the notice requirement in paragraph (d)(1) of this section, the cost of reimbursement—

(1) Must not be reduced or denied for failure to provide the notice if—

(i) The school prevented the parents from providing the notice;

(ii) The parents had not received notice, pursuant to § 300.504, of the notice requirement in paragraph (d)(1) of this section; or

(iii) Compliance with paragraph (d)(1) of this section would likely result in physical harm to the child; and

(2) May, in the discretion of the court or a hearing officer, not be reduced or denied for failure to provide this notice if—

(i) The parents are not literate or cannot write in English; or

(ii) Compliance with paragraph (d)(1) of this section would likely result in serious emotional harm to the child.

Sea Responsibility for General Supervision and Implementation of Procedural Safeguards

§ 300.149 SEA responsibility for general supervision.

(a) The SEA is responsible for ensuring—

(1) That the requirements of this part are carried out; and

(2) That each educational program for children with disabilities administered within the State, including each program administered by any other State or local agency (but not including elementary schools and secondary schools for Indian children operated or funded by the Secretary of the Interior)—

(i) Is under the general supervision of the persons responsible for educational programs for children with disabilities in the SEA; and

(ii) Meets the educational standards of the SEA (including the requirements of this part).

(3) In carrying out this part with respect to homeless children, the requirements of subtitle B of title VII of the McKinney-Vento Homeless Assistance Act (42 U.S.C. 11431 et seq.) are met.

(b) The State must have in effect policies and procedures to ensure that it complies with the monitoring and enforcement requirements in §§ 300.600 through 300.602 and §§ 300.606 through 300.608.

(c) Part B of the Act does not limit the responsibility of agencies other than educational agencies for providing or paying some or all of the costs of FAPE to children with disabilities in the State.

(d) Notwithstanding paragraph (a) of this section, the Governor (or another individual pursuant to State law) may assign to any public agency in the State the responsibility of ensuring that the requirements of Part B of the Act are met with respect to students with disabilities who are convicted as adults under State law and incarcerated in adult prisons.

§ 300.150 SEA implementation of procedural safeguards.

The SEA (and any agency assigned responsibility pursuant to § 300.149(d)) must have in effect procedures to inform each public agency of its responsibility for ensuring effective implementation of procedural safeguards for the children with disabilities served by that public agency.

State Complaint Procedures

§ 300.151 Adoption of State complaint procedures.

(a) General. Each SEA must adopt written procedures for—

(1) Resolving any complaint, including a complaint filed by an organization or individual from another State, that meets the requirements of § 300.153 by—

(i) Providing for the filing of a complaint with the SEA; and

(ii) At the SEA's discretion, providing for the filing of a complaint with a public agency and the right to have the SEA review the public agency's decision on the complaint; and

(2) Widely disseminating to parents and other interested individuals, including parent training and information centers, protection and advocacy agencies, independent living centers, and other appropriate entities, the State procedures under §§ 300.151 through 300.153.

(b) Remedies for denial of appropriate services. In resolving a complaint in which the SEA has found a failure to provide appropriate services, an SEA, pursuant to its general supervisory authority under Part B of the Act, must address—

(1) The failure to provide appropriate services, including corrective action appropriate to address the needs of the child (such as compensatory services or monetary reimbursement); and

(2) Appropriate future provision of services for all children with disabilities.

§ 300.152 Minimum State complaint procedures.

(a) Time limit; minimum procedures. Each SEA must include in its complaint procedures a time limit of 60 days after a complaint is filed under § 300.153 to—

(1) Carry out an independent on-site investigation, if the SEA determines that an investigation is necessary;

(2) Give the complainant the opportunity to submit additional information, either orally or in writing, about the allegations in the complaint;

(3) Provide the public agency with the opportunity to respond to the complaint, including, at a minimum—

(i) At the discretion of the public agency, a proposal to resolve the complaint; and

(ii) An opportunity for a parent who has filed a complaint and the public agency to voluntarily engage in mediation consistent with § 300.506;

(4) Review all relevant information and make an independent determination as to whether the public agency is violating a requirement of Part B of the Act or of this part; and

(5) Issue a written decision to the complainant that addresses each allegation in the complaint and contains—

(i) Findings of fact and conclusions; and

(ii) The reasons for the SEA's final decision.

(b) Time extension; final decision; implementation. The SEA's procedures described in paragraph (a) of this section also must—

(1) Permit an extension of the time limit under paragraph (a) of this section only if—

(i) Exceptional circumstances exist with respect to a particular complaint; or

(ii) The parent (or individual or organization, if mediation or other alternative means of dispute resolution is available to the individual or organization under State procedures) and the public agency involved agree to extend the time to engage in mediation pursuant to paragraph (a)(3)(ii) of this section, or to engage in other alternative means of dispute resolution, if available in the State; and

(2) Include procedures for effective implementation of the SEA's final decision, if needed, including—

(i) Technical assistance activities;

(ii) Negotiations; and

(iii) Corrective actions to achieve compliance.

(c) Complaints filed under this section and due process hearings under § 300.507 and §§ 300.530 through 300.532.

(1) If a written complaint is received that is also the subject of a due process hearing under § 300.507 or §§ 300.530 through 300.532, or contains multiple issues of which one or more are part of that hearing, the State must set aside any part of the complaint that is being addressed in the due process hearing until the conclusion of the hearing. However, any issue in the complaint that is not a part of the due process action must be resolved using the time limit and procedures described in paragraphs (a) and (b) of this section.

(2) If an issue raised in a complaint filed under this section has previously been decided in a due process hearing involving the same parties—

(i) The due process hearing decision is binding on that issue; and

(ii) The SEA must inform the complainant to that effect.

(3) A complaint alleging a public agency's failure to implement a due process hearing decision must be resolved by the SEA.

§ 300.153 Filing a complaint.

(a) An organization or individual may file a signed written complaint under the procedures described in §§ 300.151 through 300.152.

(b) The complaint must include—

(1) A statement that a public agency has violated a requirement of Part B of the Act or of this part;

(2) The facts on which the statement is based;

(3) The signature and contact information for the complainant; and

(4) If alleging violations with respect to a specific child—

(i) The name and address of the residence of the child;

(ii) The name of the school the child is attending;

(iii) In the case of a homeless child or youth (within the meaning of section 725(2) of the McKinney-Vento Homeless Assistance Act (42 U.S.C. 11434a(2)), available contact information for the child, and the name of the school the child is attending;

(iv) A description of the nature of the problem of the child, including facts relating to the problem; and

(v) A proposed resolution of the problem to the extent known and available to the party at the time the complaint is filed.

(c) The complaint must allege a violation that occurred not more than one year prior to the date that the complaint is received in accordance with § 300.151.

(d) The party filing the complaint must forward a copy of the complaint to the LEA or public agency serving the child at the same time the party files the complaint with the SEA.

Methods of Ensuring Services
§ 300.154 Methods of ensuring services.

(a) *Establishing responsibility for services.* The Chief Executive Officer of a State or designee of that officer must ensure that an interagency agreement or other mechanism for interagency coordination is in effect between each noneducational public agency described in paragraph (b) of this section and the SEA, in order to ensure that all services described in paragraph (b)(1) of this section that are needed to ensure FAPE are provided, including the provision of these services during the pendency of any dispute under paragraph (a)(3) of this section. The agreement or mechanism must include the following:

(1) An identification of, or a method for defining, the financial responsibility of each agency for providing services described in paragraph (b)(1) of this section to ensure FAPE to children with disabilities. The financial responsibility of each noneducational public agency described in paragraph (b) of this section, including the State Medicaid agency and other public insurers of children with disabilities, must precede the financial responsibility of the LEA (or the State agency responsible for developing the child's IEP).

(2) The conditions, terms, and procedures under which an LEA must be reimbursed by other agencies.

(3) Procedures for resolving interagency disputes (including procedures under which LEAs may initiate proceedings) under the agreement or other mechanism to secure reimbursement from other agencies or otherwise implement the provisions of the agreement or mechanism.

(4) Policies and procedures for agencies to determine and identify the interagency coordination responsibilities of each agency to promote the coordination and timely and appropriate delivery of services described in paragraph (b)(1) of this section.

(b) *Obligation of noneducational public agencies.*

(1)(i) If any public agency other than an educational agency is otherwise obligated under Federal or State law, or assigned responsibility under State policy or pursuant to paragraph (a) of this section, to provide or pay for any services that are also considered special education or related services (such as, but not limited to, services described in § 300.5 relating to assistive technology devices, § 300.6 relating to assistive technology services, § 300.34 relating to related services, § 300.41 relating to supplementary aids and services, and § 300.42 relating to transition services) that are necessary for ensuring FAPE to children with disabilities within the State, the public agency must fulfill that obligation or responsibility, either directly or through contract or other arrangement pursuant to paragraph (a) of this section or an agreement pursuant to paragraph (c) of this section.

(ii) A noneducational public agency described in paragraph (b)(1)(i) of this section may not disqualify an eligible service for Medicaid reimbursement because that service is provided in a school context.

(2) If a public agency other than an educational agency fails to provide or pay for the special education and related services described in paragraph (b)(1) of this section, the LEA (or State agency responsible for developing the child's IEP) must provide or pay for these services to the child in a timely manner. The LEA or State agency is authorized to claim reimbursement for the services from the noneducational public agency that failed to provide or pay for these services and that agency must reimburse the LEA or State agency in accordance with the terms of the interagency agreement or other mechanism described in paragraph (a) of this section.

(c) Special rule. The requirements of paragraph (a) of this section may be met through—

(1) State statute or regulation;

(2) Signed agreements between respective agency officials that clearly identify the responsibilities of each agency relating to the provision of services; or

(3) Other appropriate written methods as determined by the Chief Executive Officer of the State or designee of that officer and approved by the Secretary.

(d) Children with disabilities who are covered by public benefits or insurance.

(1) A public agency may use the Medicaid or other public benefits or insurance programs in which a child participates to provide or pay for services required under this part, as permitted under the public benefits or insurance program, except as provided in paragraph (d)(2) of this section.

(2) With regard to services required to provide FAPE to an eligible child under this part, the public agency—

(i) May not require parents to sign up for or enroll in public benefits or insurance programs in order for their child to receive FAPE under Part B of the Act;

(ii) May not require parents to incur an out-of-pocket expense such as the payment of a deductible or co-pay amount incurred in filing a claim for services provided pursuant to this part, but pursuant to paragraph (g)(2) of this section, may pay the cost that the parents otherwise would be required to pay;

(iii) May not use a child's benefits under a public benefits or insurance program if that use would—

(A) Decrease available lifetime coverage or any other insured benefit;

(B) Result in the family paying for services that would otherwise be covered by the public benefits or insurance program and that are required for the child outside of the time the child is in school;

(C) Increase premiums or lead to the discontinuation of benefits or insurance; or

(D) Risk loss of eligibility for home and community-based waivers, based on aggregate health-related expenditures; and

(iv)(A) Must obtain parental consent, consistent with § 300.9, each time that access to public benefits or insurance is sought; and

(B) Notify parents that the parents' refusal to allow access to their public benefits or insurance does not relieve the public agency of its responsibility to ensure that all required services are provided at no cost to the parents.

(e) Children with disabilities who are covered by private insurance.

(1) With regard to services required to provide FAPE to an eligible child under this part, a public agency may access the parents' private insurance proceeds only if the parents provide consent consistent with § 300.9.

(2) Each time the public agency proposes to access the parents' private insurance proceeds, the agency must—

(i) Obtain parental consent in accordance with paragraph (e)(1) of this section; and

(ii) Inform the parents that their refusal to permit the public agency to access their private insurance does not relieve the public agency of its responsibility to ensure that all required services are provided at no cost to the parents.

(f) Use of Part B funds.

(1) If a public agency is unable to obtain parental consent to use the parents' private insurance, or public benefits or insurance

when the parents would incur a cost for a specified service required under this part, to ensure FAPE the public agency may use its Part B funds to pay for the service.

(2) To avoid financial cost to parents who otherwise would consent to use private insurance, or public benefits or insurance if the parents would incur a cost, the public agency may use its Part B funds to pay the cost that the parents otherwise would have to pay to use the parents' benefits or insurance (e.g., the deductible or co-pay amounts).

(g) Proceeds from public benefits or insurance or private insurance.

(1) Proceeds from public benefits or insurance or private insurance will not be treated as program income for purposes of 34 CFR 80.25.

(2) If a public agency spends reimbursements from Federal funds (e.g., Medicaid) for services under this part, those funds will not be considered "State or local" funds for purposes of the maintenance of effort provisions in §§ 300.163 and 300.203.

(h) Construction. Nothing in this part should be construed to alter the requirements imposed on a State Medicaid agency, or any other agency administering a public benefits or insurance program by Federal statute, regulations or policy under title XIX, or title XXI of the Social Security Act, 42 U.S.C. 1396 through 1396v and 42 U.S.C. 1397aa through 1397jj, or any other public benefits or insurance program.

Additional Eligibility Requirements
§ 300.155 Hearings relating to LEA eligibility.

The SEA must not make any final determination that an LEA is not eligible for assistance under Part B of the Act without first giving the LEA reasonable notice and an opportunity for a hearing under 34 CFR 76.401(d).

§ 300.156 Personnel qualifications.

(a) General. The SEA must establish and maintain qualifications to ensure that personnel necessary to carry out the purposes of this part are appropriately and adequately prepared and trained, including that those personnel have the content knowledge and skills to serve children with disabilities.

(b) Related services personnel and paraprofessionals. The qualifications under paragraph (a) of this section must include qualifications for related services personnel and paraprofessionals that—

(1) Are consistent with any State-approved or State-recognized certification, licensing, registration, or other comparable requirements that apply to the professional discipline in which those personnel are providing special education or related services; and

(2) Ensure that related services personnel who deliver services in their discipline or profession—

(i) Meet the requirements of paragraph (b)(1) of this section; and

(ii) Have not had certification or licensure requirements waived on an emergency, temporary, or provisional basis; and

(iii) Allow paraprofessionals and assistants who are appropriately trained and supervised, in accordance with State law, regulation, or written policy, in meeting the requirements of this part to be used to assist in the provision of special education and related services under this part to children with disabilities.

(c) Qualifications for special education teachers. The qualifications described in paragraph (a) of this section must ensure that each person employed as a public school special education teacher in the State who teaches in an elementary school, middle school, or secondary school is highly qualified as a special education teacher by the deadline established in section 1119(a)(2) of the ESEA.

(d) Policy. In implementing this section, a State must adopt a policy that includes a requirement that LEAs in the State take measurable steps to recruit, hire, train, and retain highly qualified personnel to provide special education and related services under this part to children with disabilities.

(e) Rule of construction. Notwithstanding any other individual right of action that a parent or student may maintain under this part, nothing in this part shall be construed to create a right of action on behalf of an individual student or a class of students for the failure of a particular SEA or LEA employee to be highly qualified, or to prevent a parent from filing a complaint about staff qualifications with the SEA as provided for under this part.

§ 300.157 Performance goals and indicators.

The State must—

(a) Have in effect established goals for the performance of children with disabilities in the State that—

(1) Promote the purposes of this part, as stated in § 300.1;

(2) Are the same as the State's objectives for progress by children in its definition of adequate yearly progress, including the State's objectives for progress by children with disabilities, under section 1111(b)(2)(C) of the ESEA, 20 U.S.C. 6311;

(3) Address graduation rates and dropout rates, as well as such other factors as the State may determine; and

(4) Are consistent, to the extent appropriate, with any other goals and academic standards for children established by the State;

(b) Have in effect established performance indicators the State will use to assess progress toward achieving the goals described in paragraph (a) of this section, including measurable annual objectives for progress by children with disabilities under section 1111(b)(2)(C)(v)(II)(cc) of the ESEA, 20 U.S.C. 6311; and

(c) Annually report to the Secretary and the public on the progress of the State, and of children with disabilities in the State, toward meeting the goals established under paragraph (a) of this section, which may include elements of the reports required under section 1111(h) of the ESEA.

§§ 300.158 to 300.161 [Reserved]
§§ 300.158 to 300.161 [Reserved]
§ 300.162 -300.173 [omitted]

§ 300.174 Prohibition on mandatory medication.

(a) General. The SEA must prohibit State and LEA personnel from requiring parents to obtain a prescription for substances identified under schedules I, II, III, IV, or V in section 202(c) of the Controlled Substances Act (21 U.S.C. 812(c)) for a child as a condition of attending school, receiving an evaluation under §§ 300.300 through 300.311, or receiving services under this part.

(b) Rule of construction. Nothing in paragraph (a) of this section shall be construed to create a Federal prohibition against teachers and other school personnel consulting or sharing classroom-based observations with parents or guardians regarding a student's academic and functional performance, or behavior in the classroom or school, or regarding the need for evaluation for special education or related services under § 300.111 (related to child find).

§ 300.175 – 300.186 [omitted]

By-pass for Children in Private Schools

§ 300.190 By-pass—general.

(a) If, on December 2, 1983, the date of enactment of the Education of the Handicapped Act Amendments of 1983, an SEA was prohibited by law from providing for the equitable participation in special programs of children with disabilities enrolled in private elementary schools and secondary schools as required by section 612(a)(10)(A) of the Act, or if the Secretary determines that an SEA, LEA, or other public agency has substantially failed or is unwilling to provide for such equitable participation then the Secretary shall, notwithstanding such provision of law, arrange for the provision of services to these children through arrangements which shall be subject to the requirements of section 612(a)(10)(A) of the Act.

(b) The Secretary waives the requirement of section 612(a)(10)(A) of the Act and of §§ 300.131 through 300.144 if the Secretary implements a by-pass.

§ 300.191 Provisions for services under a by-pass.

(a) Before implementing a by-pass, the Secretary consults with appropriate public and private school officials, including SEA officials, in the affected State, and as appropriate, LEA or other public agency officials to consider matters such as—

(1) Any prohibition imposed by State law that results in the need for a by-pass; and

(2) The scope and nature of the services required by private school children with disabilities in the State, and the number of children to be served under the by-pass.

(b) After determining that a by-pass is required, the Secretary arranges for the provision of services to private school children with disabilities in the State, LEA or other public agency in a manner consistent with the requirements of section 612(a)(10)(A) of the Act and §§ 300.131 through 300.144 by providing services through one or more agreements with appropriate parties.

(c) For any fiscal year that a by-pass is implemented, the Secretary determines the maximum amount to be paid to the providers of services by multiplying—

(1) A per child amount determined by dividing the total amount received by the State under Part B of the Act for the fiscal year by the number of children with disabilities served in the prior year as reported to the Secretary under section 618 of the Act; by

(2) The number of private school children with disabilities (as defined in §§ 300.8(a) and 300.130) in the State, LEA or other public agency, as determined by the Secretary on the basis of the most recent satisfactory data available, which may include an estimate of the number of those children with disabilities.

(d) The Secretary deducts from the State's allocation under Part B of the Act the amount the Secretary determines is necessary to implement a by-pass and pays that amount to the provider of services. The Secretary may withhold this amount from the State's allocation pending final resolution of any investigation or complaint that could result in a determination that a by-pass must be implemented.

§ 300.192 Notice of intent to implement a by-pass.

(a) Before taking any final action to implement a by-pass, the Secretary provides the SEA and, as appropriate, LEA or other public agency with written notice.

(b) In the written notice, the Secretary—

(1) States the reasons for the proposed by-pass in sufficient detail to allow the SEA and, as appropriate, LEA or other public agency to respond; and

(2) Advises the SEA and, as appropriate, LEA or other public agency that it has a specific period of time (at least 45 days) from receipt of the written notice to submit written objections to the proposed by-pass and that it may request in writing the opportunity for a hearing to show cause why a by-pass should not be implemented.

(c) The Secretary sends the notice to the SEA and, as appropriate, LEA or other public agency by certified mail with return receipt requested.

§ 300.193 Request to show cause.

An SEA, LEA or other public agency in receipt of a notice under § 300.192 that seeks an opportunity to show cause why a by-pass should not be implemented must submit a written request for a show cause hearing to the Secretary, within the specified time period in the written notice in § 300.192(b)(2).

§ 300.194 Show cause hearing.

(a) If a show cause hearing is requested, the Secretary—

(1) Notifies the SEA and affected LEA or other public agency, and other appropriate public and private school officials of the time and place for the hearing;

(2) Designates a person to conduct the show cause hearing. The designee must not have had any responsibility for the matter brought for a hearing; and

(3) Notifies the SEA, LEA or other public agency, and representatives of private schools that they may be represented by legal counsel and submit oral or written evidence and arguments at the hearing.

(b) At the show cause hearing, the designee considers matters such as—

(1) The necessity for implementing a by-pass;

(2) Possible factual errors in the written notice of intent to implement a by-pass; and

(3) The objections raised by public and private school representatives.

(c) The designee may regulate the course of the proceedings and the conduct of parties during the pendency of the proceedings. The designee takes all steps necessary to conduct a fair and impartial proceeding, to avoid delay, and to maintain order.

(d) The designee has no authority to require or conduct discovery.

(e) The designee may interpret applicable statutes and regulations, but may not waive them or rule on their validity.

(f) The designee arranges for the preparation, retention, and, if appropriate, dissemination of the record of the hearing.

(g) Within 10 days after the hearing, the designee—

(1) Indicates that a decision will be issued on the basis of the existing record; or

(2) Requests further information from the SEA, LEA, other public agency, representatives of private schools or Department officials.

§ 300.195 Decision.

(a) The designee who conducts the show cause hearing—

(1) Within 120 days after the record of a show cause hearing is closed, issues a written decision that includes a statement of findings; and

(2) Submits a copy of the decision to the Secretary and sends a copy to each party by certified mail with return receipt requested.

(b) Each party may submit comments and recommendations on the designee's decision to the Secretary within 30 days of the date the party receives the designee's decision.

(c) The Secretary adopts, reverses, or modifies the designee's decision and notifies all parties to the show cause hearing of the Secretary's final action. That notice is sent by certified mail with return receipt requested.

§ 300.196 Filing requirements.

(a) Any written submission under § 300.194 must be filed by hand-delivery, by mail, or by facsimile transmission. The Secretary discourages the use of facsimile transmission for documents longer than five pages.

(b) The filing date under paragraph (a) of this section is the date the document is—

(1) Hand-delivered;

(2) Mailed; or

(3) Sent by facsimile transmission.

(c) A party filing by facsimile transmission is responsible for confirming that a complete and legible copy of the document was received by the Department.

(d) If a document is filed by facsimile transmission, the Secretary or the hearing officer, as applicable, may require the filing of a follow-up hard copy by hand-delivery or by mail within a reasonable period of time.

(e) If agreed upon by the parties, service of a document may be made upon the other party by facsimile transmission.

(f) A party must show a proof of mailing to establish the filing date under paragraph (b)(2) of this section as provided in 34 CFR 75.102(d).

§ 300.197 Judicial review.

If dissatisfied with the Secretary's final action, the SEA may, within 60 days after notice of that action, file a petition for review with the United States Court of Appeals for the circuit in which the State is located. The procedures for judicial review are described in section 612(f)(3) (B) through (D) of the Act.

§ 300.198 Continuation of a by-pass.

The Secretary continues a by-pass until the Secretary determines that the SEA, LEA or other public agency will meet the requirements for providing services to private school children.

§ 300.199 – 300.208 [omitted]

§ 300.209 Treatment of charter schools and their students.

(a) Rights of children with disabilities. Children with disabilities who attend public charter schools and their parents retain all rights under this part.

(b) Charter schools that are public schools of the LEA.

(1) In carrying out Part B of the Act and these regulations with respect to charter schools that are public schools of the LEA, the LEA must—

(i) Serve children with disabilities attending those charter schools in the same manner as the LEA serves children with disabilities in its other schools, including providing supplementary and related services on site at the charter school to the same extent to which the LEA has a policy or practice of providing such services on the site to its other public schools; and

(ii) Provide funds under Part B of the Act to those charter schools—

(A) On the same basis as the LEA provides funds to the LEA's other public schools, including proportional distribution based on relative enrollment of children with disabilities; and

(B) At the same time as the LEA distributes other Federal funds to the LEA's other public schools, consistent with the State's charter school law.

(2) If the public charter school is a school of an LEA that receives funding under § 300.705 and includes other public schools—

(i) The LEA is responsible for ensuring that the requirements of this part are met, unless State law assigns that responsibility to some other entity; and

(ii) The LEA must meet the requirements of paragraph (b)(1) of this section.

(c) Public charter schools that are LEAs. If the public charter school is an LEA, consistent with § 300.28, that receives funding under § 300.705, that charter school is responsible for ensuring that the requirements of this part are met, unless State law assigns that responsibility to some other entity.

(d) Public charter schools that are not an LEA or a school that is part of an LEA.

(1) If the public charter school is not an LEA receiving funding under § 300.705, or a school that is part of an LEA receiving funding under § 300.705, the SEA is responsible for ensuring that the requirements of this part are met.

(2) Paragraph (d)(1) of this section does not preclude a State from assigning initial responsibility for ensuring the requirements of this part are met to another entity. However, the SEA must maintain the ultimate responsibility for ensuring compliance with this part, consistent with § 300.149.

§ 300.210 Purchase of instructional materials.

(a) General. Not later than December 3, 2006, an LEA that chooses to coordinate with the National Instructional Materials Access Center (NIMAC), when purchasing print instructional materials, must acquire those instructional materials in the same manner, and subject to the same conditions as an SEA under § 300.172.

(b) Rights of LEA.

(1) Nothing in this section shall be construed to require an LEA to coordinate with the NIMAC.

(2) If an LEA chooses not to coordinate with the NIMAC, the LEA must provide an assurance to the SEA that the LEA will provide instructional materials to blind persons or other persons with print disabilities in a timely manner.

(3) Nothing in this section relieves an LEA of its responsibility to ensure that children with disabilities who need instructional materials in accessible formats but are not included under the definition of blind or other persons with print disabilities in § 300.172(e)(1)(i) or who need materials that cannot be produced from NIMAS files, receive those instructional materials in a timely manner.

§ 300.211 Information for SEA.

The LEA must provide the SEA with information necessary to enable the SEA to carry out its duties under Part B of the Act, including, with respect to §§ 300.157 and 300.160, information relating to the performance of children with disabilities participating in programs carried out under Part B of the Act.

§ 300.212 Public information.

The LEA must make available to parents of children with disabilities and to the general public all documents relating to the eligibility of the agency under Part B of the Act.

§ 300.213 Records regarding migratory children with disabilities.

The LEA must cooperate in the Secretary's efforts under section 1308 of the ESEA to ensure the linkage of records pertaining to migratory children with disabilities for the purpose of electronically exchanging, among the States, health and educational information regarding those children.

§§ 300.214 to 300.219 [Reserved]
§§ 300.214 to 300.219 [Reserved]
§ 300.220 – 300.299 [omitted]
§ 300.300 Parental consent.

(a) Parental consent for initial evaluation.

(1)(i) The public agency proposing to conduct an initial evaluation to determine if a child qualifies as a child with a disability under § 300.8 must, after providing notice consistent with §§ 300.503 and 300.504, obtain informed consent, consistent with § 300.9, from the parent of the child before conducting the evaluation.

(ii) Parental consent for initial evaluation must not be construed as consent for initial provision of special education and related services.

(iii) The public agency must make reasonable efforts to obtain the informed consent from the parent for an initial evaluation to determine whether the child is a child with a disability.

(2) For initial evaluations only, if the child is a ward of the State and is not residing with the child's parent, the public agency is not required to obtain informed consent from the parent for an initial evaluation to determine whether the child is a child with a disability if—

(i) Despite reasonable efforts to do so, the public agency cannot discover the whereabouts of the parent of the child;

(ii) The rights of the parents of the child have been terminated in accordance with State law; or

(iii) The rights of the parent to make educational decisions have been subrogated by a judge in accordance with State law and consent for an initial evaluation has been given by an individual appointed by the judge to represent the child.

(3)(i) If the parent of a child enrolled in public school or seeking to be enrolled in public school does not provide consent for initial evaluation under paragraph (a)(1) of this section, or the parent fails to respond to a request to provide consent, the public agency may, but is not required to, pursue the initial evaluation of the child by utilizing the procedural safeguards in subpart E of this part (including the mediation procedures under § 300.506 or the due process procedures under §§ 300.507 through 300.516), if appropriate, except to the extent inconsistent with State law relating to such parental consent.

(ii) The public agency does not violate its obligation under § 300.111 and §§ 300.301 through 300.311 if it declines to pursue the evaluation.

(b) Parental consent for services.

(1) A public agency that is responsible for making FAPE available to a child with a disability must obtain informed consent from the parent of the child before the initial provision of special education and related services to the child.

(2) The public agency must make reasonable efforts to obtain informed consent from the parent for the initial provision of special education and related services to the child.

(3) If the parent of a child fails to respond or refuses to consent to services under paragraph (b)(1) of this section, the public agency may not use the procedures in subpart E of this part (including the mediation procedures under § 300.506 or the due process procedures under §§ 300.507 through 300.516) in order to obtain agreement or a ruling that the services may be provided to the child.

(4) If the parent of the child refuses to consent to the initial provision of special education and related services, or the parent fails to respond to a request to provide consent for the initial provision of special education and related services, the public agency—

(i) Will not be considered to be in violation of the requirement to make available FAPE to the child for the failure to provide the child with the special education and related services for which the public agency requests consent; and

(ii) Is not required to convene an IEP Team meeting or develop an IEP under §§ 300.320 and 300.324 for the child for the special education and related services for which the public agency requests such consent.

(c) Parental consent for reevaluations.

(1) Subject to paragraph (c)(2) of this section, each public agency—

(i) Must obtain informed parental consent, in accordance with § 300.300(a)(1), prior to conducting any reevaluation of a child with a disability.

(ii) If the parent refuses to consent to the reevaluation, the public agency may, but is not required to, pursue the reevaluation by using the consent override procedures described in paragraph (a)(3) of this section.

(iii) The public agency does not violate its obligation under § 300.111 and §§ 300.301 through 300.311 if it declines to pursue the evaluation or reevaluation.

(2) The informed parental consent described in paragraph (c)(1) of this section need not be obtained if the public agency can demonstrate that—

(i) It made reasonable efforts to obtain such consent; and

(ii) The child's parent has failed to respond.

(d) Other consent requirements.

(1) Parental consent is not required before—

(i) Reviewing existing data as part of an evaluation or a reevaluation; or

(ii) Administering a test or other evaluation that is administered to all children unless, before administration of that test or evaluation, consent is required of parents of all children.

(2) In addition to the parental consent requirements described in paragraph (a) of this section, a State may require parental consent for other services and activities under this part if it ensures that each public agency in the State establishes and implements effective procedures to ensure that a parent's refusal to consent does not result in a failure to provide the child with FAPE.

(3) A public agency may not use a parent's refusal to consent to one service or activity under paragraphs (a) or (d)(2) of this section to deny the parent or child any other service, benefit, or activity of the public agency, except as required by this part.

(4)(i) If a parent of a child who is home schooled or placed in a private school by the parents at their own expense does not provide consent for the initial evaluation or the reevaluation, or the parent fails to respond to a request to provide consent, the public agency may not use the consent override procedures (described in paragraphs (a)(3) and (c)(1) of this section); and

(ii) The public agency is not required to consider the child as eligible for services under §§ 300.132 through 300.144.

(5) To meet the reasonable efforts requirement in paragraphs (a)(1)(iii), (a)(2)(i), (b)(2), and (c)(2)(i) of this section, the public agency must document its attempts to obtain parental consent using the procedures in § 300.322(d).

Evaluations and Reevaluations

§ 300.301 Initial evaluations.

(a) General. Each public agency must conduct a full and individual initial evaluation, in accordance with §§ 300.305 and 300.306, before the initial provision of special education and related services to a child with a disability under this part.

(b) Request for initial evaluation. Consistent with the consent requirements in § 300.300, either a parent of a child or a public agency may initiate a request for an initial evaluation to determine if the child is a child with a disability.

(c) Procedures for initial evaluation. The initial evaluation—

(1)(i) Must be conducted within 60 days of receiving parental consent for the evaluation; or

(ii) If the State establishes a timeframe within which the evaluation must be conducted, within that timeframe; and

(2) Must consist of procedures—

(i) To determine if the child is a child with a disability under § 300.8; and

(ii) To determine the educational needs of the child.

(d) Exception. The timeframe described in paragraph (c)(1) of this section does not apply to a public agency if—

(1) The parent of a child repeatedly fails or refuses to produce the child for the evaluation; or

(2) A child enrolls in a school of another public agency after the relevant timeframe in paragraph (c)(1) of this section has begun, and prior to a determination by the child's previous public agency as to whether the child is a child with a disability under § 300.8.

(e) The exception in paragraph (d)(2) of this section applies only if the subsequent public agency is making sufficient progress to ensure a prompt completion of the evaluation, and the parent and subsequent public agency agree to a specific time when the evaluation will be completed.

§ 300.302 Screening for instructional purposes is not evaluation.

The screening of a student by a teacher or specialist to determine appropriate instructional strategies for curriculum implementation shall not be considered to be an evaluation for eligibility for special education and related services.

§ 300.303 Reevaluations.

(a) *General.* A public agency must ensure that a reevaluation of each child with a disability is conducted in accordance with §§ 300.304 through 300.311—

(1) If the public agency determines that the educational or related services needs, including improved academic achievement and functional performance, of the child warrant a reevaluation; or

(2) If the child's parent or teacher requests a reevaluation.

(b) *Limitation.* A reevaluation conducted under paragraph (a) of this section—

(1) May occur not more than once a year, unless the parent and the public agency agree otherwise; and

(2) Must occur at least once every 3 years, unless the parent and the public agency agree that a reevaluation is unnecessary.

§ 300.304 Evaluation procedures.

(a) *Notice.* The public agency must provide notice to the parents of a child with a disability, in accordance with § 300.503, that describes any evaluation procedures the agency proposes to conduct.

(b) *Conduct of evaluation.* In conducting the evaluation, the public agency must—

(1) Use a variety of assessment tools and strategies to gather relevant functional, developmental, and academic information about the child, including information provided by the parent, that may assist in determining—

(i) Whether the child is a child with a disability under § 300.8; and

(ii) The content of the child's IEP, including information related to enabling the child to be involved in and progress in the general education curriculum (or for a preschool child, to participate in appropriate activities);

(2) Not use any single measure or assessment as the sole criterion for determining whether a child is a child with a disability and for determining an appropriate educational program for the child; and

(3) Use technically sound instruments that may assess the relative contribution of cognitive and behavioral factors, in addition to physical or developmental factors.

(c) *Other evaluation procedures.* Each public agency must ensure that—

(1) Assessments and other evaluation materials used to assess a child under this part—

(i) Are selected and administered so as not to be discriminatory on a racial or cultural basis;

(ii) Are provided and administered in the child's native language or other mode of communication and in the form most likely to yield accurate information on what the child knows and can do academically, developmentally, and functionally, unless it is clearly not feasible to so provide or administer;

(iii) Are used for the purposes for which the assessments or measures are valid and reliable;

(iv) Are administered by trained and knowledgeable personnel; and

(v) Are administered in accordance with any instructions provided by the producer of the assessments.

(2) Assessments and other evaluation materials include those tailored to assess specific areas of educational need and not merely those that are designed to provide a single general intelligence quotient.

(3) Assessments are selected and administered so as best to ensure that if an assessment is administered to a child with impaired sensory, manual, or speaking skills, the assessment results accurately reflect the child's aptitude or achievement level or whatever other factors the test purports to measure, rather than reflecting the child's impaired sensory, manual, or speaking skills (unless those skills are the factors that the test purports to measure).

(4) The child is assessed in all areas related to the suspected disability, including, if appropriate, health, vision, hearing, social and emotional status, general intelligence, academic performance, communicative status, and motor abilities;

(5) Assessments of children with disabilities who transfer from one public agency to another public agency in the same school year are coordinated with those children's prior and subsequent schools, as necessary and as expeditiously as possible, consistent with

§ 300.301(d)(2) and (e), to ensure prompt completion of full evaluations.

(6) In evaluating each child with a disability under §§ 300.304 through 300.306, the evaluation is sufficiently comprehensive to identify all of the child's special education and related services needs, whether or not commonly linked to the disability category in which the child has been classified.

(7) Assessment tools and strategies that provide relevant information that directly assists persons in determining the educational needs of the child are provided.

§ 300.305 Additional requirements for evaluations and reevaluations.

(a) Review of existing evaluation data. As part of an initial evaluation (if appropriate) and as part of any reevaluation under this part, the IEP Team and other qualified professionals, as appropriate, must—

(1) Review existing evaluation data on the child, including—

(i) Evaluations and information provided by the parents of the child;

(ii) Current classroom-based, local, or State assessments, and classroom-based observations; and

(iii) Observations by teachers and related services providers; and

(2) On the basis of that review, and input from the child's parents, identify what additional data, if any, are needed to determine—

(i)(A) Whether the child is a child with a disability, as defined in § 300.8, and the educational needs of the child; or

(B) In case of a reevaluation of a child, whether the child continues to have such a disability, and the educational needs of the child;

(ii) The present levels of academic achievement and related developmental needs of the child;

(iii)(A) Whether the child needs special education and related services; or

(B) In the case of a reevaluation of a child, whether the child continues to need special education and related services; and

(iv) Whether any additions or modifications to the special education and related services are needed to enable the child to meet the measurable annual goals set out in the IEP of the child and to participate, as appropriate, in the general education curriculum.

(b) Conduct of review. The group described in paragraph (a) of this section may conduct its review without a meeting.

(c) Source of data. The public agency must administer such assessments and other evaluation measures as may be needed to produce the data identified under paragraph (a) of this section.

(d) Requirements if additional data are not needed.

(1) If the IEP Team and other qualified professionals, as appropriate, determine that no additional data are needed to determine whether the child continues to be a child with a disability, and to determine the child's educational needs, the public agency must notify the child's parents of'—

(i) That determination and the reasons for the determination; and

(ii) The right of the parents to request an assessment to determine whether the child continues to be a child with a disability, and to determine the child's educational needs.

(2) The public agency is not required to conduct the assessment described in paragraph (d)(1)(ii) of this section unless requested to do so by the child's parents.

(e) Evaluations before change in eligibility.

(1) Except as provided in paragraph (e)(2) of this section, a public agency must evaluate a child with a disability in accordance with §§ 300.304 through 300.311 before determining that the child is no longer a child with a disability.

(2) The evaluation described in paragraph (e)(1) of this section is not required before the termination of a child's eligibility under this part due to graduation from secondary school with a regular diploma, or due to exceeding the age eligibility for FAPE under State law.

(3) For a child whose eligibility terminates under circumstances described in paragraph (e)(2) of this section, a public agency must provide the child with a summary of the child's academic achievement and functional performance, which shall include recommendations on how to assist the child in meeting the child's postsecondary goals.

§ 300.306 Determination of eligibility.

(a) General. Upon completion of the administration of assessments and other evaluation measures—

(1) A group of qualified professionals and the parent of the child determines whether the child is a child with a disability, as defined in § 300.8, in accordance with paragraph (b) of this section and the educational needs of the child; and

(2) The public agency provides a copy of the evaluation report and the documentation of determination of eligibility at no cost to the parent.

(b) *Special rule for eligibility determination.* A child must not be determined to be a child with a disability under this part—

(1) If the determinant factor for that determination is—

(i) Lack of appropriate instruction in reading, including the essential components of reading instruction (as defined in section 1208(3) of the ESEA);

(ii) Lack of appropriate instruction in math; or

(iii) Limited English proficiency; and

(2) If the child does not otherwise meet the eligibility criteria under § 300.8(a).

(c) *Procedures for determining eligibility and educational need.*

(1) In interpreting evaluation data for the purpose of determining if a child is a child with a disability under § 300.8, and the educational needs of the child, each public agency must—

(i) Draw upon information from a variety of sources, including aptitude and achievement tests, parent input, and teacher recommendations, as well as information about the child's physical condition, social or cultural background, and adaptive behavior; and

(ii) Ensure that information obtained from all of these sources is documented and carefully considered.

(2) If a determination is made that a child has a disability and needs special education and related services, an IEP must be developed for the child in accordance with §§ 300.320 through 300.324.

Additional Procedures for Identifying Children with Specific Learning Disabilities

§ 300.307 Specific learning disabilities.

(a) General. A State must adopt, consistent with § 300.309, criteria for determining whether a child has a specific learning disability as defined in § 300.8(c)(10). In addition, the criteria adopted by the State—

(1) Must not require the use of a severe discrepancy between intellectual ability and achievement for determining whether a child has a specific learning disability, as defined in § 300.8(c)(10);

(2) Must permit the use of a process based on the child's response to scientific, research-based intervention; and

(3) May permit the use of other alternative research-based procedures for determining whether a child has a specific learning disability, as defined in § 300.8(c)(10).

(b) *Consistency with State criteria.* A public agency must use the State criteria adopted pursuant to paragraph (a) of this section in determining whether a child has a specific learning disability.

§ 300.308 Additional group members.

The determination of whether a child suspected of having a specific learning disability is a child with a disability as defined in § 300.8, must be made by the child's parents and a team of qualified professionals, which must include—

(a)(1) The child's regular teacher; or

(2) If the child does not have a regular teacher, a regular classroom teacher qualified to teach a child of his or her age; or

(3) For a child of less than school age, an individual qualified by the SEA to teach a child of his or her age; and

(b) At least one person qualified to conduct individual diagnostic examinations of children, such as a school psychologist, speech-language pathologist, or remedial reading teacher.

§ 300.309 Determining the existence of a specific learning disability.

(a) The group described in § 300.306 may determine that a child has a specific learning disability, as defined in § 300.8(c)(10), if—

(1) The child does not achieve adequately for the child's age or to meet State-approved

grade-level standards in one or more of the following areas, when provided with learning experiences and instruction appropriate for the child's age or State-approved grade-level standards:

(i) Oral expression.
(ii) Listening comprehension.
(iii) Written expression.
(iv) Basic reading skill.
(v) Reading fluency skills.
(vi) Reading comprehension.
(vii) Mathematics calculation.
(viii) Mathematics problem solving.

(2)(i) The child does not make sufficient progress to meet age or State-approved grade-level standards in one or more of the areas identified in paragraph (a)(1) of this section when using a process based on the child's response to scientific, research-based intervention; or

(ii) The child exhibits a pattern of strengths and weaknesses in performance, achievement, or both, relative to age, State-approved grade-level standards, or intellectual development, that is determined by the group to be relevant to the identification of a specific learning disability, using appropriate assessments, consistent with §§ 300.304 and 300.305; and

(3) The group determines that its findings under paragraphs (a)(1) and (2) of this section are not primarily the result of—

(i) A visual, hearing, or motor disability;
(ii) Mental retardation;
(iii) Emotional disturbance;
(iv) Cultural factors;
(v) Environmental or economic disadvantage; or
(vi) Limited English proficiency.

(b) To ensure that underachievement in a child suspected of having a specific learning disability is not due to lack of appropriate instruction in reading or math, the group must consider, as part of the evaluation described in §§ 300.304 through 300.306—

(1) Data that demonstrate that prior to, or as a part of, the referral process, the child was provided appropriate instruction in regular education settings, delivered by qualified personnel; and

(2) Data-based documentation of repeated assessments of achievement at reasonable intervals, reflecting formal assessment of student progress during instruction, which was provided to the child's parents.

(c) The public agency must promptly request parental consent to evaluate the child to determine if the child needs special education and related services, and must adhere to the timeframes described in §§ 300.301 and 300.303, unless extended by mutual written agreement of the child's parents and a group of qualified professionals, as described in § 300.306(a)(1)—

(1) If, prior to a referral, a child has not made adequate progress after an appropriate period of time when provided instruction, as described in paragraphs (b)(1) and (b)(2) of this section; and

(2) Whenever a child is referred for an evaluation.

§ 300.310 Observation.

(a) The public agency must ensure that the child is observed in the child's learning environment (including the regular classroom setting) to document the child's academic performance and behavior in the areas of difficulty.

(b) The group described in § 300.306(a)(1), in determining whether a child has a specific learning disability, must decide to—

(1) Use information from an observation in routine classroom instruction and monitoring of the child's performance that was done before the child was referred for an evaluation; or

(2) Have at least one member of the group described in § 300.306(a)(1) conduct an observation of the child's academic performance in the regular classroom after the child has been referred for an evaluation and parental consent, consistent with § 300.300(a), is obtained.

(c) In the case of a child of less than school age or out of school, a group member must observe the child in an environment appropriate for a child of that age.

§ 300.311 Specific documentation for the eligibility determination.

(a) For a child suspected of having a specific learning disability, the documentation of the determination of eligibility, as required in § 300.306(a)(2), must contain a statement of—

(1) Whether the child has a specific learning disability;

(2) The basis for making the determination, including an assurance that the determination has been made in accordance with § 300.306(c)(1);

(3) The relevant behavior, if any, noted during the observation of the child and the relationship of that behavior to the child's academic functioning;

(4) The educationally relevant medical findings, if any;

(5) Whether—

(i) The child does not achieve adequately for the child's age or to meet State-approved grade-level standards consistent with § 300.309(a)(1); and

(ii)(A) The child does not make sufficient progress to meet age or State-approved grade-level standards consistent with § 300.309(a)(2)(i); or

(B) The child exhibits a pattern of strengths and weaknesses in performance, achievement, or both, relative to age, State-approved grade level standards or intellectual development consistent with § 300.309(a)(2)(ii);

(6) The determination of the group concerning the effects of a visual, hearing, or motor disability; mental retardation; emotional disturbance; cultural factors; environmental or economic disadvantage; or limited English proficiency on the child's achievement level; and

(7) If the child has participated in a process that assesses the child's response to scientific, research-based intervention—

(i) The instructional strategies used and the student-centered data collected; and

(ii) The documentation that the child's parents were notified about—

(A) The State's policies regarding the amount and nature of student performance data that would be collected and the general education services that would be provided;

(B) Strategies for increasing the child's rate of learning; and

(C) The parents' right to request an evaluation.

(b) Each group member must certify in writing whether the report reflects the member's conclusion. If it does not reflect the member's conclusion, the group member must submit a separate statement presenting the member's conclusions.

Individualized Education Programs
§ 300.320 Definition of individualized education program.

(a) General. As used in this part, the term individualized education program or IEP means a written statement for each child with a disability that is developed, reviewed, and revised in a meeting in accordance with §§ 300.320 through 300.324, and that must include—

(1) A statement of the child's present levels of academic achievement and functional performance, including—

(i) How the child's disability affects the child's involvement and progress in the general education curriculum (i.e., the same curriculum as for nondisabled children); or

(ii) For preschool children, as appropriate, how the disability affects the child's participation in appropriate activities;

(2)(i) A statement of measurable annual goals, including academic and functional goals designed to—

(A) Meet the child's needs that result from the child's disability to enable the child to be involved in and make progress in the general education curriculum; and

(B) Meet each of the child's other educational needs that result from the child's disability;

(ii) For children with disabilities who take alternate assessments aligned to alternate achievement standards, a description of benchmarks or short-term objectives;

(3) A description of—

(i) How the child's progress toward meeting the annual goals described in paragraph (2) of this section will be measured; and

(ii) When periodic reports on the progress the child is making toward meeting the annual goals (such as through the use of quarterly or other periodic reports, concurrent with the issuance of report cards) will be provided;

(4) A statement of the special education and related services and supplementary aids and services, based on peer-reviewed research to the extent practicable, to be provided to the child, or on behalf of the child, and a statement of the program modifications or supports for school personnel that will be provided to enable the child—

(i) To advance appropriately toward attaining the annual goals;

(ii) To be involved in and make progress in the general education curriculum in accordance with paragraph (a)(1) of this section, and to participate in extracurricular and other nonacademic activities; and

(iii) To be educated and participate with other children with disabilities and nondisabled children in the activities described in this section;

(5) An explanation of the extent, if any, to which the child will not participate with nondisabled children in the regular class and in the activities described in paragraph (a)(4) of this section;

(6)(i) A statement of any individual appropriate accommodations that are necessary to measure the academic achievement and functional performance of the child on State and districtwide assessments consistent with section 612(a)(16) of the Act; and

(ii) If the IEP Team determines that the child must take an alternate assessment instead of a particular regular State or districtwide assessment of student achievement, a statement of why—

(A) The child cannot participate in the regular assessment; and

(B) The particular alternate assessment selected is appropriate for the child; and

(7) The projected date for the beginning of the services and modifications described in paragraph (a)(4) of this section, and the anticipated frequency, location, and duration of those services and modifications.

(b) Transition services. Beginning not later than the first IEP to be in effect when the child turns 16, or younger if determined appropriate by the IEP Team, and updated annually, thereafter, the IEP must include—

(1) Appropriate measurable postsecondary goals based upon age appropriate transition assessments related to training, education, employment, and, where appropriate, independent living skills; and

(2) The transition services (including courses of study) needed to assist the child in reaching those goals.

(c) Transfer of rights at age of majority. Beginning not later than one year before the child reaches the age of majority under State law, the IEP must include a statement that the child has been informed of the child's rights under Part B of the Act, if any, that will transfer to the child on reaching the age of majority under § 300.520.

(d) Construction. Nothing in this section shall be construed to require—

(1) That additional information be included in a child's IEP beyond what is explicitly required in section 614 of the Act; or

(2) The IEP Team to include information under one component of a child's IEP that is already contained under another component of the child's IEP.

§ 300.321 IEP Team.

(a) General. The public agency must ensure that the IEP Team for each child with a disability includes—

(1) The parents of the child;

(2) Not less than one regular education teacher of the child (if the child is, or may be, participating in the regular education environment);

(3) Not less than one special education teacher of the child, or where appropriate, not less then one special education provider of the child;

(4) A representative of the public agency who—

(i) Is qualified to provide, or supervise the provision of, specially designed instruction to meet the unique needs of children with disabilities;

(ii) Is knowledgeable about the general education curriculum; and

(iii) Is knowledgeable about the availability of resources of the public agency.

(5) An individual who can interpret the instructional implications of evaluation results, who may be a member of the team

described in paragraphs (a)(2) through (a)(6) of this section;

(6) At the discretion of the parent or the agency, other individuals who have knowledge or special expertise regarding the child, including related services personnel as appropriate; and

(7) Whenever appropriate, the child with a disability.

(b) *Transition services participants.*

(1) In accordance with paragraph (a)(7) of this section, the public agency must invite a child with a disability to attend the child's IEP Team meeting if a purpose of the meeting will be the consideration of the postsecondary goals for the child and the transition services needed to assist the child in reaching those goals under § 300.320(b).

(2) If the child does not attend the IEP Team meeting, the public agency must take other steps to ensure that the child's preferences and interests are considered.

(3) To the extent appropriate, with the consent of the parents or a child who has reached the age of majority, in implementing the requirements of paragraph (b)(1) of this section, the public agency must invite a representative of any participating agency that is likely to be responsible for providing or paying for transition services.

(c) *Determination of knowledge and special expertise.* The determination of the knowledge or special expertise of any individual described in paragraph (a)(6) of this section must be made by the party (parents or public agency) who invited the individual to be a member of the IEP Team.

(d) *Designating a public agency representative.* A public agency may designate a public agency member of the IEP Team to also serve as the agency representative, if the criteria in paragraph (a)(4) of this section are satisfied.

(e) *IEP Team attendance.*

(1) A member of the IEP Team described in paragraphs (a)(2) through (a)(5) of this section is not required to attend an IEP Team meeting, in whole or in part, if the parent of a child with a disability and the public agency agree, in writing, that the attendance of the member is not necessary because the member's area of the curriculum or related services is not being modified or discussed in the meeting.

(2) A member of the IEP Team described in paragraph (e)(1) of this section may be excused from attending an IEP Team meeting, in whole or in part, when the meeting involves a modification to or discussion of the member's area of the curriculum or related services, if—

(i) The parent, in writing, and the public agency consent to the excusal; and

(ii) The member submits, in writing to the parent and the IEP Team, input into the development of the IEP prior to the meeting.

(f) *Initial IEP Team meeting for child under Part C.* In the case of a child who was previously served under Part C of the Act, an invitation to the initial IEP Team meeting must, at the request of the parent, be sent to the Part C service coordinator or other representatives of the Part C system to assist with the smooth transition of services.

§ 300.322 **Parent participation.**

(a) *Public agency responsibility—general.* Each public agency must take steps to ensure that one or both of the parents of a child with a disability are present at each IEP Team meeting or are afforded the opportunity to participate, including—

(1) Notifying parents of the meeting early enough to ensure that they will have an opportunity to attend; and

(2) Scheduling the meeting at a mutually agreed on time and place.

(b) *Information provided to parents.*

(1) The notice required under paragraph (a)(1) of this section must—

(i) Indicate the purpose, time, and location of the meeting and who will be in attendance; and

(ii) Inform the parents of the provisions in § 300.321(a)(6) and (c) (relating to the participation of other individuals on the IEP Team who have knowledge or special expertise about the child), and § 300.321(f) (relating to the participation of the Part C service coordinator or other representatives of the Part C system at the initial IEP Team meeting for a child previously served under Part C of the Act).

(2) For a child with a disability beginning not later than the first IEP to be in effect when the child turns 16, or younger if determined appropriate by the IEP Team, the notice also must—

(i) Indicate—

(A) That a purpose of the meeting will be the consideration of the postsecondary goals and transition services for the child, in accordance with § 300.320(b); and

(B) That the agency will invite the student; and

(ii) Identify any other agency that will be invited to send a representative.

(c) Other methods to ensure parent participation. If neither parent can attend an IEP Team meeting, the public agency must use other methods to ensure parent participation, including individual or conference telephone calls, consistent with § 300.328 (related to alternative means of meeting participation).

(d) Conducting an IEP Team meeting without a parent in attendance. A meeting may be conducted without a parent in attendance if the public agency is unable to convince the parents that they should attend. In this case, the public agency must keep a record of its attempts to arrange a mutually agreed on time and place, such as—

(1) Detailed records of telephone calls made or attempted and the results of those calls;

(2) Copies of correspondence sent to the parents and any responses received; and

(3) Detailed records of visits made to the parent's home or place of employment and the results of those visits.

(e) Use of interpreters or other action, as appropriate. The public agency must take whatever action is necessary to ensure that the parent understands the proceedings of the IEP Team meeting, including arranging for an interpreter for parents with deafness or whose native language is other than English.

(f) Parent copy of child's IEP. The public agency must give the parent a copy of the child's IEP at no cost to the parent.

§ 300.323 When IEPs must be in effect.

(a) General. At the beginning of each school year, each public agency must have in effect, for each child with a disability within its jurisdiction, an IEP, as defined in § 300.320.

(b) IEP or IFSP for children aged three through five.

(1) In the case of a child with a disability aged three through five (or, at the discretion of the SEA, a two-year-old child with a disability who will turn age three during the school year), the IEP Team must consider an IFSP that contains the IFSP content (including the natural environments statement) described in section 636(d) of the Act and its implementing regulations (including an educational component that promotes school readiness and incorporates pre-literacy, language, and numeracy skills for children with IFSPs under this section who are at least three years of age), and that is developed in accordance with the IEP procedures under this part. The IFSP may serve as the IEP of the child, if using the IFSP as the IEP is—

(i) Consistent with State policy; and

(ii) Agreed to by the agency and the child's parents.

(2) In implementing the requirements of paragraph (b)(1) of this section, the public agency must—

(i) Provide to the child's parents a detailed explanation of the differences between an IFSP and an IEP; and

(ii) If the parents choose an IFSP, obtain written informed consent from the parents.

(c) Initial IEPs; provision of services. Each public agency must ensure that—

(1) A meeting to develop an IEP for a child is conducted within 30 days of a determination that the child needs special education and related services; and

(2) As soon as possible following development of the IEP, special education and related services are made available to the child in accordance with the child's IEP.

(d) Accessibility of child's IEP to teachers and others. Each public agency must ensure that—

(1) The child's IEP is accessible to each regular education teacher, special education teacher, related services provider, and any other service provider who is responsible for its implementation; and

(2) Each teacher and provider described in paragraph (d)(1) of this section is informed of—

(i) His or her specific responsibilities related to implementing the child's IEP; and

(ii) The specific accommodations, modifications, and supports that must be provided for the child in accordance with the IEP.

(e) IEPs for children who transfer public agencies in the same State. If a child with a disability (who had an IEP that was in effect in a previous public agency in the same State) transfers to a new public agency in the same State, and enrolls in a new school within the same school year, the new public agency (in consultation with the parents) must provide FAPE to the child (including services comparable to those described in the child's IEP from the previous public agency), until the new public agency either—

(1) Adopts the child's IEP from the previous public agency; or

(2) Develops, adopts, and implements a new IEP that meets the applicable requirements in §§ 300.320 through 300.324.

(f) IEPs for children who transfer from another State. If a child with a disability (who had an IEP that was in effect in a previous public agency in another State) transfers to a public agency in a new State, and enrolls in a new school within the same school year, the new public agency (in consultation with the parents) must provide the child with FAPE (including services comparable to those described in the child's IEP from the previous public agency), until the new public agency—

(1) Conducts an evaluation pursuant to §§ 300.304 through 300.306 (if determined to be necessary by the new public agency); and

(2) Develops, adopts, and implements a new IEP, if appropriate, that meets the applicable requirements in §§ 300.320 through 300.324.

(g) Transmittal of records. To facilitate the transition for a child described in paragraphs (e) and (f) of this section—

(1) The new public agency in which the child enrolls must take reasonable steps to promptly obtain the child's records, including the IEP and supporting documents and any other records relating to the provision of special education or related services to the child, from the previous public agency in which the child was enrolled, pursuant to 34 CFR 99.31(a)(2); and

(2) The previous public agency in which the child was enrolled must take reasonable steps to promptly respond to the request from the new public agency.

Development of IEP

§ 300.324 Development, review, and revision of IEP.

(a) Development of IEP—

(1) General. In developing each child's IEP, the IEP Team must consider—

(i) The strengths of the child;

(ii) The concerns of the parents for enhancing the education of their child;

(iii) The results of the initial or most recent evaluation of the child; and

(iv) The academic, developmental, and functional needs of the child.

(2) Consideration of special factors. The IEP Team must—

(i) In the case of a child whose behavior impedes the child's learning or that of others, consider the use of positive behavioral interventions and supports, and other strategies, to address that behavior;

(ii) In the case of a child with limited English proficiency, consider the language needs of the child as those needs relate to the child's IEP;

(iii) In the case of a child who is blind or visually impaired, provide for instruction in Braille and the use of Braille unless the IEP Team determines, after an evaluation of the child's reading and writing skills, needs, and appropriate reading and writing media (including an evaluation of the child's future needs for instruction in Braille or the use of Braille), that instruction in Braille or the use of Braille is not appropriate for the child;

(iv) Consider the communication needs of the child, and in the case of a child who is deaf or hard of hearing, consider the child's language and communication needs, opportunities for direct communications with peers and professional personnel in the child's language and communication mode, academic level, and full range of needs, including opportunities for direct instruction in the child's language and communication mode; and

(v) Consider whether the child needs assistive technology devices and services.

(3) *Requirement with respect to regular education teacher.* A regular education teacher of a child with a disability, as a member of the IEP Team, must, to the extent appropriate, participate in the development of the IEP of the child, including the determination of—

(i) Appropriate positive behavioral interventions and supports and other strategies for the child; and

(ii) Supplementary aids and services, program modifications, and support for school personnel consistent with § 300.320(a)(4).

(4) *Agreement.*

(i) In making changes to a child's IEP after the annual IEP Team meeting for a school year, the parent of a child with a disability and the public agency may agree not to convene an IEP Team meeting for the purposes of making those changes, and instead may develop a written document to amend or modify the child's current IEP.

(ii) If changes are made to the child's IEP in accordance with paragraph (a)(4)(i) of this section, the public agency must ensure that the child's IEP Team is informed of those changes.

(5) *Consolidation of IEP Team meetings.* To the extent possible, the public agency must encourage the consolidation of reevaluation meetings for the child and other IEP Team meetings for the child.

(6) *Amendments.* Changes to the IEP may be made either by the entire IEP Team at an IEP Team meeting, or as provided in paragraph (a)(4) of this section, by amending the IEP rather than by redrafting the entire IEP. Upon request, a parent must be provided with a revised copy of the IEP with the amendments incorporated.

(b) *Review and revision of IEPs*—

(1) *General.* Each public agency must ensure that, subject to paragraphs (b)(2) and (b)(3) of this section, the IEP Team—

(i) Reviews the child's IEP periodically, but not less than annually, to determine whether the annual goals for the child are being achieved; and

(ii) Revises the IEP, as appropriate, to address—

(A) Any lack of expected progress toward the annual goals described in § 300.320(a)(2), and in the general education curriculum, if appropriate;

(B) The results of any reevaluation conducted under § 300.303;

(C) Information about the child provided to, or by, the parents, as described under § 300.305(a)(2);

(D) The child's anticipated needs; or

(E) Other matters.

(2) *Consideration of special factors.* In conducting a review of the child's IEP, the IEP Team must consider the special factors described in paragraph (a)(2) of this section.

(3) *Requirement with respect to regular education teacher.* A regular education teacher of the child, as a member of the IEP Team, must, consistent with paragraph (a)(3) of this section, participate in the review and revision of the IEP of the child.

(c) *Failure to meet transition objectives*—

(1) *Participating agency failure.* If a participating agency, other than the public agency, fails to provide the transition services described in the IEP in accordance with § 300.320(b), the public agency must reconvene the IEP Team to identify alternative strategies to meet the transition objectives for the child set out in the IEP.

(2) *Construction.* Nothing in this part relieves any participating agency, including a State vocational rehabilitation agency, of the responsibility to provide or pay for any transition service that the agency would otherwise provide to children with disabilities who meet the eligibility criteria of that agency.

(d) *Children with disabilities in adult prisons*—

(1) *Requirements that do not apply.* The following requirements do not apply to children with disabilities who are convicted as adults under State law and incarcerated in adult prisons:

(i) The requirements contained in section 612(a)(16) of the Act and § 300.320(a)(6) (relating to participation of children with disabilities in general assessments).

(ii) The requirements in § 300.320(b) (relating to transition planning and transition services) do not apply with respect to the children whose eligibility under Part B of the Act will end, because of their age, before they will be eligible to be released from prison based on consideration of their sentence and eligibility for early release.

(2) Modifications of IEP or placement.

(i) Subject to paragraph (d)(2)(ii) of this section, the IEP Team of a child with a disability who is convicted as an adult under State law and incarcerated in an adult prison may modify the child's IEP or placement if the State has demonstrated a bona fide security or compelling penological interest that cannot otherwise be accommodated.

(ii) The requirements of §§ 300.320 (relating to IEPs), and 300.112 (relating to LRE), do not apply with respect to the modifications described in paragraph (d)(2)(i) of this section.

§ 300.325 Private school placements by public agencies.

(a) Developing IEPs.

(1) Before a public agency places a child with a disability in, or refers a child to, a private school or facility, the agency must initiate and conduct a meeting to develop an IEP for the child in accordance with §§ 300.320 and 300.324.

(2) The agency must ensure that a representative of the private school or facility attends the meeting. If the representative cannot attend, the agency must use other methods to ensure participation by the private school or facility, including individual or conference telephone calls.

(b) Reviewing and revising IEPs.

(1) After a child with a disability enters a private school or facility, any meetings to review and revise the child's IEP may be initiated and conducted by the private school or facility at the discretion of the public agency.

(2) If the private school or facility initiates and conducts these meetings, the public agency must ensure that the parents and an agency representative—

(i) Are involved in any decision about the child's IEP; and

(ii) Agree to any proposed changes in the IEP before those changes are implemented.

(c) Responsibility. Even if a private school or facility implements a child's IEP, responsibility for compliance with this part remains with the public agency and the SEA.

§ 300.326 [Reserved]

§ 300.327 Educational placements.

Consistent with § 300.501(c), each public agency must ensure that the parents of each child with a disability are members of any group that makes decisions on the educational placement of their child.

§ 300.328 Alternative means of meeting participation.

When conducting IEP Team meetings and placement meetings pursuant to this subpart, and subpart E of this part, and carrying out administrative matters under section 615 of the Act (such as scheduling, exchange of witness lists, and status conferences), the parent of a child with a disability and a public agency may agree to use alternative means of meeting participation, such as video conferences and conference calls.

§ 300.500 Responsibility of SEA and other public agencies.

Each SEA must ensure that each public agency establishes, maintains, and implements procedural safeguards that meet the requirements of §§ 300.500 through 300.536.

§ 300.501 Opportunity to examine records; parent participation in meetings.

(a) Opportunity to examine records. The parents of a child with a disability must be afforded, in accordance with the procedures of §§ 300.613 through 300.621, an opportunity to inspect and review all education records with respect to—

(1) The identification, evaluation, and educational placement of the child; and

(2) The provision of FAPE to the child.

(b) Parent participation in meetings.

(1) The parents of a child with a disability must be afforded an opportunity to participate in meetings with respect to—

(i) The identification, evaluation, and educational placement of the child; and

(ii) The provision of FAPE to the child.

(2) Each public agency must provide notice consistent with § 300.322(a)(1) and (b)(1) to ensure that parents of children with disabilities have the opportunity to participate in meetings described in paragraph (b)(1) of this section.

(3) A meeting does not include informal or unscheduled conversations involving public agency personnel and conversations on issues such as teaching methodology, lesson plans, or coordination of service provision. A meeting also does not include preparatory activities that public agency personnel engage in to develop a proposal or response to a parent proposal that will be discussed at a later meeting.

(c) Parent involvement in placement decisions.

(1) Each public agency must ensure that a parent of each child with a disability is a member of any group that makes decisions on the educational placement of the parent's child.

(2) In implementing the requirements of paragraph (c)(1) of this section, the public agency must use procedures consistent with the procedures described in § 300.322(a) through (b)(1).

(3) If neither parent can participate in a meeting in which a decision is to be made relating to the educational placement of their child, the public agency must use other methods to ensure their participation, including individual or conference telephone calls, or video conferencing.

(4) A placement decision may be made by a group without the involvement of a parent, if the public agency is unable to obtain the parent's participation in the decision. In this case, the public agency must have a record of its attempt to ensure their involvement.

§ 300.502 Independent educational evaluation.

(a) General.

(1) The parents of a child with a disability have the right under this part to obtain an independent educational evaluation of the child, subject to paragraphs (b) through (e) of this section.

(2) Each public agency must provide to parents, upon request for an independent educational evaluation, information about where an independent educational evaluation may be obtained, and the agency criteria applicable for independent educational evaluations as set forth in paragraph (e) of this section.

(3) For the purposes of this subpart—

(i) Independent educational evaluation means an evaluation conducted by a qualified examiner who is not employed by the public agency responsible for the education of the child in question; and

(ii) Public expense means that the public agency either pays for the full cost of the evaluation or ensures that the evaluation is otherwise provided at no cost to the parent, consistent with § 300.103.

(b) Parent right to evaluation at public expense.

(1) A parent has the right to an independent educational evaluation at public expense if the parent disagrees with an evaluation obtained by the public agency, subject to the conditions in paragraphs (b)(2) through (4) of this section.

(2) If a parent requests an independent educational evaluation at public expense, the public agency must, without unnecessary delay, either—

(i) File a due process complaint to request a hearing to show that its evaluation is appropriate; or

(ii) Ensure that an independent educational evaluation is provided at public expense, unless the agency demonstrates in a hearing pursuant to §§ 300.507 through 300.513 that the evaluation obtained by the parent did not meet agency criteria.

(3) If the public agency files a due process complaint notice to request a hearing and the final decision is that the agency's evaluation is appropriate, the parent still has the right to an independent educational evaluation, but not at public expense.

(4) If a parent requests an independent educational evaluation, the public agency may ask for the parent's reason why he or she objects to the public evaluation. However, the public agency may not require the parent to provide an explanation and may not unreasonably delay either providing the independent educational evaluation at public expense or

filing a due process complaint to request a due process hearing to defend the public evaluation.

(5) A parent is entitled to only one independent educational evaluation at public expense each time the public agency conducts an evaluation with which the parent disagrees.

(c) Parent-initiated evaluations. If the parent obtains an independent educational evaluation at public expense or shares with the public agency an evaluation obtained at private expense, the results of the evaluation—

(1) Must be considered by the public agency, if it meets agency criteria, in any decision made with respect to the provision of FAPE to the child; and

(2) May be presented by any party as evidence at a hearing on a due process complaint under subpart E of this part regarding that child.

(d) Requests for evaluations by hearing officers. If a hearing officer requests an independent educational evaluation as part of a hearing on a due process complaint, the cost of the evaluation must be at public expense.

(e) Agency criteria.

(1) If an independent educational evaluation is at public expense, the criteria under which the evaluation is obtained, including the location of the evaluation and the qualifications of the examiner, must be the same as the criteria that the public agency uses when it initiates an evaluation, to the extent those criteria are consistent with the parent's right to an independent educational evaluation.

(2) Except for the criteria described in paragraph (e)(1) of this section, a public agency may not impose conditions or timelines related to obtaining an independent educational evaluation at public expense.

§ 300.503 Prior notice by the public agency; content of notice.

(a) Notice. Written notice that meets the requirements of paragraph (b) of this section must be given to the parents of a child with a disability a reasonable time before the public agency—

(1) Proposes to initiate or change the identification, evaluation, or educational placement of the child or the provision of FAPE to the child; or

(2) Refuses to initiate or change the identification, evaluation, or educational placement of the child or the provision of FAPE to the child.

(b) Content of notice. The notice required under paragraph (a) of this section must include—

(1) A description of the action proposed or refused by the agency;

(2) An explanation of why the agency proposes or refuses to take the action;

(3) A description of each evaluation procedure, assessment, record, or report the agency used as a basis for the proposed or refused action;

(4) A statement that the parents of a child with a disability have protection under the procedural safeguards of this part and, if this notice is not an initial referral for evaluation, the means by which a copy of a description of the procedural safeguards can be obtained;

(5) Sources for parents to contact to obtain assistance in understanding the provisions of this part;

(6) A description of other options that the IEP Team considered and the reasons why those options were rejected; and

(7) A description of other factors that are relevant to the agency's proposal or refusal.

(c) Notice in understandable language.

(1) The notice required under paragraph (a) of this section must be—

(i) Written in language understandable to the general public; and

(ii) Provided in the native language of the parent or other mode of communication used by the parent, unless it is clearly not feasible to do so.

(2) If the native language or other mode of communication of the parent is not a written language, the public agency must take steps to ensure—

(i) That the notice is translated orally or by other means to the parent in his or her native language or other mode of communication;

(ii) That the parent understands the content of the notice; and

(iii) That there is written evidence that the requirements in paragraphs (c)(2)(i) and (ii) of this section have been met.

§ 300.504 Procedural safeguards notice.

(a) General. A copy of the procedural safeguards available to the parents of a child with a disability must be given to the parents only one time a school year, except that a copy also must be given to the parents—

(1) Upon initial referral or parent request for evaluation;

(2) Upon receipt of the first State complaint under §§ 300.151 through 300.153 and upon receipt of the first due process complaint under § 300.507 in a school year;

(3) In accordance with the discipline procedures in § 300.530(h); and

(4) Upon request by a parent.

(b) Internet Web site. A public agency may place a current copy of the procedural safeguards notice on its Internet Web site if a Web site exists.

(c) Contents. The procedural safeguards notice must include a full explanation of all of the procedural safeguards available under § 300.148, §§ 300.151 through 300.153, § 300.300, §§ 300.502 through 300.503, §§ 300.505 through 300.518, § 300.520, §§ 300.530 through 300.536 and §§ 300.610 through 300.625 relating to—

(1) Independent educational evaluations;

(2) Prior written notice;

(3) Parental consent;

(4) Access to education records;

(5) Opportunity to present and resolve complaints through the due process complaint and State complaint procedures, including—

(i) The time period in which to file a complaint;

(ii) The opportunity for the agency to resolve the complaint; and

(iii) The difference between the due process complaint and the State complaint procedures, including the jurisdiction of each procedure, what issues may be raised, filing and decisional timelines, and relevant procedures;

(6) The availability of mediation;

(7) The child's placement during the pendency of any due process complaint;

(8) Procedures for students who are subject to placement in an interim alternative educational setting;

(9) Requirements for unilateral placement by parents of children in private schools at public expense;

(10) Hearings on due process complaints, including requirements for disclosure of evaluation results and recommendations;

(11) State-level appeals (if applicable in the State);

(12) Civil actions, including the time period in which to file those actions; and

(13) Attorneys' fees.

(d) Notice in understandable language. The notice required under paragraph (a) of this section must meet the requirements of § 300.503(c).

§ 300.505 Electronic mail.

A parent of a child with a disability may elect to receive notices required by §§ 300.503, 300.504, and 300.508 by an electronic mail communication, if the public agency makes that option available.

§ 300.506 Mediation.

(a) General. Each public agency must ensure that procedures are established and implemented to allow parties to disputes involving any matter under this part, including matters arising prior to the filing of a due process complaint, to resolve disputes through a mediation process.

(b) Requirements. The procedures must meet the following requirements:

(1) The procedures must ensure that the mediation process—

(i) Is voluntary on the part of the parties;

(ii) Is not used to deny or delay a parent's right to a hearing on the parent's due process complaint, or to deny any other rights afforded under Part B of the Act; and

(iii) Is conducted by a qualified and impartial mediator who is trained in effective mediation techniques.

(2) A public agency may establish procedures to offer to parents and schools that choose not to use the mediation process, an opportunity to meet, at a time and location convenient to the parents, with a disinterested party—

(i) Who is under contract with an appropriate alternative dispute resolution entity, or a parent training and information center or community parent resource center in the State established under section 671 or 672 of the Act; and

(ii) Who would explain the benefits of, and encourage the use of, the mediation process to the parents.

(3)(i) The State must maintain a list of individuals who are qualified mediators and knowledgeable in laws and regulations relating to the provision of special education and related services.

(ii) The SEA must select mediators on a random, rotational, or other impartial basis.

(4) The State must bear the cost of the mediation process, including the costs of meetings described in paragraph (b)(2) of this section.

(5) Each session in the mediation process must be scheduled in a timely manner and must be held in a location that is convenient to the parties to the dispute.

(6) If the parties resolve a dispute through the mediation process, the parties must execute a legally binding agreement that sets forth that resolution and that—

(i) States that all discussions that occurred during the mediation process will remain confidential and may not be used as evidence in any subsequent due process hearing or civil proceeding; and

(ii) Is signed by both the parent and a representative of the agency who has the authority to bind such agency.

(7) A written, signed mediation agreement under this paragraph is enforceable in any State court of competent jurisdiction or in a district court of the United States.

Discussions that occur during the mediation process must be confidential and may not be used as evidence in any subsequent due process hearing or civil proceeding of any Federal court or State court of a State receiving assistance under this part.

(c) Impartiality of mediator.

(1) An individual who serves as a mediator under this part—

(i) May not be an employee of the SEA or the LEA that is involved in the education or care of the child; and

(ii) Must not have a personal or professional interest that conflicts with the person's objectivity.

(2) A person who otherwise qualifies as a mediator is not an employee of an LEA or State agency described under § 300.228 solely because he or she is paid by the agency to serve as a mediator.

§ 300.507 Filing a due process complaint.

(a) General.

(1) A parent or a public agency may file a due process complaint on any of the matters described in § 300.503(a)(1) and (2) (relating to the identification, evaluation or educational placement of a child with a disability, or the provision of FAPE to the child).

(2) The due process complaint must allege a violation that occurred not more than two years before the date the parent or public agency knew or should have known about the alleged action that forms the basis of the due process complaint, or, if the State has an explicit time limitation for filing a due process complaint under this part, in the time allowed by that State law, except that the exceptions to the timeline described in § 300.511(f) apply to the timeline in this section.

(b) Information for parents. The public agency must inform the parent of any free or low-cost legal and other relevant services available in the area if—

(1) The parent requests the information; or

(2) The parent or the agency files a due process complaint under this section.

§ 300.508 Due process complaint.

(a) General.

(1) The public agency must have procedures that require either party, or the attorney representing a party, to provide to the other party a due process complaint (which must remain confidential).

(2) The party filing a due process complaint must forward a copy of the due process complaint to the SEA.

(b) Content of complaint. The due process complaint required in paragraph (a)(1) of this section must include—

(1) The name of the child;

(2) The address of the residence of the child;

(3) The name of the school the child is attending;

(4) In the case of a homeless child or youth (within the meaning of section 725(2) of the McKinney-Vento Homeless Assistance Act (42 U.S.C. 11434a(2)), available contact information for the child, and the name of the school the child is attending;

(5) A description of the nature of the problem of the child relating to the proposed or refused initiation or change, including facts relating to the problem; and

(6) A proposed resolution of the problem to the extent known and available to the party at the time.

(c) Notice required before a hearing on a due process complaint. A party may not have a hearing on a due process complaint until the party, or the attorney representing the party, files a due process complaint that meets the requirements of paragraph (b) of this section.

(d) Sufficiency of complaint.

(1) The due process complaint required by this section must be deemed sufficient unless the party receiving the due process complaint notifies the hearing officer and the other party in writing, within 15 days of receipt of the due process complaint, that the receiving party believes the due process complaint does not meet the requirements in paragraph (b) of this section.

(2) Within five days of receipt of notification under paragraph (d)(1) of this section, the hearing officer must make a determination on the face of the due process complaint of whether the due process complaint meets the requirements of paragraph (b) of this section, and must immediately notify the parties in writing of that determination.

(3) A party may amend its due process complaint only if—

(i) The other party consents in writing to the amendment and is given the opportunity to resolve the due process complaint through a meeting held pursuant to § 300.510; or

(ii) The hearing officer grants permission, except that the hearing officer may only grant permission to amend at any time not later than five days before the due process hearing begins.

(4) If a party files an amended due process complaint, the timelines for the resolution meeting in § 300.510(a) and the time period to resolve in § 300.510(b) begin again with the filing of the amended due process complaint.

(e) LEA response to a due process complaint.

(1) If the LEA has not sent a prior written notice under § 300.503 to the parent regarding the subject matter contained in the parent's due process complaint, the LEA must, within 10 days of receiving the due process complaint, send to the parent a response that includes—

(i) An explanation of why the agency proposed or refused to take the action raised in the due process complaint;

(ii) A description of other options that the IEP Team considered and the reasons why those options were rejected;

(iii) A description of each evaluation procedure, assessment, record, or report the agency used as the basis for the proposed or refused action; and

(iv) A description of the other factors that are relevant to the agency's proposed or refused action.

(2) A response by an LEA under paragraph (e)(1) of this section shall not be construed to preclude the LEA from asserting that the parent's due process complaint was insufficient, where appropriate.

(f) Other party response to a due process complaint. Except as provided in paragraph (e) of this section, the party receiving a due process complaint must, within 10 days of receiving the due process complaint, send to the other party a response that specifically addresses the issues raised in the due process complaint.

§ 300.509 Model forms.

(a) Each SEA must develop model forms to assist parents and public agencies in filing a due process complaint in accordance with §§ 300.507(a) and 300.508(a) through (c) and to assist parents and other parties in filing a State complaint under §§ 300.151 through 300.153. However, the SEA or LEA may not require the use of the model forms.

(b) Parents, public agencies, and other parties may use the appropriate model form described in paragraph (a) of this section, or another form or other document, so long as the form or document that is used meets, as appropriate, the content requirements in § 300.508(b) for filing a due process complaint, or the requirements in § 300.153(b) for filing a State complaint.

§ 300.510 Resolution process.

(a) Resolution meeting.

(1) Within 15 days of receiving notice of the parent's due process complaint, and prior to the initiation of a due process hearing under § 300.511, the LEA must convene a meeting with the parent and the relevant member or members of the IEP Team who have specific knowledge of the facts identified in the due process complaint that—

(i) Includes a representative of the public agency who has decision-making authority on behalf of that agency; and

(ii) May not include an attorney of the LEA unless the parent is accompanied by an attorney.

(2) The purpose of the meeting is for the parent of the child to discuss the due process complaint, and the facts that form the basis of the due process complaint, so that the LEA has the opportunity to resolve the dispute that is the basis for the due process complaint.

(3) The meeting described in paragraph (a)(1) and (2) of this section need not be held if—

(i) The parent and the LEA agree in writing to waive the meeting; or

(ii) The parent and the LEA agree to use the mediation process described in § 300.506.

(4) The parent and the LEA determine the relevant members of the IEP Team to attend the meeting.

(b) Resolution period.

(1) If the LEA has not resolved the due process complaint to the satisfaction of the parent within 30 days of the receipt of the due process complaint, the due process hearing may occur.

(2) Except as provided in paragraph (c) of this section, the timeline for issuing a final decision under § 300.515 begins at the expiration of this 30-day period.

(3) Except where the parties have jointly agreed to waive the resolution process or to use mediation, notwithstanding paragraphs (b)(1) and (2) of this section, the failure of the parent filing a due process complaint to participate in the resolution meeting will delay the timelines for the resolution process and due process hearing until the meeting is held.

(4) If the LEA is unable to obtain the participation of the parent in the resolution meeting after reasonable efforts have been made (and documented using the procedures in § 300.322(d)), the LEA may, at the conclusion of the 30-day period, request that a hearing officer dismiss the parent's due process complaint.

(5) If the LEA fails to hold the resolution meeting specified in paragraph (a) of this section within 15 days of receiving notice of a parent's due process complaint or fails to participate in the resolution meeting, the parent may seek the intervention of a hearing officer to begin the due process hearing timeline.

(c) Adjustments to 30-day resolution period. The 45-day timeline for the due process hearing in § 300.515(a) starts the day after one of the following events:

(1) Both parties agree in writing to waive the resolution meeting;

(2) After either the mediation or resolution meeting starts but before the end of the 30-day period, the parties agree in writing that no agreement is possible;

(3) If both parties agree in writing to continue the mediation at the end of the 30-day resolution period, but later, the parent or public agency withdraws from the mediation process.

(d) Written settlement agreement. If a resolution to the dispute is reached at the meeting described in paragraphs (a)(1) and (2) of this section, the parties must execute a legally binding agreement that is—

(1) Signed by both the parent and a representative of the agency who has the authority to bind the agency; and

(2) Enforceable in any State court of competent jurisdiction or in a district court of the United States, or, by the SEA, if the State has other mechanisms or procedures that permit

parties to seek enforcement of resolution agreements, pursuant to § 300.537.

(e) *Agreement review period.* If the parties execute an agreement pursuant to paragraph (c) of this section, a party may void the agreement within 3 business days of the agreement's execution.

§ 300.511 Impartial due process hearing.

(a) *General.* Whenever a due process complaint is received under § 300.507 or § 300.532, the parents or the LEA involved in the dispute must have an opportunity for an impartial due process hearing, consistent with the procedures in §§ 300.507, 300.508, and 300.510.

(b) *Agency responsible for conducting the due process hearing.* The hearing described in paragraph (a) of this section must be conducted by the SEA or the public agency directly responsible for the education of the child, as determined under State statute, State regulation, or a written policy of the SEA.

(c) *Impartial hearing officer.*

(1) At a minimum, a hearing officer—

(i) Must not be—

(A) An employee of the SEA or the LEA that is involved in the education or care of the child; or

(B) A person having a personal or professional interest that conflicts with the person's objectivity in the hearing;

(ii) Must possess knowledge of, and the ability to understand, the provisions of the Act, Federal and State regulations pertaining to the Act, and legal interpretations of the Act by Federal and State courts;

(iii) Must possess the knowledge and ability to conduct hearings in accordance with appropriate, standard legal practice; and

(iv) Must possess the knowledge and ability to render and write decisions in accordance with appropriate, standard legal practice.

(2) A person who otherwise qualifies to conduct a hearing under paragraph (c)(1) of this section is not an employee of the agency solely because he or she is paid by the agency to serve as a hearing officer.

(3) Each public agency must keep a list of the persons who serve as hearing officers. The list must include a statement of the qualifications of each of those persons.

(d) *Subject matter of due process hearings.* The party requesting the due process hearing may not raise issues at the due process hearing that were not raised in the due process complaint filed under § 300.508(b), unless the other party agrees otherwise.

(e) *Timeline for requesting a hearing.* A parent or agency must request an impartial hearing on their due process complaint within two years of the date the parent or agency knew or should have known about the alleged action that forms the basis of the due process complaint, or if the State has an explicit time limitation for requesting such a due process hearing under this part, in the time allowed by that State law.

(f) *Exceptions to the timeline.* The timeline described in paragraph (e) of this section does not apply to a parent if the parent was prevented from filing a due process complaint due to—

(1) Specific misrepresentations by the LEA that it had resolved the problem forming the basis of the due process complaint; or

(2) The LEA's withholding of information from the parent that was required under this part to be provided to the parent.

§ 300.512 Hearing rights.

(a) *General.* Any party to a hearing conducted pursuant to §§ 300.507 through 300.513 or §§ 300.530 through 300.534, or an appeal conducted pursuant to § 300.514, has the right to—

(1) Be accompanied and advised by counsel and by individuals with special knowledge or training with respect to the problems of children with disabilities;

(2) Present evidence and confront, cross-examine, and compel the attendance of witnesses;

(3) Prohibit the introduction of any evidence at the hearing that has not been disclosed to that party at least five business days before the hearing;

(4) Obtain a written, or, at the option of the parents, electronic, verbatim record of the hearing; and

(5) Obtain written, or, at the option of the parents, electronic findings of fact and decisions.

(b) *Additional disclosure of information.*

(1) At least five business days prior to a hearing conducted pursuant to § 300.511(a), each party must disclose to all other parties all evaluations completed by that date and recommendations based on the offering party's evaluations that the party intends to use at the hearing.

(2) A hearing officer may bar any party that fails to comply with paragraph (b)(1) of this section from introducing the relevant evaluation or recommendation at the hearing without the consent of the other party.

(c) *Parental rights at hearings.* Parents involved in hearings must be given the right to—

(1) Have the child who is the subject of the hearing present;

(2) Open the hearing to the public; and

(3) Have the record of the hearing and the findings of fact and decisions described in paragraphs (a)(4) and (a)(5) of this section provided at no cost to parents.

§ 300.513 Hearing decisions.

(a) *Decision of hearing officer on the provision of FAPE.*

(1) Subject to paragraph (a)(2) of this section, a hearing officer's determination of whether a child received FAPE must be based on substantive grounds.

(2) In matters alleging a procedural violation, a hearing officer may find that a child did not receive a FAPE only if the procedural inadequacies—

    (i) Impeded the child's right to a FAPE;

    (ii) Significantly impeded the parent's opportunity to participate in the decision-making process regarding the provision of a FAPE to the parent's child; or

    (iii) Caused a deprivation of educational benefit.

(3) Nothing in paragraph (a) of this section shall be construed to preclude a hearing officer from ordering an LEA to comply with procedural requirements under §§ 300.500 through 300.536.

(b) *Construction clause.* Nothing in §§ 300.507 through 300.513 shall be construed to affect the right of a parent to file an appeal of the due process hearing decision with the SEA under § 300.514(b), if a State level appeal is available.

(c) *Separate request for a due process hearing.* Nothing in §§ 300.500 through 300.536 shall be construed to preclude a parent from filing a separate due process complaint on an issue separate from a due process complaint already filed.

(d) *Findings and decision to advisory panel and general public.* The public agency, after deleting any personally identifiable information, must—

(1) Transmit the findings and decisions referred to in § 300.512(a)(5) to the State advisory panel established under § 300.167; and

(2) Make those findings and decisions available to the public.

§ 300.514 Finality of decision; appeal; impartial review.

(a) *Finality of hearing decision.* A decision made in a hearing conducted pursuant to §§ 300.507 through 300.513 or §§ 300.530 through 300.534 is final, except that any party involved in the hearing may appeal the decision under the provisions of paragraph (b) of this section and § 300.516.

(b) *Appeal of decisions; impartial review.*

(1) If the hearing required by § 300.511 is conducted by a public agency other than the SEA, any party aggrieved by the findings and decision in the hearing may appeal to the SEA.

(2) If there is an appeal, the SEA must conduct an impartial review of the findings and decision appealed. The official conducting the review must—

    (i) Examine the entire hearing record;

    (ii) Ensure that the procedures at the hearing were consistent with the requirements of due process;

    (iii) Seek additional evidence if necessary. If a hearing is held to receive additional evidence, the rights in § 300.512 apply;

    (iv) Afford the parties an opportunity for oral or written argument, or both, at the discretion of the reviewing official;

    (v) Make an independent decision on completion of the review; and

(vi) Give a copy of the written, or, at the option of the parents, electronic findings of fact and decisions to the parties.

(c) *Findings and decision to advisory panel and general public.* The SEA, after deleting any personally identifiable information, must—

(1) Transmit the findings and decisions referred to in paragraph (b)(2)(vi) of this section to the State advisory panel established under § 300.167; and

(2) Make those findings and decisions available to the public.

(d) *Finality of review decision.* The decision made by the reviewing official is final unless a party brings a civil action under § 300.516.

§ 300.515 Timelines and convenience of hearings and reviews.

(a) The public agency must ensure that not later than 45 days after the expiration of the 30 day period under § 300.510(b), or the adjusted time periods described in § 300.510(c)—

(1) A final decision is reached in the hearing; and

(2) A copy of the decision is mailed to each of the parties.

(b) The SEA must ensure that not later than 30 days after the receipt of a request for a review—

(1) A final decision is reached in the review; and

(2) A copy of the decision is mailed to each of the parties.

(c) A hearing or reviewing officer may grant specific extensions of time beyond the periods set out in paragraphs (a) and (b) of this section at the request of either party.

(d) Each hearing and each review involving oral arguments must be conducted at a time and place that is reasonably convenient to the parents and child involved.

§ 300.516 Civil action.

(a) *General.* Any party aggrieved by the findings and decision made under §§ 300.507 through 300.513 or §§ 300.530 through 300.534 who does not have the right to an appeal under § 300.514(b), and any party aggrieved by the findings and decision under § 300.514(b), has the right to bring a civil action with respect to the due process complaint notice requesting a due process hearing under § 300.507 or §§ 300.530 through 300.532. The action may be brought in any State court of competent jurisdiction or in a district court of the United States without regard to the amount in controversy.

(b) *Time limitation.* The party bringing the action shall have 90 days from the date of the decision of the hearing officer or, if applicable, the decision of the State review official, to file a civil action, or, if the State has an explicit time limitation for bringing civil actions under Part B of the Act, in the time allowed by that State law.

(c) *Additional requirements.* In any action brought under paragraph (a) of this section, the court—

(1) Receives the records of the administrative proceedings;

(2) Hears additional evidence at the request of a party; and

(3) Basing its decision on the preponderance of the evidence, grants the relief that the court determines to be appropriate.

(d) *Jurisdiction of district courts.* The district courts of the United States have jurisdiction of actions brought under section 615 of the Act without regard to the amount in controversy.

(e) *Rule of construction.* Nothing in this part restricts or limits the rights, procedures, and remedies available under the Constitution, the Americans with Disabilities Act of 1990, title V of the Rehabilitation Act of 1973, or other Federal laws protecting the rights of children with disabilities, except that before the filing of a civil action under these laws seeking relief that is also available under section 615 of the Act, the procedures under §§ 300.507 and 300.514 must be exhausted to the same extent as would be required had the action been brought under section 615 of the Act.

§ 300.517 Attorneys' fees.

(a) *In general.*

(1) In any action or proceeding brought under section 615 of the Act, the court, in its discretion, may award reasonable attorneys' fees as part of the costs to—

(i) The prevailing party who is the parent of a child with a disability;

(ii) To a prevailing party who is an SEA or LEA against the attorney of a parent who files a complaint or subsequent cause of action that is frivolous, unreasonable, or without foundation, or against the attorney of a parent who continued to litigate after the litigation clearly became frivolous, unreasonable, or without foundation; or

(iii) To a prevailing SEA or LEA against the attorney of a parent, or against the parent, if the parent's request for a due process hearing or subsequent cause of action was presented for any improper purpose, such as to harass, to cause unnecessary delay, or to needlessly increase the cost of litigation.

(2) Nothing in this subsection shall be construed to affect section 327 of the District of Columbia Appropriations Act, 2005.

(b) Prohibition on use of funds.

(1) Funds under Part B of the Act may not be used to pay attorneys' fees or costs of a party related to any action or proceeding under section 615 of the Act and subpart E of this part.

(2) Paragraph (b)(1) of this section does not preclude a public agency from using funds under Part B of the Act for conducting an action or proceeding under section 615 of the Act.

(c) Award of fees. A court awards reasonable attorneys' fees under section 615(i)(3) of the Act consistent with the following:

(1) Fees awarded under section 615(i)(3) of the Act must be based on rates prevailing in the community in which the action or proceeding arose for the kind and quality of services furnished. No bonus or multiplier may be used in calculating the fees awarded under this paragraph.

(2)(i) Attorneys' fees may not be awarded and related costs may not be reimbursed in any action or proceeding under section 615 of the Act for services performed subsequent to the time of a written offer of settlement to a parent if—

(A) The offer is made within the time prescribed by Rule 68 of the Federal Rules of Civil Procedure or, in the case of an administrative proceeding, at any time more than 10 days before the proceeding begins;

(B) The offer is not accepted within 10 days; and

(C) The court or administrative hearing officer finds that the relief finally obtained by the parents is not more favorable to the parents than the offer of settlement.

(ii) Attorneys' fees may not be awarded relating to any meeting of the IEP Team unless the meeting is convened as a result of an administrative proceeding or judicial action, or at the discretion of the State, for a mediation described in § 300.506.

(iii) A meeting conducted pursuant to § 300.510 shall not be considered—

(A) A meeting convened as a result of an administrative hearing or judicial action; or

(B) An administrative hearing or judicial action for purposes of this section.

(3) Notwithstanding paragraph (c)(2) of this section, an award of attorneys' fees and related costs may be made to a parent who is the prevailing party and who was substantially justified in rejecting the settlement offer.

(4) Except as provided in paragraph (c)(5) of this section, the court reduces, accordingly, the amount of the attorneys' fees awarded under section 615 of the Act, if the court finds that—

(i) The parent, or the parent's attorney, during the course of the action or proceeding, unreasonably protracted the final resolution of the controversy;

(ii) The amount of the attorneys' fees otherwise authorized to be awarded unreasonably exceeds the hourly rate prevailing in the community for similar services by attorneys of reasonably comparable skill, reputation, and experience;

(iii) The time spent and legal services furnished were excessive considering the nature of the action or proceeding; or

(iv) The attorney representing the parent did not provide to the LEA the appropriate information in the due process request notice in accordance with § 300.508.

(5) The provisions of paragraph (c)(4) of this section do not apply in any action or proceeding if the court finds that the State or local agency unreasonably protracted the final resolution of the action or proceeding or there was a violation of section 615 of the Act.

§ 300.518 Child's status during proceedings.

(a) Except as provided in § 300.533, during the pendency of any administrative or judicial proceeding regarding a due process complaint notice requesting a due process hearing under § 300.507, unless the State or local agency and the parents of the child agree otherwise, the child involved in the complaint must remain in his or her current educational placement.

(b) If the complaint involves an application for initial admission to public school, the child, with the consent of the parents, must be placed in the public school until the completion of all the proceedings.

(c) If the complaint involves an application for initial services under this part from a child who is transitioning from Part C of the Act to Part B and is no longer eligible for Part C services because the child has turned three, the public agency is not required to provide the Part C services that the child had been receiving. If the child is found eligible for special education and related services under Part B and the parent consents to the initial provision of special education and related services under § 300.300(b), then the public agency must provide those special education and related services that are not in dispute between the parent and the public agency.

(d) If the hearing officer in a due process hearing conducted by the SEA or a State review official in an administrative appeal agrees with the child's parents that a change of placement is appropriate, that placement must be treated as an agreement between the State and the parents for purposes of paragraph (a) of this section.

§ 300.519 Surrogate parents.

(a) General. Each public agency must ensure that the rights of a child are protected when—

(1) No parent (as defined in § 300.30) can be identified;

(2) The public agency, after reasonable efforts, cannot locate a parent;

(3) The child is a ward of the State under the laws of that State; or

(4) The child is an unaccompanied homeless youth as defined in section 725(6) of the McKinney-Vento Homeless Assistance Act (42 U.S.C. 11434a(6)).

(b) Duties of public agency. The duties of a public agency under paragraph (a) of this section include the assignment of an individual to act as a surrogate for the parents. This must include a method—

(1) For determining whether a child needs a surrogate parent; and

(2) For assigning a surrogate parent to the child.

(c) Wards of the State. In the case of a child who is a ward of the State, the surrogate parent alternatively may be appointed by the judge overseeing the child's case, provided that the surrogate meets the requirements in paragraphs (d)(2)(i) and (e) of this section.

(d) Criteria for selection of surrogate parents.

(1) The public agency may select a surrogate parent in any way permitted under State law.

(2) Public agencies must ensure that a person selected as a surrogate parent—

(i) Is not an employee of the SEA, the LEA, or any other agency that is involved in the education or care of the child;

(ii) Has no personal or professional interest that conflicts with the interest of the child the surrogate parent represents; and

(iii) Has knowledge and skills that ensure adequate representation of the child.

(e) Non-employee requirement; compensation. A person otherwise qualified to be a surrogate parent under paragraph (d) of this section is not an employee of the agency solely because he or she is paid by the agency to serve as a surrogate parent.

(f) Unaccompanied homeless youth. In the case of a child who is an unaccompanied homeless youth, appropriate staff of emergency shelters, transitional shelters, independent living programs, and street outreach programs may be appointed as temporary surrogate parents without regard to paragraph (d)(2)(i) of this section, until a surrogate parent can be appointed that meets all of the requirements of paragraph (d) of this section.

(g) Surrogate parent responsibilities. The surrogate parent may represent the child in all matters relating to—

(1) The identification, evaluation, and educational placement of the child; and

(2) The provision of FAPE to the child.

(h) SEA responsibility. The SEA must make reasonable efforts to ensure the assignment of a surrogate parent not more than 30 days after a public agency determines that the child needs a surrogate parent.

§ 300.520 Transfer of parental rights at age of majority.

(a) General. A State may provide that, when a child with a disability reaches the age of majority under State law that applies to all children (except for a child with a disability who has been determined to be incompetent under State law)—

(1)(i) The public agency must provide any notice required by this part to both the child and the parents; and

(ii) All rights accorded to parents under Part B of the Act transfer to the child;

(2) All rights accorded to parents under Part B of the Act transfer to children who are incarcerated in an adult or juvenile, State or local correctional institution; and

(3) Whenever a State provides for the transfer of rights under this part pursuant to paragraph (a)(1) or (a)(2) of this section, the agency must notify the child and the parents of the transfer of rights.

(b) Special rule. A State must establish procedures for appointing the parent of a child with a disability, or, if the parent is not available, another appropriate individual, to represent the educational interests of the child throughout the period of the child's eligibility under Part B of the Act if, under State law, a child who has reached the age of majority, but has not been determined to be incompetent, can be determined not to have the ability to provide informed consent with respect to the child's educational program.

§§ 300.521 to 300.529 [Reserved]
§§ 300.521 to 300.529 [Reserved]

Discipline Procedures

§ 300.530 Authority of school personnel.

(a) Case-by-case determination. School personnel may consider any unique circumstances on a case-by-case basis when determining whether a change in placement, consistent with the other requirements of this section, is appropriate for a child with a disability who violates a code of student conduct.

(b) General.

(1) School personnel under this section may remove a child with a disability who violates a code of student conduct from his or her current placement to an appropriate interim alternative educational setting, another setting, or suspension, for not more than 10 consecutive school days (to the extent those alternatives are applied to children without disabilities), and for additional removals of not more than 10 consecutive school days in that same school year for separate incidents of misconduct (as long as those removals do not constitute a change of placement under § 300.536).

(2) After a child with a disability has been removed from his or her current placement for 10 school days in the same school year, during any subsequent days of removal the public agency must provide services to the extent required under paragraph (d) of this section.

(c) Additional authority. For disciplinary changes in placement that would exceed 10 consecutive school days, if the behavior that gave rise to the violation of the school code is determined not to be a manifestation of the child's disability pursuant to paragraph (e) of this section, school personnel may apply the relevant disciplinary procedures to children with disabilities in the same manner and for the same duration as the procedures would be applied to children without disabilities, except as provided in paragraph (d) of this section.

(d) Services.

(1) A child with a disability who is removed from the child's current placement pursuant to paragraphs (c), or (g) of this section must—

(i) Continue to receive educational services, as provided in § 300.101(a), so as to enable the child to continue to participate in the general education curriculum, although in another setting, and to progress toward meeting the goals set out in the child's IEP; and

(ii) Receive, as appropriate, a functional behavioral assessment, and behavioral intervention services and modifications, that are designed to address the behavior violation so that it does not recur.

(2) The services required by paragraph (d)(1), (d)(3), (d)(4), and (d)(5) of this section may be provided in an interim alternative educational setting.

(3) A public agency is only required to provide services during periods of removal to a child with a disability who has been removed from his or her current placement for 10 school days or less in that school year, if it provides services to a child without disabilities who is similarly removed.

(4) After a child with a disability has been removed from his or her current placement for 10 school days in the same school year, if the current removal is for not more than 10 consecutive school days and is not a change of placement under § 300.536, school personnel, in consultation with at least one of the child's teachers, determine the extent to which services are needed, as provided in § 300.101(a), so as to enable the child to continue to participate in the general education curriculum, although in another setting, and to progress toward meeting the goals set out in the child's IEP.

(5) If the removal is a change of placement under § 300.536, the child's IEP Team determines appropriate services under paragraph (d)(1) of this section.

(e) Manifestation determination.

(1) Within 10 school days of any decision to change the placement of a child with a disability because of a violation of a code of student conduct, the LEA, the parent, and relevant members of the child's IEP Team (as determined by the parent and the LEA) must review all relevant information in the student's file, including the child's IEP, any teacher observations, and any relevant information provided by the parents to determine—

(i) If the conduct in question was caused by, or had a direct and substantial relationship to, the child's disability; or

(ii) If the conduct in question was the direct result of the LEA's failure to implement the IEP.

(2) The conduct must be determined to be a manifestation of the child's disability if the LEA, the parent, and relevant members of the child's IEP Team determine that a condition in either paragraph (e)(1)(i) or (1)(ii) of this section was met.

(3) If the LEA, the parent, and relevant members of the child's IEP Team determine the condition described in paragraph (e)(1)(ii) of this section was met, the LEA must take immediate steps to remedy those deficiencies.

(f) Determination that behavior was a manifestation. If the LEA, the parent, and relevant members of the IEP Team make the determination that the conduct was a manifestation of the child's disability, the IEP Team must—

(1) Either—

(i) Conduct a functional behavioral assessment, unless the LEA had conducted a functional behavioral assessment before the behavior that resulted in the change of placement occurred, and implement a behavioral intervention plan for the child; or

(ii) If a behavioral intervention plan already has been developed, review the behavioral intervention plan, and modify it, as necessary, to address the behavior; and

(2) Except as provided in paragraph (g) of this section, return the child to the placement from which the child was removed, unless the parent and the LEA agree to a change of placement as part of the modification of the behavioral intervention plan.

(g) Special circumstances. School personnel may remove a student to an interim alternative educational setting for not more than 45 school days without regard to whether the behavior is determined to be a manifestation of the child's disability, if the child—

(1) Carries a weapon to or possesses a weapon at school, on school premises, or to or at a school function under the jurisdiction of an SEA or an LEA;

(2) Knowingly possesses or uses illegal drugs, or sells or solicits the sale of a controlled substance, while at school, on school premises, or at a school function under the jurisdiction of an SEA or an LEA; or

(3) Has inflicted serious bodily injury upon another person while at school, on school premises, or at a school function under the jurisdiction of an SEA or an LEA.

(h) Notification. On the date on which the decision is made to make a removal that constitutes a change of placement of a child with a disability because of a violation of a code of student conduct, the LEA must notify the parents of that decision, and provide the parents the procedural safeguards notice described in § 300.504.

(i) Definitions. For purposes of this section, the following definitions apply:

(1) Controlled substance means a drug or other substance identified under schedules I, II, III, IV, or V in section 202(c) of the Controlled Substances Act (21 U.S.C. 812(c)).

(2) Illegal drug means a controlled substance; but does not include a controlled substance that is legally possessed or used under the supervision of a licensed health-care professional or that is legally possessed or used under any other authority under that Act or under any other provision of Federal law.

(3) Serious bodily injury has the meaning given the term "serious bodily injury" under paragraph (3) of subsection (h) of section 1365 of title 18, United States Code.

(4) Weapon has the meaning given the term "dangerous weapon" under paragraph (2) of the first subsection (g) of section 930 of title 18, United States Code.

§ 300.531 Determination of setting.

The child's IEP Team determines the interim alternative educational setting for services under § 300.530(c), (d)(5), and (g).

§ 300.532 Appeal.

(a) General. The parent of a child with a disability who disagrees with any decision regarding placement under §§ 300.530 and 300.531, or the manifestation determination under § 300.530(e), or an LEA that believes that maintaining the current placement of the child is substantially likely to result in injury to the child or others, may appeal the decision by requesting a hearing. The hearing is requested by filing a complaint pursuant to §§ 300.507 and 300.508(a) and (b).

(b) Authority of hearing officer.

(1) A hearing officer under § 300.511 hears, and makes a determination regarding an appeal under paragraph (a) of this section.

(2) In making the determination under paragraph (b)(1) of this section, the hearing officer may—

(i) Return the child with a disability to the placement from which the child was removed if the hearing officer determines that the removal was a violation of § 300.530 or that the child's behavior was a manifestation of the child's disability; or

(ii) Order a change of placement of the child with a disability to an appropriate interim alternative educational setting for not more than 45 school days if the hearing officer determines that maintaining the current placement of the child is substantially likely to result in injury to the child or to others.

(3) The procedures under paragraphs (a) and (b)(1) and (2) of this section may be repeated, if the LEA believes that returning the child to the original placement is substantially likely to result in injury to the child or to others.

(c) Expedited due process hearing.

(1) Whenever a hearing is requested under paragraph (a) of this section, the parents or the LEA involved in the dispute must have an opportunity for an impartial due process hearing consistent with the requirements of §§ 300.507 and 300.508(a) through (c) and §§ 300.510 through 300.514, except as provided in paragraph (c)(2) through (4) of this section.

(2) The SEA or LEA is responsible for arranging the expedited due process hearing, which must occur within 20 school days of the date the complaint requesting the hearing is filed. The hearing officer must make a determination within 10 school days after the hearing.

(3) Unless the parents and LEA agree in writing to waive the resolution meeting described in paragraph (c)(3)(i) of this section, or agree to use the mediation process described in § 300.506—

(i) A resolution meeting must occur within seven days of receiving notice of the due process complaint; and

(ii) The due process hearing may proceed unless the matter has been resolved to the satisfaction of both parties within 15 days of the receipt of the due process complaint.

(4) A State may establish different State-imposed procedural rules for expedited due process hearings conducted under this section than it has established for other due process hearings, but, except for the timelines as mod-

ified in paragraph (c)(3) of this section, the State must ensure that the requirements in §§ 300.510 through 300.514 are met.

(5) The decisions on expedited due process hearings are appealable consistent with § 300.514.

§ 300.533 Placement during appeals.

When an appeal under § 300.532 has been made by either the parent or the LEA, the child must remain in the interim alternative educational setting pending the decision of the hearing officer or until the expiration of the time period specified in § 300.530(c) or (g), whichever occurs first, unless the parent and the SEA or LEA agree otherwise.

§ 300.534 Protections for children not determined eligible for special education and related services.

(a) General. A child who has not been determined to be eligible for special education and related services under this part and who has engaged in behavior that violated a code of student conduct, may assert any of the protections provided for in this part if the public agency had knowledge (as determined in accordance with paragraph (b) of this section) that the child was a child with a disability before the behavior that precipitated the disciplinary action occurred.

(b) Basis of knowledge. A public agency must be deemed to have knowledge that a child is a child with a disability if before the behavior that precipitated the disciplinary action occurred—

(1) The parent of the child expressed concern in writing to supervisory or administrative personnel of the appropriate educational agency, or a teacher of the child, that the child is in need of special education and related services;

(2) The parent of the child requested an evaluation of the child pursuant to §§ 300.300 through 300.311; or

(3) The teacher of the child, or other personnel of the LEA, expressed specific concerns about a pattern of behavior demonstrated by the child directly to the director of special education of the agency or to other supervisory personnel of the agency.

(c) Exception. A public agency would not be deemed to have knowledge under paragraph (b) of this section if—

(1) The parent of the child—

(i) Has not allowed an evaluation of the child pursuant to §§ 300.300 through 300.311; or

(ii) Has refused services under this part; or

(2) The child has been evaluated in accordance with §§ 300.300 through 300.311 and determined to not be a child with a disability under this part.

(d) Conditions that apply if no basis of knowledge.

(1) If a public agency does not have knowledge that a child is a child with a disability (in accordance with paragraphs (b) and (c) of this section) prior to taking disciplinary measures against the child, the child may be subjected to the disciplinary measures applied to children without disabilities who engage in comparable behaviors consistent with paragraph (d)(2) of this section.

(2)(i) If a request is made for an evaluation of a child during the time period in which the child is subjected to disciplinary measures under § 300.530, the evaluation must be conducted in an expedited manner.

(ii) Until the evaluation is completed, the child remains in the educational placement determined by school authorities, which can include suspension or expulsion without educational services.

(iii) If the child is determined to be a child with a disability, taking into consideration information from the evaluation conducted by the agency and information provided by the parents, the agency must provide special education and related services in accordance with this part, including the requirements of §§ 300.530 through 300.536 and section 612(a)(1)(A) of the Act.

§ 300.535 Referral to and action by law enforcement and judicial authorities.

(a) Rule of construction. Nothing in this part prohibits an agency from reporting a crime committed by a child with a disability to appropriate authorities or prevents State law enforcement and judicial authorities from exercising their responsibilities with regard to the application of Federal and State law to crimes committed by a child with a disability.

(b) Transmittal of records.

(1) An agency reporting a crime committed by a child with a disability must ensure that copies of the special education and disciplinary records of the child are transmitted for consideration by the appropriate authorities to whom the agency reports the crime.

(2) An agency reporting a crime under this section may transmit copies of the child's special education and disciplinary records only to the extent that the transmission is permitted by the Family Educational Rights and Privacy Act.

§ 300.536 Change of placement because of disciplinary removals.

(a) For purposes of removals of a child with a disability from the child's current educational placement under §§ 300.530 through 300.535, a change of placement occurs if—

(1) The removal is for more than 10 consecutive school days; or

(2) The child has been subjected to a series of removals that constitute a pattern—

(i) Because the series of removals total more than 10 school days in a school year;

(ii) Because the child's behavior is substantially similar to the child's behavior in previous incidents that resulted in the series of removals; and

(iii) Because of such additional factors as the length of each removal, the total amount of time the child has been removed, and the proximity of the removals to one another.

(b)(1) The public agency determines on a case-by-case basis whether a pattern of removals constitutes a change of placement.

(2) This determination is subject to review through due process and judicial proceedings.

§ 300.537 State enforcement mechanisms.

Notwithstanding §§ 300.506(b)(7) and 300.510(d)(2), which provide for judicial enforcement of a written agreement reached as a result of mediation or a resolution meeting, there is nothing in this part that would prevent the SEA from using other mechanisms to seek enforcement of that agreement, provided that use of those mechanisms is not mandatory and does not delay or deny a party the right to seek enforcement of the written agreement in a State court of competent jurisdiction or in a district court of the United States.

§§ 300.538 to 300.599 [Reserved]
§§ 300.538 to 300.599 [Reserved]
§ 300.600 – 300.818 [omitted]

United Nations Convention on the Rights of Persons with Disabilities
Resolution adopted by the General Assembly
[*without reference to a Main Committee (A/61/611)*]

61/106. Convention on the Rights of Persons with Disabilities

The General Assembly,

Recalling its resolution 56/168 of 19 December 2001, by which it decided to establish an Ad Hoc Committee, open to the participation of all Member States and observers to the United Nations, to consider proposals for a comprehensive and integral international convention to promote and protect the rights and dignity of persons with disabilities, based on a holistic approach in the work done in the fields of social development, human rights and non-discrimination and taking into account the recommendations of the Commission on Human Rights and the Commission for Social Development,

Recalling also its previous relevant resolutions, the most recent of which was resolution 60/232 of 23 December 2005, as well as relevant resolutions of the Commission for Social Development and the Commission on Human Rights,

Welcoming the valuable contributions made by intergovernmental and non-governmental organizations and national human rights institutions to the work of the Ad Hoc Committee,

1. *Expresses its appreciation* to the Ad Hoc Committee for having concluded the elaboration of the draft Convention on the Rights of Persons with Disabilities and the draft Optional Protocol to the Convention;

2. *Adopts* the Convention on the Rights of Persons with Disabilities and the Optional Protocol to the Convention annexed to the present resolution, which shall be open for signature at United Nations Headquarters in New York as of 30 March 2007;

3. *Calls upon* States to consider signing and ratifying the Convention and the Optional Protocol as a matter of priority, and expresses the hope that they will enter into force at an early date;

4. *Requests* the Secretary-General to provide the staff and facilities necessary for the effective performance of the functions of the Conference of States Parties and the Committee under the Convention and the Optional Protocol after the entry into force of the Convention, as well as for the dissemination of information on the Convention and the Optional Protocol;

5. *Also requests* the Secretary-General to implement progressively standards and guidelines for the accessibility of facilities and services of the United Nations system, taking into account relevant provisions of the Convention, in particular when undertaking renovations;

6. *Requests* United Nations agencies and organizations, and invites intergovernmental and non-governmental organizations, to undertake efforts to disseminate information on the Convention and the Optional Protocol and to promote their understanding;

7. *Requests* the Secretary-General to submit to the General Assembly at its sixty-second session a report on the status of the Convention and the Optional Protocol and the implementation of the present resolution, under a sub-item entitled "Convention on the Rights of Persons with Disabilities".

76th plenary meeting
13 December 2006

Annex I
Convention on the Rights of Persons with Disabilities
Preamble

The States Parties to the present Convention,

(*a*) *Recalling* the principles proclaimed in the Charter of the United Nations which recognize the inherent dignity and worth and the equal and inalienable rights of all members of the human family as the foundation of freedom, justice and peace in the world,

(*b*) *Recognizing* that the United Nations, in the Universal Declaration of Human Rights and in the International Covenants on Human Rights, has proclaimed and agreed that everyone is entitled to all the rights and freedoms set forth therein, without distinction of any kind,

(*c*) *Reaffirming* the universality, indivisibility, interdependence and interrelatedness of all human rights and fundamental freedoms and the need for persons with disabilities to be guaranteed their full enjoyment without discrimination,

(d) *Recalling* the International Covenant on Economic, Social and Cultural Rights, the International Covenant on Civil and Political Rights, the International Convention on the Elimination of All Forms of Racial Discrimination, the Convention on the Elimination of All Forms of Discrimination against Women, the Convention against Torture and Other Cruel, Inhuman or Degrading Treatment or Punishment, the Convention on the Rights of the Child, and the International Convention on the Protection of the Rights of All Migrant Workers and Members of Their Families,

(e) *Recognizing* that disability is an evolving concept and that disability results from the interaction between persons with impairments and attitudinal and environmental barriers that hinders their full and effective participation in society on an equal basis with others,

(f) *Recognizing* the importance of the principles and policy guidelines contained in the World Programme of Action concerning Disabled Persons and in the Standard Rules on the Equalization of Opportunities for Persons with Disabilities in influencing the promotion, formulation and evaluation of the policies, plans, programmes and actions at the national, regional and international levels to further equalize opportunities for persons with disabilities,

(g) *Emphasizing* the importance of mainstreaming disability issues as an integral part of relevant strategies of sustainable development,

(h) *Recognizing also* that discrimination against any person on the basis of disability is a violation of the inherent dignity and worth of the human person,

(i) *Recognizing further* the diversity of persons with disabilities,

(j) *Recognizing* the need to promote and protect the human rights of all persons with disabilities, including those who require more intensive support,

(k) *Concerned* that, despite these various instruments and undertakings, persons with disabilities continue to face barriers in their participation as equal members of society and violations of their human rights in all parts of the world,

(l) *Recognizing* the importance of international cooperation for improving the living conditions of persons with disabilities in every country, particularly in developing countries,

(m) *Recognizing* the valued existing and potential contributions made by persons with disabilities to the overall well-being and diversity of their communities, and that the promotion of the full enjoyment by persons with disabilities of their human rights and fundamental freedoms and of full participation by persons with disabilities will result in their enhanced sense of belonging and in significant advances in the human, social and economic development of society and the eradication of poverty,

(n) *Recognizing* the importance for persons with disabilities of their individual autonomy and independence, including the freedom to make their own choices,

(o) *Considering* that persons with disabilities should have the opportunity to be actively involved in decision-making processes about policies and programmes, including those directly concerning them,

(p) *Concerned* about the difficult conditions faced by persons with disabilities who are subject to multiple or aggravated forms of discrimination on the basis of race, colour, sex, language, religion, political or other opinion, national, ethnic, indigenous or social origin, property, birth, age or other status,

(q) *Recognizing* that women and girls with disabilities are often at greater risk, both within and outside the home, of violence, injury or abuse, neglect or negligent treatment, maltreatment or exploitation,

(r) *Recognizing* that children with disabilities should have full enjoyment of all human rights and fundamental freedoms on an equal basis with other children, and recalling obligations to that end undertaken by States Parties to the Convention on the Rights of the Child,

(s) *Emphasizing* the need to incorporate a gender perspective in all efforts to promote the full enjoyment of human rights and fundamental freedoms by persons with disabilities, (*t*) *Highlighting* the fact that the majority of persons with disabilities live in conditions of poverty, and in this regard recognizing the critical need to address the negative impact of poverty on persons with disabilities,

(*u*) *Bearing in mind* that conditions of peace and security based on full respect for the purposes and principles contained in the Charter of the United Nations and observance of applicable human rights instruments are indispensable for the full protection of persons with disabilities, in particular during armed conflicts and foreign occupation,

(*v*) *Recognizing* the importance of accessibility to the physical, social, economic and cultural environment, to health and education and to information and communication, in enabling persons with disabilities to fully enjoy all human rights and fundamental freedoms,

(*w*) *Realizing* that the individual, having duties to other individuals and to the community to which he or she belongs, is under a responsibility to strive for the promotion and observance of the rights recognized in the International Bill of Human Rights,

(*x*) *Convinced* that the family is the natural and fundamental group unit of society and is entitled to protection by society and the State, and that persons with disabilities and their family members should receive the necessary protection and assistance to enable families to contribute towards the full and equal enjoyment of the rights of persons with disabilities,

(*y*) *Convinced* that a comprehensive and integral international convention to promote and protect the rights and dignity of persons with disabilities will make a significant contribution to redressing the profound social disadvantage of persons with disabilities and promote their participation in the civil, political, economic, social and cultural spheres with equal opportunities, in both developing and developed countries,

Have agreed as follows:

Article 1
Purpose

The purpose of the present Convention is to promote, protect and ensure the full and equal enjoyment of all human rights and fundamental freedoms by all persons with disabilities, and to promote respect for their inherent dignity.

Persons with disabilities include those who have long-term physical, mental, intellectual or sensory impairments which in interaction with various barriers may hinder their full and effective participation in society on an equal basis with others.

Article 2
Definitions

For the purposes of the present Convention:

"Communication" includes languages, display of text, Braille, tactile communication, large print, accessible multimedia as well as written, audio, plain-language, human-reader and augmentative and alternative modes, means and formats of communication, including accessible information and communication technology;

"Language" includes spoken and signed languages and other forms of non-spoken languages;

"Discrimination on the basis of disability" means any distinction, exclusion or restriction on the basis of disability which has the purpose or effect of impairing or nullifying the recognition, enjoyment or exercise, on an equal basis with others, of all human rights and fundamental freedoms in the political, economic, social, cultural, civil or any other field. It includes all forms of discrimination, including denial of reasonable accommodation;

"Reasonable accommodation" means necessary and appropriate modification and adjustments not imposing a disproportionate or undue burden, where needed in a particular case, to ensure to persons with disabilities the enjoyment or exercise on an equal basis with others of all human rights and fundamental freedoms;

"Universal design" means the design of products, environments, programmes and services to be usable by all people, to the greatest extent possible, without the need for adaptation or specialized design. "Universal design" shall not exclude assistive devices for particular groups of persons with disabilities where this is needed.

Article 3
General principles

The principles of the present Convention shall be:

(*a*) Respect for inherent dignity, individual autonomy including the freedom to make one's own choices, and independence of persons;

(*b*) Non-discrimination;

(*c*) Full and effective participation and inclusion in society;

(*d*) Respect for difference and acceptance of persons with disabilities as part of human diversity and humanity;

(*e*) Equality of opportunity;

(*f*) Accessibility;

(*g*) Equality between men and women;

(*h*) Respect for the evolving capacities of children with disabilities and respect for the right of children with disabilities to preserve their identities.

Article 4
General obligations

1. States Parties undertake to ensure and promote the full realization of all human rights and fundamental freedoms for all persons with disabilities without discrimination of any kind on the basis of disability. To this end, States Parties undertake:

(*a*) To adopt all appropriate legislative, administrative and other measures for the implementation of the rights recognized in the present Convention;

(*b*) To take all appropriate measures, including legislation, to modify or abolish existing laws, regulations, customs and practices that constitute discrimination against persons with disabilities;

(*c*) To take into account the protection and promotion of the human rights of persons with disabilities in all policies and programmes;

(*d*) To refrain from engaging in any act or practice that is inconsistent with the present Convention and to ensure that public authorities and institutions act in conformity with the present Convention;

(*e*) To take all appropriate measures to eliminate discrimination on the basis of disability by any person, organization or private enterprise;

(*f*) To undertake or promote research and development of universally designed goods, services, equipment and facilities, as defined in article 2 of the present Convention, which should require the minimum possible adaptation and the least cost to meet the specific needs of a person with disabilities, to promote their availability and use, and to promote universal design in the development of standards and guidelines;

(*g*) To undertake or promote research and development of, and to promote the availability and use of new technologies, including information and communications technologies, mobility aids, devices and assistive technologies, suitable for persons with disabilities, giving priority to technologies at an affordable cost;

(*h*) To provide accessible information to persons with disabilities about mobility aids, devices and assistive technologies, including new technologies, as well as other forms of assistance, support services and facilities;

(*i*) To promote the training of professionals and staff working with persons with disabilities in the rights recognized in the present Convention so as to better provide the assistance and services guaranteed by those rights.

2. With regard to economic, social and cultural rights, each State Party undertakes to take measures to the maximum of its available resources and, where needed, within the framework of international cooperation, with a view to achieving progressively the full realization of these rights, without prejudice to those obligations contained in the present Convention that are immediately applicable according to international law.

3. In the development and implementation of legislation and policies to implement the present Convention, and in other decision-making processes concerning issues relating to persons with disabilities, States Parties shall closely consult with and actively involve persons with disabilities, including children with disabilities, through their representative organizations.

4. Nothing in the present Convention shall affect any provisions which are more conducive to the realization of the rights of persons with disabilities and which may be contained in the law of a State Party or international law in force for that State. There shall

be no restriction upon or derogation from any of the human rights and fundamental freedoms recognized or existing in any State Party to the present Convention pursuant to law, conventions, regulation or custom on the pretext that the present Convention does not recognize such rights or freedoms or that it recognizes them to a lesser extent.

5. The provisions of the present Convention shall extend to all parts of federal States without any limitations or exceptions.

Article 5
Equality and non-discrimination

1. States Parties recognize that all persons are equal before and under the law and are entitled without any discrimination to the equal protection and equal benefit of the law.
2. States Parties shall prohibit all discrimination on the basis of disability and guarantee to persons with disabilities equal and effective legal protection against discrimination on all grounds.
3. In order to promote equality and eliminate discrimination, States Parties shall take all appropriate steps to ensure that reasonable accommodation is provided.
4. Specific measures which are necessary to accelerate or achieve de facto equality of persons with disabilities shall not be considered discrimination under the terms of the present Convention.

Article 6
Women with disabilities

1. States Parties recognize that women and girls with disabilities are subject to multiple discrimination, and in this regard shall take measures to ensure the full and equal enjoyment by them of all human rights and fundamental freedoms.
2. States Parties shall take all appropriate measures to ensure the full development, advancement and empowerment of women, for the purpose of guaranteeing them the exercise and enjoyment of the human rights and fundamental freedoms set out in the present Convention.

Article 7
Children with disabilities

1. States Parties shall take all necessary measures to ensure the full enjoyment by children with disabilities of all human rights and fundamental freedoms on an equal basis with other children.
2. In all actions concerning children with disabilities, the best interests of the child shall be a primary consideration.
3. States Parties shall ensure that children with disabilities have the right to express their views freely on all matters affecting them, their views being given due weight in accordance with their age and maturity, on an equal basis with other children, and to be provided with disability and age-appropriate assistance to realize that right.

Article 8
Awareness-raising

1. States Parties undertake to adopt immediate, effective and appropriate measures:

(*a*) To raise awareness throughout society, including at the family level, regarding persons with disabilities, and to foster respect for the rights and dignity of persons with disabilities;

(*b*) To combat stereotypes, prejudices and harmful practices relating to persons with disabilities, including those based on sex and age, in all areas of life;

(*c*) To promote awareness of the capabilities and contributions of persons with disabilities.

2. Measures to this end include:

(*a*) Initiating and maintaining effective public awareness campaigns designed:

(i) To nurture receptiveness to the rights of persons with disabilities;

(ii) To promote positive perceptions and greater social awareness towards persons with disabilities;

(iii) To promote recognition of the skills, merits and abilities of persons with disabilities, and of their contributions to the workplace and the labour market;

(*b*) Fostering at all levels of the education system, including in all children from an early age, an attitude of respect for the rights of persons with disabilities;

(*c*) Encouraging all organs of the media to portray persons with disabilities in a manner consistent with the purpose of the present Convention;

(d) Promoting awareness-training programmes regarding persons with disabilities and the rights of persons with disabilities.

Article 9
Accessibility

1. To enable persons with disabilities to live independently and participate fully in all aspects of life, States Parties shall take appropriate measures to ensure to persons with disabilities access, on an equal basis with others, to the physical environment, to transportation, to information and communications, including information and communications technologies and systems, and to other facilities and services open or provided to the public, both in urban and in rural areas. These measures, which shall include the identification and elimination of obstacles and barriers to accessibility, shall apply to, inter alia:

(a) Buildings, roads, transportation and other indoor and outdoor facilities, including schools, housing, medical facilities and workplaces;

(b) Information, communications and other services, including electronic services and emergency services.

2. States Parties shall also take appropriate measures:

(a) To develop, promulgate and monitor the implementation of minimum standards and guidelines for the accessibility of facilities and services open or provided to the public;

(b) To ensure that private entities that offer facilities and services which are open or provided to the public take into account all aspects of accessibility for persons with disabilities;

(c) To provide training for stakeholders on accessibility issues facing persons with disabilities;

(d) To provide in buildings and other facilities open to the public signage in Braille and in easy to read and understand forms;

(e) To provide forms of live assistance and intermediaries, including guides, readers and professional sign language interpreters, to facilitate accessibility to buildings and other facilities open to the public;

(f) To promote other appropriate forms of assistance and support to persons with disabilities to ensure their access to information;

(g) To promote access for persons with disabilities to new information and communications technologies and systems, including the Internet;

(h) To promote the design, development, production and distribution of accessible information and communications technologies and systems at an early stage, so that these technologies and systems become accessible at minimum cost.

Article 10
Right to life

States Parties reaffirm that every human being has the inherent right to life and shall take all necessary measures to ensure its effective enjoyment by persons with disabilities on an equal basis with others.

Article 11
Situations of risk and humanitarian emergencies

States Parties shall take, in accordance with their obligations under international law, including international humanitarian law and international human rights law, all necessary measures to ensure the protection and safety of persons with disabilities in situations of risk, including situations of armed conflict, humanitarian emergencies and the occurrence of natural disasters.

Article 12
Equal recognition before the law

1. States Parties reaffirm that persons with disabilities have the right to recognition everywhere as persons before the law.

2. States Parties shall recognize that persons with disabilities enjoy legal capacity on an equal basis with others in all aspects of life.

3. States Parties shall take appropriate measures to provide access by persons with disabilities to the support they may require in exercising their legal capacity.

4. States Parties shall ensure that all measures that relate to the exercise of legal capacity provide for appropriate and effective safeguards to prevent abuse in accordance with international human rights law. Such safeguards shall ensure that measures relating to the exercise of legal capacity respect the rights, will and preferences of the person, are free of conflict of interest and undue influence, are proportional and tailored to the per-

son's circumstances, apply for the shortest time possible and are subject to regular review by a competent, independent and impartial authority or judicial body. The safeguards shall be proportional to the degree to which such measures affect the person's rights and interests.

5. Subject to the provisions of this article, States Parties shall take all appropriate and effective measures to ensure the equal right of persons with disabilities to own or inherit property, to control their own financial affairs and to have equal access to bank loans, mortgages and other forms of financial credit, and shall ensure that persons with disabilities are not arbitrarily deprived of their property.

Article 13
Access to justice

1. States Parties shall ensure effective access to justice for persons with disabilities on an equal basis with others, including through the provision of procedural and age-appropriate accommodations, in order to facilitate their effective role as direct and indirect participants, including as witnesses, in all legal proceedings, including at investigative and other preliminary stages.

2. In order to help to ensure effective access to justice for persons with disabilities, States Parties shall promote appropriate training for those working in the field of administration of justice, including police and prison staff.

Article 14
Liberty and security of person

1. States Parties shall ensure that persons with disabilities, on an equal basis with others:

(*a*) Enjoy the right to liberty and security of person;

(*b*) Are not deprived of their liberty unlawfully or arbitrarily, and that any deprivation of liberty is in conformity with the law, and that the existence of a disability shall in no case justify a deprivation of liberty.

2. States Parties shall ensure that if persons with disabilities are deprived of their liberty through any process, they are, on an equal basis with others, entitled to guarantees in accordance with international human rights law and shall be treated in compliance with the objectives and principles of the present Convention, including by provision of reasonable accommodation.

Article 15
Freedom from torture or cruel, inhuman or degrading treatment or punishment

1. No one shall be subjected to torture or to cruel, inhuman or degrading treatment or punishment. In particular, no one shall be subjected without his or her free consent to medical or scientific experimentation.

2. States Parties shall take all effective legislative, administrative, judicial or other measures to prevent persons with disabilities, on an equal basis with others, from being subjected to torture or cruel, inhuman or degrading treatment or punishment.

Article 16
Freedom from exploitation, violence and abuse

1. States Parties shall take all appropriate legislative, administrative, social, educational and other measures to protect persons with disabilities, both within and outside the home, from all forms of exploitation, violence and abuse, including their gender-based aspects.

2. States Parties shall also take all appropriate measures to prevent all forms of exploitation, violence and abuse by ensuring, inter alia, appropriate forms of gender- and age-sensitive assistance and support for persons with disabilities and their families and caregivers, including through the provision of information and education on how to avoid, recognize and report instances of exploitation, violence and abuse. States Parties shall ensure that protection services are age-, gender- and disability-sensitive.

3. In order to prevent the occurrence of all forms of exploitation, violence and abuse, States Parties shall ensure that all facilities and programmes designed to serve persons with disabilities are effectively monitored by independent authorities.

4. States Parties shall take all appropriate measures to promote the physical, cognitive and psychological recovery, rehabilitation and social reintegration of persons with disabilities who become victims of any form of exploitation, violence or abuse, including through the provision of protection services. Such recovery and reintegration shall take

place in an environment that fosters the health, welfare, self-respect, dignity and autonomy of the person and takes into account gender- and age-specific needs.

5. States Parties shall put in place effective legislation and policies, including women- and child-focused legislation and policies, to ensure that instances of exploitation, violence and abuse against persons with disabilities are identified, investigated and, where appropriate, prosecuted.

Article 17
Protecting the integrity of the person

Every person with disabilities has a right to respect for his or her physical and mental integrity on an equal basis with others.

Article 18
Liberty of movement and nationality

1. States Parties shall recognize the rights of persons with disabilities to liberty of movement, to freedom to choose their residence and to a nationality, on an equal basis with others, including by ensuring that persons with disabilities:

(*a*) Have the right to acquire and change a nationality and are not deprived of their nationality arbitrarily or on the basis of disability;

(*b*) Are not deprived, on the basis of disability, of their ability to obtain, possess and utilize documentation of their nationality or other documentation of identification, or to utilize relevant processes such as immigration proceedings, that may be needed to facilitate exercise of the right to liberty of movement;

(*c*) Are free to leave any country, including their own;

(*d*) Are not deprived, arbitrarily or on the basis of disability, of the right to enter their own country.

2. Children with disabilities shall be registered immediately after birth and shall have the right from birth to a name, the right to acquire a nationality and, as far as possible, the right to know and be cared for by their parents.

Article 19
Living independently and being included in the community

States Parties to the present Convention recognize the equal right of all persons with disabilities to live in the community, with choices equal to others, and shall take effective and appropriate measures to facilitate full enjoyment by persons with disabilities of this right and their full inclusion and participation in the community, including by ensuring that:

(*a*) Persons with disabilities have the opportunity to choose their place of residence and where and with whom they live on an equal basis with others and are not obliged to live in a particular living arrangement;

(*b*) Persons with disabilities have access to a range of in-home, residential and other community support services, including personal assistance necessary to support living and inclusion in the community, and to prevent isolation or segregation from the community;

(*c*) Community services and facilities for the general population are available on an equal basis to persons with disabilities and are responsive to their needs.

Article 20
Personal mobility

States Parties shall take effective measures to ensure personal mobility with the greatest possible independence for persons with disabilities, including by:

(*a*) Facilitating the personal mobility of persons with disabilities in the manner and at the time of their choice, and at affordable cost;

(*b*) Facilitating access by persons with disabilities to quality mobility aids, devices, assistive technologies and forms of live assistance and intermediaries, including by making them available at affordable cost;

(*c*) Providing training in mobility skills to persons with disabilities and to specialist staff working with persons with disabilities;

(*d*) Encouraging entities that produce mobility aids, devices and assistive technologies to take into account all aspects of mobility for persons with disabilities.

Article 21
Freedom of expression and opinion, and access to information

States Parties shall take all appropriate measures to ensure that persons with disabilities can exercise the right to freedom of expression and opinion, including the freedom to seek, receive and impart information and ideas on an equal basis with others and through all forms of communication of their choice, as defined in article 2 of the present Convention, including by:

(a) Providing information intended for the general public to persons with disabilities in accessible formats and technologies appropriate to different kinds of disabilities in a timely manner and without additional cost;

(b) Accepting and facilitating the use of sign languages, Braille, augmentative and alternative communication, and all other accessible means, modes and formats of communication of their choice by persons with disabilities in official interactions;

(c) Urging private entities that provide services to the general public, including through the Internet, to provide information and services in accessible and usable formats for persons with disabilities;

(d) Encouraging the mass media, including providers of information through the Internet, to make their services accessible to persons with disabilities;

(e) Recognizing and promoting the use of sign languages.

Article 22
Respect for privacy

1. No person with disabilities, regardless of place of residence or living arrangements, shall be subjected to arbitrary or unlawful interference with his or her privacy, family, home or correspondence or other types of communication or to unlawful attacks on his or her honour and reputation. Persons with disabilities have the right to the protection of the law against such interference or attacks.

2. States Parties shall protect the privacy of personal, health and rehabilitation information of persons with disabilities on an equal basis with others.

Article 23
Respect for home and the family

1. States Parties shall take effective and appropriate measures to eliminate discrimination against persons with disabilities in all matters relating to marriage, family, parenthood and relationships, on an equal basis with others, so as to ensure that:

(a) The right of all persons with disabilities who are of marriageable age to marry and to found a family on the basis of free and full consent of the intending spouses is recognized;

(b) The rights of persons with disabilities to decide freely and responsibly on the number and spacing of their children and to have access to age-appropriate information, reproductive and family planning education are recognized, and the means necessary to enable them to exercise these rights are provided;

(c) Persons with disabilities, including children, retain their fertility on an equal basis with others.

2. States Parties shall ensure the rights and responsibilities of persons with disabilities, with regard to guardianship, wardship, trusteeship, adoption of children or similar institutions, where these concepts exist in national legislation; in all cases the best interests of the child shall be paramount. States Parties shall render appropriate assistance to persons with disabilities in the performance of their child-rearing responsibilities.

3. States Parties shall ensure that children with disabilities have equal rights with respect to family life. With a view to realizing these rights, and to prevent concealment, abandonment, neglect and segregation of children with disabilities, States Parties shall undertake to provide early and comprehensive information, services and support to children with disabilities and their families.

4. States Parties shall ensure that a child shall not be separated from his or her parents against their will, except when competent authorities subject to judicial review determine, in accordance with applicable law and procedures, that such separation is necessary for the best interests of the child. In no case shall a child be separated from parents on the basis of a disability of either the child or one or both of the parents.

5. States Parties shall, where the immediate family is unable to care for a child with disabilities, undertake every effort to provide alternative care within the wider family, and failing that, within the community in a family setting.

Article 24
Education

1. States Parties recognize the right of persons with disabilities to education. With a

view to realizing this right without discrimination and on the basis of equal opportunity, States Parties shall ensure an inclusive education system at all levels and lifelong learning directed to:

(a) The full development of human potential and sense of dignity and self-worth, and the strengthening of respect for human rights, fundamental freedoms and human diversity;

(b) The development by persons with disabilities of their personality, talents and creativity, as well as their mental and physical abilities, to their fullest potential;

(c) Enabling persons with disabilities to participate effectively in a free society.

2. In realizing this right, States Parties shall ensure that:

(a) Persons with disabilities are not excluded from the general education system on the basis of disability, and that children with disabilities are not excluded from free and compulsory primary education, or from secondary education, on the basis of disability;

(b) Persons with disabilities can access an inclusive, quality and free primary education and secondary education on an equal basis with others in the communities in which they live;

(c) Reasonable accommodation of the individual's requirements is provided;

(d) Persons with disabilities receive the support required, within the general education system, to facilitate their effective education;

(e) Effective individualized support measures are provided in environments that maximize academic and social development, consistent with the goal of full inclusion.

3. States Parties shall enable persons with disabilities to learn life and social development skills to facilitate their full and equal participation in education and as members of the community. To this end, States Parties shall take appropriate measures, including:

(a) Facilitating the learning of Braille, alternative script, augmentative and alternative modes, means and formats of communication and orientation and mobility skills, and facilitating peer support and mentoring;

(b) Facilitating the learning of sign language and the promotion of the linguistic identity of the deaf community;

(c) Ensuring that the education of persons, and in particular children, who are blind, deaf or deafblind, is delivered in the most appropriate languages and modes and means of communication for the individual, and in environments which maximize academic and social development.

4. In order to help ensure the realization of this right, States Parties shall take appropriate measures to employ teachers, including teachers with disabilities, who are qualified in sign language and/or Braille, and to train professionals and staff who work at all levels of education. Such training shall incorporate disability awareness and the use of appropriate augmentative and alternative modes, means and formats of communication, educational techniques and materials to support persons with disabilities.

5. States Parties shall ensure that persons with disabilities are able to access general tertiary education, vocational training, adult education and lifelong learning without discrimination and on an equal basis with others. To this end, States Parties shall ensure that reasonable accommodation is provided to persons with disabilities.

Article 25
Health

States Parties recognize that persons with disabilities have the right to the enjoyment of the highest attainable standard of health without discrimination on the basis of disability. States Parties shall take all appropriate measures to ensure access for persons with disabilities to health services that are gender-sensitive, including health-related rehabilitation. In particular, States Parties shall:

(a) Provide persons with disabilities with the same range, quality and standard of free or affordable health care and programmes as provided to other persons, including in the area of sexual and reproductive health and population-based public health programmes;

(b) Provide those health services needed by persons with disabilities specifically because of their disabilities, including early identification and intervention as appropriate, and services designed to minimize and prevent further disabilities, including among children and older persons;

(*c*) Provide these health services as close as possible to people's own communities, including in rural areas;

(*d*) Require health professionals to provide care of the same quality to persons with disabilities as to others, including on the basis of free and informed consent by, inter alia, raising awareness of the human rights, dignity, autonomy and needs of persons with disabilities through training and the promulgation of ethical standards for public and private health care;

(*e*) Prohibit discrimination against persons with disabilities in the provision of health insurance, and life insurance where such insurance is permitted by national law, which shall be provided in a fair and reasonable manner;

(*f*) Prevent discriminatory denial of health care or health services or food and fluids on the basis of disability.

Article 26
Habilitation and rehabilitation

1. States Parties shall take effective and appropriate measures, including through peer support, to enable persons with disabilities to attain and maintain maximum independence, full physical, mental, social and vocational ability, and full inclusion and participation in all aspects of life. To that end, States Parties shall organize, strengthen and extend comprehensive habilitation and rehabilitation services and programmes, particularly in the areas of health, employment, education and social services, in such a way that these services and programmes:

(*a*) Begin at the earliest possible stage, and are based on the multidisciplinary assessment of individual needs and strengths;

(*b*) Support participation and inclusion in the community and all aspects of society, are voluntary, and are available to persons with disabilities as close as possible to their own communities, including in rural areas.

2. States Parties shall promote the development of initial and continuing training for professionals and staff working in habilitation and rehabilitation services.

3. States Parties shall promote the availability, knowledge and use of assistive devices and technologies, designed for persons with disabilities, as they relate to habilitation and rehabilitation.

Article 27
Work and employment

1. States Parties recognize the right of persons with disabilities to work, on an equal basis with others; this includes the right to the opportunity to gain a living by work freely chosen or accepted in a labour market and work environment that is open, inclusive and accessible to persons with disabilities. States Parties shall safeguard and promote the realization of the right to work, including for those who acquire a disability during the course of employment, by taking appropriate steps, including through legislation, to, inter alia:

(*a*) Prohibit discrimination on the basis of disability with regard to all matters concerning all forms of employment, including conditions of recruitment, hiring and employment, continuance of employment, career advancement and safe and healthy working conditions;

(*b*) Protect the rights of persons with disabilities, on an equal basis with others, to just and favourable conditions of work, including equal opportunities and equal remuneration for work of equal value, safe and healthy working conditions, including protection from harassment, and the redress of grievances;

(*c*) Ensure that persons with disabilities are able to exercise their labour and trade union rights on an equal basis with others;

(*d*) Enable persons with disabilities to have effective access to general technical and vocational guidance programmes, placement services and vocational and continuing training;

(*e*) Promote employment opportunities and career advancement for persons with disabilities in the labour market, as well as assistance in finding, obtaining, maintaining and returning to employment;

(*f*) Promote opportunities for self-employment, entrepreneurship, the development of cooperatives and starting one's own business;

(*g*) Employ persons with disabilities in the public sector;

(h) Promote the employment of persons with disabilities in the private sector through appropriate policies and measures, which may include affirmative action programmes, incentives and other measures;

(i) Ensure that reasonable accommodation is provided to persons with disabilities in the workplace;

(j) Promote the acquisition by persons with disabilities of work experience in the open labour market;

(k) Promote vocational and professional rehabilitation, job retention and return-to-work programmes for persons with disabilities.

2. States Parties shall ensure that persons with disabilities are not held in slavery or in servitude, and are protected, on an equal basis with others, from forced or compulsory labour.

Article 28
Adequate standard of living and social protection

1. States Parties recognize the right of persons with disabilities to an adequate standard of living for themselves and their families, including adequate food, clothing and housing, and to the continuous improvement of living conditions, and shall take appropriate steps to safeguard and promote the realization of this right without discrimination on the basis of disability.

2. States Parties recognize the right of persons with disabilities to social protection and to the enjoyment of that right without discrimination on the basis of disability, and shall take appropriate steps to safeguard and promote the realization of this right, including measures:

(a) To ensure equal access by persons with disabilities to clean water services, and to ensure access to appropriate and affordable services, devices and other assistance for disability-related needs;

(b) To ensure access by persons with disabilities, in particular women and girls with disabilities and older persons with disabilities, to social protection programmes and poverty reduction programmes;

(c) To ensure access by persons with disabilities and their families living in situations of poverty to assistance from the State with disability-related expenses, including adequate training, counselling, financial assistance and respite care;

(d) To ensure access by persons with disabilities to public housing programmes;

(e) To ensure equal access by persons with disabilities to retirement benefits and programmes.

Article 29
Participation in political and public life

States Parties shall guarantee to persons with disabilities political rights and the opportunity to enjoy them on an equal basis with others, and shall undertake:

(a) To ensure that persons with disabilities can effectively and fully participate in political and public life on an equal basis with others, directly or through freely chosen representatives, including the right and opportunity for persons with disabilities to vote and be elected, inter alia, by:

(i) Ensuring that voting procedures, facilities and materials are appropriate, accessible and easy to understand and use;

(ii) Protecting the right of persons with disabilities to vote by secret ballot in elections and public referendums without intimidation, and to stand for elections, to effectively hold office and perform all public functions at all levels of government, facilitating the use of assistive and new technologies where appropriate;

(iii) Guaranteeing the free expression of the will of persons with disabilities as electors and to this end, where necessary, at their request, allowing assistance in voting by a person of their own choice;

(b) To promote actively an environment in which persons with disabilities can effectively and fully participate in the conduct of public affairs, without discrimination and on an equal basis with others, and encourage their participation in public affairs, including:

(i) Participation in non-governmental organizations and associations concerned with the public and political life of the country, and in the activities and administration of political parties;

(ii) Forming and joining organizations of persons with disabilities to represent persons with disabilities at international, national, regional and local levels.

Article 30
Participation in cultural life, recreation, leisure and sport

1. States Parties recognize the right of persons with disabilities to take part on an equal basis with others in cultural life, and shall take all appropriate measures to ensure that persons with disabilities:

(*a*) Enjoy access to cultural materials in accessible formats;

(*b*) Enjoy access to television programmes, films, theatre and other cultural activities, in accessible formats;

(*c*) Enjoy access to places for cultural performances or services, such as theatres, museums, cinemas, libraries and tourism services, and, as far as possible, enjoy access to monuments and sites of national cultural importance.

2. States Parties shall take appropriate measures to enable persons with disabilities to have the opportunity to develop and utilize their creative, artistic and intellectual potential, not only for their own benefit, but also for the enrichment of society.

3. States Parties shall take all appropriate steps, in accordance with international law, to ensure that laws protecting intellectual property rights do not constitute an unreasonable or discriminatory barrier to access by persons with disabilities to cultural materials.

4. Persons with disabilities shall be entitled, on an equal basis with others, to recognition and support of their specific cultural and linguistic identity, including sign languages and deaf culture.

5. With a view to enabling persons with disabilities to participate on an equal basis with others in recreational, leisure and sporting activities, States Parties shall take appropriate measures:

(*a*) To encourage and promote the participation, to the fullest extent possible, of persons with disabilities in mainstream sporting activities at all levels;

(*b*) To ensure that persons with disabilities have an opportunity to organize, develop and participate in disability-specific sporting and recreational activities and, to this end, encourage the provision, on an equal basis with others, of appropriate instruction, training and resources;

(*c*) To ensure that persons with disabilities have access to sporting, recreational and tourism venues;

(*d*) To ensure that children with disabilities have equal access with other children to participation in play, recreation and leisure and sporting activities, including those activities in the school system;

(*e*) To ensure that persons with disabilities have access to services from those involved in the organization of recreational, tourism, leisure and sporting activities.

Article 31
Statistics and data collection

1. States Parties undertake to collect appropriate information, including statistical and research data, to enable them to formulate and implement policies to give effect to the present Convention. The process of collecting and maintaining this information shall:

(*a*) Comply with legally established safeguards, including legislation on data protection, to ensure confidentiality and respect for the privacy of persons with disabilities;

(*b*) Comply with internationally accepted norms to protect human rights and fundamental freedoms and ethical principles in the collection and use of statistics.

2. The information collected in accordance with this article shall be disaggregated, as appropriate, and used to help assess the implementation of States Parties' obligations under the present Convention and to identify and address the barriers faced by persons with disabilities in exercising their rights.

3. States Parties shall assume responsibility for the dissemination of these statistics and ensure their accessibility to persons with disabilities and others.

Article 32
International cooperation

1. States Parties recognize the importance of international cooperation and its promotion, in support of national efforts for the realization of the purpose and objectives of the present Convention, and will undertake appropriate and effective measures in this regard, between and among States and, as appropriate, in part-

nership with relevant international and regional organizations and civil society, in particular organizations of persons with disabilities. Such measures could include, inter alia:

(a) Ensuring that international cooperation, including international development programmes, is inclusive of and accessible to persons with disabilities;

(b) Facilitating and supporting capacity-building, including through the exchange and sharing of information, experiences, training programmes and best practices;

(c) Facilitating cooperation in research and access to scientific and technical knowledge;

(d) Providing, as appropriate, technical and economic assistance, including by facilitating access to and sharing of accessible and assistive technologies, and through the transfer of technologies.

2. The provisions of this article are without prejudice to the obligations of each State Party to fulfil its obligations under the present Convention.

Article 33
National implementation and monitoring

1. States Parties, in accordance with their system of organization, shall designate one or more focal points within government for matters relating to the implementation of the present Convention, and shall give due consideration to the establishment or designation of a coordination mechanism within government to facilitate related action in different sectors and at different levels.

2. States Parties shall, in accordance with their legal and administrative systems, maintain, strengthen, designate or establish within the State Party, a framework, including one or more independent mechanisms, as appropriate, to promote, protect and monitor implementation of the present Convention. When designating or establishing such a mechanism, States Parties shall take into account the principles relating to the status and functioning of national institutions for protection and promotion of human rights.

3. Civil society, in particular persons with disabilities and their representative organizations, shall be involved and participate fully in the monitoring process.

Article 34
Committee on the Rights of Persons with Disabilities

1. There shall be established a Committee on the Rights of Persons with Disabilities (hereafter referred to as "the Committee"), which shall carry out the functions hereinafter provided.

2. The Committee shall consist, at the time of entry into force of the present Convention, of twelve experts. After an additional sixty ratifications or accessions to the Convention, the membership of the Committee shall increase by six members, attaining a maximum number of eighteen members.

3. The members of the Committee shall serve in their personal capacity and shall be of high moral standing and recognized competence and experience in the field covered by the present Convention. When nominating their candidates, States Parties are invited to give due consideration to the provision set out in article 4, paragraph 3, of the present Convention.

4. The members of the Committee shall be elected by States Parties, consideration being given to equitable geographical distribution, representation of the different forms of civilization and of the principal legal systems, balanced gender representation and participation of experts with disabilities.

5. The members of the Committee shall be elected by secret ballot from a list of persons nominated by the States Parties from among their nationals at meetings of the Conference of States Parties. At those meetings, for which two thirds of States Parties shall constitute a quorum, the persons elected to the Committee shall be those who obtain the largest number of votes and an absolute majority of the votes of the representatives of States Parties present and voting.

6. The initial election shall be held no later than six months after the date of entry into force of the present Convention. At least four months before the date of each election, the Secretary-General of the United Nations shall address a letter to the States Parties inviting them to submit the nominations within two months. The Secretary-General shall subsequently prepare a list in alphabetical order of

all persons thus nominated, indicating the State Parties which have nominated them, and shall submit it to the States Parties to the present Convention.

7. The members of the Committee shall be elected for a term of four years. They shall be eligible for re-election once. However, the term of six of the members elected at the first election shall expire at the end of two years; immediately after the first election, the names of these six members shall be chosen by lot by the chairperson of the meeting referred to in paragraph 5 of this article.

8. The election of the six additional members of the Committee shall be held on the occasion of regular elections, in accordance with the relevant provisions of this article.

9. If a member of the Committee dies or resigns or declares that for any other cause she or he can no longer perform her or his duties, the State Party which nominated the member shall appoint another expert possessing the qualifications and meeting the requirements set out in the relevant provisions of this article, to serve for the remainder of the term.

10. The Committee shall establish its own rules of procedure.

11. The Secretary-General of the United Nations shall provide the necessary staff and facilities for the effective performance of the functions of the Committee under the present Convention, and shall convene its initial meeting.

12. With the approval of the General Assembly of the United Nations, the members of the Committee established under the present Convention shall receive emoluments from United Nations resources on such terms and conditions as the Assembly may decide, having regard to the importance of the Committee's responsibilities.

13. The members of the Committee shall be entitled to the facilities, privileges and immunities of experts on mission for the United Nations as laid down in the relevant sections of the Convention on the Privileges and Immunities of the United Nations.

Article 35
Reports by States Parties

1. Each State Party shall submit to the Committee, through the Secretary-General of the United Nations, a comprehensive report on measures taken to give effect to its obligations under the present Convention and on the progress made in that regard, within two years after the entry into force of the present Convention for the State Party concerned.

2. Thereafter, States Parties shall submit subsequent reports at least every four years and further whenever the Committee so requests.

3. The Committee shall decide any guidelines applicable to the content of the reports.

4. A State Party which has submitted a comprehensive initial report to the Committee need not, in its subsequent reports, repeat information previously provided. When preparing reports to the Committee, States Parties are invited to consider doing so in an open and transparent process and to give due consideration to the provision set out in article 4, paragraph 3, of the present Convention.

5. Reports may indicate factors and difficulties affecting the degree of fulfilment of obligations under the present Convention.

Article 36
Consideration of reports

1. Each report shall be considered by the Committee, which shall make such suggestions and general recommendations on the report as it may consider appropriate and shall forward these to the State Party concerned. The State Party may respond with any information it chooses to the Committee. The Committee may request further information from States Parties relevant to the implementation of the present Convention.

2. If a State Party is significantly overdue in the submission of a report, the Committee may notify the State Party concerned of the need to examine the implementation of the present Convention in that State Party, on the basis of reliable information available to the Committee, if the relevant report is not submitted within three months following the notification. The Committee shall invite the State Party concerned to participate in such examination. Should the State Party respond by submitting the relevant report, the provisions of paragraph 1 of this article will apply.

3. The Secretary-General of the United Nations shall make available the reports to all States Parties.

4. States Parties shall make their reports widely available to the public in their own countries and facilitate access to the suggestions and general recommendations relating to these reports.

5. The Committee shall transmit, as it may consider appropriate, to the specialized agencies, funds and programmes of the United Nations, and other competent bodies, reports from States Parties in order to address a request or indication of a need for technical advice or assistance contained therein, along with the Committee's observations and recommendations, if any, on these requests or indications.

Article 37
Cooperation between States Parties and the Committee

1. Each State Party shall cooperate with the Committee and assist its members in the fulfilment of their mandate.

2. In its relationship with States Parties, the Committee shall give due consideration to ways and means of enhancing national capacities for the implementation of the present Convention, including through international cooperation.

Article 38
Relationship of the Committee with other bodies

In order to foster the effective implementation of the present Convention and to encourage international cooperation in the field covered by the present Convention:

(*a*) The specialized agencies and other United Nations organs shall be entitled to be represented at the consideration of the implementation of such provisions of the present Convention as fall within the scope of their mandate. The Committee may invite the specialized agencies and other competent bodies as it may consider appropriate to provide expert advice on the implementation of the Convention in areas falling within the scope of their respective mandates. The Committee may invite specialized agencies and other United Nations organs to submit reports on the implementation of the Convention in areas falling within the scope of their activities;

(*b*) The Committee, as it discharges its mandate, shall consult, as appropriate, other relevant bodies instituted by international human rights treaties, with a view to ensuring the consistency of their respective reporting guidelines, suggestions and general recommendations, and avoiding duplication and overlap in the performance of their functions.

Article 39
Report of the Committee

The Committee shall report every two years to the General Assembly and to the Economic and Social Council on its activities, and may make suggestions and general recommendations based on the examination of reports and information received from the States Parties. Such suggestions and general recommendations shall be included in the report of the Committee together with comments, if any, from States Parties.

Article 40
Conference of States Parties

1. The States Parties shall meet regularly in a Conference of States Parties in order to consider any matter with regard to the implementation of the present Convention.

2. No later than six months after the entry into force of the present Convention, the Conference of States Parties shall be convened by the Secretary-General of the United Nations. The subsequent meetings shall be convened by the Secretary-General biennially or upon the decision of the Conference of States Parties.

Article 41
Depositary

The Secretary-General of the United Nations shall be the depositary of the present Convention.

Article 42
Signature

The present Convention shall be open for signature by all States and by regional integration organizations at United Nations Headquarters in New York as of 30 March 2007.

Article 43
Consent to be bound

The present Convention shall be subject to ratification by signatory States and to formal confirmation by signatory regional integration organizations. It shall be open for accession by any State or regional integration organization which has not signed the Convention.

Article 44
Regional integration organizations

1. "Regional integration organization" shall mean an organization constituted by sovereign States of a given region, to which its member States have transferred competence in respect of matters governed by the present Convention. Such organizations shall declare, in their instruments of formal confirmation or accession, the extent of their competence with respect to matters governed by the present Convention. Subsequently, they shall inform the depositary of any substantial modification in the extent of their competence.
2. References to "States Parties" in the present Convention shall apply to such organizations within the limits of their competence.
3. For the purposes of article 45, paragraph 1, and article 47, paragraphs 2 and 3, of the present Convention, any instrument deposited by a regional integration organization shall not be counted.
4. Regional integration organizations, in matters within their competence, may exercise their right to vote in the Conference of States Parties, with a number of votes equal to the number of their member States that are Parties to the present Convention. Such an organization shall not exercise its right to vote if any of its member States exercises its right, and vice versa.

Article 45
Entry into force

1. The present Convention shall enter into force on the thirtieth day after the deposit of the twentieth instrument of ratification or accession.
2. For each State or regional integration organization ratifying, formally confirming or acceding to the present Convention after the deposit of the twentieth such instrument, the Convention shall enter into force on the thirtieth day after the deposit of its own such instrument.

Article 46
Reservations

1. Reservations incompatible with the object and purpose of the present Convention shall not be permitted.
2. Reservations may be withdrawn at any time.

Article 47
Amendments

1. Any State Party may propose an amendment to the present Convention and submit it to the Secretary-General of the United Nations. The Secretary-General shall communicate any proposed amendments to States Parties, with a request to be notified whether they favour a conference of States Parties for the purpose of considering and deciding upon the proposals. In the event that, within four months from the date of such communication, at least one third of the States Parties favour such a conference, the Secretary-General shall convene the conference under the auspices of the United Nations. Any amendment adopted by a majority of two thirds of the States Parties present and voting shall be submitted by the Secretary-General to the General Assembly of the United Nations for approval and thereafter to all States Parties for acceptance.
2. An amendment adopted and approved in accordance with paragraph 1 of this article shall enter into force on the thirtieth day after the number of instruments of acceptance deposited reaches two thirds of the number of States Parties at the date of adoption of the amendment. Thereafter, the amendment shall enter into force for any State Party on the thirtieth day following the deposit of its own instrument of acceptance. An amendment shall be binding only on those States Parties which have accepted it.
3. If so decided by the Conference of States Parties by consensus, an amendment adopted and approved in accordance with paragraph 1 of this article which relates exclusively to articles 34, 38, 39 and 40 shall enter into force for all States Parties on the thirtieth day after the number of instruments of acceptance deposited reaches two thirds of the number of States

Parties at the date of adoption of the amendment.

Article 48
Denunciation

A State Party may denounce the present Convention by written notification to the Secretary-General of the United Nations. The denunciation shall become effective one year after the date of receipt of the notification by the Secretary-General.

Article 49
Accessible format

The text of the present Convention shall be made available in accessible formats.

Article 50
Authentic texts

The Arabic, Chinese, English, French, Russian and Spanish texts of the present Convention shall be equally authentic.

IN WITNESS THEREOF the undersigned plenipotentiaries, being duly authorized thereto by their respective Governments, have signed the present Convention.

ANNEX II
Optional Protocol to the Convention on the Rights of Persons with Disabilities

The States Parties to the present Protocol have agreed as follows:

Article 1

1. A State Party to the present Protocol ("State Party") recognizes the competence of the Committee on the Rights of Persons with Disabilities ("the Committee") to receive and consider communications from or on behalf of individuals or groups of individuals subject to its jurisdiction who claim to be victims of a violation by that State Party of the provisions of the Convention.

2. No communication shall be received by the Committee if it concerns a State Party to the Convention that is not a party to the present Protocol.

Article 2

The Committee shall consider a communication inadmissible when:

(*a*) The communication is anonymous;

(*b*) The communication constitutes an abuse of the right of submission of such communications or is incompatible with the provisions of the Convention;

(*c*) The same matter has already been examined by the Committee or has been or is being examined under another procedure of international investigation or settlement;

(*d*) All available domestic remedies have not been exhausted. This shall not be the rule where the application of the remedies is unreasonably prolonged or unlikely to bring effective relief;

(*e*) It is manifestly ill-founded or not sufficiently substantiated; or when

(*f*) The facts that are the subject of the communication occurred prior to the entry into force of the present Protocol for the State Party concerned unless those facts continued after that date.

Article 3

Subject to the provisions of article 2 of the present Protocol, the Committee shall bring any communications submitted to it confidentially to the attention of the State Party. Within six months, the receiving State shall submit to the Committee written explanations or statements clarifying the matter and the remedy, if any, that may have been taken by that State.

Article 4

1. At any time after the receipt of a communication and before a determination on the merits has been reached, the Committee may transmit to the State Party concerned for its urgent consideration a request that the State Party take such interim measures as may be necessary to avoid possible irreparable damage to the victim or victims of the alleged violation.

2. Where the Committee exercises its discretion under paragraph 1 of this article, this does not imply a determination on admissibility or on the merits of the communication.

Article 5

The Committee shall hold closed meetings when examining communications under the present Protocol. After examining a communication, the Committee shall forward its suggestions and recommendations, if any, to the State Party concerned and to the petitioner.

Article 6

1. If the Committee receives reliable information indicating grave or systematic violations by a State Party of rights set forth in the Convention, the Committee shall invite that

State Party to cooperate in the examination of the information and to this end submit observations with regard to the information concerned.

2. Taking into account any observations that may have been submitted by the State Party concerned as well as any other reliable information available to it, the Committee may designate one or more of its members to conduct an inquiry and to report urgently to the Committee. Where warranted and with the consent of the State Party, the inquiry may include a visit to its territory.

3. After examining the findings of such an inquiry, the Committee shall transmit these findings to the State Party concerned together with any comments and recommendations.

4. The State Party concerned shall, within six months of receiving the findings, comments and recommendations transmitted by the Committee, submit its observations to the Committee.

5. Such an inquiry shall be conducted confidentially and the cooperation of the State Party shall be sought at all stages of the proceedings.

Article 7

1. The Committee may invite the State Party concerned to include in its report under article 35 of the Convention details of any measures taken in response to an inquiry conducted under article 6 of the present Protocol.

2. The Committee may, if necessary, after the end of the period of six months referred to in article 6, paragraph 4, invite the State Party concerned to inform it of the measures taken in response to such an inquiry.

Article 8

Each State Party may, at the time of signature or ratification of the present Protocol or accession thereto, declare that it does not recognize the competence of the Committee provided for in articles 6 and 7.

Article 9

The Secretary-General of the United Nations shall be the depositary of the present Protocol.

Article 10

The present Protocol shall be open for signature by signatory States and regional integration organizations of the Convention at United Nations Headquarters in New York as of 30 March 2007.

Article 11

The present Protocol shall be subject to ratification by signatory States of the present Protocol which have ratified or acceded to the Convention. It shall be subject to formal confirmation by signatory regional integration organizations of the present Protocol which have formally confirmed or acceded to the Convention. It shall be open for accession by any State or regional integration organization which has ratified, formally confirmed or acceded to the Convention and which has not signed the Protocol.

Article 12

1. "Regional integration organization" shall mean an organization constituted by sovereign States of a given region, to which its member States have transferred competence in respect of matters governed by the Convention and the present Protocol. Such organizations shall declare, in their instruments of formal confirmation or accession, the extent of their competence with respect to matters governed by the Convention and the present Protocol. Subsequently, they shall inform the depositary of any substantial modification in the extent of their competence.

2. References to "States Parties" in the present Protocol shall apply to such organizations within the limits of their competence.

3. For the purposes of article 13, paragraph 1, and article 15, paragraph 2, of the present Protocol, any instrument deposited by a regional integration organization shall not be counted.

4. Regional integration organizations, in matters within their competence, may exercise their right to vote in the meeting of States Parties, with a number of votes equal to the number of their member States that are Parties to the present Protocol. Such an organization shall not exercise its right to vote if any of its member States exercises its right, and vice versa.

Article 13

1. Subject to the entry into force of the Convention, the present Protocol shall enter into force on the thirtieth day after the deposit

of the tenth instrument of ratification or accession.

2. For each State or regional integration organization ratifying, formally confirming or acceding to the present Protocol after the deposit of the tenth such instrument, the Protocol shall enter into force on the thirtieth day after the deposit of its own such instrument.

Article 14

1. Reservations incompatible with the object and purpose of the present Protocol shall not be permitted.

2. Reservations may be withdrawn at any time.

Article 15

1. Any State Party may propose an amendment to the present Protocol and submit it to the Secretary-General of the United Nations. The Secretary-General shall communicate any proposed amendments to States Parties, with a request to be notified whether they favour a meeting of States Parties for the purpose of considering and deciding upon the proposals. In the event that, within four months from the date of such communication, at least one third of the States Parties favour such a meeting, the Secretary-General shall convene the meeting under the auspices of the United Nations. Any amendment adopted by a majority of two thirds of the States Parties present and voting shall be submitted by the Secretary-General to the General Assembly of the United Nations for approval and thereafter to all States Parties for acceptance.

2. An amendment adopted and approved in accordance with paragraph 1 of this article shall enter into force on the thirtieth day after the number of instruments of acceptance deposited reaches two thirds of the number of States Parties at the date of adoption of the amendment. Thereafter, the amendment shall enter into force for any State Party on the thirtieth day following the deposit of its own instrument of acceptance. An amendment shall be binding only on those States Parties which have accepted it.

Article 16

A State Party may denounce the present Protocol by written notification to the Secretary-General of the United Nations. The denunciation shall become effective one year after the date of receipt of the notification by the Secretary-General.

Article 17

The text of the present Protocol shall be made available in accessible formats.

Article 18

The Arabic, Chinese, English, French, Russian and Spanish texts of the present Protocol shall be equally authentic.

IN WITNESS THEREOF the undersigned plenipotentiaries, being duly authorized thereto by their respective Governments, have signed the present Protocol.